— THE —
Which? Wine Guide

Edited by ROSEMARY GEORGE MW
& CHRISTINE AUSTIN

Published by Consumers' Association

Which? Books are commissioned and researched by
The Association for Consumer Research and published by
Consumers' Association, 2 Marylebone Road, London NW1 4DF

Copyright © 1992/93 Consumers' Association Ltd
Revised edition September 1993
First published October 1992
First edition of *The Which? Wine Guide* published in 1981

Editorial consultant: Aileen Hall
Acknowledgements to: Maureen Ashley MW, Francessa Beckett, Liz Berry
MW, Jim Budd, Margaret Harvey MW, Helena Harwood, Maggie McNie
MW, Richard Mayson, Hazel Murphy, Gabrielle Shaw

Design of cover and taste wheels: Paul Saunders
Cover photograph: Tony Stone Worldwide/Stuart McClymont
Illustrations: Bina Haria-Shah

British Library Cataloguing-in-Publication Data
A catalogue record for this book is available from the British Library

ISBN 0 340 59628 7

Typesetting by Page Bros (Norwich) Ltd
Printed and bound in Great Britain by Biddles Ltd,
Guildford and King's Lynn

Contents

CONTENTS

Part III Where to buy wine

Part IV Find out more about wine

Introduction

Welcome to this revised edition of *The Which? Wine Guide*, with its fully updated wine merchants' section. Some merchants, sadly, have fallen by the wayside, but many new ventures are making an appearance in the *Guide*. Of the new names we have included, some are brand-new businesses, others have improved and now qualify for an entry, while some are existing businesses which have just come to our attention.

Many of the merchants we have contacted during 1993 tell us that there has been a shift in buying from traditional areas of France to the newer, better-value regions of the south. New World areas, particularly Australia, are still making great strides, with reliable, quality wines coming on to the shelves at very reasonable prices. South Africa is slowly emerging as a source of good-value wines.

Following on from the last edition of the *Guide*, we continue our campaign for better training for staff involved with wine, and are pleased to report a slight improvement. Independent shops are where you will tend to get the best advice, but some of the major chains have taken the plunge and started to train their wine staff. Sainsbury's has introduced a major training initiative for wine staff, which will gradually work through to all stores. Safeway, Marks & Spencer and high street chains such as Oddbins and Wine Rack are all particularly good at training. There is still a general reluctance to allow supermarket staff to taste the wines. This means that they are unable to help customers who seek the most simple reassurance with questions such as: 'Have you tried this wine? Is it dry or medium-dry?'

WHAT IF THE WINE IS OFF?

Having bought the wine, what should you do if it does not taste as you think it should? If it tastes 'off', i.e. oxidised or corked, then it is no different from any other unsatisfactory product bought from a shop, and it should be returned. But many wine drinkers are reluctant to take wine back to a shop in case they are made to look foolish. We found a number of wine merchants who take a patronising attitude to their customers' complaints, putting most of them down to 'not liking the wine'. While we agree that no sound wine should be replaced just because the customer does not like the flavour, there are some merchants who do not seem to be aware of the great many bottles on sale which are faulty through problems with corks.

The best response to our question: 'If a customer returns an opened bottle that he or she says is "off", how do you deal with the complaint?' comes from Peter Green of Edinburgh, who said: 'Like every wine seller in the UK, we get far too few wines back. It bothers us because bottles are easy to replace but customers are not.' Harrods, on the other hand, advises its staff to: 'Taste the bottle and inform the customer whether it is faulty or not.'

The majority of shops say that they will replace or refund the cost of a bottle without question if the customer is dissatisfied with it. The major chains are quickest and slickest at this, as long as the returned bottle is not empty. Many of the independents also gave us the same answer, but some went further than an automatic refund. Tasting and talking about wine, finding out what the customer likes and steering him or her to the right selection is the best option – here the one-man-bands and independents do best.

What the shops say and what they do may sometimes be different, so we checked out a few with genuine complaints. Major supermarkets and chains did refund or replace immediately, but one mail-order company took several reminders and nearly eight months to come through with a refund. Less determined customers might have given up by then.

WINES BY TASTE

As well as finding out where to buy, readers over the years have been no less interested in finding out more about the wines they buy and enjoy. *The Which? Wine Guide* has broken away from the traditional country-by-country survey of the world's wines. Broadly speaking, most of us choose our wines by flavour and price rather than by country, so our approach is to compare wines by their taste, even if they come from regions that are thousands of miles apart.

To this end we have compiled *The Which? Wine Guide* Taste Wheel, or rather Wheels – one large wheel for table wines and two smaller ones for fortified and sparkling wine. Quite simply, we have divided up the world's wines according to their different taste components, taking into account acidity, body, sweetness, tannin and so on, in order to demonstrate how seemingly disparate wines do in fact stand side by side when it comes to how they taste. Conversely, not all wines from the same grape variety fall within the same section of the wheels as provenance and method of vinification have a considerable effect on flavour.

However, the prime objective of our Taste Wheels is to encourage experimentation and to expand our readers' wine-drinking horizons. It is easy to remain faithful to the wine you know you like, but to try something new is much more exciting and palate-broadening. With our Taste Wheels for guidance, we hope to make your wine-buying decisions easier and more adventurous at the same time. In this edition, a new, more comprehensive index will help you pinpoint the wine of your choice at a glance.

Of course, taste is firmly subjective. Everyone's tastebuds are individual so you may find that you disagree with some of our suggestions. On the other hand, you will probably be surprised by similarities that would never otherwise have occurred to you.

FEATURES

Our first feature this year takes a look at merchants new to the *Guide*, merchants we have come across over the past year whom we feel merit inclusion. From Cupar to Cornwall, there are some new and exiciting names to look out for, providing even more choice than before.

Our second feature reflects on the ways in which wine-drinking habits have altered over the past few decades, as Harry Eyres looks at changing fashions in wine. He explains how supermarkets, foreign holidays and some intrepid wine merchants have all played their part.

Finally, we look at *What's on the label?*. For every bottle of wine, the label provides the first impression of quality and flavour; whether the wine is a vin de pays or a top-quality claret, it is saying: 'Buy me, drink me!' Legally, the label is required to tell you accurately just what is in the bottle, from the country of origin to the alcohol content. A considerable amount of optional information is also allowed and, as a result, wine labels can be a minefield for the consumer. We offer an introduction to wine-label jargon, providing pointers to facilitate understanding.

As in previous years, do please continue to let us have your views on the *Guide* and alert us to wine merchants – both those we know about and those new ones we may not. And enjoy your drinking.

CHRISTINE AUSTIN
ROSEMARY GEORGE

The Which? Wine Guide Awards

Once again, we have made some difficult decisions and given these awards to those merchants who have a special talent for selecting wines of a specialised region or who provide a particular service. An award for one speciality does not exclude another and any merchants of award-winning merit will have a great deal to offer their customers.

Bordeaux Specialist Award
Justerini & Brooks
A difficult decision, awarded to Justerini & Brooks for an excellent range and service

Burgundy Specialist Award
Adam Bancroft
A hand-picked selection of growers' burgundies at affordable prices

Rhône Specialist Award
Croque-en-Bouche
All the right wines, producers and vintages in glorious abundance

Italian Specialist Award
Valvolla & Crolla
For total dedication to providing a huge range from this complicated country and for going for quality every time

German Specialist Award
Adnams
There are merchants with bigger selections of German wines than here, but Adnams wins this award for making a determined effort to steer consumers back to the real quality estate wines of Germany

Spanish Specialist Award
Moreno Wines
Not just a great variety of wines, but a long list of vintages makes this London merchant the one to beat

Australian Specialist Award
Oddbins
Oddbins launched the UK's love affair with these wonderful wines, and continues to fan the flames with new wines and great-value prices

Fine Wine Specialist Award
Farr Vintners
If you are looking for special wines from special vintages then this is the place to come

Best Supermarket Award
Waitrose
A difficult choice this year. Last year's winner, Safeway, has maintained its terrific progress and Sainsbury's deserves recognition for a vastly improved range. This year, the overall winner is Waitrose for clear, stylish flavours in so much of its range and the sure-fire certainty of finding a really good wine at all price points

Best High-Street Chain Award
Thresher
For quality wines and round-the-world variety on almost every high street

Best Mail-Order Merchant Award
Lay & Wheeler
Quality wines, a great list and reliable service are all you need when you shop from home. Lay & Wheeler manages this easily and is charming with it!

Best Independent Merchant Award
D Byrne & Co
Huge variety, great enthusiasm and realistic prices at this Clitheroe merchant

Best Out-of-Town Merchant Award
B H Wines
For daring to go for a quality range without the reassurance of a huge population on the doorstep

In addition to these specialist awards, we would like to recognise particular merchants around the country who deserve a round of applause for serving their local community so well.

SCOTLAND
Peter Green
Would you ever leave Edinburgh if this were your local merchant?
We wouldn't

WALES
Tanners
Strongly challenged by Terry Platt, Tanners wins our vote for a
splendid range, quality service and a retail licence

SOUTH WEST
Averys
A stylish range of wines from a company 200 years old this year

EAST OF ENGLAND
Adnams
One of the best reasons for moving to East Anglia

Part I

Features

New merchants to the *Guide*

Christine Austin

The past twelve months have not been kind to the UK wine trade. Not only has there been a deep recession, hitting the luxury end of the market, but duty-free restrictions have been lifted, making it possible for travellers in the EC to fill their cars with wine and bring it into the country without paying duty. This will inevitably affect UK sales, but still the wine trade maintains an optimistic view of the future. All but a few of the merchants in last year's *Guide* have survived and some have taken advantage of low property prices to buy new premises and expand.

Although it is good to report on the continued progress of many of the merchants in the *Guide*, it is a particular pleasure to focus attention on merchants who are being included for the first time.

Some of these are new ventures in the wine market, others are existing businesses which have just come to our attention and a few are merchants who have now improved sufficiently to warrant space on the pages which follow.

AROUND LONDON

One of the most significant new merchants in London this year is **Harvey Nichols**, a company which has established a haven for wine lovers on the fifth floor of its Knightsbridge store, with a wide selection of quality wines from around the world.

With a much smaller range – but with the emphasis still firmly on quality – **Adam Bancroft**, Master of Wine, has brought together some small growers from Burgundy, the Loire and the Rhône. Sales are by the case, which can be mixed.

Selling on a similar basis is New Zealander Margaret Harvey, also a Master of Wine, at **Fine Wines of New Zealand**. Her small but expertly chosen selection makes this the place to go for some of the best from New Zealand.

These three merchants are described more fully in the *Where to buy wine* section of the *Guide*.

Bin Ends is perhaps not the most imaginative name in the wine trade but it does perfectly describe this new company (nothing to do with the Bin Ends listed on p. 262), which offers end-of-the-range wines, with branches in London, Oxford, Cambridge and Southampton. The business, which started less than two years ago, has grown from just one outlet to eight. More shops are planned in the near future.

There is a core range of good wines from around the world, sold at very reasonable prices, but the speciality is parcels of wine, which come and go at amazing speed. Surplus stock from châteaux, brokers and wholesalers appears on the shelves, even bankrupt stock from companies which have found the recession just too difficult. Price is crucial. Bravely, Bin Ends claims to try to beat any price. It will also try to source wines which are not actually in stock.

Some examples of the range include Grandes Marques champagnes at £3–4 less than many High Street shops, 1985 second-growth clarets at the price of a cru bourgeois, and a good collection of vins de pays at around the £3 mark.

Staff are knowledgeable and enthusiastic and there are always bottles open to taste. The disadvantage of a fast-moving business like this is that you cannot be sure of getting the same wine when you go back, but there should always be something of interest.

Bin Ends, 46 Shepherds Bush Road, London W6 (5 branches in London) *Tel* 071-602 7849; *also* 2 Mill Road, Cambridge, Cambridgeshire CB1 2AD *Tel* (0223) 301991; 193 Cowley Road, Oxford, Oxfordshire OX4 1UT *Tel* (0865) 201870; 14 Shirley Street, Southampton, Hampshire SO1 3MH *Tel* (0703) 511944

Enthusiasm and 'disarming friendliness' are features at the aptly – but coyly – named **Philglass & Swiggot** shop in Battersea, where proprietor Mike Rogers and his Australian wife Karen have a wide range of New World wines, as well as a good selection from Europe. Many of the Australian wines hover around the £5–7 mark, with Yalumba, David Wynn, Wolf Blass and Rothbury Estate featuring. For special occasions, there are wines from the splendid Tasmanian Wine Company, Mountadam, Moss Wood and Cape Mentelle. South Africa, New Zealand and Chile also provide good wines.

You can spend serious money on classed-growth clarets, but a good range of petits châteaux keeps the cost of drinking down. Also good value is the range of wines from southern France. With Torres and Berberana from Spain, Isole e Olena from Italy, Deinhard from Germany and a handful of English wines, there seems to be plenty with which to 'fill glass and swig it'!

Philglass & Swiggot, 21 Northcote Road, Battersea, London SW11
Tel 071-924 4494

Moving just a little further towards the river Thames, **Fernlea Vintners** in Balham is a fairly new business, where the emphasis is firmly on France, although its proprietor Peter Godden admits that the New-World range is growing in response to customers' demands. Australia, New Zealand, South Africa, Chile and California have joined the list, most bottles are under £10, apart from the rather grand Opus One from Mondavi.

Burgundies are the main focus for France and many are imported direct from growers such as Rossignol-Trapet and Domaine Henri Boillot. This shop is geared towards case sales, although single-bottle purchases are possible; informal Saturday tastings help steer you through the range.

Fernlea Vintners, 7 Fernlea Road, Balham, London SW12 *Tel* 081-673 0053

It is strictly unmixed-case sales only at **Charles Taylor Wines** (moving to London in October 1993). If you are seriously interested in domaine burgundy, then this company could help. Wines are selected by Charles Taylor MW and shipped direct from domaines such as Alain Geoffroy in Chablis, Yves Boyer-Martenot in Meursault and Bertrand Ambroise in the Côtes de Nuits. For days when burgundy seems a little extravagant, there are other wines from Bordeaux, Alsace, the Rhône and the south of France. Two estates from Australia provide some interest; armagnac and vintage ports round off the list. The disadvantage of a merchant who will not allow mixed cases is that it costs a fortune to sample the range. However, Charles Taylor is happy to give tutored tastings to groups, which could help you select your first case.

Charles Taylor Wines, 64 Alexandra Road, Epsom, Surrey KT17 4BZ *Tel* (0372) 728330; *From October 1993* 18 Whittlesey Street, London SE1 *Tel* 071-401 9271

New this year is a wine club in Hertfordshire, trading under the name **Australian Estates**. This mail-order company ignores the big names of Australia and concentrates on the wines of small estates which are not usually available in the UK – Charles Cimicky, Trentham Estate and the delicious Nicholson River, for example. Australian Estates works like a club, with a £20-a-year membership fee, for which you get newsletters, tasting notes and regular updates on new additions to the list. Sales are by the case, which can be mixed.

Australian Estates, 1 Magna Close, Harpenden, Hertfordshire AL5 12RH *Tel* (0582) 715949

Down the M4 from London is the **Harvest Wine Group** in Twyford. This company specialises in English wines from ten vineyards across England, all under the eye of an Australian winemaker. More details in the *Where to buy wine* section.

London always seems to have more than its fair share of good wine merchants, so it is good to be able to report on merchants around the UK who are new to the *Guide*.

THE SOUTH AND SOUTH WEST

In Dorset, a range of shops owned by brewers Hall & Woodhouse has been rescued from tenancy and is now directly managed by the brewery under the name **Woodhouse Wines**. Breweries are not always noted for their great interest in wine, but Hall & Woodhouse also runs fine wine merchants Hicks & Don (see the *Where to buy wine* section) and a degree of that professionalism spills over into the new shops.

France is represented by a reasonable selection of affordable clarets; burgundies are mainly from quality *négociants* Drouhin; the Rhône includes the lovely Châteauneuf-du-Pape from Château de Beaucastel. There is Masson-Blondelet in the Loire and a good choice of French country wines for everyday drinking. Spain, Italy and Germany all provide interesting wines, but it is California where the list stands out. Robert Mondavi wines are here, from the good-value Woodbridge range up to varietals from Napa Valley. Australia and New Zealand add variety to this Dorset discovery.

Woodhouse Wines, Head Office, Blandford Forum, Dorset DT11 9LS *Tel* (0258) 452141

In Somerset, **Châteaux Wines** is a new addition with a general selection from France plus a few wines from further afield. More details are in the *Where to buy wine* section.

Deeper into the West Country, at Falmouth in Cornwall, **Constantine Stores** started out as a general store and post office, but now sells wine as a major part of the business. Offering what he hopes is 'the largest range in the South-West,' David Rowe takes a shotgun approach to wine buying. There are 40 clarets from basics right up to first growths; burgundies include Domaine de la Romanée-Conti, as well as Faiveley, Drouhin and Bouchard Père. There is a huge range from Italy – some gems, some not quite so good. Australia rates a wide selection, featuring the big names of Penfolds, Wolf Blass and Renmano; Cape Mentelle and Peter Lehmann also manage some shelf space.

Malt whisky is a speciality in this shop, which is just about as far away from the distilleries of Scotland as you can get on mainland Britain. Nearly 200 single malts and blends include a selection of rare and aged malts going back to 1957.

Constantine Stores, 39 Fore Street, Constantine, Falmouth, Cornwall TR11 5AD *Tel* (0326) 40226

In Bristol, a traditional home of the English wine trade, **The Vine Trail** has set out to find wines from small growers in France, usually family domaines, some of whom produce no more than 1,500 bottles a year. Most regions of France are represented, with good-value wines from Hérault, Roussillon and Bergerac, as well as an unusual collection of Jurançon wines made from Gros and Petit Manseng grapes. Clarets are from small properties, with a good collection from St-Emilion, as well as the Médoc and Graves. Three wines from the Rhône, three more from Beaujolais, and some growers' champagnes round off this limited but satisfying collection. Sales here are by the case, which may be mixed; mail order is available.

The Vine Trail, 5 Surrey Road, Bishopston, Bristol, Avon B57 9DJ *Tel* (0272) 423946

WALES

Wales is not over-endowed with good wine merchants, so a new venture in Swansea is particularly welcome in this guide. **CPA's** is an unusual name for a merchant, until you realise the letters stand for Caroline (Rees), Paul (Davies) and Andrew (Hetherington). They have created a traditional wine shop at Mumbles and provide a small but well-chosen selection. Clarets run from Château Thieuley to La Lagune; burgundies are from domaines such as Leflaive, Simon Bize and Bertrand Ambroise; the Rhône and Loire provide quality drinking from good producers. There is also a reasonable collection of country wines, including Domaines

Virginie. Champagnes are from the family firm of Michael Noiret. From Australia, Henschke's Mount Edelstone packs a massive flavour and New Zealand is represented by wines from Delegats and Cloudy Bay. Much closer to home, the Llanerch vineyard, just outside Cardiff, supplies two Welsh wines to this splendid new shop.

CPA's, 44 Queens Road, Mumbles, Swansea, West Glamorgan SA3 4AN *Tel* (0792) 360707

YORKSHIRE

An old Victorian railway station is the setting for **Penistone Court Wine Cellars** in South Yorkshire. There are no trains passing the door now, but proprietor Christopher Ward is definitely on the right track with a comprehensive range of wines, available by the mixed case. He reckons that he has around 1,000 wines here but we didn't try to count them all. Highlights include a big selection of burgundies from Louis Latour, Beaujolais from Paul Sapin and a collection of clarets from basics up to first growths. Italian wines are worth considering, with a good-value collection which includes Chiantis from Pasolini and Castello Vicchiomaggio. Austrian wines are becoming a speciality here with several from Anton Wober. A big range from Australia, New Zealand and the USA makes selecting that mixed dozen more difficult. South African wines are here in a big way, with Simonsig, Fairview, Nederberg, Backsberg and Groot Constantia among the range. Sherries from Lustau and a wide selection of champagnes provide every reason to go full steam ahead for Penistone.

Penistone Court Wine Cellars, No. 5 The Railway Station, Penistone, Sheffield, South Yorkshire S30 6HG *Tel* (0226) 766037

Also in Yorkshire, at Springfield Mill in Huddersfield, is a fairly new business by the name of **Springfield Wines**, run by two former teachers, Lynda Higgs and Lesley Brook. Retail sales are available in premises that also include antique furniture and sofas – a very comfortable way to buy wine! Many of the wines here have been imported direct from France, and specialities include domaine Beaujolais, Alsace wines from Vonthron and a range of Jura wines. Germany rates special treatment with a large selection, particularly of Baden wines; wines from Italy, Spain, Australia and New Zealand provide a well-balanced choice.

Springfield Wines, Springfield Mill, Norman Road, Denby Dale, Huddersfield, West Yorkshire HD8 8TH *Tel* (0484) 864929

SCOTLAND

The Wine Byre at Cupar in Fife is home to a range of 750 wines, with another wide selection of malts, ports and beers. The shop's name refers to the 400-year-old premises, which have now been extended to provide extensive cellars and storage. The Wine Byre stocks a good, well-balanced range from around the world. Clarets hit both ends of the price scale with generic wines and a 1961 classed growth. Burgundies are more limited, but come from reliable suppliers. Prunotto provides some big flavours from Italy; the Spanish bottles include favourites from Torres and Ochoa, as well as a good selection of Riojas; the choice of wines costing less than £10 from Australia, New Zealand, South Africa and America is generous. Sales are by the single bottle and delivery for a case or more is free over a wide area.

The Wine Byre, Burnside, Cupar, Fife KY15 4BH *Tel* (0334) 53215

CHANGING FASHIONS IN WINE

Harry Eyres

Wine-drinking habits change more slowly than some other social indicators, such as hair, hemlines and musical fashions. If sexual intercourse began, according to Philip Larkin, in 1963 – belatedly enough, as he ruefully conceded – the liberalisation of wine took even longer. The big social changes which were crystallised by the Second World War, breaking down many of the hierarchies (upstairs-downstairs, officers-men) which prevailed up to the 1930s, were not immediately reflected in wine trends.

In fact, the old class system in wine remained largely unchanged up until the mid-1960s. Wine, till then, was not a people's drink in Britain. Wine drinking, or *good* wine drinking, was pretty much the preserve of the professional and upper classes – the lawyers and doctors who have appreciated the better sort of booze since time immemorial, the Oxbridge colleges, the St James's clubs, the posher regimental messes: these were the bastions of wine drinking. And as for the wine itself, it was claret, white burgundy, port, hock, sherry, Sauternes and a little bit of red burgundy. Of course, the lower orders did drink some too, but that tended to be branded wines (heavily advertised from the early 1960s onwards) such as Mateus Rosé and Blue Nun and, later, Hirondelle.

THE VINOUS REVOLUTION

Wine's equivalent of the French Revolution (fortunately, much less bloody) started to roll in the 1960s, the decade when per capita consumption (only one litre per annum in 1960) surged; the tumbrils turned into juggernauts in the 1970s, the decade when the supermarkets got the wine bit between their teeth. It is difficult to exaggerate the influence of Sainsbury's, Waitrose, Tesco, Safeway and the rest on the nation's drinking – not to mention eating – habits.

The coming of the supermarkets has also meant the empowering of women as wine buyers. The fact that women now drink a lot more wine than men may indeed be the most significant of all the changes in wine-drinking habits since the war. Perhaps this change has something to do with the move towards white rather than red wine (currently, around 70 per cent of wine sold in the UK is white) during the 1960s and 1970s; though the 1980s have seen the reversal of this trend, with red wine sales growing much faster. But here we are in danger of making unwarranted or even insulting assumptions about women's taste. My experience is that women love full red wines just as much as men do.

Women have, in the last two decades, become increasingly high-profile in the fields of professional wine buying and wine writing. Well-known women in the field – like Angela Muir, Liz Robertson, Marcia Waters, Claire Gordon-Brown, Arabella Woodrow, Jancis Robinson, Serena Sutcliffe, Rosemary George, Kathryn McWhirter and Jane MacQuitty – all show, if proof were needed, that women have acquired formidable palate- and pen-power in what used to be thought of as a very male area.

If women these days do most of the nation's wine buying, they are also responding to continental habits observed and absorbed in the course of holidays to the wine-producing countries of Europe. The continentalising of Britain is a slow process, but, from a London perspective at least, one that is gaining momentum.

On the other hand...

So has John Major's dream of a classless society actually materialised? Not quite, not quite. True, there has been a remarkable opening up of the previously mystifying and class-bound world of wine; supermarkets with their own-label wines of specific origin (rather than anonymous branded brews vigorously marketed) and user-friendly, unintimidating chains such as Oddbins, Majestic and Wine Rack offering top-quality bottles from the world's greatest producers, have helped transform Britain into an at least partly wine-drinking culture (twelve times as much table wine is consumed per head as in 1960). But if the growth in wine consumption so rampant during the 1980s has now gone sluggish, that has more to do with recession than snobbery, with cost than class.

At the top end of the wine market, however, a kind of plutocracy has developed, pushing the most famous names well beyond the reach of the middle-income professionals who used to be able to afford the odd bottle of Château Margaux or Corton-Charlemagne.

The price differentials between top-class and middle-ranking wines have widened dramatically since the 1960s.

GEOGRAPHICAL EXPANSION

The majority of wine merchants, not to mention wine writers, used to be fairly sedentary creatures. Of course, there were always exceptions, such as Charles Walter Berry, the Dornford-Yates-like character who explored what were then little-known French wine regions in the 1920s in his open-top automobile, complete with trusty side-kick. For most, however, tramping about in obscure vineyards was simply unnecessary: traditional customers could be satisfied by traditional wines acquired through importers with offices in London. And really, with the long city lunches and the social pressures of the season, there was not time to potter about in vineyards. And then, of course, the big brewers came along and gobbled most of the old wine merchants up.

The pioneers

Like so much else, it all began to change in the late 1960s. It was in 1969 that the rubicund dentist Robin Yapp began his trawls in those two most bucolic of French valleys, the Rhône and the Loire. There were also discoveries to be made in the most famous and supposedly familiar of classic French regions. When John Armit acquired the exclusivity for Château Trotanoy, on behalf of his firm Corney & Barrow, this great Pomerol was quite unknown in Britain. Even Pétrus was hardly a household name. Another Bordeaux initiative, begun in the 1960s by merchants such as my father, Philip Eyres, then of Henry Townsend, was that of offering wines *en primeur*, in the summer after the harvest. The advantage, initially, was low cost but, sadly, the Bordelais overcooked this golden goose by repeatedly inflating prices in the gilded decade of the 1980s.

Burgundy   The wines of Burgundy remained the biggest challenge. Until 1973, because French AC law did not apply in Britain, burgundy sold in Britain was heavily adulterated with southern French and north African red wine and even port. Authentic post-1973 red burgundy was pallid partly because it was genuine burgundy (not deep-coloured by nature), and also because growers at that time were using too much fertiliser and Pinot Droit, an inferior kind of Pinot Noir. Still, intrepid merchants such as Anthony Hanson visited growers in their limestone houses in their unwelcoming villages – Hanson even read them the riot act and said no one would buy their over-priced products until they improved quality. Burgundy improved markedly during the 1980s, helped by some miraculous vintages, but also by a new generation of Burgundian winemakers with at least one eye on the outside world. Merchants such as Haynes Hanson & Clark, Jasper Morris's Morris & Verdin, Bibendum and Domaine Direct shipped, directly from the growers, fine ranges of burgundy; unfortunately, because of the overwhelming demand for such scarce products, prices rocketed.

Rioja   France might be the nearest wine country to Britain, and the one with the greatest names, but it did not necessarily offer the best value. The most remarkable generic wine success story of the late 1970s and early 1980s was undoubtedly Rioja. Between 1976 and 1986 imports of Rioja increased by 1400 per cent, the kind of runaway romp later achieved by both Bulgaria and Australia.

There are a number of interesting lessons to be learnt from the Rioja boom. First, it was powered not so much by exploratory British merchants as by a well-planned and executed campaign run on behalf of the region by the national body, Wines from Spain. Secondly, it demonstrated the enormous potential popularity of wines which taste of oak. Once again, Australia and Bulgaria, and, to a lesser extent, California, were the countries to take those lessons to heart, while adding a further magic ingredient, varietal labelling (see later).

Italy   Other European countries must have looked enviously at Spain, or Rioja and the go-ahead Catalan firm of Torres at least, during the early 1980s. Italy, in particular, was finding it hard to move beyond the pasta-and-pizza, double-litre bottle of Soave and Valpolicella stage. This was largely the Italians' fault because most of the Italian wine shipped over here was of mediocre-to-execrable quality. A revelation for me was the first tasting I attended given by the Italian wine enthusiasts' club, Forum Vinorum, in 1985. Here were delectable, amazing wines, even from DOCs I thought it safe to despise – Quintarelli's sensational Valpolicellas and Amarone's and Pieropan's richly textured Soave. Tuscany shone too – Chianti from Badia a Coltibuono and Volpaia, Brunello from Altesino. And then there was Piedmont, almost a country on its own for wine, difficult and not well understood, but full of great things (Aldo Conterno, Mascarello, Vajra).

Elsewhere   Where next? Other countries seem poised to make their mark, some because of improved winemaking (Portugal), others aided by political liberalisation (Hungary, Romania). One or two casualties in this ever-expanding world must be mentioned: the great German Rieslings obstinately fail to regain the reputation they lost during the 1970s and 1980s, thanks largely to the oceans of Liebfraumilch (now beginning to recede) which flooded the British market – despite some wonderful vintages and a dedicated new generation of winemakers who, thankfully, have relaxed the policy of gum-stripping dryness pursued in the early 1980s. Fine, dry sherry – not just fino and the newly fashionable manzanilla from Sanlúcar, but also true amontillado and dry oloroso – is the most undervalued of Europe's great wines (see later). The big companies need to think of new marketing strategies.

Now we should turn our attention to the brave New World.

THE VARIETAL REVOLUTION

It is amazing to think that as recently as 1968 there was not a single Chardonnay vine in South Australia. Now South Australia has nearly half of Australia's substantial plantings of Chardonnay; but not only that, Australia has hijacked the white burgundy grape in the popular wine-drinking imagination. For many of today's wine drinkers, Chardonnay speaks in an Aussie accent almost as strong as Crocodile Dundee's.

Here, we look at two inter-related phenomena: on the one hand, the dramatic rise in success and reputation of the New World wine regions – California, Australia, New Zealand, South Africa and Chile – and, on the other, the move towards varietal labelling, with which the success of those countries' wines, as well as those from Eastern Europe, especially Bulgaria, is indelibly associated.

Old versus New

Logically, the grape varieties come first. And here we enter the great debate between strict legal regulation of what grapes are to be grown where, based on ideas of tradition and quality and *terroir* (in other words the French appellation contrôlée system), and the free and easy, free-market approach that you can grow whatever you like wherever you like and let the market decide (the approach prevalent in the New World countries).

It is a fascinatingly complex as well as deeply emotive debate, but there can be no question that most of the momentum at present is with the New World free-marketeers. The influence of the New World is being seen in the Old World. For example, coming to the fore in the Midi are Cabernet Sauvignon, Chardonnay, Sauvignon Blanc, as well as Syrah, Viognier and Mourvèdre – varietal wines, some actually made by Australians (the Hardy company, for example, with Chais Baumière), others by innovative locals such as Robert Skalli and the producers of the Val d'Orbieu.

What is happening in the Midi is what has already happened in the New World. California, with its dynamic wine industry reborn in the 1960s, deserves much of the credit. Once again, take the most fashionable of all grape varieties: California spotted the potential of Chardonnay well before Australia, not to mention before Chile, Bulgaria or South Africa, though as recently as 1959 there were no more than about 200 acres of the grape in the whole of California (many of them owned by Wente Bros). By the early 1970s, when Australia was still virtually Chardonnay-free, there were some 7,000 acres in California – and that was only the beginning of the Chardonnay gold-rush. At the last count there were over 50,000 acres of Chardonnay in California – amazingly, almost as much as in all of France.

Ripeness   The early California Chardonnays and Cabernets were big, bold, brash, ripe wines – luscious broads dolled up with obvious lashings of oak. The public, or at least the American public, loved them (since when did the public scorn patent attractions?). One of the secrets of New World success has been the abandonment of restraint. The New World varietals arriving in the shops in the late 1970s and 1980s had bags of ripe fruit flavour (and had not needed bags of sugar to make them reasonably alcoholic). They might not be terribly subtle, but who needs subtlety when they can have sheer sensual enjoyment?

And another thing: grape varieties are easier to understand than all the endless intricacies of appellations. The punter who was new or newish to wine found names like Chardonnay and Cabernet easier to handle than Puligny-Montrachet Premier Cru les Folatières (a bit cheaper, too).

Oak   You can tire of ripe fruit – it can begin to taste jammy. But ripe fruit and new oak, *there* was a winning combination. Rioja had already proved that point, and now California and Australia, with Bulgaria, Chile and South Africa in somewhat uncertain pursuit, put their money where the barrels were. And the extraordinary thing was that the fashion for oaked wines, especially Cabernet Sauvignon and Chardonnay, promoted by the New World, began to have a reverse influence on the way wines were made in France. In the old days in Bordeaux, you replaced barrels as infrequently as possible; now your percentage of new oak is more important than your place in the 1855 classification.

Terroir   On the other hand, in the New World countries, which originally proclaimed such contempt for geology, there is a marked move back towards concern for particular vineyard location and the affinities certain grape varieties have with a special *terroir*.

For better or worse?

So has the death-knell sounded for the French appellation system? In countries which have long and rich viticultural traditions, appellation contrôlée will always have at least historical relevance. Whether that guidance should be prescriptive is another matter. Might we see Pinot Noir growing by the Gironde, and Merlot braving the chill of a Burgundian spring? It might sound sacrilegious to some, but I don't see why not, as an experiment at least.

The greatest danger for the consumer of the free-market approach is that, paradoxically, it could end up reducing, not expanding, choice. However, look at Italy: a decade ago Cabernet's intrusion into Chianti and even Piedmont had some experts worrying about the betrayal of Italian tradition. That did not happen: the last few years have seen a powerful counter-revolution in favour of Italy's native grapes and styles, now vinified in a manner to win friends, not repel outsiders.

FORTIFIED AND SPARKLING WINES

The trend towards lightness is perhaps the most significant in the entire world of eating and drinking today. The past 60 years have seen, relatively, a major decline in consumption of fortified wines and an increase (absolute as well as relative) in consumption of light still wines. It is amazing to think that in Australia, now the world's most go-ahead wine country, it was only in 1971 that production of light table wines overtook that of fortified wines.

Fortified wines

The biggest casualty has been sherry, the market for which has been declining by as much as five or six per cent a year during the 1980s. This decline has been relatively sudden because, as recently as the 1970s, Harveys and others were bullishly planting great swathes of the chalky Jerez downs with new vineyards – only for these to be pulled up again and turned over to sunflowers in the late 1980s and early 1990s.

Most of the sherry consumed in Britain has always been of a sweetened, medium or dark sort never encountered in the land of its origin, where over 90 per cent of sherry is dry. Sweet, dark, heavy in alcohol, Bristol Cream was a dinosaur of a drink, more of an alternative to central heating than an appetising aperitif. An economic survey conducted on behalf of the sherry producers in the 1980s concluded that sherry's only viable future lay in the lighter, drier types, fino and manzanilla, which make up 90 per cent of sherry consumption in Spain – and which are drunk like wines, with food, not like liqueurs. The last decade or so has seen some growth in fino and manzanilla, but these still account for only 15 per cent of the sherry market.

A paradox now: all the damning comments just made about Bristol Cream apply equally to port, but port's performance, in the last decade at least, has been markedly sprightlier than that of sherry. The fairly stable overall volume figures for the UK market of recent years (a major slump in the early 1980s followed by a recovery, a further mini-slump, another recovery) conceal a strong move up-market. Cheap ruby, the mainstay of the port business before the war (the days when women of easy virtue drank port and lemon, doubtless making their virtue still easier), is declining fast, and it is now, by a tasty irony, the French who drink the bargain-basement stuff. The great port success story of the 1980s has been LBV or late-bottled vintage. This easy-to-drink style (no decanting, no waiting decades for maturity) may have caused controversy among port-trade traditionalists, but it undoubtedly represents a kind of port more and more people want to drink. Surprisingly, given its seductive lightness and nutty mellowness, aged tawny port (the style preferred in Portugal itself) remains a *recherché*, connoisseur's choice in Britain.

Vintage port, for decades considered as a rock-solid investment, suddenly, in the late 1980s, started behaving erratically as prices rose then fell. The collapse of prices for young vintage port certainly had an influence on the longest gap in vintage declarations since the war: 1991 was declared by several shippers, but not by such great names as Taylor and Fonseca.

Apart from port, other historic fortified wines such as madeira, marsala, and Màlaga just survive, thanks to the efforts of a few sterling producers, though the Symington family's involvement in the Madeira Wine Company has galvanised the marketing of that wine. It will take serious investment in the Madeira vineyards, however, to bring the quality up to the level required to make madeira once more a household name.

Champagne – on the way out?

The sparkling wine picture has consistently, and appropriately, been more effervescent. Champagne and its imitators (not to be called 'champagne') and competitors have always been associated with celebration; champagne, in particular, has also been closely linked to cycles of boom and bust. Great champagne-drinking epochs are associated with frivolity and decadence (the naughty 1890s, the roaring 1920s, the bingeing 1980s); that they also precede major wars or other catastrophies is another, ominous conclusion suggested by the historical record.

You could argue that the champagne producers have cut their own throats by establishing (often admirable) offshoots in California, Australia and New Zealand. Somehow, though, I suspect that the champagne obituaries of recent times are premature.

LOOKING INTO THE CRYSTAL BALLOON

Predicting future trends is, as we all know, a fool's game – especially now as we lurch towards another millennium in the midst of global violence and uncertainty. The optimism of forecasts in the late 1980s – predicting increasing overall wine consumption amid increasing prosperity – looks over-euphoric, even smug. Wine consumption in the UK is on the up, but at a rate that would make a tortoise look like Alain Prost.

The expanding middle classes will drink better wine – but how much will they drink? Is there a danger (some, I suppose, might think of it as a hope) of a kind of neo-Prohibitionism already present in the USA, inspired this time more by health-consciousness than by a self-denying puritanism? The passing of the draconian *Loi Evin*, limiting drinks advertising in France, of all countries, represents an ominous victory for the health puritans in Europe's wine heartland. Will low-alcohol wine become the trend of the first decades of the twenty-first century?

It is a terrifying threat, but perhaps not too likely to materialise for the time being, while low-alcohol wines taste like denatured fruit juice. Meanwhile, there will be increasing talk of units (off-putting pseudo-science or an essential adjunct to safe drinking?), but the most potent deterrent to over-indulgence will remain the boys in blue and the Breathalyser bag.

For someone who loves wine in its sacred, inescapably alcoholic nature, it may be more appropriate to end with reflections on the changing shape of the wine trade and the sources from which it will draw the wines of the future. These are hard times for the small specialist wine merchants – the pioneers of the new wave of wine drinking which began in the 1960s. The supermarkets, who learned much from those pioneers, continue to tighten their grip – offering, in general, ever more interesting wines, but also limited by the lack of specialised staff on their premises and the pressure to make economies of scale. Currently, wine merchants in the south of England are being squeezed by what seems a patently unfair advantage offered to French hypermarkets: the combination of a great increase in the duty-free allowance and the maintenance of UK duty at punitive levels.

As for up-and-coming wine countries, will South America seriously challenge Australia and California? Will the emergent countries of the former USSR (Moldova, Georgia) realise their potential? Or will Mars, the god of war, drive away Bacchus? Subject for a good mythological painting, at least.

(Harry Eyres is a wine writer who edited the excellent six-volume series on grape varietals published by Viking in 1992.)

What's on the label?

Rosemary George MW

Wine labels are like people: sometimes first impressions can be very deceptive, at other times absolutely accurate. The label is our first contact with the bottle, providing a key to its contents and an idea of its quality. Deliberately or not, the label creates an impression of style and taste. Contrast the classic, elegant design of a classed-growth claret label with a cheerful, colourful vin de pays. The first leads us to expect a serious wine of stature, the second a simple, everyday quaffing wine. And yet, this may not always be the case. Some producers attach more importance to the appearance of the label than others. In rural parts of France, the wine grower may be content with the limited possibilities offered by the local printer. In more design-conscious Tuscany, producers excel at creating an overall effect of sophistication.

The ultimate in designer labels must be those of Château Mouton-Rothschild. Since 1945, Baron Philippe de Rothschild, and now his daughter Philippine, has invited a leading artist of international standing to design the label for the new vintage. The choice of the next artist attracts the desired attention and the labels of artists such as Picasso and Chagall become collectors' pieces. This is an idea that has been followed elsewhere, but never with quite the same flair as at Mouton.

However, behind the façade of designer expertise, it must be remembered that the main object of the wine label is to tell us accurately and legally, without misleading us, where the wine comes from and what is actually in the bottle.

THE KEY FEATURES

The wine label should provide a guide to the essential components of the wine (though, unusually among food and drink products, it does not state the ingredients), the four key elements which determine its taste, namely the grape variety or varieties; the soil in which they are grown; the climate to which the vines are subjected (and vintage); and, finally, the winemaker.

The labels of the Old World – from countries like France, Italy, Spain and Portugal – assume knowledge that the New World readily tells us on the label. New World labels mention the **grape variety** as the key to flavour and choice – not so Old World labels. For example, if the label says Chablis, it is implied that we know that Chablis can only be made from Chardonnay. Indeed, with the exception of Alsace and very few other wines, French appellation laws forbid any reference to the grape variety on the label. However, grape varieties are permitted on the labels of lower-quality vins de pays, often preceded by the word *cépage* (which means, simply, grape variety). In this instance, the wine may be a pure varietal; if not, EC law allows the blend to contain up to fifteen per cent of another variety.

In the Old World, the area of an appellation generally assumes a particular type of **soil**, e.g. in Graves the soil is gravel, in Mosel it is slate. Again, the appellation also indicates indirectly what the **climate** is like. For instance, AC Chablis, a more northern vineyard, will usually be cooler than the Mâcon. In some parts of the world, **vintages** are insignificant, while on the edges of feasible viticulture, such as Northern France, Germany and parts of New Zealand, the vintage can make all the difference between a fine and an average bottle. In blended wines like sherry, madeira or non-vintage champagne, the vintage is immaterial.

Finally, there is the human factor – the **winemaker**. This is the person who has put his or her own individual mark on the wine, who can make something palatable out of less than perfect grapes in a problematic year or, alternatively, ruin healthy grapes with careless winemaking. In a region like Burgundy, a well-known vineyard will often belong to several different families or members of the same family, so that just a different forename may be the clue to a good or bad bottle.

Additional elements

Names other than that of the winemaker may also appear on the bottle. In Burgundy, you may find the name of the merchant or *négociant* who has bought the grapes, juice or newly fermented wine from the grower to be treated, matured and prepared for bottling. He or she may blend together several sources of the same wine to produce a wine that is characteristic of his or her particular style. The bottler's name – which may be the producer, or a merchant – *must* always appear on the label. The bottler may also be the producer. In the case of a fine wine, the name of the producer will be proclaimed loudly on the label, while a mere vin de table will carry a name and the postal code in the smallest permitted print size. Even the size of obligatory lettering is strictly controlled within the EC.

Moreover, for wine from countries outside the Common Market, not only must there be the bottler's name but *also* the name of the importer.

COMMON MARKET REGULATIONS

Each country has its own labelling policy, be it for wine or baked beans, though the broad guidelines for the compulsory elements of information are virtually the same worldwide for bottles on the export market and reflect the conditions of production in individual countries. EC countries follow the guidelines of Brussels, which expects conformity from those countries which export to the Common Market (the wines of over 40 different countries of origin are exported to Britain). Some degree of consistency over language is therefore required and names like champagne and Chablis are protected within the Common Market, even if they are borrowed and abused in Australia or the United States for wines sold to the home market.

EC wine law divides what is called 'light still wine', as opposed to sparkling and fortified wine, into three broad categories for wine produced within the Common Market. These are table wine, table wine entitled to a geographical name, and quality wine produced in a specified region. In France, for example, the categories are appellation contrôlée, vin délimité de qualité supérieur (or VDQS), vin de pays and, finally, basic vin de table.

For bureaucratic reasons, countries outside the Common Market are required to have two categories only: the basic wine, which is simply called 'wine' rather than 'table wine', and the better quality wine which is entitled to a geographical name.

Bottle size is also governed by Common Market rules. The legal standard size is now 75cl (750ml or 0.75l), with half-bottles at 37.5cl and magnums at 150cl. The litre, two-litre and half-litre are also allowed, as well as multiples of 75cl for giant champagne bottles. Sometimes, the letter 'e' still appears to indicate an authorised bottle size, though in fact this is no longer necessary and, since May 1988, it has been compulsory to state the alcohol content of a wine. It must be accurate to within half a degree.

Labelling regulations are designed to prevent a wine from appearing to be better than it actually is; for this reason, many words that denote quality are not allowed on the label of a basic table wine. However, once a geographical origin is mentioned, more information is allowed, such as grape variety, vintage and an estate name. And, once the wine is recognised as a quality wine, there is even greater scope as to what may be mentioned on the label. The area of origin, for example, must be stated, which may be as precise as a single vineyard or even part of that vineyard.

HOW IT WORKS IN PRACTICE

Visual examples are essential to amplify and illustrate. Let's begin with a classic example from France – the straightforward label of Château de Beaucastel. The reputation of the property is firmly established and it contains merely the minimum legal requirements: the country of origin; name of the appellation; bottle size in millilitres; alcohol level; name and address of the producer with a decorative signature and a statement that the wine is bottled at the château (the vintage would be found on an accompanying neck label).

Other terms to look out for on French labels might include *grand vin*, which in Bordeaux indicates the first and best wine of the estate as opposed to one of the growing number of second wines. *Grand cru classé, grand cru, premier cru* and *cru classé* are all terms which have different meanings depending on the area the wine comes from. They are more meaningful in some appellations than in others.

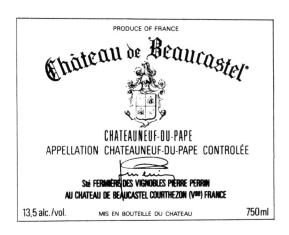

Terms like *élevé en fûts de chêne* or *cuvée bois* will describe a wine that has spent some time in wood, while *vieilles vignes* means that the wine comes from the older vines, maybe 30 or 50 years old.

Descriptions of taste may also feature; *sec, demi-sec, moelleux* or *doux. Sec,* when used for table wine, means dry; *demi-sec* is medium-dry, *moelleux* is medium-sweet and *doux* is sweet.

Except in the context of champagne, *blanc de blancs* (made from white grapes only) is virtually meaningless as all white wine is made from white grapes. (*Blanc de noirs* in champagne means that no Chardonnay has been included in the blend, only Pinot Noir and Pinot Meunier.)

Italy

In Italy, DOC (Denominazione di Origine Controllata) is the category below DOCG (Denominazione di Origine Controllata e Garantita), which has stricter regulations. Essentially, the concept is very similar to appellation contrôlée. The category below DOC, vino da tavola followed by a geographical description (e.g. vino da tavola di Sicilia), illustrates the Italian unwillingness to conform, with numerous examples of wines with no legal standing that are often *better* and certainly more expensive than the parallel DOCG (for example, the so-called Super Tuscans).

Terms that commonly appear on Italian wine labels include *messo in bottiglie*, bottled by, *classico*, the traditional heart of the vineyard area; *superiore*, like *supérieur* in French, meaning an extra degree, or half degree, of alcohol more than the minimum required for the basic DOC. *Riserva* indicates a superior wine not produced every year, one that has undergone a longer period of ageing, in bottle or cask.

Germany

German wines divide into *Deutscher Tafelwein* or German table wine; *Landwein*, which translates literally as country wine; *Qualitätswein bestimmter Anbaugebiete*, a quality wine from a specified region, commonly known as QbA; and finally *Qualitätswein mit Prädikat* (QmP), a quality wine with special attributes. The different Prädikat wines, in ascending order of sweetness, or potential alcohol, are *Kabinett, Spätlese, Auslese, Beerenauslese* and *Trockenbeerenauslese*. Spätlese comes from late-picked grapes and will be slightly sweet, unless it is followed by the word *trocken*, indicating that it is dry, or *halbtrocken*, meaning semi-dry.

If we look to the label opposite we see that there is a similar logic in the order of the names. First comes the village, in this instance Nierstein, then the vineyard, Rehbach, next the grape variety, Riesling, and finally the Prädikat, Spätlese. The AP number or *Amtliche Prüfungsnummer* shows that the wine has undergone a tasting and analytical tests. Rheinhessen is the region (as opposed to Mosel, Rheingau, etc.). *Erzeuger Abfüllung* is translated as 'estate-bottled' and the producer is the estate (or *Weingut*) of

Bürgermeister (meaning mayor) Anton Balbach and his *erben*, or heirs.

Spain and Portugal

Denominación de Origen (DO) is the Spanish quality system, with a new qualification of Denominación de Origen Calificada (DOCa), to which only Rioja is so far eligible. Colour descriptions include *tinto*, which is full red, as opposed to the lighter *clarete*; *blanco* is white and *rosado* is rosé. Maturation in oak is an essential feature of much quality Spanish winemaking, and *crianza* describes a wine that has undergone a short period of ageing, *reserva* a year or so longer, depending on the precise DO regulations, and *gran reserva* even longer. *Sin crianza*, on the other hand, refers to a wine for early drinking.

Portugal has also instituted its own system of appellations, known as Denominacão do Origem Controlada, or DOC, with the lesser IPR, or Indicaçao de Proveniência Regulamentada, for wines which have not yet been given DOC status. Vinho Verde is not only a DOC, but the term *verde* also describes a young wine, as opposed to an older *maduro* wine. The term *garrafeira* describes a producer's best wines, and denotes a minimum of three years' ageing for red wines, including one in bottle, and one year for white wines, including six months in bottle. *Velha*, meaning old, indicates three years' ageing for reds and two for whites, and *reserva* indicates half a degree more alcohol than usual.

Other table wines

In contrast to the complicated labels of western Europe, those of Eastern Europe and the New World seem positively simple and need little explanation. Bulgarian labels, for example, are usually wonderfully self-explanatory, with vintage and producer clearly marked. Other terms which may appear on a Bulgarian label include *country wine*, which roughly equates to a vin de pays, *controliran*, similar to an appellation, and *reserve*, denoting that some wood-ageing has taken place in the better wines.

English wine labels are fairly clear, too, usually giving the name of the winery and the grape variety and, perhaps, a brand name and an indication of flavour (e.g. dry or medium-dry). However, with the Quality Wine Pilot Scheme that has been in operation for the past couple of years, it has been necessary to provide an indication of region, with the result that the term *Southern Counties* is seen on some labels.

Rosé labels follow the same pattern as other labels. You may, however, see the words *White Zinfandel* or *Blanc de Cabernet Sauvignon* on the label of a wine that is distinctly pink in colour (sometimes described as *blush*). This simply implies that the grapes are red, but have been vinified as though they were white – i.e. with minimal skin contact, so that the wine has taken on a light pink colour.

Fortified wines

Fortified wines are subject to the same regulations as table wines. The use of the word *sherry* is being strictly outlawed outside of Jerez (*British sherry*, for example, will no longer be permissible after the end of 1995). On the sherry label opposite emphasis is placed on the brand name Solear, which comes from the bodega Barbadillo. The style of sherry is Manzanilla Pasada, a mature manzanilla produced in Sanlúcar de Barrameda, and classed as DO Manzanilla. Port labels describe the style, be it vintage, ruby, the wine of a single estate or quinta and so on.

Madeira is currently undergoing changes in its nomenclature as EC law demands that all grape varieties mentioned on the label must account for a minimum of 85 per cent of the wine. Most young madeira is made from the ubiquitous Negramole grape and consequently will have to be called special-dry, medium-dry, medium-rich or full-rich, while the traditional terms *sercial*, *verdelho*, *bual* and *malmsey* will be retained only for the older wines of superior quality, made from the relevant grape varieties.

Sparkling wines

The example below is a classic label from Bruno Paillard, which tells you that this is a *crémant*, indicating slightly less pressure than fully sparkling champagne, and that only Chardonnay has been used. Note that the words *appellation contrôlée* do not appear, for champagne is unique in being the only French appellation not to require them on the label. Quite simply, champagne is champagne and if the label on your bottle of fizz does not say champagne, then champagne it is not. The level of sweetness is given – in this case *brut* – from *extra-brut*, with no dosage (*see Wine glossary*), to *brut*, the most common, *extra-sec*, *demi-sec* and *doux*. Marketing terms like *Brut Zéro*, *Brut Sauvage* and *Ultra Brut* describe a champagne without any dosage.

With wines made outside Champagne, it used to be possible to describe the method of production as *méthode champenoise*, but this is no longer permitted and so other terms are being used, such as *traditional method* or *classical method*, *méthode traditionnelle* or *metodo classico*. *Mousseux* in French, *spumante* in Italy, and *espumoso* in Spain all mean sparkling, but not necessarily using the champagne method. Some appellations automatically imply that the champagne method has been used, notably those described as *crémant*, which are growing in number, from Alsace, Burgundy, Limoux, Bordeaux, the Loire and Die. *Vin mousseux* without an appellation has been made by the tank or Charmat method (*see p.211*).

Spanish cava is another champagne-method wine by implication, and may be *extra-brut*, *brut*, *extra-seco*, which is off-dry, *semi-seco*, which is more semi-sweet than semi-dry, and *dulce*, very sweet. Extra-brut and brut are the most usual.

German sparkling wine is usually described as *Sekt* or, more specifically, *Deutscher Sekt*, usually made by the transfer or cuve-close method. *Flaschengärung* means bottle fermented, while *Flaschengärung nach dem traditionallen Verfahren* means fermented in this bottle, which is very unusual in Germany. The New World has borrowed the term *champagne* indiscriminately, but not for exports to the Common Market. The term to look for is 'fermentation in *this* bottle'.

A last word...

The deciphering of the label may at first seem to present a minefield, but familiarity brings understanding. Read the small print; do not assume that something is not what it says. As with tasting, you can build up your expertise and will find that the world of wine becomes richer and more rewarding as a result.

Part II

The taste of wine

INTRODUCTION TO THE TASTE WHEELS

The country-by-country approach to wine has become too rigid and, at the same time, too confusing. Britain now imports wines from over forty different countries, from all continents, with each year bringing new wines and new flavours from hitherto undiscovered vineyards. Consequently, the consumer is presented with an ever-increasing choice. Small wonder, then, that many of us prefer to stick faithfully to the familiar old favourites and hesitate to spread our vinous wings.

Since it is the intrinsic taste that determines whether we enjoy a wine, and not the fact that it comes from such and such a grape variety or this or that vineyard, it seems more logical and useful to discuss wines by flavour rather than by country. What follows is a breakdown of the world's wines into three taste wheels – for table, fortified and sparkling wines – particularly featuring those most readily available on our wine merchants' shelves.

The taste wheels show the similarities between wines from different countries and regions and demonstrate that grape varieties, flavours and wine styles *do* cross national boundaries. They draw comparisons and contrasts between the basic taste components: acidity and body, tannin and oak. For example, if you like the firm, crisp flavour of Muscadet, you will see that you are not condemned solely to the dry whites of the Atlantic end of the Loire Valley, but can find taste parallels not only in other parts of France, but also in New Zealand, Portugal and Italy. Conversely, the identical grape variety produced in two completely different parts of the world, or indeed in two adjacent wine regions, may not taste at all the same.

Any attempt to put wine into categories of taste can only ever be purely subjective and is open to discussion. You may find that you disagree with some suggestions, but that does not matter. The aim is to provoke thought and encourage experimentation in your wine-buying. We have split the world's wine up into broad bands of flavour, determined by such fundamental factors as oak, body, acidity, sugar and tannin. There are several wines which find a place in more than one taste band. New Zealand Sauvignon Blanc is one such wine for, depending on how it is vinified, it may be crisply pungent, or ripe and full-flavoured with hints of oak. Chablis is another example which crosses the bands, depending on whether it is village Chablis or a Chablis grand cru, and whether it is fermented in stainless steel or aged in oak. The taste wheels are no more than guidelines: with something as subjective as taste in wine, nothing can be permanent, for flavours change as the wines mature and develop. Nor are our palates infallibly consistent from day to day.

THE FUNDAMENTALS

First, it is worth considering the four fundamental factors that make a wine taste the way it does. They are the grape variety or blend of grape varieties; the soil in which the vines are grown; the climate to which they are subjected; and the hand of the winemaker.

Grape varieties

An infinite number of different grape varieties can be used for making wine, although, in practice, those that make the world's finer and better-known wines are limited to perhaps a hundred. In Europe, centuries of tradition and experience have determined which are best suited to which vineyards, while parts of the New World are still experimenting with the better-known vines of France, Germany and Italy to establish which perform best and where. Efforts are concentrated above all on Cabernet Sauvignon and Chardonnay, but Riesling, Gewürztraminer, Sauvignon, Sémillon, Chenin Blanc, Cabernet Franc, Merlot, Pinot Noir, Syrah and Sangiovese all have their counterparts in other continents. In addition, there are the occasional individual grape varieties of the New World, such as California's Zinfandel and South Africa's Pinotage.

Soil and climate

Soil and climate explain, in part, why two wines from the same grape variety, grown in different parts of the world, can taste quite diverse, without any apparent similarity of flavour. Chardonnay is an obvious example, as the world's most fashionable and popular white grape. The soil components of chalk, limestone or clay may affect the flavour. In a cool climate, where the grapes find it hard to ripen, the wine will be lean with firm acidity – compared to a wine born in a hot sunny climate, where a lack of acidity in the grapes may present a problem and the wine will taste ripe and buttery. Winemakers in the New World are more cavalier in their attitude towards what the French call *terroir* – the all-encompassing term for the combination of soil and microclimate of a vineyard, as well as other factors such as aspect and altitude – and think nothing of trucking grapes for hundreds of miles to blend with other grapes grown elsewhere.

On the northern edge (in the northern hemisphere) of the band where grape growing is feasible, the annual differences in climate account for vintage variations, with rain, frost, hail, drought, sunshine – at the right or wrong time – making a wine great or merely indifferent. The permutations in climate are much less pronounced the further south you go, until you reach southern Italy and southern Spain where unlimited sunshine and unfailingly ripe grapes are assured. However, in Europe's most northern vineyards the annual differences in weather can be quite significant, and can vary quite dramatically from one region to another within the same country. For example, a great claret year does not necessarily mean a good burgundy vintage. The climatic conditions of the two regions can be quite different, for one enjoys a continental climate and the other is determined by the maritime influence of the Atlantic Ocean. The contrast between two consecutive years can be equally marked: 1990 in Bordeaux may be one of the contenders for 'the vintage of the century', while 1991 was affected by spring frosts and then by rain at the harvest, producing merely average wines.

The winemaker

Finally, the winemakers play their part. It is their decision when to pick the grapes, how to vinify them and when to bottle the wine. Tradition and experience dictate some of the choices, but experimental curiosity also features, especially in the vineyards of the New World, or in regions that are undergoing dramatic transformation, such as Tuscany or the Midi. The use of oak, of which more later, is the most obvious way in which the winemaker can directly influence the taste of the wine, but there are numerous other possible nuances of technique, all of which contribute something to the final result – the bottle on your dining-table, and the wine in your glass.

A man cannot make him laugh; but that's no marvel; he drinks no wine.

Shakespeare, *Henry IV (Part II)*

THE BASIC COMPONENTS

The basic components of taste have determined the shape of the taste wheels. For white wine, the first consideration is sweetness, or otherwise, so the initial division is between dry, medium and sweet. Body, or weight, which originates not only from sugar, but also from alcohol, must then be taken into account. A dry white wine with a high alcohol content will taste full-bodied, while a crisp wine with little alcohol will seem quite light and ethereal. There is the same difference in red wines, too, with a mouth-filling Châteauneuf-du-Pape from a warm climate contrasting with a light-bodied Pinot Noir from a much cooler region. Red wines may also have more or less weight, depending on how long the juice has spent in contact with the grape skins during fermentation: a long period of skin contact will give a wine more extract and substance than one which has spent only three or four days on the skins. Most sweet wines seem positively mouth-filling because of the high sugar content.

Acidity

Acidity is an essential ingredient in all wines, although it is most apparent to the tastebuds in light, dry, crisp whites and rosés. However, even red and richly sweet wines still need a quota of acidity, or they will taste flabby and lifeless. Acidity is mainly a function of climate: the warmer the climate, the riper the grapes, the more sugar and less acidity; conversely, the cooler the climate, the harder it is for grapes to ripen, so they are picked with higher levels of acidity which transfer to the wine. With modern vinification techniques it is possible to remove acidity from a wine, or add it, but this can sometimes be detected in the mouth as an unbalanced citric taste.

Oak

Oak is another key taste in both red and white wine. Ideally, a wine should not taste obviously of oak. It should be used in the same way that garlic is used in cooking: the taste should be well-integrated and harmonious, without dominating or overwhelming the fruit. However, without it, the wine would be that much poorer and would lack complexity or dimension. Small oak barrels have been used in parts of France for winemaking for centuries; after all, they were all that was available for storing wine before the advent of concrete and, subsequently, stainless steel. Now winemakers have a choice and many are abandoning their concrete tanks and stainless steel vats and returning to the oak barrels of their grandfathers. They are mastering the techniques required of new oak barrels; a fundamental difference is that nowadays barrels tend to be renewed at least every three or four years, whereas their grandparents continued to use the same barrels for ten, or even twenty, years.

The taste of oak from a new barrel can drown, rather than enhance, the intrinsic fruit flavour of wine and can produce what some call an infusion of oak chippings. With older barrels the effect diminishes significantly. A wine, therefore, needs to have sufficient body and structure in its own right in order to absorb the effect of the oak, without detriment to the flavour. Compare a fine white burgundy vinified in oak with a Muscadet fermented in oak. With the Muscadet there is the proverbial tisane of oak chippings, for there is insufficient structure in the wine to cope with the oak, while the burgundy takes on even greater stature and finesse. Having said that, the effect of the oak on the flavour of the wine also varies in relation to the age of the wine. A young burgundy that has just been bottled, after spending a few months in new oak, will taste ripe and buttery. It will not only have some youthful fruit, but also the vanilla flavours of the new oak, although these flavours will not yet have come together. As the wine matures it loses its youthful characteristics, and enters a rather awkward phase, when the oak overwhelms the fruit. And then, when the wine is two or three years old, it begins to take on more mature flavours, with a harmonious balance between the oak and the fruit.

Winemakers in California, Australia and elsewhere in the world, who aspire to emulate the finesse of Meursault or Puligny-Montrachet, are aware of the importance of oak barrels. They appreciate the qualities and effects of different barrels, whether they are heavily charred or only lightly so, whether they come from the Allier or the Vosges or one of the other oak forests of central France and, perhaps most important of all, who the cooper is. They have also come to realise that the flavours originating from the barrel are very much better integrated into the wine if the wine is not only aged, but also fermented, in oak. It seems that a wine put into wood for a few months will result, more often than not, in two distinct layers of flavour, oak and fruit.

Similarly, with all the great red wines, oak maturation is a vital part of the production process. While white wine can sometimes be fermented in small oak barrels, red wine is only ever matured in them, although some traditional estates may still ferment their wine in large open-topped wooden vats. However, that has little bearing on the final taste in the glass. It is the maturation in oak that is important in contributing to the ultimate quality and flavour of a red wine. Maturation in oak allows the wine to absorb some extra tannin from the wood; it also allows for a period of gentle oxidation, or rather oxygenation, which may soften the youthful tannins in a new wine. Depending on the style of the wine and the producer's aims, this period of maturation may be only a few months, or a couple of years, or even longer. While small barrels are usual in the classic regions of France, such as Bordeaux, Burgundy and the Rhône Valley, Italy has traditionally favoured large barrels, or *botti*. These have little effect in adding tannin to a wine, but provide a useful vessel for a period of gentle maturation, with some subtle oxygenation. Traditionally, Italian red wines, such as Barolo or Brunello di Montalcino, have been kept in wood for longer periods than the red wines of France.

The taste of oak in red wine is most obvious in a young wine. An immature classed-growth claret, which has only been in bottle for a few months, is likely to have the spicy vanilla flavours of new oak, combined with a powerful impact of tannin. The oak will fade as the wine matures but will have added structure and tannin rather than actual flavour. The taste of oak is also very apparent in and is essential to Rioja. Its characteristic vanilla flavour originates from American oak, traditionally used in Spain.

Age

Age is another factor which, to a certain extent, is linked with the use of oak. A very high proportion of the dry white wines available on our wine merchants' shelves are destined for consumption within a year or two of the vintage. Oak has not played a part in their vinification process and there is no virtue in laying them down as they will not improve with age. However, fuller-bodied wines, which have probably spent a little time in oak, do last longer. They have more body, originating partly from the oak, and are intended to develop with age. The prime example is, of course, white burgundy, but most Chardonnays from elsewhere in the world also benefit from a little bit of bottle age. However, their ageing ability is also determined by the amount of acidity in the wine, for acidity is one of the factors that helps a wine to retain its youth.

With red wines too, it is those most suitable for ageing that are matured in oak before bottling. Young, fruity red wines, of which Beaujolais is the most typical example, are bottled a few months after the vintage for drinking in relative youth. Wines with structure and tannin are matured in oak in order to soften the harsh, aggressive flavours of the young wine. Once bottled, they may then need several years of ageing before becoming really enjoyable. The best classed-growth clarets should age for twenty years at least, as should great Rhônes, while burgundy is a little lighter in body and not blessed with quite the same longevity.

Tannin

It is tannin that features largely in red wines, but hardly at all in white wines, and is what determines, above all, their lifespan. Tannin originates naturally from the grape skins, pips, and perhaps stalks, as well as from contact with new oak barrels, and is what gives a red wine its backbone and enables it to develop with age. However, tannin must always be balanced with sufficient fruit, for a wine with high tannin and no fruit will taste dry and puckering, while a wine with neither tannin nor acidity will seem dull and lifeless. Tannin fades with age, but enough fruit must always remain. Some wines with a tannic flavour are not worth ageing, as the austerity of the tannin is part of their character and nothing will be gained from further bottle age. Others, with a relatively high tannin content – in fact, virtually all fine red wines – benefit enormously from ageing, first in barrel in the winemaker's cellar and then in bottle, hopefully in the consumer's cellar.

A large amount of tannin is not always desirable in a young red wine. To avoid this, a vinification process has been developed, particularly designed for wines intended for early consumption, which aims to extract colour, fruit and flavour from the grapes, but not tannin. This is called carbonic maceration. Whole bunches of grapes, which have not been destalked or crushed, are put into a vat that is already filled with carbon dioxide. Some juice is released by the weight of the grapes, which begin fermenting, releasing more carbon dioxide and, at the same time, fermentation starts inside the grapes themselves. After a few days, the grapes are pressed and, whereas in most vinification it is the free-run juice that is best of all, with carbonic maceration the pressed juice is prized. In Beaujolais, they have adopted a variation of this technique called semi-carbonic maceration, where no additional carbon dioxide is added to the vat. Carbonic maceration is used particularly in the south of France to soften the flavours of the rugged Carignan. In the traditional regions of France, vinification methods are classic, with the colour, fruit and tannin coming from a period of contact between the juice and the grape skins, which may only be a few days or as much as three weeks.

Sweetness

Sweetness in wine comes about in various ways. The best sweet wines are the result of grapes affected by noble rot or *Botrytis cinerea*, which is a type of fungus which attacks the ripening grapes in the early autumn just before the vintage, causing them to dehydrate, shrivel up and become raisin-like, with an immense concentration of juice and flavour. The margin between noble and grey rot is very slender and it is all too easy for grey rot to develop rather than noble rot. Noble rot requires very special climatic conditions, ideally damp misty mornings, which must be followed by warm, sunny afternoons, to dry the grapes. Sauternes is the epitome of sweet wine made in this way. The great sweet wines of Germany and the Loire Valley also depend upon the presence of noble rot, while an increasing number of New World vineyards are producing botrytis-affected wines. Noble rot gives a wine an inimitable taste, a slightly roasted, distinctive burnt taste, which the French call a *goût de rôti*, and which ensures that the wine is sweet, but never cloying.

However, if you have very ripe grapes but no botrytis, it is still perfectly possible to make delicious sweet wine. Fermenting yeasts die when a certain level of alcohol is reached. In the case of very ripe grapes, this may happen naturally while some sugar remains in the wine or, with the increasing improvements in modern wine technology, it is feasible to stop the fermentation by chilling and filtering, in order to obtain a wine with the desired balance between alcohol and sweetness. This is often done in vineyards where botrytis is desired, but where the climate is less kind. Some medium-sweet wines are also made in this way, so that some grape sugar is retained in the wine. Alternatively, especially in Germany, they use what is called *Süssreserve*, or sweet reserve – unfermented, and therefore sweet, grape juice – which is added to the finished wine, to provide additional sweetness and richness.

The final option is to dry the grapes, either while they are still on the vines, or after they have been picked. The first procedure is favoured in Jurançon, where it is called *passerillage*. There is little or no botrytis here, for the climate of the Pyrenees is too dry. Alternatively, for vin de paille or Recioto di Soave and other traditional Italian *passiti* wines, the grapes are dried after they have been picked. Once, this was done on straw, hence the origin of the name, but it is now more usual to hang up the grapes so that they are better ventilated. The juice concentrates and the grapes become sweet and raisin-like before they are pressed, a month or two after the harvest.

THE TASTE

It must also be remembered that the taste of any wine is ultimately determined by the food with which you drink it. A simple experiment illustrates this vividly. Take a lightly tannic red wine, such as a young Bordeaux Rouge. Taste it and then take a bite of apple or carrot. Taste it again and the apple will have emphasised all the tannin and astringency in the wine. Now take a mouthful of a hard cheese, like Cheddar or Caerphilly, and taste the wine again. It will seem quite different now, for the cheese will have softened all of the rough edges in the wine and brought out all of the fruit, almost to the extent that it is hard to believe that it is one and the same wine.

This introduction has concentrated on table wines and, while some of the same factors apply to fortified and sparkling wines, the specific details are considered in the introduction to their respective wheels. With all three wheels, we hope to offer some guidance through the maze of different labels that abound on our wine merchants' shelves, thereby encouraging experimentation and enhancing your drinking enjoyment. The merchants' directory which follows will help you to decide what to buy and where.

DRY WHITE WINES

Vin Jaune and Retsina

Body	Oak	Acidity	Character	Wines
Light Body	No oak	High acidity	Crisp and fragrant	Muscadet, Côtes de Gascogne, Aligoté, Savoie, French and New World Sauvignon, Alsace Riesling, German trocken, Franconia, Austria, Vinho Verde, Galicia, Arneis, England and Wales
Light Body	No oak	High acidity	Dry and leafy	Chablis, Mâcon, Haut Poitou, Alsace Pinot Blanc and Sylvaner, Baden, German halbtrocken, Pinot Bianco and Pinot Grigio, Jurançon, Gaillac, the Loire Valley, New Zealand and Eastern Europe
Medium Body	No oak	Low acidity	Soft and grassy	Provence and the Midi, Orvieto, Verdicchio, Frascati, Galestro, Soave, Sicily and Sardinia, Rioja and Rueda, Dão, Greece, Cyprus and the New World
Medium Body	Oak	High acidity	Light and buttery	Chablis and other burgundies, New Zealand Chardonnay and Sauvignon, Australian Semillon, Graves
Full Body	Oak	Low acidity	Dry and nutty	Hermitage, Châteauneuf-du-Pape, Argentinian and Bulgarian Chardonnay, Chilean and South African Sauvignon
Full Body	Oak	High acidity	Firm and toasted	Grand cru Chablis, Puligny-Montrachet and other wines from the Côte d'Or, the New World Chardonnay
Full Body	Oak	Low acidity	Rich and buttery	North American Chardonnay, California, Fumé Blanc, Australian, South Chilean, Italian African Spanish and Chardonnay, Rioja

CRISP AND FRAGRANT (LIGHT BODY, NO OAK, HIGH ACIDITY)

Muscadet

Muscadet is the starting point for this segment of the wheel. Good Muscadet is firmly dry, with lean steely acidity, stony fruit and a lively freshness. It is light in body and, indeed, is one of the rare appellations of France to have a maximum, rather than a minimum, alcohol level – 12.3 per cent – set down in its regulations. Muscadet comes from the Atlantic end of the Loire Valley from a grape variety called Muscadet (or Melon de Bourgogne, although it has virtually disappeared from Burgundy). The area is divided into three appellations, of which **Muscadet-de-Sèvre-et-Maine** is the biggest and the best. The words *sur lie* on the label indicate that the wine has been bottled off the fine lees or sediment of the fermentation, so that the merest prickle of carbon dioxide remains in the wine, providing extra freshness and zest.

The vineyards of Muscadet suffered dreadfully in the severe spring frosts of 1991, with the result that the vintage was tiny, only a third of the normal crop. Contrary to what might have been expected, the frost damage did not have any significant impact on prices, as they had already risen with the 1990 vintage, causing a certain disenchantment with Muscadet and an appropriate drop in sales. There were no spring frosts in 1992, resulting in a generous crop, which will help the market re-establish its balance. The wines are fruity and aromatic, combining the freshness of the 1991s with the weight of the 1989s.

Good producers include Sauvion at Château de Cléray (also with its Lauréat label), Château de Chasseloir, Chereau-Carré, Marquis de Goulaine, Métaireau, Domaine des Dorices, Château la Touche, Guy Brossard, Château la Noë and Donatien-Bahuaud.

The nearby VDQS of **Gros Plant du Pays Nantais** produces wines even greener and more acidic than Muscadet.

Côtes de Gascogne

Vin de pays des Côtes de Gascogne has some characteristics in common with Muscadet: it too is light, crisp and fragrant, with a slightly smoky, stony flavour. This is a wine born of the dramatic decline in sales of armagnac, made from grape varieties like Colombard, Folle Blanche and Ugni Blanc. It does not have terrific depth of taste but, at the right price, provides good everyday drinking. There has also been a little experimentation with Gros Manseng and oak-ageing for extra flavour.

Drink the youngest vintage available. Unfortunately, the 1991 crop suffered from bad spring frosts, but things were better with the 1992 vintage. Hugh Ryman has made his mark here with numerous examples of Côtes de Gascogne: Domaine de Lian, Domaine du Biau, Domaine le Puts and Domaine Bordes, all of which are available in various supermarkets and high street shops. Other good estates include those of the pioneering Grassa family: Domaine du Tariquet, Domaine de Rieux, Domaine de la Jalousie and Domaine de Plantérieu. Domaine de San Guilhem is also good.

Bourgogne Aligoté

The appellation **Bourgogne Aligoté**, made from the Aligoté grape, fits into this section by virtue of the firm, stony acidity and crisp, dry flavour of the wine. Aligoté is often decried, but the problem is that it is usually planted in relatively unfavourable sites, resulting inevitably in less successful wine. The main exception to this is the appellation of **Bourgogne Aligoté de Bouzeron**, from the village in the Côte Chalonnaise that has made something of a speciality of Aligoté. Drink the youngest available, from Domaine Thévenot le Brun, de Villaine, Pierre Cogny and also Daniel Rion from Nuits-St-Georges.

Vin de Savoie

Vin de Savoie has a total of sixteen crus, scattered around the towns of Chambéry, Aix-les-Bains and Annecy. Most of them have little commercial significance outside of the holiday resorts of the French Alps, but the occasional one, such as Abymes or Apremont (for example, Domaine de Rocailles), makes an appearance on UK wine merchants' shelves. The main grape variety of the vineyards close to Chambéry is the little-known Jacquère, which makes some light, dry, rather stony, ethereal white wine, that is low in alcohol, with some firm acidity. Like most of the wines in this segment, there is nothing to be gained from extra maturity, so drink the youngest available. Alternatively, you may occasionally find the slightly fuller **Roussette de Savoie**, which can include a percentage of Chardonnay, or the appellation **Crépy**, with wines made from the Chasselas grape. The latter has more in common with the Swiss wines from the opposite shore of Lac Léman – it is made from the same grape variety, but like them, rarely travels.

French Sauvignon Blanc

And now back to western France, to the basic appellations of
Bordeaux Blanc and **Entre-Deux-Mers**. Both are areas where
vinification techniques have improved enormously in recent
years, making them a much more appealing choice. Once they
were oversulphured and often uncertain whether they were trying
to be vaguely sweet or indecisively dry. Now Bordeaux Blanc and
Entre-Deux-Mers are clean and fresh, positively dry, with some
vibrant fruit. Sauvignon may well be the dominant grape variety,
but sometimes some Sémillon is included to round out the wine a
little. Oak-ageing is less likely for these humble appellations,
although there are exceptions further round the wheel.

Any dry wine produced in the Sauternais or any white wine
from the Médoc is entitled only to the appellation Bordeaux Blanc,
but if it comes from a leading estate it will be treated accordingly.
There is a world of difference between Y, the dry wine of Château
d'Yquem, and Château Thieuley, for example, not only in price
but also in flavour. Generally, Bordeaux Blanc or Entre-Deux-
Mers – sometimes sold as merchants' blends, such as Sirius from
Peter Sichel or Maître d'Estournel – are intended for early
consumption. The 1991 was badly affected by spring frosts and
1992 by rain at the vintage. However, some good wine has been
made and there are still wines from the 1990 vintage around. Other
good estates include Château Ducla, Château de Sours and Moulin
de Launay.

The white wines of the South-West are based mostly on
Sauvignon and Sémillon, which means that the white versions of
appellations like **Bergerac**, **Côtes de Duras**, **Buzet** and **Côtes du
Marmandais** are very similar in taste, and again have benefited
from general improvements in vinification techniques. Buzet and
Marmandais are dominated by regional co-operatives, while
Hugh Ryman has made his mark on the Côtes de Duras, with
Domaine de Colombet and Domaine de Malardeau. For Bergerac,
look for recommended producers under red wine.

Other Sauvignons from France fit into this segment. The
obvious example is **Sancerre**, as well as the adjoining white
appellations of that part of the Loire Valley – Pouilly Fumé,
Menetou-Salon, Reuilly and Quincy. Sancerre represents the
Sauvignon grape at its most elegant and subtle, if indeed
Sauvignon can ever be described as subtle. More often than not
the pungent, somewhat brash flavours, reminiscent of
gooseberries – perhaps with feline overtones – can intrude.
However, good Sancerre, which is usually lighter in body than any

Bordelais counterparts, is refreshing and delicate with a stony flintiness. Inevitably, it is expensive, a phenomenon accentuated by the spring frost of 1991. There is little virtue in ageing it, so drink the youngest available, from producers like Vacheron, Gitton, Natter, Vatan, Bailly-Reverdy, Crochet, Cotat, Dézat and Thomas.

Pouilly Fumé is very similar to Sancerre in taste; some find the two virtually indistinguishable. Like Sancerre, Pouilly Fumé is best drunk in relative youth, from a vintage that was not too sun-soaked, otherwise the wine tends to be a little flabby, as in 1989. However, the star producer, Patrick de Ladoucette at Château du Nozet, argues the case for maturing Pouilly Fumé. His wines are generally considered the best of the appellation, but also the most expensive, especially his Baron de L. Also good, but more accessible in price, are Château de Tracey, Didier Dagueneau, Michel Redde, Jean-Claude Guyot and Guy Saget.

Menetou-Salon has been enjoying a revival in its fortunes and currently offers better-value drinking than either of its two more prestigious neighbours. The flavour is slightly less subtle, but none the worse for that. Henri Pellé and Jean Teiller are the best producers. **Reuilly** and **Quincy** are harder to find; virtually the sole representatives of the two appellations, Gérard Cordier and Denis Jaumier, feature on the list of the specialist Loire merchant, Yapp Bros.

Other comparable Sauvignons from France include **Sauvignon de Touraine**, which has some refreshingly pithy fruit. The successful co-operative of Oisly-et-Thésée is a key producer. **Sauvignon du Haut Poitou** is a touch fuller, with the regional co-operative the sole producer, while close to Chablis, the village of St-Bris-le-Vineux has a reputation for **Sauvignon de St-Bris**. Robert Defrance and Jean-Marc Brocard are good producers. All of these offer a price advantage over Sancerre and Pouilly Fumé, but do not have the same finesse.

New Zealand Sauvignon Blanc

New Zealand Sauvignon crosses the taste wheel, depending on its method of vinification – whether it has been fermented and/or aged in oak, or whether it is made in pristine stainless steel tanks. The most characteristic New Zealand Sauvignon, the wine that really brought the wines of the Antipodes to our notice, is Montana Marlborough Sauvignon. The first commercial vintage of this wine was as recent as 1980 and it quickly established a reputation for deliciously pungent, freshly vibrant Sauvignon fruit, with crisp acidity. It is eminently easy to drink, and inexpensive at around £5 a bottle. If there is a criticism to be made, the wine is perhaps a little one-dimensional, but that does not matter. Marlborough is on New Zealand's South Island and has established itself as the leading region for Sauvignon, to the extent that many of the wineries based outside Auckland either have vineyards in, or buy fruit from, Marlborough. The grapes are then either trucked to the North Island or, in a more recent development, vinified according to specifications in Marlborough by an independent winemaker.

The other key New Zealand Sauvignon is Cloudy Bay, which fits into a later taste segment, and which has partial barrel fermentation. Non-oaked New Zealand Sauvignons from Marlborough include Hunters, Matua Valley, Nobilo, Selaks, Stoneleigh, Vavasour, Jackson and Wairau River. The wines from the warmer North Island tend to be a little fuller and riper and, therefore, come into the next segment of the wheel.

Alsace Riesling

It may seem illogical to follow Sauvignon with Riesling, but there is a similarity in the fruit and balance of acidity in the two wines, making it possible to confuse the two when very young. **Riesling d'Alsace** is generally considered to be the finest, most subtle and most elegant of all the Alsace grape varieties, especially if it comes from a grand cru vineyard and a talented grower. Except in the case of Vendange Tardive and Sélection de Grains Nobles wines, Alsace Riesling is firmly dry, almost to the point of being lean and steely. Compared with German Riesling, it is much higher in alcohol as it is fermented until completely dry. Thus, it has more body and a steeliness which develops with bottle age. Wines from grand cru sites should also be a little more concentrated in flavour than a simple Vin d'Alsace.

Style varies from grower to grower; some, like Trimbach and Léon Beyer, make wines that are lean and understated, while those from Hugel are a little softer and more flowery. Riesling d'Alsace from a good vintage, such as 1990, 1989 and 1988, will age beautifully, developing slaty kerosene flavours, with considerable complexity.

Recommended producers include Trimbach (especially with Clos Ste-Hune and Cuvée Frédéric Emile), Hugel, Domaine Weinbach, Jos Meyer, Zind-Humbrecht, Domaine Ostertag, Marc Kreydenweiss, Schlumberger, Marcel Deiss, Rolly Gassmann, Léon Beyer and Kuentz-Bas.

Trocken wines from Germany

Trocken represents a broad generalisation of a relatively new and growing trend in German winemaking, and simply means dry. Some German producers have felt seriously disadvantaged by the underlying implication of sweetness in German wine, which they consider makes their wines unsuitable for drinking with food. They therefore ferment their wines until completely dry, leaving no residual sugar and ignoring the possibility of using *Süssreserve*. But, unless the grapes are fairly ripe in the first place, the result can be a rather unbalanced wine, with high acidity, low alcohol and very little body – in other words, a wine that is hollow and skeletal and decidedly unappealing compared to riper Spätlese and Auslese. However, with greater experience and expertise, some producers are making some successful trocken wines, especially those from the more southern vineyards of Germany, such as the Rheinpfalz, Rheinhessen and Baden. There the climate is warmer, the grapes are consequently riper, and the wines easily meet the criteria for Kabinett, Spätlese and even Auslese. They are better balanced, with more body, which could nudge them into the next segment of the wheel.

The taste of a trocken wine depends upon the grape variety. Usually it is firmly dry, quite light in body, slightly steely, with some austere, stony fruit. Recommended producers include Lingenfelder, Schloss Vollrads, Schloss Reinhartshausen, Schlossgut Diel, Georg Breuer and Karl Heinz Johner. These wines do not represent particularly good value. After all, there are so many other fine, dry white wines made all over the world that Germany would do better to maintain its originality by continuing with the elegantly honeyed Auslese and Spätlese that it makes so well, and which are not available elsewhere.

Franconia

The wines of **Franconia**, from vineyards in Northern Bavaria, around the town of Würzburg, fit into this segment. Traditionally, they have always been firmly dry, with some flinty fruit and they have never related quality to sweetness, as they do in the Mosel and the Rhine. Unusually, Müller-Thurgau and Silvaner, rather than Riesling, are the principal grape varieties. Franconian wines are always presented in the traditional dumpy flagons, called *bocksbeutel*, and are often referred to as Steinwein, after the most famous vineyard, Würzburger Stein. They are rarely available here, as they tend to be uncompetitive in price. The best producers are the Burgerspital, Juliusspital, Fürstlich Castell'sches Domanenamt and Weingut Hans Wirsching.

Austria

The most characteristic grape of Austria, Grüner Veltliner, fits into this category in its dry form. It crosses the border into Hungary and Czechoslovakia, but is grown nowhere else. In more commercial blends the wine sometimes has a trace of residual sugar, but it is usually firmly dry, with some fresh stony acidity and slightly smoky, slightly grassy fruit. It is usually light in body and is best drunk within a couple of years of the vintage. Occasionally, you may find it as a Spätlese, in which case it takes on a honeyed note, with some apricot fruit, but always has a dry finish. Recommended producers include Lenz Moser, Fritz Salomon and some of the supermarket own-label wines.

Vinho Verde and Bairrada

Vinho Verde, the green wine of Portugal, can be either white or red. In this instance, 'verde' means young (vinho maduro is mature wine). Although more red than white Vinho Verde is produced, it is the white that is exported. Good Vinho Verde is a crisp, dry white wine, although sometimes commercial blends have the sharp acidic edge of youth taken off them, so that they can taste very slightly sweet and rather soft.

The real thing has a crisp, pithy, lemony, stony acidity, sometimes with a hint of apples or apricots on the nose. It is very light in alcohol and can have a trace of carbon dioxide, to provide extra freshness and liveliness. In wines made from Alvarinho, the best grape variety for Vinho Verde, the apricot character is emphasised and they bear a resemblance to the wines of Galicia, just across the border in Spain.

Vinho Verde must be drunk as young and fresh as possible. For added interest, choose a single quinta or an estate wine, rather than a commercial brand, such as Solar das Bouças, Palacio da Brejoeira and Quinta da Aveleda, rather than plain Aveleda.

White **Bairrada** deserves a passing mention here. Although from slightly further south, it is still rather crisp and lemony in flavour, but perhaps slightly fuller than Vinho Verde. Most white Bairrada is sold under a supermarket own-label.

Spain

Rias Baixas, just across the border from Vinho Verde, is one of the four DOs of Galicia, in north-west Spain. Until a couple of years ago, these wines rarely travelled much outside their region, but they have recently begun to reach our wine shops. Albariño, with its slightly peachy character, is the grape which makes the best wines. They are light, fresh and delicate, low in alcohol with a gentle, refreshing, slightly peachy fragrance. Lagar de Cervera, Martin Codax and Bodegas Morgadio are the most widely exported.

The adjoining DO of **Ribeiro** includes red as well as white wines, but again it is the white wines that provide the more interesting and distinctive flavours, with Loureiro and Treixadura the main grape varieties. These wines have the same light body as Rias Baixas, but are perhaps more firmly dry, with a stonier flavour and finish. Unfortunately, most of the white wines of Galicia tend to be expensive compared with other Spanish whites, because they are sought after and can command high prices in Spain, so there is little need to export.

Viña Sol is taken as an example of the dry white wines of **Penedès**, as produced by Miguel Torres. This is characteristic of the improvement in winemaking that Torres has engineered, planting the native grape varieties of Penedès in the cooler, higher altitude vineyards of the region. Parellada is the main variety of Viña Sol, which lacks a distinctive flavour. The charm of Viña Sol lies in its dry, freshness and crisp finish, without any intrusive fruit flavour. Generally, it is a wine for drinking as young as possible. Gran Viña Sol and Gran Viña Sol Green Label feature in other segments of the wheel.

Piedmont

Arneis, an obscure Piedmontese grape variety that has been undergoing something of a revival, might also fit into this segment. The flavour is not so dissimilar from Rias Baixas. In the hands of Carlo Deltetto, for example, it has a delicate, lightly peachy flavour, with fresh fruit and a dry finish. Arneis is expensive, as is Favorita, another grape variety with a similar, but drier, flavour that is also enjoying something of a renewal of interest.

England and Wales

English wine is growing in importance as production approaches the 25,000 hectolitre mark, when some system of quality assessment, like the French appellation contrôlée, must be implemented by law. We are not yet there, but with a bumper harvest, unaffected by spring frosts, and with more vineyards coming into production each year, we are not far off. A Quality Wine Pilot Scheme was introduced for the 1992 vintage. This presents one significant problem: some of the best-performing grape varieties in England and Wales, such as Seyval Blanc, Seyve-Villard and Madeleine Angevine, are not considered suitable for quality wine under EC law. Other grape varieties, mainly German crosses like Müller-Thurgau, Reichenstein, Schönburger, Kerner and Huxelrebe, are also grown. Although there are vineyards in all but eight of England's 46 counties, as well as a growing number in South Wales, the main concentration of viticulture lies firmly in the South-West, East Anglia and the Home Counties.

As yet there are few discernable regional differences, but an overall style of fragrant, flowery, slightly spicy, ethereal wines that are light in body and low in alcohol and often high in acidity. If the producer uses Süssreserve in the German manner, the wine will be slightly sweet. There is the occasional wine that has been in oak, and which therefore features in that segment of the wheel, as well as the occasional red or pink wine. Generally, though, English wine is white.

One possible confusion must be clarified. So-called British wine has nothing to do with English or Welsh wine, and hardly merits the name of wine, for it is a manufactured product, originating from reconstituted imported dehydrated grape juice. It should be avoided at all costs by any discerning reader of this Guide.

Wineries whose wines are currently showing well include Adgestone, Three Choirs, Tenterden, Carr Taylor, Staple St James, Biddenden, Elmham Park, Wootton, Pilton Manor, Mumfords, Nutbourne, Chiltern Valley, Barkham Manor, Penshurst, Breaky Bottom, Rock Lodge, Thames Valley, Warden Abbey and a wine simply called English Vineyard, made at High Weald Winery. If in doubt, try your nearest local winery. The English Vineyards Association also awards each year a Seal of Excellence to wines which have attained the required standard: the black and gold seal on the bottle provides another guide to quality.

DRY AND LEAFY (MEDIUM BODY, NO OAK, HIGH ACID)

Chablis

Simple **Chablis** could be seen as the starting point for this section of the wheel – that is the basic village wine, or perhaps a young premier cru wine which has not seen any oak. Young Chablis, coming as it does from the most northern vineyards of Burgundy, should always have a lean streak of acidity, while the Chardonnay grape gives it a certain dry grassy character, with a touch of what the French call *pierre à fusil*, or gunflint. There is a firm stony quality to good Chablis, which will develop a little more complexity with age. However, Chablis does cross the taste wheel, depending on vinification methods and precise provenance, so a grand cru Chablis will have much more concentration than a basic Chablis. In riper vintages, such as 1990 and 1989, Chablis may be slightly lacking in acidity, while 1991 and 1988 have both made wines with a good balance of acidity; of these, 1988 is the better vintage, with more concentration of flavour.

Of the good producers who do not use wood, Louis Michel is generally considered the best. Others include Bernard Légland, Adhémar Boudin, Olivier Savary, Jean-Marc Brocard, Alain Geoffroie, Domaine des Malandes, Jean Durup at Domaine de l'Eglantière and A. Régnard. Daniel Defaix has retained his large oak vats, which have no impact on the taste of the wine.

Mâcon and Haut Poitou

It is very easy to confuse a village Chablis with a **Mâcon Blanc** or **Mâcon-Villages**. The Mâcon should also be light and grassy, with the flavour of Chardonnay, usually vinified without any contact with oak. It should be a little fuller in the mouth, especially if it comes from one of the better villages like Lugny or Viré.

Village co-operatives work well here, for example, Clessé, the aptly named Chardonnay, Lugny, Prissé and Viré; good producers include Jean Thévenet at Domaine de la Bon Gran.

The adjoining appellations of **St-Véran**, **Pouilly-Vinzelles** and the rarely seen **Beaujolais Blanc** are similar in taste, though they may be a little fuller in body, while good Pouilly-Fuissé usually has some contact with oak.

Another comparable, but lighter, Chardonnay is **Chardonnay du Haut Poitou**, which offers good value for money, but lacks some complexity of flavour. Chardonnay from further south tends to fit into lower acidity segments of the wheel.

Alsace Pinot Blanc and Sylvaner

These tend to be considered the work horse grape varieties of **Alsace**. Sylvaner is declining in importance, tending to be replaced by Pinot Blanc, which makes some soft, undemanding, grassy wines. There should be nothing aggressive or hard in the flavour, just some soft fruit, without much depth. Sylvaner, too, is lightly grassy, with even less depth of flavour.

Pinot Blanc is usually drunk as an aperitif in Alsace. The occasional producer, such as Jean Meyer, gives it more serious attention, making wine from older vines on a grand cru site.

Others may age it in oak, but that is very much the exception to the rule. Drink the youngest available, from producers like Jos Meyer, Hugel, Trimbach and the Cave Vinicole de Turckheim.

Baden

In **Baden**, Pinot Blanc is called Weissburgunder and features significantly in the vineyards of Germany's most southerly wine region, along with Müller-Thurgau, and some Riesling, Silvaner, Gewürztraminer and Ruländer (the German synonym for Pinot Gris). Most examples of wine from Baden which reach our wine merchants' shelves are simply labelled Baden, without any further indication of provenance, although there are some noted vineyard sites, such as Ortenau, Kaiserstuhl and Markgärflerland. The region is dominated by growers' co-operatives, which in turn belong to an enormous central co-operative, the ZBW or Zentralkellerei Badischer Winzergenossenschaft.

Most Baden wine is dry or trocken, without any of the residual sweetness of the wines of northern Germany. A typical Baden Dry has a soft grassy flavour, or it may be drier and stonier, perhaps with a little spice, depending on the dominant grape variety. The wines tend to be fuller in body than those from further north, for Baden is significantly warmer than the Rhine or Mosel. They have more alcohol and are not so different from those of Alsace, its French neighbour across the Rhine.

German halbtrocken

Some of the **halbtrocken** wines of Germany could also fit into this segment of the wheel. Halbtrocken, or half-dry, wines are not as searingly acidic as some trocken wines, retaining a tiny amount of sweetness to soften the sharp edges of acidity. They are usually quite soft and fruity, with some underlying acidity and perhaps a hint of honey, and are fairly light in body and alcohol. The precise flavour depends upon the grape variety and Riesling gives the most elegant, steely flavour. Good producers include those who specialise in trocken wines, such as Lingenfelder, Bürklin-Wolf, Bassermann-Jordan, Schloss Reinhartshausen, Balthasar Ress and Schloss Vollrads.

Pinot Bianco and Pinot Grigio

Pinot Bianco and Pinot Grigio are the two most characteristic grape varieties of north-east Italy and are widely grown in the vineyards of the Alto Adige, Trentino and Friuli. There has been a certain amount of confusion between Chardonnay and Pinot

Bianco in north-east Italy, but this is the one region where Pinot Bianco takes precedence over Chardonnay, the more fashionable variety. You can find Pinot Bianco from the **Alto Adige** where, thanks to the historical accidents of boundaries and language, it is also called Südtiroler Weissburgunder, and also in the DOCs of **Trentino**, **Collio**, **Colli Orientali** and **Grave del Friuli**. The flavour is not unlike a Chardonnay, with a gentle buttery taste, light and creamy, with firm acidity, originating from a relatively cool climate. However, it does not have the potential weight of good Chardonnay and therefore is rarely, if ever, put into oak.

Good producers include the Abbazia di Rosazzo, Volpe Pasini and Ronco del Gnemiz in Friuli; Tiefenbrunner, Lageder, Hofstätter and Giorgio Grai in the Alto Adige; and Jermann and Pojer e Sandri in Trentino.

Pinot Grigio from northern Italy has much less character than Pinot Gris in Alsace. It tends to be somewhat nondescript, quite light with some fruit and acidity, and perhaps a hint of varietal spice. However, in Italy itself it is rated more highly than Pinot Bianco and there are the occasional producers who manage to extract a little extra flavour, such as Marco Schiopetto, Jermann and Lageder. Like Pinot Bianco, it grows extensively in **Trentino**, **Friuli** and the **Alto Adige**, while the DOCs of **Collio** and **Colli Orientali** make some of the more characterful wines.

Another grape variety also grown extensively in north-east Italy is Tocai Friulano, also called Tocai Italico in the **Veneto**. Despite the similarity to the Alsace synonym for Pinot Gris (Tokay Pinot Gris), these two varieties are not related. However, the flavour is not dissimilar – fairly dry and neutral.

More flavour comes from the occasional example of Sauvignon which does feature in the various DOCs of north-east Italy, especially in **Collio** and **Colli Orientali**. Puiatti in Collio makes one of the best, with some pithy pungent fruit.

Jurançon and the Pyrenees

Now we go back to France, to **Jurançon**, the white wine of the Pyrenees, which can be either dry (sec) or sweet (moelleux). The moelleux version features further round the wheel. Dry Jurançon is made from the little-known Gros Manseng and Petit Manseng grapes, which provide some dry, pithy fruit, reminiscent of grapefruit, and which give it a mouth-filling flavour and some firm acidity on the finish. The best producer is Domaine Cauhapé; Château de Jolys and Clos Uroulat are good too.

Other wines of the South-West fit into this segment, with their combination of firm acidity and medium body. There is the nearby **Côtes de St-Mont**, where the regional co-operative has worked hard to put this little-known VDQS on the wine map of France. **Tursan** is another relatively obscure VDQS from the edge of the Landes, where the local co-operative has improved its vinification methods significantly in the last couple of years – making a clean fresh wine, with as much fruit as is possible from the decidedly nondescript Baroque grape. The new wines from Michel Guérard – Château de Bachen and Baron de Bachen – are both vinified in oak.

Gaillac

Gaillac, from vineyards around the town of Albi, is firm and dry, originating from a hotchpotch of different grape varieties, some of which – such as Mauzac and Loin de l'Oeil – are rarely seen outside the region. Others have a more international ring, like Sauvignon, Muscadelle and Sémillon. White Gaillac is usually made from Mauzac and Loin de l'Oeil and may retain a little carbon dioxide from the malolactic fermentation, in which case it is called Gaillac Perlé. The bubbles in the glass should look like tiny pearls, hence the name, and the wine tastes soft and dry, with hints of apples and almonds. Gaillac made with a greater proportion of Sauvignon may have more flavour, but there is no way of discerning this from the label.

The Loire Valley

The various dry white wines of the Loire Valley made from Chenin Blanc tend to have a little more body than those made from Sauvignon and therefore fit more comfortably into this segment than the previous one. **Anjou Blanc** and **Saumur Blanc**, the two basic appellations, are very similar in flavour. And while **Touraine Blanc** can be made from Chenin Blanc, the better wines are made from Sauvignon. Anjou Blanc may be dry or off-dry, with the acidity typical of Chenin Blanc. In ripe years there might be a little honey to provide some body and weight; on the other hand, in cool years, the wine can be exceedingly sour.

The star dry wine of the Loire is **Savennières**, with the smaller appellations of **Coulée de Serrant** and **Roche aux Moines**. These can be very much an acquired taste, wines to admire rather than enthuse over. There is no doubt that this is dry Chenin Blanc at its finest, always with firm acidity, but with a complex leafy flavour which develops more subtlety and depth with age. At a recent vertical tasting of Coulée de Serrant, the 1967 vintage was splendid, with innumerable nuances of flavour and a certain toasted, honeyed quality. The 1988 and 1989 were equally good vintages in the Loire Valley, and there is no reason why they too should not develop in the same way, given patience and time. While Coulée de Serrant and Roche aux Moines are single vineyards; good producers of Savennières include Domaine de la Bizolière, Château de Chamboureau and Domaine du Closel.

The remaining appellations of the Loire made from Chenin Blanc include **Vouvray** and **Montlouis** in their dry versions. Look for the word 'sec' on the label as a clue to flavour. Recommended producers of dry Vouvray include Gaston Huet, Foreau and Prince Poniatowski. Somehow, Vouvray sec just does not have the stature and complexity of the more exciting sweet wines. In **Montlouis**, Berger is the name to go for, whilst in **Touraine Azay-le-Rideau** (a sub-appellation of Touraine), there is one producer of note, Gaston Pavy, with some dry, slightly grassy wines, with that characteristic Chenin Blanc wet dog nose. **Jasnières**, on the Loir, a tributary of the larger river, is another obscurity made from Chenin Blanc, with some potential to develop with age. The Loire specialist, Yapp Bros, is the source of many of these lesser-known Loire wines.

New Zealand

With the exception of some Sauvignon and Riesling, the dry unoaked white wines of New Zealand tend to come into this category. The cooler climate gives higher acidity levels than most of the other New World vineyards, and some Sauvignons – especially those from the North Island – have a little more body than those in the previous segment, and therefore fit into the taste wheel here. Good North Island Sauvignons include Esk Valley, Collards Rothesay Sauvignon, Palliser, Morton Estate and Te Mata Castle Hill.

St Helena makes a delicious Pinot Blanc with some light grassy fruit, not unlike a good Chablis, and Collards is a winery which takes Chenin Blanc seriously – rather than putting it in a winebox. Its wine has some dry honeyed fruit, with balancing acidity.

Eastern Europe

One of the exciting new wines of recent vintages is a Hungarian
Sauvignon, made by a team of Australian winemakers under the
guidance of Hugh Ryman at the Gyöngyös estate. It has some
vibrant juicy Sauvignon fruit, with fresh herbaceous acidity, and
is extremely good value for money.

There are also examples of unoaked Chardonnay from Eastern
Europe. From Bulgaria, the Controliran wines from Varna and
Novi Pazar are made without any contact with oak, so that they are
soft and grassy, with some light fruit. The best Hungarian
Chardonnay is undisputably the Hugh Ryman wine from the
Gyöngyös estate, with its light, buttery fruit. Pinot Blanc from
Moravia is another unusual choice.

SOFT AND GRASSY (MEDIUM BODY, NO OAK, LOW ACIDITY)

The difference between the wines in this segment and those of the
previous segment lies in their acidity level. Most of the wines that
follow come from a warmer climate, resulting in less obtrusive,
lower acidity than in the wines of the previous segment. They may
still be dry, but will lack that firm acidity that can provide
backbone, so they are softer and more rounded in the mouth. Like
many of the white wines on our merchants' shelves, these are all
intended for early consumption, with little potential for ageing.

France

There are numerous appellations in the **Midi** which are better
known for their red wines, but which also make some palatable
white wines. In many instances there has been a significant
improvement in quality in recent years, originating from a better
control of fermentation temperatures and investment in new
equipment. One such wine is Picpoul de Pinet. This is one of the
crus of the **Coteaux du Languedoc**, made, as the name might
imply, from Picpoul grapes in the village of Pinet, where the main
producer is the local co-operative. The wine – marketed by
Chantovent, one of the large merchant houses of the south, under
its Contemporains label – is remarkable for its fruit and flavour.

The main problem with the white wines of the South is the
uninspiring grape varieties that feature in the appellations. Ugni
Blanc is decidedly low in flavour appeal and Macabeo and
Bourboulenc are little better, so it is hardly surprising that the

white versions of wines like **Corbières**, **Côtes du Roussillon** and **Minervois** take second place to the reds. Even **Côtes-du-Rhône Blanc** is fairly limited in appeal. All these wines do is provide some dry refreshing whites that are at their best when well chilled.

Some examples of vins de pays made from grape varieties like Terret Blanc or Grenache Blanc can offer more flavour, while Sauvignon and Chardonnay may be better still. One of the more successful examples of Chardonnay from the Midi comes from the Australian-owned Domaine de la Baume. The merchant company Skalli is also achieving some success with its Fortant de France label. The Burgundy house, Louis Latour, makes an acceptable Chardonnay de l'Ardèche.

A little more flavour comes from **Provence**. Although the best white **Côtes de Provence** is Clos Mireille from Domaines Ott, which fits into the light and buttery section of the wheel, other white Côtes de Provence tend to be dry and fresh, with slight herbal hints, and the **Coteaux d'Aix-en-Provence** might provide a little more interest with wines like Domaine de Terres Blanches. Surprisingly, the appellation of **Cassis** stakes its reputation on white wine. The grape varieties are a blend of the ubiquitous Ugni Blanc, some Clairette and Marsanne (as in the Rhône Valley) for extra flavour, and perhaps a drop of Sauvignon for additional interest. However, it is expensive for what it is – a somewhat old-fashioned white wine, with solid, nutty flavours. It lacks the pithy acidity of modern winemaking techniques, but is none the worse for that in a world of growing Chardonnay-esque uniformity.

More flavoursome is white **Bellet**, a tiny and obscure appellation in the hinterland of the city of Nice. Rolle, the main grape variety, produces a dry, leafy wine with good fruit, but Bellet is expensive. So too is the white version of **Bandol**, which is generally dry and fresh, with some fruit, although again the grape varieties are fairly unexciting.

Across the water on **Corsica**, the main white grape is Vermentino, which may be related to the Rolle, and which makes wines with a nutty, slightly almond flavour. Domaine Peraldi is one of the few imported to Britain.

And Noah he often said to his wife when he sat down to dine, 'I don't care where the water goes if it doesn't get into the wine.'

G K Chesterton, *Water and Wine*

Tuscany

From Corsica, it is but a short hop to Tuscany. In the same way that the white wines of the Midi are dominated by Ugni Blanc, the whites of Tuscany, or for that matter most of Italy, rarely escape from the influence of Trebbiano, Ugni Blanc by another name. In one form or another, this grape variety crops up in wines all the way from Soave in the Veneto down to Alcamo in Sicily. The chief virtue of many Italian whites may be that they lack real positive punchy flavours, and are more subtle and delicate in their appeal. In a recent tasting of a range of white Italians from all over the country, the most forthright wines were those that had been aged in oak; the most typically Italian were good examples of Soave, Verdicchio and Vernaccia di San Gimignano, which were delicate with some subtle fruit, the kind of wines that offer delightfully uncomplicated drinking.

Vernaccia di San Gimignano is the most original wine of Tuscany, made, as its name implies, from Vernaccia, which produces a dry nutty wine, which is occasionally aged in oak, though the oak tends to swamp the elusive and delicate flavour of the grape. Good producers include Montenidoli, Falchini, Teruzzi e Puthod, Pietraserena and Pietrafitta.

A couple of other oases of individuality are to found in Tuscany. There is **Montecarlo**, a little known DOC, which includes such grape varieties as Pinot Grigio, Roussanne and Sauvignon, as well as Trebbiano. And the tiny DOC of **Pomino**, whose production is dominated by the large Chianti house, Frescobaldi, includes Pinot Bianco, Pinot Grigio and Chardonnay to make a wine with more character than is usual in Tuscany.

Otherwise, the indigenous white wines of Tuscany are firmly based on Trebbiano, with a drop of Malvasia. Most grew in importance following the glut of white grapes in central Tuscany when Chianti became a DOCG in 1984 and the percentage of white grapes was drastically reduced. **Galestro**, a relatively new wine created from that surplus, may include grape varieties other than Trebbiano, but it still seems to remain remarkably neutral in flavour – dry, but not acidic, light in alcohol, and best drunk well chilled. Wines like Bianco Val d'Arbia, Bianco Vergine Valdichiana and Bianco della Toscana, are very similar.

There are also numerous experimental wines, sometimes labelled **Predicato del Muschio** for Chardonnay-based wines, and **Predicato del Selvante** for those with a high percentage of Sauvignon. Wines made from Chardonnay, with the rare exceptions of Villa di Capezzana and Terre di Cortona from Avignonesi, generally fit into the oaky section, as do some Sauvignons. However, the best Tuscan Sauvignon, Poggio alle Gazze from the new estate of Ornellaia in Bolgheri, is made without oak.

In Umbria, **Orvieto** offers more flavour. Coming from vineyards around the attractive hilltop town, it is made from a mixture of grapes including Trebbiano, as well as Grechetto and Verdello, which provide a little more character. There is a growing trend for single-vineyard names – which the Italians call crus – which are generally the wines from the best sites that a producer owns, probably given some extra special treatment, with a price to match. Good dry Orvieto is slightly leafy, slightly nutty, with a hint of smokiness and a gentle fragrance. For Orvieto Abboccato see further round the wheel. Good producers include Bigi with its Torricella vineyard, Berberani and Decugnano dei Barbi. Antinori owns the magnificent medieval Castello della Sala, where it makes wines which do not conform to DOC regulations, for example, Cervaro della Sala from Chardonnay and Grechetto.

Nearby is the new DOCG of **Torgiano**, which really owes its existence to one family, Lungarotti, whose white wine, Torre di

Giano, made from a substantial proportion of Grechetto as well as Trebbiano, is quite full-flavoured.

Verdicchio, or to give its full name, **Verdicchio dei Castelli di Jesi**, comes from the hills of the Marche behind the port of Ancona. Verdicchio is also the name of the grape variety unique to this part of Italy. Verdicchio is always firmly dry, but not acidic. Indeed, it can be rather boring, with some fairly neutral flavours. However, along with so many other wine regions of Italy, it has been enjoying a certain revival, with more effort being made to improve vinification methods and extract flavour. There is an increasing emphasis on single-vineyard wines, such as Casal di Serra from Umani Ronchi, Le Moie from Fazi-Battaglia, Colle del Sole and il Pallio from Monte Schiavo. They may be more expensive than simple Verdicchio, but are generally worth the extra price. They usually come in the classic Bordeaux bottle, rather than the fancy amphora shape normally associated with Verdicchio.

Frascati, drunk by the Romans, is slightly fuller and fatter. Again, Trebbiano features in the grape mix, along with Malvasia, which does not contribute much. Frascati can be plain dull, epitomising some of the worst faults of Italian winemaking, but good Frascati can be quite mouth-filling, with a flavour reminiscent of bananas. As elsewhere in Italy, things are looking up and there are some interesting wines to be found. Colli di Catone (with the single vineyard Colle Gaio), Villa Simone and Fontana Candida (with the Santa Teresa vineyard, as well as its vino da tavola, Villa Fontana) are all recommended. The nearby DOC of **Marino** is very similar. As with virtually all white Italians, these are best drunk as young as possible as there is neither enough fruit nor adequate acidity to allow the wines to develop in the bottle.

There are a couple of pure Trebbiano wines which merit a mention for the sake of completeness. Trebbiano is grown extensively in the province of **Emilia-Romagna**, and performs a useful function in producing quantities of innocuously bland white wine which is served up as bianco della casa, or house white, in Italian trattorie all over the world, and which may have a hint of almonds with a trace of acidity and a whiff of fruit. The other white wine of Emilia-Romagna, the DOCG **Albana di Romagna**, rarely travels and certainly does not deserve its elevated status in the Italian wine world.

Trebbiano d'Abruzzo, on the other hand, does have a little more character. Take, for example, the leading producer Valentini, who produces a wine with some intensity and a full earthy flavour which could be described as something of an acquired taste.

Soave

Soave is such a well-known name – forming a trio in the Veneto with Bardolino and Valpolicella – that we may tend to take it for granted. In fact, good Soave has significantly more flavour than many other Italian white wines. Again Trebbiano features, but there is also Garganega for more fruit. Look for **Classico** on the label, which indicates that the wine comes from the heart of the vineyards around the eponymous village. **Superiore** denotes nine months' ageing as well as a minimum alcohol level of 11.5 per cent. However, it is the producer's name that is really the key to quality.

Good Soave has a delicate straw colour, with a subtle grassy nose, and is full and leafy with a slightly nutty finish on the palate. There is some acidity, but it is dry rather than crisp. Wines from named vineyards tend to have a greater concentration of flavour, standing out in a sea of insipid Soave – the result of excessive yields. Good producers include Pieropan and Anselmi, as well as Boscaini, Guerrieri-Rizzardi, Masi, Tedeschi, Zenato and Santi.

There are other northern whites that are not dissimilar, such as Lugana and Bianco di Custoza. Gavi dei Gavi from the Cortese grape is also soft and grassy, but has a reputation and price that are usually unjustified. La Scolca and la Giustiniana are the best producers there.

Sicily and Sardinia

Curiously, for a hot southern island, **Sicily** makes much better white wine than red. There is the DOC of **Bianco d'Alcamo**, where Rapitalà – the best and only producer of note – makes a delicate dry wine from a typically Sicilian grape, Catarratto, blended with a hefty dollop of the ubiquitous Trebbiano. However, most of the better Sicilian wines, red or white, do not fit into the DOC system, so the key to quality is the producer's name, rather than a DOC. The new star estate is Terre di Ginestra, which hit the limelight at the Vinitaly wine fair a couple of years ago and has demonstrated just how good Sicilian whites can be, with the sensible use of modern vinification methods, as well as restrained yields. Terrale is the second wine, a cheaper and slightly diluted version, but still providing agreeable drinking.

The best-known Sicilian wine, both red and white, is Corvo, which is the brand name of the Casa Vinicola Duca di Salaparuta. It gives no more precise a regional definition than Bianco di Sicilia, which indicates simply that grapes can be bought from all over the island. The most recent vintage tastes dry and fresh with a touch of almonds. The better-quality white, Columba Platina, has some light buttery fruit. In contrast, Bianco di Valguarnera tastes like an infusion of oak chippings in a fancy bottle.

Other respectable Sicilian whites include Cellaro, Settesoli, Regaleali and Donnafugata, all from leading estates or co-operatives.

The white wine of **Sardinia** which has made the most impact on the UK market is **Torbato di Alghero**. Torbato is another fairly neutral-flavoured grape variety, which makes some dry, quite refreshing but fairly nondescript white wine. Production is concentrated in the hands of village co-operatives and the large, competent producers of the island, Sella e Mosca.

Other Italians

Italy, south of Rome, is not renowned for its white wines, with a couple of honourable exceptions, **Fiano di Avellino** and **Greco di Tufo**. Both are made by the leading, and virtually only, Campania producer whose wines reach the UK, Mastroberardino. Greco is the principal white grape variety of the south and, as Greco di Tufo, is at its most flavoursome with some dry nutty fruit. Fiano, another grape variety, is more subtle and needs some bottle age. **Lacryma Christi del Vesuvio** is memorable for its name, but certainly not for the rather earthy white wines that occasionally find their way to these shores.

Spain

The majority of white **Rioja** fits into this segment of the taste wheel, for most of the large bodegas have given up ageing their white wines in oak, and now sell them as sin crianza (without oak). However, they simply do not have as much flavour as the oak-aged wines (see further round the wheel), as the main grape variety is Viura, which is rather lacking in flavour and acidity. At best, if drunk within a year or two of the vintage, white Rioja tastes young and fresh, sometimes with the boiled-sweets flavour that originates from very cool fermentation. The best wines are clean and fresh, but it is obvious why oak was favoured in the first place.

More intrinsic flavour comes from **Rueda** and, indeed, one of the leading Rioja bodegas, Marqués de Riscal, prefers to sell a white wine from Rueda rather than from Rioja. Rueda has been transformed in the last decade or so: where once it was an oxidised, fortified sherry-like wine, it has become, with the help of a new generation of winemakers and outside investment, a dry, nutty, grassy-flavoured wine. It is dry without being acidic, with a hint of almonds and a slight bitterness on the finish, and a stony freshness. Verdejo is the main grape variety, along with Viura and a drop of Sauvignon for extra pungency. **Superiore** on the label indicates a higher percentage of Verdejo. The best producers are Marqués de Riscal, Marqués de Griñon, Los Curros and Antonio Sanz.

Portugal

Across the border in Portugal, white **Dão** might fit into this segment, as it is quite full-flavoured with lemon and honey; it is fairly acidic in its youth, but that lessens as the wine matures and it becomes fatter and richer, with a certain nutty quality. There is often an old-fashioned feel to it. It must have six months' ageing before bottling, while **garrafeira** indicates a year's ageing in both bottle and vat.

One of the better Portuguese whites comes from the Douro – **Planalto Reserva**, which is made by the Mateus Rosé company of Sogrape. The expertise is apparent in this delicately fruity, soft grassy dry white wine.

Greece and Cyprus

The most characterful white wine of Greece – apart from Retsina, which merits a segment all to itself in the taste wheel – is **Robola of Cephalonia**, made from the Robola grape. It has a dry, nutty, old-fashioned flavour to it, as does white **Patras** from the Peloponnese. Demestica is a common brand of Greek wine, with a dry, rather undistinguished flavour.

Aphrodite, the white wine from the Keo co-operative on Cyprus, is very similar. It is dry and flat, with a slightly salty tang to the finish, the kind of wine that is delicious in the island sunshine, but does not have quite the same appeal under grey British skies.

The New World

Examples of Sauvignon from the warmer New World countries – California, South America, South Africa and Australia – fit into this section, for they tend to lack the acidity of their counterparts in New Zealand or the Loire Valley. The flavours tend to be a little broader and fatter, without the crisp pungency that can be so appealing in Sauvignon.

Chile Some Chilean Sauvignon is rather dull and flat, spoilt by the use of an inferior clone called Sauvignonasse, which lacks the pungency and zest of real Sauvignon. However, with plantings of better clones, reduced yields and investment in modern technology to control fermentation temperatures, flavours are improving. Torres, Santa Rita, Caliterra, Viña Carmen, Canepa and Undurraga are amongst the best producers. Torres, in fact, makes two Sauvignons, one without oak, and one with oak, called Bellaterra, which fits alongside South African Blanc Fumé further round the wheel. Chilean Sauvignon seems to fade very quickly once the wine is more than 18 months to two years old, so drink the youngest available.

South Africa   If South African Sauvignon is aged in oak, it is usually labelled Blanc Fumé, while the unoaked wines are simply called Sauvignon. There are some good examples available, with soft, grassy, lightly pungent flavours. One of the most subtle comes from Klein Constantia, a winery that benefits from a winemaker who has worked in New Zealand. Thelema, Neil Ellis, Talana Hill, Boschendal and Villiera are also good. Usually, Sauvignon is much more successful than Chardonnay in South Africa. The other grape variety from the Cape which also fits into this segment is Chenin Blanc. South Africans tend to take it for granted as it is an easy, versatile grape variety. But, when vinified carefully, with grapes that are not diluted by excessive yields, it has some attractive fruit and flavour, medium-weight, with sufficient acidity and usually a hint of honey to make a soft, easy-to-drink, undemanding wine. The Simonsvlei co-operative makes a good, inexpensive example, generally sold under a supermarket own-label, as is Simonsig. Colombard, too, produces light, fruity wines, usually found under supermarket own labels.

Australia   Australia is not generally known for its Sauvignon: its Semillon and Chardonnay tend to be more exciting. However, one exception which does achieve some varietal pungency comes from a new winery, Shaw and Smith, run by the talented team of Michael Hill Smith and Martin Shaw. Katnook Estate and Schinus Molle are fresh and vibrant too. Other examples tend to be oaked and fit into the next segment.

USA   In California, the oaky Fumé Blanc style of Sauvignon is more popular. However, there are some Sauvignon producers who prefer to emphasise the tropical fruit flavours of ripe Sauvignon, such as Matanzas Creek. Quivira is crisp and pungent, as are Ojai, Carmenet and Konocti. Gallo is cheap, but rather fat and stewed.

   Elsewhere, there is the occasional example of Sauvignon from Washington State, such as Columbia Crest and Latah Creek, and Cordier in Texas, which makes a soft, grassy Sauvignon.

LIGHT AND BUTTERY (MEDIUM BODY, OAK, HIGH ACIDITY)

Fermentation and maturation in oak add weight and stature to a wine. However, the wine must have sufficient structure and body in order to assimilate the oak in the first place. Sometimes, where oak ageing is tried as an experiment or as a way of adding additional interest to a wine which is less than exciting, it is not always successful. One particular example of this is Muscadet. The reasons for putting Muscadet in oak, to achieve more complex flavours, can be appreciated, and the tenacity of the producers in question admired, but the success is questionable. Melon de Bourgogne is a rather light ethereal grape, with little structure. What flavour it has is drowned by the overwhelming effect of new oak, and the wine tastes just like an infusion of oak chippings. On the other hand, some grape varieties, most notably Chardonnay, lend themselves perfectly to vinification and maturation in oak, again with the proviso that there is enough structure and body in the wine in the first place.

Chablis and other white burgundies

The above is amply illustrated by **Chablis**. One or two innovative young growers, namely Jean-Pierre Grossot and Bernard Légland, have experimented with what they call a *cuvée bois* for some of their village Chablis. It is one way of extending their range of wines and adding an extra dimension to their repertoire. But, at that level, the wood can overwhelm the flinty flavour of the Chablis, making the wine less attractive than the oak-free version. William Fèvre also uses oak for his village Chablis, Champs Royaux, producing quite a rich, buttery wine.

Up a rung in the appellation ladder are those growers who put their premier cru wines in wood: that produces quite a different flavour. Good premiers crus, especially from those vineyards on the same side of the valley as the grands crus, have the structure to benefit from the effect of oak ageing. The oak gives the wine a certain richness, but there should always be a firm backbone of balancing acidity. However, it must be said that in some of the ripest years, like 1989, acidity levels were fairly low. The 1990 is balanced, with a rich concentration of flavour, and the 1988 exemplifies the underlying steeliness that is characteristic of Chablis.

Growers who do put their wine in wood include Jean-Marie

Raveneau, René and Vincent Dauvissat, William Fèvre, Jean Collet, Jean-Paul Droin, and Michel Laroche (some of his wines).

Grand cru Chablis should be significantly richer than a premier cru and so belongs to the firm and toasted segment of the wheel, along with most of the principal appellations of the Côte d'Or. Possible exceptions might be the lesser ones, like St-Aubin and St-Romain, as well as the wines of the Côte Chalonnaise, and also Pouilly-Fuissé.

The white wines of the **Côte Chalonnaise**, namely Montagny and Rully, have a firm backbone of acidity and benefit particularly from some ageing in oak. Good producers include Noël-Bouton at Domaine de la Folie, Cogny, Dury, Faiveley, Jaffelin and Delorme. The 1992, 1990, 1989 and 1988 are all good vintages.

The appellation of **Pouilly-Fuissé** can produce some good wine, but lacks the depth of a good Rully or Montagny. As an object of fashion it has been beset by prices inflated completely out of proportion to its quality. However, good estates include Domaine Corsin and Vincent at the Château de Fuissé – especially the Cuvée Vieilles Vignes, a wine made from older than average vines, which have highly developed root systems to tap into deeper minerals and provide extra flavour and concentration.

New Zealand Chardonnay

As for Chardonnay from other regions, New Zealand belongs in this segment by virtue of both the relatively high acidity levels, originating in a coolish climate, and the customary oak treatment. Although some of the richer wines stray into the next segment of the wheel, the cooler New Zealand climate avoids some of the intense tropical fruit flavours found in Australian Chardonnay, and produces more subtle flavours. Chardonnay is treated seriously in New Zealand and is virtually always given some barrel maturation, even if it is not fermented in oak. The flavours may be rich, with the deliciously toasted taste originating from charred barrels, but there is always an underlying acidity and elegance.

Good producers of New Zealand Chardonnay include Te Mata's Elston, Martinborough Vineyards, Morton Estate, Kumeu River, Villa Maria, Matua Valley (especially with its Judd Estate), Hunters, Babich, Nobilo (particularly its Dixon Vineyard Reserve),

---

Once in the bottle a cork can last for decades but eventually it becomes brittle and crumbly with age.

Cloudy Bay, Neudorf, Redwood Valley and Collards. Good recent vintages include 1992, 1991, 1990 and 1989.

Canadian Chardonnay

The occasional example of Canadian Chardonnay should also feature here, by virtue of high acidity levels and oak treatment. Hillebrand tends to be over-oaked, while Inniskillin is a little more subtle and buttery, and Château des Charmes is quite burgundian.

New Zealand Sauvignon Blanc

Some New Zealand Sauvignon also fits into this segment. There is a distinct divergence in style, depending on whether the wine has spent time in oak or not, and the label may give some indication, with the words oak aged – but not always. Perhaps the epitome of this style of Sauvignon is Cloudy Bay, one of the great success stories of the New Zealand wine industry. It is amazing to realise that the first vintage of Cloudy Bay was as recent as 1985, and yet, in some circles, this wine is now synonymous with New Zealand Sauvignon. Demand far exceeds supply; the wine is sold on quota, and the price is significantly higher than that of other New Zealand Sauvignons. Only a part of the wine is barrel aged, which prevents the taste of oak from overwhelming the flavour of the grape. A tiny proportion of Semillon also fills out the wine, making it rounded and subtle, with gentle, understated flavours.

Other riper New Zealand Sauvignons include Brookfields, Waipara Springs, Rongopai and Matua Valley Reserve.

Australian Semillon

Australian Semillon fits into this category, but the acidity level is very much more apparent on the palate than in the average Australian Chardonnay. It is Semillon that really makes the most original and distinctive white wines of Australia. In Bordeaux it is rare to find a pure Semillon – usually it is blended with Sauvignon – but in Australia it is vinified as a pure varietal. The Hunter Valley is where Semillon performs best, enjoying the warm climate to yield wines that seem rather thin, if not lean and acidic, in their youth, but which develop into something complex and subtle with bottle ageing, more than repaying patience. There is a toasted nutty quality about mature Hunter Valley Semillon, with some underlying oily richness which makes a wine refreshingly original compared with jet-setting Chardonnay.

Good producers include Rothbury, Rosemount, Lindemans and

Penfolds. The best recent vintages include 1992, 1991, 1989, 1987, and 1986.

Occasionally, you can find blends of Semillon and Chardonnay – not only in Australia but also in New Zealand – as well as the traditional Bordeaux mix of Sauvignon and Semillon. However, in Australia it is pure Semillon that works best of all.

Graves and other oaked whites

Back to France and the Graves or, more precisely, the appellation of **Pessac-Léognan** which now includes the better properties of the reduced appellation of the Graves. This is the only appellation of significance in Bordeaux that is equally important in both red and white wine production. The white wines of the Graves can cover a whole range of flavours, depending on how they are made, on whether the producer has a modern approach to winemaking or not, and on whether or not oak is used. At their most basic, the white wines of the Graves are fuller, more solid versions of Bordeaux Blanc, while at the other end of the scale, amongst the more prestigious classed growths, the flavours are much more subtle and substantial and fit in here.

These are wines that generally benefit from the use of new oak and from ageing in bottle as well as in cask. There is a toasted character that is not dissimilar to Chardonnay, but with a different dimension of flavour. The use of Sémillon makes a flavour that seems leaner and less appealing, even a little dull, in its youth, but which develops into something broader and fuller. Sometimes, the oaky overtones can be a little overwhelming, but in good Graves the oak should be well integrated. Good performers currently are Fieuzal, Olivier, Couhins-Lurton, Clos Floridène (made by Denis Dubourdieu), Domaine de la Grave, Smith-Haut Lafitte, Laville Haut Brion and Haut Brion, which makes a tiny amount of white wine. Also good are Carbonnieux, which has improved in the last few years, Domaine de Chevalier and Notre Dame de Landiras which, unusually, is a pure Sémillon. Good recent vintages are 1990, 1989, 1988, 1986, 1985, 1983 and 1982. As elsewhere in south-west France, 1991 suffered severely from spring frosts and 1992 from rain.

There are other examples of wines vinified in oak which are unusual for their appellation. In **Côtes de Provence**, there is Clos Mireille, the property of the Ott family. This is also a Sauvignon and Sémillon blend, which has something of the mature flavour of the Graves – an underlying nutty leafiness when given some bottle age. Unfortunately, but understandably, it is expensive, but delicious. Another Côtes de Provence estate, Domaine de la Courtade, made from a blend of Rolle and Sémillon, also uses oak for its white wines, which need bottle ageing for the oak to soften.

In **Tursan**, the new wines of Michel Guérard (of Eugenié-les-Bains fame), Château de Bachen, and the special cuvée, Baron de Bachen, are adding a new dimension to this overlooked VDQS on the edge of the pine forests of the Landes. Maturation in oak is a vital feature of the wine, and there is Sémillon, Sauvignon, Gros and Petit Manseng, as well as Baroque, in the blend.

A final postscript to this section is **England**, where enterprising vineyards are experimenting with oak. The most successful include Rock Lodge, Penshurst, Thames Valley, Tenterden, Lamberhurst, Chiltern Valley and Pilton Manor.

DRY AND NUTTY (MEDIUM BODY, OAK, LOW ACIDITY)

This segment covers wines made in warmer climates, such as the Rhône Valley, South America and Bulgaria, with lower acidity than in the previous segment. However, they do not quite have the weight and body of the wines further round the wheel.

The Rhône

Apart from the white wines based on Viognier, in the appellations of Condrieu and Château Grillet, and the lighter, one-dimensional Côtes-du-Rhône, other Rhône wines covered in this section are white Hermitage and neighbouring Crozes-Hermitage and St-Joseph in the northern Rhône, and Châteauneuf-du-Pape.

White **Hermitage** can age beautifully, especially when it is made by a talented grower like Gérard Chave and is given a few months' barrel ageing. It comes from two grape varieties, Roussanne and Marsanne and, in its youth, can seem a little dull and lifeless. However, it rewards patience by developing all kinds of wonderful flavours of honey and herbs, peaches and toasted nuts. In some ways it is not so different from a good white burgundy, but lacks the same acidity level or weight.

Some white Hermitage, such as Jaboulet's Chevalier de Stérimberg, is intended for earlier drinking and has a fresh lemony liveliness in its youth, but lacks the potential for further development. Good examples of traditional white Hermitage come from Chave and Sorrel. White St-Joseph and Crozes-Hermitage can at times be nothing more than slightly fuller versions of Côtes-du-Rhône, but happily this is not always so, with complex characterful wines coming from Clos de l'Arbalestrier in St-Joseph and Domaine des Remizières in Crozes-Hermitage.

White **Châteauneuf-du-Pape** can be made from Clairette, Bourboulenc, Picpoul, Picardin and Roussanne (but not Marsanne), and is not usually as flavoursome as Hermitage. Never the less, in the right hands, the taste can be distinctly leafy, with rich, herbal fruit and nutty overtones. The best producer is Château de Beaucastel.

(A **Californian** footnote to this segment is Le Sophiste from Bonny Doon, a Marsanne Roussanne blend, which is comparable both in flavour and price to white Hermitage.)

Argentina, Bulgaria and others

Both Argentinian and Bulgarian Chardonnay belong in this section as, with one or two exceptions, neither quite has the weight or body to fit into the next segment of the wheel. Chardonnay in **Argentina** is a relatively new grape variety. Like virtually every other wine-producing country, it too is joining the bandwagon of the world's most popular white grape variety, and one or two good examples are beginning to appear. The biggest producer, Trapiche, makes two Chardonnays: one, labelled Chardonnay Reserve, is without oak and is light and lemony; the other, a Chardonnay Oak Cask Reserve, has spent several months in new French oak. The price difference is quite significant: you pay about £1 (or 30 per cent) more for the oak. Trapiche is still learning about oak barrels and for the moment the wine tends to taste over-oaked. The situation will improve as the vines age and the winemakers learn to reduce the excessive yields resulting from liberal irrigation.

Bulgaria produces a range of different Chardonnays, as country wines, Controliran wines and Reserve wines. Some do not see any oak at all and fit into a previous segment of the wheel, while the Reserve wines must spend three years in wood, and the flavour is firmly oaky. The two Reserve wines are Varna and Khan Krum Chardonnay, while the Controliran Chardonnay from Preslav is also kept in new oak, and tastes of it. The value of these wines remains excellent for, despite the changes in the system, the Bulgarians are still aware of the need for foreign currency and price their wines advantageously.

In this section we should also include the occasional oaked Sauvignon from **Chile** – Miguel Torres Bellaterra Sauvignon, for example, with its firm, dry oaky flavours that rather overwhelm the fruit of the grape variety, as does Montes Fumé Blanc. The same could also be said of some of the Blanc Fumé wines from **South Africa**. These wines do not have the weight of New World Sauvignons from California or Australia, and the flavour of the grape is completely masked by the oak, with relatively low acidity.

FIRM AND TOASTED (FULL BODY, OAK, HIGH ACIDITY)

Grand cru Chablis

Grand cru Chablis is the epitome of this section. It has a richness and concentration of flavour which comes from the grape variety, Chardonnay, which is grown on the best hillsides of the village. This, combined with the backbone of firm acidity, is characteristic of all good Chablis. Grand cru Chablis, from one of seven named vineyards grouped together on the steep slopes above the river Serein, has weight, intensity and potential for ageing that is rarely seen in premier cru Chablis. Of the villages, the best known and largest is Les Clos; Grenouilles is the smallest. The others are Blanchots, Vaudésir, Preuses, Bougros and Valmur. Several producers of grand cru Chablis ferment and age their wines in wood: William Fèvre at Domaine de la Maladière is the leading exponent of new wood, as well as the largest owner of grand cru vineyards, and his example has been followed by several others. More traditional growers like Dauvissat, Pinson and Raveneau have never abandoned their oak barriques, but have favoured a limited amount of new oak. Other exponents of oak in Chablis include the producers Jean Paul-Droin, Michel Laroche, Jean Collet and Vocoret.

Amongst the 'no oak' contingent, Louis Michel remains supreme for steely grands crus that have never seen a stave of oak. The curious thing is that mature Chablis can, with bottle age, take on some of the nutty flavours that you would normally associate with oak maturation. However, Chablis that has spent some months in oak tends to be fuller in the mouth, with a greater concentration of flavour, particularly marked when it is young. With age, the differences fade.

Côte d'Or

The vineyards of the **Côte de Beaune** – there is virtually no white wine made on the Côte de Nuits – are about a hundred kilometres further south. The climate is that little bit warmer, making even richer, more concentrated flavours. Oak barrels are considered the norm here, even for the village wines of the Côte de Beaune. The classification is the same as in Chablis, with a division between grands crus, such as Le Montrachet, premiers crus, like Puligny-Montrachet, les Pucelles, Folatières or Combettes, and plain Puligny-Montrachet. A premier cru without a vineyard name is likely to be a blend from several vineyards.

Some of the village wines may not have the weight and body to justify their inclusion in this segment, but in general terms, the good wines, and certainly the great white wines of the Côte de Beaune fit in very firmly. They have complexity and richness, with a depth of flavour that develops with bottle age, and always have sufficient acidity, except, perhaps, in the very ripest years, like 1986. They are usually relatively high in alcohol, reaching 13.5 per cent, which makes them quite mouth-filling, but this should be balanced with acidity to retain the elegance that is the hallmark of great white burgundy.

The principal white wine villages of the Côte de Beaune are **Puligny-Montrachet** (the subject of a fascinating insight into Burgundian village life by Simon Loftus in his book *Puligny-Montrachet*, published by Ebury Press), with neighbouring **Chassagne-Montrachet**, as well as **Aloxe-Corton** and **Meursault**.

These are the sources of some of the most evocative names of Burgundy – Bâtard-Montrachet, Corton-Charlemagne and others. These are the wines which the producers of the New World aspire to emulate, and some do indeed come close.

The name of the producer is the all-important key to quality in Burgundy, when several families own plots of the same vineyard. Names to seek out include Domaine Leflaive and Olivier Leflaive (from the same family); also Matrot, Charton et Trébuchet, Blain-Gagnard, Sauzet, Comte Lafon, François Jobard, Simon Bize, Jean-Noël Gagnard, Henri Jayer, Henri Germain, Coche-Dury, Michelot-Buisson and Bonneau du Martray.

As in Chablis, there has been a run of good vintages – 1992, 1990, 1989 and 1988 – with 1991 making less exciting wines. The 1990 and youthful 1992 are generally very highly considered, while the 1989 and 1986 may be slightly lacking in acidity. The other good vintages of the eighties were 1982, 1983 and 1985.

New Zealand Chardonnay

Among the wines of the New World, Chardonnays from California and Australia generally fit into the next section, while the richer New Zealand Chardonnays, with their higher acidity levels, come into this segment. Included here are wines with sufficient weight, like Te Mata's Elston, Kumeu River and Matua Valley's Judd Estate, which all have rich, toasted burgundian flavours.

RICH AND BUTTERY (FULL BODY, OAK, LOW ACIDITY)

Many of the Chardonnays produced in California, Australia, Chile and South Africa fit into this segment of the wheel because their natural acidity level is often lower than in fine white Burgundy. Admittedly, however, some of the best wines from Australia and California do come close to emulating their Burgundian peers.

California and other North American Chardonnays

California Chardonnay has moved towards wines that are a little leaner and understated, with a tight, dry, nutty flavour – that is to say, wines with greater subtlety, more suitable for drinking with a meal. They no longer leap out of the glass in the exuberant way that they used to. There are still wines that are ripe and opulent with the flavours of tropical fruit, pineapples and mangoes.

However, the understated wines are more rewarding, developing, rather than fading, with age.

As with all California wines, it is the winery name on the label that is the clue to quality. Robert Mondavi, Saintsbury, Simi, Au Bon Climat, Schug Cellars, Edna Valley, Sonoma Cutrer, Kistler, Long Vineyards, Qupé, Newton Vineyard, Kendall Jackson, Grgich Hills, Far Niente, Freemark Abbey and Rutherford Hill are amongst those making fine Chardonnay. The last ten years have seen some fine vintages in California; of recent years, 1991 and 1990 are very good, while 1986 and 1985 are drinking well now.

It is surprising to realise that Chardonnay is grown in as many as 42 other American states; however, very few of these wines actually cross the Atlantic. You may find examples from **Washington State** and **Oregon**, such as Covey Run, Blackwood Canyon, Eyrie Vineyard and Ponzi, and there are also some good Chardonnays from **New York State**, from the vineyards of Long Island and from Wagner in the Finger Lakes. **Texas** is an also-ran in the Chardonnay stakes, with Llano Estacado.

The wine that Californians term Fumé Blanc might also come into this segment. The name was coined by Robert Mondavi and others have followed his example, making a Sauvignon that may be blended with a little Semillon before being aged in oak barrels. The taste, a ripe mouthful of buttery fruit and overpowering oak with low acidity, has more to do with the oak barrels than with the grape variety, and for that reason the wine fits into this segment.

Australia

The obvious comparison with California is Australia. There is no wine region in this enormous continent that does not produce Chardonnay, and usually the flavours are ripe and buttery, with overtones of tropical fruit, lychees, pineapples and peaches. In contrast to burgundy, the taste is definitely fuller and riper, with lower acidity, usually not as elegant, and perhaps a little blowsy and overstated. Sometimes the wines can be spoilt by a slightly sharp citric finish, an indication that the acidity level has been adjusted. However, Chardonnay from some of the cooler regions of Australia – such as the Yarra Valley in Victoria and even cooler Tasmania – displays some elegance and the hallmarks of good varietal character, with the toasted nuances of oak maturation and good ageing potential.

The great advantage of Australian Chardonnay for the Chardonnay enthusiast is price: the large Australian wineries seem to have more modest aspirations about price than many of their Californian counterparts. While many California

Chardonnays demand a price that is comparable with good burgundy, Australians have appreciated the virtue of value for money. The choice of a good California Chardonnay for under £10 a bottle is rather limited, compared with what is available from Australia.

As with California, the winery name is an important key to quality and style. Names to look out for include Yarra Yering, Coldstream Hills, Pipers Brook, Petaluma, Tarrawarra, Moss Wood, Smith and Shaw, Rothbury, Rosemount, Schinus Molle, David Wynn, Cullen Wines and Lake's Folly. Good recent vintages include 1992, 1991, 1990, 1988 and 1987.

Chile

In comparison with Australia and California, Chilean Chardonnay still has quite a long way to go. The flavours may be somewhat heavy-handed and unsubtle, but even in the last three or four years, there has been a marked improvement as Chilean winemakers have begun to master the intricacies of barrel fermentation and maturation. Vineyard practices are changing and, in particular, excessive irrigation is being moderated, leading to an improvement in quality. However, for the moment the best Chardonnay from Chile does not yet have the subtlety of the best from either Australia or California. Names to look for include Villa Montes, Santa Rita, Errazuriz, and Concha y Toro amongst others.

South Africa

South Africa also has a long way to go with Chardonnay. It suffered from something of a false start when some smuggled Chardonnay vines turned out to be Pinot Auxerrois, but things have been sorted out since then; problems with quarantine regulations have been overcome and Chardonnay is being planted quite extensively. For the moment, most of the vines are still very young, and barrel fermentation and oak maturation are relatively new skills for South African winemakers, who have been cut off from the many technological advances of the last decade or so. Much South African Chardonnay is still spoilt by the heavy-handed use of oak and, in general, the wines have yet to acquire the understated elegance that is the hallmark of fine Chardonnay.

Some of the better South African Chardonnays, from the cooler vineyards of the Cape, include Hamilton-Russell, Klein Constantia, Thelema, Glen Carlou and Boschendal.

Chardonnay, then, is the white grape variety that every winemaker aspires to master, with the wines of Burgundy as their examples. Just about every wine-producing country grows Chardonnay somewhere, from Israel to Mexico, and there are numerous barrel-fermented, oak-aged examples. Often they are full-bodied, with ripe buttery oaky flavours; sometimes they can lack acidity. Chardonnay has been introduced not only to the New World vineyards, but also to regions where the indigenous white grape varieties do not have the same flavour and appeal.

Italy

There are numerous examples of Chardonnay from all over Italy. Chardonnay forms part of the innovative wave of experimentation in **Tuscany**. It is given some semblance of official recognition by Predicato del Muschio (a Tuscan classification for vino da tavola based on the proportion of Chardonnay), but is usually sold with a fantasy name like Le Grance from Caparzo, I Sistri from Felsina Berardenga or Il Marzocco from Avignonesi. These wines have varying success, depending on the producer's expertise and such factors as the age of the vines. They are usually expensive, presented in a designer bottle with a fancy label, which confirms the producer's aspirations and perception of his wine. In **Piedmont**, Angelo Gaja is the leading producer of Chardonnay, while Lungarotti in Umbria makes Chardonnay di Miraduolo.

Another Italian Chardonnay is Preludio No. 1 from **Puglia**, which is ripe and full-flavoured, and somewhat lacking in acidity, originating as it does from an even warmer climate.

Other comparable Tuscan wines which have been vinified and aged in oak include the oaked version of Pomino, Il Benefizio from Frescobaldi, made from a selection of grape varieties, with its ripe buttery oaky flavours which could be confused with Chardonnay. Another example is Terre di Tufo, from Teruzzi e Puthod, which is a barrel-fermented Vernaccia di San Gimignano.

Iberia

Across the Pyrenees in Spain, there are also examples of Chardonnay. Jean León, one of the leading winemakers of **Penedès**, pairs it with Cabernet Sauvignon, while that indefatigable innovator, Miguel Torres, has also planted it in Penedès. Torres Milmanda is a pure varietal wine, while Gran Viña Sol includes a substantial amount, along with Paralleda. Green Label Gran Viña Sol, which is a blend of Sauvignon and Parellada, also deserves a passing mention here, for it is aged in oak and is ripe and buttery in flavour. The Codorníu estate of Raimat, in the new DO of **Costers del Segre**, also produces oak-aged Chardonnay.

Portugal is beginning to consider Chardonnay too, with a recently introduced example from João Pires, Cova d'Orsa.

Rioja   The final wine in this segment is the traditional, classic white Rioja, which is treated to the same ageing process as the red wine. Traditional white Rioja, made from grape varieties such as Viura, spends at least six months, if not longer, in wood and the result is firmly dry and nutty. Viura is not a particularly acidic grape variety, so the wine is low in acidity, but the flavour is firm and dry, marked by the wood, perhaps a little flat, but quite elegant. Good examples include Marqués de Murrieta, Viña Tondonia from Lopez de Heredia, and Monopole from CVNE.

VIN JAUNE

Vin Jaune needs a segment all of its own, as it is quite unlike any other table wine. The closest taste comparison is to fino sherry, which features in the fortified wine wheel, although Vin Jaune is not fortified.

   This is one of the most original and distinctive wines of France, coming from the mountainous region of the Jura, bordering Switzerland. The method of vinification contradicts all the usual oenological practices: the wine is left in small oak barrels for a minimum of six years, during which time the barrels are not topped up, but are, instead, exposed to the summer and winter variations of temperature in a cellar which must not be completely below ground. During the ageing period a flor of yeast develops, as with fino sherry, and it is this flor which gives Vin Jaune its original flavour. The grape variety is the Savagnin, which is unique to the Jura. After six years' ageing, Vin Jaune has some distinctively nutty flavours, with a firm bite of acidity and an almost savoury, salty character, again like fino sherry. The best example comes from the tiny village of Château Chalon, and the other three appellations of the Jura – Arbois, l'Etoile and Côtes du Jura – all include Vin Jaune.

   With small yields from the Savagnin grape and such a long ageing process, entailing a considerable evaporation and loss of wine, Vin Jaune is inevitably expensive. It is sold in the distinctive clavelin bottle of 62cl, the amount that 100cl reduces to in the course of six years. Château d'Arlay and Bourdy are the two examples available in Britain.

RETSINA

Retsina, most of which comes from Attica, is the best known of all Greek wines and the most individual. It maintains a centuries' old tradition of adding resin from the Aleppo pines to the fermenting wine, as a means of preserving it – a method which dates back to the days when little was understood about the damaging effects of temperature and oxidation.

Retsina has a wonderfully distinctive taste, which really has nothing at all to do with grapes, and it is the kind of wine you either love or hate. There is a sharp resinous taste, perhaps reminiscent of ginger (some might call it turpentine), which seems to complement rich Greek food. Good retsina should be light golden in colour, with a fresh lively attack of resin in the mouth. It should never be flat and lifeless and must be drunk fresh. Good producers include Kourtakis, Boutari and Tsantali.

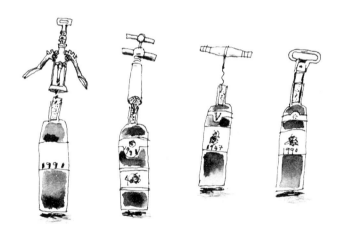

MEDIUM
WHITE WINES

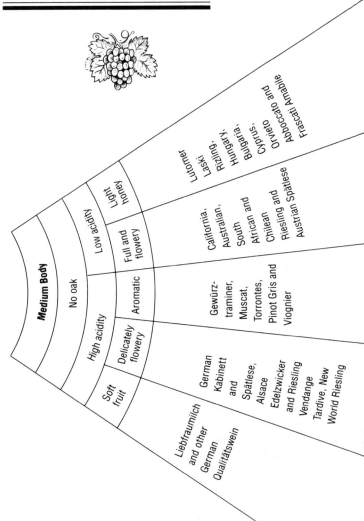

Medium Body

No oak

Low acidity

Light honey — Lutomer Laski Rizling, Hungary, Bugaria, Cyprus, Orvieto and Abboccato and Frascati Amabile

Full and flowery — California, Australian, South African and Chilean Riesling and Austrian Spätlese

High acidity

Aromatic — Gewürztraminer, Muscat, Torrontes, Pinot Gris and Viognier

Delicately flowery — German Kabinett and Spätlese, Alsace Edelzwicker and Riesling Vendange Tardive, New World Riesling

Soft fruit — Liebfraumilch and other German Qualitätswein

In broad terms, medium whites encompass all those wines that are neither firmly dry nor intensely sweet. They are wines that may contain an element of residual sugar remaining from the fermentation, or they may have had some *Süssreserve* added to them, in order to give them a soft, rounded flavour and finish. Alternatively, the intrinsic flavour may give the impression of some aromatic richness, such as an Alsace Gewurztraminer, which is essentially dry, but does not really taste so because of the particular character of the grape variety.

SOFT FRUIT (MEDIUM BODY, NO OAK, HIGH ACIDITY)

Liebfraumilch

For a soft wine with high acidity, **Liebfraumilch** is the obvious starting point. This is the wine that dominates the German export market and accounts for a considerable percentage of Britain's wine consumption. Liebfraumilch from a respectable source is a perfectly acceptable wine. Its chief virtue is that it is innocuous: slightly sweet, soft and fruity, without any harsh edges, or indeed any distinctive regional characteristics. In the minefield of confusing German names it seems a safe and pronounceable choice. The well-known brand leaders, like Blue Nun and Black Tower, are subject to meticulous attention in their production, which entails the careful blending of several different wines from diverse vineyards and grape varieties, in order to achieve a consistent style, changing only with vintage variations. Liebfraumilch must be of Qualitätswein standard and must originate from the Rheinhessen, Rheinpfalz, Nahe or Rheingau. In practice, most Liebfraumilch comes from the first two regions.

Sadly, the enormous quantity of cheap and nasty Liebfraumilch that has flooded the British market has not only damaged the reputation of Liebfraumilch but has also brought the finer German wines into disrepute. It is no secret that the German wine market is in a sorry state: Riesling, which accounts for all fine German wine, is deemed an unfashionable grape, and the better quality German wines are undervalued and simply not appreciated. However, with an elegance and subtlety which is missing from Liebfraumilch, they do not fit into this particular segment of the wheel, but are scattered elsewhere.

Liebfraumilch is an easier way of asking for a standard German wine, like Niersteiner Gutes Domtal, or Rüdesheimer Rosengarten, or one of the innumerable Bereich or Grosslage names – that group several smaller vineyards, or Einzellagen – within a village. Without any mention of Prädikat or grape variety on the label, these are wines of basic Qualitätswein standard which have some regional characteristics. Wines from the Mosel, such as Bereich Bernkastel or Piesporter Goldtröpfchen, are lighter and a little more flowery, and may fit more comfortably into the next segment of the wheel, compared with those from the Rhine, such as Bereich Johannisberg or Oppenheimer Krötenbrunnen. Rhine wines are generally a little fuller and more honeyed and are made from grapes that have reached a certain level of ripeness, measured by the sugar level in the juice.

The grape variety is unlikely to be Riesling – more likely to be Müller-Thurgau, or perhaps a blend of some of the newer crosses, like Kerner, Huxelrebe or Scheurebe, developed for their greater ripening potential in the cooler climate of Germany's northern vineyards. The overall flavour is soft and easy, with a background of high acidity which is masked by the sweetness from the *Süssreserve*. These wines lack the elegance and refinement of good Riesling, but can make pleasant enough drinking if they come from a reputable source.

Germany had a run of three superb vintages with 1990, 1989 and 1988, while in 1991 things resumed a more average standard and 1992 has produced some good wines, not unlike 1983. For recommended producers, see under Spätlese in the next segment.

DELICATELY FLOWERY (MEDIUM BODY, NO OAK, HIGH ACIDITY)

Perhaps the term 'flowery' requires some explanation. It describes a wine that is not really dry, but is certainly not at all sweet. Quite simply, it evokes a certain scented character, that is neither cloying nor pungent, but gentle and fragrant.

Kabinett and Spätlese from the Mosel and Rhine

A Mosel Kabinett or Spätlese is the epitome of floweriness. A fine Mosel has a delicate flowery quality about it, but always with a steely backbone of acidity, originating from the relatively hard climate. There is also a slatey aspect to the wine which comes from the soil, and which is emphasised by the Riesling grape. Müller-Thurgau is widely planted in the Mosel, but the better wines are always made from Riesling and can be simply delicious. As they mature, they can develop a somewhat petrolly bouquet – some say kerosene – but they never lose that flowery and, in the sweeter wines, slightly honeyed, flavour.

To explain the origins of a wine take, for example, **Bereich Bernkastel**, the most basic wine, covering an extensive area of the Mittelmosel (as opposed to the two tributaries of the Mosel, the Saar and the Ruwer). From a reputable producer, a Bereich Bernkastel can provide a simple, refreshing glass of wine. Next up the scale come the Grosslagen, which are groups of vineyards. In the town of Bernkastel, the Grosslagen are Bernkasteler Badstube and Bernkasteler Kurfürstlay, and the best-known Einzellage – single-vineyard site – is Bernkasteler Doktor.

The quality scale of German wines is linked to the sugar content and ripeness of the grapes. At the bottom there is Tafelwein, which accounts for only a tiny proportion of Germany's wine production. Most of it fits into the Qualitätswein category, above which there is Qualitätswein mit Prädikat. In ascending order of sweetness or ripeness, the Prädikat are Kabinett, Spätlese, Auslese, Beerenauslese and Trockenbeerenauslese (the last three come into the sweet section of the wheel).

Although Kabinett is the driest of the Prädikat wines, unless it is labelled trocken it is unlikely to taste absolutely dry. There will usually be an underlying flowery, or perhaps a slightly honeyed, flavour, masking the firm backbone of acidity. Much depends upon the vintage; a riper vintage like 1990 will produce somewhat fuller wines, while a cooler vintage will result in fewer Prädikat wines, as the grapes will not be so ripe, and the wines themselves will not seem so rich.

The precise origin also affects the flavour. The Mosel produces the most delicate wines of Germany, with a combination of steely acidity tempered by flowery fruit, while the wines of the Rhine are a little fuller and richer. It is indisputable that the Rheingau makes the most elegant wines of the Rhine, while those from the Rheinhessen and Rheinpfalz are fuller and riper, coming as they do from a warmer climate. The Nahe, which adjoins the Mosel, Rheingau and Rheinhessen, has characteristics of each.

Much depends too upon individual producers. As in Burgundy, what is ostensibly the same wine can be made by several different growers. For example, there are three owners of the reputed Doktor vineyard in Bernkastel. Leading estates in the Mosel include Lauerburg, Bert Simon, Deinhard, Dr Thanish, J J Prüm, Vereinigte Hospitien, von Hövel, Fritz Haag, Schloss Saarstein, Dr Fischer, Egon Müller, Höhe Domkirche, Bischöfliches Priesterseminar, Bischöfliches Konvikt, Friedrich Wilhelm Gymnasium, Weingut Klusserath, Max Ferdinand Richter and Dr

Loosen. Other good estates include: in the Rheingau, Schloss Johannisberg, Schloss Schönborn, Deinhard, Schloss Groenesteyn, State Domaine at Eltville, Schloss Reinhartshausen and Balthasar Ress; in the Nahe, State Domaine at Schlossböckelheim, Crusius and Anheuser; in the Rheinhessen, Louis Guntrum and Anton Balbach; in the Rheinpfalz, von Bühl, Bassermann-Jordan, Bürklin-Wolf, Deinhard, Fitz Ritter and Lingenfelder.

The major stumbling block to the appreciation of German wines seems to be the nomenclature, and yet it is very logical. Take an example such as **Piesporter Goldtröpfchen Riesling Spätlese**. First comes the village name, then the vineyard, then the grape variety and, finally, the Prädikat. Not only is there some difficulty in the pronunciation, but there is no way of discerning whether a vineyard name is a large Grosslage or a small, individual Einzellage.

However, the German shippers Deinhard – who are also the owners of vineyards in three main regions – are among several working to surmount this problem with what they call their Estate Wine proposition, with which they have created a new identity for the various wines from all their different vineyards in the Mosel, Rheingau and Rheinpfalz. They will continue to make Prädikat wines from their very best vineyards – Bernkasteler Doktor, Wehlener Sonnenuhr, Rüdesheimer Berg Rottland and Forster Ungeheuer – as single vineyard wines, following the traditional German pattern. However, the wines from the various other vineyards will be blended to provide classic examples of the Mosel, Rheingau and Rheinpfalz, with a simplified name – Wegeler-Deinhard Riesling Kabinett or Spätlese, plus the area. The aim is to rationalise the multiplicity of vineyard names, building on their range of village wines that were launched some time ago as classic examples of Piesport, Nierstein, Bernkastel, Johannisberg, Deidesheim and Hochheim. For anyone confused by German wine labels, these offer an easier option from a reliable source.

Alsace

Across the Rhine and the border with France lies **Alsace**, with wines that do not quite belong to Germany, but which are not entirely French in style. With several different grape varieties, the wines of Alsace fit into different segments of the taste wheel. In this delicately flowery section comes one of the best, Riesling Vendange Tardive, and one of the most basic, Edelzwicker.

Take **Edelzwicker** first. This is the most basic of Alsace wines, a blend of grape varieties – rather than a single one, like all the other

Vins d'Alsace – making a flowery, and perhaps slightly spicy, fruity wine. It may be sold under a brand name, such as Hugel's Flambeau d'Alsace or under a supermarket or wine merchant's own label. In some ways, it may be seen as the Liebfraumilch of Alsace, but it is usually slightly drier and more aromatic. Essentially, it should be a cheerful, refreshing drink, with more alcohol and body than Liebfraumilch.

At the other end of the spectrum comes **Riesling Vendange Tardive** and also **Riesling Sélection de Grains Nobles**. In Alsace, Riesling is considered to be the finest, most characteristic and stylish grape variety, with a finesse and elegance lacking in Gewurztraminer. Normally, Riesling d'Alsace is bone dry (as discussed in the dry section of the wheel) but, in the best years, notably in the recent run of good vintages – 1992, 1990, 1989 and 1988 – some richer, more concentrated Vendange Tardive and Sélection de Grains Nobles wines were made. They are not sweet in the way that German Riesling Auslese or Beerenauslese might be, for in Alsace they always ferment their wines out as dry as possible. However, in years when the grapes have been affected by noble rot, very rich wines will be made, with ripe fruit and concentration, but always with the steely acidity of good Riesling.

Producers of Vendange Tardive, and also Sélection de Grains Nobles Riesling include Hugel, Domaine Weinbach, Zind-Humbrecht, Rolly Gassmann, Marc Kreydenweiss and Marcel Deiss.

New World

Examples of Riesling from the New World (sometimes called Johannisberg, White or Rhine Riesling) may well fit more comfortably into this segment of the wheel, rather than alongside dry examples of Riesling d'Alsace in that segment. Most New World Rieslings have a ripeness and underlying sweetness, with a flowery, honeyed flavour that is neither German nor Alsatian. Indeed, these wines may even be slightly sweet or off-dry, even if they are not offered as late-harvest wines. They usually have an alcohol level comparable to those of Alsace, but with one or two exceptions, are lower in acidity.

However, the cool climate of **New Zealand** – particularly the South Island – is proving very successful for Riesling. Some of the best wines are late harvest, but Redwood Valley, Giesen and Dry River all make some delicious dry or off-dry Rieslings, which are elegantly fruity, with a relatively low alcohol level.

Cooler **Oregon** has a more suitable climate than California for producing the delicate Germanic style of Riesling, notably from

Knudsen Erath. **Washington State** also makes some good off-dry Rieslings, from Hogue Cellars and Snoqualmie.

AROMATIC (MEDIUM BODY, NO OAK, HIGH ACIDITY)

Aromatic is an adjective applied to wines made from grape varieties with a particularly characteristic aroma, wines which can be identified and enjoyed because of their bouquet, such as Muscat, Gewurztraminer or Viognier. The bouquet is not so much fruity and flowery, but pungently aromatic. They are not usually subtle wines, on either nose or palate (the one exception may be Viognier), but assail you with a powerful impact of flavour.

Gewurztraminer

Take Gewurztraminer first. This is the most typical, characteristic wine of Alsace. *Gewürz* means spice in German and the flavours of Gewurztraminer are just that, sometimes elegant, with a firm, structured backbone, but sometimes blowsy, with a vulgarly overpowering perfume. The wines can have a wealth of tropical fruit – some people mention lychees – or can be reminiscent of cold cream. Gewurztraminer is instantly recognisable and you either love it or hate it. The subtle, understated wines are best of all. In **Alsace** the wines are always fermented dry but, even so, with Gewurztraminer there is always an underlying richness, a characteristic oiliness, originating from a fairly high degree of alcohol, which packs a punch of rich flavour. Much can depend upon a producer's individual style: some enhance the opulent spiciness of Gewurztraminer, while others aim for something understated. Even then, Gewurztraminer can never really be described as elegant.

Gewurztraminer is one of the four grape varieties allowed in the grand cru vineyards of Alsace. The first 25 of these vineyards were only recognised as recently as 1983, as an addition to the basic appellation of Vin d'Alsace, and are some of the better vineyard sites in the main villages. Since then, more have been added and there are now 50 grand cru sites in all. Gewurztraminer can also be made as a Vendange Tardive or Sélection de Grains Nobles. While Sélection de Grains Nobles fits more comfortably into the sweet wine segment, Vendange Tardive is best here due to its concentrated spicy flavours, which are not actually sweet but rich. The recent vintages – 1990, 1989 and 1988 – produced some wonderful Vendange Tardive wines, while those from 1985 and

1983 are beginning to drink beautifully. Alsace wines, although rich in alcohol, always have a firm backbone of acidity which allows them to develop with bottle age.

Gewurztraminer grows in other parts of Europe and has travelled to the New World. In **Germany** a little is grown in the Rheinpfalz; one of the best examples is Weingut Fitz-Ritter's Dürkheimer Feuerberg Spätlese Trocken. **Austria** too has some Gewurztraminer in south and east Styria, close to what was the Yugoslav border.

Gewurztraminer is one of the grape varieties allowed in the DOC of the **Südtirol**, where it is called Traminer Aromatico. It is also allowed in **Friuli**, **Grave del Friuli** and **Collio**, for example. Gewurztraminer from northern Italy tends to favour the lighter, understated and more subtle style.

In **California**, Gewurztraminer has excited some interest, although certainly nowhere near as much as Chardonnay. Dry Gewurztraminer from California is sometimes spoilt by a bitter finish: it can be a difficult variety to vinify, requiring just the right balance of residual sweetness and alcohol, and the off-dry wines are more successful than those that are firmly dry.

New Zealand is probably the best source of Gewurztraminer from the New World, with some ripe spicy examples from Villa Maria, Vidal and Hunters. **South Africa** is also trying, with a full-flavoured wine from Weltevrede.

Although Gewurztraminer is grown quite extensively in **Australia**, exports to the UK seem to concentrate firmly on Chardonnay, with a few exceptions. There is a Gewurztraminer/Riesling blend in Hardys' Bird Series and Penfolds Bin 202 is another Gewurztraminer/Riesling mix, and, from Chile, Torres' Don Miguel Riesling/Gewurztraminer.

Muscat

Muscat is the one grape variety that really does taste of the grape, those succulently juicy Italian Moscatel table grapes. There are, in fact, three main varieties of Muscat – Muscat d'Alexandrie, Muscat Blanc à Petits Grains and Muscat Ottonel – which between them account for the many and various Muscat wines of the world. Moscatel is another name for Muscat d'Alexandrie, while Muscat à Petits Grains has various synonyms, such as Muscat Canelli and Muscat de Frontignan. The methods of vinification and styles of wines can vary enormously, from a table wine like Muscat d'Alsace, to a fortified wine like Muscat de Beaumes-de-Venise, or an Australian Liqueur Muscat, or even a sparkling wine, like Asti Spumante. As a table wine it can be sweet or dry.

Muscat d'Alsace is the most characteristic example of a dry Muscat. The bouquet really is reminiscent of the aroma of the grape, while the palate is drier, with a slightly pithy flavour, like bitter oranges. Muscat is one of the four grape varieties which can be grown on a grand cru site in Alsace and it is also occasionally made into Vendange Tardive or Sélection de Grains Nobles wines, but very much less frequently than either Gewurztraminer or Riesling. Muscat is best drunk as in Alsace, young, vibrantly fresh and as an aperitif. Good producers include Kreydenweiss, Zind-Humbrecht, Kuentz Bas, Becker, Trimbach, Léon Beyer, Domaine Weinbach and Muré.

Muscat grown in the warmer climate of the south tends to lack the pungent spiciness that you find in Muscat d'Alsace. Consequently, elsewhere in France the tendency is to turn Muscat into a fortified wine. One exception, however, is the growing amount of **vin de pays Catalan** or **vin de pays des Pyrénées-Orientales**, specifying 'cépage Muscat' on the label. The drop in sales of fortified Muscat de Rivesaltes has resulted in table wine being made instead.

In **Spain**, the closest comparison to table wines is Torres' Viña Esmeralda, two parts Muscat to one part Gewurztraminer. It was an illustration of Miguel Torres' inquiring mind, and is now well established in his repertoire. In **Portugal**, the talented Peter Bright produces one of the freshest and most vibrant white Portuguese wines in Setúbal – João Pires' dry Muscat – from grapes that might otherwise be used for Moscatel de Setúbal.

In north-east **Italy** the DOC of the Südtirol allows Goldmuskateller and pink Rosenmuskateller, with Tiefenbrunner the star producer. In Germany, Morio-Muscat is a variation on Muscat, grown in the Rheinpfalz to make a wine that is lighter in alcohol and a little sweeter than a Muscat d'Alsace. There are also occasional examples from Eastern Europe, notably a recent introduction from the Gyöngyös Estate in **Hungary**, where the vinification was carried out by an Australian team working with Hugh Ryman. They have succeeded in making an attractive off-dry wine, with some pithy Muscat fruit.

A diversion from the former **Czechoslovakia** comes in the form of a curious grape variety called Irsay Oliver, which is a crossing of Gewurztraminer and Muscat Ottonel, with a nose faintly reminiscent of cold cream, some Muscat and apricot fruit and firm acidity on the palate.

As for the New World, **North America** tends to favour late-harvest Muscat, as they do in **New Zealand**, while in **Australia**, Brown Brothers have a reputation for their Dry Muscat.

Torrontes

The closest that South America comes to Muscat is a grape variety called Torrontes which is grown in **Argentina**, in the vineyards of the province of Salta. Not only are they the country's most northerly vineyards, but they are also the highest, situated in the foothills of the Andes. Torrontes is not a direct import from Europe, but is said to be a mutation of Malvoisie, brought from the Canaries in the 1550s. It should be drunk as young as possible, when it has some of the aromatic qualities of Muscat, with some pithy orange flavours, tinged with a little sweetness. Bodegas Etchart, Michel Torino and Trapiche are the best producers.

Pinot Gris

Another **Alsace** grape, Pinot Gris, fits more comfortably into this segment than in the firmly dry white segment. Pinot Gris is traditionally called Tokay d'Alsace (but without any obvious connection with the Hungarian wine) and nowadays both names tend to appear on the label. It is one of the four grape varieties of Alsace that can be grown in a grand cru vineyard and is used for Vendange Tardive and Sélection de Grains Nobles. Pinot Gris has a certain spiciness that is not dissimilar to Gewurztraminer, except that the flavour is more subtle, and it complements food, particularly fish and game, very well. Like Gewurztraminer, it encaptures the quintessential flavours of Alsace. There is a similar weight and richness in the mouth and a bouquet of mushrooms, with the slightly musty smell of the undergrowth of damp woods, and perhaps a hint of apricots, or that wonderful French honey bread, pain d'épice. These flavours are emphasised all the more in the richer Vendange Tardive wines.

Alsace Pinot Gris ages splendidly; the best recent vintages are 1990, 1989, 1988, 1985, 1983 and the monumental 1976. Recommended producers include Domaine Weinbach, Muré, Schlumberger, Marc Kreydenweiss, Rolly Gassmann, Léon Beyer, Jos Meyer, Trimbach, Hugel and Zind-Humbrecht.

There are occasional examples of Pinot Gris from **Germany**, mostly from Baden, where it is called Ruländer. The slightly sweet **Hungarian** Badacsonyi Pinot Gris also fits into this segment, as does one example from **South Africa**, Van Loveren's ripe mushroomy Pinot Gris with a dry finish.

Viognier

The final aromatic grape variety in the segment is Viognier. The flavour of dried apricots is the key to the bouquet and palate, with some quite rich, in some instances almost unctuous, perfumed overtones. Viognier is a difficult, temperamental grape variety to grow. It is at its best in the tiny appellations of the northern **Rhône**, in Condrieu and adjoining Château Grillet. Both are expensive: Condrieu costs around £20 a bottle, while Château Grillet is nearer £35. It is questionable whether Château Grillet is really worth almost twice the price of Condrieu – Condrieu from a good producer like Pinchon, Georges Vernay, Château du Rozay and Dumazet certainly offers some original and appealing flavours.

Occasionally, you can find a **Côtes-du-Rhône** cépage Viognier. This may come from young vines not yet suitable for Condrieu, or simply from a grower who rises to the challenge of Viognier, such as Domaine Ste-Apollinaire. Viognier is also exciting some interest amongst the more innovative producers of the Midi. Skalli, for example, has just introduced a Viognier to its Fortant de France range. The flavour is not as intense as a Condrieu, but the wine is considerably cheaper.

Viognier has excited a little interest in **California**, amongst the band of so-called Rhône Rangers. To date, Calera is the only winery to produce a Viognier which holds its own alongside Condrieu.

FULL AND FLOWERY (MEDIUM BODY, NO OAK, LOW ACIDITY)

Most **New World Rieslings** fit into this category. They are often off-dry, but differ from Alsace and German Rieslings in their lower degree of acidity, originating from the warmer climates. That is particularly true of those from Australia, California, South America and South Africa, in contrast to those from New Zealand and Oregon, which have enough acidity and feature alongside Alsace and Germany in a previous segment of the wheel.

In California, good Riesling producers include Freemark Abbey, Joseph Phelps, Château St Jean, Firestone and Jekel. In Australia, the Barossa Valley of South Australia is generally deemed to be the best source of Riesling, with the influence of German immigrants from Silesia in the last century. Look out for Yalumba with its Pewsey Vale vineyard, Petaluma, Plantagenet in Western

Australia and Hill-Smith's Old Triangle Riesling, which offers some of the best value.

There are a couple of South African Rieslings available, notably De Wetshof and La Bri. These are clearly labelled Rhine Riesling, so as not to cause confusion with Cape Riesling or Paarl Riesling, which are Cruchen Blanc under other names.

The other contender for this segment would be from Austria, with Spätlese quality wines made from Riesling, Weissburgunder, Grüner Veltliner and other grapes. The climate is significantly warmer, giving wines with lower acidity levels. However, in practice, the Austrian wines actually available in this country seem to polarise somewhere between the rich and sweet Beerenauslese and Trockenbeerenauslese, or the firmly dry, steely Grüner Veltliner.

LIGHT HONEY (MEDIUM BODY, NO OAK, LOW ACIDITY)

Eastern Europe

It is quite extraordinary, given the phenomenal choice of wines available in Britain, that **Lutomer Laski Rizling** continues to head the list of top sellers. Laski Rizling comes largely from **Slovenia** which, as we write, has been unaffected by the turmoil in what was Yugoslavia. It is really Slovenia's answer to Liebfraumilch, soft, grassy and slightly sweet, with just enough acidity to stop it from cloying. There is nothing offensive about it, although it lacks character.

Laski Rizling is quite different from the Riesling of Germany. It lacks the depth of flavour and produces some light innocuous white wine, without much to distinguish it. It grows widely in Eastern Europe, as Welschriesling in Austria, Olasrizling in Hungary and Riesling Italico in Italy.

Comparable wines might include Austria's Welschriesling which is rarely exported, but has more fruit than its Slovenian counterpart. Hungary used to produce large quantities of a similar style of wine, but is now tending to concentrate on more Western varietals like Merlot, Cabernet Sauvignon, Chardonnay and Pinot Blanc. Bulgaria makes a basic blend of Riesling and Misket, which is soft and slightly sweet, as is Thisbe from Cyprus, produced by the large co-operative, Keo.

Central Italy

The other contenders for this segment of the wheel are the slightly sweet wines of central Italy, such as **Orvieto abboccato** and **Frascati amabile**.

Abboccato means medium-sweet. Orvieto abboccato may be made occasionally from grapes affected by noble rot – in which case it fits into the sweet wine section of the wheel – but more often it comes simply from grapes that are riper than average, left on the vines that little bit longer. The acidity level will therefore be low and the taste gentle and honeyed, with some soft fruit.

Amabile is not quite as sweet as abboccato and is therefore nearer to medium-dry than medium-sweet in flavour, with some rather bland, nondescript fruit. Dry Frascati is more satisfying.

SWEET WHITE WINES

Full Body

Rich and roasted	Botrytis	Age
Peachy elegance		
Lemony honey	Botrytis	No age
Rich dried grapes	No botrytis	Age
Late-picked elegance		
Soft and honeyed	No botrytis	No age
Grapey Muscat		

- Alsace, German and Austrian Tokaji and Eiswein; New World noble late-harvest wines
- Sauternes, Barsac; German and Austrian Trockenbeeren-auslese and Beerenauslese; Orvieto
- Sweet Loire wines, Monbazillac, Cérons, Premières Côtes de Bordeaux, Ste-Croix du Mont, Loupiac, Vouvray, Montlouis and Coteaux du Layon
- Commandaria, vin de paille, Vin Santo and Constantia
- Jurançon, Pacherenc de Vic-Bilh, Recioto di Soave, Picolit, Torcolato and New World late-harvest wines
- Monbazillac, Premières Côtes de Bordeaux, Ste-Croix du Mont and Coteaux du Layon
- Moscato Naturale d'Asti, Moscato di Pantelleria, New World Muscat and Gewurztraminer

RICH AND ROASTED (FULL BODY, AGE, BOTRYTIS)

The phenomenon of *Botrytis cinerea* (*pourriture noble* or noble rot) has already been explained in the introduction to the taste wheels; suffice to say here that its development is essential to all the really great sweet wines of the world. Noble rot adds an extra dimension of complexity, making wines with considerable concentration, a combination of intense sweetness and balancing acidity, and the characteristic *gout de rôti*, or roasted, almost burnt, flavour of the botrytis. These are wines that will enjoy a long life; a sweet wine made without noble rot does not usually have the same potential for longevity.

Sauternes

Sauternes is the classic sweet white wine. It comes from a small part of the vineyards of Bordeaux, around the village of the same name. The neighbouring village of **Barsac** also gives its name to an appellation; however, while the wines from the village of Barsac may be called Sauternes, those from Sauternes may not be called Barsac. The weather at vintage time is crucial to the production of fine Sauternes: not only must the grapes be fully ripe, but the appropriate climatic conditions must prevail – dank misty mornings to encourage the growth of botrytis, followed by brilliantly sunny afternoons to dry the grapes. On average in a decade the right conditions probably occur only three or four times, and a potentially good vintage can be ruined at the very last moment by a heavy rainstorm. The run of three consecutive fine vintages which Sauternes has enjoyed with 1990, 1989 and 1988 is virtually unheard of, with all three making some simply wonderful, rich concentrated wine.

A careful selection of the grapes – Sauvignon, Sémillon and perhaps a little Muscadelle – is made in the vineyard, with successive meticulous pickings (a process called *triage*) selecting only those grapes affected by noble rot (sometimes as many as ten times at Yquem). In years when botrytis is not prevalent it is still possible to make some perfectly acceptable Sauternes if the grapes are ripe – the wine will be sweet, but it will lack that essential flavour of botrytis and complexity that are characteristic of great Sauternes. The botrytis gives the wine a firm bite and prevents it from tasting too sweet or cloying. There is a rich unctuous quality about good Sauternes, with ripe honeyed flavours, a hint of apricots and peaches, and perhaps toffee and cream and some tropical fruit. Good Sauternes is mouth-filling, for it is relatively high in alcohol – significantly higher than German wines of comparable sweetness – and also rich in glycerine.

Inevitably, good Sauternes is expensive given the unpredictability of its production. It is said that one vine accounts for one glass of wine at Château d'Yquem and, while a vine may provide more wine in other lesser châteaux, yields are still tiny. Estates that are currently performing well include Suduiraut, de Fargues, Lafaurie-Peyraguey, St-Amand (which is also called la Charteuse), Gilette and Bastor-Lamontagne. La Tour Blanche has improved significantly in recent vintages. The other good vintages of the last decade were 1986, 1983, 1981 and 1980.

The difference between Sauternes and Barsac is not easy to discern. The consensus is that Barsac is more elegant than Sauternes, perhaps more refined, with a delicacy and a delightful honeyed, lemony character which may nudge it into the next segment of the wheel. However, the taste is so similar that it fits just as comfortably into this segment.

Barsac has enjoyed the same good run of vintages as Sauternes. Good Barsac estates include Coutet, Climens, Caillou, Doisy-Daëne, Doisy-Védrines, Liot and Suau.

Burgundy

Burgundy would certainly not spring to mind as a source of *pourriture noble*. However, very occasionally, Jean Thévenet at Domaine de la Bon Gran in the Mâconnais makes a cuvée spéciale from botrytis-affected Chardonnay. The result is quite extraordinary and the wine is very expensive, with the 1983 vintage currently costing around £50 a bottle and the 1989 around £22 a half-bottle from Adnams of Southwold. Simon Loftus of Adnams describes it as 'renowned, very rare, nectar', so what more need be said?

Alsace

A first taste of Gewurztraminer, **Sélection de Grains Nobles**, alongside a Sauternes, may reveal striking similarities, not so much in the actual taste, but in the texture of the wine. Sélection de Grains Nobles can be made only from Riesling, Pinot Gris, Muscat or Gewurztraminer – and only in the best years, when the grapes are affected by botrytis – and it has a concentrated richness of flavour. Like Sauternes, it is also relatively high in alcohol and glycerine. A Muscat Sélection de Grains Nobles is rather rare; with Pinot Gris there is a full toasted flavour, while Riesling is a little more elegant and steely. With Gewurztraminer the flavours, especially from a year like 1988, 1989 or 1990, are rich and opulent, with the essential spiciness of Gewürztraminer, and will be even better with bottle age.

Hugel were the leaders in the production of late-harvest wines in Alsace. Other houses noted for their Sélections de Grains Nobles include Schlumberger, Léon Beyer, Paul Blanck, Domaine Weinbach, Muré, Rolly Gassmann and Zind-Humbrecht.

Germany

Across the Rhine in Germany, the Riesling grape makes some stunning sweet wines and it is the sugar readings in the grapes that determine the ultimate quality category (Prädikat) of the wine. While other grape varieties have been developed for their ability to attain high sugar levels, even in a relatively cool climate – such as Kerner, Optima and Huxelrebe – there is nothing to better a fine Riesling, with its elegance combined with a firm backbone of acidity, preventing the wine ever from cloying. Other grape varieties may attain greater ripeness, but they lack the essential breed and finesse that make **Riesling Trockenbeerenauslese** the great wine that it is. The German system of Prädikat has already been explained in the medium section of the wheel; suffice to say here that Trockenbeerenauslese and **Eiswein** (see opposite) are the two categories which fit into this segment of the wheel.

Trockenbeerenauslese, which means literally individually picked dried berries, is made only in exceptional years, such as 1988, 1989 and 1990 (another extraordinary run of three fine vintages). Even in the best vintages, Trockenbeerenauslese accounts for only a minute percentage of the production of an estate. Like Sauternes, it is made from grapes that are so affected by noble rot that they have become shrivelled and raisin-like but, in contrast to Sauternes, the alcohol level is very low, with an average of only 6 per cent compared to 15 per cent for Sauternes. It seems that the German yeast has less staying power than that of Sauternes, especially in the colder winters, and this accounts for the difference. With such a tiny and uncertain production, prices are high, comparable to some of the best Sauternes.

Austria

Austria has a similar quality system, based on the sugar readings, or oechsle levels, of the ripe grapes, with an additional category called **Ausbruch**, which comes between Trockenbeerenauslese and Beerenauslese. The village of Rust is particularly renowned for its Ausbruch wines. However, Austrian dessert wines generally tend to be heavier and less elegant than those of Germany, as the alcohol levels are higher – the result of the warmer Austrian climate. Riesling is less refined in Austria than in Germany; and other grape varieties such as Bouvier, Müller-Thurgau, Ruländer, and Welschriesling are also used for sweet wines. Austrian Trockbeerenauslese is amazingly good value, for example, less than £6 for a half bottle of Bouvier Trockenbeerenauslese.

Eiswein

Eiswein is more of a German, rather than Austrian, speciality, and there are also occasional examples from Canada and Washington State. Eiswein is something of a commercial gimmick. The grapes, having already attained Beerenauslese level, are left on the vines until well into winter, December or January, becoming even more shrivelled and dehydrated. The producer is waiting for the temperature to fall to below freezing point, so that the icy grapes can be quickly picked and pressed while their water content is still frozen. This means that the sugar and acidity are all the more concentrated and, in some ways, this makes a somewhat unbalanced wine, without the usual elegance of a Beerenauslese. There is an intense concentration of flavour, with searing acidity and powerful sweet flavours. Eiswein can be made in most good vintages and, with such an acidity level, will age for as many as 20 to 50 years.

Canada also makes some good examples of Eiswein, for the climate of Niagara, with its severe winters, lends itself to its production with relative ease. The only example to reach the UK market as yet comes from Inniskillin, with a hybrid variety Vidal. However, Inniskillin's Riesling ice wine is better, as is Château des Charmes late-harvest Riesling, although these are rarely imported. The Washington State winery, Covey Run, has made some successful Riesling ice wine.

Tokaj

Tokaj is not only Hungary's most individual wine, it is also one of the world's great dessert wines. The development of noble rot is a vital factor in the final flavour and there are various levels of sweetness. **Tokaj Szamorodni** (meaning 'as it comes', implying that nothing has been added to the wine) can be either dry or sweet, depending on whether or not the grapes have been affected by noble rot. Then there is **Tokaj Aszú**, the sweetness of which is measured in putts (meaning the number of puttonyos, or tubs, of very sweet wine added to the base wine). Three, four or five putts are usual, while six is exceptional and very rich. Then there is even sweeter **Tokaj Aszú Essencia** (generally the equivalent of 5 or 6 putts but aged longer – only the best wines are used) and finally, the sweetest of all, **Tokaj Essence** (drained from the aszú fruit at 45 to 65 per cent sugar level and fermented with great difficulty), which is very rare and precious and is even attributed with life-restorative powers.

Tokaj five putts is perhaps the standard wine which fits into this category, a deliciously concentrated dessert wine. It has the amber colour of amontillado sherry, with a taste of toffee-apples and burnt sugar along with a firm, balancing bite of acidity: a really mouth-filling wine. With such a concentration of sugar and acidity, the best Tokaj will age for many years, developing some delectable roasted toffee flavours.

Until the break-up of the communist system, production had been in the sole hands of the State Cellars, but now there have been moves towards privatisation, with initiatives being taken by individual producers, as well as investment and interest from abroad, notably Peter Vinding-Diers of Notre Dame de Landiras in the Graves, who is very excited by the potential of the area. The Royal Tokaj Wine Company has been created by a group of 68 producers, but for the moment it is too early to taste the results of their investment.

New World late-harvest wines

Sweet botrytis-affected wines form part of the repertoire of most of the New World producers, with examples from South Africa, California, Australia and New Zealand. Normally, the label will specify whether a wine is botrytis affected, or merely a **late-harvest** wine, made from over-ripe grapes. The use of the word 'noble' in conjunction with late harvest always implies botrytis. The botrytis-affected wines of the New World tend to come into this category of the wheel, as they are generally quite high in alcohol, with a rich concentration of flavour.

Unfortunately, EC regulations do not at present allow table wines over a potential alcohol level of 15 per cent to be imported, which affects most of the sweet wines of the New World, although a few from Australia and elsewhere do slip through the bureaucratic net. (Australia is currently waiting for ratification of an agreement to allow the import of its dessert wines.)

The best-known botrytis-affected wine of South Africa is **Edelkeur**, which was developed by Gunter Brözel, one of the leading winemakers of the Cape, for many years responsible for the wines of the Nederburg estate. Edelkeur, made from Chenin Blanc, was his flagship; it is concentrated in flavour, with the slightly burnt taste of botrytis but, sadly, is hard to find. A Weisser

Riesling Noble late-harvest wine, from the recently renovated Neethlingshof Estate, where Gunter Brözel is now winemaker, is about to be imported for the first time.

De Bortoli in the hot Murrumbidgee Irrigation Area of New South Wales, where the vines depend upon irrigation for survival, has established a reputation for botrytis-affected Semillon, making it the leader in this style of wine from **Australia**. The wine might have neither the concentration nor the balance of Sauternes, but it does have a lovely honeyed flavour with a tang of toffee-apples. Similar wines are Petaluma's Botrytis Riesling and Yalumba's Botrytis Semillon.

In **New Zealand**, Rongopai makes something of a speciality of its botrytised wines, a blend of Chardonnay and Riesling, while Dry River Valley produces a delicious botrytis-affected Riesling, rich and concentrated. Redwood Valley in Nelson also has a late-harvest Riesling that is sometimes affected by botrytis.

California too produces some botrytis-affected wines. Château St Jean has established a reputation for its noble late-harvest Rieslings, and Robert Mondavi makes the occasional noble late-harvest wine, mainly from Riesling, and occasionally from Sauvignon. Far Niente Dolce is a superb blend of one part Sauvignon to two parts Semillon, produced like a Sauternes, and with a distinct similarity of flavour. Also look out for botrytis-affected Sauvignon and Riesling from Renaissance.

PEACHY ELEGANCE (FULL BODY, AGE, BOTRYTIS)

Sweet Loire wines – Vouvray, Bonnezeaux, Coteaux du Layon and Quarts de Chaume

The Loire Valley rivals Sauternes and Barsac as the producer of the greatest sweet wines of France, though most agree that Sauternes has the edge – just. Although the best sweet wines of the Loire also depend on botrytis, there is a fundamental difference between the regions – the grape variety. In the Loire Valley Chenin Blanc is grown and, like Sémillon and Sauvignon in Bordeaux, is particularly susceptible to noble rot in the appropriate climatic conditions. Acidity is one of the dominant characteristics of Chenin Blanc, a feature which makes it so much more appealing as a sweet wine – with honey and botrytis to balance the acidity – and better than some of the dry white appellations of the Loire Valley. The acidity also gives it immense longevity: from a good vintage, a Vouvray or Bonnezeaux could live as long as 40 years.

Coteaux du Layon is the most basic sweet white wine of the Loire, from vineyards, as the name implies, on the banks of the River Layon, a tributary of the Loire. The appellation comprises six villages, the names of which may also appear on the label. **Chaume** is generally regarded as the best. Within the village of Chaume there is a tiny vineyard called **Quarts de Chaume**, with its own appellation which, in good years, makes some particularly fine sweet wines. Also in the same valley is the small appellation of **Bonnezeaux**, producing wines with an intensity lacking in Coteaux du Layon, and nearby is the little-known, but up-and-coming, appellation of the **Coteaux de l'Aubance**, with wines that are very similar to Coteaux du Layon.

Coteaux du Layon and the other adjoining appellations are always sweet. Even if there is no botrytis, the wine is made only from very ripe grapes or, in lesser years, the juice is chaptalised in order to obtain the right balance of sugar and alcohol. In contrast, **Vouvray** is something of a chameleon for, depending on the climatic conditions of the individual year, it may be anything from very dry to lusciously sweet. **Moelleux** and **doux** are the key words on the label, indicating a sweet wine. On the opposite bank is the village of **Montlouis** which produces very similar wines, but they lack the concentration of Vouvray in the very best years, and the appellation is smaller and less well known.

Bonnezeaux or Vouvray from a great vintage is wonderful. It is deliciously honeyed, with apricots and peaches and cream, but always there is the firm backbone of acidity which makes the wine long lived as well as complex. The Loire Valley has had a terrific run of good vintages in the last decade or so, with 1990, 1989, 1988, 1985, 1983, 1982, 1978, 1976 and 1975 all making some wonderful wines. These are wines which can be drunk when they are young and obviously honeyed, but they will also develop into magnificent bottles with age.

Recommended producers include in Vouvray, Huet, Foreau, Bernard Fouquet, Champelou, Pascale Delaleu and Château Gaudrelle; in Bonnezeaux, Château de Fesles; in Montlouis, Berger; in Coteaux du Layon, Domaine de Sauveroy, Vincent Ogereau and Baumard; in Quarts de Chaume, Château de Bellerive and Château de Suronde; and in Coteaux de l'Aubance, Domaine du Bablut, Domaine Richou and Domaine de Montgilet.

Monbazillac

Monbazillac is the sweet white wine of the Dordogne, coming from vineyards just south of the town of Bergerac. In the best years, the grapes are affected by noble rot – in the same way as

Barsac or Bonnezeaux – for with its proximity to the river, there is the necessary humidity with autumnal mists. However, the years with noble rot tend to be the exception rather than the rule, and most Monbazillac fits more comfortably further round the wheel. But, when the grapes are affected by botrytis, Monbazillac makes a delicious and seriously under-priced dessert wine. Hugh Ryman has been making wine there with delicious results, in Château les Hébras and Château Monthaudes. Château Treuil de Nailhac is another excellent estate, and also Château Haut-Bernasse.

Germany and Austria – Beerenauslese and Auslese

Beerenauslese means literally 'a selection of berries' – in other words, berries affected by noble rot, which are dehydrated, with some concentrated sweet juice. Both Germany and Austria use this term. Austrian Beerenauslese is richer, with lower acidity and more alcohol, and may well fit more comfortably into the rich

segment of the wheel, while German Beerenauslese – especially if it is made with Riesling – will have a wonderful honeyed elegance, always balanced with some firm acidity that prevents a cloying finish. A good Beerenauslese will always be a perfect combination of elegance, flavour and acidity.

Auslese, which means 'selected harvest', is usually more delicate. The grapes may not necessarily be late-picked (as they are in a Beerenauslese) but the term implies a choice of the best bunches, which are particularly ripe and usually affected more than average by botrytis. The resulting wines are deliciously honeyed, not opulently luscious, but delicately sweet. The weight and body of a particular wine depends very much upon its provenance and grape variety. Riesling makes the most elegant wines, especially in the cooler Mosel valley, while wines from further south, from Rheinpfalz or Rheinhessen, may be a little heavier and fuller. If a grape variety like Scheurebe or Optima is used, the flavour will be less subtle and less elegant.

Italy

There are occasional examples of botrytised wines from Italy, which the Italians call *muffa nobile*. Antinori makes one on its Orvieto estate of Castello della Sala. Although, to all intents and purposes, the wine is a delicious **Orvieto** it can not be labelled as such: it is outside DOC regulations with the use of such grape varieties as Sauvignon, as well as Grechetto and Drupeggio, and is simply called Muffato della Sala. Other Orvieto producers also aspire to noble rot in the best vintages, most notably Decugnano dei Barbi.

LEMONY HONEY (FULL BODY, NO AGE, BOTRYTIS)

In practice, the dividing line between this segment and the previous one is very blurred. Ageing ability is the key distinction and most wines from a good vintage, made by a talented producer from botrytis-affected grapes which have sufficient acidity, have the ability to age. Those that come from lighter, lesser vintages are unlikely to be affected by botrytis and therefore may fit into the late-picked elegance segment of the wheel.

Monbazillac is an example of a wine that crosses three segments, depending on whether it has botrytis, and whether it comes from a light vintage or a more concentrated one. The best Monbazillac with botrytis, from a good vintage and a talented producer, will age for almost as long as a good Sauternes or Barsac. In lighter years, the grapes may only be partially affected by botrytis and the flavours will be less intense, with some gentle peachy honey, and the wine less suitable for ageing. The same may be said of the peripheral regions of Bordeaux such as **Premières Côtes de Bordeaux**, **Cérons**, **Ste-Croix du Mont** or **Loupiac**. In fact, more often than not these wines are not affected by botrytis.

From the Loire, a lighter, less intense **Vouvray**, **Montlouis** or **Coteaux du Layon** may fit into this section, although most of the sweet white Loire wines have an ability to age, with the firm acidity originating from the Chenin Blanc. Again, those less likely to age are without botrytis.

In other words, this segment of the wheel is a meeting point of wines that, for one reason or another, are misfits in other sections. When they are at their best, they fit more happily into other segments.

RICH DRIED GRAPES (FULL BODY, AGE, NO BOTRYTIS)

The process of drying grapes is a very simple way of increasing their sugar content. This is either done in the vineyard, with exposure to both sunshine and, more importantly, wind, or the grapes are picked and then left to dehydrate in a well-ventilated place. Whichever method is used, the grapes become raisin-like, with sweet, concentrated juice. The result is some rich, flavoursome wine, that may almost taste as though it is fortified, such are the concentration and weight.

Cyprus

Take **Commandaria**, which would not be out of place in the fortified taste wheel, alongside sweet sherry. It is the traditional dessert wine of the island of Cyprus, its name deiving from associations with the Knights Templar of the twelfth century. It is made from exotic and colourful-sounding grape varieties that are not found anywhere else, like Xynisteri, Mavron and Opthalmo. The ripe grapes are dried in the sunshine until they virtually turn into raisins, then they are pressed and the juice is slowly fermented. The resulting wine is rich and raisiny, somewhat reminiscent of Moscatel grapes, with some ripe walnuts and marmalade, but without the firm alcoholic bite of a fortified wine. However, Commandaria can be treated in exactly the same way as a cream sherry and can be drunk before or after a meal, depending upon your mood.

The main producers are the large co-operatives which dominate the wine production of Cyprus, and normally Commandaria is sold under a brand name, for example St Barnabas, Commandaria St John and Grand Commandaria.

Vin de paille

The practice of drying grapes is a very old one; often the grapes were laid on straw mats, giving rise to the term *vin de paille* in France or *Strohwein* in Germany. While Strohwein is no longer made, France still preserves the occasional pocket of tradition, with a little production of vin de paille, especially in the isolated region of the Jura mountains. While 100 kilos of grape would normally give about 70-75 litres of juice, for vin de paille the amount is drastically reduced to 20 or 25 litres. Fermentation is very slow, taking as long as four years in small barrels, and although red or white grapes can be used, the final colour of the wine is a rich brown with a taste of raisins and walnuts. This is a curiosity that rarely travels outside the region but is made by most of the growers for their family and friends.

Italy

The nearest Italian equivalent to vin de paille is **Vin Santo**, although it is not always comparable in taste. There are Vin Santi that are rich and sweet, but others that are almost shockingly dry. This uncertainty originates from the inexact, or indeed haphazard, method of production. The ripe grapes are left to dry for several weeks, with bunches either on straw mats or hanging from rafters in a well-ventilated barn. When the grapes are suitably *passiti* (dried), they are pressed and the resulting sweet juice is left to ferment in small oak barrels which are sealed, traditionally, with wax – but often more prosaically nowadays with concrete. The barrels are not completely filled, a factor which can determine the level of sweetness or not (the fuller, the sweeter). They are then left for a minimum of three years, but often longer, in an attic or somewhere that is subjected to both the summer heat and the winter cold. A considerable amount of evaporation takes place, as well as some gentle oxidation, and the resulting wine is wonderfully concentrated, with some sweet nutty flavours and a firm degree of acidity. Again, Vin Santo tastes as though it might be fortified, as the alcohol level is relatively high at 15 per cent, but genuine Vin Santo should never be fortified. Beware of any label that says Vino liquoroso, for that is not the genuine article.

Avignonesi is generally recognised as the best Vin Santo, but at a price to match. Other more accessible wines include Isole e Olena, Selvapiana, Capezzana, Antinori, Montagliari and Brolio. Although Tuscany is the most obvious source of Vin Santo, some is also made in Trentino, and a little in Umbria.

South Africa

South Africa's reputation as a wine-producing country was made with a wine called Constantia at the beginning of the nineteenth century. Today, the estate of Klein Constantia is trying to revive this old wine, but opinions vary as to whether the traditional Constantia was fortified or not. As nothing in the records of the estate says that it was fortified, the Muscat de Frontignan grapes remain on the vines until they are over-ripe. The wine is then left to age in 500-litre oak casks for a year until it turns golden amber in colour and tastes smooth and unctuous, with a flavour of orange marmalade. It is presented in an old-fashioned, irregularly shaped, 50-centilitre bottle. Avery's of Bristol is the sole importer, offering Vin de Constance at around £12 a bottle.

LATE-PICKED ELEGANCE (FULL BODY, AGE, NO BOTRYTIS)

The obvious contenders for this category are the various late-harvested wines which do not depend upon the development of *Botrytis cinerea* for sweetness and flavour. Some of the *passiti* wines of Italy may also come into this segment.

Jurançon

Jurançon, a white wine from the foothills of the Pyrenees, has already featured in the dry section of the wheel. However, the appellation also includes **Jurançon Moelleux**, which is made from grapes that have been left on the vines to dry, in a process called *passerillage* (botrytis occurs very rarely). This process relies upon the warm autumn winds – called the *froin* –that blow off the Pyrenees to keep the grapes healthy and free of rot. The grapes are usually picked some time in November and the wine is made in the classic way: a grower like Henri Ramonteu at Domaine Cauhapé ages his Jurançon Moelleux in oak barrels for a few months, and also makes a careful selection of the grapes, depending on variety and sugar levels. Like a fine Sauternes, a good Jurançon Moelleux (sometimes labelled Vendange Tardive) will develop more complex flavours with age. It can be a long-lived wine and has a significant price advantage over most Sauternes. Good recent vintages include 1990, 1989, 1988, 1986 and 1985. Reliable producers include Domaine Cauhapé, Château Jolys and Domaine Bellegard.

The nearby appellation of **Pacherenc de Vic Bilh** also includes moelleux, produced mainly by one grower, Alain Brumont at Château Bouscassé. There are wines of three different levels of quality, named according to the month in which the grapes were picked, Octobre, Novembre and Décembre. A comparative tasting clearly illustrates that the longer the grapes stay on the vine, the sweeter and more concentrated the wine. The Union de Plaimont makes a Cuvée St-Albert from grapes picked on the feast day of the saint, 15 November.

Italy

Recioto di Soave is made from grapes that could also be used for dry Soave but which are left instead to *appassire* (gently dehydrate), and are then vinified to make some deliciously elegant, honeyed sweet wine, with a concentration of fruit and balancing acidity which benefits from a little bottle age. The best producers are Anselmi and Pieropan.

Picolit was always presented as one of the great dessert wines of Italy, but it seems to have rested on its laurels, and does not now have the stature of some of its competitors. Picolit is the grape variety used, found mainly in the DOC of the Colli Orientali del Friuli. Production is tiny and demand in Friuli outstrips supply, which means that little is exported. The grapes are dried and the result is quite delicate.

Torcolato is a stylishly original Italian dessert wine, made by Maculan, the leading producers of the DOC **Breganze**. The main grape variety is the little known Vespaiolo, which may be blended with some Tocai, and again the grapes are dried out. Vinification entails some ageing in barriques to produce a lovely honeyed wine, which develops with five or six years' bottle age.

New World

The numerous late-harvest wines of the New World which depend not upon botrytis, but on the over-ripe grapes of a late harvest for their sweetness, fit into this segment of the wheel. Again, the availability is affected by the EC regulation limiting the potential alcoholic strength of these wines to 15 per cent.

California Grapes may be left on the vine in the hope of attracting botrytis in California, but if that fails to happen, a straightforward, sweet late-harvest wine is made. Riesling is the most usual grape variety, sometimes called White or Johannisberg Riesling: Firestone, Joseph Phelps, Château St Jean and Renaissance are names to look out for, while Mark West produces a Late-Harvest Gewurztraminer, which is ripe and spicy. However, in such a warm climate there is always the danger of a loss of acidity if the grapes are left on the vine for too long.

Washington State Riesling is generally more successful in cooler Washington State than in California. Not only is some steely dry Riesling produced, but also some lovely late-harvest wines, which usually have a better acidity balance and more elegance than those from the Golden State. Examples include Select Late-Harvest Riesling from Arbor Crest Wine Cellars and Stewart Vineyards Late-Harvest White Riesling – both of which are imported by Windrush Wines, who were pioneers of this part of the so-called Pacific North-West.

Australia and New Zealand Muscat seems to be the most popular grape variety for late-harvest wines from Australia, which feature further round the wheel. New Zealand too favours late-harvest Muscat, but there are also some delicious examples of late-harvest Riesling, occasionally affected by botrytis, with elegant Riesling fruit and balancing acidity; good examples come from Redwood Valley and Montana.

SOFT AND HONEYED (FULL BODY, NO AGE, NO BOTRYTIS)

One of the pleasures of sweet wines is that they have an instant appeal when they are young. Most will develop greater complexity with bottle age, but lighter wines from less prestigious appellations can offer some immediate enjoyment within a couple of years of the vintage.

Monbazillac

Monbazillac is an example of a wine that crosses two, if not three, taste segments. While the best examples of Monbazillac benefit from botrytis- affected grapes and improve with bottle age to last for some considerable time, in lighter years it is drinkable in its early youth, but may not necessarily develop.

In the past, Monbazillac had been the victim of bad winemaking, spoilt by excesses of sulphur and chaptalisation, but things are looking up, with some good producers making some lovely light honeyed, peachy wine. It may never have the subtlety of good Barsac or Sauternes, but it does offer a considerable price advantage. That roving winemaker of the south-west, the English-born, Australian-trained Hugh Ryman, has achieved great things with two estates, Château les Hébras and Château Monthaudes. Other good estates include Château Treuil de Nailhac, Château le Fage, Château Boudigand and Château Haut-Bernasse.

Some of the peripheral sweet appellations of Bordeaux are very similar to Monbazillac. The grape varieties are the same – Sauvignon, Sémillon and a drop of Muscadelle. In the finest years they may also have noble rot, but more often than not they are made from very ripe grapes and, in unripe years, may well depend upon chaptalisation for the right balance of alcohol and sufficient sweetness. However, in the better vintages, wines like **Loupiac**, **Ste-Croix du Mont** (look out for Château des Coulinats and Château Roustit), **Cadillac** and **Premières Côtes de Bordeaux** can offer some enjoyable and good-value drinking. There is also Château St-Georges in the Graves, with vineyards immediately adjoining those of Sauternes, which, contrary to the expectations of the appellation, makes a sweet honeyed wine.

The Loire

Some of the sweet wines of the Loire Valley from lighter vintages also fit into this segment. Take a wine like **Coteaux du Layon** – under ideal conditions the grapes are heavily affected by botrytis; in less than perfect conditions they are not and the producers will hope merely for ripe grapes with enough sugar to make an elegantly sweet wine, preferably without having to resort to chaptalisation. Unlike Vouvray, which is everything from very dry to very sweet depending on the condition of the grapes, Coteaux du Layon and the adjacent appellations are always sweet. For recommended producers, see the peachy elegance segment.

GRAPEY MUSCAT (FULL BODY, NO AGE, NO BOTRYTIS)

There is no doubt that the **Muscat** grape makes some delicious sweet wines; sometimes these are fortified but, in table wines, the natural sugar left in the grape emphasises the rich, perfumed flavour of the grape itself.

Italy

Asti Spumante is described in the sparkling wine wheel. The still wine of the region is **Moscato Naturale d'Asti**, refreshingly low in alcohol, at only 5·5 per cent, taking its sweetness from the grape sugar remaining after the fermentation has been stopped. It can be delicious, light, delicately refreshing and grapey. Good producers include the Viticoltori dell'Acquese, Ascheri and Chiar. Drink the youngest and freshest available.

The island of Pantelleria produces **Moscato di Pantelleria**, which can fit into two different wheels – sometimes it is fortified and sometimes not. **Moscato Passito di Pantelleria Bukkuram**, from the leading producer, Marco de Bartoli, is not fortified and is wonderfully opulent in flavour.

New World

There are numerous sweet Muscats produced in the New World, from California, Washington State, New Zealand and Australia.

In California, Robert Mondavi's **Moscato d'Oro** is the leading example, with some ripe honeyed Muscat fruit. From Washington State there is **Muscat Canelli** (which is the same grape as Muscat de Frontignan, or Muscat à Petits Grains) from the Cascade Estate Winery in the Yakima Valley, with apricots and acidity, and Château Ste Michelle, with a lovely Muscat and peach flavour.

In Australia, Brown Brothers have made a name for themselves with their Late-Picked Muscat, which has some wonderful ripe fruit (see also the Liqueur Muscats in the fortified wine wheel); while in New Zealand the best late-harvest Muscat comes from Matua Valley. A new technique called cryoextraction is applied, which concentrates the juice in the grapes, reducing the water content to make a very sweet, ripe, luscious wine.

While late-harvest Rieslings or Semillons might fit into a previous segment of the wheel, wines made from Gewurztraminer, with its spicy flavours, are more comfortable in this section. Examples include Matua Valley Late-Harvest Gewurztraminer from New Zealand, and from California, Mark West's Late-Harvest Gewurztraminer. Perhaps the flavour is not so different from a Sélection de Grains Nobles Gewurztraminer from Alsace, but it lacks the effect of the botrytis and has a lower acidity level.

ROSÉ WINES

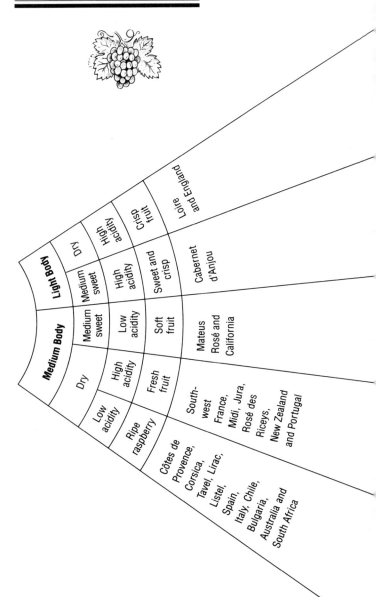

	Medium Body			Light Body		
	Dry	Medium sweet		Dry	Medium sweet	Dry
	Low acidity	High acidity	Low acidity	High acidity	High acidity	High acidity
	Ripe raspberry	Fresh fruit	Soft fruit	Sweet and crisp	Crisp fruit	
	Côtes de Provence, Corsica, Tavel, Lirac, Listel, Spain, Italy, Chile, Bulgaria, Australia and South Africa	South-west France, Midi, Jura, Rosé des Riceys, New Zealand and Portugal	Mateus Rosé and California	Cabernet d'Anjou	Loire and England	

Rosé wines are often seen as a compromise; when we are uncertain whether to drink red or white we may opt for pink instead. Essentially, the taste range of rosé is more akin to white than to red wine, though without the complexity or broad spectrum of flavours of either. Tannin and oak do not really feature and, although the best rosés are dry and fresh, there are some that are slightly sweetened; none are lusciously sweet. Acidity and body are the two main components of the pink segment of the taste wheel. Rosés are best drunk when they are young and fresh, within a year to three years of the vintage; there is nothing at all to be achieved by laying down rosés for further bottle age. Generally, light-bodied wines with high acidity come from cooler climates, while fuller-bodied wines with lower acidity originate from hotter countries.

It is rarely appreciated how difficult it actually is to make good rosé. The colour comes from contact with the grape skins: still rosé wine is never a blend of red and white wine. The key element, therefore, is in deciding how long to leave the juice in contact with the skins; the timing must be just right or the wine will be unbalanced. The visual aspect of a pretty pink in the glass is part of the charm of good rosé; too long and the colour will be too deep; not long enough and it will look pale and insipid.

Most rosés are made by what the French quite graphically call the *saignée* method of production; literally, this means that the tank of juice is bled. The red grapes are gently crushed and fermentation starts, with the juice taking on some colour until, after a few hours when it has absorbed sufficient colour, the juice is run off the skins. Fermentation then continues in the same way as for white wines, at a cool temperature. The poetic expression *vin d'une nuit* originates from the juice remaining on the skins over one night. The remaining skins are then usually added to the producer's red wine for extra colour and tannin. Alternatively, the skins may be given a gentle pressing after the juice has been run off.

'Have some wine,' the March Hare said in an encouraging tone. Alice looked all round the table, but there was nothing on it but tea. 'I don't see any wine,' she remarked. 'There isn't any,' said the March Hare.

Lewis Carroll, *Alice's Adventures in Wonderland*

MEDIUM BODY, DRY WITH LOW ACIDITY

Wines in this category originate from a warm climate, so are usually quite high in alcohol, and therefore taste quite full and rounded in the mouth. They have relatively low acidity – enough to give the wine structure, but not so much as to be obtrusive in the mouth.

Côtes de Provence and some of the other pink wines of the south of France are the obvious examples in this category. The appellation Côtes de Provence can cover white, pink or red wines. In fact, very little white is actually made and, although the red is growing in interest and quality, the most common is the pink wine, which is produced extensively in the hinterland of St-Tropez and Toulon. It is quite a full-flavoured wine, dry but not acidic, with some substantial fruit flavours, including raspberries, which makes it a good accompaniment to fish and picnics. However, the youngest available should be drunk, for it can quickly lose its freshness and charm, turn tired, flabby and a little stewed.

Domaines Ott at Château de Selle are leading producers of the appellation; but although well-made, the rosé is rather over-priced. The wines of the Vignerons du Presqu'Ile de St-Tropez are good examples of the appellation.

Neighbouring **Provençal** appellations include rosés which are very similar in flavour, coming from the same grape varieties: a mixture of Grenache, Cinsaut, Carignan, and perhaps some Syrah and other lesser known Midi varieties. In the Coteaux d'Aix-en-Provence, Château Fonscolombe makes some acceptable rosé, while within the tiny appellation of Palette, rosé accounts for only a small part of the production of the virtually sole estate of Château Simone. Likewise, Château Val-Joanis in the Côtes du Lubéron makes a wine that is full and fresh, with ripe raspberry fruit, benefiting from technical expertise and high-tech equipment. Rosé also features in the appellation of Bandol, but in tiny quantities, and also in the small VDQS of Coteaux Varois.

The island of **Corsica** also offers the occasional pink, notably from an indigenous grape variety called Sciacarello, that is grown particularly around the towns of Ajaccio and Sartène. Domaine de Peraldi is the leading Ajaccio estate, with some refreshing pink wine that is reminiscent of the herbs of the Corsican *maquis*.

The best appellation of the **Rhône Valley** for rosé is Tavel which, unlike its neighbour Lirac, is an appellation for rosé alone. It seems strange that Tavel has established a reputation for its rosé wines because the region is so much better suited to the production of gutsy reds. It lies north-west of Avignon, close to Châteauneuf-du-Pape. The rather alcoholic Grenache is the main grape variety used, so the wine tends to be quite heavy and alcoholic, lacking some of the freshness and elegance that is really desirable in a pink; it is best drunk within a year of the vintage. Reputable producers include Aqueria, Genestière, Trinquevedel, Vieux-Moulin and Forcadière.

In Lirac, which is very similar in taste, Assémat is the best producer, and Château Bouchassy is also good. Côtes-du-Rhône may also be pink, usually produced by a village co-operative; so too may Gigondas.

The other leading wine of the south of France that fits into this segment is the biggest seller from the Salins du Midi, Listel Gris de Gris, which has recently been renamed Grains de Gris. This is quite a full-flavoured fruity rosé, from a large producer that has led the way with technical developments in the cellar and virtually organic treatments in the vineyard. Grains de Gris is a vin de pays des Sables du Golfe du Lion, from phylloxera-free vineyards on the sand-dunes of the Camargue.

If we move outside France we find there are some full-bodied pink wines produced in **Spain**. Rioja rosado can be full and fruity, from producers like Marqués de Cáceres, but it is rarely aged in oak these days. The one exception here is Marqués de Murrieta, with the dry, tarry, slightly herbal flavours of traditional oak-aged Rioja. Any rosé from Navarra and Penedès is likely to be very similar to pink Rioja: Torres Casta Rosada is the most typical example. Pink wines from further south, from Jumilla, for example, which includes pink in its DO, tend to be rather heavy and over-alcoholic.

In **Italy**, the occasional DOC includes a rosato. In Bardolino, Bardolino Chiaretto is made, a lighter version of the already pale red wine. Further south, Cerasuolo d'Abruzzo makes full-flavoured, fairly alcoholic wine from the Montepulciano grape, and most of the main Sicilian producers include a pink wine in their range. Cellaro Rosato is a pleasantly quaffable pink.

One of the better Italian pinks comes from Carmignano, a wine that is poetically called Vin Ruspo, or more prosaically Carmignano Rosato. Vin Ruspo literally means stolen wine, and the name originates from the days when the peasant farmers used to keep the juice from the last picking of grapes, which were not delivered to the landowner's cellar until the following morning. The resulting wine, fermented off the skins, was pink. The occasional Chianti estate produces a rosato, which shows how suitable Sangiovese can be for pink wine, producing some fresh fruit flavours; Rosa dell'Erta from San Polo in Rosso is a good example.

Bulgarian Vintners have introduced a **Bulgarian rosé** from the Burgas region, made from Cabernet Sauvignon, which is quite full in flavour, with the merest hint of residual sugar (which could almost push it into the next segment); it is clean and fresh, and firmly eschews the idea of a blush wine.

One of the most successful pinks from outside Europe comes from **Chile**. It has a European connection: the producer is Miguel Torres of Penedès fame. His Santa Digna rosé, made from Cabernet Sauvignon, is a wonderfully fresh, but quite full, ripe raspberry-flavoured wine.

A couple of examples from **Australia** are ripe and fruity: Mount Hurtle, made from Grenache and 10 per cent Shiraz, has a ripe strawberry nose, and is reminiscent of strawberry-flavoured boiled sweets. Schinus Molle rosé is lighter and drier, with less obvious raspberry flavours.

South Africa also includes the odd rosé in its repertoire; there is a fresh Blanc de Noir from Boschendal, made from a mixture of Cabernet Sauvignon, Shiraz, Merlot and Tinta Barocca, as well as some dry, fruity rosé, made under the Fleur du Cap and Culemborg labels.

MEDIUM BODY, DRY WITH HIGH ACIDITY

Numerous appellations of France include rosé, but it is often of minimal significance and can be seen as simply a useful way of disposing of excessive juice when making red wine. This process of running off surplus juice is, to all intent and purposes, the same as the *saignée* method. Examples include Irancy rosé, Chinon rosé, Beaujolais rosé, each of which usually account for only a very small part of the appellation, but with an accordingly larger production in years of more generous yields.

Wines from the moderate climate of **south-west France** tend to have some body and weight, while retaining quite a high level of acidity. They are always firmly dry, although they may have a richness that verges on sweet, originating from the flavour of ripe fruit. The little-known appellation of the Gironde, Bordeaux Clairet, is epitomised by Château Thieuley, whose wines have some lovely raspberry fruit. Simple Bordeaux Rosé is also possible, as at Château de Sours, again with some wonderfully ripe fresh fruit.

The adjoining appellation of Bergerac also includes rosé, but only in small quantities. Château la Jaubertie makes a pleasing example, which has a surprisingly deep colour. Côtes de Gascogne rosé from Château le Puts is also good.

Rosé du Cabernet du Haut Poitou, from the excellent regional co-operative outside Poitiers, is a well-made fruity pink, from both Cabernet Sauvignon and Cabernet Franc.

Further south, the little-known appellation of Béarn owes its initial creation to the prevalence of Rosé de Béarn, made from Cabernet and Tannat. However, its appeal is limited outside the foothills of the Pyrenees. Better flavours from the same grapes come from the co-operative of Plaimont in the form of pink Côtes de St-Mont, a small VDQS around the tiny hamlet of St-Mont which is just north of the appellation of Madiran. Fresh, fruity acidity and easy drinkability are the keynotes of this wine.

Among the wines of the **Midi**, an effort is made to retain some acidity by picking the grapes before they are truly ripe, so that a refreshing crispness is part of the character of the wine. Some very successful rosé vins de pays have been produced because the producers have given the pink wines as much care and attention as their red and white wines. A pink vin de pays des Coteaux de Bessilles (one of the newer vins de pays from close to Pézenas, from a dynamic producer at Domaine St-Martin de la Garrigue) is deliciously fresh and fruity, encapsulating the essence of good rosé. So, too, Domaine de Limbardie, an innovative estate in the vin de pays des Coteaux de Murviel, produces some good rosé. Another good rosé is a vin de pays d'Oc cépage Syrah, under Skalli's Fortant de France label.

In the **Jura**, on the other side of France, close to the Swiss border, rosé is included in the appellation Côtes du Jura. In fact, neither Poulsard nor Trousseau, the two indigenous red grapes of this isolated hilly region, provides much colour – nor, for that matter, does the third red grape allowed in the appellation, Pinot Noir. The dividing line between red and pink can be somewhat blurred, with wines that are either deep pink or light red, both with quite full-bodied flavours. However, these wines tend not to travel too far from the region and so are rarely seen.

The obscure Champenois appellation of **Rosé des Riceys** also fits into this category. This is a pink wine made from Pinot Noir in the village of les Riceys in the department of the Aube. Good Rosé des Riceys is surprisingly deep in colour and full in body for such a northern climate, with ripe raspberry fruit that, in its best years, can have some of the chocolatey character of Pinot Noir. However, as far as value is concerned, it is an expensive curiosity.

Most **Portuguese rosé** is slightly sweet, but there is now one exception: from Bairrada comes Nobilis – made by Sogrape, the people who created Mateus Rosé. It may be seen as an attempt to upgrade the image of Mateus, and move away from its lightly sweet, fizzy associations. The 1991 vintage is dry and fruity with some acidity and strawberry fruit.

There is one lone example from **New Zealand**, a rosé made by Esk Valley in Hawkes Bay from Merlot and Cabernet Franc, which is quite rounded and mouth-filling, with good acidity on the finish.

MEDIUM BODY, MEDIUM-SWEET WITH LOW ACIDITY

The obvious example in this category is Mateus Rosé, a light pink, slightly sparkling, slightly sweet wine. Perhaps it should be included in the sparkling wheel, but as it is far from fully fizzy (some carbon dioxide is merely injected into the wine, and evaporates quickly once the bottle is opened), it can feature just as happily here. Mateus Rosé was one of the wine trade's great success stories, with world sales once standing at a million bottles a week. The eye-catching, instantly recognisable dumpy bottle, with a picture of the Mateus palace on the label, has probably introduced thousands of people to wine. The other key Portuguese pink wine is Lancers, made by the large company of J M da Fonseca. Both are really quite uncharacteristic of the real flavour of Portuguese wine.

Another marketing success story, though not as long-lasting or eye-catching as that of Mateus, was the ploy of renaming pink or rosé wine as blush. For some reason, this seemed to capture the consumer's imagination and it became fashionable to drink blush wine. California led the way, with numerous blush wines made from its surplus Zinfandel. White Zinfandel therefore indicates a pink wine, usually with the full, soft, slightly sweet flavour of California. The giant producers, E & J Gallo, owe their chief success in the British market to White Grenache, again a soft pink wine, with full body and low acidity.

LIGHT BODY, MEDIUM-SWEET WITH HIGH ACIDITY

Rosé is the tiniest section of the wheel, indicative of the scant attention paid to it by most British wine merchants; Simon Loftus of Adnams of Southwold is the rare exception of a wine merchant who actively enthuses about rosé, even to the extent of including it in tastings. The fact remains that pink wines represent a tiny 5 per cent of the British wine market, chiefly accounted for by Mateus Rosé, and the lightly sweet wine from the Loire Valley, Cabernet d'Anjou. The latter is made from Cabernet Franc and, less often, Cabernet Sauvignon, and is grown in vineyards around the town of Angers. It may be firmly dry, but is usually slightly sweet, over-sulphured and generally uninspiring; the dry version is usually a more interesting glass of wine. Serious producers in Anjou tend to concentrate on red wine, motivated by the relatively recent creation of the appellation Anjou Villages for the better red wines of the area.

Occasionally you may find a mature Cabernet d'Anjou, such as the 1961 Domaine de Bablut, stocked by Adnams, which has some mature herbal flavours and a hint of toffee on the finish. It is something of a rarity, not to mention a curiosity.

LIGHT BODY, DRY WITH HIGH ACIDITY

The other dry wines of the **Loire Valley** are not unlike dry Cabernet d'Anjou in flavour, but they allow a wider range of grape varieties to be used, including Groslot and Gamay, as well as both Cabernets and Pinot Noir. The appellations here are simple: Anjou Rosé is always dry; Saumur Rosé and Touraine Rosé are very similar to one another. A curiosity called Noble Joué Touraine – made from a blend of Pinot Meunier, Pinot Gris and Pinot Noir – is made by Clos de la Dorée, and is redolent of fresh raspberries, quite full on the palate with some crisp acidity on the finish. Rosé de la Loire and Chinon Rosé are two other appellations for light dry pinks. Sadly, many Loire pinks can be rather flat and dull, spoilt by an excess of sulphur.

Further east, **Sancerre** includes rosé in its appellation, as does nearby Reuilly. Both tend to be very pale in colour, the lightest of pink, and are very delicate on the palate, but usually with some crisp acidity. Beurdin in Reuilly and Vacheron in Sancerre are worth trying. However, these wines are not cheap, tending to be similar in price to the red wines of their appellation.

Across the Channel, you can find the occasional pink wine from our own **English** vineyards; Conghurst, Denbies and Tenterden rosés are the best, with fresh raspberry fruit and crisp acidity.

RED WINES

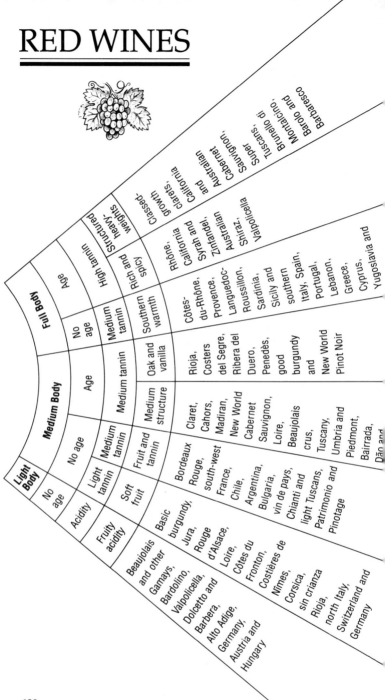

Light Body
- No age · Acidity · Light tannin · Soft fruit · Fruity acidity

Medium Body
- No age · Medium tannin · Fruit and tannin
- Age · Medium tannin · Medium structure

Full Body
- No age · Medium tannin · Southern warmth · Oak and vanilla
- Age · High tannin · Rich and spicy · Structured heavy-weights · Classed-growth

Beaujolais and other Gamays, Bardolino, Valpolicella, Dolcetto and Barbera, Alto Adige, Germany, Austria and Hungary

Basic burgundy, Jura, Rouge d'Alsace, Loire, Côtes du Fronton, Costières de Nîmes, Corsica, sin crianza Rioja, north Italy, Switzerland and Germany

Bordeaux Rouge, south-west France, Chile, Argentina, Bulgaria, vin de pays, Chianti and light Tuscans, Patrimonio and Pinotage

Claret, Cahors, Madiran, New World Cabernet Sauvignon, Loire, Beaujolais crus, Tuscany, Umbria and Piedmont, Bairrada, Dão and...

Rioja, Costers del Segre, Ribera del Duero, Penedès, good burgundy and New World Pinot Noir

Côtes-du-Rhône, Provence, Languedoc-Roussillon, Sardinia, Sicily and southern Italy, Spain, Portugal, Lebanon, Greece, Cyprus, Yugoslavia and...

Rhône, California Syrah and Zinfandel, Australian Shiraz, Valpolicella

California Cabernet Sauvignon, Australian and Super Tuscans, Brunello di Montalcino, Barolo and Barbaresco

FRUITY ACIDITY (LIGHT BODY, NO AGE, ACIDITY)

Young red wines are often dominated by acidity rather than tannin. They are light in body and are not destined for much ageing, but are best drunk within one or two years. Their immediate appeal is their fruit and easy drinkability, combined with a lack of harsh edges.

Beaujolais and the Gamay grape

Beaujolais is made from the Gamay grape and is sometimes vinified in a particular way called carbonic maceration (see introduction): whole bunches of grapes are put into a vat full of carbon dioxide, a process which brings out the youthful fruity character of the wine by emphasising the fruit flavours and reducing the tannin content. A variation on this, called semi-carbonic maceration, is more commonly used in Beaujolais: no extra carbon dioxide is added to the vat, but is retained from the fermentation. The effect is very similar, making some wonderfully fresh, lively wines, with some acidity and stacks of fruit, often reminiscent of ripe cherries. Beaujolais-Villages, a superior appellation originating from the better villages of the region, tends to have a little more body, but is still a wine for relatively early drinking.

The essential wine for early drinking is, of course, **Beaujolais Nouveau**, but this has lost some of its frivolous, popular appeal. However, it still accounts for something like half the production of the Beaujolais region, with wines that are delightfully fruity in a ripe vintage, but mean and acidic in a poorer vintage. In practice, Beaujolais Nouveau is often very much better at Christmas, or even Easter, than on its release date of the third Thursday of November.

Beaujolais Nouveau has had its imitators, inspired by its apparent success. In France there is **Gaillac Nouveau**, also made from Gamay; as well as **Côtes-du-Rhône Nouveau**, and the nouveaux wines among the vins de pays of the Midi, which can be released a month earlier than Beaujolais. As they originate from a warmer climate, they are often riper and more fruity. Italy has not escaped the craze for *vini novelli*, with Banfi's Santa Constanza, Antinori's San Giocondo and Gaja's Vinòt.

The 1992 produced good fruity wines with fresh acidity and some staying power. For wines with more structure, see Beaujolais crus in a later segment.

Good producers of Beaujolais include the range of growers in the Eventail des Vignerons Producteurs, a marketing group of such people as André Depardon, Guy Patissier, Louis Genillon and others. Georges Duboeuf is a reliable name, and so too are Loron and Chanut. The village co-operatives are also important, accounting for around 40 per cent of the production of the region. Cellier des Samsons in Fleurie is particularly fine.

The 1991 and 1990 are also good vintages in Beaujolais but, for basic Beaujolais, drink a younger vintage, and look for the crus in older vintages.

The Gamay grape rarely produces wines with any staying power. The sole exceptions are the ten Beaujolais crus, and even then, perhaps not all of them. Elsewhere in eastern France, Gamay makes deliciously accessible wines for early drinking. The nearby **Coteaux Lyonnais**, which adjoins the vineyards of Beaujolais in the south, is one of those overlooked appellations which makes an agreeable alternative to Beaujolais. Georges Duboeuf is the most easily available producer.

Other Gamay-producing regions   Mâcon, which adjoins Beaujolais, also produces a red wine made predominantly from Gamay. However, it rarely seems to have the vibrant fruitiness of good Beaujolais; the white wines of the Mâconnais are better. Gamay is also grown in the upper reaches of the Loire, and production in the **Côtes du Forez** is dominated by one of France's most modern and efficient co-operatives, the Cave Co-opérative des Vignobles Foréziens, which produces a range of wines based on Gamay, all lively and fruity and ideal for early drinking. The wine of nearby **Côte Roannaise** is very similar, though perhaps with a little more body.

Saint-Pourçain, a fairly obscure VDQS of central France, makes a red wine that is usually a blend of Pinot Noir and Gamay, in other words a type of Passe-Tout-Grain (the Burgundian appellation for wines which are a blend of Gamay and, at least a third, Pinot Noir), with some fruity acidity and light body. The wines of the local co-operative are imported by that intrepid Loire specialist, Robin Yapp of Yapp Bros, but there are numerous small producers whose wines rarely travel.

Gamay also grows along the Loire Valley in the form of **Gamay de Touraine**, as well as in the regional **vin de pays du Jardin de la France**. There is also an occasional Gamay from the **Fiefs Vendéens**, down on the Atlantic coast near the Sables d'Olonne, which is generally light and fruity, with a little more acidity and less actual fruit than good Beaujolais. **Gamay du Haut Poitou**, from the high-performance regional co-operative, has a little more structure. A more substantial Gamay from close to the Rhône Valley, is **Gamay de l'Ardèche**, again produced by a local co-operative.

Pinot Noir

Other northern French wines have the similar characteristics of fruit and acidity, but have little tannin. There are various wines made from Pinot Noir in the vineyards of Champagne, northern Burgundy and the Loire Valley, which are comparable in flavour. Pinot Noir, in a cool climate, produces some refreshing raspberry fruit, balanced with lively acidity, rather than tannin. It is only in the very ripest years that wines like Bouzy and Sancerre have much tannin and staying power and lose their fresh acidity.

Irancy, the best-known red wine appellation of the Yonne, from a village close to Chablis, usually has enough body to push it into the next segment of the wheel. Nearby **Coulanges-la-Vineuse** tends to produce wines which have a softer flavour, with some of the vegetal character of Pinot Noir; while the wines of **Epineuil**, from the third red wine-producing village of the Yonne, are fruity with a slight earthiness.

The central vineyards of the Loire Valley, Sancerre, Menetou-Salon and Reuilly, are only about 80 miles from the Yonne, so there are distinct similarities, with the same disadvantages of growing red grapes in marginal vineyards. Red **Sancerre** – like Menetou-Salon and Reuilly – is light and fruity, with acidity rather than tannin, except in very ripe years, when it might be given a little oak maturation. Generally, however, these red Loire wines are best destined for early drinking.

Bouzy, the appropriately named still red wine of Champagne, is proof that the wines of that area are so much better with bubbles, without the need to have sufficiently ripe grapes to provide enough colour for red wine. Acidity is certainly the dominant, usually excessive, taste element, with insufficient balancing fruit. Worth trying are Laurent-Perrier's red Coteaux Champenois and Bollinger's red Ay la Côte aux Enfants.

Italy

Northern Italy is the source of some light, easy-to-drink fruity reds. **Bardolino** is a pretty village on the shores of Lake Garda which produces light red and pink wine, from a mixture of grape varieties. The word '**classico**' on the label indicates that the wine comes from the heart of the vineyard area; '**superiore**' denotes a year's ageing, which does not usually improve the quality of the wine, as Bardolino is best drunk as young as possible. It is light in colour and light in body too, with some sour cherry fruit and an indefinable Italian flavour. **Chiaretto** is the pink version of the DOC, which also allows for Bardolino Novello, if you want a change from Beaujolais Nouveau.

Closest to Bardolino is **Valpolicella**, from vineyards to the north of the enchanting city of Verona, near Lake Garda. Valpolicella covers a distressingly wide quality range, resulting from an over-extension of the production area and an excessive increase in the permitted yields. However, attempts are now being made to tighten up the regulations, hopefully to some effect. Wines labelled 'classico' should have some ripe cherry fruit and should be drunk as young as possible. There is also a technique called *ripasso*, which gives fuller, richer wines, with some tannin, which places them in the rich and spicy segment of the wheel. Unfortunately for the consumer, there is rarely any indication of this on the label. Good Valpolicella producers include Allegrini, Masi, Quintarelli, Boscaini, Zenato, Tedeschi and Guerrieri-Rizzardi.

In north-west Italy, **Piedmont** – although known above all for its firmly structured wines – also makes some deliciously accessible and easy-to-drink reds from the Dolcetto and Barbera grape varieties. Dolcetto accounts for seven DOCs; Dolcetto d'Ovado, Dolcetto d'Acqui, Dolcetto d'Asti, Dolcetto di Dogliano, Dolcetto di Diano d'Alba, Dolcetto delle Langhe Monregalesi and Dolcetto d'Alba. This last one is the wine you see most often, with the highest concentration of good producers, partly because they also produce Barolo and Barbaresco. The great advantage of the Dolcetto grape is that it ripens early, and can be picked before the autumn rains.

The essence of good **Dolcetto** is ripe berry fruit, which is always balanced with some lively acidity, resulting in a deliciously refreshing bitter-sweet wine. It is rarely heavy or tannic, thus making it the most accessible of all the Piemontese reds. The key producers of the region, such as Altare, Giuseppe Mascarello, Aldo Conterno, Giacomo Conterno, Cavallotto, Prunotto and Rinaldi, complement their range with it.

Barbera also fits most happily into this segment, as the key to the taste of Barbera is acidity, rather than tannin. It is a grape variety that is grown all over Italy, both in the north and the south, but which really comes into its own in Piedmont, with three DOCs – Barbera d'Alba, Barbera d'Asti and Barbera di Monferrato. There is a quintessentially Italian flavour to Barbera, with its bitter-sweet fruit – sour cherries and plums – and a refreshingly astringent and acidic finish. Barbera d'Alba is considered the most substantial of the three DOCs, while Barbera de Monferrato is the lightest and easiest to drink. Barbera should be drunk when it is young and fresh and never more than four years old. As far as producers go, there are few who really specialise in Barbera; it forms part of the repertoire of most of the key Piedmontese estates.

There are other Italian DOCs whose key characteristics are soft ripe fruit, balanced with acidity. One is **Lagrein Dunkel**, from the Alto Adige or Südtirol, hence the Germanic ring to the name. Lagrein is the name of the grape used (*dunkel* means dark), which produces wines with masses of ripe, soft fruit, without any aggressive edges of tannin, and so is best drunk in early youth. Good producers include Grai, Lageder and Tiefenbrunner. There is a pink version too, called Lagrein Kretzer

Lago di Caldaro, or Kalterersee, is another wine from the Alto Adige. The best classico version comes from vineyards immediately around the lake of the same name, while the DOC spreads over a large area of the Alto Adige, from north of Bolzano down to Trentino. Light red fruit is its key characteristic, but with a smoky hint. Superiore indicates a half degree more alcohol, and you may see 'scelto' on the label too, which implies that the producer has made a special selection of the grapes. Good producers include Hofstätter, Schloss Schwanburg, Lageder and Tiefenbrunner.

Mountain vineyards seem to lend themselves to soft fruity reds. **Santa Maddalena** is one wine from the Alto Adige, made in exhilaratingly steep terraced vineyards outside the town of Bolzano. Schiava is the main grape variety used to make this light red wine, which has some strawberry fruit and which is for soft, easy drinking, the younger the better. Good producers include Grai, Hofstätter and Lageder.

Germany

German reds cross the boundary between the fruity acidity and soft fruit segments. Traditional German reds have the same quality categories as white wines, with the same sweetness levels. Thus, a red Spätburgunder Spätlese could be sweet, but confusingly, and happily, is not always so. A new wave of German winemakers are taking their red wines much more seriously and giving them some oak-ageing, with the aim of making wines with more stature and structure. In this instance, a Spätburgunder Spätlese would have the same level of ripeness as the sweet white wine, but would be fermented out until firmly dry; the label will indicate this with the word 'trocken'. Consequently, an increasing number of German wines fit into the following soft fruit segment.

Slovakia

Czechoslovakian, or more precisely, Slovakian wines are
beginning to make an appearance in Britain. One example which
fits into this segment is a light, fruity red wine from an indigenous
grape called Frankovka, which has fresh berry flavours.

Austria and Hungary

Red wine does not seem to be Austria's strength. However, there
are some singularly Eastern European grapes in its repertoire,
such as Blauer Zweigelt, which makes a soft fruity wine, with little
body. Blaufrankisch is also grown, mistakenly believed to be the
Gamay of Beaujolais. It is not the same grape, but there may be a
similarity in taste, with wines which have some light fruity acidity
and minimal tannin. In Hungary, the same wine is called
Kékfrankos, and in Germany, Lemberger. Examples of any of these
are pretty rare on British wine merchants' shelves.

SOFT FRUIT (MEDIUM BODY, NO AGE, LIGHT TANNIN)

Soft, ripe, juicy fruit is the key to this segment, but always with
the backbone of a light streak of tannin. These are wines to drink
in relative youth; they may age a little but that would be the
exception to the rule.

Burgundy

First comes the basic category of red burgundy, or **Bourgogne
Rouge**, which is made from Pinot Noir all over the region, from
the Yonne down to the limits of Beaujolais. In the northernmost
vineyards it tends to be light, with raspberry fruit and acidity, but
acquires more substance the further south you go. In the **Côte
d'Or**, Bourgogne Rouge comes from the less-favoured slopes:
neither grands crus, premiers crus, nor part of a village
appellation. However, in the hands of a good producer, Bourgogne
Rouge can make for an agreeable glass of wine. The grapes may
come from younger vines, which have insufficient structure for a
better appellation. The wine may even be given a little barrel
ageing for extra backbone and weight, though that is unlikely.
Usually, Bourgogne Rouge is the result of standard red-wine
vinification in a steel or cement vat, with a few days' maceration
on the skins.

Pinot Noir is a sulky grape variety, both temperamental in the vineyard and difficult to vinify in the cellar. It depends very much on the conditions of the vintage; Burgundy has been blessed with an excellent run of vintages in 1988, 1989, 1990 and then 1992, all of which are currently available. They are ripe fruity wines, with a little more body than is sometimes the case. This means that wines like Irancy and Coulanges-la-Vineuse (featured in the previous segment) may also have a little more structure than usual. Irancy, made from Pinot Noir and, occasionally, a very tiny amount of César and Tressot for extra body, tends to be a little sturdier than neighbouring Coulanges.

Good producers of Bourgogne Rouge include the Cave de Buxy in the Côte Chalonnaise and almost any top burgundy producer.

Further south, the new appellation of **Bourgogne Côte Chalonnaise** has been created to distinguish the vineyards of the Côte Chalonnaise, which do not fit into the village appellations of Rully, Givry, Montagny and Mercurey, from Bourgogne Rouge produced elsewhere. Previously, the only clue to the more precise origins of the wine was the postal code of the producer. Generally, at this level, the red wine of the Côte Chalonnaise is very similar to, but a little lighter in body than, that of the Côte d'Or. All over Burgundy the key to quality is the producer's name on the label. Good producers of Bourgogne Côte Chalonnaise include the dynamic Cave de Buxy, as well as Michel Goubard, Michel Juillot and Roger Narjoux.

The hinterland of the Côte d'Or is the source of two lesser, but increasingly popular, Burgundian appellations, **Hautes Côtes de Beaune** and **Hautes Côtes de Nuits**. As their names imply, the vineyards are on the upper plateau, behind the main slope of the Côte d'Or, where the climate is distinctly cooler. The wines tend to be lighter, with a little more acidity, and have some stalky tannin. In warmer years they should have some raspberry fruit.

Bourgogne Passe-Tout-Grain is a blend of Pinot Noir and Gamay (usually in the proportion of two to one), and can be attractively fruity, with a bit of acidity and tannin. The other lesser appellation of Burgundy, **Bourgogne Grand Ordinaire**, is anything but grand. It is decidedly ordinary, usually made from Gamay, and perhaps a little Pinot Noir, and is best forgotten.

Jura

The red wines of the Jura are covered by two appellations: **Arbois**, which includes the vineyards around the town (its one claim to fame is that it is the birthplace of Louis Pasteur), and the broader appellation of **Côtes du Jura**. The grape varieties used for red wine include Pinot Noir, as well as the indigenous Trousseau and Poulsard, both of which are peculiar to the Jura. Wines may be a blend of all three, or you may find pure Pinot Noir or Trousseau – but there will be little indication given on the label. They have a soft ripeness that can be reminiscent of light burgundy and, when they are made from Pinot Noir, they take on some of the soft vegetal characteristics, as well as the ripe fruity flavours, of that grape variety.

Unfortunately, the wines of the Jura are not widely available in Britain. Worth trying, if you can find them, are those from the Château d'Arlay, Christian Bourdy, Rolet Frères, Sylvie and Luc Boilley, and also those from Henri Maire's four different estates.

Rouge d'Alsace

Pinot Noir is the sole red grape variety of Alsace. Sometimes it makes a wine that is more pink than red, for in cooler years it suffers from the difficulties of ripening in relatively northern vineyards. Until recently, it had not really been treated seriously, with insufficient maceration to extract colour, nor any barrel-ageing to add structure. The general aim was a soft, light, fruity, easy-to-drink wine that was not sure whether it was trying to be pale red or deep rosé. Now, amongst some producers – such as Hugel, the Cave de Turckheim, Ostertag, Zind-Humbrecht and Muré – there is a trend towards producing a more structured **Rouge d'Alsace**, but it will always be a fairly light wine, with a light streak of tannin at the most, and some soft raspberry fruit. The recent run of fine vintages, notably 1988, 1989, 1990 and also 1992, has helped produce some good wines. Occasionally an older wine turns up tasting remarkably like a lesser burgundy.

Chinon, Bourgueil and the wines of the Loire

Chinon and **Bourgueil**, the two key red appellations of the Loire Valley, could cross the taste segments and fit into two categories. They may have light tannin and need no maturation or, depending on the vintage, produce a more structured wine that does need ageing. The soil also determines the style of wine: gravel, close to the river bank, makes light fruity wines; while a mixture of clay and flint gives wines structure and tannin. The grape variety used is Cabernet Franc and, while Cabernet Sauvignon is included in the appellations, in practice it is rarely used. The problem is that on the label there is little indication of the style of wine: you have to know the right grower and vintage, and both can change. Both 1990 and 1989 were good vintages; 1990 made rich, fruity wines, whilst those of 1989 are sturdier, with more staying power. Good Chinon producers include Couly-Dutheil, Charles Joguet, Bernard Baudry, Domaine de la Perrière and Clos du Saut au Loup.

Bourgueil, and the small enclave of **St-Nicolas de Bourgueil**, may fit more easily into the medium structure segment, but **Anjou Rouge** and the slightly more robust **Anjou Rouge Villages** come into this eminently fruity segment. They should have a little tannin, and ripe cherry and plum fruit should dominate the taste – what the French call *fruits rouges*, or red fruits, an all-embracing term for summer fruits, or a glorious summer pudding. Anjou Rouge is rarely worth keeping, except in the very ripest and hottest years. Similarly, **Saumur Rouge**, which is a lighter version of Anjou Rouge, from vineyards around the town of Saumur, rarely warrants keeping. However, the small enclave of **Saumur-Champigny** sometimes has a little more weight and body in riper years. Good producers include Domaine Richou, Château du Breuil and the Château de Chamboureau in Anjou; and Filliatreau, Château du Hureau and the Château de Targy in Saumur-Champigny. Amongst noted Bourgueil producers are Caslot-Galbrun and Lamé-Delille-Boucard, with Taluau and Jean-Claude Mabilleau in St-Nicolas de Bourgueil. The best Touraine Rouge comes from the vineyards of the famous Château de Chenonceau.

Côtes du Frontonnais

The **Côtes du Fronton** is one of the appellations of south-west France. It is not completely overshadowed by Bordeaux, but has some original flavour of its own, coming from the Négrette grape, which must account for a minimum 50 per cent of a wine, along with Cabernet Franc, Cabernet Sauvignon and Merlot, among others. Négrette is distinguished by its lack of tannin; this means that it produces deliciously easy-to-drink soft fruit, but needs blending with other grapes to give the wine body. Côtes du Fronton has a soft immediate appeal, in wines like Château Bellevue-la-Forêt, which is the largest estate. Other producers include Château Baudare, Château Flotis and the Cave de Fronton.

Costières de Nîmes

This is one of the newest appellations of the Midi, created in 1986. It was originally called Costières du Gard, but the name was changed in 1989 to avoid any possible confusion with vin de pays du Gard. The grape varieties are the usual Midi mixture – Carignan, Cinsaut, Grenache, as well as some improving Mourvèdre and Syrah – but the wines are very much lighter and easier than elsewhere in the south. There is an attractive spiciness, with a hint of southern warmth, but not much body. Village co-operatives dominate the appellation, but there are some good individual estates too, such as Château de la Tuilerie.

Corsica

There are three strands to Corsican viticulture: the grape varieties of North Africa and the Midi – Grenache, Cinsaut and Carignan – brought to the island by the *pieds noirs* leaving Algeria; the more recently introduced varieties like Cabernet Sauvignon and the white grapes, Chardonnay and Chenin Blanc; and, most colourful of all, the indigenous Corsican grape varieties, such as Nielluccio and Sciacarello. Nielluccio may be related to Sangiovese, and has some structure and backbone, while Sciacarello produces some wonderfully soft spicy, herbal fruit. In wines like Ajaccio, and some of the crus of **Vin de Corse** (such as Sartène, Calvi and Porto Vecchio), or in some of the **vins de pays de l'Ile de Beauté** (the evocative vin de pays that covers the whole island), Sciacarello is blended with Nielluccio and Grenache and can provide some delightfully spicy, original flavours, reminiscent of the Corsican countryside. These Corsican wines are rarely heavy or structured, but have a light, fruity character, with enough tannin to provide backbone, but no ageing potential.

Rioja

Rioja is the wine that put Spain on the world wine map. It comes from northern Spain, from vineyards around the town of Logroño, situated on the river Ebro. The wines divide into three distinct areas of production, with different soil and climatic conditions, namely, Rioja Alta, Rioja Baja and Rioja Alavesa. Most Rioja is a blend of two, if not all three, areas. The grape varieties are a mixture too: Tempranillo (in other regions largely responsible for some of Spain's best red wines) blended with Grenache, or Garnacha, as well as some Mazuelo, (otherwise known as Cariñena or Carignano) and perhaps a drop of Graciano.

There are four categories of Rioja, three of which benefit from oak ageing and one that does not. The latter is the wine that concerns us here, namely **sin crianza Rioja**, as opposed to crianza, reserva and gran reserva. Whereas the others come into the oak and vanilla segment of the wheel, sin crianza Rioja (which literally means 'without nursing', or in other words, ageing) depends upon the fruit flavour of the grapes for its taste and so fits in here. In fact, it does not have a very strong personality; it is a youthful fruity wine, with a touch of spice, but without any great individuality.

For information on producers and vintages look under gran reserva Rioja.

Other northern Spanish reds that have not been aged in wood have a similar flavour. As the nearby DO of **Navarra** produces wines from the same grape varieties, the flavours are comparable. **Toro**, which is further south on the Duero river, is made mainly from Tinto de Toro (otherwise known as Tempranillo), as well as Garnacha, so that the sin crianza version is not unlike a young Rioja. Bodegas Fariña is the best producer.

Italy

Cabernet, both Sauvignon and Franc, is widely grown all over north-east Italy. Usually, where Cabernet is included in a DOC, the label simply says Cabernet without specifying which one, and more often than not the wine is a blend of both. The taste is generally ripe and fruity, soft and plummy, with a little tannin to allow for two or three years' ageing, and occasionally it has the slightly herbaceous character that you can find in Cabernets from the Loire Valley.

Other north Italian reds have a similar fruity character, with a little tannin. One example is **Franciacorta Rosso** from Lombardy, which comes mainly from Cabernet Franc, with some Cabernet Sauvignon and Merlot, and which has some ripe berry fruit flavours, with a little tannin. **Teroldego Rotaliano**, a curious grape variety from Trentino, with its own DOC, produces ripe cherry fruit flavours, with a little tannin; Gaierhof is one of the few such wines to leave the country.

Switzerland

Swiss wines make a very occasional appearance on our shelves. Most of them are drunk by the thirsty Swiss themselves and the few wines that are available represent seriously bad value for money. More white than red wine is produced in Switzerland; the reds that we may find go under the name of **Dôle**, or may simply be labelled as Gamay or Pinot Noir. Generally, the colour tends to lack depth, and the palate definition, though they may have some of the vegetal flavour and raspberry fruit of Pinot Noir.

Germany

The better red German wines come into this segment of the wheel. The principal grape varieties are Pinot Noir (otherwise known as Spätburgunder) as well as Trollinger, Lemberger and Dornfelder. The Ahr Valley is considered to be the prime source of red German wines, but Baden and Württemberg are also important. The wines that we see most often are likely to come from Baden, or the Ahr Valley, with the occasional example from Rheinpfalz. Tesco, for instance, has a Baden Red to partner its Baden White, which is a light, fruity, slightly jammy Pinot Noir, with some raspberry fruit and acidity.

The more serious red German wines are given some oak ageing, but although this may not be obvious on the palate, the oak does provide more structure and backbone. The intrinsic taste, however, is the soft, vegetal flavour of Pinot Noir. Lingenfelder in Rheinpfalz makes some good Pinot Noir, with some ripe vegetal fruit and just enough tannin; Kessler in the Rheingau produces a slightly more austere Pinot Noir, while Weingut Meyer Nakel makes a Pinot Noir with some sweet fruit. Wines made from the Dornfelder grape tend to be a little drier and more solid, but with some ripe berry fruit. This is a relatively new German crossing that is becoming more popular, especially in southern Germany. It shows potential, both in the vineyard, where it is easy to grow, and in the bottle, with some good flavours.

FRUIT AND TANNIN (MEDIUM BODY, NO AGE, MEDIUM TANNIN)

If there is a grape variety that dominates this section, it must be Cabernet Sauvignon, blended perhaps with some Cabernet Franc and Merlot. Some grape varieties naturally produce more tannin from their skins than others, irrespective of whether they are then aged in oak, and assimilate more tannin from the wood – Cabernet Sauvignon is one of those. Although the tannin may be more obvious than in wines featured in the previous segment, it must always be balanced by sufficient fruit to make a harmonious wine. A backbone of tannin is an intrinsic part of the character of the wine; there is no virtue in keeping it on the assumption that the tannin will fade. It may well do, but so will the fruit, and then the wine is dead.

Bordeaux Rouge
Bordeaux Rouge is the most basic appellation of the Gironde, along with **Bordeaux Supérieur**, which simply denotes an extra half degree of alcohol and therefore a little more body. It covers all the vineyards outside of the better village and area appellations and is claret at its simplest and most accessible. Bordeaux Rouge is the house claret or own-label claret of wine merchants and

supermarkets. The wines inevitably vary with the vintage, but are generally ready for drinking within one to three years. There was a run of good vintages in Bordeaux, so that Bordeaux Rouge from 1988, 1989 and 1990 is drinking well, with plenty of ripe blackcurrant fruit, while the wines of 1991 and 1992 are generally lighter. A good Bordeaux Rouge has all the characteristics of a greater wine from the region, but less so. The blend of Cabernet Sauvignon, Cabernet Franc, Merlot (and perhaps Malbec, depending on the vineyard) makes a wine with some cassis fruit, perhaps a hint of spinach (the slight vegetal character of Merlot – not the same as the rotting vegetation of Pinot Noir), with a sturdy streak of tannin to provide some backbone.

There is not so much difference between a good Bordeaux Rouge and the wines of some of the peripheral areas of Bordeaux, such as **Premières Côtes de Bordeaux**, **Côtes de Castillon**, **Côtes de Bourg** or **Côtes de Blaye**. Those that adjoin St-Emilion, such as **Canon Fronsac** and the up-and-coming **Côtes de Francs**, have more affinities with St-Emilion, with a little more flesh and richness; while those that face the Médoc across the estuary of the Gironde have a lean, sturdier character.

Oak rarely features in the vinification of these wines. The economics of production simply do not permit such an indulgence; oak barrels are expensive and the price that Bordeaux Rouge fetches certainly does not warrant the outlay. Concrete or steel vats, lined with epoxy resin – not even stainless steel – are usual. Some Bordeaux Rouge is produced by a *négociant* who has bought wine, must or grapes from numerous small growers; if it comes under a château name, the so-called château will be a simple farmhouse, with a shed for the winemaking, and certainly not a handsome edifice, complete with *chai*. Much Bordeaux Rouge comes from the vineyards of Entre-Deux-Mers, which only have a specific appellation for white wine, although both colours are produced.

In Britain, much Bordeaux Rouge is sold under a wine merchant's own label such as The Society's Claret, Tanners' Claret, Harvey's No. 1 Claret, or under a brand name like Mouton Cadet, or the substantially better Sirius Rouge.

Amongst the so-called petits châteaux, the lesser estates that provide the basis of any good claret list, try de Sours, Bonnet, Thieuley, Méaume, de Tourtigeac, la Gardéra, all with the appellation Bordeaux or Bordeaux Supérieur.

From more precise appellations try: in Canon-Fronsac, Moulin Pey Labrie and Canon-Moueix; in the Côtes de Bourg, de Barbe, du Bousquet, la Croix-Millorit; in Fronsac, la Rivière, la Vieille Cure, Richotey; in the Côtes de Francs, Puyguéraud; in Côtes de

Castillon, Pitray; in Premières Côtes de Blaye, Haut-Sociondo; and in Premières Côtes de Bordeaux, du Juge, Reynon, Cayla and Tanesse.

South-west France

The appellations of south-west France have close affinities with Bordeaux. Until the region of Bordeaux was delimited in 1911, much of the wine from Bergerac, Duras and Buzet was simply blended with that of the Gironde. The grape varieties are the same, with Cabernet Sauvignon, Cabernet Franc and Merlot forming the basis. It is only as you travel further from Bordeaux that there are distinct changes, notably in Cahors and Madiran, but they come into the next segment. It is the wines of the appellations closest to Bordeaux that are generally ready for drinking within one to three years of the vintage.

The appellation of **Bergerac** was certainly overshadowed by Bordeaux for many years and only in the last decade has it really striven to create a separate identity. The vineyards on the western edge of the appellation touch those of St-Emilion and there are certain affinities of taste between the two. **Côtes de Bergerac** covers the same area, but indicates an extra degree of alcohol, while **Pécharmant** is a small enclave to the east of the town of Bergerac, where the wines are a little more structured and sturdy.

Co-operatives are important in Bergerac, and there are also some good individual estates. Best known is Château La Jaubertie, which has benefited from some Australian influence in the wine-making techniques; the wines are a little fuller and richer than others in the appellation. Other good estates include Château la Raz, Château Belingard, Château Richard and Château Court-les-Mûts. Try also Château Tiregand in Pécharmant.

The vineyards of the **Côtes de Duras** are separated from Entre-Deux-Mers simply by the departmental boundary. The differences between Bordeaux Rouge from Entre-Deux-Mers and red Côtes de Duras are therefore negligible; climate, soil and vinification methods are similar and the flavours are comparable. Two large co-operatives dominate the production of the Côtes de Duras, one of which is actually within Entre-Deux-Mers and makes both appellations. The other is outside the town of Duras. There are numerous small estates too, such as Domaine la Grave-Béchade, Domaine de Ferrant and Château de Conti.

A little further south are the **Côtes du Marmandais**, situated around the town of Marmande, which is better known in France for its tomatoes than for its wine. Flavours again are similar to Bordeaux Rouge, with similar weight, but with a streak of originality in the inclusion of the Abouriou grape, which can add an extra dimension of perfume. In practice, however, it is usually overwhelmed by Cabernet and Merlot, so that Côtes du Marmandais tastes very similar to a young Bordeaux. Two co-operatives account for almost the total production of the area.

The final Bordeaux Rouge taste-alike of the south-west is **Buzet**, formerly Côtes du Buzet. Once again, the grape varieties are Cabernet Sauvignon, Cabernet Franc and Merlot. A large and efficient co-operative, unusual in having its own cooperage, dominates the appellation, so that the better wines of Buzet are all given some oak ageing. However, this is not obvious on the palate and merely provides the wines with the subtle addition of some tannin, as well as some gentle oxidation. The best wines from the co-operative go under the châteaux of individual members, namely Château de Gueyze and Château de Padère. Vintages in this part of France follow those of basic Bordeaux very closely, so that the wines of 1988, 1989 and 1990 are all good vintages in the south-west, with wines that are already drinking well.

Gaillac, the appellation with vineyards around the Toulouse-Lautrec city of Albi, has improved the quality of its wines steadily over the last few years. However, it does suffer from something of an identity crisis in its red wines, for the regulations allow a considerable mixture of grape varieties. There are those of Bordeaux, as well as Gamay, Duras (no connection with the appellation), Fer Servadou, Négrette and Syrah, with various restrictions as to minimum and maximum percentages in the blend. The veritable hotchpotch of flavours produced makes it very difficult to define the quintessence of Gaillac, but it seems that Duras is the most characteristic grape variety, and most Gaillac Rouge includes a significant proportion. If it is blended with the Bordeaux grape varieties, the result is a red wine with some of the characteristics of the Médoc, with some tannin as well as fruit. However, if Syrah and Fer Servadou are used, the result is a little more spicy. Co-operatives dominate the production of Gaillac, notably Labastide-de-Lévis, whose wines have improved considerably in recent vintages, as well as the Cave de Técou. There are some good individual producers too, such as Château Clément Termes.

The flavours of the south-west meet those of the Midi in the twin VDQS of **Côtes de la Malepère** and **Cabardès**, which are situated on either side of the city of Carcassonne. The vineyards are a melting pot of grape varieties; those of the Midi mingle with those of Bordeaux to produce some original flavours which owe something to Bordeaux and something to the Languedoc. However, they retain a structure and a degree of leanness that has more in common with Aquitaine than with the Midi, so they fit quite happily into this taste segment. In the search for good value, it is the lesser-known regions of France that are coming into their own and there is no doubt that the value offered by a Côtes de la Malepère or Cabardès is far greater than a comparable petit château. Producers include Château Ventenac, Château de Rayssac, Château Troncin-Capdevila and Château de Pennautier in Cabardès, and Château de Routier and Château de Malviès in the Côtes de la Malepère.

Another lost area of the south-west is the **Côtes de St-Mont**, a small VDQS lying in the foothills of the Pyrenees, to the north of the appellation of Madiran. The local Plaimont co-operative is one of the best in France, in terms of equipment, expertise and motivation, and has worked hard for its place on the wine map of France. Red Côtes de St-Mont has a sturdy flavour, originating from the local Tannat grape, which is softened by some Cabernet and Fer Servadou. It generally provides good-value drinking.

Chilean Cabernet Sauvignon

Chile continues to make an impact. After the first flush of enthusiasm, when it was hailed as the next exciting discovery of the wine world, things have settled down somewhat, but there has been a steady improvement in both vineyard and cellar techniques. Chile does not yet produce a Cabernet Sauvignon to compete with a classed-growth claret – good cru bourgeois is about as near as it comes – but there is plenty of sound Chilean Cabernet Sauvignon which makes a very acceptable alternative to a Bordeaux Rouge or an unknown petit château.

There is no reason why Chile should not be able to produce ripe healthy grapes. The country has the major advantage of being phylloxera-free – how fortunate it was that the first vine cuttings from France crossed the Andes before phylloxera had reached Europe. The climate is superb for viticulture and there are virtually no problems with rot or disease. Irrigation is essential, with water supplied by the melted snows of the Andes. In the past there has been a tendency to over-irrigate in order to encourage generous yields; now they are learning to control growth in the vineyard and reduced yields will undoubtedly make for more concentrated flavours.

Some better Chilean Cabernet Sauvignons, such as Santa Rita Medalla Real and Errazuriz Don Maximiano, may fit more comfortably into the medium structure segment of the wheel, but basic Chilean Cabernet Sauvignon, often sold under a

supermarket own label, makes an original diversion from
Bordeaux Rouge.

Argentina

Argentina has lagged behind Chile, but is trying hard to catch up.
It is one of the big producers in the world league table, but most of
the wine produced, from the insipid Criolla grape, is destined for
its own domestic market. There are European grape varieties, such
as Chardonnay and Cabernet Sauvignon, but so far they represent
a minute percentage of the total production. The majority of the
vineyards of Argentina are on the sandy soils of the province of
Mendoza where again irrigation is essential and, although there is
phylloxera, it does not pose a threat in such sandy soil, so the
vines remain ungrafted. Yields in Argentina have been rather
excessive in the past, but they are being reduced, with the result
that the occasional good Cabernet is beginning to appear, notably
from Trapiche. As yet, they are without the depth of flavour of the
best of the Chileans. Merlot and Malbec from Trapiche are good
too, and the wines of Etchart and Michel Torino are also well
worth a try.

Bulgaria

Bulgaria is the one country of Eastern Europe that has successfully
adapted its wines to western taste and commercial demands. The
state-controlled wine industry was subsidised so that it could offer
competitive prices and thereby earn much sought-after foreign
currency. Bulgarian Cabernet Sauvignon was one of the great
success stories of the 1980s and it continues to represent very
good-value drinking, despite problems within Bulgaria,
originating from the dismantling of the systems of the Communist
era. Somehow, the taste of Bulgarian Cabernet Sauvignon will
never be very refined for it has a certain rustic earthiness about it.
The country's vineyards are divided up into *controliran* regions
which, more or less, equate to appellations. The best for Cabernet
Sauvignon are **Svischtov**, **Yantra Valley** and **Oriachovitza**. The
word 'reserve' on the label indicates three years' ageing in wood,
including a short time in new American oak and a longer period in
large Slavonic oak casks, with Reserve Cabernet Sauvignon from
Suhindol and Oriachovitza showing well. Sometimes Cabernet
Sauvignon is blended with **Merlot**. Stambolovo Merlot is also
good. Production is generally in the hands of large anonymous co-
operatives.

Two indigenous Bulgarian grape varieties also fit into this
section, namely Melnik and Mavrud. Both are fairly sturdy, rugged

varieties. Assenovgrad is the best area for Mavrud, while Melnik comes from the village of the same name. With some oak ageing it can have more body and substance than Mavrud.

And after this meander around the comparable Cabernet Sauvignons of the world, it is back to France, for vin de pays.

Vin de pays

There are vins de pays all over viticultural France, covering a multitude of flavours. The greatest concentration is in the Midi, particularly in the four departments of the **Gard**, **Hérault**, **Aude** and **Pyrénées-Orientales**. Vins de pays were created about twenty years ago, as a category below appellation contrôlée and VDQS, in order to give some kind of identity to the lake of anonymous vin de table – or plonk – that was produced in the south of France. Regulations are not as strict as for an appellation, allowing a much greater flexibility of grape varieties, and thus a considerable range of quality. There are vins de pays that compete with, or even out-perform, their neighbouring appellations, and there are others that are really no better than ordinary plonk and do nothing more than continue to contribute to the diminishing wine lake of the Midi.

The charm of the vins de pays is that they provide an outlet for creativity for the imaginative experimental producer. A producer is not compelled to plant the grape varieties of an appellation but can experiment pretty freely. It is true that there are regulations as to what can be planted, but if a grape variety is planted which is not authorised but which proves to be successful, the chances are that a blind eye will be turned. The most basic vins de pays come from Carignan and Cinsaut, and perhaps from crossings like Aramon and Alicante Bouschet, which were developed in the last century with the sole aim of boosting the colour in high-yielding vineyards. Syrah and Mourvèdre are increasingly planted, as are the grape varieties of Bordeaux, the Cabernets and Merlot, with some success. A winemaker may not put Merlot in his Minervois, but there is nothing to stop him experimenting with Merlot in his vin de pays.

Unlike appellations, all the vins de pays (with one exception, vin de pays des Sables du Golfe du Lion) depend upon administrative geography for their delimitation, usually in the form of a department (such as vin de pays de l'Aude), or a zone within a department covering several villages (such as vin de pays de la Vallée du Paradis). The Sables du Golfe du Lion are limited by the sand dunes of the Camargue, while there are four other larger vins de pays that cover several departments. The relevant one for the Midi is vin de pays d'Oc, covering Languedoc-Roussillon. The Comté Toloson accounts for a large part of south-west France, while the Comtés Rhodaniens relates to the northern part of the Rhône Valley and the Jardin de la France covers the whole of the Loire Valley. This last vin de pays is usually a white wine; the others fit quite happily into this taste segment.

The Midi is one of the most exciting regions of France, for a wind of experimentation has blown through the region at near gale force and continues to do so. There are constant changes, new developments, innovative techniques and new producers coming to the fore. Outside interest has been excited, not just from other parts of France but from other continents. Hardys, the large Australian company, has established a super new winery at Béziers and is encouraging local growers to plant more Cabernet Sauvignon, Sauvignon Blanc and Chardonnay, to which Australian vinification techniques are being applied. Domaine de la Baume from the Chais Baumière is the result.

Skalli, a long established *négociant* in the port of Sète, realised the changing role of the local merchants and has created a series of varietal wines under the Fortant de France label, mainly for Cabernet Sauvignon and Chardonnay, but for other grape varieties as well, such as Syrah, Merlot and Viognier.

There are numerous estates with imaginative, far-sighted owners who are seeking to achieve the best from their vineyards. They are pulling up their old Carignan and Aramon vines and replacing them with Syrah and Cabernet. The older generation is giving up its vines, in which its children have no interest, so that many of the old vineyards on the plains of the Midi are gradually being abandoned. Village co-operatives account for a considerable part of the production of the south; some are good, some are bad. Amongst individual estates worth seeking out are Domaine de St-Martin de la Garrigue, Domaine de l'Arjolle, Mas Jullien, Domaine de l'Abbaye de Valmagne, Domaine de Limbardie, Domaine Anthéa, Mas Chichet and Domaine Pech de Celeyran.

All of the above make good sturdy vins de pays, with a good balance of fruit and tannin. Sometimes the wines may benefit from a little bottle age, but, generally, vins de pays are best drunk at most within three to four years of the vintage. The main exception to this rule is Mas de Daumas Gassac, which fits more comfortably into the structured heavyweights segment of the wheel. Generally, however, most vins de pays – whether they are based on Cabernet, Carignan or Syrah – fit into this segment.

Chianti and other Tuscan reds

The epitome of Tuscany is Chianti, from vineyards covering a large part of the region. The DOCG of Chianti breaks down into several sub-zones. The most important is **Chianti Classico**, between the two cities of Siena and Florence. Then there is **Rufina**, the tiniest zone, which lies in a small valley north-east of Florence. **Montalbano** comes from the slopes of the Monte Albano, to the west of Florence (adjoining the more structured wine of Carmignano). **Colli Fiorentini** lies to the south and west of Florence; the **Colli Senesi** is a large area, encompassing the vineyards of Montalcino, Montepulciano and San Gimignano. The vineyards of the **Colli Aretini** are mixed up with suburbs of Arezzo and the **Colline Pisane** are contained in a small group of hills south-east of Pisa.

Essentially, there are two styles of Chianti: Chianti normale and Chianti riserva. The normale is for early drinking, while the riserva is not sold until it is at least three years old, and therefore comes in the next segment of the wheel. It is **Chianti normale** that concerns us here. The Chianti Classico Consorzio has gradually extended the ageing period of Chianti Classico normale; previously it was available in the June following the vintage, but this has now been extended a further seven months so that the 1993 vintage, for instance, will not be available until January 1995. In contrast, most other Chianti normale is available in the March following the vintage. The motives behind this lie in the Consorzio's attempt to make Chianti Classico appear a more serious, structured wine than light-hearted simple Chianti. It aims to cast off the image of frivolity attached to Chianti, along with the dumpy straw-covered bottle, and to demonstrate that Chianti deserves more serious attention. It also wants to distinguish Chianti Classico from the other Chiantis, in anticipation of Chianti Classico being given its own separate superior DOCG. Apparently all that is needed is the appropriate signature on the decree.

There are other differences between Chianti Classico and the other zones: for example, yields are lower and the required proportion of white grapes is smaller. None the less, Chianti normale, Classico or otherwise, is a delicious wine for relatively early drinking. The mainstay of Chianti, and all the wines of central Italy, is Sangiovese. Basically, there is good and bad Sangiovese, originating from a variety of different clones. Chianti has suffered from an influx of the wrong clones and some unfortunate plantings, but things are now looking much brighter, with considerable improvements, not only in the vineyard, but also in the cellar. As well as Sangiovese, a small percentage of a lighter grape, Canaiolo, is included, along with the statutory percentage of white grapes, Trebbiano and Malvasia, often ignored by the better producers.

Good Chianti Classico normale does have more structure than the other Chianti normale. It can age, but the general aim is to produce a wine for earlier drinking. Sangiovese produces a firm streak of tannin and an element of astringency that simply demands wonderful Tuscan olive oil to balance it. If the wine and food of a region are the natural complement to each other, then this is the perfect example. The flavour of Chianti Classico is of ripe but sour cherries, whereas Chianti from the other areas, with the possible exception of Rufina, tends to be lighter, a little softer, with less body, but none the worse for that. Drinkability is its essence and it does not merit much ageing.

Vintages do vary quite considerably in Tuscany. The 1990 was one of the great Chianti vintages, a year in which everything went right and some first-class wines were produced. The 1988 was also an excellent vintage; the 1985 and 1986 were good too, while the 1987, 1989, 1991 and 1992 were lighter. (For recommended producers see under Chianti riserva.)

There are other Tuscan wines in the style of Chianti. In the wake of the creation of the DOCGs of **Vino Nobile di Montepulciano** and **Brunello di Montalcino** came two new DOCs, **Rosso di Montepulciano** and **Rosso di Montalcino**. These are from the same vineyards as the finer wines, but are lighter, without the ability to age. Rosso di Montepulciano is available in the April following the vintage, while Rosso di Montalcino can be bottled a year afterwards. With Sangiovese the principal, or indeed only, grape variety in the case of Rosso di Montalcino, there is a distinct similarity to young Chianti, especially Chianti Classico, which has a moderate amount of tannin to provide sufficient structure, but which lacks the depth and body for long ageing. Rosso di Montalcino offers particularly good-value drinking, and is a very acceptable and much more accessible alternative to the often overpriced Brunello di Montalcino.

Morellino di Scansano is another Tuscan wine that is based on Sangiovese. Quite simply, Morellino is the local name for Sangiovese, in the town of Scansano in the heart of the Maremma in southern Tuscany. The mix of grape varieties is similar to that of Chianti – allowing Canaiolo, and also Malvasia Nera and some Ciliegiolo – and the taste is similar. You can also find a riserva version, which may even have been kept in *barriques* for a few months, in which case it would fit into the next segment. That is particularly true of the wines of Erik Banti. Le Pupille and Montelassi are two other good estates.

Brief mention can also be made of the small estate of **La Parrina**, which is virtually synonymous with the DOC of the same name. It is situated on the hills near the town of Orbitello and, with similar grape varieties to Chianti, is fairly alike in taste, with some sour cherry fruit and the typical Tuscan bite of astringency. The Italian specialist, Winecellars, is the sole importer.

Patrimonio

It is but a short hop across the water from Tuscany to Corsica, to a grape variety called Nielluccio which is the mainstay of **Patrimonio**, and which is said to be related to Sangiovese. As Corsica belonged to the city state of Pisa from the eleventh to the thirteenth century, this may well be true. Certainly there is a similarity in the wines: Patrimonio has an underlying astringency and a firm streak of tannin that is indeed not unlike Sangiovese in flavour, but it lacks the aromatic perfume of the lighter wines of the island, featured in the previous segment. However, it rarely travels; nor does it have much ageing potential. It does bear a slight resemblance to some of the wines of the south of France, such as those from Coteaux du Languedoc or from Minervois, which come under the southern warmth segment.

South Africa

Pinotage is the most individual of all the South African wines. A cross between Pinot Noir and Cinsaut, created in the 1920s by a Professor Perold from Stellenbosch University, it has been seen as the red workhorse grape variety of the vineyards of the Cape. It is easy to cultivate and to vinify, generous in its yields and adaptable in the cellar. It can produce light red, blush, or even sparkling, wine, but is at its best when given a serious red wine vinification, with grapes from low-yielding vines. Then, it has some structure and tannin and a balancing amount of fruit; it may even benefit from a little ageing in large, rather than small, oak barrels, but that should not be apparent on the palate. It is not usually a wine for ageing, but is best drunk in relative youth. Sometimes it can be spoilt by rather rubbery overtones. Good producers include Simonsig, Kanonkop and Vriesenhof (with a second label, Paradise Vale).

MEDIUM STRUCTURE (MEDIUM BODY, AGE, MEDIUM TANNIN)

Again Bordeaux is the starting point for this segment of the wheel, but with wines that are the next rung up the quality ladder.

Bordeaux

This is a broad section that excludes only the basic claret of the previous section and the very best clarets, which feature in the structured heavyweights segment. It does include the crus bourgeois and lighter classed growths of the Médoc, with the communes of Listrac and Moulis. It also includes some Graves, many of the wines of St-Emilion and its satellites, and Pomerol.

To a certain extent, the 1855 classification still holds good today. There have been changes: one or two châteaux have disappeared, their vineyards absorbed into other estates. Mouton-Rothschild is the only property to have achieved an actual change in status, while other châteaux are generally acknowledged to be in the wrong category. Quality is never static; winemakers come and go; châteaux change hands; vines are replanted; vinification methods alter; all of these affect the ultimate quality of the wine in the glass. The best classed growths fit into the structured, heavyweights segment, and the lighter wines, perhaps the fourth or fifth growths, come into this segment.

These are wines with good structure as well as a considerable amount of tannin, which enables them to age for a few years. They will probably have been kept in oak for some months before bottling, but this should not be too obtrusive on the palate.

In the hierarchy of the **Médoc** châteaux, the **crus bourgeois** is the category below the classed growths, although some of the better ones, such as Chasse-Spleen and Fourcas-Hosten, are generally considered to be of classed-growth quality. A syndicate of crus bourgeois lays down certain quality criteria which must be satisfied in order to meet the membership requirements.

The wines of the Médoc are the most elegant of Bordeaux, perhaps the leanest, with more austerity than those of Graves. Certainly, they are not as fleshy as those of St-Emilion and Pomerol: the generally high proportion of Cabernet Sauvignon and the gravelly soil are the reasons for this difference.

St-Emilion and **Pomerol** both contain a much larger proportion of Merlot, as well as more Cabernet Franc, rather than Cabernet Sauvignon. This makes richer, fleshier wines, which could be confused with burgundy, except for the firm streak of tannin which gives them a certain structure. However, although Merlot has a youthful plummy character, it can develop deceptive vegetal overtones as it matures, especially in lighter-bodied wines.

Pomerol, which was a rural backwater until the Moueix family of Pétrus fame established it firmly on the world's wine map, does not have any form of classification. St-Emilion, on the other hand, has a plethora of grands crus classés, perhaps too many to have any real meaning. The most significant part of the classification system of St-Emilion is premier grand cru, with two châteaux, Ausone and Cheval Blanc in category A, and another nine estates in category B, representing some of the better wines of St-Emilion, which might fit better into the structured heavyweights segment of the wheel.

Graves, or **Pessac-Léognan**, comes between the previous two in style and character. Good Graves is typified by a *goût de terroir*, a certain smoky character which is said to originate from the soil, from the gravel pebbles of the appellation. Even good Graves generally has neither the richness of St-Emilion, nor the elegance of the Médoc. Again the better wines of the Graves come into the structured heavyweights segment.

In this category are wines of medium structure and medium ageing ability, such as Magence, Landiras, Domaine la Grave, Domaine de Gaillat, Chicane, de Chantegrive, Montalivet, Rahoul and de Roquetaillade-la-Grange. They all offer good medium-term drinking and several of them bear the mark of two leading winemakers of the region, Peter Vinding-Diers and Pierre Coste.

South-west France

Two of the wines of the south-west have some capacity for ageing: Madiran and Cahors. Both can be compared to Bordeaux.

The appellation of **Cahors** is centred on vineyards in the Lot Valley close to the medieval town of the same name. It is an area that has evolved considerably over the last decade or so, with major investment by growers and *négociants*, and vineyards planted on the arid plateau above the valley. The principal grape variety is Auxerrois, which is the rather insignificant Malbec in Bordeaux. In Cahors it makes lean, sturdy wine, with a rugged quality, softened by some Merlot, while extra structure is added by Tannat which, as the name implies, is thick-skinned and tannic. Surprisingly, perhaps, Cahors does not contain a drop of Cabernet Sauvignon.

The wine of Cahors can vary in style; traditionally it was the black wine of the last century, so thick and tannic that it was barely drinkable. Today, it has become significantly more accessible, to the extent that some Cahors is made for fairly early drinking, although wines from good estates repay some bottle-ageing. There is a sturdy fruitiness to the wine, a certain stalky character which comes from the harshness of the Auxerrois. Some oak ageing softens this, but only in the best estates are the barrels new, and only for the best wines from those estates, such as Clos Triguedina's Prince Probus. Other serious estates include Château de Chambert, Rigal, Prieuré de Cenac, Domaine de Gaudou, Domaine d'Eugénie, Château de Cayrou and Clos la Coutale. The regional co-operative works well for its appellation, making sound wine under the label of les Côtes d'Olt, and also under several individual châteaux names.

Madiran is the red wine of the Pyrenees, from vineyards around the sleepy village of the same name, north of Pau. The dominant grape variety is Tannat, which, as mentioned earlier, makes wines that are deep-coloured and firmly tannic; it can be softened with some Merlot and Cabernet Franc and perhaps some Cabernet Sauvignon. Madiran needs ageing, in vat or in wood, depending on the means and wishes of the producer. Good Madiran will have spent a few months in oak, perhaps even in new oak, and the result is a structured wine, with more flesh and weight than Cahors. It repays keeping. Vintages generally follow those of Bordeaux.

Good producers include Château Montus and Domaine du Bouscassé from Alain Brumont, and also Domaine Teston, Château d'Aydie and Château Arricau-Bordes.

Cabernet Sauvignon from North America

Cabernet Sauvignon is generally considered to be the most successful red grape variety of **California**. It is treated in the same way as in Bordeaux, except that it is not always blended with Merlot or Cabernet Franc. The varietal name on the label implies a minimum of 75 per cent, but it may well be 100 per cent. Merlot is the grape variety that is usually added; Cabernet Franc is a much more recent and experimental innovation. California Cabernet Sauvignon has a more immediate impact than the somewhat reticent wines of Bordeaux: it tends to leap out of the glass, reeking of blackcurrants, with instant appeal. Recently, however, its producers have begun to aspire to some subtlety as well, making wines with rich, ripe cassis fruit, tannin, and occasionally some herbal minty hints.

The better California Cabernet Sauvignons fit into the structured heavyweights segment. More accessible wines, which need only four or five years' ageing, such as Mondavi's Woodbridge label, Sebastiani, Konocti and Sutter Home, are included here. There are some good Merlots, too, such as Newton and Rutherford Hill, but they very much take second place to Cabernet Sauvignon.

Washington State is making respectable Cabernet Sauvignon and Merlot – perhaps lacking the depth of the best California wineries, but good none the less. Arbor Crest and Chinook Merlot, and Cabernet Sauvignon from Hogue Cellars and Columbia Crest, are all wines to look out for.

Perhaps this is the place to mention the red wines of **Long Island**, which is now deemed to be the best viticultural region of New York State, even though the first vines were planted on the island as recently as twenty years ago. Perhaps the reason is that the climatic conditions of the North Fork of Long Island are very similar to those of Bordeaux, with a mild maritime influence. Merlot may be marginally more successful than Cabernet Sauvignon, but there are some excellent results as the vines grow older and the winemakers gain experience. Hargrave, Palmer and Bridgehampton are the leading wineries.

Australian Cabernet Sauvignon

Cabernet Sauvignon grows successfully all over the viticultural regions of this vast continent, from the Hunter Valley and Mudgee in New South Wales to the Margaret and Swan rivers of Western Australia, and even in the vineyards of Château Hornsby in the semi-desert of Alice Springs. However, it is indisputably at its best in the vineyards of **Coonawarra** in South Australia, where the famous iron-rich terra rossa soil produces the most complex examples. As with California, ripe blackcurrant fruit is the theme. The wines are full and ripe, sometimes with minty, eucalyptus flavours, as well as a sweetness that you do not find in Bordeaux. There is usually enough tannin to allow the wines to age for a few years, although the acidity is usually lower than in a claret.

Cabernet Sauvignon may be blended with Merlot, but Shiraz (the Australian name for Syrah), is the more common choice and adds a little extra spice to the wine. Again, the best wines fit into the structured heavyweights segment of the wheel. The easier to drink styles of Australian Cabernet Sauvignon include Brown Brothers Koombahla label, Wolf Blass Yellow Label, Hill-Smith and Yalumba.

New Zealand Cabernet Sauvignon

New Zealand Cabernet Sauvignon is coming of age. Until very recently it was very much an also-ran in the mammoth annual New Zealand tasting, but the emphasis has gradually shifted. White wines will always dominate the New Zealand wine scene, but there is now an ever-growing number of serious red wines. New Zealand Cabernet is sometimes spoilt by a vegetal, herbaceous character, which is a defect of the cool climate, but when it is good, it can be very good indeed, to the extent that it may also fit into the next segment. A notable example is Te Mata's Coleraine Cabernet Sauvignon, which has a firm impact of tannin, making a wine that will age for several years.

The better New Zealand Cabernets, such as the wines from Villa Maria, Vidal, Pask and Vavasour, contain a moderate amount of tannin, balanced with some attractive fruit. They have enough structure to enable them to age for three or four years, but are medium, rather than full-bodied. However, the cooler climate of New Zealand, with its long ripening season, makes more elegant wines than California and Australia. Vintages inevitably vary, but 1992, 1991, 1990 and 1989 have all produced some good wines.

South Africa

Cabernet Sauvignon is quite widely planted in South Africa, especially in the cooler Coastal Region that includes Stellenbosch and Paarl. Sometimes it is a pure varietal, although the varietal name on the label indicates a minimum of 75 per cent. The quality is not yet very consistent; there are some good South African Cabernet Sauvignons with cedarwood and blackcurrant fruit, but sometimes the wines can be just a little too high in alcohol and are spoilt by earthy, rubbery flavours, and by watery fruit. A recent tasting left an impression that high yields, stemming from excessive irrigation, had simply diluted the fruit.

Things can only improve and there is no doubt that South African winemakers are working hard to bring their wines back into the mainstream. The Bordeaux blends of Cabernet Sauvignon, Cabernet Franc and Merlot generally seem much more successful. The addition of Merlot and Cabernet Franc rounds out the fruit and gives the Cabernet Sauvignon more flesh. Often, these wines are sold under fantasy names, like Paul Sauer, Trilogy, Rustenberg Gold. There is much less vintage variation in the Cape than in northern Europe. Good producers include Rustenberg, Warwick Farm, Overgaauw, Klein Contantia, Simonsig and Vriesenhof.

Chinon, Bourgueil and St-Nicolas de Bourgueil

Chinon and **Bourgueil**, two **Loire** appellations, feature largely in the soft fruit segment, but there are exceptions to every rule, and this is one of them. Depending on the soil in the vineyard and the conditions of the vintage, as well as the winemaker's particular philosophy and method, Chinon and Bourgueil, and even more so, the smaller appellation of **St-Nicolas de Bourgueil**, will age. With the right climatic conditions, most recently in 1989, these appellations produce wines that are structured, with a firm backbone of tannin, that benefit considerably from some bottle age. This was amply illustrated by bottles of 1964 and 1955 Chinon from Couly Dutheil: in the summer of 1991 they were both delicious glasses of wine, with elegant cedarwood flavours, more reminiscent perhaps of a classed-growth claret, and quite belying the view that all red Loires are made for drinking young.

The Beaujolais crus.

Again, **Beaujolais** may not be an obvious choice for inclusion in this taste segment, but when it is made in the traditional way, with a classic red wine vinification, rather than by carbonic maceration, it has more tannin, body and guts and can indeed age very successfully. Of the ten crus, some are distinctly lighter than others. The newest, Régnié, has yet to prove that it is really any better than a Beaujolais-Villages, while others, notably Moulin-à-Vent and Morgon, develop more complexity in better vintages, such as 1991. They start life with a tannic streak, with some ripe plum and cherry fruit, and develop considerable finesse with age. Ironically, mature Beaujolais behaves like a vinous chameleon. taking on the vegetal character of Pinot Noir, with a flavour that quite belies its origins.

Beaujolais has suffered in the past year or two from excessively inflated prices, but these have now returned to a more reasonable level, making cru Beaujolais relatively good value for money. Like much of France, Beaujolais enjoyed a run of good vintages; 1990, 1989 and 1988 were good, while 1991 was a very much better vintage in Beaujolais than elsewhere in France. Good producers include Georges Duboeuf, Château de Chénas, Château du Moulin-à-Vent, Brac de la Perrière, Geoffray and members of the Eventail des Vignerons Producteurs.

Chianti Riserva

Many **Tuscan** wines come into this segment. The first, Chianti, crosses two segments of the wheel: Chianti normale has some tannin but is not really intended for ageing, while a **Chianti riserva**, especially a **Chianti Classico riserva**, is kept for three years before it is released for sale. A riserva is only produced in better vintages, from the better wines of an estate. Very little will have been made in the rather patchy vintages of 1992, 1991 and 1989, but plenty in the excellent years of 1990 and 1988, with their rich, structured wines. The decision is generally made in the vineyard; the producers know which vineyards are more likely to produce riper grapes and more concentrated wine. They follow the evolution of the wine in barrel, ensuring that it will be able to sustain maturation, not only in cask, but also in bottle.

Some Chianti riserva might be criticised for being prematurely mature and dilute in flavour. There has, however, been a considerable improvement in the quality of Chianti, with Chianti Classico in particular proving its ability to age, perhaps for eight or ten years. A good Chianti riserva has a firm backbone of tannin and structure, with enough balancing fruit to develop into a fine bottle with age. The sharp reduction in the percentage of white grapes included in Chianti, following its elevation to DOCG status, brought about a considerable change in its personality, gradually turning it into a wine that merits serious attention.

The current vintages of Chianti riservas generally available are 1990, 1988, and 1986. All three are good, but 1990 is undoubtedly the best. The wines from the good estates will never be cheap, but they will reward patience. There are numerous producers to recommend: Felsina Berardenga, Volpaia, San Polo in Rosso, Fontodi, Fonterutoli, Selvapiana, Vecchie Terre di Montefili, Ama, Villa Cafaggio, Le Masse, Badia a Coltibuono, Montagliari, Pagliarese, Il Palazzino, San Giusto a Rentennano, Riecine, Rampolla and Vicchiomaggio. While Isole e Olena does not make a Chianti riserva as such, Cepparello, labelled as vino da tavola because it is pure Sangiovese, is similar in style and quality.

Vino Nobile di Montepulciano

Vino Nobile has been criticised for being little more than a superior Chianti, and in some instances it was doubtful whether it was even that. The grape varieties are virtually identical to Chianti: Sangiovese is the mainstay, with a particular clone called Prugnolo in Montepulciano. There is Canaiolo too, perhaps Mammola, and a maximum ten per cent of white grapes. However, there is no minimum percentage, so the most serious producers have omitted the white grapes altogether from their wines. Two years' ageing is mandatory, while three years denotes a riserva quality. Generally, the wines are richer than Chianti normale, and more comparable to Chianti riserva.

Vino Nobile di Montepulciano has benefited from the dramatic improvement in winemaking all over Tuscany. The pacesetters were two estates, Avignonesi and Poliziano, but others have followed in their wake. Good Vino Nobile has a firm structured texture, with some ripe plummy fruit, good tannin, and the firm streak of astringency from Sangiovese that gives it backbone. Other good estates include Boscarelli, le Casalte and Il Cerro.

Brunello di Montalcino

Brunello di Montalcino is generally considered to be the Tuscan wine with the most stature. The Biondi Santi family placed it firmly on the wine map of Italy and created a red wine that was a hundred years ahead of its time, by making it from just one grape variety alone, the Brunello (which was their particular clone of Sangiovese), rather than from the customary mish-mash of grapes used all over Tuscany. Thus, they preceded the vogue of the Super Tuscans and established the potential for pure Sangiovese. Three years' ageing in large wood (what the Italians call *botti*) forms part of the production regulations. Small Bordeaux *barriques* cannot be used as they give a flavour that is quite foreign to Brunello. Originally, the statutory ageing period was four, then three and a half years, now reduced to three years in recognition of the fact that an excessively long period of wood ageing can sometimes destroy the fruit flavour of the wine.

Young Brunello has the sour cherry fruit of Sangiovese, which develops with bottle age, acquiring much greater complexity and a flavour that is sometimes reminiscent of the cedarwood of St-Julien. Sometimes it has a hint of herbs and perhaps some spice and smoky overtones, but always with a firm backbone of tannin. Good Brunello is beautifully balanced and elegant. It may be very tannic in its early youth, in which case it fits more happily into the structured heavyweights section, in the same way that the young, better classed-growth clarets do. Some producers, the so-called 'new school', aim to make their wines ready for drinking earlier, while other, more traditional producers aim for considerable longevity.

Good producers include Altesino, Caparzo, Il Poggione, Talenti, Col d'Orcia, Lisini and Banfi. Biondi Santi is expensive.

Carmignano

Carmignano is the newcomer to the line-up of Tuscan DOCGs. At first it was lost in a sea of Chianti, but then – thanks to the efforts of one family, the Bonacossis of Villa di Capezzana – it was awarded its own DOC, with the distinguishing feature of an obligatory percentage of Cabernet Sauvignon. It is thought that Cabernet Sauvignon was first brought to these hills west of Florence by the Medici, when they were dukes of Florence. This means that Cabernet Sauvignon is no upstart newcomer, as in other parts of Tuscany, but has long-standing credentials. However, Sangiovese still remains the principal grape variety, with some complementary Canaiolo and the usual drop of white wine.

With DOCG status, the proportion of Cabernet Sauvignon was increased from 10 to 15 per cent in order to distinguish Carmignano still more from Chianti. The ageing period is two years, and three for a riserva. The best-known producer is Villa di Capezzana, while Villa di Trefiano belongs to Vittorio, the son of the family. Fattoria di Ambra is another tiny, but highly recommended estate. The taste of Carmignano is a little softer and richer than Vino Nobile, and is a little more accessible than Brunello di Montalcino.

Torgiano

The other new DOCG of central Italy is **Torgiano**, which was essentially the creation of one man, Giorgio Lungarotti, whose family controls virtually the entire production of the vineyards surrounding this small Umbrian village. His red wine, made principally from Sangiovese, is sold under the name of Rubesco, while Rubesco riserva, cru Monticchio, is a stylish wine, capable of considerable longevity.

North-west Italy

Barolo and Barbaresco are the two great red wines of Piedmont, but there are numerous other Nebbiolo-based reds which have fruit and tannin, but which do not quite have the same stature or potential for longevity. **Gattinara** is a new DOCG, in some ways the least deserving amongst the Piedmontese wines. There are two good producers, Travaglini and Antoniolo, but other neighbouring wines, such as **Roero** and **Carema**, often offer more exciting flavours. The co-operative of Carema works well and Luigi Ferrando is a good private producer.

In nearby Lombardy, **Valtellina**, which borders Switzerland, produces wines which are also based on Nebbiolo. The DOC is simply Valtellina or, for better wines, **Valtellina Superiore**, which has four sub-divisions with the evocative names of Inferno, Grumello, Vargella and Sassella. Nino Negri and Rainoldi are the best producers here.

Portugal – Bairrada

Bairrada was seen as a rising star amongst Portuguese wines, but the question must be asked: has it fulfilled its promise? It comes from vineyards in central Portugal, south of the city of Oporto. While it can be red, white or sparkling, red accounts for the largest part of the production and this is the wine most usually found outside Portugal.

The main grape variety of red Bairrada is Baga, a tough-skinned variety that can make unyielding, astringent, tannic red wines, which require several years' ageing in both barrel and bottle. However, changes in vinification methods have made the wine more approachable; destalking the grapes before fermentation softens the tannin; experiments with new oak have improved the flavour, allied with a better understanding of the effects of oxygenation, as opposed to fruit-destroying oxidation. This softer style of Bairrada is ready to drink early – in a year, say.

Good Bairrada, that is not dried-out and tired, has a backbone of tannin, with a certain spiciness – a cross between a claret and a Côtes-du-Rhône, with some pepperiness and blackcurrant. In youth it has the stalky taste of young claret, but will develop more mellow flavours with age.

Good producers include Luis Pato, Caves São João, Sogrape and Caves Alianças.

Dão

Dão, Portugal's best-known red table wine, has undergone some of the same changes as Bairrada. It comes from northern Portugal, from hillsides around the town of Viseu, to the south of the Douro river. It too can be either red or white, but is more commonly red, made from a hotchpotch mixture of indigenous grape varieties, with quite unmemorable names.

Red Dão requires a minimum of 18 months' ageing, while **garrafeira** wines, which the producer deems to be his very best, must spend two years in vat and one in bottle. Often it is longer, and sometimes too long: the tendency has been to keep Dão in wood for so long that the fruit has disappeared long before it ever reaches the bottle. Dão is firmly tannic and certainly needs some ageing, but not too much. Mature Dão is medium-weight, with a rugged, dry, peppery character but it never quite loses that puckering edge of tannin. Sogrape's Grão Vasco is one of the best available examples, along with their new Duque de Viseu.

Other parts of Portugal produce table wines that are growing in importance. It is debatable whether they always have enough ageing potential to fit into this segment, or whether they belong to the previous segment, or in the category of southern warmth. **Arruda**, from one successful village co-operative in the Estremadura, is a combination of fruit and tannin, but lacks the staying power of either Bairrada or Dão. However, at a competitive price, it is a good introduction to the flavours of Portugal. The better table wines of the Douro, those not used for port, are well worth trying; they have fruit and tannin, with a hint of the liquorice overtones of port. The best and most expensive is Barca Velha, produced by the port house Ferreira, while Quinto do Côtto is also good.

Other Portuguese garrafeira wines also come into this segment, such as Romeira Garrafeira, as well as some of the wines of the leading Setúbal company, J M da Fonseca. Periquita, the name of the grape, but also meaning parrot in Portuguese, combines tannin with a certain indefinable Portuguese flavour. Quinta da Camarate, which includes some Cabernet with Periquita, is also distinctly Portuguese in flavour, while Quinta da Bacalhôa, made from Cabernet Sauvignon by the talented Australian, Peter Bright, at João Pires, has some New World blackcurrant fruit, balanced with tannin.

Israel

An unexpected postscript to this section might be Cabernet Sauvignon from Israel. Yarden from the Golan Heights produces Merlot, but the Cabernet Sauvignon is better. With some attractive cassis fruit, it is a well-made wine of medium staying power.

OAK AND VANILLA (MEDIUM BODY, AGE, MEDIUM TANNIN)

As explained in the introduction, countless wines benefit from the effects of oak maturation, but the taste should not always be apparent in the mouth; wines that have an obvious oaky flavour in their youth mellow with age, so that the strong taste of new oak disappears, leaving fruit and tannin. One wine in which the taste of oak is especially noticeable, forming a vital component of the flavour, is Rioja, which gets its distinctive vanilla overtones from American oak. Rioja wines, therefore, dominate this section, and other northern Spanish wines are included as they are very similar, also benefiting from the influence of American oak.

It may seem illogical, contradictory or perverse also to include fine red burgundy and good Pinot Noir from elsewhere but, although the use of oak should be less marked in these wines, there is a similarity of taste, a certain sweetness, with some ripe flavours that is not so unlike a good Rioja.

Rioja

Rioja is the wine that first put Spain on the international wine map, preparing the way for other Spanish wines. It comes from northern Spain, from vineyards around the town of Logroño. There are three distinct areas of production, with differences in soil and climate: the Rioja Alta, the Rioja Baja and, the one which is considered to be best of all, Rioja Alavesa. Most Rioja is a blend from all three areas, or at least from two. The concept of a single-vineyard Rioja was unknown in the area, but there is now a handful of estates making wine from their own grapes, namely

Contino, Remélluri, Baron de Ley and Amezoladella Mora. The large bodegas that dominate the production of Rioja may own vineyards in the different areas and also buy in a large proportion of grapes from numerous small farmers.

Rioja is the first Spanish wine to be given a higher qualification than DO; as from 1991 it is DOCa (Denominación de Origen Calificada), which entails stricter controls – including bottling at source – for all Rioja. Although the Denominación covers all three colours, Rioja is known primarily for its red wines. There are four different categories, beginning with **sin crianza**, without any wood ageing, which features in an earlier segment. Then there are **con crianza, reserva** and **gran reserva**, all of which entail some time in oak – from twelve months for a crianza wine to a minimum of two years for a gran reserva, or perhaps longer, depending on the individual bodega style. In any case, a gran reserva must be aged for a total of five years altogether before sale, and a reserva for a minimum of three years, of which at least one must be in cask. Crianza Rioja also requires one year's ageing in cask, but only a further year of ageing in tank or bottle before release.

Tempranillo is the key grape variety which gives Rioja its fruit and flavour, as well as featuring in many of the better DOs of northern Spain. There may be a link with Pinot Noir, but that remains unproven. Grenache or Garnacha is the other important variety, as well as Mazuelo, and a drop of Graciano, which is currently enjoying something of a revival in the vineyards.

Oak maturation for Rioja is always done in small American oak barrels of 225 litres, the same size as the classic Bordeaux *barrique*. Oak, therefore, is a dominant feature of the taste of Rioja and it is only wines with a sufficient inherent structure in the first place that can cope with a long period in wood. Otherwise, the smoky fruit of the Tempranillo grape is lost. Leading producers include Marqués de Riscal, CVNE, Contino, Remélluri, Marqués de Cáceres, Olarra, La Rioja Alta, Bodegas Riojanas, Berberana, Olarra and Muga.

Costers del Segre

Raimat is a remarkable estate in the province of Lérida in northern Spain, which belongs to the Raventos family of Codorníu fame (see sparkling section). As well as white grapes for cava, there are plantings of Tempranillo, Cabernet Sauvignon and Merlot, in semi-desert land where the vines depend upon irrigation for survival. The energy of the company was responsible for the creation of a new DO, **Costers del Segre**, to cover the wines of the Raimat estate. These include three reds: a Tempranillo, a Cabernet

Sauvignon and Abadia, which is a blend of Cabernet Sauvignon and Merlot. Although the grape varieties of the last wine may be French in origin, there is something distinctly Spanish about the flavour, with the pronounced influence of American oak, some rich spicy fruit and a soft velvet finish.

Ribera del Duero

Ribera del Duero became a DO as recently as 1982. Until then there was just one estate of any note in the region, namely Vega Sicilia, whose wines are fabulous, both by reputation and in price. As well as Tempranillo, which they call Tinto Fino, the Bordeaux grape varieties, Cabernet Sauvignon, Merlot and Malbec, are grown. The resulting wines are known for their considerable richness and longevity, and ageing in both French and American oak is an important part of the production process. In the case of Vega Sicilia Unico, the key wine of the estate, made from the oldest vines, ageing could be for as long as ten years. There is also an extraordinary Reserva Especial, which is a blend of old vintages, some from the 1950s. While the 1980 vintage of Vega Sicilia Unico costs around £40 from Spanish specialists Laymont & Shaw, the Reserva Especial costs roughly twice as much. There are also two slightly more accessible wines from the same estate, called Valbuena, released in the third and fifth years of maturation, which have some wonderful complex flavours, equating to fine Rioja.

Apart from Vega Sicilia, the production of Ribera del Duero (literally, the banks of Duero, better known in Portugal as the Douro) was, until recently, dominated by co-operatives. That was until the wines of Pesquera, made by Alejandro Fernandez, hit the limelight after their discovery by an American wine merchant. Other bodegas have caught the public eye, following in the wake of Pesquera – Viña Pedrosa and Bodegas Mauro, for example. Unfortunately, prices have escalated, following the demands of fashion. Tinto Fino remains the principal grape variety used and, given some ageing in small barrels, makes some wonderfully rich, complex, smoky wines.

Penedès

Penedès is known, above all, for cava (see the sparkling wine wheel). However, still wines are made too and production is dominated by one family – Torres – who have put their region and their own name firmly on the world wine map. Miguel Torres was the first to plant grape varieties that are not Spanish, and to experiment with Cabernet Sauvignon, Merlot and Pinot Noir. He has done the same with white grape varieties too. The range of Torres wines continues to expand, with a rich plummy Merlot called Las Planas, and Mas Borras, which is a single-vineyard Pinot Noir. Other stalwarts include Tres Torres and Gran Sangredetoro, both made from Grenache and Carignan; Coronas, made from Tempranillo; Gran Coronas, which includes some Cabernet Sauvignon along with the Tempranillo; Mas la Plana, which replaces the former Gran Coronas Black Label, made from pure Cabernet Sauvignon; and Viña Magdala, a blend of Pinot Noir and Tempranillo. The flavours produced are a combination of the fruit of the grape, whether it is the blackcurrants of Cabernet Sauvignon or the vegetal overtones of Pinot Noir, with the Spanish influence of American oak barrels. These are wines that may mislead us as to their origins.

There are other producers of still wines in Penedès, such as Masia Bach, now part of the Codorníu group, who produces some serious red wines, including Cabernet Sauvignon.

The other star of Penedès is Jean León, known for his Cabernet Sauvignon as well as his Chardonnay (see further round the wheel). The Cabernet Sauvignon is rich and oaky, blended with a little Cabernet Franc and Merlot, and has plenty of ripe fruit. The oak places it in this segment of the wheel, but with its firm tannin, it could also fit into the previous section.

Another Spanish Cabernet Sauvignon comes from the Marqués de Griñon, Carlos Falco, who had the imagination to replant the vineyards of his family estate near Toledo with Cabernet and Merlot, rather than the ubiquitous Airén of the Spanish plains. A good Marqués de Griñon red can be rich in blackcurrant fruit and oak, but is generally not a long-lived wine.

This is also the place to include the wines of an up-and-coming DO in Aragon, namely Somontano, which literally means under the mountain. The wines of a new company, Covisa, with the brand name Viñas del Vero are worth seeking out. The Duque de Azura crianza, made from Moristel and Tempranillo, and aged for a few months in American oak, has some spicy vanilla flavours and a backbone of tannin. The basic Tinto, with its plummy fruit, as well as tannin, fits more comfortably into the fruit and tannin section, while the Val de Uga, made from Pinot Noir with some sweet vanilla fruit, bridges the gap between Spain and Burgundy.

Burgundy

When Pinot Noir is great it is sublime, and there is nowhere it performs as well as on the best sites of the **Côte d'Or**, in the grand cru vineyards of the best villages of the **Côte de Beaune** and the

Côte de Nuits. There is an initial sweet oaky flavour in Pinot Noir when it is young, mixed with raspberry fruit. In some years the fruit will taste ripe; in leaner years, there may be a stalky overtone. In the best vintages, the oak and tannin will fade, leaving some ripe vegetal fruit, as should happen in the unparalleled run of good vintages in 1988, 1989 and 1990. The 1988 vintage was the best since 1985, with wines that are quite firm and tannic. In contrast, 1989 produced ripe, fleshy wines, which may lack structure. The best of the three is undoubtedly 1990, with both tannin and body and, better still, prices are lower than the 1989 level. These are wines that will age into great bottles, especially from leading producers like Joseph Roty, Domaine Dujac, Armand Rousseau, Trapet, Daniel Rion and Marquis d'Angerville.

The wines of the **Côte Chalonnaise**, especially from Rully, Givry and Mercurey, are similar to those of the Côte d'Or, but lighter in style and less elegant. They lack the refinement of the best red burgundies, but if there are bargains to be had anywhere in Burgundy, the Côte Chalonnaise may provide one. Good producers include Noël-Bouton at Domaine de la Folie, Cogny, Dury and Delorme.

New World Pinot Noir

Pinot Noir is the Holy Grail of the New World; Chardonnay and Cabernet Sauvignon have proved fairly easy to master, there are good Merlots and Rieslings too, but the essential quality of Pinot Noir has proved infuriatingly elusive. It is a temperamental grape that hitherto has only performed well on one small hillside in northern France. Things, however, have begun to change, with a growing feeling that the New World growers might just be on to a winning streak.

California   There has been an enormous improvement in California Pinot Noir. There have been more plantings of better clones in the cooler parts of the State, notably at the southern end of the Napa and Sonoma Valleys in Carneros, where temperatures are moderated by the maritime influence of the Pacific Ocean. Pinot Noir needs a long, cool growing season; it does not like to ripen quickly. There are numerous different clones – some good, some distinctly inferior – and there is still much to be learnt about them. The other problem is that Californians have tended to make Pinot Noir in the same way that they make Cabernet Sauvignon, with some unhappy results. Now that they have realised that it needs completely different treatment, things are definitely looking up, and there are some good California Pinot Noirs around.

Successful producers include Robert Mondavi, Saintsbury, Au Bon Climat and Kent Rasmussen. The flavours may not yet be as subtle as the best red burgundies, but at about £10 a bottle the price is distinctly attractive.

Oregon Further north, in cooler Oregon, Pinot Noir may have even greater potential than in California, and it is certainly proving more successful there than Cabernet Sauvignon. David Lett first set the pace at Knudsen-Erath. After a period of excitement, things fell into the doldrums, but are now looking up again, with interest excited by the first vintage from Robert Drouhin's estate. Other good estates that have captured something of the elusive qualities of Pinot Noir include Ponzi, Eyrie Vineyard and Bethel Heights.

New Zealand New Zealand boasts of the advantages of its cool climate and Pinot may well provide the next success story of the Antipodes. St Helena, a winery outside Christchurch, on the South Island, first caught the limelight with its 1986 Pinot Noir. About the same time, Pinot Noir was being planted in the Wairarapa, north of Wellington, around the village of Martinborough. The first vintage of Martinborough Vineyards was a Pinot Noir, made by a Pinot Noir fanatic, Larry McKenna, and it met with instant acclaim. Others have followed his example: Ata Rangi, Dry River and Te Kairanga.

Back on the cooler South Island, Pinot Noir is planted as far south as the 45th parallel, at Rippon Vineyards on Lake Wanaka in Central Otago. St Helena, after a hiccup or two, is continuing its initial success, along with Waipara Springs and Omihi Hills, from two more Pinot Noir enthusiasts, Mark Rattray and Danny Schuster. In the tiny area of Nelson, Tim and Judy Finn at Neudorf Vineyards, and Hermann and Agnes Seifried from Redwood Valley, are also achieving some exciting flavours. Perhaps New Zealand Pinot Noir does not quite have the subtlety of the best burgundies, but a consistency of flavour and quality is beginning to develop – something you do not always find in burgundy – and there is a distinct price advantage to boot.

Australia Much of Australia is simply too hot for Pinot Noir. Murray Tyrrell, in the Hunter Valley of New South Wales, was the first to produce some rather jammy Pinot, but it is now generally agreed that the best areas for it are the coolest – the hills south of Adelaide, the Yarra Valley of Victoria, and Tasmania, the most temperate of all the Australian Vineyards. Pipers Brook is achieving good things in Tasmania, while James Halliday, a lawyer-turned-wine-writer and now winemaker, has made some successful Pinot Noir at Coldstream Hills. Mountadam in south Australia and Dromana Estate in Victoria are good too.

South Africa   South Africa has tended to concentrate on Pinotage and Cabernet Sauvignon. However, there is some growing interest in Pinot Noir, which in any case was a parent of Pinotage. Tim Hamilton-Russell, of Hamilton-Russell Vineyards in Hermanus, was the first to take Pinot Noir seriously; he looked long and hard for suitably cool conditions where he could plant it and now makes one of the most successful wines from the Cape, with some lovely vegetal fruit and rich flavours.

His ex-winemaker, Peter Finlayson, has recently joined forces with Paul Bouchard, and together they have planted vineyards close to the Hamilton-Russell Vineyards, which are not yet in production. However, Bouchard-Finlayson will be a name to watch out for. Meanwhile, Peter's brother, Walter, is responsible for Glen Carlou, which produces another stylishly oaky Pinot Noir. Meerlust is another estate to make a commendable example; with some ripe but elegant vegetal fruit and good oaky flavours.

Italy, Austria and Romania   There are occasional examples of Pinot Noir from Italy. So far, the best one to come out of Tuscany is Ruffino's Tondo del Nero. Although Pinot Noir is one of the permitted grape varieties of the DOCs of the Alto Adige, Trentino and Friuli, the wines produced are rarely exciting.

In Austria, George Stiegelmar is almost alone in making an oaky raspberry-flavoured Pinot Noir, while in Romania the Pinot produced is rather hot and jammy, with the merest hint of farmyards.

SOUTHERN WARMTH (FULL BODY, NO AGE, MEDIUM TANNIN)

Perhaps the idea of southern warmth needs some explanation: it is a term which should conjure up thoughts of wines that are born in warm sunshine, which are redolent of the scents and herbs of the Midi and the flavours of the Mezzogiorno of Italy. Generally, these wines are full-bodied, for sunshine produces sugar and thereby alcohol. Usually, they have some structure and a backbone of tannin, but not enough to merit a lengthy amount of ageing; they are usually best drunk within three to four years of the vintage but, as with any well-made red wine, especially if from a good vintage and a talented producer, there are always exceptions that last longer.

Côtes-du-Rhône

The **Côtes-du-Rhône** is a good starting point; this is the basic appellation of the Rhône Valley, with the greatest concentration of vineyards in the south, around Avignon. Although Côtes-du-Rhône can be white and pink, the best wines are red. **Côtes-du-Rhône-Villages**, usually with the name of one of the 17 villages on the label – Chusclan, Beaumes-de-Venise or Sablet, for example – has stricter production regulations, making wines with a little more substance and body. Where no village name is given, the wine is generally a blend of wines from more than one of these villages.

A good Côtes-du-Rhône tastes of the south, providing a warm mouthful, scented with herbs of the Midi, lavender, thyme and rosemary, as well as a touch of spice and liquorice. A mixture of different grape varieties is allowed, with Grenache, Syrah, Mourvèdre, Cinsaut and Carignan the most common. Grenache is the most important, making wine that is quite high in alcohol, full-bodied and mouth-filling. Sadly, modern trends have sometimes lightened Côtes-du-Rhône, turning it into a feeble shadow of its former self. However, a wine like the 1988 Côtes-du-Rhône from Guigal is a superb example of the appellation.

Other good producers include Pascal, Jaboulet (especially with Parallèle 45), Château du Grand Moulas, Cru du Coudoulet, Chapoutier, Domaine St-Gayan and Château Ste-Estève. The recent vintages of 1988, 1989 and 1990 offer some delicious drinking.

Vacqueyras was once a Côtes-du-Rhône-Villages, but it now has an appellation in its own right. The grape varieties are the same, the flavours warm and fruity, with perhaps a little more body. The nearby **Côtes du Ventoux** also compares with Côtes-du-Rhône, but is a little lighter; again, southern warmth prevails with a large helping of Grenache in the grape mix. For Côtes du Ventoux, try Domaine des Anges; whilst Jaboulet and Pascal both make good Vacqueyras, as does the village co-operative.

Gigondas, with vineyards dominated by the dramatic skyline of the Dentelles de Montmirail, is a lighter version of a Châteauneuf-du-Pape, with some warm, southern fruit. Domaine du Grand Montmirail and Domaine St-Gayan are reputable estates.

Côtes de Provence

Contrary to what its name might imply, this appellation covers a relatively small part of Provence, but with vineyards scattered over quite a wide area. They are mostly in the department of the Var, including the coastal region south of the Massif des Maures and a large area to the north of the mountains. On the west side, the **Côtes de Provence** are limited by the **Coteaux Varois**, a relatively recently created VDQS. Although pink wine accounts for a larger percentage of the appellation, red Côtes de Provence is an infinitely more interesting wine.

There have been moves to improve the blend of grape varieties allowed for both pink and red wine. The high-yielding Carignan used to be the principal variety, making some singularly dull and uninspiring wine. Nor did lengthy ageing in old oak barrels improve matters. The percentage of Carignan has now been significantly reduced, and replaced by Grenache, which makes some warm, fruity, full-bodied wine. However, it is Syrah and Cabernet Sauvignon that have attracted the most interest in the vineyards, with their role as improving grape varieties, although neither must exceed 30 per cent in the wine. Serious producers are adamant that they do not want to make a Provençal claret, but there is no doubt that a little Cabernet Sauvignon does wonders for the aroma, and provides backbone in a wine that has sometimes lacked structure. Syrah, although more commonly associated with the vineyards of the northern Rhône, is encroaching on the south and undeniably provides fruit and flavour, without detracting from the true character of the appellation.

All over the south of France, vinification methods are improving significantly – and Provence is no exception. Carbonic maceration is generally considered to have a beneficial effect on Carignan; it extracts fruit without too much tannin, and gives some warm vibrant flavours. Small oak barrels, as opposed to large casks, are another fashionable trend, and certainly benefit the wine, provided that care is taken that the oak does not dominate.

A good Côtes de Provence is not so different from a Côtes-du-Rhône. It may be a little meatier in character, but it has the same full-bodied warmth of the south. Good producers include the Vignerons du Presqu'Ile de St-Tropez, with their flagship estate, Château Pamplonne; Domaines Ott, a new up-and-coming estate; Domaine de la Courtade, on the island of Porquerolles; also Domaine de St-Baillon, Domaine Richeaume and Château Rimauresq.

Coteaux d'Aix-en-Provence

The nearby appellation of **Coteaux d'Aix-en-Provence**, with the sub-region of the **Coteaux des Baux**, is a more serious red wine appellation than Côtes de Provence. Its advantage, which seemed rather a slight at the time, was not to be made an appellation at the same time as the Côtes de Provence, in 1977. This, however, provoked a considerable improvement in the quality of the wines, with greater concentration on red wines – rewarded with an appellation in 1985. Indeed, the wines of the better producers of the area fit more comfortably into the next segment of the wheel.

As with Côtes de Provence, a considerable mixture of grape varieties is allowed – including Carignan, Cinsaut, Counoise, Grenache, Syrah, Mourvèdre and Cabernet Sauvignon. The maximum allowance of Carignan will be reduced to 30 per cent by 1995, while 40 per cent is the maximum for the other red varieties. However, not everyone conforms to the regulations. Indisputably, the best Coteaux d'Aix-en-Provence comes from vineyards at the foot of the Alpilles of les Baux, at Domaine de Trévallon, where Eloi Dürrbach obstinately refuses to plant any Grenache, but continues to make his wine from Cabernet Sauvignon and Syrah alone. The results are majestic, and the wine fits into the next segment. The wines of his neighbours around the Alpilles are softer and fruitier, with a higher percentage of Grenache and with the wonderful warm herbs of the south; wines like Mas de la Dame, Domaine des Terres Blanches, Domaine du Gourgonnier. Organic viticulture is widely practised here; the growers have a considerable advantage over colleagues from more northern climates, for the drying winds of the Mistral provide a wonderful anti-rot treatment.

Other good estates in the appellation include Château du Fonscolombe, whereas the estate that was once seen as the flagship of the appellation, Château du Vignelaure, has been through an unsatisfactory period, with changes of ownership. However, it has recently been bought by the Shivdasani family, which also owns Domaine du Galoupet in the the Côtes de Provence, so things may look up.

Other appellations of Provence provide winter-warming wines, although the red version of Cassis is not better than a rather undistinguished Côtes de Provence. The **Côtes du Lubéron**, produced from vineyards on the foothills of the Montagne du Lubéron, became an appellation in 1987 and is an area where tradition and innovation lie side by side. The Chancel family at Château Val Joanis made a considerable investment in its new estate, redesigning the contours of the landscape with bulldozers and diggers, replanting vineyards with experimental as well as traditional varieties, and installing the latest technology in the cellar. The wines are widely available, not only under the name of Château Val Joanis, but also as Domaine Chancel and Domaine des Blancs.

In contrast, the wines of Château la Canorgue are made on a much smaller scale, with more elementary equipment but with some good results. The Côtes du Lubéron adjoins the Côtes-du-Rhône, but the wines are a little lighter and more aromatic, but with the same southern warmth.

Côtes du Roussillon

On the other side of the French Mediterranean coast are the vineyards of **Côtes du Roussillon** and **Côtes du Roussillon-Villages**, with two named villages – Caramany and the poetic-sounding Latour de France. The reason that these two were singled out had more to do with commercial clout than quality. As throughout the Midi, the principal grape varieties are Carignan, Cinsaut and Grenache, with more recent plantings of Syrah and Mourvèdre. Carignan does better here in the sun-soaked arid hills of Roussillon than anywhere else in the Midi. None the less, it is generally accepted that it needs an additional boost of flavour from Syrah and Mourvèdre. There is not the same interest in Cabernet Sauvignon here as elsewhere in the Midi. Village co-operatives dominate the production of the appellation and their wines are usually marketed by one of the large growers' unions, such as the Vignerons Catalans.

There are some individual estates setting the pace in the appellation, such as Château de Jau, which has done good things, replanting vineyards and modernising equipment. Château de Corneilla is another leading estate whose wines are worth seeking out for their warm flavoursome fruit. Cazes Frères is another company working well for the appellation.

Fitou

The oldest appellation of this part of France is **Fitou**, dating back to 1948. Again, co-operatives dominate the production, although two individual estates of note are Château de Nouvelles and Château l'Espigne. The Vignerons du Val d'Orbieu had considerable success with their Madame Claude Parmentier label, which resulted in shortages and price rises, but things have now stabilised. The flavour of Fitou is solidly warm and rustic. The co-operative des Producteurs de Mont Tauch is one of the more innovative, making not only good Fitou, but also Corbières and Rivesaltes, with various levels of quality.

Nearby **Collioure**, with vineyards that are adjacent to those of Banyuls, also offers some warm southern fruit. In the hands of a meticulous producer like Alan Parcé it is indeed a serious wine with some stature as well as warm spice.

Corbières and Minervois

Further north, the twin appellations of **Corbières** and **Minervois** are enjoying renovations in vineyard and cellar. Both became appellations in 1985 and the grape varieties for each are similar, with Carignan, Cinsaut and Grenache forming the backbone of the wine. Some Syrah and possibly Mourvèdre may be added to give an extra injection of flavour as *cépages améliorateurs* (improving grape varieties). Growers who have Cabernet and Merlot in their vineyards here use them, in theory, for vin de pays, but perhaps not always in practice.

The vineyards of Corbières lie on the first foothills of the Pyrenees, while those of Minervois are on the north side of the valley of the Aude, on the very first foothills of the Massif Central. Much depends on individual producers here. There are those who are making a great effort to improve the quality of their wine, reducing their yields, planting better grape varieties, and improving vinification methods in efficiently equipped cellars. There has been investment and interest from Bordeaux, from Peter Sichel in Domaine du Révérend and the late Bernadette Villars of Château Chasse-Spleen in the Château de Cabriac.

Both appellations cover quite large areas and there are moves towards further sub-divisions to recognise differences in microclimate and soil. However, in choosing the wine in the glass, it is the producer's name that counts. Good Corbières producers include Château les Ollieux, Château de Caraguilhes, Domaine de Fontsainte, Château de Cabriac, Domaine du Révérend, Château St-Auriol and Château de Lastours. For Minervois, try Domaine de Ste-Eulalie, Château de Paraza, Domaine Maris and Château de Gourgazaud. Although expensive, best of all is Clos Centeilles, which is stocked by Corney & Barrow and Adnams of Southwold.

Coteaux du Languedoc

Further east, the wines become progressively lighter until you reach Côtes-du-Rhône and Coteaux d'Aix-en-Provence. However, the **Coteaux du Languedoc** fits more happily into this segment than anywhere else. The wines may not quite have the weight of some of the others of the Midi, but the best do have a certain southern warmth. Several crus are included in the appellation – the best are **St-Chinian** and **Faugères**. Originally, they were appellations in their own right, but have since been incorporated into the larger appellation. There are both individual producers and co-operatives working well for their area, such as Cave de Berlou with its brand name Schisteil, Château Coujan, Gérard Alquier and the Château de Haut Fabrègues.

The other crus include **St-Georges d'Orques**, which is mainly produced by one go-ahead co-operative. Other good individual producers include the Prieuré de St-Jean de Bébian, just outside Pézenas, where Alain Roux grows all thirteen grape varieties of the appellation of Châteauneuf-du-Pape, as he claims that the soil in his vineyards is identical.

Italy

The islands and the south dominate Italy's input into this section.

Sardinia What the French call Grenache the Italians call Cannonau – grown, above all, in Sardinia, as **Cannonau di Sardegna**. Sometimes it is used to make a port-like dessert wine, but as a table wine it has some southern warmth and fruit, with a dry finish. Sella e Mosca are leading producers.

Sicily Sicily provides some sturdy warm flavours, not only from the widely available Corvo – which is the trading name of the Casa Vinicola Duca di Salaparuta – but also from other producers such as Rapitalà, Regaleali, COS (who make the DOC wine Cerasuola di Vittoria) and Donnafugata. The newest claim to fame in Sicily is Terre di Ginestra, which makes more exciting whites than reds. Its reds fit a little uneasily into this segment as they are relatively light, with a little spice and tannin. Corvo's latest introduction, Duca Enrico, is over-oaked and over-priced to match. Surprisingly, for a southern island, Sicily makes much better white than red wine.

Mezzogiorno On mainland Italy, many of the wines of the southern part of the country fit into this category. **Montepulciano d'Abruzzo** is a warm, rather earthy wine made from the Montepulciano grape, and has nothing to do with Vino Nobile. The leading producers are Valentini, Cornacchia, Illuminati, Casal Thaulero and Tollo.

Cirò, the principal DOC of Calabria, is a pretty hefty red wine, made from a little-known grape variety called Gaglioppo. It has the warmth and herbs of the south, with a rather dry earthy finish and alcoholic body; Librandi is the key producer.

Spain

Many of the red table wines of southern Spain fit into this segment too. The warm sunshine makes heady, alcoholic wines, which are then aged in large oak barrels for several months or longer. Take **Jumilla**, for example: a full-bodied alcoholic red wine from vineyards in the arid hills behind the town of Alicante in south-east Spain, made mainly from the grape variety Monastrell. Old-style Jumilla was kept for several months, if not years, in large oak vats, with the result that the fruit flavours tended to disappear and a rather dry, tarry, even oxidising, red wine was left. High alcohol was its dominant characteristic. But there has now been a gradual change in the winemaking, so that Jumilla has become just a little lighter in body, with a little more fruit, while still retaining its southern warmth.

Good producers include Ascensio Carcelén, Bodegas Juvinsa, Señorio del Condestable and the San Isidro co-operative. Vintages are of little significance. Other wines from the south of Spain also appear occasionally on our shelves, such as the adjoining DOs of **Yecla**, **Almansa**, **Utiel Requeña**, as well as **Valdepeñas**, which is a hilly enclave in the vast plains of La Mancha. The red wine of the latter has improved considerably over the last few years, benefiting from better winemaking techniques. The main grape variety is Cencibel (the Tempranillo of Rioja); when aged in oak for a few months, it provides some ripe flavours, with a hint of southern warmth and a mellow fruitiness. Thus, Valdepeñas straddles two segments of the taste wheel. The leading producer is Bodegas Felix Solis, under the brand name Viña Albali, a wine which offers some delicious good-value drinking.

Two other Spanish wines fit into this segment. The first is **Priorato** in southern Catalonia, a full-bodied gutsy red wine made from Cariñena and Garnacha, with some liquorice spice and an alcoholic finish. Masia Barril is the estate to follow. The other wine to look out for is **Lar de Barros**, from Tierra de Barros, an aspiring DO to the west of La Mancha, which has some warm fruit, a hint of vanilla and some gamey overtones.

Portugal

Some of the table wines of Portugal have a warmth about them that brings them into this category. Mention has already been made of Arruda and the Douro, as well as leading producers, such as J M da Fonseca and João Pires, in the medium structure segment. However, some of these wines could also fit equally well into this segment. Periquita, for example, has both structure and warmth, while Tinta da Anfora from João Pires is a warm, rugged red. Other wines from southern Portugal are beginning to appear. The co-operative of Borba in the Alentejo has begun to improve winemaking techniques significantly and now produces some acceptable wines. In some instances the winemaking leaves much to be desired, but at best there are some warm, spicy flavours.

Lebanon

Château Musar is virtually the only estate of the war-damaged Lebanon. The wine is produced with considerable determination by Serge Hochar, who trained at Bordeaux university and planted Cabernet Sauvignon as the main grape variety of his vineyards. Vinification methods follow those of Bordeaux, with ageing in small barrels, and yet the wines have a warmth and spiciness that has more in common with the south of France than with Bordeaux. The Cabernet is blended with some Syrah and Cinsaut, but not too much, and results in some warm, meaty flavours. Musar tends to release its wines when they are ready for drinking; the 1986 is the current vintage, which is drinking beautifully.

Greece

Although the Greek wine scene is still dominated by Retsina, there are a growing number of wineries producing wines with flavour and individuality. Domaine Carras, made from the indigenous Limnio grape, is warm and spicy, with a Rhônish quality to it; while Château Carras, made in the Côtes de Meliton from a Bordeaux blend, based on Cabernet Sauvignon, has established a reputation for its red wines and would fit more comfortably into the medium structure segment of the taste wheel. But it is the exception among Greek wines. Semeli, another up-and-coming estate, makes red Nemea, with some warm, raisiny fruit from the Agiorgitiko grape. Another full-bodied Greek wine is Naoussa, from the Xynomavro grape.

Cyprus

Othello is the standard Cypriot red wine that UK buyers are most likely to encounter. It is produced by Keo, one of the large co-operatives that dominate the island's wine production. The grapes are a blend of indigenous island varieties like Mavron and Ophthalmo, grown in the arid foothills of the Troodos mountains. In summer, temperatures can be searingly hot and this can be tasted in the wine, with its dry, tarry flavour and warm alcoholic finish.

Other wines from Cyprus include the brands from other co-operatives, like Afames, Domaine d'Ahéra and one private estate, Laona, where efforts are being made to improve vinification methods, especially on a smaller, more individual scale. Vintage variations are insignificant.

Macedonia

At the time of writing, the country that was once Yugoslavia is currently beset by civil strife, with trade sanctions in force against Serbia. However, its best-known wine, Lutomer Laski Rizling, comes from Slovenia, which remains unaffected by the unrest. Macedonia, too, is untroubled, and that is one of the sources of **Vranac**, which is sold as a varietal wine and provides originality. Vranac makes full-bodied, warm, robust red wine that is quite high in alcohol, with some southern warmth, which is characteristic of the southern Rhône. Sometimes there is a slight bitterness on the finish, not unlike some of the southern Italian reds. Vintages do not vary.

There are also examples of French grape varieties, like Merlot and Cabernet Sauvignon, from Slovenia. Otherwise, some of the more individual grapes and flavours, like Postup, Prosek and Dingac, come from the Dalmatian coast and are currently unobtainable.

Mexico

A postscript to this section is a newcomer to our wine shelves, **Petite Sirah** from Mexico. It is no relation at all to Syrah, but is the little-known Durif of France, although it has virtually disappeared from French vineyards. However, in California it is grown quite extensively as Petite Sirah and has travelled south into Mexico. An example from L A Cetto provides some ripe brambly fruit, with a hint of spice, some tannin and a warm finish.

RICH AND SPICY (FULL BODY, AGE, HIGH TANNIN)

This section covers full-bodied, rich spicy wines with tannin and ageing potential, wines like the 1990 **Rhônes**, which epitomise, above all, the characteristics of this segment of the wheel. This is especially true of the northern Rhônes – the appellations of Côte Rôtie, Hermitage and Cornas, whose wines are made from the Syrah grape, which is redolent of spice. Young Syrah is deep-coloured, rich and peppery, intense and full-bodied, with the ability to age into more elegant wines; the blackcurrant gums and peppery aromas of its youth develop into more meaty flavours with maturity. The Rhône Valley has been blessed with an incredible run of vintages – 1988, 1989, 1990 – and even 1991, decried in most other parts of France, has produced some superlative wines.

Côte Rôtie

The most northern of the Rhône appellations is **Côte Rôtie**, which literally means the roasted slope. The vines are grown on steeply terraced hillsides behind the town of Vienne, but recently have also been allowed to spread on to the less favourable plateau behind. Syrah is the main grape variety, but it is sometimes softened by a little Viognier, 10 per cent at the most. The flavours, from the best growers, are always rich and concentrated, demanding several years of bottle ageing and, although the wines spend several months in cask in the cellar, oak is not immediately apparent to the taste buds.

1990 was a difficult year in Côte Rôtie; many of the vines suffered from problems linked to the extensive drought, so a careful selection is essential. Some growers, such as Jamet, have made truly great wine. The 1989 is also very good, with more consistent quality. Other good producers include Chapoutier, Jaboulet, Guigal, Barge, Champet, Gentaz and Jasmin.

Hermitage

Hermitage is the next red appellation down the valley. It too is made from Syrah, which in this instance can be softened with a little Rousanne and Marsanne. Tightly knit, concentrated blackcurrant is the key to Syrah – not the ripe juicy fruit of Cabernet Sauvignon, but the rubbery flavour of fruit gums, with masses of pepper and tannin. Young Hermitage is a solid mouth-puckering wine that requires several years of ageing, at least five for a light vintage and a minimum of ten for a good vintage, to soften it out into a wonderfully spicy bottle, with liquorice fruit and herbs.

Gérard Chave remains the star of the appellation, producing serious and long-lasting wines. He is, however, challenged by others, such as Sorrel and Grippat, as well as two *négociants*, Jaboulet (with Hermitage la Chapelle) and Chapoutier. Vintages to lay down include 1991, 1990, 1989 and 1988, while 1986 and 1983 are just beginning to drink well. 1985 is still too young.

Sadly, the peripheral appellation of **Crozes-Hermitage** is often no more than a shadow of the main appellation, for the vineyard area has been extended to include land that is not really worthy of the appellation. At worst it is barely distinguishable from a Côtes-du-Rhône, but at best – and there are some good wines – it can provide satisfyingly spicy fruit, and in a more accessible form than Hermitage itself. The wines are softer, with less stature, but still with enough tannin in their youth to merit ageing. For example, Jaboulet's 1983 Domaine Thalabert has just reached its peak in the summer of 1993. Other good producers include Desmeure, Pochon at Château de Curson, Fayolle, Graillot and Chapoutier.

St-Joseph

St-Joseph is another northern Rhône appellation that can vary considerably in quality. Sometimes it has little more depth than a Côtes-du-Rhône, but in the hands of a producer like Dr Emile Florentin from Clos de l'Arbalestrier, it takes on a different stature. This is winemaking at its most traditional and meticulous. The

1990 vintage is packed with flavour and will not be ready for drinking for years. Other reliable producers include Chapoutier, Grippat and Coursodin.

Cornas

Cornas is the other great red appellation of the northern Rhône. In some respects it is very similar to nearby Hermitage, with vineyards of Syrah on steep, granite hillsides. There is the same rich, blackcurrant-gum fruit in early youth which will develop into complex, elegant, meaty bottles with maturity. Thierry Allemande is a young grower in the appellation, with just two hectares in the best sites. His 1990 Vieilles Vignes can only be described as monumental, with intense fruit and considerable structure. Noël Verset is another serious producer, as are Auguste Clape, de Barjac, Juge, Michel and Voge.

Châteauneuf-du-Pape

Châteauneuf-du-Pape is the principal appellation of the southern Rhône. Unlike the northern half of the valley, with its concentration on just one grape variety, here there may be as many as 13 used, but in practice the most common varieties are Syrah (as in the north), as well as Grenache and Mourvèdre. While Syrah gives spice, and Mourvèdre weight and backbone, Grenache provides ripe fruit and alcohol. Indeed, the minimum alcohol level is a heady 12.5 per cent (sometimes significantly higher). You only have to see the huge stones in the vineyards in the heart of the appellation – that reflect heat on the ripening grapes in the height of summer, and retain warmth during the cooler nights – to appreciate how Châteauneuf-du-Pape can be as rich and full-bodied as it is. However, as Grenache does not have the staying power of Syrah and Mourvèdre, the wines soften earlier than those of the north.

There is a perfumed scent in good Châteauneuf-du-Pape, with wines redolent of the herbs and spices of the south – the thyme, lavender and rosemary that defined the original vineyard area. Sadly, there have been less than conscientious producers who have been content to dilute the flavours of their wine, making anaemic Châteauneuf-du-Pape that is not worthy of the appellation. But, in the right hands, it is a rich, full-flavoured wine with tannin, requiring some years of bottle age to reach maturity, especially in good vintages like the 1990 (truly great in the southern Rhône), which is comparable to the fabulous 1961.

Leading estates include Château de Beaucastel, Clos des Papes, Château Rayas, Vieux Télégraphe and Château Fortia. The vintages of the mid-eighties, 1986, 1985 and 1983, are drinking well now.

Bandol

Bandol is a rich spicy red wine from the terraced vineyards behind the eponymous Mediterranean port. Serious Bandol is red (there are white and pink Bandol too, but they are of infinitely less significance). It has something in common with the southern Rhône, a certain warmth as well as a distinctly meaty quality, from the Mourvèdre grape, which must account for a considerable percentage of the wine. The appellation laws dictate a minimum of 50 per cent, but serious growers are using even more. Eighteen months' oak-ageing in large oak casks is mandatory and the result is some wonderful rich wine, with meaty complex flavours, animal overtones and a firm backbone of tannin.

Domaine Tempier is the star producer, for its owner, Lucien Peyraud, did much to resurrect a flagging appellation. Domaine du Pibarnon is serious in stature, while other slightly softer, more accessible wines include those of the Bunan family at Mas de la Rouvière and Moulin des Costes, as well as Domaine de Terrebrune and Château Vannières. Vintages tend to follow those of the southern Rhône.

Palette

The tiny appellation of **Palette** deserves a passing mention in this segment. This is one of the smallest appellations of France, situated just outside the enchanting town of Aix-en-Provence. There is just one serious producer, Château Simone, whose red wines are made from an extraordinary mixture of grape varieties – the classic Mourvèdre, Grenache and Cinsaut, as well as other relatively unknown Provençal varieties. Methods here are firmly traditional, resulting in some structured, meaty wines, with the spices of the south, that merit some bottle age.

Coteaux d'Aix-en-Provence

Undeniably, the best red wine of the appellation of **Coteaux d'Aix-en-Provence** fits firmly into this segment, rather than with the wines of the rest of the appellation. Eloi Dürrbach at Domaine de Trévallon breaks the rules by refusing to plant the necessary small percentage of Grenache that is required to make his wine a true Coteaux d'Aix-en-Provence. He persists with a highly successful blend of Cabernet Sauvignon and Syrah, which is aged in small oak barrels, to make one of the most individual wines of Provence.

California Syrah

Syrah, or Shiraz, from other parts of the world also fits into this segment. Over the last few years California has seen an increasing trend of growers intent on trying to perfect Syrah and Mourvèdre: Cabernet Sauvignon is deemed to be boring; everyone else is growing it all over the world, so Syrah (not to be confused with the Californian grape Petite Sirah) and Mourvèdre present a much more exciting challenge. The group of wineries in question have been dubbed the Rhône Rangers; Qupé, Jade Mountain, Ojai and Bonny Doon are the leaders in the British market. They follow the vinification methods of the Rhône Valley, with long maceration periods and oak-ageing. Bonny Doon is known for using flamboyant names: Le Cigar Volant – the French for flying saucer – refers to an occasion in 1954 when the village council of Châteauneuf-du-Pape issued an ordinance to forbid the landing of flying saucers in the vineyards of the village. The back label tells all and, appropriately, the wine is a classic Châteauneuf-du-Pape blend of more or less equal parts of Grenache and Mourvèdre, with a little Syrah, while Ca' del Solo Big House Red has different proportions of the same grape varieties and is a little lighter in body. Jade Mountain makes pure Mourvèdre, while Qupé Syrah, from the Central Coast, has good blackcurrant gum spice, as does Ojai, with some sturdy fruit.

California Zinfandel

Zinfandel is the one California grape variety that is not obviously borrowed from the Old World. It may be the Primitivo of southern Italy – cuttings of which were brought to north America by Agoston Haraszthy, the Hungarian nobleman who did so much for the blossoming wine industry – but this theory is unsubstantiated. A hundred or so years later, Zinfandel has acquired its own individuality.

Zinfandel is eminently versatile. It can make all manner of wines, from pink blush, often labelled White Zinfandel, through light, fruity Beaujolais taste-alikes and jug wines to medium-bodied reds and more heady, alcoholic and tannic wines. It can even be used for fortified wine, with pretensions towards ruby port. It is an easy grape to grow and a generally undemanding vine in the vineyard, although it can ripen unevenly; in the cellar, versatility is the name of the game. As a result, it is often taken for granted and rarely given the serious treatment it deserves.

However, when Zinfandel is given due consideration, with low yields from a coolish vineyard, careful vinification and some oak-ageing, the resulting wine is rich and individual. At its best, Zinfandel has ripe berry flavours, with a substantial amount of tannin and some meaty, liquorice and spicy fruit that is not so different from Syrah. Good Zinfandel is mouth-filling, with weight and concentration.

Ridge is generally considered to make the best Zinfandel, with individual vineyard names like Paso Robles and Geyserville. Other good producers include Frog's Leap Wine Cellars, Lytton Springs and Sutter Home.

Outside California, there is the odd example: notably in Australia, from David Hohnen at Cape Mentelle in Western Australia, as well as the occasional Zinfandel from South Africa. However, neither travels much as yet and so our perception of Zinfandel remains firmly Californian.

Australian Shiraz

What the French call Syrah is called Shiraz in Australia. The grape variety is identical and the taste can be very similar too. Shiraz grows all over the continent, from the warm vineyards of the Hunter Valley of New South Wales, to the cooler regions of Victoria and South Australia. Like Zinfandel in California, it can be exceedingly versatile in flavour, ranging from the light fruity wines that are more like young Beaujolais, to substantial, full-bodied wines with depth and flavour. The best of these is indisputably Grange – formerly called Grange Hermitage – which was created by the talented Max Schubert, the winemaker of Penfolds, back in the 1950s. Grange demonstrates just how good an Australian Shiraz can be. It is a wine that is comparable in stature, if not exactly in flavour, to some of the great Syrahs of Hermitage.

Young Shiraz has the characteristic nose and palate of blackcurrant gums, the hallmark of all good Shiraz; sometimes there is an almost sweet, minty eucalyptus taste that is typical of some New World Shiraz. A good example will be deep in colour, with masses of fruit and tannin, really packing a punch of flavour, with a long finish.

Cabernet Sauvignon is sometimes blended with Shiraz, or vice versa, and the Cabernet generally adds some elegance and more subtle blackcurrant fruit. Much, however, depends upon the producer's individual style.

Grange is expensive, but deserves to be. Luckily, Penfolds produces other good, but more price-friendly Shiraz, such as Kalimna Shiraz Bin 28. Other serious producers of Shiraz include

David Wynn, Bannockburn Vineyards, Henschke, Peppertree
Vineyard, Plantagenet, Rouge Homme, Rothbury, Montrose, Kies
Estate and Cape Mentelle.

Italy

The sole example of **Syrah** in central Italy is from Paolo de Marchi
of the Chianti estate, Isole e Olena. He originally planted vine
cuttings, obtained from Guigal, as an alternative to Cabernet
Sauvignon, to boost the flavour of his Chianti. He now makes a
pure varietal, under the Collezzione dei Marchi label, with some
ripe spicy fruit; it is good, but expensive.

Another Italian oddity which may just fit into this category is
Sagrantino di Montefalco, and the even more individual
Sagrantino passito. Sagrantino is a peculiarly Umbrian grape
variety, grown particularly around the village of Montefalco,
which has a spicy, bitter-sweet, berry fruit flavour. Alternatively,
the grapes are dried, in a process that the Italians call *passito*, to
make a richer, port-like wine that is usually drunk as a dessert
wine. It is an interesting curiosity.

Valpolicella

Italy's best-known red wine, after Chianti, features at both ends of
the taste spectrum. Everyday **Valpolicella** is light and fruity, while
serious Valpolicella is quite a different animal. There are two
vinification processes that transform its flavour and character.
Look for **Recioto** or **Amarone** on the label. Recioto means that the
wine has been made from grapes that are left to dry and dehydrate
so that the juice becomes rich and concentrated. If the subsequent
fermentation is stopped before all the sugar has turned to alcohol,
the wine will be sweet and rich. If, on the other hand, it is
fermented until it is completely dry, it takes on an entirely
different stature, with a rich, concentrated flavour, reminiscent of
sour cherries and plums with meaty, smoky overtones. In this
instance it is called Amarone de la Valpolicella.

Another way of obtaining additional flavour in Valpolicella is a
technique called *ripasso*, where the fermenting juice is put into a
vat containing the lees of the previous year's Recioto. This adds
fruit and intensity to the young wine, as well as structure and
tannin. A ripasso wine is quite different from everyday
Valpolicella – it has a deep colour, a ripe nose of plums and
cherries with, on the palate, tannin and plenty of rich cherry fruit,
as well as spice. The taste is rich rather than sweet. Unfortunately,
the bureaucrats of the EC forbid the use of the word ripasso on a
DOC wine, though not on a vino da tavola, with the result that it is

impossible to identify a ripasso Valpolicella. Masi's Campo Fiorin is the best-known example, for it is labelled as a table wine.

Try also Allegrini, Le Ragose, Quintarelli (who makes some of the most individual wines of the DOC), Serègo Alighieri, and Tedeschi's Capitel San Rocco (which is another table wine), plus Boscaini's Le Canne, Santi's Castello d'Illasi and Bolla's Jago. The price is considerably higher than basic Valpolicella, but that is more than compensated for by additional flavour. Particularly good recent vintages in the Veneto were 1990 and 1988.

STRUCTURED HEAVYWEIGHTS (FULL BODY, AGE, HIGH TANNIN)

This segment covers the very biggest wines, mainly from France, Australia, California and Italy. We begin with Bordeaux.

Claret

The best **classed-growth claret** is the epitome of this segment. The blending of Cabernet Sauvignon, Cabernet Franc and Merlot in varying proportions –perhaps with a little Malbec and Petit Verdot – makes wines of great distinction and style. It is these wines that winemakers all over the world aspire to emulate with their own Cabernet Sauvignon and Bordeaux blends, and now do so with increasing success. However, there is a certain indefinable quality to fine claret which makes it arguably the greatest of all red wines. Advocates of red burgundy will disagree, for it is true that when red burgundy is great, it is truly sublime, but top-quality Bordeaux has a very much lower disappointment rate than supposedly fine burgundy. Claret in its youth is rich and intense in fruit, flavour and tannin. It requires at least 18 months in small oak barrels, probably a high proportion of them new oak – if not entirely new oak in the most prestigious châteaux – to soften the tannins, followed by several years of bottle age before the wine becomes an enjoyable drink.

Cabernet Sauvignon always makes a deep-coloured wine, which allows for development with maturity so that it gradually acquires a delicate brick-orange rim. Blackcurrant is the main aroma, often tempered with the vanilla or the toasted character of new oak. In its youth, a good claret is mouth-puckeringly tannic: it needs to be if it is to develop in the bottle for 20 years, or perhaps more. There is some intense blackcurrant fruit on the palate, which mellows into softer fruit flavours and more elegant cedarwood subtlety.

The differences between the various village appellations of Bordeaux can be hard to define; perhaps **St-Estèphe** may be more austere, **Pauillac** more opulent, **St-Julien** more elegant, while **Margaux** comes somewhere between. **Pomerol** and **St-Emilion** are richer and plummier, with a higher percentage of Merlot and Cabernet Franc, while the **Graves** has the distinctive *goût de terroir* of the appellation.

The Bordeaux market is not in a happy state. Whereas we used to see a flood of *en primeur* offers, with excitement at the opening prices of the big names, last year and again this year things have been decidedly quiet. After a run of three good vintages in Bordeaux, 1991 was a difficult year, with spring frosts causing considerable damage. The 1992 was badly affected by heavy rain at the vintage, resulting in a bumper-sized crop. At the time of writing, in the spring of 1993, very few châteaux have announced an opening price, and those that have are asking for prices well below the 1990 average.

While 1989 was seen as a great vintage almost before the grapes were picked, 1990 enjoyed less hype and is now being re-evaluated as perhaps a potentially finer vintage than 1989. *En primeur* prices were lower for 1990 than 1989, and these may well increase as the economic situation improves. For those wishing to buy claret for laying down, 1990 would be the choice. However, for a relatively inexpensive, enjoyable glass of wine for current drinking, the wines of the 1987 vintage from St-Emilion and Pomerol are the ones to consider. The 1987 vintage was a better year for Merlot, while Cabernet Sauvignon in the Médoc was rather diluted. The 1983s are more forward than 1982s and are beginning to make enjoyable bottles, as are the 1985s from lighter châteaux. Generally, 1985s are better in St-Emilion and Pomerol, while 1986s are more successful in the Médoc.

It is difficult to recommend estates in this category. There are the great names of the 1855 classification, which have the prestige of fine claret. But there are other estates which, for one reason or another, are not included and deserve to be, such as d'Angludet and Chasse-Spleen. Reputations come and go: currently Montrose is improving; so is Baron Pichon-Lalande, after some considerable investment by its new owners. Rausan-Ségla has also been enjoying a revival in its fortunes. Other good wines from the Médoc include Palmer, Beychevelle, Grand-Puy-Lacoste, Léoville-Las Cases, Léoville-Barton, Langoa-Barton, Ducru-Beaucaillou and Lynch-Bages, and on the right bank, Pavie, Trottevieille, Figeac and Magdeleine.

Mas de Daumas Gassac

The other French example appropriate to this segment is a unique vin de pays from the Hérault, **Mas de Daumas Gassac**, which has excited over the years an enormous amount of interest and has been given such epithets as the Lafite of the Languedoc. That may be rather far-fetched, but there is no doubt that, for a mere vin de pays, it has a stature and weight quite outside its class. The principal grape variety is Cabernet Sauvignon, grown in unusual glacial soil; the renowned Professor Peynaud advised on vinification methods and his advice has been strictly followed. The result is undeniably very bordelais in character, a wine that improves both in the bottle, and with every vintage, as the vines themselves age. The current available vintage is the 1990 and, at around £10 a bottle, the price has more in common with classed-growth claret than a vin de pays.

Australia and California

Winemakers in Australia and California see classed-growth claret as the standard towards which they strive with their Cabernet Sauvignon. Some are near to success. Cabernet Sauvignon grows easily all over Australia, from the warm vineyards of the Hunter Valley and Mudgee to Western Australia. However, it is in cooler Coonawarra, with its famous terra rossa – the iron-red soil – that Cabernet Sauvignon really excels. The wines have a richness, but with perhaps less elegance than Bordeaux, with plenty of soft tannins to allow for ageing, although probably not for as long as the finest clarets.

Great **Australian** producers of Cabernet Sauvignon include Wynns with the John Riddoch label, Katnook Estate, Lindemans St-George, Rouge Homme and Petaluma in Coonawarra, while the best recent vintages are 1992, 1991, 1990 and 1988. From elsewhere on this vast continent try Henschke, Yarra Yering, Cape Mentelle, Montrose Wines, Tim Knappstein, Hungerford Hill, Rothbury, Rosemount, Penfolds, Chittering Estate and Parker Estate.

The trend in **California** is now towards more subtle flavours. Where once California Cabernet Sauvignon had instant appeal, leaping out of the glass to greet you, it is now more reticent in its approach. The climate is generally warmer than in Bordeaux, which produces some rich, ripe blackcurrant fruit, with plenty of tannin, and sometimes some herbaceous minty overtones, as in Joseph Heitz Martha's Vineyard.

One of the main differences from Bordeaux, and this applies to Australia too, is that less attention is paid to the precise provenance of the grapes: wineries in both California and Australia think nothing of trucking grapes across states in refrigerated containers to blend them with grapes from other vineyards. While California does have the elements of an appellation system, in the form of the Authorised Vineyard Areas or AVAs – of which there are now close to a hundred – this is purely an indication of provenance, with no quality tag attached to it. The choice of a wine depends very much upon the winery name on the label.

The Rutherford Bench, in the Napa Valley, is generally deemed to produce some of the best California Cabernet Sauvignons. It includes wineries which have established a particular reputation for that grape variety, notably Robert Mondavi, Heitz, Joseph Phelps and Freemark Abbey. Opus One is the result of a joint venture between Robert Mondavi and Baron Philippe of Château Mouton-Rothschild, while Dominus takes advantage of the expertise of Christian Moueix of Pétrus fame. Clos du Val, Simi, Beaulieu Vineyards, Stag's Leap and Newton are other names to look for.

Italy

The one other place where Cabernet Sauvignon really excels, and where wines of comparable stature to classed-growth claret are made, is Tuscany – but more often than not it is blended with that very Tuscan grape variety, Sangiovese.

Sassicaia and Tignanello were the pacesetters here. The Marchese Niccolò Incisa della Rochetta planted Cabernet Sauvignon, with a little Cabernet Franc, on his estate in Bolgheri, close to the Tuscan coast, for no other reason than that he liked the taste of claret and wanted to make his own. For several years **Sassicaia** was produced by Giacomo Tachis, the talented oenologist from Antinori, who thereby gained the experience of the first small Bordeaux *barriques* to be used in Tuscany. At the end of the 1960s, Tuscan viticulture was in a sorry state, without reputation or standing. Antinori, among others, decided that something had to be done and **Tignanello** was created, intended as a wine with international appeal, but with a Tuscan flavour. The main grape variety is Sangiovese, but with a fluctuating percentage of Cabernet Sauvignon, and the method is that of Bordeaux, with ageing in small oak barrels, which are regularly replaced. The impact was immediate, following in the wake of the success of the 1968 Sassicaia which brought the wine to the attention of the world's wine connoisseurs. However, it was Tignanello that really showed just what could be achieved with

Sangiovese if it was vinified properly, with Cabernet Sauvignon used to add a little extra body and structure.

Numerous others have followed the example. Tuscany is now awash with expensive designer bottles, adorned with appropriate labels. Sometimes the contents are superb; sometimes they leave much to be desired. It is not enough to put an indifferent wine into new oak barrels for a few months in the hope of turning it into something exceptional – you have to start in the vineyard and that is what the better Tuscan producers have realised. A man like Paolo de Marchi at Isole e Olena is working hard on improving the overall quality of his Sangiovese, seen at its best in his vino da tavola Cepparello (see also the medium structure segment). This wine takes the place of a riserva Chianti, but cannot be called Chianti because it breaks the rules by being pure Sangiovese. De Marchi is working on Cabernet Sauvignon, too, but it is Sangiovese which excites him most.

The Italian wine law is such that these wines, many of them the best that an estate produces, do not conform to the regulations so must remain classed as supposedly inferior vini da tavola, or what are sometimes called Super Tuscans or alternative wines. The Predicato system, which has been developed by a handful of the larger companies, attempts to give them some form of order, but in fact has a very limited acceptance. To read a Tuscan wine list, you virtually need a specialised glossary.

However, among the vini da tavola which fit into this segment, try Sassicaia, Tignanello, Ornellaia, Balifico, Cepparello, Coltassala, Elegia, Fontalloro, Montesodi, Le Pergole Torte, Rancia, Sammarco and Vinattieri. They may include some Cabernet Sauvignon or not. None is cheap, but they are amongst the best that Tuscany has to offer.

There are plantings of Cabernet Sauvignon in other parts of Italy too, with the quality attaining the same level as some of the Super Tuscans. Angelo Gaja, of Barbaresco fame, is achieving successful flavours with Darmagi. As an illustration of the idiosyncrasy of nomenclature of these alternative wines in Italy, Darmagi (what a shame!) was his father's comment on seeing one of the better vineyard sites of the family estate planted with Cabernet Sauvignon rather than Nebbiolo. The wine is, however, impressive, with an impressive price to match.

Brunello di Montalcino   Brunello di Montalcino has been discussed in some detail under the medium structure segment but, in fact, it is a borderline wine and several of the better Brunellos di Montalcino come within the structured high tannic category. Sometimes there is little difference between a Brunello and a pure Sangiovese vino da tavola, possibly only in the ageing process. Usually the vino da tavola has been in small new Bordeaux *barriques*, while the Brunello must spend three years in the traditonal large *botti* of Slavonic oak. The difference is apparent on the palate. Depending on the producer, the body varies between medium and full; usually a good Brunello di Montalcino is quite full-bodied in its youth, but matures into a wine with more elegance, sometimes something akin to a St-Julien.

Barolo   Barolo is the great red wine of northern Italy. It is produced in vineyards around the village of the same name in the Langhe hills, south-east of the town of Alba. The tough-skinned Nebbiolo grape is the sole variety, producing wines that are high in tannin, extract and acidity. In the right hands, the results can be amongst the best that Italy has to offer, but Nebbiolo is not always easy to vinify. Long fermentation, adding even more extract and tannin, means that the wine requires a long ageing period in wood even to begin to soften. This is the traditional style of Barolo, with maturation in large Slavonic oak barrels which may even be 100 years old. The modern trend, however, is towards something softer and more accessible, with subtle changes in vinification, a short period of maceration and more bottle- rather than barrel-ageing. None the less, Barolo is still required by DOCG regulations to spend a minimum of two years in wood, plus another one in vat before sale. Riserva on the label indicates four years of ageing, and riserva speciale five years.

In its youth, Barolo is tough and unyielding, a sturdy, structured wine with masses of colour, tannin, acidity and extract. The harsh tannin is tempered by some fruit, liquorice and prunes, but still leaves an underlying austerity, with a dry tarry finish. However, this initially unapproachable quality is what turns Barolo into great wine when it is ten, if not twenty, years old. With age, it mellows, developing a rich nose that is reminiscent of Christmas cake, with a wonderful fruity, cinnamon and nutmeg taste on the palate. Some associate it with truffles, for Piedmont is the home of some of the finest white truffles; others talk of violets. There is no doubt that it is a serious, attention-demanding glass of wine. Great Barolo can be sublime, but to some it is very definitely an acquired taste.

Good producers include Aldo Conterno, Giacomo Conterno, Mascarello, Altare, Cavalotto, Ceretto, Pio Cesare, Ratti, Prunotto, Vietti. The best recent vintages include 1990, 1989, 1988, 1986, 1985 and 1982.

Barbaresco   In comparison with Barolo, Barbaresco, the second long-standing DOCG wine of Piedmont, is more accessible. It too is made purely from Nebbiolo, grown in vineyards around the village of the same name. The clue to the difference lies in the soil, which is much lighter than that of Barolo and makes a less substantial wine. Consequently, Barbaresco requires a shorter ageing period – two years in barrels and bottle, three years for a riserva and four for a riserva speciale.

Like Barolo, Barbaresco is tough and unyielding in its youth, though it is perhaps the less aggressively tannic of the two. The wine is still intense, with plenty of extract. With ageing it develops some lovely aromas of rich fruit-cake, liquorice, prunes and raspberries and, with increasing maturity, it can take on almost burgundian overtones, some vegetal sweetness, but never loses the firm tannic backbone.

Like Barolo, Barbaresco has enjoyed a similar run of good vintages. The key producers are Gaja, making good, but expensive, wine, Marchesi de Gresy, Bruno Giacosa, and some of the leading Barolo producers, such as Pio Cesare, Rinaldi, Ceretto, Oddero and Mascarello.

There are a handful of wines from southern Italy that have the same tannic, sturdy character, with structure and backbone. Aglianico is the grape variety responsible, sometimes described as the Nebbiolo of the south, with a similar tannic character, as well as acidity and extract. It is at its best in the dramatic-sounding wine of the Basilicata, **Aglianico del Vulture**, the Vulture being an extinct volcano. This is a DOC of growing interest, as vinification methods improve. Fratelli d'Angelo is the best producer, followed by Paternoster and Sasso.

Aglianico is also the grape variety of **Taurasi**, a DOC from Campania, produced mainly by the leaders of the region, Mastroberardino. Like young Barolo and Barbaresco, young Taurasi can disappoint: bottles should be stored away and forgotten about for at least five, if not ten, years.

Portugal

Some sturdy, tannic examples of Dão and Bairrada could also creep into this segment of the wheel, but have been discussed at greater length under the medium structure segment, which is where they sit most comfortably.

FORTIFIED WINES

All the wines in this wheel (see inside back cover) have one thing in common: the addition of grape brandy has featured at some stage during the production process. Although the precise moment when the brandy is added may vary from wine to wine, its use always accounts for the higher level of alcohol, taking the wine above the 15 per cent that generally constitutes the highest alcohol level in a table wine.

The range of flavours of fortified wines is as rich and varied as with table wines, from light and elegant to rich and luscious, and everything in between. Some are aged, in some instances for many years; others are best drunk in early youth. The appropriate moment to drink them varies too: some make excellent aperitifs; others are very much better after a meal, or make delicious pudding wines.

DRY AND LIGHT

Fino sherry

Fino sherry is a highly underrated aperitif in Britain. Its austere tang is the perfect foil for the mouth-watering range of tapas eaten in its native Spain – olives, roasted almonds, chorizo sausage and other more exotic flavours. One of the reasons for the immense drinkability of fino sherry on its home ground may be that it is not fortified to the same extent for consumption in Spain itself, so that it is only marginally more alcoholic than a table wine. Also, it may well be much fresher and therefore more appealing – the problem with fino is that it begins to lose its freshness the moment it is bottled, and the time-lag between bottling in Jerez and consumption in Britain may amount to several weeks, if not months. The only solution is to be sure to buy your fino from a wine shop with a fast turnover, not from an emporium where it has gathered dust on the shelves. Consider, too, the advantage of a half-bottle, which provides a generous glass, and maybe a top-up, for three or four people at one time.

Good fino sherry should be pale in colour and light in body, absolutely bone dry, with a firm, almost austerely dry finish. It should never be heavy or clumsy. The flavour depends upon the development in cask of a film of yeast, called flor, which looks rather like a veil of cotton wool and accounts for the distinctive taste. Contrary to most winemaking practice, oxidation through contact with the air plays an essential part in the development of a good fino. As with all sherry, a period of ageing in a *solera* system is an important part of the production process. A *solera* consists of a series of tiers, or scales, of sherry barrels containing the same wine, with each tier being younger than the one below. As the wine is drawn off from the oldest barrels for bottling they are refreshed with a slightly younger wine, and so on up the tiers, and the youngest tier is replenished by a wine that has not yet been aged at all. The *solera* system depends upon the fact that the younger wine takes on the characteristics of the older wines.

Most fino sherry is sold by the large sherry bodegas under brand names like Garvey's San Patricio, Gonzalez Byass' Tio Pepe and Domecq's La Ina. Finos from Lustau and Don Zoilo are good, and look out too for Waitrose's own-label fino in half-bottles.

Manzanilla

Manzanilla is very similar to fino sherry, but with an extra distinctive nuance of flavour, a firm salty tang, that is not found in fino. This salty characteristic is said to originate from its maturation by the sea; it is matured in barrels in the warehouses of the port of Sanlúcar de Barrameda. Good manzanillas, from the large sherry bodegas, include Hidalgo's La Gitana, Barbadillo and Don Zoilo. Sainsbury's own-label manzanilla is available in half-bottles.

Montilla

Montilla also comes from southern Spain, not far from Jerez de la Frontera, but it has acquired something of a tarnished reputation as a poor man's sherry. The term amontillado literally means 'in the style of montilla' but generally it is montilla which is the less exciting and cheaper drink. The grapes tend to be riper, making wine that is low in acidity, as well as higher in alcohol and therefore needing less fortification. The final alcoholic strength is slightly lower than that of sherry, which makes it cheaper on the shelf. Also, montilla undergoes a shorter ageing period than amontillado. It tends to be rather soft and rarely has the firm dry backbone of good fino – indeed, virtually all montilla imported into Britain is not fortified at all. What would be a fino montilla in Spain is sold as montilla dry in Britain. Bodegas Alvear is the best producer, but most montilla is sold under a supermarket's or merchant's own label.

Madeira: sercial

Sercial is the driest style of all the wines from Madeira, the Portuguese island that is closer to Africa than to Europe, and it has an original taste all of its own. The production of all madeira involves a process of heating the wine in what is called an *estufa*, which may be a tank or a heated warehouse. This 'cooking' of the wine is said to imitate the days when Madeira was the last port of call for ships crossing the Atlantic, or rounding the Cape of Good Hope on their way to India. The wine was taken on as ballast, and as such was literally cooked in the hold of the ship during the long sea voyage; amazingly, it was found to be much improved in flavour on its arrival at its destination.

Sercial takes its name from the grape used, although until very recently it was made predominantly from Tinta Negra Mole, as were most other madeiras. However, as EC regulations now require a wine to contain 85 per cent of any grape mentioned on the label, the Portuguese have had to conform, and much young, so-called sercial, will now be sold as Special Dry or Light Dry. Older wines will contain the required amount of Sercial. Sercial is not quite as bone dry as fino sherry, although it has a very high acidity level and a certain fullness in the mouth which can be likened to a cheesy character. The Madeira Wine Co. dominates the island's production, controlling many of the famous old names like Cossart Gordon, Rutherford & Miles, Leacock and Blandys. The handful of other producers includes Barbeito and Henriques & Henriques. Sercial is very rarely sold as a vintage wine; more often it has an indication of age, such as 5-year-old or 10-year-old. Even better, and more expensive, is Cossart Gordon's Duo Centenary Celebration. Very occasionally you may find a *solera* madeira.

MEDIUM-SWEET

Pale cream sherry

It seems appropriate to include **pale cream sherry** under the medium section, for it is simply fino sweetened with cane sugar, and therefore does not have the weight of a standard cream sherry. Basically, it panders to the snobbery of wanting to be seen to drink dry, while actually drinking sweet. The colour is that of deep fino, but the flavour is somewhere between an amontillado and a cream sherry, although it lacks the body of either. A few pale cream sherries are marketed as commercial brands, of which Croft Original Pale Cream is the brand leader.

Amontillado sherry

Amontillado is the term commonly used to describe medium-sweet sherry, but the truth is that as such it is a complete travesty of the real thing (discussed later under 'dry and heavy'). Commercial amontillado is quite soft and sweetish, with some body and alcohol and a dryish finish. Like all sherry it has gone through the *solera* system of ageing, but it is then blended with some sweetening agent, usually concentrated Pedro Ximénez, to bring the wine to the required specification of sweetness. It is undemanding and fairly undistinguished and is sold under numerous shippers' brand names, such as Dry Fly, Dry Sack, Harvey's Club Amontillado. These are the wines that have done little to enhance the declining fortunes of the sherry trade. For real sherry, turn to the dry segments of the wheel.

Cyprus and South Africa

Cyprus and South Africa both produce medium-sweet sherry-style wines, but have a price advantage over Spanish sherry. South Africa now has a very small share of the market, and brand names are used, like Cavendish Cape Medium Dry. Illogically, Cyprus is still allowed to use the term sherry, but the wines bear little relationship to the real thing, and lack alcohol and bite. Mosaic and Emva are the two main brands.

Montilla

Montilla, which gave its name to amontillado sherry, also has a medium-sweet, amontillado category. As with the fino or dry style, it is paler and lighter than sherry with less bite and generally labelled medium-dry.

Verdelho

After sercial, **verdelho** (or Medium Dry madeira) is next on the madeira sweetness ladder. It is fuller and richer than sercial, with more body and, like all madeira, it has a firm backbone of acidity. It benefits from ageing in cask for an absolute minimum of 18 months and usually for considerably longer. This makes a medium-bodied wine with a nutty flavour and a trace of sweetness or, more accurately, richness. The members of the Madeira Wine Co. are the principal names to look out for.

All madeira has a wonderful capacity for ageing: the exceptionally high level of acidity, not to mention the heating of the wine during the production process, makes it virtually

197

indestructible. Madeira never seems to oxidise once a bottle has been opened and old bottles of madeira can be bought without any fear of deterioration.

The occasional bottle of Rainwater, another medium-dry style, and Terrantez, made from a less common grape variety, also fits into this taste category. Rainwater is not really as poetic as it sounds. There are various stories on the origin of its name – most common is that the contents of some caskets of madeira were diluted with rain and that the result became a popular style of madeira in America in the eighteenth century. Today it is a commercial blend of different grapes, and varies from shipper to shipper in weight and flavour.

Port: white, ruby, tawny, colheita, single quinta, late-bottled vintage, crusted and vintage-character

'Port' covers a multitude of qualities: most is medium-sweet, but with variations in depth of flavour, richness, nuttiness and staying power (or length in the mouth). It is aged in either bottle or cask and the best bottle-aged port is vintage port, which comes into the rich and heavy segment of the taste wheel. All other styles of port fit more or less into the medium-sweet segment of the taste wheel – or should it really be medium-dry? The distinction is rather blurred. In any case, the sweetness of port comes from the natural sugar in the grape juice, which remains in the wine because the fermentation is stopped at the appropriate moment by the addition of grape spirit.

Take **white port** first of all – this accounts for a minuscule proportion of the port trade, to the extent that some houses do not bother to produce it at all. The vinification process is the same as for standard ruby port and the taste is dryish rather than bone dry, with a softness, a hint of liquorice and a lightly mouth-filling flavour. Taylor's Chip Dry is the best known; and Delaforce and Cockburns also produce white ports. It provides an original aperitif, but lacks the finesse of an elegant fino or manzanilla.

Moving on, **ruby port** describes a young wine that is sold after two or three years' ageing in wood. It is deep in colour, with the typical liquorice fruit flavour of port, but with a rather spirity, alcoholic burn to the finish, as the brandy is not properly integrated into the taste. Cheap **tawny**, which is generally a blend of white and ruby, is lighter in colour and body, but not dissimilar in taste.

However, **mature tawny** port is quite another story. It has been aged for ten, twenty or maybe as long as forty years in cask, so the colour has turned tawny-red as part of the natural process of maturation. The taste is mellow and nutty, redolent of liquid walnuts, with an underlying elegance and sweetness. A newcomer to the British market is a 10-year-old tawny from Quinta da Ervamoira, an estate which belongs to Ramos Pinto, and in which Louis Roederer now has a controlling interest

While a 20-year-old tawny, for example, gives only an indication of the average age, a **colheita** port is a single vintage tawny, that is, a wine that is treated in the same way as a blended tawny but comes from only one vintage. It must be aged in cask for a minimum of seven years and, in practice, often for much longer. The label gives not only a vintage date but also a bottling date. Colheitas seem to be the preserve of the Portuguese port houses and have been neglected by the English shippers like, for example, Taylors or Cockburns; while Cálem, a leading Portuguese house, makes something of a speciality of its Colheitas, as does Niepoort; Souza is another name to look out for. The taste, depending on the vintage, is not unlike that of a 10- or 20-year-old tawny, with similar nutty overtones. Pricewise they compare with tawny ports of a similar age.

There is a growing trend for port shippers to produce what they call a **single quinta** port, which is a wine from their best estate or vineyards, in years in which a port vintage is not generally declared (otherwise this wine would be used for the vintage port). Generally, it is a lighter version of vintage port, with some ripe liquorice fruit and an underlying sweetness and richness, but without the body of a vintage port. Wines like Taylor's Quinta de Vargellas, Graham's Quinta do Malvedos, Delaforce's Quinta da Corte all provide a vintage-style wine, at a much more affordable price than a true vintage port. Usually, a single quinta is sold at the moment that it is ready for drinking so, for instance, 1979 Quinta do Malvedos is on sale at about £15 a bottle at the moment, while the currently most accessible vintage port from Grahams, the 1975, costs about £24 a bottle, a good deal more expensive.

A newcomer to the ranks of port producers is Quinta la Rosa, from a small family estate, launched with the 1988 vintage. It has potential, with some ripe liquorice fruit but, needless to say, it needs some bottle age before it will make an enjoyable drink.

Interesting, but of less depth of character, are the **late-bottled vintage** wines, LBV for short. As the name implies, this is the wine of a single vintage, which is bottled later than is normal for a true vintage port (between four and a half and six years, instead of eighteen months or so after the vintage). The idea behind the concept is that the wine, from a lighter year than a true vintage, ages more quickly in cask than in bottle. In theory there is some trace of vintage style, although the wines are somewhat lighter, albeit with some liquorice fruit. Late-bottled vintage wines are generally ready for drinking once they are bottled, with little to be gained from giving them further ageing in bottle. Taylors were the trendsetters here, while others, such as Warre, Sandeman, Graham, Fonseca and Dow, have followed suit.

Wines labelled **vintage-character** are really only one step up from basic ruby, with little real aspiration to emulate vintage port. **Crusted**, or crusting, port, on the other hand, which is produced only for the British market, is a blend of wines from two or three quite good – but not great – years, which are aged in cask for three or four years before bottling. The result can be quite flavoursome and also presents some good-value drinking.

New World tawny and ruby

Not so long ago the wine industries of Australia and South Africa concentrated on dessert wines, mainly port and sherry lookalikes and, although there has been a definite shift of emphasis towards table wines in the last ten or twenty years, fortified wines are still produced in some quarters. Sometimes the grape varieties are the same as for European wines, sometimes quite different. In California, ruby styles are made with Zinfandel and Cabernet Sauvignon. In Australia, the traditional Portuguese port varieties, such as Touriga Nacional and Bastardo, are sometimes used.

Australia produces some remarkably good port-style wines. Of course, the export label must not mention the word port, but the terms tawny and ruby are permitted. Yalumba's Galway Pipe is a delicious old tawny, with some rich, sweet walnut fruit. Seppelt's Mount Rufus Finest Old Tawny is a little drier, but with a similar walnut flavour. In California, Quady makes a joke of the fact that it cannot mention the word port on the label by calling its ruby-style wine Starboard. It is rather sweet, with a taste of raisins, rather than the more classic liquorice flavour of ruby port.

In South Africa, Allesverloren makes some of the best port styles with some ripe liquorice fruit, albeit a trifle coarse, but these wines are not yet available in Britain.

Vin doux naturel from Rivesaltes, Banyuls, Maury and Rasteau

The **vins doux naturels** feature amongst France's undiscovered vinous delights, although those made from Muscat (see next segment) are well-known. Other wines which are based on Grenache and other red grapes are aged in large oak casks and then left for six months or more in glass demijohns outside in all weathers, giving them a distinctive individuality. The term vin doux naturel is something of a misnomer. What it really means is that the sweetness in the wine is natural, originating from the grape, not from sacks of sugar, and that sweetness is retained in the wine by the addition of brandy at the appropriate moment during vinification to stop further fermentation. With some lengthy ageing in cask the wines take on rich, nutty flavours, redolent of walnuts, liquorice and prunes. Walk into a cellar of old casks in Rivesaltes and there is the wonderfully enticing aroma of fruitcake.

Rivesaltes is the most important vin doux naturel of the Midi in terms of volume. The vineyards cover a wide area around the town of the same name and intermingle with those of the Côtes-du-Roussillon. Moving on, **Banyuls** is a small village almost on the Mediterranean border with Spain, and its vineyards are the same ones that make the gutsy red wine Collioure. The third name to look out for, **Maury**, is made in one tiny village in the heart of Roussillon. Mas Amiel is the only producer of any importance and a 15-year-old Maury is certainly worth seeking out.

The village of **Rasteau** is in the Rhône valley and is better-known for being a part of the appellation of Côtes-du-Rhône-Villages. Its Grenache-based fortified wine forms a pair with Beaumes-de-Venise's Muscat, from another village of the Côtes-du-Rhône-Villages.

There is an element of obscurity in all these wines: they have suffered with the fall from fashion of sweet aperitif wines. However, they can make delicious after-dinner drinks in place of the more conventional port, and have the added advantage of being a little lighter in alcohol.

Recommended producers include Cazes Frères with their Vieux Rivesaltes, which makes a wonderful alternative to tawny port; the competent Rasteau village co-operative and the leading Banyuls producer, Domaine du Mas Blanc.

SWEET MUSCAT

Muscat-based vin doux naturel from Beaumes-de-Venise, Frontignan and Rivesaltes

Muscat de Beaumes-de-Venise, from one of the Côtes-du-Rhône-Villages, established the popularity of Muscat-based vin doux naturel as a delicious dessert wine, the essence of which is the fresh, ripe flavour of the Muscat grape. The skill in the vinification is judging the exact moment to stop the fermentation by the addition of grape brandy: too soon and the wine is sweet and heavy; too late and some of the fresh fruit flavour is lost. Producers even sleep in their cellars at night in order not to miss the vital moment.

Good producers include Domaine de Durban, Domaine de Coyeux and the village co-operative. The wine should be drunk as young as possible, within a year or two of the vintage, before its fresh grapey flavour fades. There are other Muscat-based vins doux naturels in France that are similar in taste, but they are less popular and therefore offer better value. For example, **Muscat de Frontignan** comes from the town of Frontignan on the Mediterranean coast, where Château la Peyrade makes the most delicate wine.

Muscat de Rivesaltes, from the large appellation in the foothills of the Pyrenees behind the town of Perpignan, is just beginning to re-emerge from a period in the doldrums, with a handful of producers struggling to make their wines better known. It has the characteristic taste of Muscat, with lemon and honey flavours, and hints of ripe apricots and pithy oranges. Domaine de Sarda-Malet, Cazes Frères, and the Arnaud de Villeneuve label are all worth trying.

A handful of other little-known Muscat-based vins doux naturels occasionally find their way across the Channel, for example **Muscat de Lunel** (a tiny appellation near Montpellier), **Muscat de Mireval** (the next-door appellation to Muscat de Frontignan) and **Muscat de St-Jean-de-Minervois** (from one village within the appellation of Minervois). Sainsbury's has the imagination to sell Muscat de St-Jean-de-Minervois in half-bottles.

In addition, there is the occasional vin doux naturel which does not have an appellation, such as the José Sala label, which originates from somewhere near Pézenas and which offers unrefined and cheerful good value.

Valencia, Málaga, Samos and Pantelleria

Parts of southern Spain also grow Muscat, or Moscatel as they call it, and it is treated in much the same way as when making the vins doux naturels of the Midi. **Moscatel de Valencia** is a cheap and cheerful fortified Muscat made in vineyards behind one of the largest cities of Spain, a city which is generally better known for the production of large quantities of increasingly quaffable but undistinguished table wine. It is heavier and infinitely less elegant than its French counterparts, but has some ripe, grapey fruit, offers excellent value for money and can stand up to rich sweets, even mince pies.

Málaga wine, from southern Spain, comes in many guises, and one of the forms it takes is a **Moscatel de Málaga**. Scholtz is the leading Málaga producer.

The Greek island of Samos is also known for its fortified Muscat wines, as are Patras and Lemnos; these wines are similar in flavour.

Southern Italy, or more precisely the tiny island of Pantelleria, lost in the Mediterranean between Sicily and Tunisia, produces a **Moscato di Pantelleria**. Depending on the producer it may or may not be fortified. The best wines are not generally fortified and therefore feature in the sweet section of the table wine wheel. However, the Marsala producers Florio have recently begun to take an interest in the island and have introduced a new fortified Moscato di Pantelleria called Morse di Luce.

USA and South Africa

Most sweet Muscats from California tend to be unfortified, late-harvest wines, which fit into the sweet segment of the table wine wheel. The one exception comes from Quady, a small Californian winery, which makes a speciality of fortified wines and whose Essensia Orange Muscat has the pithy orange fruit of the Muscat grape.

Some of the early traditions of South Africa are based on fortified wines from Moscatel. Often the sweet grape juice was simply fortified to prevent any fermentation. However, Muscat de Montac is made in the same way as the vins doux naturels of the south of France, with a little fermentation prior to fortification, thus retaining the grapey flavour.

Neither Australia nor New Zealand ever seems to have vinified Muscat in this way. Both countries make some deliciously grapey late-harvest Muscats, which feature in the sweet segment of the table wine wheel, and Australia also boasts some wonderful Muscat-based fortified wines, in the form of Liqueur Muscat, which is described below.

RICH AND HEAVY

Australian liqueur Muscat and tokay

Liqueur Muscat must be Australia's most original wine. It is produced around the town of Rutherglen in the north-east corner of the state of Victoria. It is made from Muscat grapes that are left on the vines until they are over-ripe and raisin-like; the fermentation is stopped by the addition of brandy and the wine is then matured in oak barrels, often for several years and sometimes even in a *solera* system, like sherry. The result is magnificent, rich and luscious, the essence of liquid walnuts and orange marmalade; older wines become more toffee-like, losing some of the orange flavour of the Muscat grapes. Colours range from amber-orange to mahogany-brown.

The best producers include Chambers, Campbells, Stanton & Killeen, All Saints, Seppelts and Baileys. Sadly – but inevitably – these wines are expensive, given the small yields and long periods of maturation, but they are well worth it, making a dessert wine or after-dinner drink with a taste of Australian individuality. They partner Christmas pudding and chocolate triumphantly.

Baileys also produces what it calls Founder Liqueur Tokay, which is very similar to Liqueur Muscat in taste, wonderfully smooth and unctuous, with a flavour of marmalade and cinnamon. The method of production is virtually identical, using very ripe grapes, and extensive maturation in old oak barrels, with the main difference in taste coming from the grape variety, which is Muscadelle. The price is comparable too.

Cream sherry

Cream sherry or sweet oloroso sherry covers a multitude of flavours. Not to put too fine a point on it, there are cream sherries that are rich and luscious and simply delicious whilst others – commercial blends, well-laced with sweet grape concentrate – are of little distinction. However, there is nothing better than a real cream sherry on a cold winter's night by an open log fire, wonderful to sip with a bowl of walnuts. The best-known commercial brand may be Harvey's Bristol Cream, but there are many wines with infinitely more depth of flavour and character. Look out for Gonzalez Byass Matusalem, Lustau's Old East India and Sandeman's Royal Corregidor. (For dry oloroso see under the dry and heavy segment.)

The use of the name sherry is now controlled on labels with increasing severity. South Africa may no longer use the term, while Cyprus may, and, for some nonsensical reason, although British wine is not even acceptable as real wine because it is based on reconstituted grape juice, the term British sherry is still permissible until the end of 1995. From Spain, Montilla cream is not dissimilar to a commercial cream sherry, nor is cream Cyprus sherry, usually sold under a brand name like Mosaic. The same style of wine from South Africa is sold simply as cream under a brand name such as Cavendish Cape and Ouzerust.

Moscatel de Setúbal

The Setúbal peninsula, south of Lisbon, is a source of some delicious Moscatel-based wines, as well as greater quantities of table wine. The grapes used (a blend in which Moscatel is the most important but does not always amount to the 85 per cent necessary for it to feature on the label) are fermented and grape brandy is added at the appropriate moment. The grape skins are then left to macerate in the young fortified wine until the following spring, in order to extract even more aroma and flavour. Then the wine is kept in first large, then small, wooden barrels. Sometimes the wine has a vintage, sometimes merely an indication of age.

The best **Moscatels de Setúbal** are those that have been aged for several years, perhaps as many as 20 or 25, so that they take on rich toffee-like flavours, reminiscent of fruitcake, nuts and treacle. Alternatively, the younger wines, usually sold when they are about four years old, are fresh and grapey, with a somewhat spirity finish, and have more in common with Muscats from the Midi or Spain.

Vintage port

Vintage port stands apart from other ports, for in early youth it is very rich and concentrated, with mouth-filling flavours of liquorice, prunes, tannin and spirit, none of which have quite blended together yet. It needs several years in the bottle before it is ready to be enjoyed. The idea of laying down vintage port for the coming of age of a child demonstrates that 21, or at least 18, years is an appropriate period of maturation.

As it ages, vintage port mellows, becoming smooth and elegant, losing any rough spirity edges and developing some complex flavours of prunes and spice, with an underlying rich sweetness. It will always have more body, concentration and colour than a tawny port of similar age.

Vintage port is not made every year. The decision to declare a vintage depends not only on the quality of the grapes, but on the economic health of the port trade. An extreme example was when the depression of the 1930s stopped every shipper but Noval from declaring the fabulous 1931 vintage. Similarly, only three shippers declared the good 1987 vintage, as it followed too closely after the 1985. The decision belongs to each house individually; some years are declared almost universally and others not. Sometimes, when there are two comparable years side by side, the shippers may be almost equally divided between the two, for example, in 1982 and 1983. In fact, 1983 is now generally considered to be the better year of the two.

The most recent generally declared vintage is 1991, the first since 1985. It is just being offered for sale in autumn 1993. Port shippers, like champagne houses, have a house style that is individual to them, so personal taste should be a guide when reading our recommendations. A generalisation which is not totally founded is that the Portuguese houses, such as Ferreira, Niepoort and Cálem, make wines that are a little lighter in style, while the wines from the English shippers are richer and more full-bodied. This may be something to do with the indisputable fact that a lighter tawny is an infinitely more attractive drink in the hotter climate of Portugal than a full-bodied vintage wine, which is more appealing in a colder northern clime.

Among currently available vintages, 1966 and 1970 are drinking well; the underrated 1980 is also beginning to show well; 1975 is not really fulfilling its promise, while 1977 should be kept for a few years more, as can 1963. After madeira, vintage port is the most long-lived fortified wine, as a sip of Taylors 1865, offered recently on the occasion of the company's 300th anniversary, well demonstrated.

Madeira: bual and malmsey

Bual is the next stage up the sweetness scale after verdelho (younger wines will now be sold as Medium Rich). It is fairly sweet and nutty, with the slightly cooked flavour of all madeira. The older it is, the better. Compare Cossart Gordon's Good Company which is cheesy on the palate, with its 5-Year-Old Reserve which is sweeter and nuttier, and then with the Duo Centenary Celebration Bual which is smooth and rich, with a dry caramel nose, a firm bite of acidity and a powerful mouthful of flavour.

Malmsey, as the fourth wine on the sweetness scale, otherwise to be labelled as Full Rich, is so rich and sweet that it is positively unctuous, with rich burnt caramel flavours, nuts and fruit, and a firm bite of acidity to counter-balance the sweetness. Good madeira will never be cheap, but it deserves greater attention. It is the most long-lived of all wines, with the unique advantage that an open bottle does not deteriorate.

Málaga

At the height of the Victorian era, Málaga was eminently fashionable; today the name tends to conjure up images of sun-soaked package holidays. The grape varieties grown in the vineyards behind the town in southern Spain are Pedro Ximénez and Moscatel. A wide range of styles is possible, from seco to dulce (dry, sweet) and, sometimes classified by colour, from blanco, to dorado, rojo-dorado, oscuro and negro (white, golden, tawny, dark and black). However, there are three styles that are worth seeking out; first is the Moscatel de Málaga, mentioned earlier under fortified Muscat.

Next is **Lágrima**, a wonderful, rich dessert wine, made only from free-run juice, matured in wood for several years. It has an intense dark chocolate colour, with hints of Bovril on the nose and a rich and concentrated taste. The wine is so unctuously thick that you could almost stand a teaspoon in it, but it is wonderfully soothing to the throat and has a dry finish so it does not cloy.

More common is a Málaga which is aged in a *solera*, like sherry. The most popular is Solera Scholtz 1885 (1885 refers to the year in which that particular *solera* was started, so that the wine may contain only the tiniest drop of wine from 1885), which is deep brown in colour, with rich Moscatel flavours, as well as walnuts. It is smooth with a firm finish: with wines like these, Málaga deserves a return to popularity.

DRY AND HEAVY

Sherry: oloroso, amontillado and Palo Cortado

British tastebuds are so attuned to expect sherry to be sweet (unless it is fino or manzanilla) that we forget that in Spain all sherry begins life as a dry wine, and more often than not stays that way. We glibly equate oloroso to cream sherry, but the word oloroso actually means fragrant, so that an oloroso sherry is usually a rich, aromatic wine. **Oloroso seco** is a firmly, sometimes searingly, dry wine, with a concentration of flavour reminiscent of nuts and prunes. It is fortified to a higher degree than either fino or amontillado, to 18 or 20 per cent, and is aged for several years in a *solera* system. Real olorosos include Gonzalez Byass Apostoles, which is very slightly sweetened; Williams & Humbert's Dos Cortados Old Dry Oloroso; Rio Viejo from Domecq and the olorosos in Lustau's Almacenista range. The words seco (dry) and muy viejo (very old) are the clue to quality.

Authentic **amontillados**, rather than the commercial variety, are wines that were once finos, but have lost their flor character and developed with age. They are fortified to a higher degree than fino but they do not quite have the weight of an oloroso, and so are more delicate, dry and nutty. Good examples include Garvey's Tio Guillermo, Gonzalez Byass Amontillado del Duque, Principe from Barbadillo and Napoleon from Hidalgo.

Palo Cortado is something of an anomaly, coming somewhere between amontillado and oloroso in style. Like oloroso, it does not develop flor, and it is possibly best described as an elegant oloroso. Genuine Palo Cortado is rare and tends to be quite expensive; take Harvey's 1796 as an example, which costs around £10.

Also worth seeking out are the **almacenista** sherries, which are the particular speciality of Emilio Lustau. The term almacenista describes a small amount of a particularly fine unblended sherry purchased from a small stockholder.

With wines like these, dry olorosos and aged amontillados, sherry takes on another dimension of flavour and quality. Inevitably these wines seem expensive compared to commercial blends, for the years of maturation in a lengthy *solera* system have to be sustained. But in reality they represent exceptional value for money in terms of flavour and quality.

The sherry industry has not been without its problems. In the past couple of years, large tracks of vineyards have been pulled up in an attempt to solve the problems of over-production which stem from the sharp decline in sales over recent years. This is proving successful and resulting in a greater concentration of quality, helping to retain sherry's position as one of the great wines in a world that is increasingly polarised between Chardonnay and Cabernet Sauvignon.

Marsala

Last in this wheel is **marsala**, which crosses taste bands from sweet to dry and traverses the quality range from fairly dire to sublimely delicious. Once upon a time it held its place amongst the great fortified wines of the world, proudly taking its position alongside sherry, port and madeira. But then the decline set in. You could find marsala flavoured with egg, coffee, even bananas, designed for making zabaglione. Happily these travesties of the real thing have now been relegated to the category of cremova. The classification of marsala is far from simple and is determined by wood-ageing – a minimum of one year for fine and two for a superiore (up to ten years old or more). Colour represents another possible category of classification: oro, ambra or rubino. Then there is sweetness, or otherwise, to consider; dry, semi-dry and sweet. Vergine marsala with five years' ageing is dry, and depends upon small amounts of older wine for its character.

The best marsalas are firmly dry. Take as a guideline the distinctive and individual wines of Marco de Bartoli, who has done more than any other producer to restore the tarnished reputation of marsala. Often his wines do not conform to the DOC regulations, but that does not affect the taste. De Bartoli's 10-year-old Vecchio Samperi is not, in fact, fortified, which means that technically it is not marsala at all, but it comes from the two key grape varieties of marsala – Grillo and Inzolia – and has a wonderful dry nutty flavour with great depth of flavour and complexity. Other marsala producers of note include Curatolo, Rallo and Florio.

SPARKLING WINES

Champagne (see the wheel on the inside of the back cover) is the pacesetter: the sparkling wine that all the others aspire to emulate, if not actually to imitate. There is no doubt that a really good champagne is sublime, an incomparable drink full of bubbles and festivity, but in reality not all champagne is so good. It is also expensive and, consequently, there are a growing number of equally (if not more) enjoyable, and certainly more affordable, alternatives. These may take champagne as their bench mark, but the individual taste of each is adapted to the specific conditions of the region of production, particularly taking into account climate and grape varieties.

Champagne at its best is undeniably unique. The particular method of making sparkling wine in Champagne has evolved through years, if not centuries, of experience and is unquestionably accepted to be the best way of making sparkling wine. The second fermentation, which takes place in the bottle, gives the wine greater finesse, with a finer, lighter mousse and more staying power, as well as a greater depth of flavour, originating particularly from the contact of the wine with the lees of the second fermentation. This allows for yeast autolysis, where the wine takes on more complex flavours (which can be described as yeasty, or bready) from the dead yeast remaining from the second fermentation.

A blind monk, Dom Pérignon, the renowned cellarmaster of the Abbey of Hautvillers outside Epernay, was the first to appreciate the art and skill of blending wines from different vineyards. Aided by the development of cork as a bottle-stopper and the new possibility of producing glass bottles strong enough to withstand pressure, he worked out how to retain the bubbles of carbon dioxide. Then Madame Veuve Clicquot, one of the great ladies of champagne, invented the technique of *remuage*, or riddling, in order to remove from the bottle the sediment resulting from the second fermentation. This has subsequently been refined by the use of modern machinery, automatic giropalettes, which consist of a metal frame in which the bottles are placed neck downwards and rotated daily, manually or mechanically, or even by computer programme. Meanwhile, Moët & Chandon are working on more sophisticated techniques, which will completely remove the need for *remuage*.

The grape varieties used in champagne production are Chardonnay, Pinot Noir and Pinot Meunier. Chardonnay generally provides delicacy and elegance, while Pinot Noir contributes body and backbone. Pinot Meunier lacks the finesse of the other two, but contributes some flavour; it has the disadvantage of ageing faster than either Chardonnay or Pinot Noir, but this, on the other hand, could benefit someone aiming to make a young champagne taste more mature. Pinot Meunier has not travelled much outside the Champagne area, while Pinot Noir and Chardonnay are grown extensively for sparkling wine, especially in the New World.

What singles out champagne from other sparkling wines is the soil, a type of chalk called *Belimnita quadrata* that is found extensively in the land around Reims and Epernay. Climate also plays a part, for the vineyards of Champagne – with the exception of those of the little known Côtes de Toul – are the most northerly in France and are subject to all the climatic vagaries which that entails. This results in wines with lean steely acidity. If you have ever tasted the *vin clair*, or base wine, of champagne, it is obvious why bubbles are essential to render it palatable. The same might also be said of the occasional bottle of still Coteaux Champenois produced in the region.

The **champagne method** is used all over the world for making any sparkling wine with pretensions to quality. It is used elsewhere in France, in such appellations as Blanquette de Limoux and Crémant d'Alsace; for cava in Spain; in Italy; in the New World; and even in England. The Champenois are very anxious to protect their name from pale imitations, with the result that the use of the words 'méthode champenoise', or similar, has been banned from September 1993. Alternative terms such as 'méthode traditionnelle', or 'metodo classico', or 'second fermentation in *this* bottle' are now being used instead.

For cheaper sparkling wine, the most common method of production is variously called '**cuve close**', 'the Charmat method', after the man who invented it, or 'the tank method'. The essential difference from the champagne method is that the second fermentation takes place not in a bottle, but in a tank. The wine is then filtered and bottled under pressure. The resulting mousse is infinitely less subtle, with larger bubbles and less staying power; with a far greater volume of wine in contact with the lees, there is less effect of yeast autolysis. In addition, the wine generally has contact with the lees for a much shorter period of time, a matter of weeks rather than months, or even years. However, for cheerful bubbles, this is a perfectly acceptable way of making sparkling wine.

Somewhere between the champagne and Charmat methods comes what is called the **transfer method**, or *transvasage*, where the second fermentation takes place in a bottle, but the wine is then emptied into a tank under pressure before filtration and subsequent rebottling. This avoids the labour-intensive processes of *remuage* and *dégorgement* (ejection of sediment).

Another variation in method is to stop the first fermentation and then allow it to take off again, but this time retain the bubbles of carbon dioxide, as in the case of Asti Spumante, where a quantity of unfermented grape sugar enhances the lusciously sweet flavour of the wine.

Finally, the cheapest method of all for making sparkling wine is to inject bubbles of carbon dioxide into the finished wine. This could be termed the bicycle pump method, for the technique is somewhat similar to pumping up a bicycle tyre. The bubbles have no staying power at all and are large and coarse. Needless to say, this is used only for cheap wines which are not usually fully sparkling.

CHAMPAGNE

Champagne is the world's greatest sparkling wine. However hard its competitors may try to emulate it, there is a certain indefinable quality about champagne that ensures that they never quite succeed. They may come very close; they may even make better wines than some champagne. Yet when champagne is great, it is very great indeed. This is not to say that there are no poor champagnes; unfortunately there are. And there are times when an alternative to champagne is the preferable choice – when the occasion does not justify the price or when quantity rather than quality may be a consideration – but when the best is what is needed, champagne is the only choice.

After slow champagne sales in 1991, in some measure a result of the unhappy inflationary economic climate, but also in response to the excessive price increases demanded by the Champenois and the growing range of alternatives to champagne, sales have picked up again, so that the market is more buoyant.

Dosage is an essential part of the process of champagne production. When the *liqueur d'expédition* is added after *dégorgement*, the champagne can be sweetened according to taste. Most non-vintage champagne is **brut** which contains no more than

15 grammes of sugar per litre, and allows for a certain flexibility to show a house style; an **extra sec** contains between 12 and 20 grammes of sugar per litre; and the very rare **doux** more than 50 grammes per litre. There has been a certain vogue for ultra-dry champagnes without any dosage. These can be so steely and austere that it is immediately apparent why champagne benefits from a gentle dosage. For some austerely dry bubbles, look for names like Brut Zéro, Brut Sauvage and Ultra Brut. The best come from Besserat de Bellefon, Laurent Perrier and Piper Heidsieck.

Non-vintage

The most basic category of champagne is the standard **non-vintage brut** wine, which demands a minimum of 12 months' ageing on the lees of the second fermentation. This is the wine which illustrates the particular house style of the producer, and upon which reputations are based. There should be no difference in taste from one year to the next, with the maintenance of a consistency of style. The large champagne houses, or *grandes marques*, hold reserves of wine of previous years which enable them to blend the still wines, the *vins clairs*, taking annual differences into account, balancing wines with low acidity with some of an earlier year with higher acidity, or fuller wines with leaner wines. A non-vintage champagne will certainly contain a dozen or so different wines and perhaps as many as 50, from different villages and vineyards scattered over the appellation, mainly from the Montagne de Reims, the Côte des Blancs and the valley of the Marne, and perhaps the outlying vineyards of the Aube. A permutation of grape varieties is possible too, with greater or smaller percentages of white or red grapes.

The great advantage of the large champagne houses is the wide choice that they have in the provenance of their wines. Although most own some vineyards, these supply only a small proportion of their needs and so they buy grapes from growers. Until 1990 the price of a kilo of grapes was set each year, according to the quality and size of the vintage. Now a free market prevails, with individual agreements between growers and merchants, which may prove better for the region in the long term.

Some smaller growers have been encouraged to make their own champagne, rather than sell their grapes to a large house. This gives rise to a much wider choice of relatively unknown and potentially good-value names. Some are very good, but have one big disadvantage – a small grower relies upon the grapes from his own vineyards and therefore does not have the resources or reserves to maintain the same consistency of style. He is much more at the mercy of the climatic vagaries of the region. Good small growers include Vilmart and Alain Cossins.

The choice of a non-vintage champagne, therefore, depends upon preferred style; some are lighter and creamier, with a higher percentage of Chardonnay; others include more Pinot Noir and are heavier with more body and weight. Bollinger, Roederer and Veuve Clicquot tend towards the richer style, while Charles Heidsieck, Laurent Perrier, Pol Roger, Pommery and Deutz all favour the lighter style.

Choice also depends upon the price that you are prepared to pay, and there has been some very cheap champagne on offer. A non-vintage *grande marque* champagne from one of the prestigious names of the area can cost around twice as much as an unknown name, perhaps a small grower or a BOB – Buyer's Own Brand champagne. A wine merchant or supermarket goes to one of the large houses or co-operatives in Champagne and chooses the wine it would like for its own label. Sometimes it is difficult to tell what is what, but a judicious look at the small print on the label can help, for each producer must be registered, with a number and a category: NM, CM, RM or MA. NM is a *négociant manipulant*, a merchant who makes and sells champagne under his own name; CM is a co-operative; RM is a *récoltant manipulant*, a grower who produces and sells his own champagne; while MA is a *marque auxiliaire*, in other words, a secondary brand name.

Numerous factors determine the final cost of a bottle of champagne. The vineyards and villages are graded in what is called the *échelle des crus*, including grand cru at 100 per cent and premier cru from 90 to 99 per cent. Ratings are according to the quality of the grapes produced, so the wine of a producer who uses only grands crus and premiers crus will be significantly more expensive than a wine from vineyards with a lower rating, as their grapes will have cost more in the first place; you do occasionally see the terms grand cru and premier cru on a bottle. There are other differences in price: a wine that has spent longer on the lees of the second fermentation is likely to be more expensive and taste better than one which has had the barest minimum of 12 months. Houses that maintain large stocks of reserve wines have to finance them; manual *remuage* is more costly in manpower than mechanical *remuage*. Basically, you tend to get what you pay for. Although a cheap champagne may prove to be a delicious bargain, it could well turn out to be a decidedly disappointing experience, and you could have had infinitely more drinking pleasure from a comparably priced bottle of bubbles from elsewhere in the world.

Bottle age also affects the taste of a champagne quite

214

significantly. All champagne improves with some bottle age, be it only six months or so, so that the flavours mellow and develop. While champagne needs a fairly neutral base wine with firm acidity, its true flavour comes from the second fermentation, with the effects of yeast autolysis creating a delicately nutty, creamy, yeasty – some call it bready – flavour. However, when a young champagne is first disgorged, it can still taste quite lean and acidic. A few months of bottle age can change the taste quite dramatically, allowing the flavour to fill out and the acidity to tone down. Some champagne houses give their wines some bottle age before they leave the cellars; others do not.

Vintage

Vintage champagne, the wine of a particular year and that year alone, requires a minimum of three years on the lees before disgorgement. While at one time vintage champagne was made only in exceptional years, it now seems to be produced in most years. The decision depends upon individual houses but 1984 is the one rare exception of the last decade and, in the 1970s, only 1972 was missed completely. A vintage champagne accentuates the characteristics of the year. The current vintage that is generally available is 1985, which is a fine vintage that yielded wines with good fruit and balance; 1986 will follow shortly, but at the time of writing was not generally available for tasting; 1982 and 1983, both big vintages, producing some good wines, can still be found. Of the last two, acidity levels were slightly higher in 1983, which might make the wines longer lived, while the 1982 may have a greater concentration of flavour. Inevitably, they will always be compared to one another, while 1979 stands alone and is drinking beautifully. Again, vintage champagne often benefits from some bottle maturation, depending on the character of the vintage.

Blanc de Blancs and Blanc de Noirs

Champagne is the one wine where the over-used term **Blanc de Blancs** has any real meaning. When it appears on a white table wine it is nonsensical, for a white table wine is always made from white grapes, unless it happens to be a blush wine, coming from red grapes. However, as it is possible to make champagne from both red and white grapes, the term Blanc de Blancs does indeed describe a wine that comes from Chardonnay alone. The taste is usually delicate and creamy, light and flavoursome and, with age, a good Blanc de Blancs develops some of the rich, nutty aromas of mature Chardonnay. Good examples include Ruinart, Taittinger, Pol Roger, Salon, Jacquart, Joseph Perrier and Mumm de Cramant, which was formerly Crémant de Cramant, but has been renamed in response to the change of regulations, limiting the use of the term Crémant to the other sparkling wine appellations of France.

In contrast, **Blanc de Noirs**, which is quite rare, is made from Pinot Noir and Pinot Meunier, without a drop of Chardonnay. This makes a wine with backbone and body and with more substance and weight than a Blanc de Blancs or even a straight non-vintage champagne. Good examples include Bollinger and Bruno Paillard.

Cuvée de prestige

The most expensive of all champagnes are the so-called **cuvées de prestige** or de-luxe champagnes. These are the absolute flagships of the champagne houses, to which are attached glamour and prestige. Generally, these wines come from the very best vineyards and from the very best vintages; they are always vintage wines. They are made in small quantities and are appropriately expensive, usually double the price of a vintage champagne.

Amongst the leading cuvées de prestige feature Dom Pérignon and Roederer Cristal (in its unusual clear bottle, intended to imitate the crystal bottle that was produced for the Tsarist court). Bollinger makes what it calls Bollinger RD, a mature wine that has been recently disgorged – the current vintage is 1982. Its Vieilles Vignes, from two tiny vineyards of pre-phylloxera vines in the villages of Ay and Bouzy, might also be considered a de-luxe cuvée; Dom Ruinart Blanc de Blancs is wonderfully rich and full; Perrier Jouët's Belle Epoque comes in the bottle of the period; and look out too for La Grande Dame, as well as Salon le Mesnil; the latter is only made in good vintages – 1982 is currently on sale.

In general

The flavours of champagne cover a wide spectrum of the taste wheel, with variations according to house style, amount of dosage, blend of grape varieties and the age of the wine. However, a broad generalisation can be made between wines that are delicate and creamy, and those that are fuller-bodied and richer with nuttier and more yeasty, bready flavours. Bottle age, as well as house style, certainly plays a part in this.

Young champagne should have a lightly creamy, delicately bready nose, but nothing too pronounced and rich. Try Pol Roger, Perrier Jouët, Deutz, Billecart-Salmon, Henri Abelé and Canard Duchêne.

More mature wines have developed richer, fuller flavours. A mature Dom Ruinart is a fine example, for, as a Blanc de Blancs, it has the ripe nutty flavour of mature Chardonnay, with considerable depth of flavour. A few suggestions for good, rich, full-flavoured wines include Bollinger, Krug, Salon, Roederer, Joseph Perrier and Alfred Gratien.

COMPETITORS TO THE REAL THING

Sparkling wine producers all over the world aspire to emulate champagne, and there are several sparklers which are more than acceptable alternatives, with flavours near enough to be confused with the real thing. The key grape varieties, Pinot Noir and Chardonnay, have travelled the world with some success. When they are grown in a cool climate, they produce base wines without too much positive flavour and with fairly high acidity – essential to the production of good sparkling wine. The techniques of the champagne method have been perfected, with Champenois acting as consultants in various parts of the world.

Moët & Chandon were the first to spread their wings outside Champagne. Their activities include the production of sparkling wine in many parts of the world, as diverse as South America, Austria, Australia, Germany and California. Domaine Chandon in **California** is the wine that has made the most impact; it is destined for the domestic market, and is not intended to be an imitation of champagne. However, the grape varieties and method are identical and, but for a fullness of flavour that is absent in champagne, it could be seen as a competitor. The same may be said for some of the other sparkling wines produced by subsidiaries of champagne houses in the Golden State, such as Mumm's Cuvée Napa, Roederer Estate, Maison Deutz and Piper Sonoma. Most of these have vineyards in Carneros, at the coolest end of the Sonoma and Napa valleys.

However, California has a distinct disadvantage over northern France in that the climate is usually much too warm to make the base wines with the almost searing acidity necessary for champagne. The one country in the New World that comes closest is **New Zealand**. A joint effort between Montana, one of the two giants of the New Zealand wine industry, who provided money, equipment and grapes, and Champagne Deutz, who contributed expertise, has produced Cuvée Deutz from Marlborough, on the cooler South Island. The result is a stylish, elegant, creamy sparkling wine, with finesse and flavour, at approximately half the price of a *grande marque* champagne. Production for the moment is small, while larger quantities are made of a lesser cuvée, Lindauer, which has sound, flavoursome bubbles, but is without the elegance of the Cuvée Deutz.

Another name to look out for from New Zealand is Daniel le Brun, who originally came from Champagne. Now he is applying his expertise in Marlborough, with Pinot Noir, Chardonnay and, unusually for the New World, Pinot Meunier. The range includes a non-vintage Brut, as well as a 1989 Blanc de Noirs.

The closest contender to champagne to come out of **Australia** is generally considered to be Croser, named after its creator, the talented Brian Croser, who benefits from an input from Bollinger at his Petaluma winery. The grape varieties used are Chardonnay and Pinot Noir and the flavour is definitely elegant, lightly yeasty, fresh and very stylish. However, Croser may well have a contender for its prime position with the launch of Green Point from Domaine Chandon. The first release comprises a 59 per cent Chardonnay and 41 per cent Pinot Noir blend from the cool Yarra Valley and it certainly has that imperceptible, indefinable something that makes champagne the wine that it is, with a light nutty flavour and a hint of attractive yeastiness.

Seppelt Sallinger benefits from a high altitude and cool climate provenance, with some elegant, dry nutty fruit. Yalumba D also has a touch of class, with some lemony acidity and just a hint of yeasty fruit.

The most obvious champagne look-alike from France is **Crémant de Bourgogne**. After all, the vineyards are closest to Champagne, so the climate is similar; the grape varieties, mainly Pinot Noir and Chardonnay, are original to the area and the method did not have far to travel. Good Crémants de Bourgogne compare favourably with cheaper champagnes.

LIGHT AND CREAMY

Light and creamy describes a category of sparkling wine that comes close to emulating champagne, but which lacks the richness of some champagnes. These are wines with a delicacy of flavour, a certain yeasty creaminess that usually, but not always, originates from the Chardonnay grape. The champagne method is an essential part of the quality, as is some firm acidity to give the wine bite and backbone.

Crémant de Bourgogne is the most obvious example in this category, although it also fits into the competitors-to-the-real-thing segment. Chardonnay is often the dominant grape variety, blended sometimes with Pinot Noir, to make some creamy, fruity, sparkling wines. Sparkling burgundy is produced all over the region, from near Chablis right down to the Mâconnais. One producer, the Cave de Bailly, dominates production in the Yonne with both white and pink wines, sold under the brand name of Meurgis. Nuits-St-Georges is the historic centre for sparkling wine in the Côte d'Or, as is Rully in the Côte Chalonnaise. In addition, some of the co-operatives of the Mâconnais, such as Viré and Lugny, produce some good-value sparklers, with some creamy fruit and yeasty, bready overtones.

The Jura may not be an obvious source of sparkling wine, although the appellation **Côtes du Jura** does include mousseux made by the champagne method. Chardonnay is the usual grape variety and there are some good producers, such as Hubert Clavelin. Although Henri Maire is the largest and best-known producer of the Jura, his mass-produced Vin Fou is not at all the same thing, but a branded wine of indefinite origins. Other curiosities from France are the sparkling wines of **Gaillac**, based on Mauzac and usually made according to the champagne method by the occasional producer, such Robert Plageoles.

Crémant d'Alsace is a relatively recent appellation, created in 1976, although the history of sparkling wine in Alsace is much older. The main grape variety here is Pinot Blanc, while others such as Riesling, Pinot Noir and Tokay Pinot Gris can also be used. Riesling can make some elegant, stylish wines, with a slatey finish, while Pinot Blanc produces some soft creamy wines, with good fruit. Dopff 'au Moulin' is the leader in the market with Cuvée Julien, and other producers of note include Dopff & Irion and the village co-operatives of Turckheim and Eguisheim. For the moment, Crémant d'Alsace enjoys more success in France than it does in Britain.

A much newer appellation is **Crémant de Bordeaux**, made from the white grapes of the Gironde. That of Patrick Boudon at Domaine du Bourdieu is a blend of Sémillon and Ugni Blanc, with some attractive creamy fruit.

NEUTRAL

Neutrality in sparkling wine fulfils a purpose if you are looking for a drink that is innocuously festive, with clean, fresh bubbles. It is cheap and cheerful but has no real flavour, which makes it an ideal foil for orange juice or cassis liqueur – or indeed other flavours like blackberry or peach. There are numerous sparkling wines without any specific regional definition; their virtue is a clean but anonymous flavour. Sometimes the grapes are grown in one place and the base wine turned into sparkling wine elsewhere: for example, Henkel in Germany buys a lot of wine from Corovin, a large co-operative in Emilia Romagna. Sparkling wine of this nature is considered to be a manufactured industrial product rather than the result of a combination of grape varieties, soil, climate and technical expertise.

The second fermentation takes place in a tank, which is ideal for mass-production. The base wine should be clean and fresh with some acidity, but with as little intrinsic flavour as possible. High-yielding, low-acidity grapes like Ugni Blanc often provide the backbone. These wines have no regional denomination or appellation; the clue to the place of production may lie in the postal code, but generally there is nothing more precise than the country of origin on the label. Veuve du Vernay, produced in Bordeaux and Kriter from Burgundy are the two most obvious examples on the British market. Cavalier from Wissembourg, north of Strasbourg, is better than average; it is a cheap and refreshing wine, which is all it sets out to be. Flutelle, a mousseux from south-west France, has a hint more flavour and body, as does Blanc de Chardonnay made from grapes grown in Corsica and turned into sparkling wine in Salon de Provence by Auran.

Some **Sekt** may also come into this neutral category, especially where the wine is bought from another country, such as Henkel Trocken. Essentially, this segment of the taste wheel is filled by various branded sparkling wines, sold under fantasy names.

DUSTY, LEMON AND HONEY FLAVOURS

Low acidity

Various wines fit into this segment because they lack a certain acidity.

Blanquette de Limoux   Blanquette de Limoux claims a history even older than that of champagne. The wine was first made by the monks of the Benedictine monastery of St-Hilaire, near the city of Carcassonne, perhaps as early as the sixteenth century. Blanquette is the local name for a somewhat dull grape variety called Mauzac, which can be enlivened with some Chenin Blanc and Chardonnay. A new appellation, **Crémant de Limoux**, created in 1990, denotes an even higher percentage of these two additional grape varieties, namely a maximum of 40 per cent rather than the 30 per cent maximum in Blanquette de Limoux. But here lies the problem with the sparkling wines of Limoux – Mauzac can lack charm; it makes rather flat, dry, even slightly bitter, white wine. While it is true that the base wine for a sparkling wine must not be too characterful, it does help if there is some elegance and fruit. Coming as it does from the south of France, Blanquette de Limoux can also be quite low in acidity. It can have a soft southern dustiness about it, while the addition of Chenin Blanc and Chardonnay provides a definite touch of creaminess and fruit.

The co-operative of Limoux is the main producer, using high-tech equipment for efficient production by the champagne method (although it does not say so on the label, the appellation automatically implies the use of the champagne method). The wines are available under various brand names, such as Aimery and Sieur d'Arques. In addition, there are a handful of individual estates, such as Domaine des Martinolles and Domaine de Froin.

Cava Most Spanish cava fits into this segment of the taste wheel, for it too can lack a certain acidity, and the grape varieties used in its production are not the most exciting. The base is provided by Parellada, Macabeo and Xarel-lo, while one or two more of the innovative estates are growing Chardonnay in the search for additional flavour and elegance. The DO of cava automatically implies that the champagne method is used. Geographically, it covers a large part of northern Spain, mostly Catalonia, with the centre of the cava industry in the town of San Sadurní da Noya, as well as in villages in areas as far apart as Rioja, Cariñena, Costers del Segre and Tarragona.

The principal grape varieties are rather flat and bland. More significantly, they can lack acidity and, consequently, tend not to age well – sometimes even the minimum nine months on the lees can seem too long. This can produce a somewhat earthy or dusty flavour, with a hint of pepperiness. More exciting are the occasional cavas made from Chardonnay, notably from Raimat and Codorníu, which have quite ripe, full, buttery flavours and fit into the fuller-flavoured segment of the taste wheel. The charm of the better cavas can be their soft, slightly flowery, lightly honeyed flavours. They are also significantly cheaper than any champagne, not to mention some of the French or Italian alternatives.

Amongst more traditional cava producers, Codorníu is the biggest, with some sound, reliable wines; Freixenet's Cordon Negro is an innocuously pleasant drink, undemanding with refreshing bubbles. In addition, Cavas Hill, Ferret i Mateu, Juvé y Camps and Marqués de Monistrol are all worth trying. Sometimes a vintage wine or better cuvée offers more interest, such as the recently introduced Cuvée DS from Freixenet, which has more complexity after four years on the lees, with some creamy fruit and a yeasty finish.

Russia   Sparkling wine has a long tradition in the former Soviet Union; Tsarist Russia was a big consumer of champagne in the nineteenth century. The republics bordering the Black Sea, namely Russia itself, the Ukraine and Moldova, all produce wine. André Roederer, of the champagne family, even built a winery in Odessa in 1896. Today, Russian sparkling wine is made, not by the champagne method, but on a much more economical variation of the cuve-close method involving a series of tanks that turn the base wine into a sparkling wine within a month. Two Russian sparkling wines are available here: Grand Duchess Brut, made mainly from Aligoté, and rather lemony and yeasty, and the better Grand Duke Vladimir making an unusual choice.

High acidity

Crémant de Loire, Saumur, Vouvray and other wines from the Loire Valley   The Loire Valley has the ideal conditions for the production of sparkling wine, so much so that Saumur has been an important centre for wine production since the beginning of the last century. The tufa rocks provide ideal cellar conditions, like the chalk cellars of Champagne. But the principal difference between champagne and the sparkling wines of the Loire lies with the grape variety – in the Loire Valley Chenin Blanc predominates rather than Pinot Noir and Chardonnay. Chenin produces a base wine with the firm acidity essential for good sparkling wine but, unfortunately, when Chenin is not fully ripe, it displays the somewhat unattractive overtones of wet dogs or wet wool. This is more noticeable in still wine, but can also feature in the sparkling wine. Good sparkling Loire wine, be it Crémant de Loire, Saumur or Anjou, should have some delicate honey and yeasty flavours with firm acidity.

The appellations of the Loire can all be grouped together within this same taste segment. They include **Crémant de Loire**, which covers the whole valley and which has stricter production regulations than either Saumur or Anjou; **Saumur**, from the vineyards around the town of the same name, where most of the large producers are based; and **Anjou**, which is really only distinguished from Saumur by geography. In addition, sparkling **Vouvray** is made in years when the Chenin Blanc grapes have not ripened fully, when to produce sweet Vouvray would be an impossibility. **Montlouis**, across the river, is similar, but not so well known.

Good Loire fizz producers include some of the big names like Gratien & Meyer (who own the champagne house of Alfred Gratien), Bouvet-Ladubay and Langlois-Château (who both belong to champagne houses), as well as Marc Brédif and Gaston Huet in Vouvray and the Château de Chenonceau.

Savoie On the other side of France, the town of Seyssel, which straddles the Rhône, is a centre for sparkling wine, notably with the company of Varichon et Clerc. Its Seyssel Mousseux is a blend of two peculiarly Savoyard grape varieties, Molette and Roussette, with firm acidity and some light dusty, lemony fruit.

In the Rhône Valley, the small appellation of **St Péray** includes sparkling, as well as still, wine from a blend of Rousanne and Marsanne. However, it is rarely seen outside the region.

England The occasional sparkling wines of England fit into this segment by virtue of their high acidity. David Carr Taylor, of Carr Taylor vineyards outside Hastings, is a pioneer who uses the champagne method. Others have followed his example; one of the most successful is Rock Lodge in Sussex with Impresario.

German Sekt To be blunt, Sekt rarely excites. Until quite recently the base wine for what was labelled 'Deutscher Sekt' did not even have to come from Germany, but was more often than not a dull white wine imported from central Italy, to be turned into Sekt in Germany. It was the production process, not the grapes, that was German. Now plain Sekt indicates this dual country origin, while **Deutscher Sekt** is purely Germanic. The best examples are made from Riesling, but are generally made by the transfer method, with the second fermentation taking place in a bottle, but not in *the* bottle in which the wine is subsequently sold. If more specific details of origin are given, this indicates a more serious wine, such as Deinhard Lila Imperial Riesling. Although the most common Sekt, Henkel, comes into the neutral segment of the wheel, with grapes grown in such a northerly clime, there will always be a firm acidity in German Sekt. There may be a hint of honey too, especially if the base is ripe Riesling, but more often than not there is a none-too-inspiring dusty quality about the wine.

FULLER FLAVOURED

One of the keys to the elegance of champagne is the acidity in the base wine. Wines coming from warmer regions are automatically handicapped without the natural advantage of the Champagne region. Their producers may use the same grape varieties as champagne; they may believe the soil to be similar to that of Champagne and the production method identical – perhaps even performed by Champenois who have learnt their skills in Reims and Epernay – but the flavour will not be the same, for the one thing that is different is the climate. Longer hours of sunshine make riper grapes, with lower acidity and richer flavours, all of which translate into a wine with fuller, riper flavours. These producers may try to compensate by picking the grapes before they are fully ripe or by seeking out particularly cool vineyard sites, often at higher altitudes, with sharp contrasts between day and night-time temperatures. Some are successful, others not. Perhaps the dividing line between this segment and competitors to the real thing is somewhat blurred, for the origins of both may be the same.

There is no doubt that acidity is a key flavour factor. The fuller-flavoured wines tend to be lower in acidity and lack the intrinsic elegance that should be present in good champagne. But this does not mean that they are not worthwhile drinks in their own right, and they sometimes have a significant price advantage.

Italy

Asti Spumante and Lambrusco may be Italy's best-known sparkling wines, but there are numerous examples of dry sparkling wines, especially in the north-eastern part of the country. Sometimes the grape varieties are indigenous, like Prosecco; sometimes they are more recent introductions, like Chardonnay or Pinot Noir. The method is usually, but not always, that of Champagne, which the Italians call metodo classico. Sometimes these wines come from a region where there is a long tradition of sparkling wine; sometimes they are the result of an attempt to diversify within a DOC, alongside a still wine, such as Verdicchio; and sometimes they provide yet another challenge or source of experimentation to satisfy the curiosity of an eager winemaker.

The main DOCs for sparkling wine, apart from Lambrusco and Asti Spumante, are **Oltrepò Pavese**, **Trentino**, **Prosecco di Conegliano di Valdobbiadene**, which tends to be lightly sparkling or frizzante, as opposed to fully spumante, and **Franciacorta Spumante** (as opposed to the still wines), but more often than not it is simply the producer's name on the label that provides the clue to choice and quality, for much spumante is made without any reference to regional DOC regulations. Names to watch for include Berlucchi, Ca'del Bosco and Bellavista from Franciacorta, Carpené Malvolti from Conegliano and Ferrari and Equipe 5 from Trentino.

Cava

Although **cava** comes into another taste segment, there is one exception, namely the occasional cava made from Chardonnay rather than the indigenous grape varieties of Penedès. Wines like Raimat's and Codorníu's Chardonnay have a rich, full-flavoured taste. They are ripe and buttery and can be blowsy and overblown, but what they may lack in elegance, they make up for in flavour, compared with the average, traditional cava.

Australia

There is no doubt that **Australia** is one of the best sources of good-value quaffable bubbles. Take a wine like Yalumba's Angas Brut or Penfold's Killawarra Brut: they may not be subtle and refined, but they are fresh and well made. Angas Brut, based on Semillon and made by the transfer method, is a reliable and inexpensive glass of bubbles; it is full of flavour, slightly biscuity, low in acidity and eminently drinkable.

Other Australian bubbles have more pretensions to finesse. Some succeed, while others remain in the full-flavoured category, lacking that indefinable touch of elegance that puts them above the others. Wines that remain firmly in this segment of the wheel include Seppelt's Imperial Brut, Orlando's Carrington with its ripe easy-to-drink fruit, Seaview Brut and Rosemount Brut, all with fresh, well-made bubbles, some weight and flavour.

California

Just about every **California** sparkling wine that crosses the Atlantic aspires to emulate champagne, usually not only in flavour but also in price. Some succeed better than others. However, in general, they all tend to have a richness and lack of acidity that separates them from champagne; there is a full-flavoured biscuity character that detracts from their elegance, but they may on occasion be infinitely more appealing than a lean, acidic champagne.

Schramsberg Winery set the pace in California. Older established houses like Hans Kornell and Korbel had made little impact outside the domestic market until, in 1965, Jack and Jamie Davies bought the historic Napa Valley winery which has links with Robert Louis Stevenson. They planted Chardonnay and Pinot Noir and established a reputation for excellent champagne-method sparkling wine, capped by their new prestige cuvée, J. Schram.

About the same time, Domaine Chandon was set up in the Napa Valley, representing the first investment in California by a champagne house. In the past 15 years numerous others have followed their example, namely Roederer, Mumm, Deutz, Piper Heidsieck, Taittinger, as well as a couple of cava producers, Codorníu and Freixenet.

Iron Horse has also come on the scene as another true California sparkling wine, as well as Schaffenberg, which has a link with Lanson. There is no doubting the expertise, with so many wines master-minded by champagne houses, but many of them lack that indefinable something that separates them from champagne. They are richer and fuller, with less acidity, riper more biscuity flavours – they may even verge on the clumsy. The better ones, however, do offer an alternative to the real thing.

South Africa

Like Australia and California, South African sparkling wine appears in various segments of the wheel. The better wines, such as Charles de la Fère from the Villiera Wine Estate, have some fresh, lightly yeasty fruit, while others are not as distinguished, and suffer from the disadvantage of a warm climate.

India

India is a highly unlikely source of sparkling wine, or any wine, for that matter. However, high in the hills of the Maharashtra region near Bombay, vineyards of Chardonnay, Pinot Blanc and Ugni Blanc have been planted, and sparkling wine is produced under the guidance of a former winemaker of Piper Heidsieck. The resulting wine, Omar Khayyam, is remarkably good under the circumstances, with some ripe fruit and fat yeasty flavours. The quality can be a little inconsistent, but it makes up for that in curiosity value.

Once in the bottle a cork can last for decades but eventually it becomes brittle and crumbly with age.

SWEET WINE

Asti Spumante

Good **Asti Spumante** is wonderfully luscious and fresh. It is made from Muscat grapes and should really taste of the grape. As with all good Muscat wines, it is the flavour of the grape itself that gives the wine its intrinsic appeal. With no aspirations whatsoever to imitate champagne, unlike most other Italian sparklers, Asti (from vineyards around the eponymous town, near Turin, in Piedmont) is the most individual of all Italian spumante. It is unashamedly sweet, but it should never be cloying and must always be drunk as young and fresh as possible – within a year or two at the most. It has the advantage of being low in alcohol, for no sugar or yeast are added to induce the second fermentation. Instead, the first fermentation is stopped, leaving some sugar in the wine, and the carbon dioxide from the first fermentation is retained in the tank, as a variation on the cuve-close method.

Good producers include the Viticoltori dell'Acquese who makes some perfectly delicious Asti. Fontanafredda is good too, while some of the big vermouth houses (Turin is the vermouth capital of Italy) also make respectable Asti, namely Gancia, Martini & Rossi and Cinzano. Freshness and youth are the keys to enjoyment, along with the right balance of grapiness and sweetness.

Moscato d'Asti is similar, but not quite as fizzy. Sparkling **Moscadello di Montalcino**, from producers like Banfi and Col d'Orcia, also has the same appealing grapiness.

Lambrusco

White **Lambrusco** fits into the sweet, low acidity, cuve-close segment of the wheel. However, its charm is pale compared to Asti. The wine lacks the real luscious depth of flavour of Asti, for it is made from red Lambrusco grapes and vinified off the skins so that no colour is retained in the wine. Fermentation takes place in a tank, and the sweetness comes from the judicious addition of grape concentrate. The result is pretty bland, quite sweet and fairly neutral, with low acidity. It is easy to drink if well chilled, and then instantly forgettable.

The other sweet Italian sparkler comes from **Soave**. Although Soave is known principally as a dry white wine, a traditional technique of drying the grapes makes sweet **Recioto di Soave**, which may be either still or sparkling. Usually it is still, but the occasional sparkling version is quite full and flavoursome, with some richness.

Clairette de Die Tradition

This wine comes from a tiny appellation situated on a tributary of the Rhône. Muscat is the principal grape variety, sometimes blended with a small amount of Clairette, producing a fresh, lightly grapey sweet wine, with a fresh juicy vitality. The method is similar to Asti in that no extra sugar is added for the second fermentation, which takes place in the bottle. The regulations are in the process of changing, so that Clairette de Die will always include Muscat, while the new appellation, Crémant de Die, will cover wines made from Clairette alone. Virtually the sole producer is the village co-operative.

Champagne

We are so accustomed to drinking dry **champagne** (usually labelled brut) that we tend to overlook the fact that the need to add the dosage to champagne allows the level of sweetness or otherwise to be significantly altered. The wording on the label, at first glance, has little bearing on the actual taste in the bottle for, while brut may indeed mean very dry, confusingly it is drier than extra dry, and sec is medium-dry and demi-sec positively sweet. Doux is very sweet, indeed intensely so, but is rarely made these days. Most sweet champagne is likely to be labelled demi-sec, and in reality it represents only a tiny percentage of the champagne market and is hardly ever seen, except occasionally in France served with dessert, or in Eastern Europe where people generally have a sweeter tooth.

PINK WINE

Champagne

Pink champagne is underrated, for it is fiendishly difficult to make. Great skill lies in obtaining just the desired depth of colour: not too pale or the wine will seem wishy-washy, and not too dark or it will be heavy and clumsy. There are two ways to make pink champagne; either you leave the juice in contact with the grape skins long enough for it to absorb the required amount of colour; or you can blend a tiny proportion of still red wine into the white base wine. This is one of the very rare instances when it is permitted to blend red and white wine together in order to make pink wine and it is the more common way to make pink champagne because it provides a closer control of the colour. Even so, account must be taken of the effect of the second fermentation on the depth of colour, for some colour is generally lost during the fermentation.

Most of the major houses include a pink champagne in their repertoire, and occasionally even a pink vintage wine, but some take it more seriously than others. Names to look out for are Alfred Gratien, Louis Roederer, Bruno Paillard, Laurent Perrier and Billecart-Salmon. Pink champagne is always more expensive than the non-vintage brut from the same house, for the simple reason that it is more difficult and therefore more expensive to produce.

As for taste, pink champagne should have a delicate flavour of raspberries, with the dry yeasty tang which is characteristic of champagne. The extra dollop of red grapes in the blend provides backbone and body, but it should not be heavy or coarse. Instead, it should be subtle and flavoursome, though sometimes with a little more weight than a normal champagne.

Champagne method

The **Loire Valley** is the major source of pink sparkling wine in France. All the main producers, such as Gratien & Meyer, Bouvet-Ladubay and Langlois-Château include it in their ranges. The grape varieties may include Pinot Noir (but not Pinot Meunier) and, more likely, Cabernet Franc and Gamay, and perhaps Cabernet Sauvignon and Groslot. Rather than blending red and white juice, the colour tends to come from a limited period of skin contact. The two principal appellations are **Saumur** and **Crémant de Loire**, and the wines are generally crisp and fresh, with good acidity and delicate raspberry or strawberry fruit, and are perhaps even firmer and fuller bodied than pink champagne. Prices are distinctly competitive with champagne.

The appellation **Crémant de Bourgogne** also encompasses rosé, originating in this instance from Pinot Noir or Gamay. The main centres of sparkling wine production in Burgundy include Nuits-St-Georges, the tiny hamlet of Bailly, just outside the appellation of Chablis, and Rully in the Côte Chalonnaise. Pink Crémant de Bourgogne is the closest alternative in taste to pink champagne because of some similarity in grape variety, but it never quite has the finesse and elegance of good pink champagne. Good examples come from the Cave de Bailly, sometimes under the brand name Meurgis, and also from André Delorme in Rully. There is also the occasional **Crémant d'Alsace** rosé.

Across the Pyrenees, a small amount of pink **cava** is made by blending Garnacha Tinta and Monastrell with the usual cava grapes, Parellada, Macabeo and Xarel-lo. The flavour is slightly dusty, heavier and less acidic than anything from France.

Northern **Italy** has a flourishing sparkling wine industry, with producers like Berlucchi in Franciacorta making some very acceptable pink spumante. Other names to look out for include Bellavista, Ca' del Bosco, also in Franciacorta, as well as Equipe 5 from Trentino and Monsupello from Oltrepò Pavese. Again the champagne method is used and the resulting wine is quite full and fruity, with less acidity than French counterparts, but usually with a little more elegance than Spanish cava.

There is the odd example of pink bubbles made by the champagne method from the **New World**, such as California's Cuvée de Pinot from Schramsberg, which has some soft raspberry fruit, and Mumm's Cuvée Napa Rosé . However, the most popular Australian pink sparkler is Yalumba's Angas Brut which is made *not* by the champagne method but by the transfer method. The result is a wine that is full-bodied, with soft, ripe raspberry fruit, and which is excellent value for money. It may lack acidity and elegance, but proves immensely quaffable when well chilled. Killawarra Rosé from Penfolds is comparable in flavour and price, as is Orlando Carrington Brut Rosé, while Taltarni Brut Taché is a little drier and crisper. From New Zealand, Montana makes a pink version of its Lindauer sparkling wine which is dry and fresh.

England, too, makes some pink sparkling wine: Tenterden produces a sparkling rosé with some raspberry fruit and fresh acidity.

Cuve close

Traditionally, **Lambrusco** is a sparkling red wine. However, with the extension of its commercial popularity, the colour range has been widened to include pink Lambrusco, made by the cuve close method from the same Lambrusco grapes that are used for the red wine, but with minimal skin contact. Often it is lightly sweet and lacking in acidity. Its chief virtue is that it is innocuous.

RED WINE

Cuve close

Red bubbles are a pretty unusual, not to mention an acquired, taste. The most obvious example is **Lambrusco**, which is considered a bit of a joke, partly because the true traditional Lambrusco has been distorted to include pink or blush, as well as white. In addition, some producers have pandered to commercial taste and have turned Lambrusco into a sweet wine, when traditionally the real thing is garnet-red and firmly dry.

Lambrusco takes its name from the grape of the same name, which is grown in the region of Emilia-Romagna. A variety of different Lambruscos are produced, some that are DOC, and some that are not. It can all be rather confusing – the best Lambrusco is Lambrusco de Sorbara, Sorbara being both a sub-variety of the grape and also the name of the particular area in the centre of the province of Modena where it is grown. It has perfumed cherry fruit, fresh acidity and a firm, bitter finish which goes remarkably well with the rich regional cuisine of Bologna and Modena. Good producers include Cavicchioli, Chiarli and Giacobazzi. Other good examples are Lambrusco Grasparossa di Castelvetro and Lambrusco Salamino di Santa Croce, and you can also find Lambrusco di Modena and Lambrusco Reggiano, or just plain red Lambrusco, which is probably best avoided. Lambrusco is not fully frothy, but gently fizzy, and above all it must be young and fresh.

Champagne method

A tiny amount of sparkling red **burgundy** is still produced from Pinot Noir and Gamay, and it tends to be rather dry and heavy. The same goes for red **Crémant de Loire** and **Saumur**, made from Cabernet Franc, Cabernet Sauvignon, Gamay and Groslot. These are definitely of minority interest, with some cherry fruit and acidity and more body than is usually appealing in a sparkling wine. Gratien & Meyer's Noir de Noirs Cardinal goes particularly well with a bowl of strawberries.

Australia is an unexpected source of red bubbles, but Seppelt has indeed added a sparkling Shiraz to its range which is distinctive and original in flavour, reminiscent of blackcurrant fruit gums and frothy blackcurrant juice – which is perhaps something of an acquired taste (but as a talking point...).

Part III

Where to buy wine

Symbols

 Denotes generally low prices and/or a large range of modestly priced wines.

 A merchant given this symbol offers exceptionally good service. We rely on readers' reports in allocating service symbols; this means that there may be merchants offering first-class service who appear here with no symbol because such distinction has gone unreported. Readers, please report!

 A merchant awarded this symbol makes a special effort to train staff to a high standard in wine knowledge, so advice from behind the counter should be particularly reliable. Other merchants without this symbol may also offer good advice – please report.

 Indicates high-quality wines across the range.

 This award is given for a wide range of wines from around the world.

Best buys

These are the Editor's choice of four out of a group of wines selected by the merchant in question as being distinguished in terms of value for money, or offering very fine quality regardless of price. In most instances, two wines at under £5 and two at over £5 have been selected. A very few merchants were unwilling to nominate any wines as their best buys and so the recommendations here may be restricted.

A & A Wines

Smithbrook Kilns, nr Cranleigh, Surrey   *Tel* (0483) 274666
GU6 8JJ

Case sales only   **Open** Mon–Fri 9.30–5.30; Sat 10–2   **Closed** Sun, public
holidays   **Credit cards** Access, Visa; personal and business accounts
Discounts On 6–19 cases and 20+ cases   **Delivery** Free to Surrey, Sussex,
Hampshire, Middlesex; London (min 5-case order); mail order available
Glass hire Free; breakages charged for   **Tastings and talks** 2 large wine tastings
in June and Oct/Nov; 6 smaller tutored tastings; themed months featuring a
particular country or region   **Cellarage** £2.50 per case per year

With walls six feet thick and no natural daylight, the old brick
kilns at Cranleigh are ideal for wine storage. The kilns are home
to A & A Wines, run by Andrew Connor and Andrew
Bickerton. Regular tastings are held in these fairly unusual
surroundings, often hosted by winemakers.

Most wine areas of the world are represented on the list, but
the main emphasis is on Spain. Ten bodegas, including
Espanolas and AGE, provide a range of red and white Riojas;
Penedès wines are from Torres and the small family-owned
Bodega Alsina & Sarda. A clutch of wines from Gutierrez in
Valladolid provides interesting and good-value drinking. A new
development this year is the addition of some old Riojas from
leading Bodegas, some going back to the 1950s.

Italy and Germany have reasonable selections, although the
pattern does not seem to change much from year to year. A
collection of vintages from Cissac looks interesting in the
Bordeaux section; burgundies are from good producers.
Australian wines come from two big, yet good, producers –
Seppelt and Wyndham – and South Africans now include a
range from the Avontuur Estate as well as the usual KWV
wines.

A & A also arranges annual trips to the vineyards.

Best buys

Ardèche Chardonnay 1992, Louis Latour, £
Moyston Semillon/Chardonnay 1992, Australia, £
Marqués de Riscal Reserva 1988, Rioja, ££
Frank Phélan 1986, second wine of Ch. Phélan-Ségur, ££

Best buys
   £ denotes a bottle costing under £5
   ££ denotes a bottle costing over £5

Abbey Cellars (Chard Fine Wines)

19A High Street, Chard, Somerset TA20 1QF   *Tel* (0460) 62546

Open Mon–Sat 10–8 **Closed** Sun, public holidays **Credit cards** Access, Visa
Discounts Available depending on quantity **Delivery** Free within 20-mile radius
of Chard (min order 1 case); £5 per case outside van area **Glass hire** Free
Tastings and talks Tastings held twice a year; in-store tastings throughout the
year **Cellarage** £5 per case per year

New premises and a new name for this business, which has
moved half an hour's drive away from Yeovil to Chard. The
name over the door is Chard Fine Wines, but if you normally
deal with this company over the phone then it is still known as
Abbey Cellars.

The range has increased to take in the existing stock of the
shop and new lists will keep customers up to date with
additions and special offers. The basic range is well-chosen,
with the emphasis on getting good flavour for your money;
wines rarely stray over £10 and only then with good reason.
Clarets are represented by an impressive selection of petits
châteaux, with St-Emilion being a favourite area. Burgundies
provide enough choice to sample the flavour of the region and
the Rhônes include La Vieille Ferme from the Côtes du Ventoux.
French country wines look worth spending some time on, most
of them costing under £5. Italy includes a couple of wines from
the much-neglected Trentino region and Spain provides a few
fresh faces from Somontano.

The New World range is extensive, with Australia, New
Zealand, South Africa and South America well represented.

Yeovil's loss would seem to be Chard's gain.

Best buys

Señorio de los Llanos Reserva 1988, Valdepeñas, £
Domaine de Pensées Sauvages 1990, Corbières, £
Sauvignon de Touraine 1992, Marrionet, ££
Gewurztraminer 1989, Médaille d'Or, Heyberger, Alsace, ££

Adnams Wine Merchants

The Crown, High Street, Southwold, Suffolk IP18 6DP	*Tel* (0502) 724222
The Cellar & Kitchen Store, Victoria Street, Southwold, Suffolk IP18 6DP	*Tel* (0502) 724222
The Grapevine, Cellar & Kitchen Store, 109 Unthank Road, Norwich, Norfolk NR2 2PE	*Tel* (0603) 613998

Open (The Crown) Mon–Fri 9–5; (Cellar & Kitchen Store) Mon–Sat 10–6 (Southwold), 9–9 (Norwich) **Closed** Sun, public holidays **Credit cards** Access, Visa; personal and business accounts **Discounts** 5% on 12 cases **Delivery** Free on UK mainland (min 2 cases); otherwise £5 (1 case); mail order available **Glass hire** Free **Tastings and talks** To groups on request; 6 public tastings a year (London, Suffolk and Cheshire in May, London, Cheshire and Norwich in autumn) at £7.50 per person (£5 refundable against purchase); up to 40 bottles always available in Southwold store **Cellarage** £5 per case per year

---

Adnams is not only stylish in its wines but in appearance too. In addition to the exuberant ties and waistcoats launched last year, there now comes a blazer, striped in vinous colours. This will become essential wear during the cricket season or at any languid summer gathering where a glass of wine, a straw hat and good conversation are the main features.

Adnams has shops in Southwold and Norwich as well as a pub and a hotel, but most of its customers know the company via the list which thuds on to the doormat every May. It is a user-friendly list packed with information about vintages, winemakers and wines, all written about in the enthusiastic style of Adnams' director and buyer, Simon Loftus. It is the kind of list that whets the appetite and encourages you to try the many new additions to the range. No wine gains its place here just by having the right name on the label. Each wine has been selected by Loftus and his team for character and style. They sell the wines they like to drink themselves, and while this can leave some areas a little bare – such as Eastern Europe – their obvious enthusiasm for good wine, at all price levels, brings dividends.

The French country section has grown again this year. Ozidoc is the Adnams name for wines made in Languedoc by Australian winemakers and last year's excellent Sauvignon Blanc has been joined by Syrah, Merlot and Chardonnay. All have great character and are under £5. Ch. Routas from the Coteaux Varois is another splendid discovery.

Classic French wines are good, particularly burgundy. Italy is introduced with an appraisal of the *passito* (dried grape) style of winemaking and then takes a gentle stroll around the best and the most interesting flavours this country can offer. The Australian section has grown yet again, making it one of the best selections around. Germany looks set to follow.

Half-bottles and magnums are a speciality, as are mixed 'sample' cases from each of the regions. New this year is a partnership with Haughton Fine Wines in Cheshire which will benefit mail-order customers in the north-east.

If your only contact with Adnams is by phone, help and advice are always available, but if you should decide to head off for some bracing east-coast sea air, the tasting room at the Cellar & Kitchen store has a huge collection of wines open and ready for tasting.

Best buys

Ozidoc Sauvignon Blanc 1992, Vin de Pays d'Oc, £
Ozidoc Syrah 1992, Vin de Pays d'Oc, £
Domaine de la Bon Gran 1990, Mâcon-Clessé, Thévenet, ££
Rioja Crianza, Remelluri 1989, ££

David Alexander

69 Queen Street, Maidenhead, Berkshire   *Tel* (0628) 30295
SL6 1LT

Open Mon 10–7; Tue–Thur 10–8.30; Fri–Sat 10–9; Sun 12–2 **Closed** Public holidays **Credit cards** All accepted; personal and business accounts **Discounts** 5% on 1 case **Delivery** Free in Maidenhead and M4 corridor to west London (min 1-case order) **Glass hire** Free with order **Tastings and talks** In-store tastings once every three months; to groups on request **Cellarage** Available (charges on request)

This well-stocked shop in Maidenhead offers something from everywhere, with the focus on quality and individuality. From France, the range of clarets is surprisingly wide – there are good petits châteaux, a few second wines and some older vintages from the 1970s. Burgundies have been strengthened recently with a collection of wines from Simon Bize and Domaine Moillard. The Rhône section has dwindled a little but plans are afoot to build it up again. Elsewhere in France there is plenty of choice, and it is encouraging to see a few unusual wines, such as a Pinot Noir from Jura and half-bottles of Vin Jaune.

Germany provides estate wines from Dr Loosen, Italy has a tasty selection from some well-known names and Spain includes the splendid wines of La Rioja Alta. Australia has changed a lot this year with Tarra Warra, Seppelts, Langi Ghiran and Cape Mentelle now giving great flavours for your money. With more wines from the USA, Canada, Chile and South Africa, it is not surprising that the shelves and racks of this shop are stuffed full. The two partners, David Wright and John Leech, claim to have the hottest delivery service on two cylinders – we presume they mean speed not temperature – and with one case delivered free along the M4 corridor from Reading to west London they are not only hot but diligent, too.

Best buys

Rioja Tinto 1991, Navajas, £
La Parrina Rosso 1990, Italy, £
Riesling Trocken, Dr Loosen 1990, Mosel-Saar-Ruwer, ££
Ch. Beaumont Cru Bourgeois 1989, Haut-Médoc, ££

Ameys Wines

83 Melford Road, Sudbury, Suffolk CO10 6JT   *Tel* (0787) 377144

Open Tue–Sat 10–7 **Closed** Sun, Mon, public holidays **Credit cards** Access, Visa **Discounts** 5% on 1 case **Delivery** Free delivery within 20-mile radius of Sudbury (min order £50+) **Glass hire** Free **Tastings and talks** Free tastings most Saturdays **Cellarage** Not available

High business rates drove Ameys out of Colchester four years ago, but what was Colchester's loss was definitely Sudbury's gain. This retail shop has a wide, well-structured range which could keep the local populace supplied for quite some time. New additions arrive as Peter Amey finds room for them.

Australian wines seem to do well in this part of East Anglia, and the choice of over 80 includes not only the big names of Rosemount, Seppelt and Hardy but also some small producers such as Mountadam and Coldstream Hills. There is even an organic Tasmanian wine from Buchanan. Other New World areas, such as California and Chile, are represented by a small but good selection, including the super Montes wines from Chile. South Africa is strangely absent from this cosmopolitan collection. Italy has seen some recent additions, with Chiantis from Felsina Berardenga and Fattoria di Vetrice and Barco Reale from Villa Capezzana. Spain's contribution includes quality wines from Torres and Berberana. The French section covers all the regions well – a reasonable choice of petit-château wines, with a few classed growths for when the occasion demands. Rhônes include classy Châteauneuf-du-Pape from Font de Michelle and Chante-Cigale, as well as good-value domaine-bottled Côtes-du-Rhônes. Wines from south-west France and Languedoc-Roussillon provide further choice for under £5.

Free tastings are held in the shop most Saturdays, which seems like a pleasant way to avoid doing the family shopping.

Best buys

Miguel Torres Sauvignon Blanc 1992, Chile, £
Barbera d'Asti Ceppi Storici 1990, Italy, £
Taltarni Shiraz 1990, Australia, ££
Alsace Gewurztraminer 1991, Léon Beyer, ££

Les Amis du Vin

(Mail order only)
430 High Road, London NW10 2HA   *Tel* 081-451 1135
Shops
The Winery, 4 Clifton Road, London W9 1SS   *Tel* 071-286 6475
Les Amis du Vin, 51 Chiltern Street, London   *Tel* 071-487 3419
W1M 1HQ

Open (W9) Mon–Fri 10.30–8, Sat 10–6.30; (W1) Mon–Fri 10.30–7; (office) Mon–Fri 9.15-5.15 **Closed** (W1 and office) Sat, Sun, public holidays **Credit cards** All accepted; personal and business accounts **Discounts** 5% per unmixed case **Delivery** Free on UK mainland (min 3 cases); otherwise £3.95 to Greater London, £5.50 elsewhere on UK mainland, £10 to Scottish Highlands and offshore UK deliveries **Glass hire** Usually free with order **Tastings and talks** Regular (usually fortnightly) tastings at Chiltern Street; prestige Les Amis du Vin tastings at London venues 3–4 times a year **Cellarage** Not available

The confusion of last year has been sorted out and Les Amis du Vin is now the main name for this operation, with Wine Growers Association fading into the background. Membership is free, and it works just like many other mail-order companies, with the added attraction of a couple of London shops and fairly regular tastings which give more of a 'club' feel.

The range is wide and good. Many of the wines have come through an associated company – Geoffrey Roberts – which is a major importer and wholesaler to the trade. The emphasis on California is particularly strong, with a terrific range from Acacia, Calera, Edna Valley, Ridge, Sanford and Schramsberg, to mention but a few.

Other new world areas are covered well – Australia includes the wines of Tim Knappstein, Petaluma, Rothbury and the complete range from Yalumba. New Zealand has Delegat's, Cloudy Bay and a rather unusual Cabernet Sauvignon from Stonyridge on Waiheke Island. Chile has joined this list with a selection from Cousiño Macul.

From Europe, Italy and France are the stars. Italy boasts nine vintages of Barolo and six of Barbaresco. Chiantis come from Frescobaldi and Pagliarese, with a clutch of Super Tuscans adding to the variety. A round-up of good-value wines from the south finishes off the Italian section. France provides a wide range of clarets from Cru Bourgeois to Ch. Latour. Burgundy, the Rhône and Loire regions are covered with a satisfying selection from quality names. The south in particular offers good value.

The shops don't always have everything in stock but anything from the list can be ordered. Chiltern Street tends to have more from California, while The Winery has a stock of fine and rare wines which are not on the list. Regular mailshots have special offers at reduced prices.

Major tastings are notified to all members but there are some select gatherings in Chiltern Street for which you have to indicate an interest.

Best buys

Domaine de Capion Cabernet/Merlot 1988, Vin de Pays d'Oc, £
Fetzer Gewurztraminer 1991, Mendocino, California, £
Calera Jensen Vineyard Pinot Noir 1990, California, ££
Patriglione 1977, Rosso di Brindisi, Taurino, Italy, ££

John Armit Wines

5 Royalty Studios, 105 Lancaster Road,   *Tel* 071-727 6846
London W11 1QF

Case sales only   Open Mon–Fri 8.30–7   **Closed** Sat, Sun, public holidays
Credit cards Access, Visa; personal and business accounts   **Discounts** Not available   **Delivery** Free for 3+ cases; otherwise £10 for 1 case, £15 for 2 cases; mail order available   **Glass hire** Not available   **Tastings and talks** Tastings held 3 times annually; regular special dinners   **Cellarage** Approx £6.90 per case (inc insurance)

A slight change of image (and change of address) here at John Armit. Last year's extravagant brochure apparently gave the wrong impression and so the latest list has a few elegant drawings but is definitely a working document.

France is the mainstay of this list, with clarets introduced vintage by vintage and accompanied by good notes for each region and wine. Classed growths tend to gather on the bin-end list where in-bond prices appear startlingly good, and even with duty and VAT added they are still very reasonable. New this year is a section entitled 'Inexpensive Wines' containing six whites and 18 reds under £6, with a much bigger selection between £6 and £10. Among these value wines is a handful of vins de pays, petits châteaux from Fronsac and Bourg and Chilean wines from Montes and Los Vascos.

The Burgundy section has also been rearranged this year. Now organised vintage by vintage, instead of by domaine, it lists wines from quality growers and *négociants* such as Dujac, Tollot-Beaut, Olivier Leflaive and Faiveley.

The rest of France is fairly limited, four Loire whites and

three from Alsace, but the Rhône has a little more choice with astute selections from Guigal and Jaboulet. There is nothing from Italy, Portugal or Germany, but the New World gets some acknowledgement – Groth, Hess, Ravenswood and the Dominus wines from California. Australia is limited to Eden Ridge, Cape Mentelle and the delicious wines of the small Nicholson River winery.

John Armit is one of the few merchants included in the *Guide* to sell only by the unmixed case. While we believe that mixed cases should be available to customers, the regular programme of tastings and dinners does mean that many wines can be tasted before purchase.

Best buys

Ch. Philippe 1990, Gaillac, £
Réserve du Révérend Rouge 1990, Corbières, £
Bourgogne Rouge Mont Avril 1989, Domaine Goubard, ££
Groth Sauvignon Blanc 1991, Napa, California, ££

Arriba Kettle

Mail order

Buckle Street, Honeybourne, Evesham, *Tel* (0386) 833024
Hereford & Worcester WR11 5QB (24-hour telephone
answering service)

Case sales only **Open** 24-hour telephone answering service **Credit cards** None accepted; business accounts **Discounts** From £1.75 on 3 cases to £3.25 on 11+ cases; £2 per case collected (by prior arrangement) **Delivery** Free on UK mainland (min 2 cases) **Glass hire** Free with order in West Midlands and north Cotswolds **Tastings and talks** For mail-order customers in November **Cellarage** Not available

Good news on the Spanish front from this merchant. The peseta has held up better against the pound than the French franc, so prices of Spanish wines are virtually unchanged this year. Despite an increasing range from elsewhere, this is still very much a Spanish list and deliciously so.

Riojas are here in force from Bodegas Marqués de Cáceres, Marqués de Riscal, Martínez Bujanda, Berberana, Rioja Alta and others. Still in Spain, Torres represents the Penedès region and wines from Chivite provide the Navarras. New this year is a pair of Spanish table wines under the name of Don John which offer great value for money.

Sherries have pride of place at the start of the list. Five almacenista sherries from Lustau offer concentrated flavours as different from commercial sherry as farmhouse-matured cheddar is from the supermarket mousetrap variety.

French wines are mainly from the Loire and Bordeaux; Pouilly Fumé comes from Domaine Cailbourdin and Vouvray from Le Clos Baudoin. Barry Kettle has also found room for an estate Vieilles Vignes Bourgueil in the range. Clarets are limited but well chosen. Ch. Cissac is here, as is Les Gravières, a wine made by Cissac from vines grown nearby. Other clarets include La Tour du Mirail from the Haut-Médoc and Ch. Victoria from Graves. Babich from New Zealand and Hill-Smith from Australia are recent additions to the list, and some South African wines may soon join this very personal selection.

Delicious recipes acquired on trips to the vineyards give this list an added attraction.

Best buys

Don John Red Vino de Mesa nv, £
Ch. d'Astros 1990, Provence, £
Vouvray, Le Clos Baudoin 1985, Prince Poniatowski, ££
Lustau Almacenista Sherries, ££

ASDA

Head office
ASDA House, South Bank, Great Wilson   *Tel* (0532) 435435
Street, Leeds, West Yorkshire LS11 5AD
Approximately 205 branches nationwide

Open Mon–Fri 9–8 (Sat 8.30–8); Sun (selected stores) 10–5; selected stores also open on public holidays **Credit cards** Access, Visa **Discounts, delivery, glass hire** Not available **Tastings and talks** Approximately every four weeks (in specified stores) a selection of wines can be sampled **Cellarage** Not available

---

With wide aisles and artistic labels, ASDA is one supermarket where browsing becomes a pleasure. The range in bigger stores is huge and includes a sizeable fine-wine section. As with most multiples, not all the stores have all the range, but even if your nearest store is a small one, there is still enough choice to make life interesting.

ASDA's main strength is its own-label wines. In some supermarkets this would mean downmarket packaging but not here. The artistic design reflects each wine and each country; they are distinctive without shouting ASDA in large letters. But you can't drink the label, so what of the wines? Value is the key word among the own-labels and, in general, each wine is good quality and individually reflects its grape and region. Many of these own-labels sell for less than £3.50, which makes their quality and style even more amazing. Particularly good is the range of French regional wines and the pair of own-label Chilean wines.

At the other end of the scale, ASDA is always worth checking out for finer wines which are displayed horizontally in racks. Not all are hugely expensive. The Australian Oxford Landing wines are available, both priced under £5. The racks are also where you will find a fine range of champagnes, a sparkling Scharffenberger Brut from California and some up-market burgundies.

In between the two extremes of fine wine and own-label is a reasonable selection of wines which are well worth a try: organic Muscadet from Bossard, South African Sauvignon Blanc from Van Loveren, and a clutch of good-value Italian reds.

ASDA has a wine-training manual but, like many supermarkets, there is often no one around to give help. Informative back labels are a distinct bonus in this case.

Best buys

ASDA Chilean Cabernet/Merlot 1992, £
ASDA South Australian Chardonnay 1991, £
Goundrey Windy Hill Cabernet Sauvignon 1988, Western Australia, ££
Scharffenberger Brut nv, Mendocino, California, ££

Askham Wines

Askham, Newark, Nottinghamshire   *Tel* (0777) 838659
NG22 0RP

Case sales only **Open** Mon–Fri 9–6; Sat 9–12 **Closed** Sun, public holidays
Credit cards None accepted; personal and business accounts
Discounts Available **Delivery** Free within 5-mile radius of Askham (min order
1 case) **Glass hire** Free with order **Tastings and talks** Two tastings per year
(entrance charge discounted against orders) **Cellarage** Not available

Any wine merchant who attempts to run a business in this isolated area deserves a medal. Askham is a tiny (really tiny) village which you may come across as you drive from Lincoln to the A1. The area is known as the salesman's graveyard – there is no passing trade, no big towns, just lots of fields, pheasants and farms. In fact, it is rather pleasant. People who enjoy good wine are thin on the ground, and to survive a wine merchant must know his stuff and provide a good service. That is just what Andrew Brownridge does. He doubles as a prep-school headmaster during the day while his wife Elspeth keeps the business going. Between them their customers get pretty good service.

The range is small but well chosen. The emphasis is on individual growers and producers rather than the big names. Bordeaux is mainly affordable petits châteaux, burgundies are

245

sparse but good, and Alsace wines come from the co-operative at Turckheim. Portugal is a particular enthusiasm and provides quality drinking at a reasonable price. South Africa is a fairly new addition to the range with four wines from Groot Constantia and the Fairview Pinot Noir.

When time permits, Andrew can be persuaded to give talks about his wines. His style is good (years of practice at the chalk-face) but you have to listen properly or you could find yourself staying in at play-time!

Best buys

Ch. de Routier 1988, Côtes de la Malpère, £
Domaine de Maisonneuve 1991, Vin de Pays des Côtes de Gascogne, £
Cabernet Sauvignon 1989, Stag's Leap, California, ££
Chardonnay, Hawk Crest 1991, California, ££

The Australian Wine Centre

| 'Down Under', South Australia House, | *Tel* 071-925 0751 |
| 50 Strand, London WC2N 5LW | *Tel* 071-839 9021 |

Open Mon–Fri 10–7; Sat 10–4 **Closed** Sun, public holidays **Credit cards** Access, Amex, Visa; business accounts **Discounts** 5% on 1 case (to be collected) **Delivery** Free to mainland UK (min order £75); smaller orders £5; mail order available **Glass hire** Free **Tastings and talks** Winemakers' dinners and tastings to coincide with visiting Australian winemakers; Great Australian Wine Tastings held annually for members of The Australian Wine Club **Cellarage** Not available

---

If the thought of row upon row of Aussie wines just waiting to be bought excites you, experience a real thrill by taking a dive off the Strand into the Australian Wine Centre. There you will find the biggest range of Australian wines in the UK in a big, high-ceilinged cellar under South Australia House. Craig Smith and his team (Aussies, naturally) are chatty and helpful, and will happily steer you through the assembled 300 wines, from good-value Jacobs Creek right up to the various vintages of Grange Hermitage which slumber in racks in the centre of the floor space.

With such a wide range, it is hard to pick out strengths, but Penley Estate, Mountadam, Tarrawarra, Willows and St Hallett are just some of the delights. A range of wines from Charles Melton includes the sensational Nine Popes and there are plenty of winter-warming Liqueur Muscats and Tawnies.

Conveniently for central London, there is a loading bay at the back of the building, and for those who don't want to battle through the traffic, the Australian Wine Centre has a mail-order service. Delivery is free anywhere in mainland UK for orders over £75. Once on the mail-order list, customers receive regular newsletters with details of new lines and special offers. The annual tasting is a splendid bash with hundreds of wines open for tasting and many visiting winemakers available for a chat.

The New Zealand Wine Club, which used to operate from the same address, is 'on the back burner for the moment'. Not because it wasn't successful, far from it, it was so successful that getting hold of enough stock became a problem. Some New Zealand wines are available in the shop.

Best buys

St Hallett 'Poachers Blend' 1992, Barossa, Australia, £
Queen Adelaide Chardonnay 1991, South East Australia, £
Buckleys Coonawarra Cabernet Sauvignon 1991, South Australia, ££
Charles Melton Sparkling Shiraz nv, South Australia, ££

Averys of Bristol

7 Park Street, Bristol, Avon BS1 5NG   *Tel* (0272) 214141

Open Mon–Sat 9–7; Sun and public holidays 12–3 **Credit cards** Access, Visa; personal and business accounts **Discounts** Available **Delivery** Free within a 5-mile radius of Bristol; otherwise £5.50 if less than 2 cases ordered; mail order available **Glass hire** Free with orders **Tastings and talks** To groups on request **Cellarage** £4.09 (inc VAT) per case per year

Averys celebrates its bicentennial in 1993, although, to be absolutely accurate, it is the company it acquired around 1867 that was founded way back in 1793. Still, anyone's anniversary is a good excuse for celebration and Averys has really pushed the boat out. The list is remarkable, packed with information about the history of the company, the family and Bristol. Who would believe that this illustrious family could be related, however tenuously, to a seventeenth-century pirate, but it makes a good story to be told over a glass of port.

Averys has always done the classics well. Clarets are here in depth – a good range of affordable generics and petits châteaux is followed by three pages of classier châteaux. Against each wine is an indication of whether it is ready to drink or whether it should be kept. This theme continues into the burgundies, of which there are many, mainly from Remoissenet and Lupé-Cholet. The Rhône is fairly restrained while the Loire boasts no fewer than five Muscadets and also has some good Bourgueils and Chinons from Jacques Morin. French country wines and vins de table provide reasonably priced drinking while you wade through the rest of this heavyweight list.

The New World is splendid. Tyrrells, Rouge Homme and Penfolds are the main players from Australia, with Piper's Brook Chardonnay from Tasmania making an appearance. New Zealand is represented (mainly) by Nobilo; California is a delight, with wines from Belvedere, Swanson, Far Niente and many more; and South African wines include the excellent Rustenberg, Hamilton-Russell and Klein Constantia. (Old and rare wines such as vintage madeiras, aged ports and pre-Seventies clarets are not on the main list and have to be asked for separately.)

Averys operates a Bin Club, members of which pay in a regular amount each month and the credit is used to build up a cellar at discounted prices. There are also *en primeur* and special mixed-case offers, details of which are in the regular informative newsletters.

Averys is a traditional merchant which does not try to compete at the £3 level with high-street supermarkets – instead, it offers a quality range, traditional service and helpful advice, as befits a merchant established 200 years ago.

Best buys

Undurraga Sauvignon Blanc 1992, Chile, £
Averys Club Red Vin de Table, £
Averys Fine Claret 1990, ££
Tyrrells Old Winery Shiraz 1990, Australia, ££

Look after your glasses by storing them upright so that air can circulate. Wash them by hand and rinse thoroughly. Decanters should always be stored without stoppers.

All love at first, like generous wine,
Ferments and frets until 'tis fine;
But when 'tis settled on the lee,
And from th'impurer matter free,
Becomes the richer still the older,
And proves the pleasanter the colder.

Samuel Butler, *Miscellaneous Thoughts*

Adam Bancroft

57 South Lambeth Road, London SW8 1RJ *Tel* 071-434 9919

Case sales only **Open** Mon–Fri 9–6 **Closed** Sat, Sun, public holidays
Credit cards None accepted; personal and business accounts **Discounts** Not
available **Delivery** Free in London (min 1 case); in south-east, free (min 3 cases),
£7.64 for 1 case, £9.99 for 2 cases; mail order available **Glass hire** Free
Tastings and talks Regular tastings **Cellarage** £5.50 per case per year

A personal service and a range of hand-picked wines are
available from this Master of Wine. Sales are by the case, which
can be mixed, and there should be no problem finding an
assorted dozen here.

Classic French wines are the main feature but, instead of a
full frontal assault on Bordeaux, the list first investigates the
Loire. A range of domaine wines from Muscadet to Sancerre is
the theme, with individual growers, such as Pierre Girault in
Sancerre, Henri Beurdin in Reuilly and Masson-Blondelet in
Pouilly Fumé. There is a super selection of Loire reds, Menetou-
Salon, Chinon, two from Saumur-Champigny and three
different vineyard wines from Pierre Breton in Bourgueil.

Burgundy has the same kind of feel, with a fairly wide
selection of wines providing a good range under £20. Chablis,
Côtes de Nuits, Côtes de Beaune, Chalonnais and Mâconnais all
have separate listings and good variety. Armand Girardin,
Maréchal-Jacquet and Claude Nouveau are just some of the
names here. Some notes about the growers and their wines help
decision making.

Between these two major areas of interest there are some
Rhône wines, including a full-flavoured Côtes-du-Rhône Syrah
from René Sinard and a handful from elsewhere. Jurançon rates
three wines from Domaine Castéra, and Savoie includes a wine
from the Mondeuse grape.

And Bordeaux? That stalwart of so many lists is limited to just
three reds and a white. A tiny range compared with many
merchants who offer page after page of Bordeaux wines, but in
this haven of Loire, Rhône and Burgundy, there is plenty to
drink through before you even notice the lack of claret.

Best buys

Sauvignon de Touraine 1992, Alain Marcadet, £
Merlot, Vin de Pays de l'Ardèche 1992, Domaine des Terriers, £
Valréas Côtes-du-Rhône-Villages 1990, Sinard, ££
Bourgogne Rouge 1990, Daniel Chopin-Groffier, ££

Barnes Wine Shop

51 Barnes High Street, London SW13 9LN   *Tel* 081-878 8643

Open Mon–Sat 9.30–8.30; Sun 12–2 **Closed** Public holidays and Chr period
Credit cards Access, Visa; personal and business accounts **Discounts** 5% on 1
mixed case (payment by credit card); 7% on payment by cash/cheque
Delivery Free locally (min 2 cases); elsewhere negotiable; mail order available for
5 cases **Glass hire** Free with order **Tastings and talks** Regular in-store tastings
(Sats); occasional private tastings **Cellarage** £6 per case per year

Francis Murray of the Barnes Wine Shop sees a trend away from
the New World and back to traditional European wines. Even
so, his New World list makes good reading, with Moss Wood,
Shaw and Smith and Ryecroft Estate among the Australians,
Martinborough and Hunters weighing in for New Zealand and
a wide choice from South Africa and Chile, including the
delicious Louisvale Chardonnay. The resulting effect is variety,
quality and style.

Back amongst the Europeans, Italy looks particularly
impressive with a full countrywide range reflecting the terrific
variety available. Umani Ronchi, Mascarello and Altesino are
just some of the highlights; all are worth exploring.

The French list is equally enjoyable. Quality wines within a
realistic price range is the key, with a good selection of Rhônes,
clarets and burgundies slipping well under the £10 price band.
A further selection of fine wines gives plenty of opportunity to
push the boat out.

Barnes Wine Shop does not issue a full list, but twice a year it
points out certain interesting wines. Tastings are held every
Saturday; it is by far the best way to find out what is in stock.
Expansionist plans are still in the pipeline. For the sake of
Barnes drinkers we hope that these plans are more than pipe
dreams.

Best buys

Copertino DOC Riserva 1989, Italy, £
Côtes-du-Rhône 1991, 'Serre de Lauzière', £
Pinot Grigio 1991, Silvio Jermann, Italy, ££
Overgaauw Merlot 1989, South Africa, ££

A man cannot make him laugh; but that's no marvel; he drinks no wine.

Shakespeare, *Henry IV (Part II)*

Augustus Barnett

Head office
3 The Maltings, Wetmore Road, Burton-on-Trent, Staffordshire DE14 1SE   *Tel* (0283) 512550
Approximately 570 branches nationwide

Open Varies from store to store; most outlets open Mon–Sat 10–10; Sun, public holidays 12–2, 7–9.30 **Closed** Chr Day **Credit cards** Access, Amex, Visa; personal and business accounts **Discounts** 5% on 1 case **Delivery** Free locally from outlets (min 1 case) **Glass hire** Free **Tastings and talks** At selected branches **Cellarage** Not available

With 26 new shops this year and a programme of refurbishment, this chain of neighbourhood wine shops is still thriving. Like all the big chains, the range of wines you will find in your local shop is tailored to match the demand. The down side of this is that if you live near a shop that is expected to sell just beer, fags and Liebfraumilch, then that is pretty much what you will get. The up side is that any good wines that are in your local store will not have been gathering dust under fluorescent lights for years. The stock is tailored to demand, and if you require something which is not normally stocked you can order it by the single bottle. The manager we spoke to said he could get most items within a day or two.

The range is quite surprising: despite the 1.5-litre bottles of Lambrusco crowding the bottom shelves, there are some reasonable labels lurking above. France is well represented with a good supply of petit-château wines from £3.99 upwards. Parent company Bass owns Ch. Lascombes in Margaux and so there is a choice of vintages from this property. Burgundy, Alsace and the Loire provide a further choice of reasonable drinking, and the French regional range has some good wines from Minervois, Ardèche and the Côtes de Gascogne.

The New World range is fairly strong, with Coldridge Estate, Hardy, Lindemans, Orlando and Penfolds supplying variety for between £3 and £7 a bottle. Wolf Blass President's selection and Black Label wines add a few top-notes. Santa Rita from Chile and several Bulgarians also have big flavours and small price-tags.

With local delivery, glass loan and occasional tastings in some branches, Augustus Barnett is beginning to look like a serious act in the wine business.

Best buys

Undurraga Chardonnay 1992, Chile, £
Augustus Barnett Cava Brut, £
Ch. Lascombes 1986, Margaux, ££
Domaine Chandon Green Point nv, Australia, ££

Bedford Fine Wines

Faulkners Farm, The Marsh, Carlton, *Tel* (0234) 721153
Bedford, Bedfordshire MK43 7JU

Case sales only   Open During office hours or by appointment only
Credit cards None accepted; personal and business accounts
Discounts Negotiable **Delivery** Free within 15-mile radius of Bedford (min value
£80); elsewhere £5 per case on 1–2 cases, £3 per case on 3–4 cases
Glass hire Free **Tastings and talks** Regular tastings **Cellarage** Not available

A fairly limited but well-chosen range is on offer from Bedford
Fine Wines, with France being the main feature. A few
respected properties form the core of the claret list: Palmer,
Angludet, Chasse-Spleen and Ch. de la Rivière, with a
sprinkling of others here and there depending on the vintage.
Burgundies are selective rather than being present in force but
the names are good: Jaboulet-Vercherre, Faiveley, William Fèvre
and Moillard. The Rhône's representative is essentially Guigal
and the Alsace range comes from Caves de Turckheim and
Dopff 'Au Moulin'.

Outside France, the complete works from Torres lead the
Spanish entry, with wines from Australia, New Zealand, Chile
and California also making an appearance.

Tastings are held frequently in the modern barns at this farm-based business. Pre-shipment and *en primeur* offers from Bordeaux and Burgundy add to the attractions. At the same address (and run by the same people) is another outfit called the Real Burgundy Company. This range is a real treat of domaine wines from classy growers; William Fèvre, Armand Rousseau and Jean Grivot are just some of the names available in unmixed cases. Unfortunately, this stock is not kept on site and has to be ordered.

Best buys

Dry Muscat Resplandy 1992, Vin de Pays d'Oc, £
Simonsig Chenin Blanc 1992, South Africa, £
Ch. d'Angludet 1987, Cantenac-Margaux, ££
Condrieu 1990, Guigal, ££

Belfast Wine Company

130 Stranmillis Road, Belfast BT9 5DT   *Tel* (0232) 381760

Open Mon–Sat 9.30–9 **Closed** Sun, public holidays **Credit cards** Access, Visa; personal and business accounts **Discounts** Available **Delivery** Free in Greater Belfast; mail order available **Glass hire** Free with 1-case order
Tastings and talks Free tastings approximately once a month by invitation
Cellarage Not available

There is no list available at this Belfast shop so customers have to go along and take a look at the shelves.

The range has changed considerably this year but there is still a good selection of clarets at both ends of the price scale, from affordable petits châteaux to first growths. Burgundies are mainly from *négociant* Patriarche, and Chablis comes from the large producer Jean Durup. The Loire sports a selection of Muscadets and Coteaux du Layon.

Spain goes for value with Riojas from Campo Viejo, and there are some wines from small producer Marqués de Puerto. Italian wines include Chiantis from Rocca delle Macie and a range of Trentino wines from the North East of the country.

Australia sounds more interesting with selections from Hardy, Haughton, Peter Lehmann, Mitchelton and Taltarni, and California provides basic wines from Gallo and top-notes from Simi and Clos du Val.

Best buys

Bellingham Pinotage 1990, South Africa, £
Eileen Hardy Chardonnay 1990, Australia, ££
Mas de Daumas Gassac 1989, Vin de Pays de l'Hérault, ££

Benedict's

28 Holyrood Street, Newport, Isle of Wight
PO30 5AU

Tel (0983) 529596

Open Mon–Sat 9–5.30 **Closed** Sun, public holidays and the Chr–New Year
period **Credit cards** Access, Visa; personal and business accounts **Discounts** 5%
on mixed case of table wines (payment by cash/cheque only) **Delivery** Free on
Isle of Wight (min 1 case); otherwise £1 per delivery; mail order available
Glass hire Free; 80p per breakage **Tastings and talks** Two tastings per month
from Sept to Apr **Cellarage** £3 per case per year

From the sound of this shop on a busy Saturday morning, the
customers come in waves to Benedicts, which presumably
makes former Royal Naval Officer Malcolm Rouse feel quite at
home.

The range takes in most of the world, but there is a distinct
Iberian flavour with 30 Spanish wines and another dozen from
Portugal, not counting a fair selection of ports. Riojas come from
CVNE, Muga and Berberana; other wines come from Torres and
sherries from Garvey and Hidalgo. Portuguese wines feature
Fonseca's Quinta de Camerate and the wines of João Pires made
by Australian winemaker Peter Bright.

Clarets range from the basics to classed growths; burgundies
include wines from Bouchard and Chanson on the *négociant* side
and Jean Thévenet and Etienne Sauzet for the growers. Stars
from the Rhône include Ch. Fortia in Châteauneuf-du-Pape,
Guigal in Hermitage, Chapoutier in Crozes, with Ch. du Grand
Moulas making a very satisfactory Côtes-du-Rhône. Italy
includes Chiantis from Castello di Volpaia and Badia a
Coltibuono, top-notch Valpolicella from Quintarelli and Barolo
from Fontanafredda.

The New World rates a reasonable selection with Mitchelton,
Brown Brothers and the full-flavoured Eileen Hardy range from
Hardy representing Australia, Te Mata doing the same job for
New Zealand, and a full range of Caliterra wines from Chile.

Benedict's is also a delicatessen, so you can buy tempting
foods to go with your wines. Regular wine tastings are a
feature, and once a year a happy band of travellers escapes from
the Isle to tour the vineyards of France.

Best buys

Sauvage de la Bri 1990, Blanc Fumé Franschhoek Valley, South
Africa, £
Ochoa Tinto 1990, Navarra, £
Barton Manor 1989, Sparkling Wine, England, ££
Ch. Plagnac 1987, Cru Bourgeois Médoc, ££

Bennetts Wines and Spirits

High Street, Chipping Campden, *Tel* (0386) 840392
Gloucestershire GL55 6AG

Open Mon–Fri 9–1, 2–5.30; Sat 9–5.30 **Closed** Sun, public holidays
Credit cards Access, Visa; business accounts **Discounts** 5% on 1 case, 7.5% on 5–
9 cases, 10% on 10+ cases (apply to orders collected from premises only)
Delivery Free nationally for 2 cases or more; mail order available **Glass hire** Free
with order **Tastings and talks** Large free public tastings twice a year in town hall,
also regular wine dinners with local restaurants and hotels **Cellarage** Not
available

Charles Bennett decided not to follow up a career in music
despite training as a pianist; instead, he seems to have found
his *forte* in wine. He runs a tiny shop in Chipping Campden,
with a wonderful range from classic French regions and small
New World properties.

The clarets are good. A couple of AC Bordeaux wines start off
the bidding before the list climbs rapidly to the classed growths.
White burgundies come from a collection of top-name growers:
Chablis from Fèvre; Chassagne-Montrachet from Leflaive and
Puligny-Montrachet from Sauzet; among the reds, the names
Drouhin, Jean Gros and Domaine Dujac stand out from a pretty
impressive crowd. Alsace wines are mainly Schlumberger and
Hugel, with Jaboulet featuring from the Rhône.

The New World selection is huge. From Australia there are
Petaluma, Taltarni and Bannockburn in depth, with Rothbury
Estate, Cape Mentelle and Yarra Yering providing sufficient
choice to last for months. Representing California are Bonny
Doon, Qupé and Calera, among others. The Italian section has
seen a lot of work recently with Barolos from Mascarello and
Soaves from Pieropan. Quality sherries are provided by Lustau
and Don Zoilo.

Bennetts is full of excellent quality and famous names but the
everyday drinker is not neglected. Heading up the list is a wide
selection of wines under £6, including a new range of French
estate varietals.

Best buys

Cuvée du Cépage Cabernet 1992, Vin de Pays d'Oc, £
Salisbury Estate Sauvignon 1992, Victoria, Australia, £
Mâcon Viré 'Domaine Emilian Gillet' 1990, Jean Thévenet, ££
Bannockburn Pinot Noir 1989, Geelong, Victoria, ££

Benson Fine Wines

96 Ramsden Road, London SW12 8QZ   *Tel* 081-673 4439

Open Mon–Fri 9–5.30 **Closed** Sat, Sun, public holidays **Credit cards** None accepted; personal and business accounts **Discounts** Not available
Delivery Free in London **Glass hire** Not available **Tastings and talks** To groups on request **Cellarage** Not available

This specialised company run by Clare Benson has a specialised list. There is an 1874 Ch. Léoville-Poyferré and a 1980 Ch. Arnauton and in between these vintages there are enough wines to launch a hundred anniversary or birthday parties. The selection is essentially classic – claret and sweet white Bordeaux, red burgundy plus port and a few spirits, some from the nineteenth century. The stock is cellared at Ramsden Road but can also be purchased in the city by prior arrangement.

Best buys

Your best buy depends on which anniversary you want to celebrate

Bergerac Wine Cellar

37 Hill Street, St Helier, Jersey JE2 4UB   *Tel* (0534) 70756

Open Tue–Sat 10–1, 2–6 **Closed** Sun, public holidays **Credit cards** All accepted; personal and business accounts **Discounts** 10% on 1 case **Delivery** On Jersey only (min 1 bottle) **Glass hire** Free; breakages charged for
Tastings and talks Available **Cellarage** Not available

VAT-free prices make any Jersey wine-list seem attractive, but the Bergerac list is worth a second look for its range as well as for its prices. It is a small but reliable selection and, despite Jersey's proximity to France, it includes choices from around the world. Clarets are fairly classic – lots of classed growths with prices at the top end of the range seeming to benefit most from the VAT-free status. Burgundies are mainly from Faiveley and Mommessin. The Rhône is not exciting, but Alsace and the Loire provide a wide choice of whites to chill and enjoy in the Jersey sunshine. Spanish wines also seem popular: a good range of Riojas is topped off by five vintages of Vega Sicilia. The Australian selection includes wines mainly from big producers Hardy and Rosemount, with a handful from Yarra Yering at the top end of the price range. Wines from Rothbury Estate, Bannockburn and a Rhine Riesling from Petaluma add a touch more variety to the list.

Port is a popular choice, with vintages stretching back to 1935. Delivery is free for just one bottle around Jersey, but with a 10 per cent case discount you might think it worthwhile selecting a mixed dozen.

Best buys

Viña Real Rioja Tinto 1988, CUNE, £
Barramundi Red nv, Australia, £
Ch. Musar 1983, Gaston Hochar, Lebanon, ££
Ch. Lyonnat 1988, Lussac St-Emilion, ££

Berkeley Wines

See Cellar 5

Berkmann Wine Cellars

See Le Nez Rouge

Berry Bros & Rudd

3 St James's Street, London SW1A 1EG

Tel 071-396 9600
Tel (answering machine
071-396 9644)

The Wine Shop, Houndmills, Basingstoke,
Hampshire RG21 2YB

Tel (0256) 23566

Open (London) Mon–Fri 9–5.30; Sat 9–1 (Dec only), (Basingstoke) Mon–Fri 9–5;
Sat 9–1 **Closed** Sat (London, exc Dec), Sun, public holidays **Credit cards** Access,
Diners Club, Visa; personal and business accounts **Discounts** 3% on 3 cases, 5%
on 5 cases, 7.5% on 10+ cases **Delivery** Free on UK mainland (min 1 case);
mail order available **Glass hire** £3.30 per 30 glasses (inc cleaning)
Tastings and talks Tastings in June and November in Basingstoke at £7.50
per person refundable against purchase; tastings to groups on request;
tastings by invitation **Cellarage** £4.56 per case per year

For those used to choosing wine from a supermarket shelf and wheeling it to the checkout, the service at one of the last bastions of the traditional wine trade might come as a pleasant surprise. But, despite the museum air of its St James's Street premises, Berry Bros & Rudd is well in tune with the twentieth century. The London shop is an experience not to be missed. Do not try to have your suitcase weighed on the famous scales, or even yourself: such a privilege is reserved for eminent personages. One which was noted in the famous book was a Sumo wrestler who had to be weighed in cases of Cutty Sark because they ran out of weights. Even without the scales, this wine shop is unlike any other you may encounter. No serried ranks of wine and a check-out counter, the service here is pure Dickensian drama.

But the London shop is only half the story; much of the business has relocated to Basingstoke. This is hardly the centre of the wine trade, but with a purpose-built temperature-controlled warehouse and easy distribution it seems very sensible. To get there you have to negotiate Basingstoke's many roundabouts to one of the industrial sites on the outskirts of the town. Parking is right outside and there is a discreet sign directing you to the shop (not really a shop, more of an office with a few wines on show). Not all the range is displayed but, as in St James's Street, courtesy is everything. Take a seat and a charming chap will advise you on the right wines for the right occasion and then take your order. It may take a little time for the wines to be brought to you but at least you know that they have been stored properly in that modern warehouse. Pleasant members of staff even carry the cases out to your car; in circumstances like these, spending serious money becomes a real pleasure.

The range at both venues is comprehensive with a tendency to excel in the traditional areas – Bordeaux, Burgundy and classic German wines. The New World is not neglected, though, with Australian wines from Henschke, Wynns, Petaluma and Peter Lehmann. Italy and Spain are good, but if there is a weak area Portugal could be it. Still, there is plenty of choice from other regions to provide a lifetime's drinking.

Once you have made a purchase you will go on to Berry's mailing list and receive the delightful list (chunky, pocket-sized), the magazine (stiff-backed, pleasant post-prandial reading) and lots of special offers. We have had good reports of the mail-order service and delivery is free anywhere in the UK for 12 assorted bottles or more.

Best buys

Good Ordinary Claret, Berry's Own Selection, £
Berry's Mâcon Rouge, £
Crozes-Hermitage, Les Meysonniers 1989, ££
Berry's Own Selection Vintage Character Port, ££

Cork was used by the Romans to stopper jars and amphorae but after the Romans its use was forgotten until the middle of the sixteenth century.

B H Wines

Boustead Hill House, Boustead Hill,
Burgh-by-Sands, Carlisle, Cumbria CA5 6AA   *Tel* (0228) 576711

Case sales only   Open 'All reasonable hours', but advisable to phone before
calling   **Credit cards** None accepted   **Discounts** Occasionally   **Delivery** Free
within Carlisle/North Cumbria, Newcastle upon Tyne, Durham areas and the
Scottish Borders (depending upon quantity ordered)   **Glass hire** Free; breakages
charged at 75p   **Tastings and talks** Free pre-Christmas tasting; monthly meetings
to wine-society members (from £5 per person); talks to groups on request
Cellarage Not available

'Visitors beware!' says B H Wines – not an unfriendly lot, just
warning customers that the road to Boustead Hill sometimes
floods at high tide. Once you do make it to the lovely Georgian
house on the edge of the Solway Firth you can while away the
hours until the waters retreat by playing croquet on the back
lawn with proprietor Linda Neville and her husband Richard.

B H's list may take some getting used to, but it is worth the
effort. Laid out differently from most lists, it tackles reds, then
dry whites, medium and sweet whites followed by sparklers
and fortifieds; within each section the choice is alphabetically
by country from Argentina to USA. This layout is just the start
of B H's sensible approach. Each wine is accompanied by
detailed tasting notes and mentions of the various medals it has
recently acquired.

The range is wide with no real gaps anywhere. There are
good French wines from the south as well as from the classic
regions; no endless columns of classed-growth clarets here. Just
a few well-chosen top-notes to a good collection of crus
bourgeois and petits châteaux.

Further afield, Italy deserves special mention with a trio of
wines from Umani Ronchi, including three vintages of Cumaro.
Chiantis are from Frescobaldi and Farneta. California is a
delight with wines from Simi, Firestone, Trefethen and others,
including the glorious Saintsbury Pinot Noir. Among the
Australians the names Dromana, Mountadam and Vasse Felix
are outstanding.

This is a dedicated company – it not only trades in wine sales
but in advice, knowledge and appreciation and customers seem
to be well served.

Best buys

Undurraga Cabernet Sauvignon 1989, Chile, £
Fleur 1989, Union des Producteurs de Rauzan, Bordeaux, £
Viña Hergabia Reserva 1982, Navarra, Spain, ££
Wairau River Sauvignon Blanc 1992, New Zealand, ££

Bibendum

113 Regent's Park Road, London NW1 8UR	*Tel* 071-722 5577

Associated outlet

Yorkshire Fine Wines, Sweethills,	*Tel* (0423) 330131
Nun Monkton, York, North Yorkshire	
YO5 8ET	

Case sales only Open Mon–Sat 10–8 **Closed** Sun, public holidays
Credit cards Access, American Express, Visa; personal and business accounts
Discounts Negotiable **Delivery** Free within M25 and north of England from
Yorkshire Fine Wines (min 1 mixed case); mail order available **Glass hire** Free
with order **Tastings and talks** Regular tutored tastings held in tasting room
Cellarage 45p per month or part thereof

'Bibendum is a pursuit of excellence.' That's how this list starts out and although it's a tall order, Bibendum works very hard towards reaching its goal.

Operations in London are in a splendid warehouse in Primrose Hill. Case sales only but, with a superb range on show, you will have no trouble choosing an assorted dozen to take home. Like all the best lists, this one is focused on growers: small, independent, often family concerns that are mostly exclusive to Bibendum. Buying Director Simon Farr introduces each one in a way that makes you feel that you have just arrived at the vineyard gate on a bicycle. From the Rhône, Marc Sorrel provides the Hermitage, Paul Avril the Châteauneuf-du-Pape and the Côtes-du-Rhône-Villages is the splendid one by Gérard Meffre from Ch. la Courançonne.

In general, burgundy and value are terms which don't go together, but this range has been well chosen to provide interesting, quality wines that are worth forking out the money for. Bibendum is not just a French specialist. The Italian range is a delight, worth several weekends' research; California has wines from Saintsbury, Chalk Hill and Konocti. New this year is a range of wines from the Duxoup Wineworks in Somoma, where the proprietors grow an almost extinct grape variety, Charbono, and, somewhat oddly, they name the barrels after opera singers. Australia has no such quirks and concentrates on wines that give big flavours and good value; Basedow, Redcliff and Katnook. Chile has the super Santa Rita wines.

You don't have to go to Regent's Park to take advantage of all these goodies. Bibendum has a massive, fast, free-delivery service, which includes the M25 area and the north of England from the Wash to the Borders. Outside that area you pay for delivery by the consignment, not by the case.

Regular tastings cover such topics as 'Cabernet Sauvignon: New World versus Old World' (£15) and Château Cheval Blanc (£50). This year, up-market clarets and vintage port have been included in the main list but there is still a Fine Wine list that concentrates on special parcels of wine as they occur.

Yorkshire Fine Wines operates out of Nun Monkton and has the same splendid range.

Best buys

La Croix 1992, Vin de Pays d'Oc, £
La Serre Sauvignon Blanc 1992, Vin de Pays d'Oc, £
Mâcon Rouge 1990, Domaine du Vieux St Sorlin, ££
Ch. Villegeorge 1987, Haut-Médoc, ££

Bin 89 Wine Warehouse

89 Trippet Lane, Sheffield, South Yorkshire   *Tel* (0742) 755889
S1 4EL

Case sales only   Open Sat 10.30–2   **Closed** Mon–Fri, Sun, public holidays
Credit cards None accepted   **Discounts** Available   **Delivery** Free in Sheffield and North Derbyshire (min 3 cases); elsewhere at cost   **Glass hire** Free with order
Tastings and talks Two in-store tastings per year   **Cellarage** Not available

You have to be quick: this business is open on Saturdays between 10.30am and 2pm only, but regulars know that they can leave messages at Jonathan Park's other enterprise, Trippet's Wine Bar.

The emphasis in this list is on value for money. Most of the wines are under £10, with many hovering around the £5 mark. Italy has a wider range than others with Teroldego, Rosso Cònero and Brusco di Barbi joining the more familiar names of Soave and Chianti. Spain and Portugal also offer big flavours from reliable producers.

Jonathan has worked hard to get Australia accepted in conservative (with a small 'c') Sheffield. The wines of Woodstock, Pirramimma and Mount Helen all deserve their places in this range. The USA fares less well, with just one producer representing this huge area. From South America, Chile is rewarded with wines from Viña Carmen and the South American branch of Torres. South Africa is a fairly new addition with wines from Drostdy-Hof, L'Ormarins and Meerlust.

France has a few clarets, mainly petits châteaux, but there are good stocks of '82 and '83 cru classé wines at the warehouse. A wide choice of regional French wines should make up an interesting mixed case.

Vintages are totally missing from this list, which doesn't make life easy.

Best buys

Castillo de San Diego, Barbadillo, £
Drostdy-Hof Pinotage, South Africa, £
Marrano, Vino da Tavola del'Umbria, ££
Woodstock Shiraz, Southern Vales, Australia, ££

Bin Ends

Toone House & Cellars, 83–85 Badsley Moor Lane, Rotherham, South Yorkshire S65 2PH	*Tel* (0709) 367771
Associated outlet	
(By the case only) Patrick Toone Personal Wine Merchant, Pavilion House, Oswaldkirk, York, North Yorkshire YO6 5XZ	*Tel* (04393) 504

Open Mon–Fri 10–5.30; Sat 9.30–12.30 **Closed** Sun, public holidays
Credit cards Access, Visa; personal and business accounts **Discounts** 5% on 1
unmixed case (still wines) (2.5% on all other wines); 7.5% on 3+ mixed cases (still
wines) (5% on all other wines) **Delivery** Free within 25-mile radius of Rotherham
(min 1 case) **Glass hire** Free with order **Tastings and talks** Monthly tastings for
general public; tutored tastings to groups on request **Cellarage** Not available

The name Bin Ends doesn't really do this company justice. It
implies a hotch-potch of assorted wines or the dregs of
someone's cellar. In reality, this is a well-structured list with
wines from a variety of good producers.

Refreshingly, the list is arranged alphabetically: Australia
comes first, quickly followed by California, Chile and China –
China? The two good Tsingtao wines, Riesling and Chardonnay,
are included – bound to get the conversation going at any
dinner party! Chilean wines are from Montes, the Australians
are mainly Brown Brothers and New Zealand is represented by
Cloudy Bay, Vavasour and Aotea.

From France, representing the burgundies, is the splendid
range from Faiveley; Chablis is from William Fèvre. A full range
of Vidal-Fleury wines from the Rhône is listed in addition to
four Châteauneuf-du-Pape and three white Rhônes from other
producers. Garvey's sherries are here in depth and it is good to
see finos and manzanillas in half-bottles. More halves and a few
magnums are grouped together at the end of the list.

Retail sales are available from the Rotherham shop. Patrick
Toone 'Personal Wine Merchant' operates from Oswaldkirk on a
mixed-cased basis only.

Once in the bottle a cork can last for decades but eventually it
becomes brittle and crumbly with age.

Best buys

Domaine de la Hitaire 1992, Vin de Pays des Côtes de
Gascogne, £
Chianti, Landozzi 1988, DOCG, £
Sancerre, Croix d'Ursin 1991, Sylvain Bailly, ££
CVNE Viña Real Gran Reserva 1985, Rioja, ££

Booths

Head office
4–6 Fishergate, Preston, Lancashire PR1 3LJ   *Tel* (0772) 51701
20 branches in Cumbria, Cheshire and Lancashire

Open Varies from store to store   **Closed** Sun, public holidays
Credit cards Access, Visa   **Discounts** Available   **Delivery** Not available
Glass hire Free   **Tastings and talks** Customer tastings limited – on application;
occasionally bottles available in-store   **Cellarage** Not available

Booths is not an ordinary supermarket group when it comes to
wine. Fine clarets are thick on the shelves with top-weight
wines, such as Mouton and Latour, here in a choice of vintages.
For a little variety on Saturday nights you could also be tempted
by Pavie, Palmer or Pétrus. The prices are not outrageous, in
fact, many are pounds less than might be asked by more serious
merchants. For weekday evenings you could content yourself
with a stroll through the cheaper clarets: Beychevelle,
Lynch-Bages and Beau-Séjour Bécot.

Burgundy is slightly less extensive, but selections from
Drouhin, Leflaive and Moillard make appearances on the
shelves. This is possibly the only supermarket to list wines from
Domaine de la Romanée-Conti. Alsace wines are from
Schlumberger, with Guigal providing some of the Rhônes. Italy
includes some gems amongst the Lambrusco, such as
Tignanello, Sassicaia and Conterno's Barolo. Australia has a fine
spread from Jacobs Creek to Grange, with interesting excursions
to Mountadam, Yarra Yering, Vasse Felix and Cape Mentelle.

As with all multiples, not all the range is in all the stores, but
apparently Knutsford has the best choice.

> When opening a bottle cut through the capsule just below the lip of
> the bottle, then wipe the lip with a damp cloth. This is particularly
> important for bottles with lead capsules since wine can pick up lead
> contamination from the bottle rim as it is poured.

Best buys

La Volière du Ch. Ollieux 1990, Corbières, £
Ch. de Violet Blanc 1992, Minervois, £
Ch. Gaillard 1990, Morgon, ££
Ch. de Meursault 1983, Meursault, ££

Bordeaux Direct

Mail order

New Aquitaine House, Paddock Road,
Reading, Berkshire RG4 0JY

Tel (0734) 481711
(enquiries)
Tel (0734) 471144
(orders)

5 Bordeaux Direct shops in Reading, Windsor,
Beaconsfield, Bushey and Woking

Open Mon–Fri 9–7; Sat, Sun 10–4 **Closed** Chr Day, Boxing Day, public holidays
Credit cards All accepted; business accounts **Discounts** Available **Delivery** Free
nationally for orders over £50; mail order available **Glass hire** Free
Tastings and talks Weekly tastings through retail outlets on request
Cellarage Not available

This is one of the faces of Direct Wines of Windsor, the other
being the Sunday Times Wine Club. It operates as a mail-order
club but also has five retail shops within easy reach of Reading.
The shops are staffed by enthusiasts who will talk you through
the range, which is probably a good thing as the names on the
labels are not the familiar ones you might see in other wine
shops.

Bordeaux Direct is innovative. It is spearheaded by Tony
Laithwaite who tends not to buy what is available but makes
available what he wants to buy. Long before it was the
fashionable thing to do he had a group of 'flying winemakers',
usually Australians, who took their techniques to the more
remote parts of France to make wine the way they wanted it –
fruity, full-flavoured and with character. Bordeaux Direct
discovered many of the southern French wines which are now
to be found on other merchants' shelves. This flying-
winemakers approach has now been extended to take in Chile,
Czechoslovakia and Spain.

The monthly mailshots are full of enjoyable hype, describing
the endless quest to find the best flavours and value in the
vineyards of the world. The Douro in Portugal is one of the
latest regions to come in for this treatment, with purple prose
whetting the appetite for the arrival of new wines later in the
year. South Africa, Australia and California have also been
scoured to bring the right wines to your doorstep. If you prefer,
you can always stick with the 'house wine', which is a Côtes de
Castillon from Ch. Clarière Laithwaite. The name says it all.

Bordeaux Direct shops always have bottles open for tasting and if you get on the shop mailing-list you will be invited to more specialised tastings as well. Much of the range is shared with the Sunday Times Wine Club, although Ch. Laithwaite is exclusive to Bordeaux Direct. Some of the mailshots are identical, including prices, which is nice to note – some organisations charge different prices to people on different lists.

Wine buying here is fun. Prices are around the middle range, cheap enough not to worry about comparing values and expensive enough to let you know this is something worth having.

Best buys

Marcillac Cave de Valady 1989, £
Sauvignon Blanc 1991, Archioni, Czechoslovakia, £
Cabernet Sauvignon 1991, Domaine Caperana, Chile, ££
Domaine de Cassagnoles 1992, Vin de Pays des Côtes de Gascogne, ££

Bottoms Up

See Thresher

The Broad Street Wine Company

Emscote Mill, Wharf Street, Warwick,   *Tel* (0926) 493951
Warwickshire CV34 5LB

Case sales only   **Open** Mon–Fri 9–6; Sat 9–1   **Closed** Sun, public holidays
Credit cards Access, Visa; personal and business accounts   **Discounts** By
negotiation   **Delivery** Free in UK (min 6 cases); otherwise £6 surcharge; mail
order available   **Glass hire** Free   **Tastings and talks** To groups on request
Cellarage 4p per case per week

Spirits are a speciality at this company, but not just any spirit
will do. Vintage cognacs roll back through the years as far as
1820, a year when Napoleon, who has lent his name to many a
good cognac, was still alive and kicking. The armagnacs come
from small domaines – such as Domaine Laberdolive where the
grapes, distilling and even the oak for the casks are controlled
by one family. English brandy, from Lamberhurst in Kent, is
another unusual spirit.

Returning to wine, the regions of France are well covered but
there is a fondness for old vintages here too. Among a quality
selection of Rhône wines lurks a 1923 Châteauneuf-du-Pape,
and a 1904 Romanée-St-Vivant rounds off a respectable choice of
burgundy from Drouhin, Faiveley and others. The German
selection starts at 1983 and works back to 1963, including on the
way a few gems from the glorious 1976 vintage. The New World
has plenty of drinking wines: the superb wines of Rongopai
and Cloudy Bay represent New Zealand; and Australia shows a
western bias with three Margaret River wines and only two,
Rouge Homme and Taltarni, from the south-eastern corner.
There are nods in the directions of Washington State, Chile and
Spain, while the vintage port section spans 50 years from 1935
to 1985.

Mixed cases are available, but you have to be fairly thirsty to
qualify for free delivery, which is available on orders of six
cases or more.

Best buys

Los Vascos Cabernet Sauvignon 1990, Chile, £
Cuvée Georges Blanc/Rouge Vin de Table, £
Rongopai Sauvignon Blanc 1991, New Zealand, ££
Rongopai Chardonnay 1991, New Zealand, ££

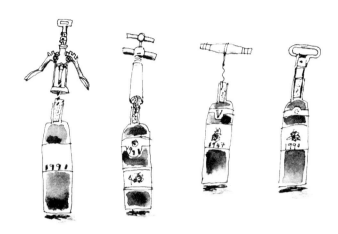

Bute Wines

Mount Stuart, Rothesay, Isle of Bute
PA20 9LR

Tel (0700) 502730

Associated outlet

2 Cottesmore Gardens, London W8 5PR

Tel 071-937 1629

Case sales only   **Open** Mon–Fri 8–6   **Closed** Sat, Sun, public holidays (skeleton staff only)   **Credit cards** None accepted; personal and business accounts
Discounts Occasionally   **Delivery** £8.50 for 1 case, £10.50 on 2 cases
Glass hire Available with wines   **Tastings and talks** Tastings and talks by invitation only   **Cellarage** £5 per case per year

This most aristocratic of wine companies is run by Jennifer, Marchioness of Bute. It has a huge range of clarets, burgundies and other wines, and you don't have to live in the Scottish Highlands and Islands to take advantage of it. Delivery is available nationwide.

This year the list is more manageable at around a third of its usual thickness. It means that not everything is listed but still the variety is impressive. A good selection of clarets from recent vintages starts off the range, with 70 or so from the 1989 vintage. All the good burgundy names are here: Rousseau, Voarick, Dujac, Domaine de la Romanée-Conti and lots more.

Rhônes are also here in depth. Guigal's top vineyard wines are available in a choice of vintages. There is a huge range of Hermitage and Châteauneuf-du-Pape from Jaboulet, Perrin,

Chapoutier and Paul Avril. White Rhônes include three vintages of Condrieu. From Alsace the pattern is the same – Lady Bute has concentrated on buying the good names and good wines of Trimbach, Zind Humbrecht and Faller.

The classic wines of Antinori, Torres and Hochar represent Italy, Spain and Lebanon. Australia includes Lindemans, Cape Mentelle and a selection from Rosemount.

South African wines have sold so well that a major restocking exercise is taking place. Backsberg, Neethlingshof and Simonsvlei will soon join the range. The new emphasis at Bute is on good value from around the world rather than sheer devotion to grand names. This is a welcome change.

Best buys

Ryecroft Flame Tree Cabernet Merlot 1992, Australia, £
Los Vascos Cabernet Sauvignon 1989, Chile, £
Bourgogne Passe-Tout-Grains 1989, Volpato, ££
Gigondas 1988, Domaine du Terme, Rolland Gaudin, ££

The Butlers Wine Cellar

247 Queen's Park Road, Brighton, East Sussex   *Tel* (0273) 698724
BN2 2XJ

Open Tue–Wed 9–5.30; Thur–Sat 9–7   **Closed** Mon, Sun, public holidays
Credit cards Access, Visa; business accounts   **Discounts** Not available
Delivery Free within 10-mile radius (min 1 case); elsewhere at cost (3+ cases free); mail order available   **Glass hire** Free with case order   **Tastings and talks** Regular tastings   **Cellarage** Not available

If you are looking for a special vintage to celebrate a particular anniversary then this is the place to start your search. Burgundies and Bordeaux wines go back through the years, often with only one or two bottles of each vintage available. Ch. Calon-Ségur 1945 or Pétrus 1958 could recall a magic moment in someone's life.

However, Butlers is not just a museum – there are plenty of wines which can be drunk without the accompanying strains of the Anniversary Waltz. The range is wide, if slightly unusual. Russian wines feature heavily with a choice of vintages of Moldovan Cabernet Sauvignon. With names like Red Stone, South Coast and Negru de Purkar, these wines might take some getting used to, but they are well worth the effort.

French regional wines are here in depth and are keenly priced with good tasting notes to help you make your choice. Wines of the Rhône are included, with a few oldies providing a touch of interest. There are some well-chosen wines from the rest of the world, including the good-value Peteroa range from Chile and Dieu Donné Chardonnay from South Africa.

Butlers runs regular tasting evenings, each with a different theme – they sound like fun.

Best buys

Marius Oak-Aged White 1990, Almansa, Spain, £
Chasan 1991, Vin de Pays des Côtes de Thongue, £
Buena Cepa 1989, Ribera del Duero, Spain, ££
Ch. d'Issan 1985, Margaux, ££

Anthony Byrne Fine Wines

88 High Street, Ramsey, Cambridgeshire   *Tel* (0487) 814555
PE17 1BS

Open Mon–Sat 9–6 (Sat till 5) **Closed** Sun, public holidays **Credit cards** Access, Visa; personal and business accounts **Discounts** 5% on 1 case **Delivery** Free on 5+ cases; otherwise £6 per delivery **Glass hire** Not available **Tastings and talks** Tastings on request **Cellarage** Not available

This company is a major wholesaler to the trade but it does have a retail shop and offers mail order to private customers. The range is huge – not everything is on show in the shop, but the warehouse is only 600 yards down the road, and we are assured that anything a customer wants can be obtained quickly.

The list is not for light bedtime reading: there is no chatty introduction, no descriptions. The only pointers to quality are a few stars dotted against those wines which are particularly recommended. Prices are given in four columns, the price charged depending on whether you are a private customer buying a mixed case or a retailer buying a pallet-load. VAT has to be added to all prices.

The French section is by far the biggest, with good names, many of them exclusive agencies, crowding the pages. Burgundies are a major interest with wines from Gagnard-Delagrange, Michelot-Buisson, Etienne Sauzet, Tollot-Beaut, Armand Rousseau and more – the spending potential is limitless. Alsace features with what must be the most comprehensive choice of Zind Humbrecht wines anywhere in the UK. The Loire, Rhône and Bordeaux regions are well represented; the only area which might be thought a little sparse is the south of France.

Penfolds, Delatite and Brown Brothers are the main players from Australia, exhibiting comprehensive selections from each. Wolf Blass and Lindemans feature in addition. With a fair range from California and a few from South Africa and Chile, it is unlikely that anyone could ever manage to work through the entire list.

We have had one reader's report that the shop is not the easiest place in which to browse, and the vast list is certainly not very user-friendly. But, do the advantages of dealing with such a major wholesaler outweigh the disadvantages? Please let us know.

Best buys

Côtes de Gascogne 1992, André Daguin, £
Beaujolais-Villages 1992, Cellier des Samsons, £
Ch. Lyonnat 1988, Lussac St-Emilion, ££
Pinot Blanc 1991, Domaine Zind Humbrecht, Alsace, ££

D Byrne & Co

12 King Street, Clitheroe, Lancashire BB7 2EP   *Tel* (0200) 23152

Open Mon–Sat 9–6 (Thur, Fri till 8)   **Closed** Sun, Easter holidays
Credit cards None accepted; personal and business accounts   **Discounts** £1 on mixed case, £1.20 on unmixed case, 5% on orders over £250   **Delivery** Free within 50-mile radius of Clitheroe (min 1 case)   **Glass hire** Free with orders
Tastings and talks Free annual tasting; to groups on request   **Cellarage** Free

What a gem! Do the good people of Clitheroe realise how lucky they are? This shop aims to have the most comprehensive stock in Lancashire and in most counties it would succeed with ease, but this is Lancashire, where determination and competition are strong. As it is, this merchant still provides one of the most varied ranges of any independent in the business.

This is still a family business, but Michael Byrne has retired and handed over the reins to his two sons, Andrew and Philip. They have set about adding even more wines to the already huge stock and that is why they did not publish a list this year. Another change has been the long-awaited acquisition of the old postal sorting office which has now become a warehouse. This cleared some space in the King Street shop which the two brothers are busy filling up again.

Focus of this new attention is the Italian range, which has doubled in size. New arrivals include four new Chiantis, a handful of wines from Aldo Conterno, Valpolicella from Allegrini and a big selection from Sardinia, Sicily and the southern parts of Italy. Eastern Europe is also under intensive review.

Classic parts of the range are good. Bordeaux manages a fine selection of classed growths supported by a good crop of petits châteaux. Unfashionable vintages of the great and good are here at reasonable prices, one of the few ways most of us can afford to drink these top wines. Burgundy wines are available in depth: Armand Rousseau, Bruno Clair and Mongeard-Mugneret feature among the reds, while William Fèvre, Sauzet and Leflaive crowd the white burgundy section – the choice goes on and on. The Rhône section has grown to include twenty red Châteauneuf-du-Papes and five whites. Hermitage, Côte Rôtie and Condrieu add to the distractions. The Loire follows in the same way – famous names, vintages and wines are all here. Ninety well-chosen wines from the south and south-west of France complete the Gallic picture, but then it's time to hold your breath and plunge into the rest of Europe and the world beyond – Germany, Spain, Italy, California, Chile, Australia and New Zealand are all represented – with a relentless enthusiasm for providing the best selection of well-made wines from everywhere.

If you tire of the selection of wine, D Byrne can offer you 150 beers, 35 coffees and 50 teas, and it is probably the only place within 50 miles where you can have your own blend of 'baccy' mixed. This shop acts as a magnet for many miles around, attracting customers with a taste for variety and value. Apparently they also come for the famous local sausages sold nearby!

Best buys

Pinot Noir Bourgogne Rouge 1991, Louis Alexandre, £
L A Cetto Cabernet Sauvignon 1986, Mexico, £
Villa Montes Alpha Cabernet Sauvignon 1988, Chile, ££
Palliser Estate Sauvignon Blanc 1992, New Zealand, ££

Bywater & Broderick

Lime Trees, 7 Main Street, Nether Poppleton,   *Tel* (0904) 793540
York, North Yorkshire YO2 6HS
44 The Calls, Leeds, West Yorkshire LS2 7EW   *Tel* (0532) 452281

Case sales only (Leeds shop by bottle) **Open** Mon–Fri 8–6 **Closed** Sat, Sun, public holidays **Credit cards** Access, Amex, Visa; personal and business accounts **Discounts** 1.5% on 5+ cases, 2.5% on 10+ cases **Delivery** Free in Yorkshire and orders of 5+ cases; elsewhere £4.50 per case; mail order available **Glass hire** Free **Tastings and talks** Regular tastings **Cellarage** Not available

---

Good news for customers of David Bywater and the elusive Mr Broderick – they have opened a retail outlet in the centre of Leeds. Now you can buy by the mixed case as before or visit the shop and choose from the full range. Bottles will always be open for tasting in the shop and a series of regular organised tastings is planned.

The list has grown this year but still maintains the policy of sticking to good producers in any area. From France, there is no attempt to compete in the classed-growth claret market, just a few petits châteaux, with a 1987 Vieux-Château-Certan hitting the high note. A separate list of older clarets, including crus classés, is available. Burgundy is much more adventurous, with a few gems such as the wines of Emmanuel Rouget, nephew of now-retired Henri Jayer in Vosne-Romanée. Small producers, tiny quantities and moderate prices are the key to this section of the list. You will not go far wrong with other French wines, which again focus on small estates in the Loire and Rhône. The choice from the rest of the world is good. Italy provides Pieropan's Soave, Isole e Olena's Chianti and two delicious wines from Ornellaia; Australia, New Zealand, California and South Africa continue the good work. Free delivery of a mixed case throughout that big county of Yorkshire is an added bonus here at Nether Poppleton.

Best buys

Ch. de Violet 1991, Minervois, £
Ch. Castelneau Blanc 1992, Entre-Deux-Mers, £
Bourgogne Passe-Tout-Grains 1990, Rouget, ££
Sancerre 'Chavignol' 1992, Cotat, ££

Cachet Wines

Lysander Close, Clifton Moor, York, North   *Tel* (0904) 690090
Yorkshire YO3 4XB

Case sales only   Open Mon–Fri 9–5.30; Sat 9–12.30   **Closed** Sun, public holidays   **Credit cards** Access, Visa; business accounts   **Discounts** Not available **Delivery** Free in Yorkshire and Derbyshire (min 1 mixed case); elsewhere at cost **Glass hire** Free   **Tastings and talks** Three/four tastings per year (£7–£15 per person inc food)   **Cellarage** Not available

---

It is case sales only from this York-based merchant. Nevertheless, there is a good choice within the middle price range from most parts of the globe to fill your mixed case.

The New World pages have seen some work recently. From Australia there is the complete works from Yalumba as well as some from Montrose, Haughton and Balgownie Estate. California is represented by Fetzer and the Sanford Winery, and Chilean wines come from Viña Carmen, a second label of Santa Rita. Fairly new is a small range of South African wines from Simonsig Estate. Italy has Barolo from Giacomo Ascheri and the delicious Parrina from Tuscany. Spanish wines are mainly Riojas from CVNE and Martínez Bujanda.

France is still the major part of the list, focusing on small reliable producers. Clarets are grouped by vintage and nearly all are petits châteaux or crus bourgeois under £10, including the delicious Ch. Côtes Daugay from St-Emilion. The burgundies are mainly property wines from Domaine Parent, Vallet Frères and Domaine Jean Germain – an unusual wine is the Chardonnay de Jura from the latter. There is an interesting collection of wines from the South-West, including Clos Guirouilh from Jurançon, three good-value wines from Producteurs Plaimont and three from English winemaker Hugh Ryman.

We have had encouraging reports on the service at Cachet. Regular tastings and special offers keep customers informed about the range.

Best buys

Domaine de Galipouy 1992, Vin de Pays des Côtes de Gascogne, £
Domaine de la Fadèze Syrah 1991, Vin de Pays de l'Hérault, £
Taltarni Brut Taché nv, Australia, ££
Georges Gardet Brut Champagne nv, ££

Cairns & Hickey

17 Blenheim Terrace, Woodhouse Lane, Leeds, West Yorkshire LS2 9HN	*Tel* (0532) 459501
Outlet	
856 Leeds Road, Bramhope, Leeds, West Yorkshire LS16 9ED	*Tel* (0532) 673746

Open (Woodhouse Lane branch) Mon–Fri 9–6; Sat 9–1; Sun 9–1 in Dec; (Leeds Road branch) Mon–Sat 10–9; Sun 12–2, 7–9 **Closed** Sun, public holidays **Credit cards** Access, Visa; personal and business accounts **Discounts** 5% on 1 case **Delivery** Free within 40-mile radius of Leeds (min 1 case); mail order available **Glass hire** Free if collected and washed by customer **Tastings and talks** Annual customer tasting **Cellarage** £3 per case per year

Cairns Junior has taken over some of the buying this year and the range is all the better for it. Lots of new faces crop up, particularly from the New World, such as Roo's Leap and Jamieson's Run from Australia, and Cooper's Creek from New Zealand. But there is still room for improvement. The Italian section remains rather bland and California is restricted to the good-value Sutter Home Winery – eminently drinkable but hardly top drawer.

Better news comes from the Spanish section, where Torres, Murrieta and Rioja Alta provide big, reliable flavours; Chile has Villard and Viña Linderos.

From France there is the usual range of standards. Clarets include some classy names but still manage a few affordable choices. Burgundies are mainly from Chanson, Louis Latour and Bouchard Père. Alsace is exclusively Dopff and Irion.

As with any merchant, it is always worth checking out prices before you buy.

Best buys

Señorio de Los Llaños Reserva 1987, Valdepeñas, £
Vin de Pays des Côtes de Gascogne 1992, Lou Magret, £
Cooper's Creek Sauvignon Blanc 1992, New Zealand, ££
Fleurie, Domaine de la Presle 1992, ££

Cantina Augusto

91–95 Clerkenwell Road, London EC1R 5BX   *Tel* 071-242 3246

Open Mon–Thur 9–6; Fri 9–6.30; Sat 9.30–12.30   **Closed** Sun, public holidays
Credit cards Access, Visa; personal and business accounts
Discounts Approximately 10% on 1 case   **Delivery** Free in central London for orders over £50; otherwise £5 delivery charge; mail order available
Glass hire Free with order   **Tastings and talks** In-store tastings Fri lunchtimes (during most of year)   **Cellarage** Not available

Cantina Augusto sounds like an Italian specialist but in fact the range is much broader than that. Good clarets and burgundies, a few Spanish wines – all well chosen – and a selection of Australians from Chapel Hill, Cape Mentelle and Wolf Blass give this list a well-managed, enthusiastic feel. This year there is an increased range from South Africa, Romania and Chile.

But Italy is the main focus of the list, which is now arranged region by region. From the top of Italy to its toe, it gathers together some of the best flavours that this fascinating country offers. There are some unusual names such as Refosco and Picolit from Venezia, Inferno from Lombardy and Per'e Palummo from Ischia, but there are well-known, reliable names too. Antinori, Prunotto, Tedeschi and Lungarotti give weight and style to this interesting list.

Regular tastings add to the attractions here.

Best buys

Cabernet Sauvignon nv, Murfatlar, Romania, £
Chianti Colli Fiorentini 1991, Tenuta Lanciola, £
Gattinara Numerata 1985, Travaglini, ££
Terrici 1988, Guarnieri, ££

Cape Province Wines

1 The Broadway, Kingston Road, Staines,   *Tel* (0784) 451860/455244
Middlesex TW18 1AT

Open Mon–Sat 9–9 **Closed** Sun, public holidays **Credit cards** Access, Visa
Discounts On South African wines collected from stores **Delivery** £5.75 per
consignment in London; otherwise £5.90 for 1 case, £5.45 per case on 2–5 cases,
£4.90 per case on 6+ cases **Glass hire** Free with order **Tastings and talks** In-
store tastings **Cellarage** Not available

Through all the threatened sanctions and general public
opposition to South Africa, Cape Province Wines' managing
director Peter Loose battled on, stocking the good wines of the
region. Now, as that country emerges from its political isolation,
so interest in the wines is growing.

The shop claims to have one of the biggest ranges of Cape
wines outside South Africa. This is difficult to check out but the
list extends to 150 and there are a few more available in
quantities too small to include. The real gems are the estate
wines, with names such as Meerlust, Fairview, Neethlingshof
and Twee Jongegezellen. It will take some time before the
drinking public becomes familiar with these strange names and
spellings, but in wine-quality terms the potential is there for
South Africa once again to become a leading light in the world
of wine.

The Nederburg annual auction is a major event and Peter
Loose goes there each year to buy some unusual and rare wines
for his shop – wines such as the Nederburg Private Bins and
the sweet wine Edelkeur. If you are interested in these
specialities ask for the separate list. Generally, prices for South
African wines are still very reasonable. This could be the right
time to try a few.

Wines are available by the single bottle at the shop and by
the mixed case by mail order.

Best buys

Nederburg Sauvignon Blanc 1991, £
Nederburg Baronne 1988, £
Neethlingshof Cabernet Sauvignon 1988, ££
Laborie Blanc de Noirs, Sparkling Wine, ££

A 125ml glass of wine, a 170ml glass of sherry and half a pint of beer
all contain approximately the same amount of alcohol called a 'unit'.
The Health Education Authority's recommendations for sensible
drinking limits are 21 units per week for men and 14 units per week
for women.

A Case of Wine ('Pigs 'n' Piglets')

Harford, Pumpsaint, Llanwrda, Dyfed *Tel* (05585) 671
SA19 8DT

Open Mon–Sat 9–9 **Credit cards** Access, Visa **Discounts** 2.5% on 1 unmixed
case (payment by cash/collected from shop) **Delivery** Free in Dyfed (min 1
case) **Glass hire** Free with order; breakages charged for
Tastings and talks Tastings on Mons in next-door restaurant; to groups on
request **Cellarage** Charges by arrangement

The story behind the 'Pigs 'n' Piglets' sous-name of this
company is fairly long and complicated but, since no one forgets
a name like that, proprietors Jennifer Taylor and Aldo
Steccanella have decided to stick with it. This is a young
business adjacent to an Italian restaurant run by the same
people. The range is gradually changing, with Italy becoming a
bigger force, while still retaining a healthy selection from
elsewhere.

France kicks off with an affordable range of clarets, followed
by a limited selection from Burgundy, the Loire and Rhône.
Most notable from France is the splendid variety of regional
wines such as Mas de Daumas Gassac and Mas de Gourgonnier.

Italy runs to three pages and the aim is to become an Italian
specialist without losing the rest of the range. So far, there is a
fine Tuscan selection, good Barolos and a collection of whites
from producers such as Pieropan, Puiatti and Ca' dei Frati.

Australia includes big-flavoured Shiraz wines from Mount
Langi Ghiran and St Hallett. Spanish wines come mainly from
Bodegas Navajas and there is local interest with Croffta from
neighbouring Glamorgan. Organic wine is taken seriously, with
a separate listing for around 20 wines.

A mail-order operation is at the planning stages but,
meanwhile, you have to live within Dyfed to take advantage of
this tasteful range. Olive oils and assorted Italian specialities are
also available.

Best buys

Salice Salentino Riserva 1988, Candido, £
Barbera d'Asti 'Ceppi Storici' 1990, Cantina Nizza di
Monferrato, £
Poggia alle Gazze, Antinori 1991, ££
Cepparello 1989, Isole e Olena, ££

Cellar 5

Head office
China Lane, Warrington, Cheshire WA4 6RT   *Tel* (0925) 444555
493 branches

Open Mon–Sat 10–10; Sun and public holidays 12–2, 7–10 (with some local variations) **Closed** Chr Day **Credit cards** Access, Visa; personal and business accounts **Discounts** 5% on 1 case; negotiable on larger orders **Delivery** Free from selected branches (generally within a 5-mile radius) **Glass hire** Free with order **Tastings and talks** Upon application **Cellarage** Not available

With around 500 shops in the north of England, this could be one of the major names in wine, but it isn't. The range is strictly limited according to the grade of shop, and only the top 70 shops get anything like a decent selection. Berkeley Wines is the name given to the top handful of shops and here there is a reasonable choice.

The range includes some clarets – Ch. Monbousquet from St-Emilion and the reliable Ch. Cissac among them. There are quite a few burgundies, although the all-important producers' names were missing from our list. Other highlights include Campo Viejo Rioja and Chianti from Ricasoli. Australia is represented by Mitchelton, Lindemans and Coldridge; other producers are Christian Brothers from California, Errazuriz Panquehue from Chile and Bodegas Weinert from Argentina.

It is a shame that these few good wines are presently stocked by only a handful of shops within the Cellar 5 group. Come on Cellar 5 customers, the range is there, demand it in your local shop.

Best buys

Christian Brothers Zinfandel 1986, California, £
Coldridge Estate Semillon/Chardonnay nv, Australia, £
Ch. Haut-Marbuzet 1988, St-Estèphe, ££
Mitchelton Reserve Chardonnay 1988, Australia, ££

The Celtic Vintner

73 Derwen Fawr Road, Sketty, Swansea,   *Tel* (0792) 206661
West Glamorgan SA2 8DR

Case sales only **Open** Mon–Fri 9–5.30; Sat by arrangement **Closed** Sun, public holidays **Credit cards** Personal and business accounts **Discounts** Negotiable for quantity discounts **Delivery** Free in south and south-west Wales (min 5 cases unless on regular delivery run); elsewhere at cost **Glass hire** Free (refundable deposit) **Tastings and talks** Large annual tasting in Swansea; to groups on request **Cellarage** Possible

This company has been acquired by Stedman Ltd, a family-run wholesaler in Caerleon and, while the stock is now at its new home, orders will continue to be taken in Swansea by the old team of Brian Johnson and his daughter Clare Croft. They will both have a lot more time to devote to selecting and extending the range of wines.

The range has all the hallmarks of being a personal selection of wines, with quality and individuality the main considerations. From Australia, there are wines from Hardy and Yalumba, but, in addition, there is a liberal sprinkling of small producers such as Coldstream Hills, Moss Wood and Fermoy Estate. New Zealand follows suit with Palliser and Vavasour adding to the Selak's selection. South Africa has seen a rapid expansion with wines from Klein Constantia, Nederburg and Fairview Estate. Argentina provides the full-flavoured wines of Bodegas Weinert.

From France there is a fine selection of wines from traditional areas, but the Loire and southern France are particular specialities. Chais Baumière from the south produces French wine in the Australian style; Château Baudare and the Hugh Ryman range both provide good flavours at reasonable prices.

Best buys

Ch. Bauduc 1990, Entre-Deux-Mers, £
CUNE Tinto 1990, Rioja, £
Jacksons Sauvignon Blanc 1992, New Zealand, ££
Cabernet Sauvignon Bodegas Weinert 1983, Argentina, ££

A man may surely be allowed to take a glass of wine by his own fireside.

Sheridan (on being encountered drinking a glass of wine in the street, watching his theatre, the Drury Lane, burn down)

The Champagne House

Office only
15 Dawson Place, London W2 4TH   *Tel* 071-221 5538

Case sales only **Open** Mon–Thur 9–6 **Closed** Fri–Sun, public holidays, Sept and early Jan **Credit cards** None accepted **Discounts** Available **Delivery** Free in Kensington & Chelsea, Westminster and City of London and for orders of 4+ cases; otherwise at cost **Glass hire** Not available **Tastings and talks** On an occasional basis for established customers **Cellarage** Not available

'Has champagne become too expensive?' asks Richard Freeman of the Champagne House. 'Quite simply, yes,' is the answer he gives himself. He then goes on to give a summary of the state of the market and the way forward – quality.

The Champagne House specialises in just that one product – champagne – and it is commendable that it has survived the boom and the subsequent fall in popularity that champagne has suffered.

The list is well put together; an overview of the region, a summary of the process, profiles of the producers and statements about how the Champagne House selects its range. It is really quite substantial. The vintage champagnes and specialities are largely from the major houses such as Bollinger, Pol Roger, Krug and Roederer. It is in the non-vintage range that small family producers appear, names such as Albert le Brun, Barnaut and Selosse. Here is the chance to taste wines not found on many shelves. Prices for this range seem reasonable as far as champagne prices go. For the better-known names, they are roughly the same as those found elsewhere.

Best buys

Richard Freeman declined to indicate that any of his wines were of better value than others. 'The whole purpose of the Champagne House is to list wines which we are totally happy with.'

Châteaux Wines

(Not a shop)
11 Church Street, Bishop's Lydeard,   *Tel* (0454) 613959
Taunton, Somerset TA4 3AT

Case sales only **Open** Mon–Fri 9–5.30; Sat 9–12.30 (most Sats) **Closed** Sun,
public holidays **Credit cards** Access, Delta, Visa; personal and business accounts
Discounts Available **Delivery** Free on UK mainland (min 1 case); mail order
available **Glass hire** Not available **Tastings and talks** Annual tasting and lunch
in London **Cellarage** £4.33 per case per year (inc insurance)

Service and value for money are the features that David Miller
and wife Cheryl aim to offer with their range from Châteaux
Wines, a small operation run from home.

The list is essentially French with just a handful from
Australia, New Zealand and Lebanon. Another major feature of
the list is that it is like looking at somebody else's holiday
snaps. On almost every page there is a beaming David (DGM),
wife (CM) and assorted growers. But enough of the pictures,
what of the wines?

Clarets are the affordable kind. They start with basic Bordeaux
Supérieur, and then rise in gentle steps through petits châteaux,
Potensac, Cissac, Chasse-Spleen and up to la Lagune. These are
arranged in price order rather than by vintage. There is a
vintage guide at the back of the list but it might be more
helpful to indicate drinkability alongside the wines.

Burgundy vintages are also confusing but the wines look
good. Growers such as Ampeau, Yves Rossignol and Simonnet
feature here. There is a single Rhône wine, a Muscadet, a special
page devoted to two wines from Ch. Pierrail in Bordeaux and
four Alsace wines which appear to come from the co-operative
at Orschwiller.

From further afield, Ch. Musar in Lebanon rates special
treatment. There are six vintages listed plus another eight
vintages which are not priced. New Zealand features wines
from Lincoln Vineyards, with a particularly good Cabernet/
Merlot. Australia provides a selection from Rosemount,
including the single vineyard Roxburgh Chardonnay.

Best buys

Domaine des Garrigues 1992, Côtes-du-Rhône, £
Juliénas 'Les Envaux' 1991, Pelletier, ££
Chablis 1991, Simonnet-Febvre, ££

Chard Fine Wines

See Abbey Cellars

Chennell & Armstrong

Manor Lane, Shipton Road, York, North
Yorkshire YO3 6TX

Tel (0904) 647991

Case sales only **Open** Mon–Fri 8–5 **Closed** Sat, Sun, public holidays
Credit cards None accepted; personal and business accounts
Discounts Available **Delivery** Free within Yorkshire (min 1-case order);
elsewhere by arrangement; mail order available **Glass hire** Free; breakages
charged for **Tastings and talks** Two annual tastings in May and Sept
Cellarage Not available

There is a strong trade-only feel about the Chennell &
Armstrong list – with ex-VAT prices and hefty discounts if you
buy 100 cases or more. Even so, we are assured that the private
customer is welcomed and gets a good deal here. Good service
is the key, we are told, and this includes decanting your vintage
port for you.

Claret is a speciality: there is a long list of vintages and bottle
sizes. The rest of France is fairly classic, although Alsace looks a
little sparse. Traditional German wines still seem popular, and a
1976 Riesling Beerenauslese appears on the list at a very
reasonable price. Australian wines hinge on a selection from
Best's, with a few from Penfolds and Brown Brothers to add
variety. Champagne includes the delicious Barancourt range.

Mixed cases are available, presumably at no extra cost, but
there is also a small range of tasting cases arranged around
different themes. Delivery is free for one case within Yorkshire;
outside that area costs begin to climb.

Best buys

Best's Victoria Colombard 1993, £
Domaine de Bose-Long Gaillac Rouge 1991, £
Best's Great Western Shiraz 1989, Australia, ££
Best's Great Western Chardonnay 1989, Australia, ££

---

*By insisting on having your bottle pointing to the north when the cork is
being drawn, and calling the waiter Max, you may induce an impression
on your guests which hours of laboured boasting might be powerless to
achieve. For this purpose, however, the guests must be chosen as carefully
as the wine.*

Saki (Hector Hugo Munro), *The Chaplet*

Chippendale Fine Wines

15 Manor Square, Otley, West Yorkshire   *Tel* (0943) 850633
LS21 3AP

Open Mon–Tue, Thur–Fri 10–5.45; Sat 9.30–5   **Closed** Wed, Sun and public
holidays   **Credit cards** Access, Visa; personal and business accounts
Discounts 5% on mixed and unmixed cases   **Delivery** Free within 3-mile radius
of Otley, and within 15-mile radius of Otley for orders of 6+ bottles; elsewhere at
cost   **Glass hire** Free (min order 6 bottles); 75p charge per breakage
Tastings and talks Free in-store tastings (Sat); 2 major tastings in May/October by
invitation only   **Cellarage** Not available

Just in case you were wondering, this company is named after
the master furniture maker, Thomas Chippendale, who was
born in Otley; it does not refer to the group of American
beefcakes who take their clothes off for a living! Not that
proprietor Michael Pollard isn't entertaining in his own way.
Send for a list, settle down with a glass of wine and prepare to
be amused. There are tirades against the government, the
economy, the EC and travel writers, all best read in a deliberate,
dry, Yorkshire tone.

And what of the wines? For a fairly new company (just three
years old), surprisingly good. Australia is a speciality with an
increased selection this year. The range is focused on a few
really good growers, including Adam Wynn with his
Mountadam range, the David Wynn label and the organic Eden
Ridge wines. Tim Adams is a newcomer with his terrific Shiraz,
and Peter Lehmann, Normans and Pikes add more variety. The
New Zealand range includes Martinborough and Babich;
Californians are from Newton.

French treats include Domaine de la Bon Gran from Jean
Thévenet, a compact selection of petits châteaux from Bordeaux
and a terrific range of regional French wines which could keep
Otley drinkers busy for a few weekends. More expensive clarets,
burgundies and Rhônes are available for special occasions. Most
other regions are represented by a few wines; each producer,
wine and even the state of the market are commented on in
Mike Pollard's inimitable style.

With reasonable prices and free in-store tastings every
Saturday, Chippendale seems to have carved a niche in this
Otley market.

Best buys

Les Terrasses de Guilhem 1992, Vin de Pays de l'Hérault, £
Periquita 1989, Fonseca, £
Pikes Polish Hill River Estate Shiraz 1992, Australia, ££
Mas de Daumas Gassac Blanc 1991, Vin de Pays de l'Hérault, ££

Christchurch Fine Wine

1–3 Vine Lane, High Street, Christchurch,   *Tel* (0202) 473255
Dorset BH23 1AB

Open Tues 10–1; Fri 10–6; Sat 10–5   **Closed** Sun, Mon, Wed, Thur, public
holidays   **Credit cards** Access, Visa; personal and business accounts
Discounts 5% on 1+ case to Club members   **Delivery** Free within 10-mile radius
of Christchurch (min order 1 case); mail order available   **Glass hire** Free with
order   **Tastings and talks** 9 tastings per year for club members   **Cellarage** Free for
2 years to customers

There is no better place for a wine business than Vine Lane. No
vines there now, just lots of super wines in a former stable and
coach-house in the centre of Christchurch. The business is run
by former restaurateur John Carter and this list has a definite
'good restaurant' feel about it.

France is the main area of interest. Clarets tend to be biased
towards the £20-plus bracket, with Latour, Mouton, Lafite and
Margaux heading the classed growths. Older vintages are
scattered throughout the list: a clutch of 1966 wines, some 1970s
and a few from the 1950s. The Sauternes are a delight, with
older vintages including a 1966 Yquem for a mere £126.

Red burgundies are mainly from Prosper Maufoux and his
sous-marque Marcel Amance, and there are some splendid whites
from Louis Latour. Particularly interesting is a collection of
wines from the Hospices de Beaune. The Rhône and Loire
wines are good – with Chave's Hermitage and Clos les Perrières
Sancerre from Vatan. These sections also provide plenty of
'drinking' wines as well as special-occasion bottles. Two wines
from the Savoie are a pleasant distraction from the classic areas
and a big collection of German wines, many from Wegeler-
Deinhard, rounds off the list.

Tastings are a feature at Christchurch. Membership of the
Wine Club costs £5 and entitles you to a 5 per cent discount on
purchases of five or more cases a year. The shop is well laid out
but the list takes some getting used to – it is close-typed and
has no clear groupings within a region. A few tasting notes
might help too.

Best buys

Côtes du Roussillon Rouge 1991, Villeneuve, £
Côtes-du-Rhone Blanc 1992, Brunel, £
Sauvignon de St-Bris 1990, Lamblin, ££
Vieux Château Chambeau 1989, St-Emilion, ££

City Wines

221 Queens Road, Bracondale, Norwich, Norfolk NR1 3AE	*Tel* (0603) 617967
305 Aylsham Road, Norwich, Norfolk NR3 2RY	*Tel* (0603) 405705

Open Mon–Sat 9–9; Sun and public holidays 12–2, 7–9 **Closed** Chr Day, Boxing Day **Credit cards** Access, American Express, Visa; personal and business accounts **Discounts** 5% on 1 case **Delivery** Free in Norwich (min 1 case); elsewhere at cost; mail order available **Glass hire** Free
Tastings and talks Available on request **Cellarage** Not available

'Great Wine is a Work of Art,' declares the City Wines list and, while we agree with this sentiment, the wines in this collection are less National Gallery standard and more the kind of thing you can enjoy without worrying about the price. The range is not huge but has been assembled with care and shows a clear intention to provide positive, reliable flavours for less than £10.

Australia merits a fairly large section with good-value, well-made wines from Hardy, Brown Brothers and Penfolds. Lindemans and Rosemount make an appearance, too. The New Zealand list is limited to Montana and we are told that there is increasing interest in South Africa. So far only four KWV wines are listed, but more are on their way.

France provides a reasonable selection of drinkable clarets but burgundy does not really go much beyond generics. French regional wines are a strong point, with good Corbières, Cahors and Madiran. Sweet wines are collected together and include Australians, Californians and a choice of Tokajis, as well as an interesting pair of Jurançon wines from Domaine Cauhapé.

City claims to give excellent service to its customers. Can readers confirm this?

Best buys

Ch. Bastide Durand 1990, Corbières, £
Taichat 1992, Côtes du Roussillon Réserve, £
Finages Monopole nv, Vin de Table, ££
Ch. Peyros 1986, Madiran, ££

Classic Wine Warehouses

Unit A2, Stadium Industrial Estate,   *Tel* (0244) 390444
Sealand Road, Chester, Cheshire CH1 4LU

Open Mon–Fri 7.45–6; Sat 9–5   **Closed** Sun, public holidays   **Credit cards** All
accepted; personal and business accounts   **Discounts** Negotiable   **Delivery** Free
nationwide (min 1 case); mail order available   **Glass hire** Free
Tastings and talks Bottles open on premises; occasional regional tastings
Cellarage Free

With John Lennon and James Dean as directors of this company
all they really need is Elvis to show up and sing a song or two
to make it truly an 'all-time classic'.

The majority of Classic's business is selling into the trade,
hence the VAT-exclusive list, but the company does have a
retail licence which means that you can pick up a single bottle
from the Unit A2 address. Champagne is a speciality, with
endless vintages and labels. France is fairly classic, with
burgundies from Drouhin, Bouchard Père and Faiveley. The
New World has Cooks and Stoneleigh from New Zealand,
Rosemount, Wolf Blass and Penfolds from Australia, lots of
Mondavi from California and Santa Rita from Chile.

There is a reasonable selection of half-bottles, particularly
among the champagnes. Classic hopes to move to a bigger
warehouse soon – check by phone before you set out.

Best buys

Domaine de la Hitaire 1991, Vin de Pays des Côtes de
Gascogne, £
Claret 'Louis XIV' nv, Nathaniel Johnson, £
Bourgogne 1990, 'Les Caves de la Tour Blondeau', Bouchard Père
et Fils, ££
Chapin Landais nv, Sparkling Saumur Rosé, ££

The Clifton Cellars

22 The Mall, Clifton, Bristol, Avon BS8 4DS   *Tel* (0272) 730287

Open Mon–Fri 9.30–6.30; Sat 9–6   **Closed** Sun, some public holidays
Credit cards Access, Visa; personal and business accounts   **Discounts** 5% on 1
unmixed case   **Delivery** Free within 20-mile radius of Bristol   **Glass hire** Free
Tastings and talks To groups on request   **Cellarage** £2.05 per case per year

Bristol is already home to two of the big names in wine – John
Harvey and Averys – but there is still room for this
independent merchant, Clifton Cellars. Founded just as long ago
as the big shots, the business is now in its second year under
Alan Wright and the range just keeps on growing.

Clarets are good, with most choice among the 1985 vintage, although there is a fair sprinkling from the 1970s. Burgundies are fewer in number, but Faiveley, Bouchard and Tollot-Beaut are among the high-class names here. Champagne appears to be a speciality, with 25 non-vintage and 17 vintage wines to choose from. Outside France, Spain looks impressive: Riojas from Muga, Contino and Berberana; Torres wines are a feature as well as the superb Cabernet Sauvignon from Marqués de Griñon. Portugal has a small but interesting collection; Italy is also worth taking some time over.

Germany might be worthy, but the pages of the list do not seem long enough to cope with the names of the producers. This is the only blot on an otherwise well-produced list. South Africa contains some interest from Neethlingshof, Backsberg and Overgaauw Estate. Australia now includes Mount Hurtle and Brown Brothers as well as Wyndham and Hunter Estate.

A spendid collection of half-bottles, plus sherries, ports and over 100 malt whiskies gives even more reasons to call in at this historic shop.

Best buys

Torres Coronas 1989, Penedès, Spain, £
Hill-Smith Cabernet Sauvignon 1991, Australia, £
Recioto della Valpolicella Amarone 1985, Tedeschi, Italy, ££
Ch. Musar 1981, Lebanon, ££

Colombier Vins Fins

Ryder Close, Cadley Hill Industrial Estate,   *Tel* (0283) 552552
Swadlincote, Burton on Trent, Derbyshire
DE11 9EU

Case sales only **Open** Mon–Fri 8.30–5; Sat on request **Closed** Sun, public holidays **Credit cards** None accepted; personal and business accounts **Discounts** 5% on 10 cases **Delivery** Free in Leicestershire, Birmingham, Nottingham, Northamptonshire, Peterborough, Lincolnshire and Derby; free elsewhere (min 5 cases); otherwise £9 per case **Glass hire** Free with orders **Tastings and talks** Organised tastings on premises every month **Cellarage** £3.80 per case per year (£7.60 if wine bought elsewhere)

Colombier has the feel of a trade-only wholesaler. There are three catalogues of varying delightful shades, one specially for Italy, another for the New World and one for everything else. All prices are given ex-VAT and we do wonder how well the occasional order for one mixed case is received.

The main catalogue starts off with France – the speciality here is small growers, many of whom are exclusive to Colombier.

Burgundy has a comprehensive range: a number of wines come through the French arm of Colombier which is based in the region. Bordeaux has a fine selection of classed growths and this year there is an increased choice of petits châteaux and crus bourgeois. The choice of Rhônes is fairly limited but the Loire expands to include four Bourgueils, a Saumur Champigny and two Chinons. The range from the South of France has increased a little this year.

The Italian collection rates a separate catalogue and is impressive – plenty to work through there. Piemonte wines come from Poderi Anselmi and Tuscan wines are from Avignonesi. The New World list has a wide selection from South Africa and a very limited Australian range, but it does include Garry Crittenden's Schinus Molle. A sprinkling from New Zealand, California, Chile and Israel rounds off the rest.

With such a heavy emphasis on ex-VAT prices and complicated lists we would be interested to find out from customers of Colombier just how easy it is to buy wine there.

Best buys

Ch. la Rose Chevrol 1989, Fronsac, £
Cannonau del Parteola 1988, Dolianova, Sardinia, £
Backsberg Estate Pinotage 1988, South Africa, ££
Rosso di Montepulciano 1989, Avignonesi, Italy, ££

Connolly's

Arch 13, 220 Livery Street, Birmingham,   *Tel* 021-236 9269
West Midlands B3 1EU

Open Mon–Fri 9–6.30; Sat 9–2 **Closed** Sun, public holidays **Credit cards** Access, American Express, Visa; personal and business accounts **Discounts** 10% on 1 case if collected **Delivery** Free within 15-mile radius of Birmingham (min 1 case); mail order available **Glass hire** Free with order **Tastings and talks** Two free major tastings per year; monthly tutored tastings; wine club **Cellarage** Not available

With a 'quantum leap forward', Chris Connolly has changed the style of his list and introduces it with a little ditty about Postman Pat. This may be too frivolous for some staid members of the drinking public, but at least he sounds as if he enjoys his job!

Why not club together with friends to enjoy volume discounts and free delivery?

His selection of wine is a fine mixture of new and old faces. Clarets come from well-known properties – Palmer, Angludet, Haut-Bages-Libéral and so on – in a variety of recent vintages. Burgundies are from Faiveley and Bouchard with a sprinkling from Robert Arnoux. French regionals are from small estates and apparently there are always a few extra lines available in the shop.

The Italian range has expanded this year and now includes Cappello di Prete from the south, Ascheri's Barolo and a good-value collection under the Via Nova label. Spain also looks after value with Don John, Agramont and Señorio de los Llanos, but then starts to climb with CUNE Riojas and a sizeable range from Torres. Australian wines include the super Mount Edelstone from Henschke and Pipers Brook from Tasmania. De Redcliffe is a new addition from New Zealand, while Fairview Estate from South Africa joins this well-chosen selection. A wide collection of malt whiskies rounds off the list. Monthly tutored tastings sound like good value and fun.

Best buys

Merlot del Veneto, Via Nova 1992, Italy, £
Pinotage, Fairview Estate 1990, South Africa, £
Grove Mill Sauvignon Blanc 1992, New Zealand, ££
Viña Ardanza 1985, La Rioja Alta, ££

Corney & Barrow

12 Helmet Row, London EC1V 3QJ	*Tel* 071-251 4051
194 Kensington Park Road, London W11 2ES	*Tel* 071-221 5122
Belvoir House, High Street, Newmarket,	*Tel* (0638) 662068
Suffolk CB8 8OH	

Open Mon–Fri 9–6; Sat 10.30–8 (Kensington) **Closed** Sat (City), Sun, public holidays **Credit cards** Access, Visa; personal and business accounts
Discounts Negotiable **Delivery** Free within London (min 2+ cases) and outside London (min 3+ cases); elsewhere £7 per delivery; mail order available
Glass hire Free (charged then credited on return) **Tastings and talks** Regular tastings; regular wine course; to groups on request **Cellarage** £4.95 per case per year

Any merchant who has been established since 1780 and is the proud holder of three royal warrants is bound to be a classy organisation. That much is obvious as soon as you get the list: a chunky publication with discreet gold-block lettering that would enhance anyone's social standing when left on a coffee table.

French wines start at the very top with Pétrus, expensive, exclusive and here in a variety of vintages going back to 1966. Corney & Barrow holds the UK agencies for all the wines of Ets. J J Moueix and so Pétrus is joined by other right-bank properties including La Fleur-Pétrus, Latour à Pomerol, Magdaleine and Trotanoy. Just in case millionaire customers prefer burgundy, Corney & Barrow also handles the superb wines of Domaine de la Romanée-Conti. Ordinary mortals with smaller bank accounts might feel intimidated by all this but there is no need. Refreshingly, right at the front of the list are sections with wines under £5 and under £10. There is also a fine selection of French Regional Wines and all the petit-château wines from J P Moueix, most of them under £7. The rest of France has been selected with care, with Rhônes from Jaboulet, Alsace wines from Cattin and Heydt, and a delicious selection of domaine burgundies.

Customers here are clearly Francophiles, but Spain, Italy, North and South America are all acknowledged with quality, reliable wines. From Coonawarra in Australia comes the rather exclusive Parker Estate and New Zealand provides Aotea, Palliser and Cloudy Bay.

In the City, Corney & Barrow has a string of wine bars, including the champagne bar at Lloyds. The West London shop is also allowed a few little luxuries which don't feature on the main list, such as a few more Italians and a wider choice of New World wines, as well as excellent olive oils. Downstairs is 'The Strongroom' where treasures such as 50 vintages of armagnac, 36 vintages of assorted claret and the occasional jeroboam of Pétrus may be found.

The mail-order operation works from the Helmet Row offices. A separate company, Corney & Barrow Broker Services, can arrange to sell any surplus wines you bought here and still have in store at the warehouse.

Best buys

Corney & Barrow's House Claret, £
Merlot, Domaine de Puget 1991, Vin de Pays de l'Aude, £
Ch. Richotey, Fronsac Ets. 1989, J P Moueix, ££
Parker Estate Terra Rossa Cabernet Sauvignon 1989, Coonawarra, ££

'Have some wine,' the March Hare said in an encouraging tone. Alice looked all round the table, but there was nothing on it but tea. 'I don't see any wine,' she remarked. 'There isn't any,' said the March Hare.

Lewis Carroll, *Alice's Adventures in Wonderland*

Cornwall Wine Merchants

Chapel Road, Tuckingmill, Camborne, *Tel* (0209) 715765
Cornwall TR14 8QY

Case sales only Open Mon–Fri 9–1, 2–5; Sat 10–1 **Closed** Sun
Credit cards Access, Visa; personal and business accounts **Discounts** Quantity
discounts **Delivery** Free locally; elsewhere at cost; mail order available
Glass hire Free to customers **Tastings and talks** Regular tutored tastings; bottles
open on premises **Cellarage** Available

They have a big new sign saying Wine-By-The-Case here in
Tuckingmill, but this is really an office where you place your
order and your case is assembled downstairs. A new list with
VAT-inclusive prices helps to make this merchant a little more
user-friendly.

The range is good, with a reasonable collection from
Bordeaux. Burgundy shows enthusiasm, with wines from Louis
Latour and Chablis from William Fèvre. There is a full range
from Antinori in the Italian section, and from Chile, the wines
of Concha y Toro take the spotlight. Australian wines include an
interesting range from Basedow, Willespie and McGuigan. A big
range of Bulgarians gives easy drinking at value prices.

Best buys

Jarrah Ridge Shiraz/Cabernet 1991, South Eastern Australia, £
Rioja Crianza Conde Albalat Guia Real 1989, £
Willespie Margaret River Verdelho 1990, Western Australia, ££
Monbazillac Tête de Cuvée 1989, Domaine de Chantalouette, ££

Côte d'Or Wines

88 Pitshanger Lane, London W5 1QX *Tel* 081-998 0144

Open Mon–Tue and Thur–Sat 9.30–6 (Thur, Fri till 8) **Closed** Wed, Sun, public
holidays **Credit cards** Access, Visa; personal and business accounts
Discounts 5% on 1 unmixed case; negotiable on larger orders **Delivery** Free to
south-east England (min order 1 case); elsewhere at cost; mail order available
Glass hire Free with order **Tastings and talks** To groups on request
Cellarage £3 per case per year

There is a pleasant round-the-world selection from Gavin
Whitmee of Ealing-based Côte d'Or Wines. Despite the name,
there is no particular focus on Burgundy; if anything, Bordeaux
is more of a speciality with a good range of petit château wines
and some top-notch 1983 clarets. From the rest of the world
there is a sprinkling of everything, although it wouldn't take
more than a few weekends in Ealing to run through most of the

range. Spain has some good Riojas, and Italy provides Chiantis from Antinori and Ricasoli. Seppelts and Orlando from Australia, and Stoneleigh from New Zealand add to the variety.

A new idea is a 'Gourmet Club' with regular tastings, including food. These look fun and are reasonably priced.

Best buys

Côtes-du-Rhône, Le Mistral 1990, £
Cuvée Jean Paul Vin de Table, £
Stoneleigh Sauvignon Blanc 1992, New Zealand, ££
Magenta Champagne nv, ££

County Wines of Hagley

2 The Mews, Hagley Hall, Stourbridge, West   *Tel* (0562) 882346
Midlands DY9 9LG

Open Mon–Fri 9–5.30; Sat 10–4   **Closed** Sun, public holidays
Credit cards Access, Visa; personal and business accounts   **Discounts** Between 5% and 10% depending on volume   **Delivery** Free in Midlands area (min order 1 case); elsewhere £7.50   **Glass hire** Free   **Tastings and talks** Monthly themed programme of tastings (Sats)   **Cellarage** Not available

There is a short, select range from this company operating from the mews at Hagley Hall. Clarets remain in the affordable petit-château category, apart from a solitary Lafite 1978 which looks almost out of place. Red burgundies are from reliable *négociants* such as Faiveley and Chauvenet, and whites come from Domaine Laroche. Beaujolais gets a good airing, but the Rhône has not yet been fully explored. Alsace wines are from quality producers Dopff & Irion.

This year, the selections from Spain and Italy look rather forlorn with just a handful of wines from each. Chile has a new range from Torres and there are new Australian wines from Oakwood, as well as the Rosemount Show Reserve wines.

This list would not hold the attention of an adventurous wine drinker for too long, but the selection is sound, although it would be nice to see a few more producers' names included, particularly in the Italian and German sections. A wine club operates with regular tastings which are based around a particular theme.

Best buys

House Claret, Beau Rivage, Borie-Manoux, £
Domaine de Valmagne Cabernet Sauvignon 1990, Languedoc, £
Grove Mill Sauvignon Blanc 1993, New Zealand, ££
Ch. Lamothe 1989, Premières Côtes de Bordeaux, ££

Croque-en-Bouche

221 Wells Road, Malvern Wells, Hereford & Worcester WR14 4HF

Tel (0684) 565612

Case sales only **Open** Any reasonable time, by arrangement
Credit cards Access, Visa **Discounts** 4% on 4+ cases (cash/cheque and collect)
Delivery Free locally (min 2 cases); elsewhere £5 on orders of £350+; mail order available **Glass hire, tastings and talks** Not available **Cellarage** Short term only

Like a good deed in a naughty world the Croque-en-Bouche wine-list shines out with beacon brightness for sheer mouthwatering variety. If you plan to eat at this restaurant, since that is what it is, then you will need to allow an hour or two to read through all 1000 wines. The list comes complete with hand-drawn maps and sensible tasting notes and you can even buy a take-home version so you can plan ahead for your next visit.

But this is not a restaurant guide, so why is this establishment included? The simple reason is that if you like the wine you had with dinner, you can buy a case to take home. Prices are discounted by a set amount, £4 off for bottles up to £10, £5 for bottles up to £20, and so on. New this year is proprietor Robin Jones' first attempt at a comprehensive retail list, but he also has a heavily pruned version for customers who are short of reading time.

The choice here is amazing. The Rhône is a particular speciality and rates its own additional list. Where else can you get Côte Rôtie from a choice of growers such as Jasmin, Gentaz-Dervieux and Guigal across 12 vintages? Hermitages spill down the page – Chave, Jaboulet, Guigal and Chapoutier – again in vintage after vintage. Each section introduces the growers and their styles.

The clarets run to 12 pages, while red burgundies are comparatively sparse on only six. All the classic areas are comprehensively covered with wines from the best growers and vintages; this is the kind of list to get lost in. But New World areas are here as well. California takes in Mondavi, Au Bon Climat, Phelps, Simi and many more. Australia majors in the great wines from Henschke, Penfolds and Parker, but is not too proud to include the very drinkable and reasonable Jacob's Creek.

A new departure for this business is to break into the rich seam of young wines that have been maturing gently behind the scenes here in Malvern Wells. Yet another list is being prepared for retail sales.

Sales are by the case, which can be mixed. If you have trouble choosing your wines, at least you can get a meal while you make up your mind!

Best buys

Coddington Vineyard Bacchus 1990, England, £
Señorio de Los Llanos Gran Reserva 1984, Valdepeñas, £
Kumeu River Chardonnay 1991, New Zealand, ££
Hogue Cellars Cabernet 1987, Washington State, ££

Cumbrian Cellar

1 St Andrew's Square, Penrith, Cumbria   *Tel* (0768) 63664
CA11 7AN

Open Mon–Sat 9–5.30   **Closed** Sun, Chr Day, Boxing Day, Good Friday
Credit cards Access, Visa; personal and business accounts   **Discounts** 5% on 1
mixed case   **Delivery** Free in Cumbria (min 1 case); mail order available
Glass hire Free with order   **Tastings and talks** Bottles available on premises from
time-to-time; to groups on request   **Cellarage** Not available

---

A wide range is available for Penrith drinkers at the Cumbrian Cellars. Ex-RAF navigator Kenneth Gear has steered his way around the wine world, collecting examples from Peru, Brazil, China and Russia, as well as from the more classic regions. Australia is a special interest with a complete range from Rosemount and wines from Orlando, Seppelt and Houghton. Bosanquet Estate wines from the Southern Vales provide even more variety. Italy includes the standard names, with interest added by Venegazzù and Teroldego, and Chiantis from Rocca delle Macie and Ricasoli. France is handled competently, but it seems that the residents of Penrith do not go in for classy clarets or expensive burgundies. There are a few organic wines, including Bossard's Blanc de Blancs. Sales of sherry in this area, bucking national trends, are booming. The range includes Valdespino, Williams & Humbert and Burdon, whose Heavenly Cream probably goes down a treat when the westerlies are blowing a gale.

The emphasis in this little shop is on drinkable wines at reasonable prices, which is as good a reason as any to navigate your way here.

Best buys

Barramundi Shiraz/Merlot nv, South-East Australia, £
Cismeira Douro Red 1990, £
Ch. Musar 1986, Lebanon, ££
Muscat de Frontignan, Ch. de la Peyrade, ££

Davisons Wine Merchants

Head office
7 Aberdeen Road, Croydon, Surrey CR0 1EQ   *Tel* 081-681 3222
79 branches in London and South-East

Open Generally Mon–Sat 10–2, 5–10; Sun 12–2, 7–9; public holidays 10–2,
5–10 **Credit cards** Access, Visa **Discounts** 8.5% on full or mixed cases
Delivery Free locally (min 1 case); otherwise charges by arrangement; mail order
available **Glass hire** Free with order **Tastings and talks** Tastings in-store
Cellarage Not available

Davisons is a familiar sight on local shopping parades in the
Home Counties, but to think of this chain as just another 'offie'
would be a mistake. On the shelves is a good round-the-world
range with particular strengths in Bordeaux, burgundy and port.
Most of these classic wines were bought *en primeur* and prices

are generally fair or, indeed, very fair. If you are thinking of investing in a few bottles of claret it would be wise to check out the price on the Davisons list before you buy. Mixed cases qualify for an additional 8.5 per cent discount which makes some of the fine wine prices unbeatable. From Bordeaux there are over 120 châteaux wines, dating from 1989 back to 1966, including some interesting second wines from Ducru-Beaucaillou and Beychevelle. Davisons is also one of the few high-street shops where you can get a good bottle of Sauternes (often Rieussec) at a moment's notice. Friendly staff will even chill bottles ready for collection later.

Burgundies are from individual growers such as Machard de Gramont, Pavelot and Jean Grivot. Still on the classic wines, the range of vintage ports is terrific: all the major names and lots of vintages going back to 1963. Not every shop has every wine from this range but you will certainly find a few gems on the racks and others can be ordered.

Outside these areas the Davisons range is less exciting. Rhônes are lumped together with French country wines; there is only one Châteauneuf-du-Pape and no Hermitage. Loires, too, are fairly predictable. If Davisons stores can sell classed growths, couldn't they also try a Bourgueil or Chinon? The Chilean range is short but includes the lovely Montes wines; Australia has seen some work this year and now includes Penfolds, Rothbury, Cape Mentelle and Krondorf.

Under the same parent company as Davisons is the Master Cellar Wine Warehouse in Croydon. It operates from the same list but, being a warehouse, has considerably more stock available. In addition, manager Keith Nanson buys a few extras, such as the Super Tuscans Sassicaia, Tignanello and Ornellaia, and Barolos from Prunotto. A retail licence at this warehouse means that you can buy single bottles as well as by the case.

Best buys

Cape Cellars Colombard 1992, South Africa, £
Terras d'El Rei Tinto 1991, Portugal, £
Bricco Mileui, Vino da Tavola 1990, Matteu Ascheri, Italy, ££
Wirra Wirra Church Block 1990, Australia, ££

Come, Come; good wine is a good familiar creature if it be well used; exclaim no more against it.

Shakespeare, *Othello*

Dennhöfer Wines

47 Bath Lane, Newcastle upon Tyne,   *Tel* 091-232 7342
Tyne & Wear NE4 5SP

Open Mon–Fri 8.30–5.30; Sat 9.30–1.30   **Closed** Sun, public holidays
Credit cards Access, Visa; personal and business accounts   **Discounts** Not
available **Delivery** Free locally (min 1 case); elsewhere at cost **Glass hire** Free
with order **Tastings and talks** Available **Cellarage** Free

There's a reasonably well-balanced selection from this merchant,
with a slight emphasis on Germany but still plenty to choose
from other areas. Bordeaux takes in a quick round-up of cru
bourgeois and classier clarets, while the burgundies indicate
sound buying with names such as Alain Geoffroy and Domaine
Laroche. The Loire and Rhône are adequate if not exciting.
Further afield, Italy is worth a browse with Chiantis from
Frescobaldi; Spain has Riojas from Bodegas Montecillo.
Delicious Pipers Brook from Tasmania adds to a limited
Australian selection. The two wines from Hamilton-Russell in
South Africa are well worth a try.

Best buys

Niersteiner Spiegelberg 1991, Riesling Kabinett, J Flick, £
Goundrey Langton Mount Barker Semillon/Sauvignon Blanc
1992, Western Australia, £
Fleurie 1991, Domaine de la Bouroniere, Lescure, ££
Mâcon-Vinzelles 1991, Cave des Grands Crus Blancs, ££

Rodney Densem Wines

Office
Stapeley Bank, London Road, Stapeley,
Nantwich, Cheshire CW5 7JW
Retail
4 Pillory Street, Nantwich, Cheshire
CW5 5BD

Tel (for both addresses)
(0270) 623665

Open Mon–Tue 10–6; Wed–Fri 9–6; Sat 9–5.30 **Closed** Sun, public holidays
Credit cards Access, Visa; personal and business accounts **Discounts** 5% on 1
mixed case **Delivery** Free within 25-mile radius (min 1 case); elsewhere
approximately £8 per case; mail order available **Glass hire** Free with order
Tastings and talks Available **Cellarage** Not available

A range 950-plus items strong is the claim for this retail shop,
while the wholesale business operates a more manageable
selection from nearby premises. A new feature this year is a
retail list to help those who are bewildered by the choice.

The southern hemisphere features strongly, with a good set of
Australians (Brown Brothers, Rosemount, Lindemans and
Hardy) and de Redcliffe Estates, Cooks and Cloudy Bay batting
for New Zealand. Chile is fairly sparse: just a few wines from
Torres.

In Europe, France holds most interest – clarets (mainly in the
affordable class) and a few special-occasion top-notes.
Burgundies are from a number of reliable *négociants*, Viénot and
Drouhin among them. With Pascal in the Rhône and a handful
of worthwhile vins de pays there is enough to keep the interest
going. One special feature is a separate section of wines priced
at £4 and under.

Education is taken seriously here, with even the delivery staff being encouraged to take Wine and Spirit Education Trust courses.

Best buys

Claret AC Bordeaux, Borie Manoux, £
Jarrah Ridge Semillon/Chardonnay 1992, South Australia, £
Ch. Lamothe 1988, 1er Cuvée, Premières Côtes de Bordeaux, ££
De Redcliffe Chardonnay 1989, New Zealand, ££

Direct Wine Shipments

5/7 Corporation Square, Belfast, Co Antrim   *Tel* (0232) 238700/243906
BT1 3AJ
Associated outlet
Duncairn Wines, 555 Antrim Road, Belfast,   *Tel* (0232) 370694
Co Antrim BT15 3BU

Open Mon–Sat 9.30–6 (5pm on Sat, 8pm on Thur)   **Closed** Sun, Chr for 3 days, Easter for 2 days, 12–13 July   **Credit cards** Access, Visa; personal and business accounts   **Discounts** Available on request   **Delivery** Free in Northern Ireland (min 2 cases)   **Glass hire** Not available   **Tastings and talks** 6-week courses; to groups on request   **Cellarage** Free with purchase

Refurbishment work continues at Direct Wine Shipments' lovely old building in the dock area of Belfast. This business is well named: shipping direct to Northern Ireland from major producers around the world has given DWS an edge on range and value. Most areas and countries are represented by two or three quality names whose ranges are held in full.

France starts off with a fine collection of clarets. If you want to spend £120 on a 1982 Ch. Latour you can, but there is plenty of drinking available at less than £10 a bottle, too. Burgundy is from good names such as Faiveley, Olivier Leflaive and Domaine Laroche. The Rhônes are almost all from Chapoutier. Hugel represents Alsace, and the German range stays firmly in the quality area with wines from Bürklin-Wolf and Prüm. From Spain, the wines of Torres, Marqués de Cáceres and Chivite are stocked and there are five vintages of Vega Sicilia. Italian wines are here from top to toe: Soave and Valpolicella from Masi, Chianti from Antinori and Sicilian Regaleali. From outside Europe, Arunda from Australia and Hunter Estate from New Zealand are new additions to the range.

Most wine merchants will supply wine for parties on a sale or return basis.

Education ranks high on DWS's list of priorities. Customers can take a six-week in-house course with an examination at the end, and the company hosts 'Winemaker's Dinners' with distinguished guests.

Best buys

Santa Rita 120 Cabernet Sauvignon 1988, Chile, £
Gran Fuedo Crianza 1989, Chivite, Navarra, £
Saint Romaine 1991, Olivier Leflaive, ££
Hermitage 1990, Chapoutier, ££

Domaine Direct

29 Wilmington Square, London WC1X 0EG   *Tel* 071-837 1142

Case sales only   Open Mon–Fri 8–6   **Closed** Sat, Sun, public holidays
Credit cards None accepted; personal and business accounts   **Discounts** Not available   **Delivery** Free in central London and Home Counties (min 1 case) and on UK mainland (min 3 cases); otherwise 1 case £8, 2 cases £11; mail order available   **Glass hire** Free   **Tastings and talks** 2–3 free tastings a year
Cellarage £5.75 per case per year (inc insurance and VAT)

Domaine Direct has branched out in a modest way and its range now includes wines from Australia, New Zealand and California, as well as Burgundy. The principle is the same for all its wines: take a quality wine region and find the good or even the best growers. This comes over clearly in Burgundy where wines from Michel Juillot, Tollot-Beaut, Guy Roulot and Comte Lafon are just the start of the story. From the whole of the Côte d'Or there is tremendous choice of vineyards, growers and vintages and informative notes to help you decide. As befits a true specialist, many of the wines are available in magnums and if you like your burgundy in smaller packages, this is the place to come. Nearly 50 wines are available in half-bottles, from Beaujolais to Chassagne-Montrachet.

The New World selection is from a variety of sources: Australia features Leeuwin Estate, Capel Vale and Penfolds; New Zealand wines are from Redwood Valley and Nobilo; while California supplies wines from Stag's Leap, Hawk Crest and Sonoma-Cutrer. Particularly interesting is the Spottswoode Cabernet Sauvignon from a tiny vineyard in the Napa Valley and the same winemaker's Pinot Noir, called Etude.

All prices are quoted ex-VAT, which could indicate that most of Domaine Direct's customers are restaurants and businesses. The minimum quantity is one mixed case which is delivered free in central London and the Home Counties.

Best buys

Leeuwin Estate Chardonnay 1986, Margaret River, Australia, ££
Beaujolais-Villages 1992, Jean Charles Pivot, ££
There are no wines available from Domaine Direct for under £5

Eaton Elliot Winebrokers

15 London Road, Alderley Edge, Cheshire   *Tel* (0625) 582354
SK9 7JT

Open Mon 9.30–6.30; Tues–Fri 9.30–8.30; Sat 9.30–7   **Closed** Sun, public
holidays   **Credit cards** All accepted; personal and business accounts
Discounts 5% on 1 case   **Delivery** Free within 25-mile radius of Alderley Edge
(min 1 case); elsewhere at cost; mail order available   **Glass hire** Free with order
Tastings and talks Four formal tastings per year; regular informal in-store
tastings   **Cellarage** Not available

A well-sourced, individual range of wines is on offer from this
Cheshire merchant. Within France the emphasis is on domaines,
particularly in the 'regional' section, which includes Madiran
from Ch. Peyros, four Jurançon wines from Domaine Cauhapé
and an unusual vin de table from La Chablisienne co-operative.
Bordeaux wines are good but Burgundy holds more interest
with domaine wines again taking centre-stage. In the Loire,
Bourgueil from Clos la Gaucherie and Reuilly from Henri
Beurdin look interesting.

Outside France there is little more than a nod in Germany's
direction, but Italy is worth spending some time on: Chiantis
from Castello di Volpaia, Barolo from Giacomo Ascheri and
some full-flavoured wines from the south and Sardinia. Spain is
set to increase this year, but for the moment has some good
Riojas (CUNE and Cáceras) and Navarras from Ochoa. There are
interesting wines from California and a trio from Nederburg in
South Africa.

Australian wines come from reliable producers Rosemount,
Ryecroft, Cape Mentelle and the lovely Plantagenet of Western
Australia. Ngatarawa is a challenge to pronounce in the New
Zealand section.

Champagnes from Nicolas Feuillatte and sherries from Lustau
round off the wines, but a range of 26 malt whiskies provides
further attraction.

Wine is best stored in a cool, dark place where the temperature is
steady at around 11°C. If you intend to keep the wine for more than
three months store the bottle on its side so that the cork and the
wine remain in contact.

Best buys

Salice Salentino Riserva 1988, Puglia, £
Ch. Malvies, Côtes de la Malpère 1991, £
Jurançon Sec, Domaine Cauhapé 1991, ££
Pinot Gris 1991, Schlumberger, Alsace, ££

Eldridge Pope

Head office
Weymouth Avenue, Dorchester, Dorset   *Tel* (0305) 251251
DT1 1QT
13 wine shops/Wine Libraries

Open Generally Mon–Sat 9–5.30 (varying half-days); (Reynier) Mon–Fri 11–6.30
(Sat also Exeter branch); (Bristol) 9.30–6.30 **Closed** Sat (Reynier, London and
Bristol), Sun, public holidays **Credit cards** Access, Visa; personal and business
accounts **Discounts** 5% on mixed or full cases **Delivery** Free within 20-mile
radius of Dorchester and local area of branches (min £35 order) and UK mainland
(min 2+ cases); smaller orders £5 delivery charge **Glass hire** Free
Tastings and talks Regular tutored tastings at Wine Libraries; tutored tastings
for Dorset Wine Society (£10–£14 per person, inc supper) **Cellarage** £3 per case
per year

A delicate shade of fudge makes this an easy list to find on the
bookshelf. The colour changes annually – bright pink, pale
blue...

Eldridge Pope is a major wholesaler of wine to the trade but
also has nine retail shops and four additional outlets – the
Reynier Wine Libraries. It would be nice if these libraries
operated like book libraries where you could borrow a bottle
and return it later, having sampled the contents. Surprisingly
enough they don't work like that. They are really off-licences,
with eating areas attached, where you can buy your wine at
normal prices, pay a £1 corkage and enjoy a simple fixed-price
meal. It is a splendid idea. In the evenings the Libraries are
used for pre-arranged tutored tastings. There are Wine Libraries
in London (SW1 and EC3), and in Bristol and Exeter.

The nine Eldridge Pope shops are spread mainly around
Dorset, with the Dorchester one being the biggest. The same
range is available in all shops, although space may sometimes
limit the stock. Anything not immediately available can be
ordered. The list is a magnificent production. A thumb index
takes you straight to the page you need and each region is
introduced with a well-written essay. Joe Naughalty, a Master of
Wine for 25 years, is the buyer and his experience shows in the
quality of the wines listed. The range has a heavy bias towards
France. Good traditional clarets are listed (page after page) and
not all of them are hugely expensive. The younger vintages
include quite a few reasonably priced petits châteaux. The

Chairman's Claret (one of an extensive range of Chairman's wines) is from young vines at Ch. Cissac. Burgundies are equally comprehensive; single-line descriptions point punters in the right direction.

The Rhône selection includes top-notes from Chapoutier but the basics are good too. Côtes-du-Rhône from Ch. la Renjardière is soft, peppery and excellent value, while the Châteauneuf-du-Pape, Domaine de Monpertuis from Paul Jeaune, is concentrated and full. The 'Tradition' wines are made from 100-year-old vines and reek of pepper, plums and spice – delicious.

Germany and Italy are well represented but the rest of the world is banished to a small section at the back of the list. Australia has blossomed a little this year with wines from Mountadam, Shaw and Smith and Dalwhinnie. New Zealand manages just four wines, including two delicious examples from Redwood Estate. South Africa is a fairly new addition with wines from Rheedeberg and Backsberg.

Best buys

Ch. la Renjardière Côtes-du-Rhône 1991, £
Domaine de Monpertuis nv, Vin de Pays d'Orange, £
The Chairman's Traditional Mature Claret 1987, ££
The Chairman's White Burgundy 1991, ££

Ben Ellis and Associates

Brockham Wine Cellars, Wheelers Lane,   *Tel* (0737) 842160
Brockham, Surrey RH3 3HJ

Case sales only   **Open** Mon–Fri 9–6.30 (telephone beforehand); Sat 9–1; other times by arrangement   **Credit cards** Access, Visa; personal and business accounts **Discounts** Not available   **Delivery** Free in Surrey and central London (min 1 case) and nationally (min 5+ cases); otherwise £9.40 per consignment; mail order available   **Glass hire** Free with order   **Tastings and talks** To groups on request; major customer tastings in May and November   **Cellarage** £4.70 per case per year

---

There is a new outlet this year for Ben Ellis and his associates, Mark Pardoe, Master of Wine, and Martin Sheen. The company has moved to Brockham, and converted some old milking sheds into a warehouse and tasting room. It is still case sales only from here but outside there is room to park and inside there is space to browse.

For those who can't get to Brockham, the list remains a friendly point of contact, and the free delivery area takes in Surrey and Central London. Comments such as 'We try to arrange a mutually convenient delivery point to avoid carriage charges' get full marks for trying harder!

The range takes in both ends of the market: inexpensive

everyday wines and top-quality fine wines. From France, generic Bordeaux and petits châteaux are topped off by a classy selection of clarets, including a fair number from the 1985, 1983 and 1982 vintages and a few half-bottles. Burgundies are from a variety of quality producers, the range of prices and vintages ensuring there is something for everyone in this expensive area. Good wines from the Rhône, Loire and Alsace are introduced page by page with a chatty commentary about each region. The selection of French regional wines has been put together with care. Many are single-domaine wines priced under £5.

The Italian range has grown this year. New additions include a good-value Soave from Rocca Sveva and Aldo Conterno's Barbera d'Alba. Spain has classy Riojas from La Rioja Alta and a Gran Reserva Valdepeñas, Pata Negra. The partners moan about the moribund state of the German market and do their best to get interest going with some quality wines from Lingenfelder and Bürklin-Wolf.

Australia manages four wines from St Hallett in Barossa, Tarrawarra Chardonnay and the lovely Moss Wood Pinot Noir, plus a round-up from elsewhere. California is limited to just a handful of wines from Qupé and Au Bon Climat, plus a stunning Nebbiolo under the Il Podere label.

Best buys

Ch. Haut-Rian 1992, Bordeaux Blanc Sec, £
Salisbury Chardonnay 1992, Victoria, Australia, £
Champagne Georges Goulet Extra Quality Brut nv, ££
Jackson Estate Marlborough Dry 1992, New Zealand, ££

English Wine Centre

Alfriston Roundabout, Alfriston, East Sussex   *Tel* (0323) 870164
BN26 5QS

Open Mon–Sat 10–5; Sun 12–4 **Closed** 25 Dec–2 Jan; Sun Nov–Mar
Credit cards Access, Visa; personal and business accounts **Discounts** Available
Delivery Free within 20-mile radius (min order 2+ cases); elsewhere at cost; mail order available **Glass hire** Free with order **Tastings and talks** Series of free Chr tastings; regular tutored tastings **Cellarage** Not available

English wines are now gradually making their way into supermarkets but it is still good to deal with a specialist. At the English Wine Centre, Christopher Ann has brought together a

See the back flap for an explanation of the symbols used in the *Guide*.

wide range of wines from across the south of England, including a *méthode traditionnelle* sparkling wine and a choice of English reds. These are available on a retail or wholesale basis and there are always a few bottles open for tasting if you call in. The Centre operates not only as a shop but has vineyards and cellars of its own. There is a museum of English winemaking, and tours, tastings and dinners can be arranged. It is also the venue for the English Wine Festival which is held in September each year.

Best buys

Cuckmere Selected Dry 1990, £
Downers 1990, £
Breaky Bottom Seyval Blanc 1990, ££
Staple St-James Huxelrebe 1990, ££

Philip Eyres Wine Merchant

The Cellars, Coleshill, Amersham,   *Tel* (0494) 433823
Buckinghamshire HP7 0LW   (enquiries)

Case sales only   **Open** Personal callers by appointment; telephone enquiries during office hours Mon–Fri 8–10, Sat, Sun 9–10   **Closed** Public holidays and during annual holiday   **Credit cards** None accepted; personal and business accounts   **Discounts** 2.5% on unmixed cases   **Delivery** Free within surrounding areas; central London charged at £6.50 for 1 case, 2 cases or more free; other parts of UK mainland, 1 case £10, 2–3 cases £6.50, 4 cases or more free   **Glass hire** Free **Tastings and talks** Tastings given at various locations   **Cellarage** Customers introduced to Octavian, Corsham, Wilts

Philip Eyres and his four associates run this business which operates in the south Buckinghamshire and north Berkshire areas as well as in Aylesbury and Bicester. There is no shop; instead there is an extensive list and wines can be bought by the mixed case supplemented by *en primeur* and special offers. Recent offers include a vastly increased range of Italian wines, which are available in straight cases or in pre-selected mixed dozens. Producers such as Aldo Conterno for Barbera and Le Casalte for Vino Nobile give confidence to this selection. In the main list France provides plenty of choice: Jaboulet, Florentin and Guigal in the Rhône, good clarets and burgundies, and even Domaine Cauhapé from Jurançon. French country wines supply good-value drinking below £5. Only the Loire seems a bit thin.

Further afield, Germany is well researched with wines from Dr Loosen, Friedrich-Wilhelm-Gymnasium and Lingenfelder and not a drop of Liebfraumilch in sight. Spain provides good flavours from Torres and La Rioja Alta, including the magnificent Reserva 904.

The New World selection is extensive: Moss Wood, Cape Mentelle and others from Australia, Trefethen and good-value Fetzer from California, plus wines from Chile, New Zealand and South Africa.

We have heard good reports of the service here. Annual tastings keep customers in touch with the range.

Best buys

Cortese dell'Alto Monferrato 1992, Italy, £
Don John Vino de Mesa, Spain nv, £
Carignano del Sulsis Riserva 'Rocca Rubia' 1989, Sicily, ££
Spätburgunder Tafelwein 1989, Rheinpfalz, Lingenfelder, ££

Farr Vintners

Mainly mail order
19 Sussex Street, London SW1V 4RR   *Tel* 071-828 1960

Minimum order £250 (exc VAT)   **Open** Mon–Fri 10–6   **Closed** Sat, Sun, public holidays   **Credit cards** Access, Visa; business accounts   **Discounts** Variable (orders over £2,500)   **Delivery** £8.50 per consignment within London; elsewhere at cost; mail order available   **Glass hire** Not available   **Tastings and talks** Regular tastings and dinners   **Cellarage** £5 per case per year

'Thank you for introducing me to Farr: it has saved me a lot of money,' wrote one of our readers; we have heard similar sentiments from others. This specialised merchant offers *en primeur* claret at prices that look like printing errors. You end up double-checking the small print just to make sure that there are no colossal extras (there aren't, apart from normal shipping and duty). The only stipulation is a minimum order of £250 excluding VAT, with delivery charges extra. They even think for you and don't bother to offer vintages which are just not worth buying ahead.

En primeur is only a small part of this merchant's business, which acts mainly as a clearing house for some of the world's finest and rarest wines. If you are looking for a special wine from a special vintage, this is the place to come. Pétrus, Mouton, Latour, Margaux and Yquem are available in endless vintages and bottle sizes. Many have been bought from private cellars, and Farr does a surprisingly brisk trade in selling older vintages back to Bordeaux where they are difficult to find. It even has a retail licence so you can buy a single bottle of 1900 Margaux (only £1250) without upsetting the licensing magistrates.

For merchants who sell a minimum of twelve bottles, we say 'Case sales only' in the details at the head of an entry.

The range is not just First Growths, there is a wonderful selection of cru classé wines dating from recent vintages back through the years, mostly in unbroken cases. Overall, prices are very reasonable.

Away from Bordeaux, Burgundy merits detailed attention, with wines in a variety of vintages from some of the best domaines, including Leroy, Comtes Lafon and Domaine de la Romanée-Conti; the Rhône is represented by Jaboulet, Chave and Ch. de Beaucastel. Vintage ports roll back through the years to 1908. A clutch of wines from New Zealand (Wairau and Redwood Valley) adds a New World touch to this essentially Old World selection.

Farr is run by Stephen Browett and Lindsay Hamilton who, together with Jonathan Stephens in sales, have tasted most wines from most vintages this century. With quality tasting practice of that kind, their advice can only be good.

Best buys

Ch. de Beaucastel 1990, Châteauneuf-du-Pape, ££
Ch. Gruaud Larose 1986, ££

Farthinghoe Fine Wine and Food

The Old Rectory, Farthinghoe, Brackley, *Tel* (0295) 710018
Northamptonshire NN13 5NZ

Open Mon–Fri 9–5; Sat, Sun, public holidays by arrangement only
Credit cards None accepted; personal and business accounts **Discounts** 6–10 cases £1 per case, 11+ cases £2 per case **Delivery** Free on UK mainland (min 3 cases); otherwise 1 case £6, 2 cases £3 per case; mail order available
Glass hire Available with charge (£2.50 for 48 glasses cleaning charge)
Tastings and talks Occasional customer tastings **Cellarage** By arrangement

There is no longer a cookery school linked to this merchant but the name stays the same just for continuity. A legacy of this arrangement is that there is a retail licence here and, although no-one ever turns up to buy a single bottle, it is possible. Mixed cases are also allowed despite the list remaining resolutely wholesale.

The range is a personal selection from Master of Wine Simon Cox. It concentrates on France, with just a handful of wines from elsewhere. Tasting notes are given for most of the wines to help selection.

There are Alsace wines from Gisselbrecht and a few specialities from Trimbach. Clarets include a reasonable selection of petits châteaux, with a few classier 1982 wines recommended for laying down, although some should be

drinkable now. Burgundies are from Domaines Thénard and
Corsin, with a few representatives from Armand Rousseau and
Tollot-Beaut.

Rhônes include wines from Jaboulet and the good-value
Vieille Ferme wines from Perrin of Ch. de Beaucastel fame. The
two non-French wines, Brown Brothers Shiraz from Australia
and Villa Montes Cabernet Sauvignon from Chile, seem rather
lonely but are terrific wines and perhaps more southern
hemisphere wines will eventually join them.

Best buys

Johnston Reserve Claret nv, £
La Vieille Ferme Blanc 1992, Côtes du Lubéron, £
Ch. de Sours 1992, Bordeaux Rosé, ££
Domaine Petit Château, Chardonnay 1992, Vin de Pays du
Jardin de la France, ££

Ferrers le Mesurier

Turnsloe, North Street, Titchmarsh,   *Tel* (0832) 732660
Kettering, Northamptonshire NN14 3DH

Case sales only   **Open** (Best to telephone before calling) Mon–Fri 8–8; Sat, Sun,
public holidays by arrangement   **Credit cards** None accepted; personal and
business accounts   **Discounts** By arrangement (min 1 case)   **Delivery** Within a
50-mile radius of Kettering and London (min 1 case); elsewhere at cost
Glass hire Not available   **Tastings and talks** Annual Cambridge college tasting
Cellarage Free for up to two years if wine purchased from premises

Ferrers le Mesurier (the name of the company and the man who
runs it) offers a personal selection of wines from well-chosen
growers. The choice is restricted to just over 50 wines, mainly
French but this year the range has expanded to take in five from
the New World. That Mr le Mesurier has included a Tasmanian
Pinot Noir in this tiny selection is typical of his search for
interesting, quality wines.

That same dedication shows in the choice of French domaine-
bottled wines. Burgundy is the main treat, with the splendid
1990 vintage very much in evidence, but selections from the
Rhône and Loire are equally good. A new section offers wines
under £5. Highlight of the year is the annual tasting in a
Cambridge college.

Best buys

Domaine la Taste 1992, Vin de Pays de Gascogne, £
Côtes-du-Rhône 1990, Delorme, £
Marsanny 1990, Vieilles Vignes, Bouvier, ££
Savigny lès Beaune 1990, Serpentiers, Guillemont, ££

Alex Findlater

Vauxhall Cellars, 86 Goding Street, London SE11 5AW	*Tel* 071-587 1644

Office

Heveningham High House, Halesworth, Suffolk IP19 0EA	*Tel* (0986) 798274

Case sales only **Open** Mon–Fri 10–6 **Closed** Sat, Sun, public holidays
Credit cards Access, Visa; personal and business accounts **Discounts** Available
Delivery Free locally (min 1 case); mail order available **Glass hire** Free with
order **Tastings and talks** To groups on request **Cellarage** £5.28 per case per year

Alex Findlater was one of the first merchants to specialise in Australian wine. While the rest of the world was dipping a toe in 'Kangarouge', Alex was busy sorting out the Wirra Wirra from the Tarrawarra and helping his customers to do the same. His range of Australian wines is still huge, including those from the big companies such as Penfolds, Orlando, Wynns and Wolf Blass, but also the smaller properties such as Crabtree, Tarrawarra and Lake's Folly. Sadly missing this year is the comprehensive list that used to act as a guide to the regions and the wineries.

New Zealand comes in for much the same treatment as Australia: all kinds of producers, all grape varieties. The South African section of the list stands at around 30 wines but is set to increase steadily.

As an alternative to the southern hemisphere, you can buy other wines from Alex Findlater. He has a range from France consisting of domaine burgundies, good clarets and wines from the Rhône and Loire. Germany gets quite serious treatment with wines from Armin Diel, Dr Loosen and Georg Breuer.

Alex operates out of the same address as the London Wine Emporium and sells mainly to the trade, however, private customers wanting a mixed case are equally valued.

Best buys

Vin de Fin de la Terre Rouge, Alex Findlater & Co, £
Ch. la Ressaudie 1989, Bergerac, £
Bongoverno 1988, Tenuta Farneta Vino da Tavola, ££
Crabtree's Shiraz/Cabernet 1988, Clare Valley, Australia, ££

Findlater Mackie Todd

Deer Park Road, Merton Abbey, London   *Tel* 081-543 0966
SW19 3TU

Case sales only   **Open** Mon–Fri 9–5; Sat also, during December   **Closed** Sun,
public holidays   **Credit cards** All accepted; personal and business accounts
Discounts Available   **Delivery** Free on UK mainland (min 3 cases); mail order
available   **Glass hire** Available   **Tastings and talks** Tastings vary in size,
frequency and venue   **Cellarage** £5.50 per case per year

This mail-order wine company was taken over by the John
Lewis Partnership during 1993. It now operates with a
combined selection from Findlater and Waitrose. Now Findlater
customers can enjoy the skills of the Waitrose buying team, and
it means that John Lewis customers around the country can buy
Waitrose wines by mail order.

So far, wines are offered as pre-selected mixed cases, unmixed
cases at special prices, or a selection of wines to mix freely. This
is a tremendous step forward for Findlater and Waitrose and
great news for customers.

Fine Wines of New Zealand

PO Box 476, London NW5   *Tel* 071-482 0093

Case sales only   **Open** Call for details   **Credit cards** None accepted; personal and
business accounts   **Discounts** Available   **Delivery** Delivery service available in
inner London   **Glass hire** Not available   **Tastings and talks** Tastings given on
request   **Cellarage** Not available

The name says it all. This company is run by Margaret Harvey,
a New Zealander who did the Master of Wine examinations the
hard way. In the time-honoured tradition of the independent
wine trade, she worked at a day job (pharmacy) while
developing her wine business, then switched to wine full-time a
few years ago. Somehow she also managed to find time to pass
the MW exams – determination indeed!

New Zealand wines have grown in popularity over the last
few years from being a bit of an oddity to the point where
almost everyone has tried and liked a New Zealand wine.
Margaret Harvey seeks out good quality, but also keeps an eye
on value. The range includes Aotea, Redwood Valley, Vidal,
Matua Valley, Rippon, Mills Reef and St Nesbit. Ata Rangi has a
stunning Pinot Noir at a fairly stunning price. Célèbre is
another great wine from this company.

There are lots more New Zealand wines just waiting to be
discovered. It is quite likely that this specialist will get to them
first.

Best buys

Vidal Sauvignon Blanc 1992, Hawkes Bay, ££
Rippon Pinot Noir 1991, Wanaka, ££
Redwood Valley Chardonnay 1991, Nelson, ££

Le Fleming Wines

9 Longcroft Avenue, Harpenden,   *Tel* (0582) 760125
Hertfordshire AL5 2RB

Case sales only   **Open** 24-hour answerphone   **Credit cards** None accepted;
business accounts   **Discounts** Occasionally   **Delivery** Within a 25-mile radius
Glass hire Free   **Tastings and talks** Regular tastings every 4 months; to groups on
request   **Cellarage** Not available

It is case sales only and just local delivery from this one-woman
band operating from Harpenden, but the range is good and
choosing a mixed dozen should pose no problems.

The Australian section is extensive and reflects Cherry
Jenkins' enthusiasm following a trip to Oz in 1992. It includes
the good-value Orlando range, Eden Ridge organics, Oxford
Landing, Schinus Molle and Shaw and Smith. St Hallett Old
Block Shiraz and Charlie Melton's Nine Popes reveal what
glorious flavours the old Barossa vines can produce. Other New
World wines include Rongopai from New Zealand and Newton
from California.

Back in Europe, the Spanish selection is limited but worthy,
Italy includes the vino da tavola Sangioveto from Badia a
Coltibuono and Portugal provides three good-value reds with
individual character. The French range is well chosen and most
wines are well under £10, although you can let out the purse
strings on some classier clarets and domaine-bottled
burgundies, particularly Daniel Rion's Vosne-Romanée. The
French country section features a Bourgogne Passe-Tout-Grains
from Jean Musso and the peppery, spicy Mas de Gourgonnier
Tradition, Coteaux d'Aix en Provence – both wines are
organically grown.

Best buys

Les Terrasses de Guilhem 1991, Vin de Pays de l'Hérault, £
Eden Ridge Dry White, Adelaide Hills, South Australia, £
Ch. Malescasse 1988, Cru Bourgeois Médoc, ££
Mas de Daumas Gassac 1990, Languedoc, ££

John Ford Wines

8 Richardson Road, Hove, East Sussex   *Tel* (0273) 735891
BN3 5RB

Open Mon–Sat 9–9; Sun 12–2, 7–9; public holidays 10–2, 6–9
Credit cards Access, American Express, Visa   **Discounts** 10% per case if paying
by cash or cheque; 5% per case if paying by credit card   **Delivery** Free locally
(Mon–Sat only)   **Glass hire** Free   **Tastings and talks** Regular free in-store tastings
and talks   **Cellarage** Not available

At present there are two names for this South Coast business.
John Ford is the name which has been over the door for five
years but new owners, Ken and Liz Rollings, will shortly change
it to 'York House Wines'. That was the name of the shop that
for fifty years operated from these converted mews premises.

With the switch in ownership has come a change in range,
now with the emphasis firmly on quality under £10. From
France, a good selection of petits châteaux leads up to a few
classier wines, including Ch. Monbousquet from St-Emilion and
Ch. Beychevelle. Jaboulet and Chapoutier appear in the Rhône
section and a good crop of French regional wines keep flavour
up and costs down. Only in Burgundy do prices soar with a
range of wines from Drouhin and the Hospices de Beaune.

Further afield, Australia provides big flavours from the Wolf
Blass range, with some good standards from Brown Brothers,
Mitchelton and Rosemount. New Zealand wines are mainly
from Nobilo and a good selection from South Africa includes
the excellent Hamilton-Russell wines.

Monthly newsletters and regular tastings add to the
attractions here.

Best buys

Kapfontein Pinotage 1992, South Africa, £
Concha y Toro Cabernet Sauvignon 1987, Chile, £
Wolf Blass Shiraz 1988, South Australia, ££
Ch. Monbousquet 1989, St-Emilion, ££

Fortnum & Mason

181 Piccadilly, London W1A 1ER   *Tel* 071-734 8040

Open Mon–Sat 9.30–6 **Closed** Sun, public holidays **Credit cards** Access,
American Express, Visa; personal and business accounts **Discounts** 5–10% (min 1
case) **Delivery** Free in Greater London (min £40 order, exc account holders);
otherwise £4 per order; mail order available **Glass hire** Not available
Tastings and talks Promotional tastings of champagne and port; regular tastings of
sherry, Italian and Spanish wines; tastings and talks given only by private
arrangement **Cellarage** £4.50 per case per year

No one who strolls by chance into Fortnum's Piccadilly
emporium could mistake it for a bargain-basement warehouse.
The stiff collars and splendid tailcoats of the staff clearly let you
know that this is a Quality Establishment.

The wine department is not vast, just the right size to spend
ten minutes or so browsing around before going on to partake
of one of Fortnum's famous afternoon teas. Pick up a list as you
do so and you will have some interesting reading. As you might
expect, the range is well chosen and provides everything that
the well-heeled clientele of London and the Home Counties
could require in the way of wine.

There is a wide range of quality champagnes (many of them
available in half-bottles and magnums), clarets through the
vintages and the price bands and, of course, a good selection of
port. Half-bottles are a speciality with vintage champagne,
classed-growth clarets and an enticing choice of quality
Sauternes, including four vintages of Yquem, joining a well-
established range of own-label wines. Most of the classic areas
have an own-label wine at the bottom of the price range – but
in no way are these poor relations. The crusted port comes from
Dow, the Mosel from Dr. Loosen, and the clarets from well-
known châteaux hiding behind anonymous labels.

Fortnum's choice does not end with the classics. There are
interesting pockets of wine from the rest of the world: Shaw
and Smith Chardonnay and Yarra Yering Cabernet Sauvignon
from Australia, for example. It is pleasing to see the Hamilton-
Russell wines from South Africa but you would need friends at
Fort Knox to pull the cork on Tokaji Essencia 1947 at over £600 a
bottle. Fortnum has expanded beyond the level of just a wine
section in a department store. The range qualifies it as a wine
merchant in its own right and it obviously adds a certain
something to have liveried vans plying to and from the suburbs
laden with their excellent comestibles. Fortnum will never be a
cheap place to buy wine, but it is so very solid, reliable and
reassuring to deal with.

Best buys

Fortnum & Mason Claret 1990 (produced by Ch. Chapelle Maracan), £
Fortnum & Mason Côtes-du-Rhône 1990, £
Fortnum & Mason Chablis 1991, ££
Fortnum & Mason Pauillac 1989 (second wine of Ch. Pichon Longueville Lalande), ££

John Frazier

Warehouse

Stirling Road, Cranmore Industrial Estate, Shirley, Solihull, West Midlands B90 4XD	*Tel* 021-704 3415

Associated outlets

252 Longmore Road, Shirley, Solihull, West Midlands B90 3ER	*Tel* 021-745 4303
4 Trinity Court, Stoke Road, Aston Fields, Bromsgrove, Hereford & Worcester B60 3EJ	*Tel* (0527) 579911
New Inn Stores, Stratford Road, Wootton Wawen, Solihull, West Midlands B95 6AS	*Tel* (0564) 794151
618 Yardley Wood Road, Billesley, Birmingham, West Midlands B13 0HW	*Tel* 021-441 3888
56 Thornhill Road, Streetly, Sutton Coldfield, West Midlands B74 3EN	*Tel* 021-353 7352

Open Mon–Sat 10–10; Sun 12–2, 7–10 **Credit cards** Access, American Express, Visa; personal and business accounts **Discounts** Negotiable **Delivery** Free within a 50-mile radius (min 4 cases); mail order available **Glass hire** 45p per dozen **Tastings and talks** Available **Cellarage** Free

---

There are five retail shops and a wholesale warehouse in this Midlands-based family business. The range takes a general look at the wines of the world, picking out a few well-known names from each region.

From France comes a good choice of Bordeaux wines, mainly crus bourgeois with a few second wines of grander châteaux. In Burgundy, the wines are mainly from reliable *négociants* such as Louis Latour, Chanson and Drouhin. The Rhône section is strong, with wines from Jaboulet, Chapoutier and Guigal. At basic Côtes-du-Rhône level, Ch. du Grand Moulas provides robust flavours at good-value prices. French country wines include Domaine du Révérend from Corbières and Domaines Virginie. Outside France, Spain has a wide choice of Riojas, while Italy includes Chiantis from Antinori and Rocca delle Macie. The New World is well represented with Taltarni, Penfolds and Lindeman in Australia, Mondavi and the classy Cuvaison from California and Concha y Toro from Chile.

Prices at the warehouse in Solihull tend to be a bit cheaper than at the retail shops so it might be worth taking a drive there or ordering four cases to qualify for free delivery. Definitely worthwhile is the bin-end sale with substantial reductions.

Best buys

Domaine de Rieux 1992, Vin de Pays des Côtes de Gascogne, £
Trois Mouline Sauvignon 1992, Vin de Pays d'Oc, £
Ch. Beaumont 1986, Haut-Médoc, ££
Mâcon-Clessé, Domaine de la Bon Gran 1990, Thévenet, ££

Friarwood

26 New Kings Road, London SW6 4ST   *Tel* 071-736 2628

Open Mon–Fri 9–7; Sat 10–5 **Closed** Sun, public holidays **Credit cards** All accepted; personal and business accounts **Discounts** 5% per case **Delivery** Free inside M25; mail order available **Glass hire** Free **Tastings and talks** Free twice monthly tastings to customers and general public **Cellarage** 12p per case per week

---

Although very willing and with bags already packed, we were unable to check out the two off-shore retail outlets of Friarwood, one in Barbados and the other in Antigua. Perhaps our well-travelled readers could let us know more about them.

Meanwhile, Friarwood is busy retailing wine in the slightly cooler climate of Fulham. The range is classic French, although there is a slight nod in the direction of New Zealand, Australia and South Africa. Clarets are strong with a long list going back to 1970. The 1985 collection is good with 21 wines, many classed growths. Jeroboams (6-bottles) and Imperials (8.5 bottles) are a speciality of the 1982 vintage. There is also a good selection of Barsacs and Sauternes going back to 1967 Ch. d'Yquem.

Burgundies are from some fairly classy growers but outside these areas the list begins to look a little sparse: one Alsace wine, a few from the Loire and the Rhône. Cognac and armagnac are available under bond or duty-paid and include venerable spirits under the Lafite-Rothschild label.

A small selection of French regional wines provides low-cost drinking while saving up for the classy stuff.

Best buys

Cabernet Sauvignon 1990, Bergerac Rouge, £
Abbaye Sainte-Hilaire Rouge 1990, Coteaux Varois, £
Ch. Millet 1989, Graves, ££
Domaine St Anne 1989, Côtes-du-Rhône, ££

The Fulham Road Wine Centre

899/901 Fulham Road, London SW6 5HU   *Tel* 071-736 7009

Open Mon–Sat 10–9   **Closed** Sun, public holidays   **Credit cards** Access, Visa;
personal and business accounts   **Discounts** 5% on 1 mixed case   **Delivery** Free in
central London (by arrangement); mail order available   **Glass hire** Free
Tastings and talks Wine school in purpose-built tasting room; regular in-store
tastings on Sat   **Cellarage** Available

Angela Muir, Master of Wine and proprietor of the Fulham
Road Wine Centre, is busy these days sourcing wines and
improving their quality in various parts of the world, such as
Slovakia, Moldova and Spain. These wines are gradually
appearing on the shelves of the major multiples and sometimes
at the Fulham Road Wine Centre.

Good winemaking is the key to the range at Fulham Road.
You are just as likely to be bowled over by an Australian, Italian
or Chilean wine as by a French one. There are top-notch
burgundies, delicious Gevrey-Chambertin from Trapet and
Volnay from Jean-Marc Bouley, but for those who like to afford
to eat as well as drink there are terrific wines, particularly in the
£5 to £10 range, which all have the stamp of quality.

The New World is well represented with Rothbury, Tarra
Warra and Shaw and Smith from Australia. Chile sports the
Undurraga range; there is Bodegas Etchart from Argentina;
Inglenook, Trefethen and Sonoma-Cutrer are from California.

The Italian range brings together classic names and some
lesser-known but good vini da tavola – all well made and
packing splendid flavours. France majors on good-value vins de
pays as well as taking in a cross-section from the regions.

But this is not just a shop. If you want to learn about wine in
a more structured way, enrol for one of the courses at the Wine
School (underneath the shop). You can work though 'What's My
Wine', 'Grape Varieties', 'Regions of France', all tutored by well-
qualified visiting speakers. With regular tastings in the shop on
Saturdays and a variety of wine books, maps, prints and
antique decanters available, there is every reason to call into
this part of the Fulham Road.

Best buys

Irsay Oliver 1992, Slovakia, £
Domaine de San Guilhem 1992, Vin de Pays des Côtes de
Gascogne, £
Laurel Glen Cabernet Sauvignon 1987, Sonoma Mountain,
California, ££
Redwood Valley Chardonnay 1991, New Zealand, ££

Fullers (Fuller, Smith & Turner)

Head office
Griffin Brewery, Chiswick Lane South, *Tel* 081-994 3691
London W4 2QB
Approximately 60 shops in Home Counties

Case sales only **Open** Mon–Sat 9.30–9.30; Sun and public holidays 12–3, 7–9
Credit cards Access, Visa; personal and business accounts **Discounts** Available; 1
free bottle with every unmixed case; larger orders attract further discounts
Delivery Free locally **Glass hire** Free; 50p deposit per glass
Tastings and talks Free, fortnightly on Saturdays from March to November; also at
managers' discretion **Cellarage** Not available

Fullers' managers are a talented lot. Once again, Shepperton
shop manager, James Burton, has adorned the wine-list with
some amusing cartoons which could be just the start of a whole
new career for him.

Fullers is more than just an 'offie' that stays open late; it is
part of the Fuller, Smith & Turner brewing operation of which
you might get a delicious malty whiff if you are ever stuck at
the Hogarth roundabout in Chiswick, west London. Fullers has
a chain of shops in London and the Home Counties which is
gradually expanding and becoming increasingly serious about
the wine business. You may know the company better as a
place to pick up the excellent London Pride bitter, but while
you are there take a look at the wine shelves as well. The range
covers most parts of the world but is particularly strong in
Bordeaux and Burgundy, with a good selection of Home-
Counties-dinner-party wines at the £5 to £15 mark. Ch.
Cantenac-Brown 1988 and Faiveley's Savigny lès Beaune 1990
should go down well. The Rhône is represented by plenty of
fine names – Chapoutier, Jaboulet and Chave – while at the
cheaper end, a Côtes-du-Rhône-Villages from Cairanne provides
decent drinking. French country wines rate a big section – all
under £5 – and the rest of Europe provides plenty of choice. The
Australian range is a major feature, with the spotlight on good-
value, well-made wines, many under £5 and all but Penfolds
Grange under £10. Rosemount, Brown Brothers, Nottage Hill
and Rothbury are some of the better-known names, but a
Tasmanian Chardonnay adds variety. New Zealand is worth a
look with Montana, Babich, Nobilo and Cloudy Bay.

With a good emphasis on reasonable ports and a few
Rutherford and Miles madeiras, a Fullers store makes a welcome
addition to any high street. The managers we have come across
are pleasant, never pushy and know their stock well. Certainly
well worth checking out.

Best buys

Ch. du Cèdre 1990, Cahors, £
Berticot Sauvignon Blanc 1992, Côtes de Duras, £
Señorio de Sarria Cabernet Sauvignon 1987, Navarra, ££
Tasmanian Wine Company Chardonnay 1991, ££

Garrards Wine Merchants 🖙

Mayo House, 49 Main Street, Cockermouth,   *Tel* (0900) 823592
Cumbria CA13 9JS

Open Mon, Tues 9.30–5.45; Wed–Sat 9.30–8; some public holidays **Closed** Sun, some public holidays **Credit cards** Access, Visa; personal and business accounts
Discounts 5% on 1 case (not with credit-card payment) **Delivery** Free within 10-mile radius (min 1 case); mail order available **Glass hire** Free
Tastings and talks Tastings through the Cockermouth Wine Club; to groups on request **Cellarage** Not available

This small family business manages to squeeze quite a lot into its long thin shop in Cockermouth. New World wines are gaining popularity and Garrards has responded with a good Australian selection from Orlando, Rosemount, Brown Brothers and Tyrrells. New Zealand sees a few new faces with Nobilo and Montana joining Cooks and Cloudy Bay. South African wines have expanded to include Fairview Estate, Backsberg and Nederburg, as well as a range from KWV. The Chilean branch of Torres joins Undurraga and Santa Carolina from South America and Torres crops up again from Spain, along with Ochoa and a selection of Riojas. German wines are good, mainly from Sichel and Deinhard. From France, clarets include a fair range for under £13 and then shoot up-market to the heights of Palmer 1978 and Pichon-Lalande 1970. Alsace wines are from Hugel, Beaujolais comes from Duboeuf and burgundies are provided by Louis Latour and Chanson.

Once again, prices seem quite reasonable in this little shop. Perhaps that is what they mean by the motto 'Your astonishing good fortune'.

Best buys

Undurraga Sauvignon Blanc 1992, Chile, £
Vin de Table Blanc, Georges Duboeuf, £
Ch. Fombrauge 1986, St-Emilion Grand Cru, ££
Late Harvest Orange Muscat and Flora 1990, Brown Brothers, Australia, ££

Un bon buveur doit au premier coup reconnaître le cru, au second la qualité, au troisième l'année.

[At the first sip a good drinker will recognise the vineyard, at the second the quality, and at the third the year.]

Alexander Dumas, *La Dame de Monsoreau*

Gateway/Somerfield

Gateway House, Hawkefield Business Park,
Whitchurch Lane, Bristol, Avon BS14 0TJ
Approx 700 branches nationwide

Tel (0272) 359359

Open Mon–Sat 8.30–6; selected stores open Sun **Closed** Public holidays
Credit cards Access, Visa **Discounts** Not available **Delivery** Within 10-mile
radius of Somerfield stores at Christmas only **Glass hire** Not available
Tastings and talks Monthly in-store tastings of approx 6 wines **Cellarage** Not
available

With nearly 700 branches from Aberdeen in Scotland to Ystrad
Mynach in Wales it is quite likely that there is a Gateway store
near you. The range of wine in these neighbourhood shops has
been undergoing a transformation in the past few years under
the direction of wine buyer Angela Mount. Now, with basic
lines radically improved and a huge selection of new lines,
Gateway looks as if it is going places. Its particular strength is
in wines under £5. Among the French reds there is a young
stylish claret, a fruity Côtes de Duras, and a big-flavoured Côtes
de Castillon from Ch. la Chapelle Paradis. Inexpensive French
whites include a fresh and lively Côtes de Gascogne and the
Australian-style wines of Chais Baumière.

Value comes from other parts of the world too. Hugh Ryman's
Gyöngyös Estate wines from Hungary, Seaview Cabernet/
Shiraz, a buttery Chardonnay from Australia and a rich,
plummy Carignano del Sulcis from Sardinia. There are more up-
market wines in all sections – St-Joseph from the Rhône, Viña
Ardanza from Rioja and Ch. Reynella Cabernet Sauvignon from
Australia. New this year is a range of English wines, with
Lamberhurst Sovereign available nationally and a further seven
wines restricted to stores nearest the vineyards.

Larger Gateways are being transformed into Somerfield stores
with a bigger range and more up-market image. Small Gateways
have a fraction of the range, but there should be some
representatives from all regions. Many of the wines can be
bought more cheaply from the related Food Giant stores.

Best buys

Somerfield Australian Chardonnay 1991, £
Philippe de Baudin Cabernet Sauvignon 1991, Vin de Pays
d'Oc, £
Ochoa Tempranillo 1988, Navarra, ££
Somerfield Chablis 1990, La Chablisienne, ££

Gauntleys of Nottingham

4 High Street, Exchange Arcade,   *Tel* (0602) 417973
Nottingham, Nottinghamshire NG1 2ET

Open Mon–Sat 9–5.30   **Closed** Sun, public holidays   **Credit cards** Access, Visa;
personal and business accounts   **Discounts** 5% on 1–5 cases; 10% on 5–10 cases
Delivery Free in Nottingham, Derby, Southwell, Newark and Leicester (min 1-case
order); mail order available   **Glass hire** Free with order
Tastings and talks Monthly tutored tastings; specific tastings by growers
Cellarage Not available

'Hints of tobacco' would be a reasonable tasting note for this
shop. We are not talking about some up-market Médoc wine
but the premises themselves, infused with the heady aroma of
Gauntleys other product, high-class cigars. The wine business
started out in a small way as John Gauntley's hobby but now
occupies the basement of his high street shop.

Because of new wines constantly being added to the range, a
main list became impracticable. Now John issues monthly
offers, concentrating on one region at a time and giving
excellent, readable information about the region, the wines and
the vintages.

Quality producers are the keynote here, a recent Rhône offer
included wines from Auguste Clape, Yvonne Verset and René
Rostaing. The Rhône is very much a speciality at this shop with
no less than 19 Côtes Rôties from 8 growers in a variety of
vintages. This pattern is repeated in Hermitage, Cornas,
St-Joseph and Châteauneuf-du-Pape. The Loire is also put under
the spotlight but is focused on sweet wines such as Vouvray,
Quarts de Chaumes and Coteaux de Layon. Burgundy has seen
some work in the past year and now provides some very classy
wines from domaines such as Lafon, Simon Bize, Patrice Rion
and Charles Rousseau. Bordeaux is strangely neglected by
comparison but Alsace is a delight with wines from Trimbach,
Domaine Weinbach and Ostertag.

Spanish and Italian wines are well chosen, with a fine
selection from good growers, while Germany is almost ignored
apart from four wines from Prüm.

The New World presents a collection of up-market wines,
including Rockford, Wynns and Lindemans from Australia,
Mondavi and Beringer from California and a wide and varied
choice from South Africa.

This is a high-class list with a great many wines sailing by at
over £20, although there are just a few that could qualify for
weekday drinking. Tutored tastings are a speciality here and
could serve as a good introduction to this classy range.

Best buys

Domaine Fontaine du Clos Syrah 1990, Provence, £
Domaine de Joy 1991, Vin de Pays des Côtes de Gascogne, £
Domaine Ernest Burn Pinot Blanc 1990, Alsace, ££
Domaine Gramenon, 1991, Côtes-de-Rhône, ££

General Wine Company

25 Station Road, Liphook, Hampshire   *Tel* (0428) 722201
GU30 7PW

Open Mon–Sat 9–9; Sun and public holidays 12–2, 7–9   **Closed** Chr Day, New
Year's Day   **Credit cards** Access, Visa; Switch; personal and business accounts
Discounts 5% on 1 mixed case, 10% on 4+ cases   **Delivery** Free within 20-mile
radius; mail order available   **Glass hire** Free with order; breakages charged for
Tastings and talks Three tutored tastings a year   **Cellarage** Not available

The little list that this company produces is just a taster for the
much bigger range in the shop. The focus this year is on the
South of France, with a range of domaine wines providing
quality drinking at good-value prices. Claret is another
speciality: a small range of petits châteaux leads on to much
grander wines, such as Mouton Rothschild 1970 and a clutch of
Ch. Latour vintages rolling back to 1937. Burgundies are mainly
from *négociants* Chanson and Louis Latour.

Spain has seen some work this year with 20 new wines, most
of them at the good-value end of the price range, including
Agramont from Navarra, Pata Negra from Valdepeñas and
Campo Viejo from Rioja.

South Africa continues to look good. Nederburg, Fairview and
Neethlingshof are the main producers, along with KWV, but
new wines from Groot Constantia are on their way.

From Australia, the familiar names of Mitchelton, Lindemans
and Penfolds give reliable flavours at reasonable prices. Palliser
Estate Pinot Noir plus Stoneleigh and Cooks are the attractions
from New Zealand.

With Santa Rita and Torres representing Chile and L A Cetto
adding variety from Mexico, this range should be enough to
keep Liphook throats lubricated.

Best buys

Ch. Grand Moulin 1991, Corbières, £
Neethlingshof Gewurztraminer 1991, South Africa, £
Monte Real 1985, Rioja Blanco, ££
Mount Helen Chardonnay 1990, Australia, ££

Matthew Gloag & Son

Bordeaux House, 33 Kinnoull Street, Perth, Perthshire PH1 5EU

Tel (0738) 21101

Open Mon–Fri 9–5 **Closed** Sat, Sun, public holidays **Credit cards** Access, Visa; personal and business accounts **Discounts** Not available **Delivery** Free on mainland Scotland (min 1 case); free in England & Wales (min order 2+ cases); single-case orders £7.05; mail order available **Glass hire** Free
Tastings and talks Two large tastings per year; tutored tastings throughout the year **Cellarage** Not available

Matthew Gloag & Son has been supplying the Scots with their whisky and claret for nearly 200 years. The list is a rather modest pocket-notebook size which contrasts dramatically with the expensive and hefty publications that some merchants issue. But good things come in little packages and this one has a rounded and reliable choice.

Gloag's Reserve house claret is from Ch. Cissac and the main wine from that château features through the vintages in the list. Other clarets include a good round-up of cru bourgeois wines with a few classed growths. The red burgundy section had a complete overhaul this year with wines from Domaines Bachelat and Machard de Gramont appearing. Chablis is from Domaine Servin. French country wines were also extended and give good-value drinking. Italian wines now include Umani Ronchi's Cumaro Vino da Tavola, among others, and Spain manages to hold some interest despite being limited to just six wines.

Australia and New Zealand sport a few fresh faces this year, such as Preece from Victoria and Mills Reef from the Bay of Plenty, while South Africa adds style with L'Ormarins Sauvignon and Middelvlei Pinotage.

Central heating for winter-time is provided by a fine collection of wood and vintage ports, including examples from 1963 and 1966. Sherries are from the splendid Barbadillo range.

Best buys

Sauvignon de la Tour Signy 1992, Haut Poitou, £
Drostdy-Hof Steen 1992, South Africa, £
Mitchelton Reserve Chardonnay 1990, Australia, ££
Ch. La Tuilerie 1986, Graves, ££

If all be true that I do think,
  There are five reasons we should drink;
  Good wine – a friend – or being dry -
  Or lest we should be by and by –
  Or any other reason why.

Henry Aldrich, *Reasons for Drinking*

Gordon & MacPhail

58–60 South Street, Elgin, Moray IV30 1JY   *Tel* (0343) 545111

Open Mon–Fri 9–5.15; Sat 9–5 **Closed** Wed pm (Jan, Feb, May, June, Oct, Nov),
Sun, public holidays **Credit cards** Access, Visa; personal and business accounts
Discounts 5% on 6 bottles; 10% on 12 bottles **Delivery** Free within 30-mile
radius (min 1 bottle) **Glass hire** Free with 1-case order **Tastings and talks**,
cellarage Not available

Any merchant who is prepared to deliver a single bottle within
a radius of 30 miles deserves a round of applause. The business
at Gordon & MacPhail is aimed mainly towards the wholesale
trade but there is a retail shop and nationwide mail order is
available. The real attraction of this company is the totally
unrivalled range of whiskies. These come in a list twice as fat as
the wine-list and include dated whiskies, specially bottled
whiskies and several pages of miniatures.

The wine-list takes in the world with a surprising emphasis
on the southern hemisphere. KWV provides many of the South
African wines but there is a good selection of estate wines from
Neethlingshof, Groot Constantia and Fairview. Chilean wines
are from the old-style Santa Carolina bodega, Australia provides
a good selection from Mitchells, Tyrrell's and Wynns, with Cooks
and Stoneleigh from New Zealand. German wines are obviously
still selling well in Elgin – producers names tend to disappear
in this section but von Simmern, Bischöflichen Weingüter Trier
and Prüm feature occasionally.

A good range of clarets, burgundies and Rhônes caters for
more traditional tastes, and a fine selection of vintage ports,
dating back to 1948, should keep out the worst of the winter
weather.

Best buys

Rowland's Brook Shiraz/Cabernet 1990, Australia, £
Cape County Chardonnay nv, South Africa, £
Mitchells Peppertree Shiraz 1991, Australia, ££
Pask Sauvignon Blanc 1992, New Zealand, ££

But that which most doth take my Muse and me,
Is a pure cup of rich Canary wine,
Which is the Mermaid's now, but shall be mine:
Of which, had Horace or Anacreon tasted,
Their lives, as do their lines, till now had lasted.

Ben Jonson, *Epigrams: Inviting a Friend to Supper*

Grape Ideas

3/5 Hythe Bridge Street, Oxford, Oxfordshire OX1 2EW	*Tel* (0865) 791313/724866
Associated outlet	
Grape Ideas, 2a Canfield Gardens, London NW6 3BS	*Tel* 071-328 7317

Open Mon–Sat 10–7 **Closed** Sun, public holidays **Credit cards** Access, Visa; personal and business accounts **Discounts** 5% on 1 unmixed case, 2.5% on 1 mixed case; larger orders by negotiation **Delivery** Free locally, approx 10-mile radius of Oxford (min order £50); elsewhere free on 3+ cases; mail-order available **Glass hire** Charge for breakages and unclean glasses only **Tastings and talks** Tutored tastings on request; large annual tasting **Cellarage** Not available

Grape Ideas in Oxford may look like a warehouse but you can buy single bottles as well as by the case (mixed cases qualify for a smaller discount). Part of the warehouse is in fact a different company (Fine Vintage Wines), although this is not apparent to the casual customer. That means there are two ranges available but since all bottles go through the same till-point we are considering them together. Just in case you are not totally confused, there is a shop in London, also called Grape Ideas, which is part of the same operation. That shop has access to pretty much everything that is available in Oxford, although it may take a day or two to be delivered.

The range is fairly comprehensive with a good spread of New World wines. Australians are from Leasingham and Plantagenet, as well as the widely available Rosemount and Wyndhams. New Zealand wines are a mixture of familiar names like Cooks, Cloudy Bay and Delegat's, with some less well-known wines from Vidal and Redwood Valley. Chile sports a full range from Viña Carmen, while Argentina provides the big flavours of Trapiche. New this year are Fetzer and Sutter Home from California and a South African range from Zonnebloem. Also new is a range of five wines from Château des Charmes, a small winery near Niagara in Ontario.

Italy has good Chiantis from Isole e Olena, Villa di Vetrice and Frescobaldi. Spain provides a full range from Campo Viejo as well as Torres and Marqués de Riscal. In France, Bordeaux and burgundy are the major sections, with a surprising choice of white Mâcons under £8. The Fine Vintage Wines list provides the top-notes to this range, with clarets, burgundies and ports from recent and not so recent vintages. Some of these wines are available by the straight case only, so check before setting your heart on a particular bottle.

Best buys

Domaine de la Présidente 1992, Vin de Pays de la Principauté d'Orange, £
Mount Barker Red 1990, Plantagenet, Western Australia, £
Moutere Valley Sauvignon 1991, Nelson, New Zealand, ££
Trapiche Medalla Cabernet/Malbec 1991, Argentina, ££

Great Northern Wine Company

Granary Wharf, The Canal Basin, Leeds,	*Tel* (0532) 461200
West Yorkshire LS1 4BR	
The Warehouse, Blossomgate, Ripon,	*Tel* (0756) 606767
North Yorkshire HG4 2AJ	

Open Mon–Fri 9–6; Sat 9.30–5; Sun 12–3; public holidays 9–5 **Closed** Chr Day, Boxing Day, New Year's Day **Credit cards** Access, Visa; personal and business accounts **Discounts** 8% on 1 case **Delivery** Free within 30-mile radius of Leeds (min 1 case); otherwise at cost; mail order available **Glass hire** Free with order **Tastings and talks** Speciality tastings; monthly tutored tastings; annual wine fair; Ripon wine club **Cellarage** £2.50 per case per year

We are sad to note the loss of one of the wine trade's best addresses. Dark Arches, Leeds Canal Basin has given way to Granary Wharf – very nineties but it sounds a lot less atmospheric. Great Northern has also opened another outlet in Ripon and has gone for a good address again – Blossomgate. With shelves well stocked from around the world, but with a particular enthusiasm for New World wines, Great Northern provides good drinking throughout the price range.

Australia is particularly strong, with big names such as Brown Brothers, Seppelts and Penfolds leading the team. A worthy selection from smaller wineries, such as Tarra Warra (great Pinot Noir) and Mountadam (excellent Chardonnay), adds individuality and style. Some of the prices seem a little out of line with the competition, for example Wirra Wirra Church Block is £9.05 here but only £6.70 from the Wine Society, but others are pretty much the same as elsewhere. As usual it is always worth checking around before you buy. New Zealand offers a fine selection, with wines from Nobilo, Delegat's and Kumeu River amongst others. Chile sports the splendid Montes and Undurraga wines. The USA range has been expanded to show the various styles and grape varieties available: Mondavi, Oak Knoll, Statton Hills and Sonoma-Cutrer are some of the prestigious names.

Spain includes a wide range of Riojas (CUNE, Berberana and La Rioja Alta among others) plus Torres, Ochoa and a couple of wines from Somontano. France takes in a good round-up of the classic areas: Alsace has wines from Gisselbrecht, clarets stay well within the affordable range and burgundies are largely through Drouhin and Jaffelin. Particularly good is the wide range of French regional wines.

Best buys

Rolleston Vale Red 1992, Australia, £
Ch. Tour des Gendres, Bergerac Sec 1991, £
Gonnet Champagne nv, ££
Muscat d'Alsace, Gisselbrecht 1990, ££

Great Western Wine Company

2–3 Mile End, London Road, Bath, Avon *Tel* (0225) 448428
BA1 6PT

Case sales only **Open** Mon–Sat 9–7 **Closed** Sun, public holidays
Credit cards Access, Visa; business accounts **Discounts** Available; up to 10% on
selected wines **Delivery** Free within 20-mile radius of Bath (min order 1 mixed
case); elsewhere at cost **Glass hire** Free **Tastings and talks** Regular tastings
Cellarage £2.50 per case per year

This is yet another wine company named after a railway (see
Great Northern). Perhaps the trend will continue and soon we
will be able to buy wine from the Trans-Siberian Wine Cellar or
small bottles from the Hornby Double 'OO' Wine Company.

Great Western does not operate out of railway sidings but
from offices in Bath. There is a shop which, despite all
appearances, does not have a retail licence, so purchases have to
be made by the mixed case. This is no real problem since the
range is wide enough to hold the interest for quite some time.

France takes in all the classic areas. Good basic clarets are
mainly under £10 and are supplemented by a grand cru section
which will explore the inner recesses of your wallet more
thoroughly. Burgundies try hard to stay affordable, with basics
from reliable *négociants* and a quick flurry among the better
domaines. The south of France has new attractions, including a
range of vins de pays from small domaines, all under £5, apart
from the splendid Mas de Daumas Gassac.

Italy has also seen some work. Highlights include Capello di
Prete from the south, Chianti from Isole e Olena and good-value
Valpolicella from the co-operative in Soave.

Spain looks good with reliable names – CUNE, Torres and
Ochoa provide much of the action. Australia, New Zealand,
California, Chile and South Africa are also worth a browse.

Best buys

Ch. de la Reynardie 1990, Vin de Pays des Coteaux de
Murviel, £
Viña los Vascos Cabernet Sauvignon 1991, Chile, £
Ch. Picque Caillou 1988, Pessac-Léognan, ££
Matua Valley Sauvignon Blanc 1992, Marlborough, New
Zealand, ££

Peter Green

37a/b Warrender Park Road, Edinburgh   *Tel* 031-229 5925
EH9 1HJ

Open Mon–Fri 9.30–6.30; Sat 9.30–7   **Closed** Sun, public holidays
Credit cards None accepted; personal and business accounts   **Discounts** 5% on
unmixed cases   **Delivery** 50p per trip in Edinburgh; mail order available
Glass hire Free   **Tastings and talks** Regular tastings; to groups on request
Cellarage Not available

Does your local wine merchant give you a choice of ten Alsace
Rieslings and 11 Gewurztraminers? Is there a terrific selection of
clarets and four vintages of Quarts de Chaume among a tongue-
tingling array of Loire Chenin Blancs? And is delivery within
city limits supposedly charged at 50p but isn't really (that's only
a threat in case someone wants a bottle of lemonade delivered)?
If all this has a familiar ring then you must live in Edinburgh,
within sight and sound of Peter Green.

This independent merchant is run by Michael and Douglas
Romer who appear to be extremely modest of their buying
skills. 'We are lucky to have such interested customers, they
teach us a lot,' the brothers tell us. Well, luck cuts both ways
here and if you needed a reason to live in this lovely city, Peter
Green would rate pretty high on anyone's list. The collection is
not just good, it is very good. Germany seems to be taken
seriously: a letter 'e' or 'g' alongside each wine tells you
whether it is from a single vineyard (*Einzellage*) or a collection of
vineyards (*Grosslage*). Since even the Germans get muddled over
their vineyards this devastatingly simple idea seems a good way
to dispense information. Italian wines are worth several
weekends' research. Not only are the super-expensive Super
Tuscans here but an enticing range of Italian grapes from
excellent producers, too. Spain, Portugal and the New World
have been explored with great enthusiasm. Thirty Chilean
wines, nine Argentinians and one wine from Mexico provide a
vinous tour guide of South and Middle America. An extensive
range of Californians and two Inniskillin wines from Canada
continue the journey northwards. With a couple of Swiss wines,
five Greek, two from China and a fistful of vintages from the
Lebanon's Musar, an explorer's pith helmet may be needed to
map out the range fully.

A variety of half-bottles is available – particularly good in the
sweet-pudding direction. If you fancy a drop of the hard stuff,
over 100 whiskies could prolong decision-making indefinitely.

Best buys

Undurraga Sauvignon Blanc 1992, Chile, £
Vine Vale Chardonnay 1992, Lehmann, Australia, £
Hunter's Marlborough oak-aged Sauvignon 1991, New
Zealand, ££
Ch. Chasse-Spleen 1988, Moulis, ££

Greenwood & Co

See Nickolls & Perks

Guildford Wine Market/The Vintner

216 London Road, Burpham, Guildford, Surrey GU4 7JS	*Tel* (0483) 575933

Vintner shops

51 Queen Victoria Street, London EC4	*Tel* 071-236 1758
4 Angel Gate, High Street, Guildford, Surrey GU1 3DP	*Tel* (0483) 451214
4 The 1st Floor Gallery, The Peacocks, Woking, Surrey GU2 1GA.	*Tel* (0483) 765470

Open Mon–Sat 10–9; Sun, public holidays 12–2, 7–9 (may vary from store to store) **Closed** Chr Day, Boxing Day, Jan 1 **Credit cards** All accepted; personal and business accounts **Discounts** 10% on 1 case; Vintner Club discount
Delivery Free locally **Glass hire** Free with suitable case order
Tastings and talks In-store tastings at weekends; tastings for groups on request
Cellarage Not available

Guildford Wine Market is the name over the door but, since the last edition of the *Guide*, Nicholas Brougham, who built up this business, has joined forces with James Rackham in a small chain of four shops, now known as the Vintner. The Guildford Wine Market is one of this chain but retains its original name.

Much of the range is shared with the Arthur Rackham shops (*q.v.*) but the emphasis is definitely on the finer wines in the range. All the shops in the Vintner group will be run in the

proprietorial style, developing good customer relations and building confidence in the range.

There is also the Vintner Wine Club, accessible through these shops and Arthur Rackham for an annual fee of £18. For this you get discounts on all purchases, and the opportunity to go to gourmet dinners, tastings and visits to the vineyards.

Best buys

Domaine de l'Ile St Pierre Rouge, Vin de Pays des Bouches-du-Rhône 1991, £
Niersteiner Louis Philip 1992, Guntrum, £
Côtes de Nuits Villages 1990, Gérard Julien, ££
Marqués del Puerto Reserva 1985, Rioja, ££

Half Yard Wines

Regatta View, River Road, Taplow,   *Tel* (0628) 24155
Buckinghamshire SL6 0BE

Case sales only   Open Mon–Fri 9–6; always available for telephone orders
Credit cards None accepted; personal and business accounts   **Discounts** 5% on
10+ cases   **Delivery** Free within 25-mile radius (min order 10+ cases)
Glass hire Free with order   **Tastings and talks** Four tastings a year; two tutored
tastings per year   **Cellarage** Not available

Maggie Richardson continues the fine tradition of many sole traders in the wine business – she has a day job, too. As a change from all the doctors, dentists and teachers who juggle two jobs until the wine side gets big enough to rely on, Maggie is a purser with British Airways. With a new baby now joining the juggling act, Maggie still manages to find time to give talks and tastings when asked.

The list is limited but good, and whatever deficiencies there are in the range, Maggie makes up for in the boundless enthusiasm she shows for the subject. Prices are keen, reflecting her low overheads. Most wines fit comfortably under the £10 mark, only the champagnes and a handful of wines creep above this level. There is a fine collection from Spain and Italy, Bordeaux stays firmly in the petit-château range, apart from a grand cru St-Emilion – Ch. Haut-Sarpe – while burgundies are of the white variety, no reds! The Loire shows no such prejudice, including two impressive reds among a small collection of whites. The range from the New World demonstrates a talent for picking out value and variety.

Best buys

St Nicolas de Bourgueil Rosé 1991, Max Cognard, Tacuau, £
Ch. de Berbec 1990, Premières Côtes de Bordeaux, Brun
Camille, £
Puerto Fino Sherry, ££
Gigondas Ch. Respail 1989, ££

Hall Batson Wine Importers

168d Wroxham Road, Sprowston, Norwich,   *Tel* (0603) 415115
Norfolk NR7 8DE

Case sales only   **Open** Mon–Fri 8.30–6; Sat 9–1   **Closed** Sun, public holidays
Credit cards None accepted; personal and business accounts
Discounts Available   **Delivery** Free within 50-mile radius of Norwich; elsewhere
at cost   **Glass hire** Free; breakages charged for   **Tastings and talks** Regular
tastings; in-store tastings   **Cellarage** Not available

Despite a brief flirtation with a retail outlet, Hall Batson remains
a case-sales-only operation in Norwich. Buying wine here seems
to be a fairly civilised process. Customers go along to the
warehouse and instead of pushing a trolley around they can sit
in the tasting room and discuss their requirements with a
member of staff. Bottles are always open for tasting to help
make decisions easier.

The range has grown since last year. Whiskies are now a
speciality with over 100 single malts listed alphabetically from
Aberfeldy to Tullibardine. Blends, Irish Whiskey and Bourbon
bring the selection up to a massive 155 varieties.

The wine range is equally comprehensive. From France,
clarets are the affordable type with a good sprinkling of crus
bourgeois among some classier wines. Burgundies are
represented by a wide variety of villages, vintages and
producers. Chapoutier joins Père Anselme in providing many of
the Rhônes, while Zind Humbrecht features in Alsace. Château
Chalon from the Jura is one of the more unusual offerings from
this firm. Quality producers among the Italian range include
Antinori, Prunotto and Masi; Spanish activity is centred on
Berberana and CUNE. With Mondavi among the Californians
and a fine collection from Australia, this range could provide
interesting drinking for quite some time.

Best buys

Sauvignon Blanc, Duc de Berticot 1992, Côtes de Duras, £
Ch. de Corneilla Rouge 1990, Côtes du Roussillon, £
Mâcon-Clessé 1990, Domaine des Gandines, Robert
Dananchet, ££
Rockford Basket Press Shiraz 1989, Australia, ££

Halves

Wood Yard, off Corve Street, Ludlow,   *Tel* (0584) 877866
Shropshire SY8 2PX
(See also C A Rookes)

Case sales only **Open** Mon–Fri 9–6; Sat 10–1 **Closed** Sun, public holidays
Credit cards Access, Amex, Visa **Discounts** 4% on 1 unmixed case; £2.35 per
order on 2+ cases; 7.5% on specific mixed cases on list **Delivery** To UK mainland
(charge inc in price quoted) **Glass hire** Not available
Tastings and talks Periodic tastings on a nationwide basis; dinners at restaurants
on a nationwide basis **Cellarage** Not available

Halves was a good idea just waiting to happen, but it took Tim
Jackson to do it. The principle is simple: thousands of people
would like to drink decent wine but don't want to open a full
bottle. Restaurants are an obvious market but, for home
drinkers too, there are many occasions when it is more fun to
open two different half-bottles.

Some producers are more amenable than others to the idea of
half-bottles. In Jerez everyone drinks sherry from half-bottles
and, accordingly, Halves has a good range of Hidalgo sherries.
Champagne producers are already used to the idea of halves;
the house champagne here is the delicious Bruno Paillard.
Burgundy in half-bottles is less usual but Tim Jackson has
managed to get some splendid Gevry-Chambertin from Alain
Burguet as well as wines from Trapet, Prosper Maufoux and
Chablis from Louis Michel. Clarets are limited in number but
include Chx Sénéjac, Potensac and a 1985 Léoville-Poyferré.
There are interesting wines among the Rhônes, with Château de
Beaucastel and a clutch of wines from Guigal. The New World
has obviously taken this company to heart and bottled a
surprising range of Australian and California wines in the
smaller version.

Halves has set up a cash-and-carry warehouse in Stratford-
upon-Avon in conjunction with C A Rookes. Customers can
make their choice at the warehouse (retail licence) or order
through the Ludlow office in the usual way.

To avoid your half-bottles slipping through the holes in your
normal-sized wine rack, Tim Jackson can arrange for half-size
racks to be made. This sounds like a clever idea, as is free
delivery of a case (24 halves) within mainland UK.

Best buys

Manzanilla La Gitana, Hidalgo Sherry, £
Ch. Lamothe de Haux Rouge 1989, Premières Côtes de
Bordeaux, £
Bruno Paillard Champagne Rosé nv, ££
Quivera Cabernet Sauvignon 1989, California, ££

Hampden Wine Company

Jordan's Courtyard, 8 Upper High Street,   *Tel* (0844) 213251
Thame, Oxfordshire OX9 3ER

Open Mon, Tue, Sat 9.30–5; Wed 9.30–5; Thur, Fri 9.30–5.30 **Closed** Sun, public
holidays **Credit cards** Access, Visa; Switch; personal and business accounts
Discounts 5% on 1 case; quantity discounts negotiable **Delivery** Free within 20-
mile radius of Thame (min 1 case); free elsewhere for larger orders; mail order
available **Glass hire** Free with order **Tastings and talks** Eight tastings per year
with dinner at around £30 per person **Cellarage** Free for customers

The Hampden Wine Company is run by Lance Foyster and Ian
Hope-Morley, and it is one of Ian's ancestors whose face stares
at you from the cover of the wine-list. He was Puritan John
Hampden who apparently refused to pay ship-tax to Charles I.
What he would think of his descendant making a living from
something as enjoyable as wine doesn't bear thinking about.
Hampden shares a shop with a delicatessen called Jordans – you
have to walk through the deli to get at the wine. In 1991 radical
expansion increased the wine area by two-and-a-half times, so
now it looks more like a proper wine shop instead of a bit
bolted on. Supermarkets provide the main competition in this
area but Ian and Lance counter them by providing an intelligent
selection of hand-picked, good-value wines. Lance is a Master of
Wine so you can be sure of getting some pretty competent
advice.

In all areas of the list there are quality wines at reasonable
prices. A selection of vins de pays starts off the range, and
among the clarets there are some decent petits châteaux.
Portugal is well worth exploring, exhibiting some traditional
wines from small quintas. New World areas have a fair cross-
section of well-priced drinking, including Cousiño Macul and
Concha y Toro from Chile. But this is not just a cheap list; there
is plenty available to encourage customers to climb the quality
ladder. Among the Rhônes, a single vineyard wine from Marius
Gentaz allows you to try just the Côte Brune part of the
normally blended Côte Rôtie, and there are some very special
madeiras lurking at the back of the list for when the occasion
demands. A separate list of fine and very fine wines is also
available.

Tutored tastings with dinner are a regular feature and there are always a few bottles open in the shop, especially on Saturdays. The motto of this establishment is 'Life is too short to drink bad wine', a sentiment with which we agree wholeheartedly.

Best buys

Quinta de la Rosa 1991, Douro, Portugal, £
Salisbury Estate Chardonnay 1992, Victoria, Australia, £
Gentaz-Dervieux 1990, Côte Rôtie, ££
Quinta do Cotto, Grande Escolha, Douro, Portugal, ££

Harcourt Fine Wine

3 Harcourt Street, London W1H 1DS   *Tel* 071-723 7202

Open Mon–Fri 9–6; Sat 10.30–5 **Closed** Sun, public holidays **Credit cards** All accepted; personal and business accounts **Discounts** From 5% per case **Delivery** In central London and the City (charges depend upon value); mail order available **Glass hire** Free **Tastings and talks** One free annual tasting; bottles normally open to try **Cellarage** 10p per case per week

Harcourt Fine Wine tackles the tricky end of the market – German wines (including a fine collection of reds), English wines and fine vintage brandies. These three areas are handled with great skill, although it is encouraging to see a few other wines on the list – a relief to regular customers who might fancy a change now and then.

English wine is still a difficult concept to put over. There are still a few people who have not yet grasped the difference between imported grape juice diluted with tap water and fermented into something fairly second-rate (British wine) and the product of an English vineyard, carefully nurtured through fermentation and bottling (English wine). This list explores vineyards from Breaky Bottom in Sussex to Sharpham in Devon, a total of 45 properties, most of them sporting two or three wines in various styles. There are a few English red wines and four *méthode traditionnelle* sparklers – interesting conversation pieces as well as being good wines. The German range is estate-based and from quality producers, including Lingenfelder and Schloss Reinhartshausen. The German wines of Karl Heinz Johner make an appearance, and he must feel particularly at home in this list as he used to make wine at a major English vineyard and still acts as consultant to some. The range of brandies includes cognac, armagnac, calvados, eaux-de-vie and marc, all from a variety of vintages and companies.

Best buys

Hambledon Dry 1990, Hampshire, £
Rock Lodge Ortega 1990, Sussex, £
Beenleigh Manor Cabernet/Merlot 1990, Devon, ££
Staple St James Müller-Thurgau 1990, Kent, ££

Harpenden Wines

68 High Street, Harpenden, Hertfordshire *Tel* (0582) 765605
AL5 2SP

Open Mon–Fri 10–10; Sat 9–10; Sun 12–3, 7–9; public holidays 12–8.30
Closed Chr and New Year   **Credit cards** All accepted; personal and business
accounts   **Discounts** 5% on 1 case for credit card or 7.5% for cheque/cash;
negotiable on 5+ cases   **Delivery** Free within 10-mile radius of Harpenden
Glass hire Free   **Tastings and talks** To groups on request   **Cellarage** By
arrangement

Just one retail outlet for this company remains but the range is
as dependable as ever. Good choice, honest advice and reliable
service are the key words. Australia seems to be a favoured
region: Coldridge, Mitchelton and Brown Brothers are the main
players but there are wines from Mountadam and Heggies
Vineyard as well as three organics from Buchanan in Tasmania.
New Zealand provides a basic range from Montana but there
are some additional treats from Te Mata, Millton and Vavasour.
Other New World areas covered include Guenoc Vineyards from
Lake County and Foppiano from Sonoma in California. Chilean
wines are the full-flavoured Montes range.

Italy is worth spending some time browsing through.
Pagliarese Chianti, Barco Reale from Capezzana and Barolo from
Borgogno are featured. Two wines from Puglia and a couple
from Sardinia and Sicily add to the variety. France includes a
fair selection of clarets, burgundies and Loire wines, although
the Rhône looks a bit thin. A good selection of vins de pays
makes up for this deficiency.

There are also 15 organic wines grouped together at the back
of the list and a good selection of malt whiskies available in the
shop.

Best buys

Ch. Lamothe 1992, Bordeaux Blanc, £
Les Terraces de Guilhem 1992, Vin de pays de l'Hérault, £
Ch. Haut Piquat 1988, Lussac St-Emilion, ££
Châteauneuf-du-Pape 1985, Pascal, ££

Gerard Harris Fine Wines

2 Green End Street, Aston Clinton, *Tel* (0296) 631041
Buckinghamshire HP22 5HP

Open Mon–Wed 9.30–6.30; Thurs–Sat 9.30–8 **Closed** Sun, public holidays
Credit cards Access, Visa; personal and business accounts **Discounts** Not
available **Delivery** Free within an area bordered by the M1/M25 in the East and
Buckingham in the West, and from the M40 in the South to Milton Keynes in the
North (min order 1 case); mail order available **Glass hire** Free
Tastings and talks Two major wine fairs each year; the Bell Fine Wine Society
organises 6 tutored tastings per year **Cellarage** Not available

The new list from this merchant is just a shadow of its former
self, but that is good news. Apparently, the old range, with its
huge variety of the great and the good, had become massively

depleted. Now, a new retail-shop manager has been appointed and the list tidied up. The range is restricted but at least the wines are actually available and there is continuity.

Many customers have reacted well to this change, and with time the list will grow again. Meanwhile, if customers want a particular wine of a particular vintage, it can be ordered.

The range first takes a look at the classic areas. Clarets are from a collection of well-known châteaux – Cissac, Angludet, Batailley and so on. There are quite a few below £10 before prices climb up to second- or third-growth levels. Interestingly, there are still a few older vintages lurking here, going back to 1978.

Burgundies are well chosen and show that quality is still an important factor at Gerard Harris. Jayer Gilles, Dujac and Domaine Voarick are some of the growers, with *négociants* Bouchard Père, Chanson and Faiveley also appearing.

Alsace wins are mainly from quality producer Kuentz-Bas, a Grand Cru Gewurztraminer showing just how concentrated this wine can get. From the Rhône, Ch. de Beaucastel provides lots of flavour, but good Côtes-du-Rhônes keep the cost of everyday drinking down.

Outside France, Spain manages a good variety within a small range. Riojas include the massively flavoured Gran Reserva 904 from La Rioja Alta and wines from CUNE and Marqués de Murrieta. Torres also features here. Portugal gives good value with wines from Fonseca and Tinta da Anfora from João Pires. Italy concentrates on classic areas and good producers such as Rocca delle Macie and Frescobaldi.

The New World has a fairly restrained look to it. Brown Brothers and Normans from Australia, Riverside and Mondavi Oakville from California and a handful from South Africa. New Zealand shows some independence with a Pinotage from Nobilo among the reds and the splendid Elston Chardonnay among the whites. Ports were always a feature here – there are apparently still limited stocks of vintages back to 1963.

This range has been pruned back hard, but the cuts seem to have been made by a well-trained hand, and future growth should be good.

The Bell Fine Wine Society costs £15 for life membership and gives access to tastings, dinners and special offers.

Best buys

Dry Plains Cabernet/Shiraz 1991, Australia, £
Chardonnay, Vin de Pays d'Oc 1992, J&F Lurton, £
Domaine de Vignemont, St-Véran 1991, Thévenet, ££
Ch. Lamothe 1987, 1er Côtes de Bordeaux, ££

Roger Harris

Loke Farm, Weston Longville, Norfolk
NR9 5LG
Tel (0603) 880171

Case sales only   **Open** Mon–Fri 9–5   **Closed** Sat, Sun, public holidays
Credit cards All accepted; personal and business accounts   **Discounts** 2 cases at
£2 per case, 3 cases at £2.50 per case, 5 cases at £3 per case   **Delivery** Free on UK
mainland (min 1 case); mail order available   **Glass hire** Not available
Tastings and talks To groups on request   **Cellarage** Not available

If your only contact with Beaujolais tends to be of the Nouveau
variety, send for a copy of Roger Harris's list and prepare to
have your eyes opened and your tastebuds awakened.

Roger Harris is a Beaujolais specialist. He admits that what
started out as a simple enjoyment of the wine has now
developed into a passion, and this enthusiasm comes across in
his list. For a start, it is not just a list. First, you study the
booklet. This is a detailed story about the area, the soil, people,
vintages and villages and is full of the kind of information you
can get only if you spend years researching just one area. There
are even recommendations for hotels and restaurants should you
decide to visit the source of this interest. Next comes the list,
again no half-hearted effort. The growers and their wines are
introduced: 11 Beaujolais-Villages, four Juliénas, the same
number from Chénas, then comes Chiroubles, Morgon, St-
Amour and so on. Some of the wines are available in a variety
of vintages – undoubtedly the most comprehensive collection of
Beaujolais you will come across.

In addition to these major documents come regular mailshots
with special offers, new vintages and mixed-case offers. If,
perish the thought, you might want to drink something other
than Beaujolais, Roger Harris takes care of that, too. There is a
small range from the Mâconnais, a couple of vins de pays, a
grower's champagne, and a marc made from the Beaujolais
grape skins. Loke Farm is the best place to start your Beaujolais
education.

Best buys

Vin de Pays des Côtes de Gascogne 1991, Cuvée Louis XI, £
Vin de Pays du Vaucluse 1991, Cuvée Louis XI, £
Moulin-à-Vent 1989, Château Moulin-à-Vent, ££
Morgon, oak-aged 1991, Domaine Noël Aucoeur, ££

Harrods

Knightsbridge, London SW1X 7XL   *Tel* 071-730 1234

Open Mon, Tues, Sat 10–6; Wed–Fri 10–7; public holidays 10–6 **Closed** Sun
Credit cards All accepted; personal and business accounts **Discounts** 1 free bottle
per case **Delivery** Free in central London (min order £25) and within 25-mile
radius of M25 (min £50 order); £5 charge for orders under £50; mail order
available **Glass hire** Not available **Tastings and talks** Weekly tastings to
customers **Cellarage** Not available

There's a brand new range in the hallowed halls of Harrods,
with new emphasis on wines with individuality and style. Wine
buyer Alun Griffiths MW has spent the last year or so clearing
out the endless *négociant* wines and replacing them with quality
growers. There are also new wines under Harrods' own-labels,
and there seems to have been a rethink on prices. This
gloriously extravagant emporium will never be the cheapest
place to buy wine, but it is no longer just for the seriously rich.
There are some very drinkable wines under £6, although, if you
have a fortune to spend, they can certainly help you do so.

Among the clarets there is a fair selection of classed growths
but there are also drinkable petits châteaux which would go
down well at a Knightsbridge dinner party. Burgundies come
from names such as Rousseau, Dujac, Voarick and Jayer-Gilles,
with a sprinkling from Drouhin and Faiveley. The rest of France
is good; Chave in the Rhône, Trimbach in Alsace and some
affordable wines from the South.

Italy has plenty to keep the interest going. It is possible to
spend serious money on up-market vini da tavola but you don't
have to, with decent Chianti from Rocca delle Macie and
Montepulciano di Abruzzo from Umani Ronchi.

Australia starts with Aldridge Estate and climbs via Leeuwin
Estate and Cape Mentelle up to Grange. New Zealand, South
Africa and the Americas keep the interest going.

A huge variety of champagnes, from half-bottles up to
Nebuchadnezzars, could provide the toasts for any number of
celebrations.

Best buys

Minervois, Ch. de Violet 1991, £
Somontano Macabeo 1987, Montesierra, £
St Joseph, Les Grisiers 1990, Perret, ££
Ch. Tour Haut Caussan, Moulis 1989, ££

Harvest Wine Group

Clocktower Mews, Stanlake Park, Twyford,   *Tel* (0734) 344290
Reading, Berkshire RG10 0BN

Open Mon–Fri 11–6   **Credit cards** Access, Visa; business accounts
Discounts Between 5% and 10% depending on quantity purchased
Delivery Reading postcodes RG1–10, 1 case £3.50, 2+ cases £2.95; nationwide
delivery, free for 11+ cases, prices vary from £2.95–£6.75 for smaller amounts
Glass hire Not available   **Tastings and talks** Regular tastings on and off site;
group talks and tastings on and off site   **Cellarage** Not available

The name of this company is new, but it grew out of Great
English Wines, which more clearly explains its business.
Harvest Wines is the marketing arm of a group of English
vineyards – all under the carefully trained eye of Australian
winemaker John Worontschak.

There are ten vineyards in the group; the main base is at
Thames Valley Vineyards, but John travels to all the vineyards
in the group to oversee the grapes and winemaking. The quality
of some wines has improved enormously as a result. The range
includes crisp lively whites, such as Pilton Manor Dry, or oak-
fermented fuller wines such as Sharpham's Barrel-Fermented
Madeleine Angevine. There is even a selection of reds and some
Traditional-Method sparkling wines.

English wine has had a patchy reception from wine drinkers,
but these wines are some of the best around.

Best buys

Valley Vineyards Regatta 1991, Berkshire, £
Boze Down Skippetts 1992, Berkshire, £
Valley Vineyards Fumé 1991, Berkshire, ££
Pilton Manor Fumé 1991, Somerset, ££

John Harvey & Sons

Order office and shop
31 Denmark Street, Bristol, Avon BS1 5DQ   *Tel* (0272) 268882

Open Mon–Fri 9–6; Sat 9–1   **Closed** Sun, public holidays   **Credit cards** All
accepted; personal and business accounts   **Discounts** £2 on 2–5 cases, £3 on 6–10
cases, £3.50 on 11+ cases   **Delivery** Free within 30-mile radius (min 1 case/£5
order)   **Glass hire** Free with order   **Tastings and talks** Free autumn tasting for
customers; gourmet wine tastings and dinner from £50 per person; special tastings
with supper/lunch £7.50 per person   **Cellarage** £3.80 per case per year

Major changes here in Bristol as John Harvey reviews its
business. The company has decided to concentrate on local
customers, with a range that is much more restricted than in the

past. They also have decided not to offer a national mail-order service.

The range is still big on claret. Classy names are here but so are good-value cru bourgeois wines, such as Lamothe-Cissac and La Tour St Bonnet. Ch. Latour, its second wine Forts de Latour and the fairly anonymous third wine, Pauillac de Ch. Latour, are also featured. There is a good selection of burgundy, mainly Jadot wines, from a basic Bourgogne Blanc right up to Le Montrachet. Other producers include Trapet, Mongeard-Mugneret and Tollot-Beaut. The Rhône, Loire and Alsace all contain good wines but would not hold the attention for too long. French country wines are a reasonable choice under £5.

Spain, Chile, South Africa, Australia and New Zealand are all represented by a handful of wines from each. Only Germany and Italy manage a selection of more than half a dozen.

The Denmark Street shop always used to carry extra lines and bin ends and we hope this continues to add a little more variety to this good but restricted list. Gourmet wine tastings took off in a big way last year and the second series look attractive. Winemakers, such as Anthony Barton of Léoville-Barton, lead a tasting of their wines, which is followed by dinner. Not cheap at around £60 per person, but definitely An Occasion.

Best buys

Domaine de Haut Carizière, Muscadet de Sèvre et Maine 1991, £
Domaine de Bosc Sauvignon 1991, Vin de Pays de l'Hérault, £
Pauillac de Ch. Latour 1990, ££
Ch. Fombrauge 1986, St-Emilion, ££

Richard Harvey Wines

Not a shop

Bucknowle House, Bucknowle, Wareham, *Tel* (0929) 480352
Dorset BH20 5PQ
71 Avenue Carnot, Cherbourg, France *Tel* (010 33) 33 43 3979
Mainly telephone and mail order

Case sales only Open Mon–Fri 9–6 **Closed** Sat, Sun, public holidays
Credit cards None accepted; personal and business accounts **Discounts** 5% on
7+ cases **Delivery** Free within 30-mile radius (min 3 cases); free delivery on 7+
cases elsewhere; otherwise £6 per consignment **Glass hire** Free with order
Tastings and talks Major annual tasting by invitation; tutored tastings, dinners,
etc. by arrangement **Cellarage** £4 per case per year (plus insurance)

There is a choice from Richard Harvey. Either you ring him up at his Dorset number and order wine in the UK or you can get on a boat and go along to his shop in Cherbourg and bring the bottles back yourself.

The two ranges are similar but not identical. If you choose the French route, you will save considerably on the total bill and, rather than just buying in a French supermarket, you will have the reassurance of choosing from a range selected by a Master of Wine.

The range includes some good vins de pays from the south, a few small-scale clarets and a handful of Rhône and Loire wines. Particularly interesting is the range of wines from Australia, New Zealand, Chile and Spain, all available to homeward travellers at attractive prices.

Best buys

Cabernet Sauvignon 1991, Vin de Pays d'Oc, Yves Gau, £
Ch. Bauduc, Bordeaux Blanc 1992, £
Moulin à Vent 1990, Paul Janin, ££
Le Mesnil, Blanc de Blancs Champagne nv, ££

Harvey Nichols

Knightsbridge, London SW1X 7RJ   *Tel* 071-235 5000

Open Mon–Fri 10–8; Sat 10–6; public holidays   **Closed** Sun, Chr period
Credit cards All cards accepted   **Discounts** 5% on one case   **Delivery** Free for
account-card customers or orders over £50 in inner London; mail-order available
Glass hire Not available   **Tastings and talks** In-store tastings on Sats; by
arrangement   **Cellarage** Not available

Knightsbridge wine-lovers have a new haunt – the fifth floor of this up-market store, where a new food market is also home to 850 or so wines. Its job is not only to sell wine over the counter but also to supply the restaurants on that floor. From a standing start, the buyers at Harvey Nichols have done well. There is a fine selection here, with a strong French influence, but it takes a good long look at the rest of the world as well.

Burgundies are a feature. Among the white wines there are basics from Chablis, Côtes Chalonnais and Mâconnais, all from reliable producers, but the range quickly leaps up the price scale to classier wines. Meursault from five different producers, Puligny-Montrachet from Leflaive, Sauzet and Drouhin and, at the very top of the heap, a choice of three vintages of Le Montrachet from Domaine de la Romanée-Conti. It is the same story among the reds. Affordable Bourgogne Rouge is closely followed by selections from quality growers and topped with La Tâche, Richebourg and other glorious wines. Clarets are slightly less extensive but there are some reasonably priced châteaux wines, as well as a 1961 Ch. Latour which could do serious damage to the bank balance.

The rest of the world has a confident touch. Italy has a classy collection from Avignonesi, Antinori, Ceretto and more; Spain relies on Torres, Ochoa and CUNE, with Vega Sicilia adding weight. Australia has all the right names – Pipers Brook, Petaluma, Henschke – but also manages some good-value Ryecroft and Peter Lehmann.

With America, north and south, New Zealand, Lebanon and even a trio of wines from Switzerland, Harvey Nichols looks like it is seriously in the wine business.

Best buys

Harvey Nichols Blanc House Selection, £
Champagne Deutz-Cuvée Harvey Nichols nv, ££
Il Vignola 1990, Avignonesi, Italy, ££

Haynes Hanson & Clark

Head office and wholesale warehouse
17 Lettice Street, London SW6 4EH   *Tel* 071-736 7878
Retail
36 Kensington Church Street, London   *Tel* 071-937 4650
W8 4BX

Open Mon–Sat 9–7 **Closed** Sun, public holidays **Credit cards** None accepted; personal and business accounts **Discounts** 10% on 1 unmixed case
Delivery Free in central London, Gloucestershire, M4 valley, Newmarket area (min order 5+ cases); otherwise 1 case £6.35, 2 cases £4 per case, 3–4 cases £3 per case; mail order available **Glass hire** Free **Tastings and talks** 6–10 free tastings per year by invitation only **Cellarage** Not available

If you are looking for quality, particularly from Burgundy, then this is the place to start. Anthony Hanson MW is a burgundy specialist who has written the definitive book on the subject. He is responsible for the selection of the range and his choice of wines cannot be faulted – he knows the growers and their wines well. The list is a collection of the good and the great: Simon Bize, Philipe Rossignol, Méo-Camuzet and more. But there are sound choices lower down the price scale which will not demand a second mortgage. St-Véran from Domaine des Deux Roches and Côtes de Brouilly from André Large both provide stylish drinking at prices considerably below heart-attack level.

Outside Burgundy, the same search for quality has continued. The Bordeaux section is not an endless list of well-known châteaux but a selected group of wines from good winemakers. There is a high proportion of second wines here: Lady Langoa, Ch. l'Hospitalet and Fiefs de Lagrange among them. Most clarets are of recent vintages – 1989s and 1990s with a few from 1985.

An indication of when these wines will be ready to drink would be an improvement to the list, although advice is only a phone call away. There are interesting wines to try from the Rhône and Loire sections and the New World beckons with Murphy-Goode and Saintsbury from California and the delicious Merlot from Matanzas Creek. Pierro, Dromana and Plantagenet are the highlights from Australia. New Zealand has wines from Palliser and Dashwood. Spain, Italy, Chile and South Africa all contribute good selections to this quality range.

HH&C operates a national mail-order business but you can buy by the case from the warehouse in Lettice Street. The retail shop in Kensington is small and not everything is immediately available.

Best buys

Ch. la Chapelle 1989, Bordeaux Supérieur, £
Domaine de l'Ameillaud 1992, Vin de Pays de Vaucluse, £
St-Véran 1992, Domaine des Deux Roches, ££
Bourgogne Pinot Noir 1990, Michel Lafarge, ££

The Heath Street Wine Co

See La Réserve

Cork was used by the Romans to stopper jars and amphorae but after the Romans its use was forgotten until the middle of the sixteenth century.

Hedley Wright

10–11 The Twyford Centre, London Road,   *Tel* (0279) 506512
Bishop's Stortford, Hertfordshire CM23 3YT

Case sales only **Open** Mon–Wed, Sat 10–6; Thur and Fri 10–7 **Closed** Sun,
public holidays **Credit cards** Access, Visa; personal and business accounts
Discounts By arrangement **Delivery** Free within 15-mile radius of Bishop's
Stortford **Glass hire** Free with 1-case order **Tastings and talks** Selection of
wines always available in-store; to groups on request; approx 4 tutored tastings
per year **Cellarage** £3.95 per case per year

With new supermarkets mushrooming in the Bishop's Stortford
area, Hedley Wright has to work hard to hold on to its
customers. It rises to this challenge by offering interesting
wines, personal service as well as the usual (but vital) sale-or-
return and glass-hire facilities that supermarkets cannot cope
with. In addition, the list is chatty, informative and well laid
out and the regular mailshots will keep you informed about
special offers.

Hedley Wright is a case-only merchant, but this means a
dozen assorted bottles and there is plenty to choose from. Vins
de pays start off the list, none over £5 and among them the
Troisgros Blanc – house wine for the 3-star restaurant of the
same name. South Africa has been visited this year and
provides a number of new wines, including the splendid Danie
de Wet Chardonnays and a selection of wines from Dr Julius
Laslo under the name Monastell. Chile is a speciality with the
splendid Montes wines in strength. Hedley Wright is also the
agent for Cellier le Brun (based in Marlborough, New Zealand)
who make quality sparkling wines. The clarets on the list are
affordable and Martin Wright's buying notes direct you to the
best bargains in the different price bands. Alsace wines are
provided by the co-operative in Kientzheim, and the
Australians include Heggies Vineyard from Hill-Smith and
James Halliday's Coldstream Hills.

Hedley Wright may be surrounded by supermarkets but it
looks as if it can rise to the challenge and win.

Best buys

Domaine de Pomes 1992, Vin de Pays des Côtes de Gascogne, £
Chardonnay, Domaine Petit Château 1992, Vin de Pays du
Jardin de la France, £
Daniel le Brun Brut nv, Sparkling, New Zealand, ££
Montes Alpha Cabernet Sauvignon 1989, Chile, ££

Douglas Henn-Macrae

Not a shop
81 Mackenders Lane, Eccles, Aylesford, Kent   *Tel* (0622) 710952
ME20 7JA

Case sales only   Open Telephone enquiries welcome Mon–Sat up to 10pm
Closed Sun, Chr & Easter   **Credit cards** Access, Visa   **Discounts** Not available
Delivery Free on UK mainland (min 10 cases); otherwise £8 per order; mail order
available   **Glass hire** Not available   **Tastings and talks** Tutored tastings to
societies on request   **Cellarage** Not available

'We like to deal with countries where we speak the language,'
says German teacher Douglas Henn-Macrae, and so it is easy to
understand why half his range is from Germany. How he also
came to stock Texan wines is a little more difficult to
comprehend unless DHM goes around in a stylish stetson.

Here in Aylesford, for 'German wines' read 'fairly unusual
German wines' (no Liebfraumilch and Piesporter). DHM
concentrates his attention on a few small family estates and local
cooperatives. He has a fondness for German reds, rosés and for
drier styles of wine. Exclamation marks note medal-winning
wines and these are scattered through the list with enthusiasm.

Texas is the other main area of interest, with wines from four
estates, including Sanchez Creek where Larry Hagman once
helped with the harvest. The last few cases of 'Ivanhoe' are here,
from a massive pile of bankrupt stock bought some years ago,
and Llano Estacado, as served to the Queen when she visited
the Lone Star State. Oregon and Washington State wines also
feature in this very personal selection.

Prices (quoted ex-VAT) seem reasonable and the list is worth
reading just for DHM's vigorous attack on 'sugar-water' German
wines.

Best buys

Texas Vineyards Johannisberg Riesling 1986, £
Llano Estacado Cabernet Sauvignon 1987, Texas, £
Trittenheimer Altärchen Riesling Spätlese 1990, Hubert
Clüsserath, ££

---

*Drink no longer water, but use a little wine for thy stomach's sake and
thine often infirmities.*

New Testament Timothy 5:23

Charles Hennings (Vintners)

London House, Lower Street, Pulborough, West Sussex RH20 2BW	*Tel* (0798) 872485/873909
10 Jenger's Mead, Billingshurst, West Sussex RH14 9TB	*Tel* (0403) 783187
Golden Square, Petworth, West Sussex GU28 0AP	*Tel* (0798) 43021

Open Mon–Thur 8.30–6; Fri 9–7; Sat 8.30–6 **Closed** Sun, public holidays **Credit cards** Access, Visa; personal and business accounts **Discounts** 10% on 1 case; negotiable on larger orders **Delivery** Depends on distance and size of order **Glass hire** Free with suitable order **Tastings and talks** Free in-store tastings on Fridays and Saturdays **Cellarage** Not available

There are some good wines lurking on the shelves at this small independent Sussex merchant. The New World range has increased dramatically this year with Australia providing a complete line of Penfolds, from basics right up to Grange. Rosemount and Brown Brothers add to the variety. New Zealand has the wines of Dashwood, Jackson Estate and Cloudy Bay, as well as Montana. Two California wines from Wente provide refuge from Gallo, while Backsberg and Hamilton-Russell are just a couple of the many names from South Africa.

In Europe, Spain has a splendid collection of Riojas, with Ochoa, Chivite and Torres adding a few well-chosen extras. It is surprising, therefore, to see Portugal languishing with just Mateus and a Vinho Verde. France is extensive, with good clarets and a long list of burgundies, although the Rhône is still rather thin; champagne is obviously popular in this part of Sussex. Nutbourne Manor wines from the nearby vineyard add a touch of local interest.

Best buys

Cette Nuit Blanc/Rouge Vin de Table, £
Montes Cabernet Sauvignon 1988, Chile, £
Imperial Gran Reserva Rioja 1982, CUNE, ££
Cloudy Bay Sauvignon Blanc 1992, New Zealand, ££

The Hermitage

124 Fortis Green Road, Muswell Hill, London N10 3DU	*Tel* 081-365 2122

Open Mon–Sat 10.30–8; Sun 12–2.30 **Closed** Public holidays **Credit cards** Access, Visa **Discounts** 5% on mixed cases; further discounts negotiable **Delivery** Free locally; elsewhere at cost **Glass hire** Free with orders **Tastings and talks** Free monthly in-store tastings **Cellarage** Not available

We have heard good reports of this shop in Muswell Hill. Proprietor Gill Reynolds has been in business since July 1989 and has built up a remarkable range based on the quality of wine rather than on convenient sourcing. From France there is a splendid selection of Alsace wines – Schlumberger, Humbrecht and Domaine Weinbach. Burgundies are a good mixture from Faiveley, Jayer Gilles, Mongeard-Mugneret and others. The Rhônes are equally well chosen. Italy shows a particular enthusiasm with a few of the more unusual upper-class vini da tavola, including Coltassala and Balifico, as well as Barolos from Mascarello. The New World selection should keep Muswell Hill residents busy. Australia, New Zealand, Chile, California and Washington State all have the same quality theme running through the range.

For a small one-woman business with no major buying muscle, prices are quite reasonable. One reader described this as an 'uncompromisingly serious wine shop'. We agree, and hope it attracts plenty of serious wine customers.

Best buys

Marius Riserva 1986, Almansa, Bodegas Piqueras, Spain, £
Domaine de Rieux 1992, Vin de Pays des Côtes de Gascogne, £
Domaine Richou 1991, Anjou Blanc, ££
Dolcetto d'Alba 1990, Bricco Ravera, Guiseppe Mascarello, ££

Hicks & Don

Order office

Blandford St Mary, Dorset DT11 9LS	*Tel* (0258) 456040
The Old Bakehouse, Alfred Street, Westbury, Wiltshire BA13 3DY	*Tel* (0373) 864723
Park House, North Elmham, Dereham, Norfolk NR20 5JY	*Tel* (0362) 668571
Mainly mail order	

Case sales only **Open** Mon–Fri 9–5 **Closed** Sat, Sun, public holidays **Credit cards** Access, Visa; personal and business accounts **Discounts** By negotiation **Delivery** Free for 3+ cases on mainland Britain; delivery rates to offshore islands negotiable; 1–2 cases, add £3 per case; mail order available **Glass hire** Free **Tastings and talks** To groups on request; several tastings a year **Cellarage** Available

Hicks & Don is now part of brewers Hall and Woodhouse based in Blandford St Mary; Messrs Hicks and Don (both Masters of Wine) continue to be involved and are responsible for buying, along with Angus Avery.

There is no shop and the business revolves around the list and special offers – *en primeurs* are particularly strong. This year, it has changed its policy and now allows a wide range of wines, all under £5, to be sold in mixed cases. This is a welcome move, but the bulk of the list remains straight case-sales only and to sample it all would cost a fortune. The keynote throughout the list is quality – good producers and growers prevail in every section and each wine is described in loving detail.

Clarets are mainly reliable petits châteaux, with a handful of classier wines for special occasions. Burgundies have been sourced from a variety of domaines and the Loire and Rhône both look good. The Australian and New Zealand selections have expanded this year and now include wines from Adam Wynn, Mount Helen, Hunters and Matua Valley. The Spanish range is a disappointment since most wines are available in the high street by the single bottle at the same price or even less.

Ex-cellar offers from this company are good, although a minimum order of 3 cases on most offers could be a deterrent.

Best buys

Domaine de la Salette 1992, Vin de Pays de Gascogne, £
Merlot, Vin de Pays des Coteaux de l'Ardèche 1992, £
Manzanilla de Sanlúcar, Barbadillo, ££
Elmham Park Madeleine Angevine 1991, Norfolk, England, ££

High Breck Vintners

Cellars

| Bentworth House, Bentworth, nr Alton, | *Tel* (0420) 562218 |
| Hampshire GU34 5RB | |

Case sales only   **Open** Mon–Fri 9.30–5.30; Sat, Sun by appointment
Credit cards Access, Visa; personal and business accounts   **Discounts** Not available   **Delivery** Free locally to London, Hampshire, Surrey and Berkshire (min 3+ cases); nationwide 4 cases (min value £250); otherwise £6   **Glass hire** Free with case order   **Tastings and talks** 5 to 6 tastings per year   **Cellarage** Not available

Mixed cases are allowed only if you choose a maximum of three different wines or spirits (not so very mixed, really). That is the disadvantage of buying from High Breck Vintners, but once you get over that problem it is good news all the way. The company is owned by Howard Baveystock and run by manager Wilf Nelson. Mr Baveystock claims his wine qualifications to be '40 years' dedicated consumption', which suggests that his wines are there to be enjoyed and are not just names to bolster the ego. The range is a personal selection from France, Italy, Rioja and South Africa. All are selected for 'backbone and character, with that all-important rapport between quality and price,' to quote the proprietor. Small growers are the keynote here: single-estate Beaujolais, bottled by the Eventail producers, a collection of vineyard Sancerre and Pouilly Fumé wines, three domaine red burgundies for under £11 and four good-value

Rhône wines from Wilf Nelson's cousin, who happens to be an oenologist, are among the attractions. This is an individual list and the result of much hard work.

Clarets include a few vintages of Domaine la Grave from Peter Vinding-Diers, with the white available as well. A full range from Henry Ryman at Ch. la Jaubertie makes up the Bergerac section. Antinori from Italy, Berberana from Rioja and Lustau's wonderful sherries add variety. Mr Baveystock claims that visitors seldom leave thirsty, which makes High Breck Vintners sound like an enjoyable place to buy wine.

Best buys

Ch. de Campuget Blanc 1989, Costières de Nîmes, £
St-Chinian 1989, Rouanet, £
Chablis 1990, Alain Pautré, ££
Gigondas, Domaine des Tourelles 1988, ££

George Hill of Loughborough

59 Wards End, Loughborough, Leicestershire
LE11 3HB
Tel (0509) 212717

Open Mon–Sat 9–5.30 **Closed** Sun, public holidays **Credit cards** Access, Visa; Switch; personal and business accounts **Discounts** Approximately 10% on 1 case
Delivery Free within 50-mile radius (min 2 cases) **Glass hire** Free
Tastings and talks Customer tastings available; tutored tastings for groups
Cellarage £5 per case per year

Last year's list from this company was illustrated with amusing cartoons from Bill Tidy on the subject of wine. If this streak of humour continues through the company it must make buying wine here quite good fun. The range is a well-balanced selection from around the world, and might just bring a smile to the face of anyone planning to drink some of it.

France is strong but does not dominate the list. Bordeaux provides a good selection at all prices; particularly interesting is a Margaux Private Reserve which is the second wine of Ch. Kirwan. There are burgundies, mainly from *négociants* Parent, Faiveley and Chanson, with the range starting at good-value Mâcon Rouge and climbing steadily up to grand cru level. The Rhône section contains some good wines – Michel Mourier and Jaboulet are included here. German wines feature large in this list but apparently their popularity in Loughborough has fallen – a shame because most of these are quality estate wines from Guntrum and Prüm. The Italian section provides some excitement, with Bolla's Recioto Amarone and the lovely Sassicaia from Tuscany. Australia includes the Bosanquet Estate wines and some from Pirramimma. New Zealand's contribution is mainly from Cook's and Nobilo. South Africa provides some choice from Fairview Estate and KWV, and there are additional wines from places as far apart as Moldova, California, Chile and Mexico.

Best buys

Chardonnay, Casillero del Diablo 1991, Concha y Toro, Chile, £
Côtes-du-Rhône-Villages 'Rasteau' 1990, Mourier, £
Mercurey 1989, Domaine Jean Maréchal, ££
Shiraz Reserve, Fairview Estate 1990, South Africa, ££

J E Hogg

61 Cumberland Street, Edinburgh EH3 6RA   *Tel* 031-556 4025

Open Mon, Tue, Thur, Fri 9–1, 2.30–6; Wed, Sat 9–1 **Closed** Sun, public holidays **Credit cards** None accepted **Discounts** Not available **Delivery** Free in Edinburgh (min 12 bottles); £1 per consignment for less than 6 bottles; 60p for 6–12 bottles **Glass hire** Free; breakages charged for **Tastings and talks** To groups on request **Cellarage** Not available

No one could accuse James Hogg of wasting money when he comes to produce a list. It is basic, utilitarian, close-typed on A4 paper and you almost need a magnifying glass to read the list of whiskies. However, we suspect that the customers of J E Hogg (nicely old-fashioned, and the shop closes for lunch) would rather enjoy prices at these levels than have a glossy brochure on their coffee tables.

The prices are excellent – not only a match for most independents but undercutting a lot of the multiples by pence and sometimes by pounds. And since customers know they are getting a good deal, we hope it encourages them to be adventurous. Specialities include Alsace – a terrific range from basics up to grands crus and vendanges tardives from no fewer than six producers. Sweet Loire wines merit a separate section, three vintages of Quarts de Chaumes from Jean Baumard look enticing. White burgundies are not just for the seriously wealthy: there are good Mâconnais wines – with change from £6. Outside France, Germany is taken fairly seriously with trockens as well as traditional styles from respected producers such as Prüm, Deinhard and Bürklin-Wolf. Clarets are represented by affordable châteaux below £10 before the list goes on to explore further up the price scale. Italian reds are worth investigating, as is the wonderful range of sherries. With over 100 wines available in half-bottles, presumably at keen prices too (they do not fit on to the crowded list), Edinburgh drinkers could confine themselves to little bottles and still not run out of choice.

With high-quality leaf tea and coffee beans as new additions to the range, J E Hogg could be your one-stop-shop for all beverages.

Best buys

Deinhard Hanns Christof Kabinett 1988, £
Ch. Guionne 1990, Côtes de Bourg, £
Gewurztraminer Jubilee 1988, Hugel, Alsace, ££
Don Zoilo Palo Cortado, ££

Holland Park Wine Company

12 Portland Road, London W11 4LA   *Tel* 071-221 9614

Open Mon–Fri 10–8.30; Sat 9–8.30 **Closed** Sun, public holidays
Credit cards Access, Amex, Visa; personal and business accounts **Discounts** 5%
on 1 case **Delivery** Free locally (min 1 case); otherwise at cost; mail order
available **Glass hire** Free with case order **Tastings and talks** Regular in-store
tastings; to groups on request **Cellarage** £5 per case per year

Any company that is prepared to deliver your wine order within three hours (locally) deserves all the customers it can get. It is that level of service which puts the Holland Park Wine Company ahead in a very competitive market. The list has a friendly 'handwritten' feel about it with background notes and tasting comments scattered liberally around. It starts off with everyday reds and whites, ranging in price from just over £3 to nearly £7, pleasant selections that would be welcome any time. Then there are the special suggestions such as 'Dinner Party Wines', 'Celebration' and even 'Curios', which includes a New Zealand Chenin and a Navarra Cabernet Sauvignon.

In the main part of the list, clarets occupy a full page and, while there are some grand names to catch the eye, many of them are petits châteaux with prices below £12. Five Loire reds add a touch of style to the list and burgundies try hard to stay affordable.

Further afield, Spain shows good value and flavour, Italy manages to be interesting without launching into large numbers of Super Tuscans and Germany is short and confined to quality. Australian wines concentrate on value, with Nottage Hill and Dry Plains, but Cape Mentelle is available for more special occasions. New Zealand, South Africa and Hungarian Tokaji round off this splendid selection.

Best buys

Gran Feudo 1989, Navarra, £
Butterfly Ridge Colombard/Chardonnay nv, Australia, £
Campillo Reserva 1985, Rioja, ££
St-Véran 1990, Louis Latour, ££

House of Townend

Head office

Red Duster House, 101 York Street, Hull, *Tel* (0482) 26891
Humberside HU2 0QX
14 branches in Humberside and Yorkshire

Open Mon–Sat 10 am–10.30 pm; Sun 12–2.30, 7–10.30   **Closed** Chr Day and Good
Friday   **Credit cards** Access, Visa; business accounts   **Discounts** On request
Delivery Free within 60-mile radius of Hull   **Glass hire** Free
Tastings and talks Monthly wine club tasting (£6 per head); wine tasting for clubs
on request   **Cellarage** £2.60 per case per year

The head office and main outlet of House of Townend is in Hull
with 13 additional shops around Humberside, including one at
the Willerby Manor Hotel which also happens to be Townend-
owned. This merchant claims to have the largest range of wines
in the county, but holding on to that title if and when this part
of Humberside reverts back to Yorkshire could provide it with
an exciting challenge.

The classic areas are handled very well at House of Townend.
The range of burgundies is extensive, with good growers and
producers well represented. Clarets tend to be the well-known
names that go down well in board rooms: there is a lot more
emphasis on wines at above £10 a bottle than below. The Rhône
provides more affordable drinking, including splendid
Vacqueyras and Gigondas from Roger Combe. Alsace appears to
find little favour in this part of Humberside, which is a shame
since this limited range includes wines from Blanck and
Schlumberger. German wines are here in variety from quality
producers, Italy and Spain are both trying hard, and Portugal
has livened up this year. Australian and New Zealand wines
seem a good bet, with reliable names at reasonable prices.

A fee of £5 a year entitles you to membership of the Townend
Wine Club which meets monthly at Willerby Manor; this is also
the venue for the School of Wine.

Best buys

Portal del Alto Cabernet Sauvignon 1990, Chile, £
Ch. de Bonnefond 1989, Côtes de Bourg, £
Ch. Caronne Ste-Gemme 1986, Haut-Médoc, ££
Mâcon Chardonnay 1991, Cuvée Joseph Talmard, ££

Ian G Howe

35 Appleton Gate, Newark, Nottinghamshire   *Tel* (0636) 704366
NG24 1JR

Open Mon–Sat 9–7; Good Friday 12–3, 7–9 **Closed** Sun, public holidays exc
Good Friday **Credit cards** Access, Visa; personal and business accounts
Discounts 2.5% for 1–2 cases (may be mixed), 3.5% for 3+ cases **Delivery** Free
locally (min 1 case) and within 20-mile radius (min 2 cases); elsewhere by
arrangement; mail order available **Glass hire** Free with orders
Tastings and talks Four themed tastings a year **Cellarage** Not available

This is very much a family business: Ian Howe and his wife
Sylvia are always to be found in the shop except when they
head off to France to find a few more interesting goodies for the
shelves. They have built up this business from scratch and in
the small market town of Newark have survived only by
offering quality wines and quality service. Delivering the right
wine to the right venue at the right time may sound trite but it
is a reputation like this which brings repeat custom.

The shop is interesting to browse around and there is always
some new discovery or special offer on the racks just inside the
door. If you have time, Ian will talk about his wines and he may
sprint up the stairs to the stockroom to search out an interesting
bottle. The list is not huge – it covers France only – but it has
grown over the years to the point where it really needs an
index. Chablis is a speciality with a fine collection of premier
and grand cru wines from vignerons Droin, Grossot and Boudin
as well as *négociant* wines from Moreau, Laroche and Drouhin.
The Loire is another area of keen interest, with wines from
Tinel-Blondelet, Joseph Renou and others. The Rhônes include a
super selection of Châteauneuf-du-Papes.

Ian Howe now offers a national mail-order service;
meanwhile, for East Midlands wine drinkers, this shop remains
a welcome oasis.

Best buys

Coteaux du Tricastin Rouge 1990, Pascal, £
Coteaux du Giennois Rouge 1989, I.N.R.A., £
Chardonnay 1990, Côtes du Jura, Jean Germain, ££
Rasteau, Domaine la Soumade 1989, Côtes-du-Rhône-
Villages, ££

Victor Hugo Wines

Head office
Longueville Road, St Saviour, Jersey JE2 7SA   *Tel* (0534) 32225
3 retail outlets around Jersey and a cash & carry at Longueville Road

Open Mon–Sat 9–6 **Closed** Sun, public holidays **Credit cards** Access, Amex, Visa; personal and business accounts **Discounts** Available **Delivery** Free in Jersey **Glass hire** Free **Tastings and talks** Regular tastings **Cellarage** Free

A good, balanced range from Victor Hugo on the sunshine island of Jersey, available either from its retail shops or its cash-&-carry warehouse. The warehouse has a retail licence so you can buy by the single bottle at all outlets. As you might expect, the range has a French bias with good clarets (a particularly wide selection from the 1985 vintage), burgundies are mainly from Louis Latour and Domaine Laroche and Alsace wines from Schlumberger and the Turckheim co-operative. German wines are from quality producers such as Guntrum, Prüm and Prinz Zu Salm and a couple of wines from Robert Weil give a taste of the drier German style.

The choices from Italy are reliable, with Rocca Delle Macie in Chianti and Fontanafredda in Barolo. Jermann wines from the North East include oak-aged Tunina. Spain offers well-made Navarra wines from Chivite and a good range of Riojas. The Australian selection is restricted, but good – Brown Brothers, Penfolds and Cape Mentelle are the main players. New Zealand, California and South Africa add to the variety. Two local wines are included in the list: Clos de la Mare and Ch. la Catillon provide the true taste of Jersey.

Delivery is free across the island and the untaxed prices look attractive to those of us on the mainland.

Best buys

Cuvée Jean Paul Vin de Table, £
Chardonnay de l'Ardèche 1991, Louis Latour, £
Cuvée Grand Siècle 1985, Laurent Perrier Champagne, ££
Vintage Tunina 1990, Jermann, Italy, ££

Best buys
  £   denotes a bottle costing under £5
  ££ denotes a bottle costing over £5

Hungerford Wine Company/The Claret Club ✎

Head office
Unit 3, Station Yard, Hungerford, Berkshire   *Tel* (0488) 683238
RG17 0DY
Shop
24 High Street, Hungerford, Berkshire   *Tel* (0488) 681201
RG17 0NF
(Call head office for details of the Claret Club)

Open Mon–Fri 10–6.30; Sat 9.30–5 **Closed** Sun, public holidays
Credit cards Access, Amex, Visa **Discounts** By negotiation **Delivery** Free within
15-mile radius of Hungerford **Glass hire** Free to customers
Tastings and talks Tutored tastings available on request **Cellarage** £7.99 per case
per year (inc insurance)

Hungerford Wines is run by Nick Davies, a music graduate who
started as a van driver in 1978 and, to borrow a phrase, liked
the business so much he bought the company. There are major
changes going on at Hungerford at the time of writing, but the
end result could be interesting.

The shop in Hungerford High Street has undergone a
'revamp'. The range here is heavily biased towards claret,
starting at petit-château wines and building up through the
price range to reach a crescendo with Latour, Lafite and Pétrus.
Vintages range from recent years back to 1952, but there are rich
seams of 1985s and 1988s. A selection of 130 clarets is pretty
good for any wine merchant but finding one with that range on
the shelves makes it worth a detour.

Other wines fighting for shelf space include a reasonable
selection of burgundies – names like Faiveley, Louis Latour and
Jaffelin feature here, with La Chablisienne providing its lovely
Vieilles Vignes Chablis. There are good-value vins de pays, a
handful of Rhônes and Loires and even a glance outside France
to other wine-producing countries.

Germany provides an interesting Gewürztraminer Spätlese,
there are CUNE Riojas from Spain, a couple of Portuguese
wines and a Recioto della Valpolicella from Italy. Sections on
Australia and New Zealand are also well worth a browse.

The part of the business that many people associate with
Hungerford Wines, mail order wine – in particular, claret – is
no more. In its place is The Claret Club, a venture which
members join for the princely sum of £45 a year and then have
access to a series of special offers from Bordeaux. By making it a
'members only' operation, Nick Davies reckons he can keep
prices very low. Profiles of the châteaux, vintage reports and
even wine weekends are all part of the package. The Claret Club
is still in the process of accepting members and offers are
expected to start in the autumn.

Best buys

Merlot, Vin de Pays d'Oc 1991, Vanel, £
Chardonnay, Vin de Pays d'Oc 1991, Vanel, £
Ch. Mouton-Rothschild 1964, Pauillac, ££
Ch. Filhot 1949, Sauternes, ££

Ingletons Wines

Head office and warehouse
Maldon No 1 Bond,   *Tel* (0621) 869474
Beckingham Business Park, Tolleshunt Major,
Maldon, Essex CM9 7NF
Cash-&-carry outlet
Station Road, Maldon, Essex CM9 7LF   *Tel* (0621) 852433

Open (Cash & carry) Mon–Fri 9–5; Sat 9–12.30 **Closed** Sun, public holidays
Credit cards None accepted **Discounts** Not available **Delivery** Not available
Glass hire Available **Tastings and talks** To groups on request **Cellarage** Not available

Ingletons is a major supplier to the trade but it also has a cash-&-carry warehouse. The company have been expanding this year, with new outlets in the Midlands and north but as far as we could find out these will be just for the trade. The list is worth getting hold of, despite being definitely trade-orientated (prices ex-VAT and listed in columns depending on your quantity discount). Apparently all the wines are available in the cash & carry, although we would welcome readers' confirmation of this.

Classic French is the theme of the list: page after page of wonderful burgundies from the good growers and domaines of the region, with Domaine Sauzet, Mongeard-Mugneret and Daniel Senard featuring most prominently. From Bordeaux the range runs from the basics to Mouton, with a fine collection from the 1985 vintage. For less extravagant days there is a good choice of regional French wine. The rest of the world tends to be focused on one or two suppliers from each country. So Spanish wines are mainly from Bodegas Olarra, Chileans from Caliterra and South Africans from Cape Selection. Only Italy and Australia are relieved of this supplier straitjacket.

Some bottles are open for tasting at the cash & carry.

Best buys

Sauvignon Blanc, Vin de Pays d'Oc, Domaines Virginie, £
Montauriol Merlot d'Oc, Domaines Virginie, £
Chablis Vieilles Vignes 1990, La Chablisienne, ££
Corton, Clos des Meix 1989, Daniel Senard, ££

Christopher James & Co

White Hart Vaults, 64 South Street, Exeter,   *Tel* (0392) 73894
Devon EX1 1EF

Open Mon–Fri 10–7.30; Sat 9.30–6.30   **Closed** Sun, public holidays
Credit cards All accepted; personal and business accounts   **Discounts** 7% on a
mixed case   **Delivery** Free within 5-mile radius of Exeter (min 1 case)
Glass hire Free with order   **Tastings and talks** Three tastings a year (£15 per
person inc buffet)   **Cellarage** Not available

Everyday drinking wines start off this list and the names of
Jarrah Ridge and Gamay de Touraine leap off the page for style
and value. There is also a good selection of country reds and
whites to attract you to this part of Exeter.

Better-quality wines are here in depth too. Within the small
selection of only 12 clarets, Mr Ward manages to encompass
both ends of the price scale with a range of petits châteaux and
cru bourgeois wines and then effortlessly hits the high notes
with Châteaux Beychevelle and Lafite. Red burgundies are good;
the names of Louis Latour, Faiveley and Remoriquet indicate
sound buying here.

The Italian range has seen some work but sticks to good-value
basics rather than exploring the upper reaches of vini da tavola.
Sound, reliable flavours from Torres, CUNE and Murrieta
appear in the Spanish range.

The New World provides most excitement with a fine
collection from Australia, New Zealand, California and South
Africa. Prices stay well under £10 here and give variety and
value. A good range of ports, Lustau sherries and madeiras from
Henriques & Henriques are well worth a browse.

Best buys

Jarrah Ridge Semillon/Chardonnay 1992, Australia, £
Rioja Tinto 1991, Navajas, £
Ch. des Jaubertes 1989, Graves Supérieur, ££
Canard-Duchêne nv, Champagne, ££

Do you remember an Inn, Miranda?
  Do you remember an Inn?
  And the tedding and the spreading
  Of the straw for a bedding,
  And the fleas that tease in the High Pyrenees
  And the wine that tasted of tar?

Hilaire Belloc, *Tarantella*

Tony Jeffries Wines

69 Edith Street, Northampton,   *Tel* (0604) 22375
Northamptonshire NN1 5EP

Open Tue–Fri 10–3; Sat 9–5; public holidays 12–3   **Closed** Mon, Sun
Credit cards Access, Visa; personal and business accounts   **Discounts** 10% on 1
case if payment by cash/cheque; 5% on 1 case if payment by credit card
Delivery Free within 15-mile radius of Northampton town centre (min 2+ cases);
less than two cases by arrangement   **Glass hire** Free with order
Tastings and talks In-store tastings (2nd Sun and 3rd Wed each month from May
to Oct) at £2 per person   **Cellarage** Not available

Australia is still the favourite region for Tony Jeffries, with well
over 100 wines listed, which must give Northampton residents
one of the best selections for miles around. Penfolds, Peter
Lehmann, Rosemount and Charlie Melton are just some of the
delights in store. Other regions have been extended: the New
Zealand range now includes Cloudy Bay, Vidal, Palliser Estate
and Vavasour; South Africa is tipped as the region to watch for
quality and some new Hungarian wines are planned.

Tony Jeffries admits he is a recent convert to Rhône wines
and regrets all the Hermitage and Gigondas he has missed in
the past. Now he is making up for lost time with a splendid
array from Châteauneuf-du-Pape, Cornas, Côte Rôtie and more,
all from quality producers such as Jaboulet, Chapoutier, Guigal
and Perrin.

Claret is also an interesting area on his list, with a high
preponderance of good St-Emilion wines. The delightful Ch.
Monbousquet, made by one of the region's more colourful
characters, Alain Querre, is here, as well as Châteaux Carteau,
Pavie, Rozier and Grand Mayne. All are well worth exploring.
Good selections from the Loire, Burgundy, Southern France,
Spain and Portugal are included; only Italy is strangely
neglected.

Regular tastings provide an opportunity to sample the range
and seem like a friendly way to learn about wine.

Best buys

Bull's Blood of Eger 1989, Hungary, £
Normans Chenin Blanc 1992, South Australia, £
Gigondas 1990, Respail Ay, ££
Mas de Daumas Gassac 1990, Vin de Pays de l'Hérault, ££

S H Jones

Shop

27 High Street, Banbury, Oxfordshire
OX16 8EW

Tel (0295) 251177

Open Mon–Fri 9–5.30; Sat 9–5 **Closed** Sun, public holidays **Credit cards** Access,
Visa; personal and business accounts **Discounts** Available **Delivery** Free in
Banbury and district; mail order available **Glass hire** £1 per dozen or free with
large wine orders **Tastings and talks** 5 to 6 tastings per year, 4 of which are
tutored **Cellarage** £3.50 per case per year

Despite a diploma in malting and brewing, Michael Jones has
decided to eschew the grain and take to the grape as wine
buyer for this family business. S H Jones operates from a
wonderful old building in Banbury, dating from 1537. The shop
is well laid-out, as is the list which is printed on recycled paper
(it is easy to start liking this company). Sadly, the summary of
recent vintages from various regions has been dropped from the
list but against each wine is a code indicating when it will be
ready to drink.

The range is fairly classic: good clarets with a fine selection
from the 1985 vintage; Sauternes seems to be a bit of a
speciality with five vintages of Ch. Rieussec going back to 1975;
the Rhône is a delight showing examples from Guigal, Chave
and Chapoutier and four vintages of Domaine de Vieux
Télégraphe; also worth trying are the Vacqueyras wines from
Roger Combe. Still in France, a collection of burgundies from
good growers and *négociants* such as Henri Prudhon, Domaine
Leflaive and Latour provide affordable drinking.

The German section is also clearly laid out with producers'
names diligently included. Spain now has the value Don John
wines, while new wines from Italy include Salice Salentino and
Antinori's Vin Santo. With a big range from Australia, New
Zealand and California and some new additions from South
Africa, this list should keep Banbury residents busy for some
time. Half-bottles are a particular speciality: 28 clarets, 7 Chablis
and a very good selection of pudding wines.

Best buys

Les Hauts de Bergelle 1991, Côtes de St-Mont, £
Ch. de Cabriac 1991, Corbières, £
Vacqueyras 'Maître de Chai' 1990, Roger Combe, ££
Sancerre, Domaine de Montigny 1991, Henri Natter, ££

Justerini & Brooks

61 St James's Street, London SW1A 1LZ	*Tel* 071-493 8721
45 George Street, Edinburgh EH2 2HT	*Tel* 031-226 4202
Rokehay Farm, Furley, Membury, Axminster,	*Tel* (040488) 766
Devon EX13 7TS	

Open Mon–Fri 9–5.30; Sat 9.30–1 (Dec only in London) **Closed** Sun and public holidays **Credit cards** Access, Amex, Diners, Visa; personal and business accounts **Discounts** 2–4 cases £1 per case; 5–7 cases £2 per case; 8+ cases £3 per case **Delivery** Free in London (min 2 cases), otherwise £8; UK mainland free (min 2 cases), otherwise £9; mail order available **Glass hire** Free
Tastings and talks Regular tastings to existing customers by invitation
Cellarage £5.20 per case per year (inc insurance)

With shops in London and Edinburgh and a sales office in the West Country, Justerini & Brooks has got the country covered. The London face of J&B is in up-market St James's, and with a string of royal warrants going back to the reign of George III you might be forgiven for thinking that this is an exclusive, expensive company. But even here they have found that customers like to find good value, so, new this year is a separate supplement to the main list devoted to wines under £6.50. Among this selection is a fine range of French country wines, including the lovely wines of Domaines Virginie, and a collection of petit-château wines from Bordeaux. Côtes-du-Rhône, generic burgundy and a clutch of rosé wines complete the French section. From further afield, the wines of Australia, South Africa and South America add variety to this good value list.

If you do feel extravagant turn the pages of the main list to find any number of ways to take the weight off your bank account. Clarets are a speciality – this must be one of the finest selections available on a retail basis: 66 wines from the 1989 vintage alone, ranging from Bordeaux Supérieur to Haut-Brion. The 1985 range gives a choice of 20 châteaux, each one with an indication of its maturity. Sweet Bordeaux wines are also here in abundance, including the ultimate for a sweet-toothed millionaire, *impériales* (8 bottles' worth) of Ch. d'Yquem. Burgundies follow suit with all the best growers and domaines – the same goes for the Rhône, with a choice of 19 Côte Rôtie wines and, from the Loire, a fine selection from Gaston Huet. The rest of the world is covered reasonably well, Germany in particular. Italy has seen some work this year with some new faces from the North East and from Tuscany. New Zealand includes the Jackson Estate wines and Australia has the Scotchman's Hill Pinot Noir.

J & B operates a cellar plan whereby it takes care of your short-term and long-term drinking requirements. The regular mailshots are also worth having and mixed cases and special offers make the job of acquiring a stock of good bottles almost painless. This will never be a bargain basement place to buy wine, but prices are roughly comparable with many merchants, the range is excellent and the London tastings seem well worth trying.

Best buys

Aroona Valley Estate Shiraz/Cabernet 1990, South Australia, £
Domaine du Vieux Chêne 1992, Vin de Pays de Vaucluse, £
Auxey Duresses, Clos du Val 1990, Prunier, ££
Scotchman's Hill Pinot Noir 1992, Geelong, Australia, ££

King and Barnes

The Horsham Brewery, 18 Bishopric,   *Tel* (0403) 270870
Horsham, West Sussex RH12 1QP

Open Mon–Sat 9–5.30 **Closed** Sun, public holidays **Credit cards** Access, Visa
Discounts 5% on 1 mixed case **Delivery** Free in Horsham and surrounding
villages (min 2 cases) **Glass hire** Free with order **Tastings and talks** Tastings on
most Sats; thematic tastings for the 'Case & Cellar Club'; tutored tastings to groups
on request **Cellarage** Not available

This shop is the retailing arm of brewers King and Barnes and, unlike some brewery-owned wine shops, this one has a range selected for quality and variety and not just for ease of sourcing.

The list takes a general look at all the classic French regions. Burgundies are mainly from growers rather than the large *négociants* and there is a reasonable collection of petits châteaux from Bordeaux at well under £10. The Rhône includes a splendid St-Joseph from Dr Emile Florentin and from Corbières you can support the work of a hospital for the handicapped with the wine of Ch. Lastours which tastes very good. With Alsace wines from Gisselbrecht and champagne from Georges Goulet, this French range is looking impressive. Further afield, the main areas of interest are Spain – a reliable range of Riojas and Navarra wines – and Australia, with Seppelt, St Hallett and two wines from the Willows. South America contributes the flavoursome wines of Bodegas Weinert from Argentina and Santa Helena from Chile.

Best buys

Ch. Haut-Rian 1992, Bordeaux Blanc, £
Pearl Springs Colombard 1992, South Africa, £
St Hallett 'Old Block' Shiraz 1990, Australia, ££
Weinert Cabernet Sauvignon 1985, Argentina, ££

Lay & Wheeler

Head office and wine shop
The Wine Market, Gosbecks Road, Shrub
End, Colchester, Essex CO2 9JT

Tel (0206) 764446

Culver Street Wine Shop, 6 Culver Street
West, Colchester, Essex CO1 1JA

Tel as above

Open (Wine Market) Mon–Sat 8–8; (Wine Shop) Mon–Sat 8.30–5.30 **Closed** Sun,
public holidays **Credit cards** Access, Amex, Visa; personal and business
accounts **Discounts** 5% on 120 bottles and above; supplement on less than a
case **Delivery** Free within 60-mile radius (min 1 case); free nationwide on 2+
cases; otherwise £5.05 per 1 case; mail order available **Glass hire** Free
Tastings and talks Tasting workshops with meals; food and wine workshops with
dinners ranging from 2–5 courses; general tastings and prestige workshops
Cellarage £4.95 per case per year plus insurance

Lay & Wheeler sets the standard by which all wine lists are
measured: attractive (colour photographs), interesting
(introductions to the regions) and informative (tasting notes for
all the wines) – students of wine would do well to get a copy
and study it as there is a wealth of up-to-date information to be
gleaned from its pages. It is a pleasure to sit down and read this
list, preferably with a good glass of wine to hand, and plan the
cellar of your dreams.

But Lay & Wheeler is more than a list. It has two retail outlets
and a trade cash & carry, and also organises probably the best
programme of tastings and wine workshops available in the UK,
as well as an efficient mail-order service.

The range runs to over 1000 wines, apparently all in stock and
ready to be plucked from the shelves at the Wine Market. The
strengths of the range are really too many to list but classic
areas such as Bordeaux, Burgundy, Rhône, Alsace and Loire are
very good. There is also quality, variety and value. It is possible
to buy top-growth clarets from a number of vintages but you
also get a good choice of wines from less well-known châteaux.
The style of the list and this company makes you feel that as
much consideration has gone into selecting these wines as for
the classier bottles. Outside France, the choice is virtually
limitless. Australia, New Zealand, California, Germany and Italy
are all here providing typical flavours from excellent producers.
Only the Eastern European selection looks a bit thin but, even
so, some glorious wines from the Russian Massandra collection
could tempt the cash from your pocket. If this compendium of
delight becomes too difficult to choose from then managing
director Richard Wheeler and his colleagues have selected their
own short list. These should be as interesting an introduction to
the range as any.

Once you are on the mailing list, Lay & Wheeler will send you its regular newsletter with special offers, *en primeur* offers and details of the wine workshops. Telephone queries about the range and services always meet with an informed and intelligent response.

Best buys

Domaine Condamine l'Evêque Syrah 1992, Vin de Pays des Côtes de Thongue, £
Domaines Virginie Sauvignon Blanc 1992, Vin de Pays d'Oc, £
Cyril Henschke Cabernet Sauvignon 1988, Adelaide Hills, Australia, ££
Martinborough Chardonnay 1990, Wairarapa, New Zealand, ££

Laymont & Shaw

The Old Chapel, Millpool, Truro, Cornwall   *Tel* (0872) 70545
TR1 1EX

Case sales only   **Open** Mon–Fri 9–5   **Closed** Sat, Sun, public holidays
Credit cards None accepted; personal and business accounts   **Discounts** Available on 2+ cases   **Delivery** Free (min 1 case); mail order available   **Glass hire** Free with order   **Tastings and talks** Rarely   **Cellarage** £2.50 per case per year

---

If you try to imagine a convenient place to set up a company distributing wine around the country then Truro, on the very tip of Cornwall, is probably the last place you would think of. But way back in the Seventies it really wasn't such a bad idea. Boats left Plymouth for Spain laden with Cornish china clay and returned empty. That is, until china clay executive John Hawes had the brilliant idea of putting a container of wine aboard. With the help of a Señor Montelay in Spain and a little shuffling of their combined names the wine merchant Laymont & Shaw was born. The wine no longer travels the same route but the company, based in an old chapel in the shadow of Truro cathedral, continues to stock one of the widest and most interesting ranges of Spanish wines.

Rioja was on the first boat-load and it still continues to be a major part of the range. Wines from eight bodegas are listed but the most prominent is La Rioja Alta with its delicious Viña Ardanza and massively flavoured Reserva 904, which has now been given its more accurate name of Gran Reserva. Neighbouring Navarra provides good value for under a fiver, but if money is no object there are seven wines from Vega Sicilia. Penedès is represented by the elegant wines of Jean León and a full range from Torres. From further inland, Raimat proves that irrigation does not mean poor quality, with its fine range of varietal wines. Wines from Toro, Priorato, Rueda and

Jumilla add more variety, while the range from Majorca, blessed with the new name of Binissalem, keeps the interest going. The red Don John launched last year has now been joined by a white. New this year is a range of Spanish country wines made from local grape varieties.

Sherries are from Hidalgo, Lustau, Barbardillo and Gonzalez Byass while the Málaga selection from Scholtz Hermanos is excellent. Mixed cases are available, prices include UK delivery and, once on the mailing-list, regular mailshots and special offers will land on your doorstep.

Best buys

Don John Tinto/Blanco Vino de Mesa nv, £
Señorio de Los Llanos 1987, Valdepeñas, £
Viña Ardanza Rioja 1985, La Rioja Alta, ££
Lagar de Cervera 1992, Rias Baixas, ££

Laytons   ❀ ❦

20 Midland Road, London NW1 2AD	*Tel* 071-388 5081
André Simon outlets	
14 Davies Street, London W1Y 1LJ,	*Tel* 071-499 9144
50/52 Elizabeth Street, London SW1W 9PB,	*Tel* 071-730 8108
21 Motcomb Street, London SW1X 8LB	*Tel* 071-235 3723

Case sales only   **Open** Mon–Fri 8–6; Sat 9.30–4   **Closed** Sun, public holidays
Credit cards All accepted; personal and business accounts   **Discounts** Not available   **Delivery** Free on UK mainland (min £100 order); mail order available
Glass hire Free with certain orders   **Tastings and talks** Regular free tastings
Cellarage £6 per case per year

Laytons and André Simon are just two different trading names for the same company. Graham Chidgey is the man behind the long-established Laytons and also has the three André Simon shops in the smarter parts of London. The shops sell by the bottle while Laytons continues to operate on a case-sales basis (which can be mixed).

If you are addicted to expensive burgundy then this is the place to get your fix. A page of grands crus of the Côtes de Beaune lists wines at prices that would give most of us a heart attack. A choice of vintages and growers of Le Montrachet is available at prices veering either side of £100, but this is a tiny fraction of the range and the emphasis is on good wines at whatever price you can afford to pay. France is the hub of the list, with clarets and particularly burgundies as the focus. Burgundy has been a passion for Graham Chidgey for many years and here the range expands to take in small growers and some that are even smaller than small. The only names missing are those of the major *négociants* that appear everywhere else. This is a personal list with tasting comments scattered around to add character. Clarets start off with Laytons' own 'Jolly Good Claret' and steadily climb the quality ladder. *En-primeur* claret, burgundy and even champagne are all part of the service. Outside the classic areas there are little nuggets of interest from further afield. Spain has Pesquera and Riojas from Bodegas Olarra; Italy includes some good Tuscans, particularly Chiantis from the Nozzole estate, and Moldova presents a clutch of older wines.

There is a small selection of Australian producers here (Len Evans and Taltarni are two), with some new additions from New Zealand.

A special mention must go to Angela Chidgey who designs the stunning list covers (the regular one, not the broadsheet specials) and, if you want to learn more about wine, there is a tasting club called the Circle of Wine Tasters at Laytons.

Best buys

Ch. Petit Boyer 1989, Côtes de Blaye, £
Cortenova Merlot 1991, Pasqua, Italy, £
Chardonnay Rancho Sisquoc 1991, California, ££
Deutz Blanc de Blancs Champagne 1988, ££

Lea & Sandeman

301 Fulham Road, London SW10 9QH   *Tel* 071-376 4767
211 Kensington Church Street,   *Tel* 071-221 1982
London W8 7LX

Open Mon–Fri 9–8.30; Sat 10–8.30   **Closed** Sun, public holidays, 2 January, Easter Sat   **Credit cards** Access, Visa; personal and business accounts
Discounts Quantity discounts (by the case)   **Delivery** Free in central London, and west to Reading and Basingstoke; mainland England, Scotland south of Perth and most of Wales free delivery on any order of £120+; mail order available
Glass hire Free with suitable order   **Tastings and talks** Approximately once every two months   **Cellarage** Not available

Lea & Sandeman is the kind of shop that most wine enthusiasts would like to have in their neighbourhood, namely, one that specialises in wines that reflect the quality of the grapes and the excellence of winemaking. Happily, there are now two neighbourhoods who have this advantage, with the opening of a new shop in Kensington Church Street. Burgundy is especially good, with a fine collection of growers' wines from Bourgogne Rouge to Chambertin. Many of these wines are exclusive to Lea & Sandeman and are shipped direct from the vineyards to Fulham Road. These are wines from small, individual growers who are introduced and described in the list. Bordeaux has a worthy collection of classed growths but there is a clear effort to provide less expensive, quality wines such as Ch. la Grenière from Lussac St-Emilion, Ch. Laujac from the Médoc, and Ch. Ludeman La Côte from Graves. There is a huge choice from Alsace, all from Domaine Marcel Deiss; the Rhônes and Loires are less extensive but still good. Eight regional French wines manage to creep in under £5.

Italy has seen some work this year with a range from Bricco Maiolica in Piemonte. There are also the wines of Foradori from Trentino and Querciabella in Chianti Classico. The Australian section is a collection of wines from good producers: Shaw and Smith, Langi Ghiran and Taltarni. California follows suit with Swanson, Niebaum-Coppola, Edna Valley and Dry Creek.

Sweet wines merit a section to themselves, many in half-bottles, including Vin Santo from Isole e Olena. Ports, sherries and vintage armagnacs round off this classy selection. Although firmly based in London, Lea & Sandeman has a less blinkered view of delivery than some other merchants.

Best buys

Montestell 'Cygnet' Chenin Blanc 1992, Dr Julius Laslo, South Africa, £
Domaine du Fraisse Merlot 1991, Vin de Pays de l'Hérault, £
Chablis 1991, Domaine Adhémar Boudin, ££
Meursault 1989, Domaine Charles Jobard, ££

Leo's ⌒?

CRS Head Office, National Office, 29 Dantzic Street, Manchester M4 4BA	*Tel* 061-832 8152

111 outlets in England and Wales, 12 Pioneer stores and 271 licensed Stop & Shop outlets

Open Generally Mon–Sat 8–8; some public holidays **Closed** Generally Sun, public holidays **Credit cards** Access, Visa **Discounts**, **Delivery**, **Glass hire** Not available **Tastings and talks** Occasional in-store tastings **Cellarage** Not available

The organisation of the Co-op is fairly complicated and not suited to these pages; however, Leo's is a national chain of supermarkets, part of the Co-op family but run as a separate group. It also trades under the name of Pioneer, a rapidly expanding chain of discount stores.

Most wine merchants will supply wine for parties on a sale or return basis.

Leo's buys some of its wines centrally from the Co-operative Wholesale Society, mainly generic own-label wine, and some are bought independently for Leo's. Like any large chain, the range available at your local store ultimately depends on its size, but some stores are willing to order bottles that are not normally stocked.

Leo's is not the place to come for the finest wines you may ever want but the range is steadily improving and now provides a reasonable selection of good-value drinking wines. The Australian section is well worth a try, with wines from Peter Lehmann, Hardys and Orlando. From New Zealand, Cooks and Montana are reliably good and from Chile the Errazuriz Cabernet packs plenty of flavour. Eastern Europe is another source of a lot of bargains. Spain has a wide variety, particularly under £5; Italy has Chianti from Rocca delle Macie, whilst among the French wines is a very tolerable 1982 Ch. Cissac.

Leo's has started to train all its staff in wine, which must be good news for customers.

Best buys

Hardy's Nottage Hill Chardonnay 1991, Australia, £
Hungarian Pinot Blanc, Nagyrede, £
Errazuriz Don Maximiano Cabernet Sauvignon 1988, Chile, ££
Co-op Sparkling Saumur, ££

London Wine Emporium

86 Goding Street, Vauxhall Cross, London   *Tel* 071-587 1302
SE11 5AW

Case sales only   Open Mon–Fri 10–7; Sat 10–5; Sun 11–4   **Closed** Public holidays (exc Good Friday 10–4)   **Credit cards** All accepted; personal and business accounts   **Discounts** Available   **Delivery** Free within M25 (min 1 case) or nationwide (min 3 cases); otherwise 1 case at £5.95, 2 cases at £4.95 each; mail order available   **Glass hire** Free; breakages charged for
Tastings and talks Available   **Cellarage** Not available

A slight change of address for this Emporium which has moved a few doors up the road to be on the corner and now has parking outside. The new address is also shared with Alex Findlater's London office (*q.v.*) and there is still an association between the two companies, with some of the wines sourced from the same growers.

There is a strong Australian influence, with wines from all regions, grape varieties and styles. New Zealand is also here in huge variety – 16 Sauvignon Blancs, 26 Chardonnays and a rich seam of delicious Pinot Noirs.

South Africa takes on the same comprehensive look with a vast range, 100 wines in all, including a fair selection of sparkling wines. Estates such as Fairview, Simonsig and Hamilton-Russell feature here plus quite a few more. Spain and Italy are less intensive but still good, Moldova, Turkey, Greece and Mexico are interesting diversions.

France offers a reasonable choice, particularly from Burgundy.

Best buys

Domaine de Rieux 1991, Vin de Pays des Côtes de Gascogne, Grassa, £
Bairrada 1983, Garcia Pulido, Portugal, £
Grove Mill Sauvignon Blanc 1991, Marlborough, New Zealand, ££
Thelema Cabernet Sauvignon 1989, South Africa, ££

Lorne House Vintners

Gomshall Cellars, Gomshall, Surrey GU5 9LB   *Tel* (0483) 203795

Open Mon–Sat 10–6 (Fri till 8)   **Closed** Sun, public holidays
Credit cards Access, Visa; Switch; personal and business accounts
Discounts 10% on 1 case; negotiable on larger orders   **Delivery** Free locally (min 1 case); mail order available   **Glass hire** Free   **Tastings and talks** Monthly tastings   **Cellarage** Available; call for details

Lorne House has moved out of the industrial estate in Cranleigh and into much better premises in Gomshall. There is now a retail licence so you don't have to buy a case, although there are good discounts if you do. The range has expanded a little, still concentrating on good wines from quality growers.

The Loire is one area where choice is not so wide. In the past, Lorne House has specialised in domaine Muscadets but, because of odd legislation in the region and a general hike in prices, the range is down to three. Meanwhile, a small collection of Vouvray, Menetou-Salon and Sancerre wines provides refreshment. Bordeaux is much more serious. Starting with a collection of petits châteaux, the range climbs up to second- or third-growth level, with prices staying mainly under £20.

Burgundies keep a similar eye on prices, with individual growers or Louis Latour providing much of the selection. French country wines include Ch. Eugenie from Cahors and a Pinot Noir Vin de Pays. Rhône wines are good – among the whites is a fairly rare Sablat, and a Viognier Côtes-du-Rhône.

Spanish wines feature CUNE, Colegiata and Pata Negra, the top-weight Valdepeñas from Señorio de los Llanos. Italy looks to value wines such as Barbera from Ceppi Storici and Candido's Salice Salentino.

With Salisbury Estate wines joining Petaluma, Moss Wood and Langi Ghiran from Australia and New Zealand, and South Africa and Chile adding to the range, Gomshall seems worth a visit.

Best buys

Señorio de Los Llanos Reserva 1988, Valdepeñas, £
Ch. de Juge 1992, Bordeaux Sec, £
Menetou-Salon Morogues 1991, Pelle, ££
Prunaio 1988, Vino da Tavola Landini, ££

Wm Low & Co

PO Box 73, Baird Avenue, Dryburgh   *Tel* (0382) 814022
Industrial Estate, Dundee DD1 9NF
67 branches

Open Mon–Sat 9–8 (till 9 on Thur; some regional variations); Sun 10–5
Closed Chr Day, New Year's Day **Credit cards** Access, Visa **Discounts**,
delivery Not available **Glass hire** Free **Tastings and talks** Tutored tastings for wine clubs, etc. on request **Cellarage** Not available

---

The range at Wm Low stands at over 300 wines. Not bad progress for buyer Kevin Wilson who, in two years, has taken the range from a standing start to a fairly balanced, good-value selection.

The Australians continue to grow, Eden Ridge, Nottage Hill, Penfolds and Salisbury Estate are just some of the names. It is good to see Pikes' splendid Cabernet Sauvignon making an appearance here. In comparison, the New Zealand selection is small but Montana, Stoneleigh and Martinborough make good foundations. Chile, South Africa and California all provide a reasonable choice, with most wines under £5.

Spain and Italy are greatly improved. Two wines from Raimat, a couple from Torres and a Rioja from Bodegas Beronia give much of the Spanish flavour, while Italians from Umani Ronchi, Rocca delle Macie and Frescobaldi show that this range is heading in the right direction. Even Germany has had a change of heart. Last year it was floating in a sea of Liebfraumilch, now it is tidied up and offers a small selection of better quality wines.

It is the French country wines that really deserve a round of applause. Réserve du Révérend, Chais Baumière and Domaine du Bosc are examples from this selection of 35 wines, only one of which creeps over the £5 mark. Good clarets, even with the occasional 'second' wine, round off this range.

Top marks for achievement here – let's hope progress can be maintained.

Best buys

Eden Ridge Dry White 1993, Australia, £
Rioja Bodegas Navajas 1991, £
Ch. Potensac 1987, ££
Champagne Le Brun de Neuville, ££

Majestic Wine Warehouses

Head office

Odhams Trading Estate, St Albans Road,   *Tel* (0923) 816999
Watford, Hertfordshire WD2 5RE
42 branches

Case sales only   **Open** Mon–Sat 10–8; Sun and public holidays 10–6   **Closed** 25–27 Dec, 1 Jan   **Credit cards** All accepted; business accounts   **Discounts** Available on large orders; 15% discount on cases of champagne   **Delivery** Free in London and within a 10-mile radius of stores outside London (min order 1 case); mail order available   **Glass hire** Refundable deposit of £9 per dozen
Tastings and talks Themed tastings throughout the year; tutored tastings to groups on request; all stores have free tasting counters during shop hours
Cellarage Not available

The bright-green and black colours of Majestic are now familiar at 42 sites around the country. Once inside, the operation of these branches is just what you would expect from the pioneer of wine warehouses: good prices, lots of variety and lots of enthusiasm.

There is a list, but at any one time there will be additional parcels of wines available which come and go too quickly to make it into print. Among the regulars there is a hefty reliance on good-value and well-made wines with big, positive flavours. The Australian section demonstrates this in particular, with 20 wines under £5 and nothing over £9. The wines are all from favoured names: Wyndhams, Rouge Homme, Brown Brothers and Penfolds. All are reliable wines sold at reasonable prices. California has expanded this year, Eastern Europe supplies those easy-to-drink gluggers and New Zealand, Chile and South Africa are all represented. The Spanish range is full of old friends – Riojas from CUNE, Ochoa Navarra and Toro Colegiata. Portugal includes the chunky Tinta da Anfora from Peter Bright and Bairrada Reserva from Caves Aliança. The range from France majors on regional wines, again at the good-value end of the market; prices are higher in the claret section with some classy wines between £10 and £20, before reaching Premier Grand Cru St-Emilion. Burgundies are mainly from Faiveley, Alsace wines from Kintzheim and Rhônes from Chapoutier and Jaboulet.

Prices seem good throughout. All branches have bottles open for you to try, and weekend themed tastings seem like a good idea. Enthusiastic and informed help is usually available from staff. Mail order has resumed for those who cannot get to a branch and delivery is free within ten miles.

Best buys

Domaine Fouletière 1991, Coteaux du Languedoc, £
Ch. Deville 1992, Bordeaux Blanc, £
Montes Alpha Cabernet Sauvignon 1988, Aurelio Montes, Chile, ££
Trittenheimer Altarchen Riesling Kabinett 1990, Weingut Grans-Fassian, ££

Marks & Spencer

Head office
Michael House, 57 Baker Street, London *Tel* 071-935 4422
W1A 1DN
269 licensed branches nationwide

Open Varies from store to store but generally 9–6 **Closed** Sun, public holidays (some stores) **Credit cards** Marks & Spencer Chargecard **Discounts** 12 bottles for the price of 11 **Delivery** Mail order available **Glass hire** Not available **Tastings and talks** Tastings of new ranges **Cellarage** Not available

---

M&S occupies a unique niche in the shopping trolleys of the nation. Very few people buy all their food here but many will happily load up a basket or two with the specialist items that M&S do so well. Things like ready-made meals, baby vegetables, smoked salmon starters and, of course, wine. Quality and M&S go together like a well-matched set of their silky undies. A team of technologists makes sure that the products, whether wine or food, are made in the best way to give a quality result. Wineries and bottling lines are inspected to make sure they come up to standard. Compared with many high street merchants, the range is tiny, around 150 wines. There is no depth, no duplication, but what is on the shelves is usually good. Reliable is a word that springs to mind when thinking about this company.

A reliable range might be boring if it is not changed around a little, so new products come on to the shelves and others disappear around a strong core of basics.

French Full Red, French Dry White, Jeunes Vignes, Italian Table Wines, Hock and a few more are the stalwarts of the range, always consistent, apart from the occasional change of label. Ch. Notton has also become one of the faithful, a last remainder from a classy range of 'second' wines from Bordeaux châteaux. Added to these is a South African range – fresh, clean varietal wines at good-value prices. The Australian selection of nine wines provides big fruity flavours from a number of producers. Israeli wines are a recent addition, then there are two from Chile, three from New Zealand and one each from California, Bulgaria and Lebanon.

New this year is a splendid range of wines from Domaines Virginie in the Languedoc region of France. Made by an Australian winemaker, the wines – two whites, a rosé and two reds – show regional style with a touch more fruit, flavour and sunshine.

For a retailer who has a reputation for not being exactly cheap there are some good-value wines in the range: Montepulciano d'Abruzzo, House Red and White, French Country wines. Going up in price, the Chablis is one of the most reliable buys in the high street and the range of champagnes is extremely good. But whether the range of wines matches the flair and innovation of a company that also introduced Ciabatta bread, superb sandwiches and top-class meat to the nation is doubtful.

Welcome this year has been a new training initiative with major stores each having a trained 'wine advisor' who passes on information to the rest of the team. Even so, pronunciation of some of the wine names is a problem, even in such a small range. Also welcome is the new wave of stylish labels that banishes the St Michael logo to the back label. Now a bottle no longer has to go to the table emblazoned with the name of the shop where it was bought.

A mail-order service operates for M&S card holders, offering various mixed cases delivered to your door.

Best buys

Jeunes Vignes nv, La Chablisienne, £
Tyrrell's Hunter Valley Chardonnay/Semillon 1992, £
Chablis 1990, La Chablisienne, ££
Serge Hochar 1989, Lebanon, ££

Master Cellar Wine Warehouse

See Davisons

Wine is best stored in a cool, dark place where the temperature is steady at around 11°C. If you intend to keep the wine for more than three months store the bottle on its side so that the cork and the wine remain in contact.

Mayor Sworder & Co

381 Kennington Road, London SE11 4PT *Tel* 071-735 0385

Open Mon–Fri 9–5 **Closed** Sat, Sun, public holidays **Credit cards** None
accepted; personal and business accounts **Discounts** Possible by arrangement
Delivery Free within radius of M25; otherwise £5.50 per consignment; mail order
available **Glass hire** Free **Tastings and talks** Annual tasting for customers on
mailing list **Cellarage** £4.80 per case per year

A good introduction to the wines of Mayor Sworder could be
through its own wine bar, Cuddefords in Duke Street Hill,
where the day's tasting samples often end up. Last year the
company moved out of its cellars next to the wine bar because
of the impending arrival of the new Jubilee Line extension; the
new multi-level storage facility in Kennington, south London is
probably more efficient but perhaps has less atmosphere than
the old railway arches. A great deal of Mayor Sworder's
business is with the City and corporate institutions, but free
delivery within the M25 and a nationwide mail-order service
extends the customer network. The range is predominantly
French, a great many wines selected from individual growers by
buyer and Master of Wine Martin Everett. The list is well
written, with each area and wine being carefully described.
Who could resist Philippe Brenot's Bourgogne Chardonnay
when you have been introduced to the winemaker through
Martin Everett's detailed notes?

The traditional areas of claret and burgundy are the main
strengths, but Alsace, the Rhône, Loire and French country
wines have again been well chosen and specially selected to
provide individual character and flavour. The Spanish and
Italian ranges are small; one Argentinian wine (from Bodegas
Weinert) and two Californians provide a little more choice. The
Australian and New Zealand representatives are slightly more
encouraging, and two South African wines from Zonnebloem
have been added this year. The special offers seem good value
and prices are gradually converting to VAT-inclusive. The
annual tasting is one of the highlights of the year.

STOP PRESS: As we went to press, Mayor Sworder had just
taken over Russell & McIver.

Best buys

Domaine de la Serre Merlot 1990, Vin de Pays des Côtes de
Thongue, £
Le Chardonnay de Gibalaux 1992, Vin de Pays des Coteaux de
Peyriac, £
Ch. du Moulin Rouge 1989, Cru Bourgeois, Haut-Médoc, ££
Mâcon-Clessé, Domaine Emilian Gillet 1991, Thévenet, ££

Mi Casa Wines 🗁

77 West Road, Buxton, Derbyshire SK17 6HQ   *Tel* (0298) 23952

Open Mon–Fri 3–10; Sat 11–10; Sun 12–2, 7–10; Chr Day 12–1   **Credit cards** None accepted   **Discounts** 5% on 1 case   **Delivery** Free within 10-mile radius of Buxton (min 1 case)   **Glass hire** Free with 1-case order   **Tastings and talks, cellarage** Not available

Anthony Moore has stopped printing an annual list because he likes to ring the changes on his limited shelf space. From the name of the shop you might guess he is a Spanish specialist, and wines from Rioja, Navarra, Jumilla, Valdepeñas and Penedès take up most of the space. There is a corner where other wines are allowed, inhabited by wines from the southern hemisphere, a range from Romania and a full set of English fruit wines. Kopke port, Blandy's madeira and Spanish brandy provide fortification after taking the local Buxton waters.

Best buys

Pinot Noir, Romanian Cellars, 1987, £
Cook's Pinot/Cabernet 1991, New Zealand, £
Tempranillo 1988, Ochoa, Navarra, ££
Rioja Contino Reserva 1986, ££

Midhurst Wine Shippers 🐷

The Wine Shop, Elsted Marsh, Midhurst,   *Tel* (0730) 812222
West Sussex GU29 0JT   *Tel* (0243) 513109

Case sales only   **Open** Mon–Fri 10–6; Sat, Sun, public holidays 10.30–1
Credit cards None accepted; personal and business accounts
Discounts Negotiable   **Delivery** Free within 10-mile radius of Midhurst (min 1 case)   **Glass hire** Free   **Tastings and talks** To invited guests and to groups on request   **Cellarage** Not available

There is a very personal selection here at Midhurst, based around wines from small, family-run vineyards. To keep overheads low, these wines are imported direct and sold on at very reasonable prices.

The range is small, but beautifully presented in an illustrated catalogue. One St-Emilion, one Listrac-Médoc and a Pauillac make up the Bordeaux section. There is a single red burgundy from Mercury and a couple of Beaujolais wines, which almost seems extravagant. South-west France is where much of the interest lies, with Cahors from Domaine de Fages, Madiran from Ch. de Duisse and a handful of other reasonably priced wines.

This year, the net has been cast even further afield and now includes wines from estates in Spain, Portugal, Chile and Argentina. There are even some Australian wines, although the small-estate theme seems to have been abandoned here with one of Australia's largest wineries, Berri Estates, as supplier.

Best buys

Domaine Amblard 1992, Côtes de Duras, £
Domaine Las Bruges-Mau Michau 1989, Côtes de Duras, £
Pouilly Fumé 1991, Gilles Cholet, ££
Listrac-Médoc 1985, Ch. Moulin du Bourg, ££

Milton Sandford Wines

Head office
The Old Chalk Mine, Warren Row, Knowl   *Tel* (0628) 829449
Hill, Reading, Berkshire RG10 8QS

Case sales only **Open** Mon–Fri 9–6 **Closed** Sat, Sun, public holidays
Credit cards None accepted; personal and business accounts **Discounts** Available
on 10+ cases **Delivery** Free by arrangement to Oxfordshire, Berkshire,
Buckinghamshire and Wiltshire (min order 1 case) **Glass hire** Not available
Tastings and talks Tutored tastings to groups on request **Cellarage** £3 per case
per year

It may be that the name Milton Sandford sounds familiar: it was
the name of a top restaurant just outside Reading run by
Richard Sandford. He sold the restaurant a few years ago but
carried on the wine-importing business which had supplied the
restaurant. Now this has expanded, selling mainly to
restaurants, but also to the public (mixed cases). The range is
limited and has a definite New World slant but there are sound
choices from France, too. Burgundies are from quality producers
such as Comte Lafon in Volnay and Guy Roulot in Meursault.
There is a fine collection of red and white Loire wines and a
handful of Rhônes, mainly from Guigal. The number of clarets is
not extensive but there are a few well-chosen wines at all points
of the price scale, and half-bottles are here in force.

Only in Australia does the list really get into its stride, with
wines from Basedow, St Hallett and Rouge Homme. Western
Australia has a more than fair representation: Capel Vale,
Chateau Xanadu, Leeuwin and Pierro. Five vintages of Penfolds
Grange add to the variety. The Californian range goes for
quality with its selection from Sonoma-Cutrer, Stag's Leap and a
good-value range from the same winery, Hawk Crest.

An old chalk mine in Berkshire is the latest acquistion by
Richard Sandford. This provides ideal storage conditions for
wine and the eventual aim is to open a tasting- and dining-
room. The ex-VAT list looks very reasonable and, even with the
tax added on, prices are competitive.

Best buys

Stewart Point Semillon/Chardonnay 1992, Australia, £
Côtes de St-Mont 'Les Hauts Bergelle' 1991, £
Vidal Cabernet/Merlot 1989, New Zealand, ££
Leeuwin Chardonnay 1986, Western Australia, ££

Mitchell & Son

21 Kildare Street, Dublin 2 *Tel* (010 3531) 6760766

Open Mon–Fri 10.30–5.30; Sat 10.30–1 **Closed** Sun, public holidays
Credit cards All accepted; personal and business accounts **Discounts** 10% on
1 case **Delivery** Free in Dublin (min 2 cases); otherwise £3.50 per consignment;
elsewhere £2 per case; mail order available **Glass hire** 10p per glass
Tastings and talks Customer tastings held in Cellars restaurant on request
Cellarage Not available

If you ever go across the sea to Ireland, take plenty of money.
With duty at IR£1.56 a bottle and VAT at 21 per cent, prices for
even the most modest wines sail over the IR£5 mark. This
affects all merchants equally but Mitchells in Dublin does a
reasonable job of providing variety for your money. This fairly
classic list takes most of its wines from France. Prosper Maufoux
and Mommessin feature within the burgundy section, and also
crop up in the Rhône. Mitchell is the agent for these wines but
even so it would be encouraging to see a touch more inspiration
in the selection. Clarets stay in the affordable range, apart from
a quick flurry among the top names. German wines remain
popular and include the Deinhard Heritage selection and a
Charta wine from the Rheingau.

Spain offers wines from Bodegas AGE (including the full-
flavoured Marqués del Romeral) and Portugal is well
represented with a range from Fonseca. So far, Mitchells has
only dipped a toe in the Australian wine scene but California
looks interesting with Sequoia Grove and Concannon Vineyard.
Irish whiskey outnumbers Scotch significantly but they are both
outweighed by vintage armagnac going back to 1940.

Organised tastings are held downstairs in the cellar restaurant
and there are bottles open frequently for tasting in the shop.

Best buys

Mommessin 1992, AC Côtes du Ventoux, £
Olivier de France White 1991/Red 1990, AC Bordeaux, £
Wollombi Creek Shiraz 1990, Australia, ££
Ch. de Sours Rosé 1992, AC Bordeaux, ££

Mitchells Wine Merchants

Head office and main outlet
354 Meadowhead, Sheffield, South Yorkshire   *Tel* (0742) 740311/745587
S8 7UJ
Branches
148 Derbyshire Lane, Sheffield, South   *Tel* (0742) 583989
Yorkshire S8 8SE
25 Townhead Road, Dore, Sheffield, South   *Tel* (0742) 366131
Yorkshire S17 3GD

Open Mon–Sat 8.30–10; Sun, public holidays 12–3, 7–9 **Closed** Chr Day
Credit cards Access, Visa; personal and business accounts **Discounts** 5% on 1
unmixed case; 2.5% on 1 mixed case **Delivery** Free in Sheffield, parts of South
Yorkshire and north Derbyshire; elsewhere at cost; mail order available
Glass hire Free to customers **Tastings and talks** In-store tastings Fri and Sat;
various events held for club members; new product launches; tutored tastings to
groups on request **Cellarage** £2.40 per case per year (under bond only; 50p per
case in/out)

'In line with the current state of play, we have vastly increased
our range of wines under £5 at the expense of those over £10,'
says John Mitchell, once again showing that this Sheffield
merchant never stands still.

Lots of shelf space, which is used to the full, means that the
range stands at 750 wines from around the world, with 250
under £5. This is a great place to come for good-value drinking.
Among the cheaper wines there is a good selection from
southern France, including Ch. Val-Joanis from the Côtes du
Lubéron and house wines from Georges Duboeuf. There are
Caliterra and San Pedro from Chile and a whole range of
Eastern Europeans. Interesting too is a range of wines from
Chiddingstone Vineyard in Kent.

Sheffield is well served with Mitchells' collection of wines at
£5 plus. Clarets kick off the list with a good selection of petits
châteaux and crus bourgeois, and around 30 cru classé wines,
with Lafite and Haut-Brion among them, provide the high-
notes. There is a potted version of the 1855 classification on the
clarets page and this pattern of informing customers continues
throughout the list. Burgundy's representatives are mainly from
Chanson and Moillard, with smatterings of Faiveley, Lupé-
Cholet and Domaine de la Romanée-Conti.

Spain remains a speciality, with Riojas in depth: ten reservas
and 11 gran reservas as well as viños de crianza and Rioja
Blanco complete the picture. Australia is represented by Peter
Lehmann, Hunter Estate, Penfolds, Coldridge Estate and others,
with Vidal, Stoneleigh and Cloudy Bay from New Zealand. Also
in this section is the wine from a tiny island just off Auckland,

Goldwater Estate. California and the rest of the world are handled well.

Mitchells now boasts a tasting room where local wine groups can meet and tutored tastings are held. The Wine Club has taken off in a big way and now has 400 members who receive mailshots and special offers. There is also a Wine Brokers Club which restocks members' cellars automatically. Mitchells is not a traditional stuffy wine merchant, but friendly, enthusiastic and fun. More power to its corkscrew!

Best buys

Lindemans Bin 50 Shiraz 1990, Australia, £
Navajas Rioja Tinto 1990, £
Ch. Guionne 1990, Côtes de Bourg, ££
Mills Reef Sauvignon Blanc 1991, Hawkes Bay, New Zealand, ££

Moffat Wine Shop

8 Well Street, Moffat, Dumfriesshire   *Tel* (0683) 20554
DG10 9DP

Open Mon–Sat 9–5.30   **Closed** Sun; Wed pm from Oct to Mar
Credit cards Access, Visa   **Discounts** 5% on 1 case (may be mixed)
Delivery Free in Dumfriesshire; mail order available   **Glass hire** Free with order
Tastings and talks Available   **Cellarage** Free

There has been a definite shift in emphasis north of the border in Moffat. The canny Scots, who are not ones to miss a good thing when they taste it, have turned towards Australia for their drinking. Tony McIlwrick caters for their tastes with a select range of well-made wines. Moondah Brook, Cape Mentelle and Peter Lehmann are just some of the attractions, with Mitchelton's splendid wines joining the shelves soon. Morris' Rutherglen Liqueur Muscat also goes down well. A full range from Montana represents New Zealand.

Spain is another favourite here in Moffat, with the complete works of Torres providing reliable, classy flavours. Four vintages of the top-price Gran Coronas Mas la Plana would be exceptional in a busy city, but in this sparsely populated area they indicate a real determination to stock good wine. Navarra sports the full-bodied wines of Chivite and sherries include the top end of the Gonzalez Byass range, with medal winners Apostoles and Matusalem.

France has not been forgotten. Highlights include a full range of Beaujolais Crus from Drouhin and Fessy, two organic Alsace wines and two new vins de pays from the south. A good selection from Italy, Portugal, Chile and California adds to the variety.

Best buys

Torres Cabernet Sauvignon Rosé 1990, Chile, £
Orvieto Classico Secco 1992, Antinori, £
Moondah Brook Verdelho 1990, Western Australia, ££
Chénas, Sylvain Fessy, 1989, ££

Moreno Wines

2 Norfolk Place, London W2 1QN   *Tel* 071-706 3055
11 Marylands Road, London W9 2DU   *Tel* 071-286 0678

Open (Norfolk Pl) Mon–Fri 10–9, (Marylands Rd) 10–9; (Norfolk Pl) Sat 10–8, (Marylands Rd) 10–9; (Marylands Rd) Sun 12–2 and public holidays – generally **Closed** Sun and public holidays (Norfolk Pl)   **Credit cards** Access, Visa; Switch; business accounts   **Discounts** 5% on 1 case; 10% on 5+ cases   **Delivery** Free in central London (and in UK on 5+ cases); otherwise £8 on 1 case, £7 on 2 cases, £5.50 on 3 cases, £4 on 4 cases; mail order available   **Glass hire** Free with order **Tastings and talks** Monthly tutored tastings through The Wine Club **Cellarage** Not available

When we asked merchants what trends they saw in the market, most managed a few words on the effect of the recession on their sales. Not so Moreno. Instead, we received a detailed forecast of winemaking trends such as an increase in Cabernet-based wines, less ageing in oak and more in bottle, use of French oak instead of American and an increasing use of the Tempranillo grape. It is this level of information, hopefully passed on to customers as well as to us, which separates true wine merchants from mere sellers of bottles.

Moreno is a Spanish specialist, with a few extras from Portugal and Chile. There are two retail shops in London and a nationwide mail-order service. The list takes a long and lingering look at Rioja (from 27 bodegas) varying in style from traditional Lopez de Heredia to lighter and more fruity Berberana. Most bodegas provide a range of qualities – sin crianza, crianza, reserva and gran reserva – and some have wines going back to the 1970s and beyond. Penedès comes under close scrutiny, with a full range from Torres and Jean León's Cabernet Sauvignon. Raimat provides well-made wines from Lerida. Navarra wines come from Ochoa, Chivite and Vinicola Navarra. Other regions are touched on too: Alella, Valencia and Somontano, while Toro, Cariñena and Priorato are explored in some depth. From Rueda come the wines of Marqués de Griñon as well as the local outpost of Marqués de Riscal. The dazzling wines of Ribero del Duero come from Vega Sicilia and the co-operative at Peñafiel.

With a wide choice of cavas, including the family firm of Juvé y Camps, and sherries from Barbadillo, Bobadilla, Garvey and Gonzalez Byass, there is enough here to keep even the most fervent Hispanophile amused. Should the attention wander, a selection from Portugal will keep the tastebuds occupied. Also included are ports from the House of Osborne, a company better known for its sherries. A monthly wine club provides tasting opportunities.

Best buys

Rioja Tinto Sin Crianza 1991, Navajas, £
Armonioso Blanco Seco nv, Valdepeñas, £
Protos Tinto Gran Reserva 1979, Ribera Del Duero, ££
CUNE Blanco Reserva 1985, Rioja, ££

Morris & Verdin

28 Churton Street, London SW1V 2LP   *Tel* 071-630 8888

Case sales only **Open** Mon–Fri 8–6 **Closed** Sat, Sun, public holidays
Credit cards None accepted; personal and business accounts **Discounts** By negotiation on large orders **Delivery** Free in central London and Oxford; otherwise £7.05 per consignment elsewhere for orders less than £500
Glass hire Free with 1-case order **Tastings and talks** To groups on request
Cellarage £5 ex-VAT per case per year (inc insurance)

There are two ways to buy a decent bottle of burgundy: the first is to start off with a wallet full of money and work through a lot of bottles until you find one that really merits its price; the other way is to go to a specialist such as Morris & Verdin. There you will find a collection of individual domaine wines, each one selected by Master of Wine, Jasper Morris.

In Burgundy it is not enough to know the vineyard and the vintage, you also have to know who the grower is and the style of his wines – you may even have to keep up with family inheritances as vineyards are split up and winemakers change. Jasper Morris does all this for you. He knows the region and the people and is not afraid to change suppliers if quality dips. His range includes ten Meursaults from four different producers, eight Volnays and endless Gevrey-Chambertins, each with individual style and quality. But it is not just the top wines that are good – basic Bourgogne Rouge from Jean Philippe Fichet, Mâcon La Roche Vineuse from Olivier Merlin and Chablis from Vincent Gallois are all first-class wines at affordable prices. Most burgundies in this range are from recent vintages, so cellaring may be needed for the top wines.

Although this company is a burgundy specialist, it does not confine its activities to just this narrow strip of territory. Loire wines include a fine selection from Coteaux du Layon and Vouvray. The Rhône heads straight for quality with wines from Condrieu and a fascinating array from Côte Rôtie. Alsace wines are from quality producers Domaine Ostertag, and a selection of French country wines provides fine drinking in between financial windfalls. Clarets, particularly the recent vintages, are here in depth.

California is the only other region explored to any real degree in this list and here the focus is on new-wave winemakers such as Jim Clendenen of Au Bon Climat, Bob Lindquist of Qupé and Randall Grahm of Bonny Doon.

Best buys

Quinta de la Rosa Red Wine 1991, Douro, £
Domaine de Limbardié Rosé 1992, Coteaux de Murviel, £
Ch. Routas 'Truffière' 1992, Coteaux Varois, ££
Au Bon Climat Pinot Noir 'La Bauge Vineyard' 1990, California, ££

Morrisons

Head office

Hilmore House, Thornton Road, Bradford,   *Tel* (0924) 821234
West Yorkshire BD8 9AX
Approximately 70 branches

Open Variable Mon–Sat **Closed** Sun, some public holidays **Credit cards** Access, Visa **Discounts** Selected promotional lines **Delivery** Not available **Glass hire** Free at all stores **Tastings and talks**, **cellarage** Not available

This group of supermarkets is growing steadily and by the end of 1993 there will be 70 stores based in the Midlands and the north of England. Wine-buyer Stuart Purdie has continued last year's philosophy of offering a sound range of good-value wines but, occasionally, some more extravagant wines sneak into the selection.

French regional wines have always been strong at Morrisons, even before the South of France became the fashionable place to make wine. Now the range includes Chais Baumière and Vieille Ferme among a list of almost 50. Many of these wines are under £3 and all but one are under £5. Bordeaux stays firmly in the shallow end with generic wines and some petits châteaux, burgundy is fairly restricted, but there are rays of sunshine from Bouchard and Chanson, with a handful of better reds and whites. Duboeuf provides a fair selection of Beaujolais, and the

Rhône is worth a second look. Spain goes for reliable names such as Raimat, Torres and Campo Viejo. It is good to see the splendid Murrieta white appearing in such a small selection. The Italian section has grown in the last year – Rocca delle Macie Chianti and Fontanafredda's Barolo join a wide range of own-label wines.

From Australia, reliable flavours and value are the keynotes. Lindemans, Penfolds and Wyndham feature here. New Zealand, South Africa and Chile add to the variety.

This range survived drastic surgery around a year ago. It seems that the patient is recovering well.

Best buys

Morrison Rioja Tinto, £
Lindemans Bin 45 Cabernet/Shiraz 1990, Australia, £
Paul Herard Brut Champagne, ££
Jamiesons Run Red 1989, Coonawarra, Australia, ££

Nadder Wine Company

The Wine Cellars, 2 Netherhampton Road,   *Tel* (0722) 325418
Harnham, Salisbury, Wiltshire SP2 8HE

Case sales only   Open Mon–Fri 9–7; Sat 10–3   **Closed** Sun, Chr Day, Boxing Day, Good Friday, Easter Day   **Credit cards** Access, Visa; personal and business accounts   **Discounts** 5% for orders of £100+; 7.5% on orders of £500+; 10% on orders over £1,000 (less 2.5% credit-card commission)   **Delivery** Free within 30-mile radius of Salisbury and Central London (min 1 case with a value of £50) and UK mainland and Isle of Wight (min 5 cases); otherwise at cost; mail order available   **Glass hire** Free with order   **Tastings and talks** Regularly to groups on request   **Cellarage** Not available

Case-sales only from this cash-&-carry warehouse in the old village school in Harnham, on the outskirts of Salisbury. Here the whole range is spread out over two floors, less expensive wines downstairs, more expensive upstairs. Tastings are a feature with six bottles open every day.

The range is fairly wide, but the Australian section in particular is good. Rosemount, Hunter Estate, Tisdall, Eden Ridge, Coldstream Hills and Mount Helen are just some of the new additions to the list. The New Zealand selection is joined by a full range from Hunter's, including the delicious Pinot Noir.

Among the South African wines is the good-value Drostdy-Hof range and the more expensive Meerlust wines, including the full-flavoured Meerlust Rubicon.

From Europe, the emphasis is on wines from small but quality growers such as Domaine des Dorices in Muscadet and Domaine Martin in the Rhône. Burgundies come from Faiveley and Labouré-Roi, clarets include a good selection under £10, as well as some classier wines.

The rest of the list is an interesting mix of wines from Italy and Spain, and once again these focus on small producers rather than the big names. Chris Gilbey likes his customers to have some say in what the company stocks. With frequent local tastings for wine societies, yacht clubs and the like, there are plenty of opportunities to let him know what you think.

Best buys

Domaines Virginie Sauvignon 1992, Vin de Pays d'Oc, £
Montecillo Tinto Rioja 1988, £
Ch. Loudenne 1987, Médoc, ££
Hunter's Sauvignon Blanc 1992, New Zealand, ££

Le Nez Rouge

12 Brewery Road, London N7 9NH   *Tel* 071-609 4711

Open Mon–Fri 9–5.30; Sat 10–2 **Closed** Sun, public holidays
Credit cards Access, Visa; personal and business accounts **Discounts** £1 per case collected **Delivery** In London, 1–2 cases (or less than £200 ex-VAT) £3, 3+ cases free; in Home Counties, 1–2 cases (or less than £200 ex-VAT) £6; 3–4 cases £4, 5+ cases free **Glass hire** Free **Tastings and talks** Regular in-store tastings; annual tastings to Nez Rouge Club members; occasional tutored tastings **Cellarage** £2.60 per case per year

Le Nez Rouge is the retail arm of Berkmann Wine Cellars and as such has access to the huge range of agency wines that Berkmann supplies to the trade. Last year Le Nez Rouge underwent radical surgery and emerged slimmer, but during 1993 it regrew and now works from the same list as Berkmann, with additional costs for mixed cases and delivery. Single bottles can be purchased from the shop.

A man cannot make him laugh; but that's no marvel; he drinks no wine.

Shakespeare, *Henry IV (Part II)*

The list is not particularly user-friendly, with prices given for unmixed cases, but if you can cope with this there are lots of goodies worth trying.

Burgundies occupy a hefty section, with wines from a wide variety of good domaines: Tollot-Beaut, Rossignol, Sauzet and Trapet are just a few of those available. Beaujolais is another Berkmann speciality and the Duboeuf domaine wines are here, most costing less than £6. Some Rhônes are also from the Duboeuf stable. A good selection of French regional wines helps keep costs down.

The New World range is a mixture of new names and familiar faces. Argentina provides wines from Bodegas Norton, who grow Italian grape varieties as well as Cabernet Sauvignon. Australia has the Rosemount range, Coldstream Hills and Petersons from the Hunter Valley. With Morton in New Zealand and Montestell from Julius Laszio in South Africa you are unlikely to run out of choice.

Best buys

Beaujolais Villages, Ch. de Grande Grange 1992, Duboeuf, £
Picpoul de Pinet 1992, Huges de Beauvignac, Coteaux du Languedoc, £
Crémant d'Alsace, Cuvée Prestige, René Muré, ££
Malbec, Bodegas Norton 1991, Argentina, ££

James Nicholson Wine Merchant

27a Killyleagh Street, Crossgar, Co Down   *Tel* (0396) 830091
BT30 9DG

Open Mon–Sat 10–7   **Closed** Sun, Chr Day, Boxing Day, Easter Mon, 12 July
Credit cards Access, Diners Club, Visa; business accounts   **Discounts** Available
Delivery Free in UK on 1+ case; mail order available   **Glass hire** Free, breakages
charged at £1 per glass   **Tastings and talks** In-store monthly tastings; supper
evenings bi-monthly; themed dinners quarterly with guest speaker
Cellarage Limited cellarage, prices on application

The retail part of this company is only four years old but has settled into the marketplace with ease. It was while James Nicholson was a restaurateur that he realised how difficult it was to get hold of better-quality wines. Now, as Northern Ireland agent for some of the great names, he has solved that problem.

From France none of the wines of Jaboulet, Guigal, Duboeuf or Drouhin would disappoint. Châteauneuf-du-Pape is from Beaucastel but the delicious Coudoulet de Beaucastel provides drinking at almost half the price while you wait for the main wine to mature. From Bordeaux the emphasis is on wines over £10 rather than under – classed-growth clarets obviously go down well in Crossgar. A selection of French regional wines including Ch. la Jaubertie and Ch. Bellevue-la-Forêt from Côtes du Frontonnais provides quality drinking at lower cost.

The Spanish clutch includes Riojas from Martínez Bujanda and Marqués de Murrieta, with Pesquera and six vintages of Vega Sicilia from Ribero del Duero. Italian choices would be the wines of Umani Ronchi and Rocca delle Macie, while from Lebanon seven vintages of Château Musar demonstrate that Serge Hochar's wine really does go on maturing and developing for twenty years. James Nicholson has winkled out good wines from all parts of the New World – Australia, New Zealand, South Africa and California – with two or three companies representing each region.

To introduce such a wide range, he keeps bottles open in the shop for customers to try and lays on informal monthly tastings and supper evenings with guest speakers. Mail order for one case is free throughout the UK.

Best buys

Quinta de la Rosa 1991, Douro, Portugal, £
Ch. Tour du Mirambeau 1992, Bordeaux Blanc, £
San Lorenzo Rosso Conero 1990, Umani Ronchi, ££
Gigondas 1989, Guigal, ££

Nickolls & Perks

37 High Street, Stourbridge, West Midlands DY8 1TA	*Tel* (0384) 394518
Greenwoods, 178 High Street, Lye, West Midlands DY9 8LH	*Tel* (0384) 422217
Windmill Hill, Cradley, West Midlands DY7 6DI	*Tel* (0384) 394518

Open Mon–Sat 9–10 **Closed** Sun, public holidays **Credit cards** Access, Amex, Visa; personal and business accounts **Discounts** Available **Delivery** Free within 12-mile radius (min 1 case); mail order available **Glass hire** 10p per item
Tastings and talks Regular tutored tastings **Cellarage** Available (charges vary)

This company is housed in a lovely old building which dates from Elizabethan times. Wine trading has gone on here for nearly two hundred years so it is not surprising that this company takes a fairly traditional view of the world of wine, with just a brief glimpse over the wall to the New World.

Bordeaux is the gem of the list. Page after page of the great and the good are here, a dazzling array of first growths from 1961 Latour to six vintages of Haut-Brion. Lesser cru classé wines are also here but there is a disappointing range of petits châteaux under £10. Burgundies are sound with a good cross-section from the region, including some wines from the Domaine de la Romanée-Conti. Safe *négociant* names are supplemented by a few domaine wines found in a separate section at the front of the list.

Port is an area to be drooled over. Bottles start at 1904 and climb rapidly through the '20s and '30s towards a real abundance of 1963 wines and beyond. The rest of Europe is not neglected; for instance, good Riojas make up most of the Spanish range, while Italy is covered, although, surprisingly, Tuscany is ignored completely. Australia, New Zealand, California and Chile are listed rather than featured.

Best buys

Côtes de Brouilly 1988, Dépagneaux, £
Côtes-du-Rhône 'Vieilles Vignes' 1990, Roger Perrin, £
Morey St Denis 'Clos Les Ormes' 1983, Georges Lignier, ££
Chablis 1990, Bacheroy-Josselin, ££

Nicolas

(Head office) 71 Abingdon Road, London W8 6AW	*Tel* 071-937 3996
98 Holland Park Avenue, London W11 3RB	*Tel* 071-727 5148
157 Great Portland Street, London W1N 5FB	*Tel* 071-436 9636
6 Fulham Road, London SW3 6HG	*Tel* 071-584 1450
282 Old Brompton Road, London SW5 9HR	*Tel* 071-370 4402
17 Kensington Church Street, London W8	*Tel* 071-937 5232
10 Kew Green, Kew, Surrey TW9 3BH	*Tel* 081-332 6771

Open Mon–Fri 11–10; Sat 10–10; Sun 12–2, 7–9 **Closed** Public holidays
Credit cards Access, Visa; personal and business accounts **Discounts** 5% on 1 mixed case **Delivery** Free locally (min 1 case); negotiable nationwide and in France; mail order available **Glass hire** Free with purchase
Tastings and talks Occasionally **Cellarage** Small quantities only in UK

As you might expect, the London outposts of the French-based Nicolas empire can come up with a fine range of French wines.

Once in the bottle a cork can last for decades but eventually it becomes brittle and crumbly with age.

The list shows a selection of around 200, each one identified according to taste as well as region of origin. So a vin de pays de Gascogne is given a symbol which describes it as 'lively and fresh', while Madiran is definitely a 'spicey and fleshy wine'. Regrettably, there are no producers' names included on the list so you have to go along to the shop and look at the bottles.

This regular range of wines comes from all parts of France, most of them under £10 and a big chunk under £5. There is also a splendid collection of fine wine. Clarets are here in depth – 20 from the 1982 vintage, including four first growths and Pétrus – and there is even a choice of seven wines from the 1928 vintage. Also available is a splendid collection of vintage armagnacs rolling back to 1921.

A newsletter (in French and English) keeps you up to date with the range.

Best buys

Cépage Merlot nv, Vin de Pays d'Oc, £
Bordeaux Réserve Nicolas 1988, £
Ch. Rahoul 1987, Graves Blanc, ££
Savigny lès Beaune 1987, Noirot, ££

The Nobody Inn

Doddiscombsleigh, nr Exeter, Devon
EX6 7PS

Tel (0647) 52394

Open Mon–Sat 11–11; Sun and public holidays 12–2 **Credit cards** Access, Visa; personal and business accounts **Discounts** 5% on 1 case **Delivery** Free within 20-mile radius (min 1 case); mail order available **Glass hire** Free with order **Tastings and talks** Monthly tutored tastings (Oct–Apr); other tastings by invitation **Cellarage** Not available

To look at, proprietor Nick Borst-Smith appears perfectly sane, but glance at the wine-list and you might begin to have your doubts. Remember that the Nobody Inn is essentially a pub in a tiny Devon village, not far from Exeter. It is a pretty sixteenth-century place with beams and horse brasses – the sort of venue to have a quiet drink while down in Devon on holiday. Ask for a glass of wine and, shock, horror, unlike 99 per cent of the licensed trade you are not offered a glass of tepid red or a glass of tepid (and oxidised) white. No fewer than 15 wines are open to try by the glass, all kept in perfect condition under nitrogen.

When you have sampled the open bottles, move on to the rest of the range – and this is where the wonderful sense of insanity creeps in. The list is huge and is available either in a drink-in or take-away version. The difference between the two prices is refunded if you decide to buy a mixed case. There is no region unexplored, no style left undescribed in this dedicated journal of wine, though Australia is the region of the moment after Nick's recent trip to the vineyards. The big names are here but so too are the smaller ones: the Red from Mountadam, Mount Edelstone from Henschke, even a Zinfandel from Cape Mentelle. We would echo his comment: 'Do the Americans know?'

The Americas, North and South, are explored in a similarly thorough manner. Greece, Israel, Bulgaria, Corsica and China... the list goes on and on. In France, the Loire comes in for special treatment, particularly the sweet wines. We are asked not to reveal that these wines are under-rated and excellent value because that only drives the prices up. And so we won't! We merely point out that the range of 12 Coteaux du Layon, 11 Quarts de Chaume and six Vouvrays is probably the best you will come across. With only two pages devoted to it, red burgundy takes on an almost sparse look compared with other regions; Bordeaux is more of an assault course. Sales are by the bottle or case; delivery is free within 20 miles of the inn, but nationwide mail order is available. Prices seem pretty much in line with elsewhere. Tutored tastings during the winter months make this the best venue for miles around.

And, when you have eventually decided on the wine, why not turn your thoughts to the cheese list. There are 40 varieties, all from Devon and lovingly described, with names like Ticklemoor, Colespark, Vulscombe, Meldon and Devon Oke. Now, where's the straitjacket?

Best buys

Béarn 1988, Domaine Cauhapé, £
Ch. Freysse 1989, Bordeaux Supérieur, £
Zinfandel Cape Mentelle 1990, Western Australia, ££
Coteaux du Layon, St-Aubin, Cuvée Privilège 1989, Banchereau, ££

Always open sparkling wines with care. Hold the bottle in one hand and the cork with the other. Turn the bottle while holding the cork and resist the pressure from the cork as it begins to come out of the bottle. A flying champagne cork may look impressive but it can be dangerous.

Oddbins

Head office
31–33 Weir Road, London SW19 8UG   *Tel* 081-944 4400
177 branches

Open (Generally) Mon–Sat 10–10; Sun 12–3, 7–10; public holidays 10–10
Closed Chr Day   **Credit cards** Access, Amex, Visa; business accounts
Discounts 5% on mixed cases; 'seven for the price of six' on champagne and
sparkling wine at £5.99 or above   **Delivery** Free within locality of shop (min 1
case)   **Glass hire** Free with order; deposit required   **Tastings and talks** Regular
in-store tastings on Saturdays (2–5) in all branches; to groups on request
Cellarage Not available

One of the more painful forms of torture is to tell wine drinkers
who live in remote parts of the country just how good Oddbins
is. Stranded in the sticks they have no way of taking advantage
of the terrific range of wines offered by this lively chain. Should
a rumour get around that Oddbins might be moving in, the
established merchants dive for cover while residents start
planning their cellars. Some dedicated drinkers even plan
picnics and excursions with an eye to taking in the nearest
Oddbins as one of the tourist attractions. So what is it about
this operation that inspires such reactions?

You notice an Oddbins shop as soon as you drive up the
High Street. Garish front windows are the norm (do shop
managers take a course in graffiti painting before starting the
job?). The shops manage to look busy even when there are few
customers, with piles of cases, special never-to-be-repeated
offers, up-to-date pithy tasting notes and big tickets asking low
prices. The staff deserve a mention, too. Does Oddbins have a
monopoly on engineers taking a year off or out-of-work pilots?
These people are keen, work long hours and are invariably
studying for the next wine exam on the qualifications ladder.
New lines are tasted as they come into the range and shops
band together to organise staff tastings so that the people
behind the counter actually know the range they are selling.
There are Saturday tastings in all shops and a new event is the
Consumer Wine Fair, where you get a chance to meet some of
the winemakers and taste around 400 wines. So far, London and
Edinburgh are the venues.

The range is outstanding – 800 wines is the claim (although
few shops have everything in at any one time). It is a dynamic
organisation with new lines constantly arriving. Australia is one
of the high points: most of the names you have ever heard of
crowd the shelves. They start with the good-value wines of
Tolley's and Killawarra and slowly climb via Penfolds,
Lehmann, Petaluma, Merrill and many more right up to Grange
Hermitage. Devaluation has made California wines 'about as

popular as the flagman at Aintree' but even so, the eccentrically named wines of Bonny Doon should not be missed.

Despite a slump in interest everywhere else, Oddbins has held faith with German wines, seeking out the good winemakers and tastiest wines. Lingenfelder is joined by Müller-Catoir and Kurt Darting this year. From France, the Rhône selection deserves a round of applause – Beaucastel, Auguste Clape and Guigal are the star attractions. Clarets manage to balance affordable drinking among the crus bourgeois with value for money in the classy section. The sparkling range is huge, particularly from outside Champagne, and with seven bottles for the price of six on many lines, Oddbins must rate as one of the best places to stock up on fizz.

Burgundy has livened up this year with a bigger range and better value. The new Oddbins Fine Wine Shop in Farringdon has parcels of wines from smaller domaines which just won't spread around all the shops. Also new this year is *The Catalyst*. This is a quarterly publication giving details of new developments, new wines, special offers and now, even trips to the vineyards. No quiet visit to France, they plan a full frontal assault on Australia!

If you have an Oddbins nearby, then you know how good they are. If you don't, why not move house?

Best buys

Cockatoo Ridge Chardonnay 1992, Australia, £
The Cataclysm 1989, J Lohr, Napa Valley, California, £
Scheurebe Spätlese Halbtrocken 1990, Müller-Catoir, Rheinpfalz, ££
Vino da Tavola!, Rocca di Castagnoli, Italy, ££

Pallant Wines

Apuldram Manor Farm, Appledram Lane, Chichester, West Sussex PO20 7PE *and*	*Tel* (0243) 788475
17 High Street, Arundel, West Sussex BN18 9AD	*Tel* (0903) 882288

Open Mon–Sat 9–5.30; Sun, public holidays 12–2 **Closed** Some public holidays **Credit cards** Access, Visa; business accounts **Discounts** 50p on 5+ cases, £1 on 10+ cases **Delivery** Free within 40-mile radius of Chichester (min 1 case); elsewhere by arrangement; mail order available **Glass hire** Free with order **Tastings and talks** 4 invited wine tastings to clubs per year **Cellarage** Not available

There is a new high street base for this merchant with a retail shop in Arundel to add to the business at Apuldram Manor

Farm. As well as wine, the shop will carry some delicatessen lines and will hold regular wine tastings.

The range here at Pallant is not huge but some confident buying has brought together a few highlights from around the world. France looks best among the Bordeaux petits châteaux and a selection of regional wines. Italy includes two wines from Villa di Capezzana and a good example of Vernaccia di San Gimignano from Teruzzi e Puthod. Spain contributes a few reliable wines from Rioja, Navarra and Penedès, and the South Africans extend beyond the ubiquitous KWV wines to the Simonsig Estate. With big names from Australia (Penfolds, Mildara, Rosemount) and the Undurraga range from Chile, choosing a single bottle or a mixed dozen should be no problem. Gift hampers are also big business down Appledram Lane, and when you have bought your wine you can always go and look at the Spitfire parked outside, courtesy of the local D-Day museum.

Best buys

Ch. Le Livey 1991, Bordeaux Sec, £
Gewurztraminer 1992, Villány, Hungary, £
Ch. Le Livey 1990, Bordeaux Supérieur, ££
Mâcon-Clessé 1990, Caves de la Vigne Blanche, ££

Pease & Wrightson Wine Merchants

Hill House, Gainford, Darlington,   *Tel* (0325) 730320
Co Durham DL2 3EY

Case sales only   Open Mon–Fri 9–6   **Closed** Sat, Sun, public holidays
Credit cards Access, Visa; personal and business accounts   **Discounts** Not available   **Delivery** Free within 50-mile radius of Gainford; mail order available   **Glass hire** Free; breakages charged for   **Tastings and talks** To groups on request; two tastings in Yorkshire and two in London   **Cellarage** Between £2.50 and £4.50 per case per year

This list still wins the prize for the strangest layout. French wines are mainly grouped together, but Oregon makes an appearance between the Rhône and Bergerac, while Washington State is between South Africa and sherry. California is somewhere else altogether. Welcome this year are single-bottle prices. Still, once you have mastered this merry-go-round system there is plenty to look at. Page after page of clarets provide a reasonable collection of petits châteaux and classed growths. Burgundies include some important names – Armand Rousseau, Sauzet and Tollot-Beaut – as well as wines from Olivier Leflaive. His Bourgogne Blanc Les Setilles is hinted to be somewhat grander than its appellation declares. The remainder of the list dots about, with just a few wines from each region.

Italy is limited to two wines: Prunotto's Barolo and Sassicaia, serious wines but hardly doing justice to the tremendous variety available here. Oregon provides two wines from Oak Knoll, including the splendid Pinot Noir. Ports are big at Hill House, with vintages rolling back to 1912 and a fair clutch from 1960 and 1963 still available.

Best buys

Undurraga Sauvignon Blanc 1991, Maipo, Chile, £
Ch. de Jonquières 1989, Corbières, £
Ch. Pechaurieux Blanc 1990, Montravel, ££
Oak Knoll Pinot Noir 1989, Willamette Valley, Oregon, ££

Thos Peatling

Head office
Westgate House, Bury St Edmunds, Suffolk   *Tel* (0284) 755948
IP33 1QS
28 branches throughout East Anglia (including Peatlings Wine Centre in London)

Open Hours vary from branch to branch **Credit cards** Access, Amex, Visa; personal and business accounts **Discounts** 5% on 1 case **Delivery** Free in East Anglia; mail order available **Glass hire** Free with order
Tastings and talks Weekly informal tastings at most branches; monthly tutored tastings at wine centres **Cellarage** £4 per case per year

This 28-strong chain of shops is owned by a brewery – sometimes the kiss of death when it comes to decent wine. Not so here at Thos Peatling with its owners Greene King, who are committed to maintaining a 'proper wine merchant' image in these retail shops.

Claret is the major area of interest. You could spend weeks just working through the 1985 vintage – 66 wines in all, ranging from the most petit of the petits châteaux to first growths. It is the same story for other vintages, although the big guns are matured before making their debut on the list.

French Country wines offer a wide choice at reasonable prices. Twenty reds all under £5 include Réserve du Révérend from the Sichel family in Corbières. The whites take in a good clutch of vins de pays and a Jurançon Sec. Burgundies are almost as impressive as the clarets. Individual estate wines – all the right names – and the prices seem well in tune with the current market.

Elsewhere, German wines are comprehensive and good quality; Spain includes good-value Jumilla and Toro as well as a full set from Torres, and Gran Reserva 904 Rioja. Australia brings together some of the best names. Brown Brothers get a good airing, with Mountadam, Cape Mentelle, Hardy and Capel

Vale adding to the variety. New ranges this year are from California, Italy, Australia and New Zealand.

Staff training is taken seriously, so advice from behind the counter should be knowledgable. In-store tastings, *en primeur* offers and special reductions add to the attractions.

Best buys

Ch. la Bourgette 1986, Bordeaux Supérieur, £
Chardonnay, Cave du Haut Poitou 1991, £
Ch. le Pin 1985, Pomerol, ££
Ch. Lafaurie-Peyraguey 1985, Sauternes, ££

Le Picoleur

See La Réserve

Christopher Piper Wines

1 Silver Street, Ottery St Mary, Devon
EX11 1DB

Tel (0404) 814139

Open Mon–Fri 9–1, 2–6; Sat 9–1, 2.30–5 **Closed** Sun, public holidays
Credit cards Access, Visa; personal and business accounts **Discounts** 5% on 1 mixed case, up to 10% on 3+ mixed cases **Delivery** Free in South-West (min 4 cases) and rest of UK (min 6 cases); otherwise £6.90 per consignment; mail order available **Glass hire** Free **Tastings and talks** Three to four large tastings per year; smaller regular tutored tastings; 2 wine weekends at Thurlestone, South Devon **Cellarage** £3.90 per case (inc insurance)

Don't let the size of Christopher Piper's shop in Ottery St Mary fool you. It may be too small and cramped to swing a corkscrew but the range available is huge. Apart from extensive sales to hotels and restaurants in the area, there are apparently two main groups of customers in this rural part of the world. The tourists come and buy traditional or fashionable wines while the resident agricultural community prefers to register its opposition to the EC by buying anything good as long as it doesn't come from Europe.

For the tourists, France is a treat: good clarets with plenty of crus bourgeois at under £10 a bottle and burgundies from a variety of quality growers and *négociants*. This year there is a brand new range of domaine-bottled Beaujolais and Mâconnais, and boring vins de tables have been swept away and replaced with varietal vins de pays. The rest of France cannot be faulted. Every region is well represented, as are Germany, Italy and Spain.

If you are in sympathy with the farmers, Australia is not a bad place to start. From here Christopher Piper has selected some super wines from Langi Ghiran, Taltarni and Petaluma.

He has also gone for the complete set from Brown Brothers, with New Zealand, California and South Africa available as well. These should provide enough choice to be able to steer clear of EC wines for ever. Half-bottles are a feature, including 22 from Bordeaux and a whole clutch from Burgundy, the Loire, Australia and Alsace.

This business adds a totally new meaning to the term 'house wine'. Christopher Piper is oenologist and winemaker at Ch. des Tours in Brouilly and the shop stocks several vintages in various bottle sizes.

Best buys

Aldridge Estate Chardonnay 1991, Australia, £
Sauvignon Blanc, Domaine de Breuil, 1992, Vin de Pays du Jardin de la France, £
Mâcon Blanc Villages, Domaine des Maillettes 1991, ££
Chénas, Domaine Champagnon 1991, ££

Terry Platt Wine Merchant

Ferndale Road, Llandudno Junction,   *Tel* (0492) 592971
Gwynedd LL31 9NT

Case sales only **Open** Mon–Fri 8–5.30 **Closed** Sat, Sun, public holidays
Credit cards Not accepted; personal and business accounts **Discounts** Available
Delivery Free to North and Mid-Wales, Cheshire and Shropshire (min order 1 case); mail order available **Glass hire** Free with order
Tastings and talks Tastings and lunches throughout the year **Cellarage** Not available

Good independent wine merchants in Wales are like gold dust, but when you do find them, they sparkle. This is a family business and while most of its trade is with hotels and restaurants of the area, private customers are welcome; mixed cases are available and the list is user-friendly, with VAT-inclusive prices.

The range has a personal feel about it. Most regions offer a choice from small domaines or well-known larger suppliers. In Burgundy there are domaine wines from Emile Chandesais, Jean Germain and Machard de Gramont, with a good range too from Louis Latour and Antonin Rodet. New this year is an increased range from South and South-West France, including Ch. Terre Blanche Figeac from Côtes de Duras and Domaine de Montmarin from Côtes de Thongue. Bordeaux presents an affordable range of crus bourgeois, with just a sprinkling of classed growths among the older vintages. Domaines feature again in the Loire and in the Arbois and Jura, where the bottles include a Vin de Paille, a Vin Jaune and a Pinot Noir from the Côtes du Jura.

Italy and Spain are both sound but Portugal seems to have been overlooked. German wines are mainly from family firm Michel Schneider in Zell on the Mosel. In California, Platt has followed the trail of nineteenth-century gold-diggers to the Sierra foothills and the Monteviña winery, whilst in Mudgee, New South Wales, its Australian namesake provides a selection of good-value varietals. Other Australians include d'Arenburg and Delatite.

Half-bottles are listed together and regular tastings are arranged throughout the year. Delivery is free for one case over a wide area – good news for those in North and Mid-Wales and in Cheshire.

Best buys

Fumé Blanc 1990, J Wile, Napa Valley, California, £
Ch. Terre Blanche Figeac Blanc Sec 1992, Côtes de Duras, £
Ch. Trignon Viognier 1992, Rhône Blanc, ££
Platt Chardonnay 1990, Mudgee, Australia, ££

Playford Ros

Middle Park House, Sowerby, Thirsk, North   *Tel* (0845) 526777
Yorkshire YO7 3AH

Open Mon–Sat 8–6 **Closed** Sun, public holidays **Credit cards** None accepted;
personal and business accounts **Discounts** 2.5% on 6+ cases; a further 5%
discount on settlement within 10 days **Delivery** Free to Yorkshire,
Northumberland and Derbyshire and nationwide on 4+ cases; otherwise £5 for 1
case, £7 for 2 cases, £7.50 for 3 cases; mail order available **Glass hire** Free
Tastings and talks Approx 8 trade and private tastings per year **Cellarage** £2.75
per case per year

This is a fairly new company, run by Nigel Munton, which operates out of restored old buildings in Sowerby. A lot of Playford's business is to the hotels and restaurants of the area but they are prepared to mix cases and will deliver one case free within Yorkshire, Northumberland and Derbyshire, which sounds like a pretty good deal.

The list has a definite trade feel to it. Prices are ex-VAT and there are two columns depending on how many cases you buy. The range takes a fairly traditional look at France, with a hefty listing of clarets, most under £10. This part of the north likes burgundy, so Nigel responds by listing a fine collection from small domaines and *négociants*. Names such as Leflaive, Trapet and Mommessin are here, as is the lesser-known Domaine Marshall, an estate in Nuits-St-Georges, run by Yorkshireman Tim Marshall.

Outside France, it really is just a handful of wines from each region. Italy is very restrained, there is Montes from Chile, and Spain would not take much working through. Portugal merits just one wine, Quinta de Camerate.

Only the New World seems to get into its stride with Cape Mentelle, Mountadam, Yarra Yering and Pikes from Australia; New Zealand and South Africa add to the variety.

Best buys

Domaine de la Salette 1992, Vin de Pays des Côtes de Gascogne, £
Domaine de Malardeau 1992, Côtes de Duras, Ryman, £
Mâcon Uchizy 1991, Domaine Talmard, ££
Cabernet Sauvignon 1985, Bodegas Weinert, Argentina, ££

Portland Wine Company

16 North Parade, Sale Moor, Manchester, Greater Manchester M33 3JS	*Tel* 061-962 8752
Associated outlets	
82 Chester Road, Macclesfield, Cheshire FK8 8DL	*Tel* (0625) 616147
79 Scotland Road, Nelson, Lancashire BB9 7YP	*Tel* (0282) 603382
152a Ashley Road, Hale, Manchester WA15 9SA	*Tel* 061-928 0357

Open Mon–Sat 10–10; Sun and public holidays 12–3 **Credit cards** All accepted; personal and business accounts **Discounts** 10% on mixed cases (except on special offers) **Delivery** Free to central and south Manchester, and north Cheshire (min 1 case); quantity discounts on large orders **Glass hire** Free
Tastings and talks Monthly tutored tastings (Tue, £5–10 per person); monthly shop tastings (Sun, free); to groups on request **Cellarage** Not available

---

There is a surprisingly wide range of good-value wines at this small chain of four shops in the North-West. Very few stray over the £10 mark and those that do form a reasonable selection for special occasions – champagnes, a handful of top burgundies and clarets, and the upper reaches of the Penfolds range.

Australia features large in the list. The range explores the basics from Tollana and Jacobs Creek and then climbs the quality ladder via Rosemount, Rothbury and Rouge Homme. There are over 50 ways to spend a fiver in this range, plus another 60 wines under £10, all of them eminently drinkable. Ten Aussie sparklers compete for attention among a range from France, California and Spain.

Spain is another favoured region with the reds in particular coming in for special attention. Here the approach is the same as Australia, a carpet-bombing of good-value wines, each one hitting the mark and full of flavour; Ochoa from Navarra, a collection of Riojas and a full set from Torres, rising to Vega Sicilia and Jean León. Italy is worth spending some time on, as is Eastern Europe, where the range includes reserve wines from Moldova as well as the inexpensive Bulgarians. France continues the theme of good-value drinking with a fine selection from all regions – country wines are particularly good.

Long opening hours, discounts on mixed case sales and delivery around Manchester and north Cheshire make this business well worth trying.

Best buys

Barbera d'Asti 'Ceppi Storici' 1990, £
Ch. la Bastide Vieilles Vignes 1990, Corbières, £
Chablis, Louis Alexandre 1992, ££
Morgon Vieilles Vignes 1991, Janodet, ££

Arthur Rackhams

Head office and cellars
Winefare House, 5 High Road, West Byfleet,   *Tel* (0932) 351585
Surrey KT14 7QE
9 branches in London and Surrey

Open Some outlets Mon–Sat 10–6; Sun, public holidays 12–2; other outlets Mon–Sat 10–10; Sun, public holidays 7–9 **Credit cards** Access, Visa; personal and business accounts **Discounts** Members' Club discount (The Vintner Wine Club) **Delivery** Free on UK mainland (min 5 cases) for wine club; mail order available for wine club **Glass hire** Free **Tastings and talks** Tastings in-store every weekend; monthly tutored tastings **Cellarage** Not available

There are nine shops in this group, all based around London and the leafy bits of Surrey but that is only part of the operation. Equally important is the Vintner Wine Club, a mail-order business that also holds tastings, events and trips to the vineyards. Membership costs a hefty £18 a year but entitles you to generous discounts on the retail prices, whether by mail order or for single bottles through the shops. At the core of the list for both the Wine Club and the shops is a collection of wines based on individual winemakers. These have been selected by MD James Rackham and he concentrates on family domaines and winemakers where quality and individual style are taken seriously. This works well in France, where the term 'Viticulture' describes the collection. Many of these growers are not widely known but some worth trying are Châteauneuf-du-Pape from Domaine Robert Sinard and Alsace wines from Domaine Neumeyer – however, there is a tremendous variety to work through here. The Spanish and Rest of the World collections tend to come from larger concerns, although there are some smaller producers among them, such as Tarrawarra in Australia.

Chile, California, Bulgaria, Germany, Italy and South Africa are all here in the range, with good selections of wine.

Confusingly, there is a group of shops, also called The Vintner, just like the wine club, but under slightly different ownership. Nick Brougham of the Guildford Wine Market (*q.v.*) has joined forces with James Rackham to form The Vintner shops, four in all, which have a similar but slightly wider range than Arthur Rackhams. Overall, the range is good and interesting, although the set-up of the shops/club can get a little confusing.

Advice over the counter should be good as this company takes training seriously.

Best buys

Côtes-du-Rhône, Domaine Didier Charavin 1991, £
Domaine de l'Ile Saint-Pierre Blanc, Vin de Pays des Bouches-du-Rhône 1992, £
Mâcon-Clessé 1989, Fûts de Chêne, Domaine René Michel, ££
Châteauneuf-du-Pape 1988, Domaine St Laurent, ££

Raeburn Fine Wines

21/23 Comely Bank Road, Edinburgh EH4 1DS	*Tel* 031-332 5166
The Vaults, 4 Giles Street, Leith, Edinburgh EH6 6DJ	*Tel* 031-554 2652

Open Mon–Sat 9.30–6; Sun, public holidays 10–5 **Credit cards** Access, Visa; personal and business accounts **Discounts** 5% on unmixed cases, 2.5% on mixed cases **Delivery** Free in Edinburgh (min 1 case); elsewhere negotiable; mail order available **Glass hire** Free with order **Tastings and talks** Two free annual tastings **Cellarage** £5 per case per year (under bond)

If you walk past these premises in Comely Bank Road, you could be forgiven for thinking that this is a flower shop. Until last year it was also the local grocery shop so you could have bought your baked beans along with your claret. Now the shop concentrates on flowers and wine, but, despite that odd combination and the rather cramped surroundings, Raeburn is very serious about being in the wine trade. The business is run by the Mohamed family who came to Edinburgh in 1967 from India via Kenya. Zubair Mohamed is the force behind the wine business and he has built up an impressive range, most of which he ships direct to Edinburgh from the growers. This shows particularly in the burgundy section, where a fine array of domaine wines competes for attention in the crowded shop. Echézeaux, Le Montrachet, Volnay and Chambolle-Musigny are all here, as well as respectable Passe Tout Grains and Bourgogne Rouge.

Classed-growth clarets feature in the list but the main focus is on properties where Raeburn has exclusive or privileged access to the wines, such as those from the Lucien Lurton stable, Brane-Cantenac, Villegeorge, Bouscaut and Climens. The Rhône takes a similar approach, wines from Jaboulet stand among those from Emile Florentin, Noël Verset and Desmeure. Only Alsace has just the one supplier and that is the excellent Rolly Gassmann.

Outside France, Italy concentrates on estate wines from quality producers such as Quintarelli and Monsanto. Australia contributes the wines of Cape Mentelle, Moss Wood, Seville Estate and Balgownie. The USA is a delight of individuals such as Randall Grahm's Bonny Doon and La Jota from the Howell Mountain area of the Napa. Portugal, Chile and Eastern Europe are the only regions lacking in this list of delights, but the sheer weight of variety and quality from elsewhere more than makes up for these omissions.

At last Zubair has some much-needed extra space for his stock. New premises in Leith (formerly Wines from Paris) at the Vaults will be used for storage, tastings and possibly sales. Watch this space.

Best buys

Sauvignon de Touraine 1992, Marionnet, £
Domaine les Embols Cépage Syrah 1992, Coteaux du Languedoc, £
Zinfandel 1988, Joseph Swan, Sonoma, California, ££
Seville Estate Cabernet Sauvignon 1988, Yarra Valley, Australia, ££

Ravensbourne Wine Company

6.0.2 Bell House, 49 Greenwich High Road,   *Tel* 081-692 9655
London SE10 8JL

Case sales only   **Open** Mon–Fri 9–5; Sat 10–1   **Closed** Sun, public holidays
Credit cards None accepted; personal and business accounts   **Discounts** Variable
Delivery Free in Greater London and surrounding boroughs (min 1 case);
elsewhere small charge; mail order available   **Glass hire** Free with order
Tastings and talks Tasting tutorials; bottles open on premises   **Cellarage** Not
available

With a heading of 'Independent Bespoke Vintners' Ravensbourne sounds like a snooty St James's operation run by public school types. It is refreshing to discover instead that the two directors, Steven Williams and Terry Short, hail from Wales and the outfit is run from a business centre in Greenwich.

They started seven years ago after a number of years with Oddbins and set out to provide good-value wines and spread the word with a series of tastings. The range includes BBC (as they call Bordeaux, Burgundy and Champagne) with some very good wines among them, but particular effort has gone into seeking out quality wines from rapidly-rising stars in the Rhône and South-West France. Ch. Perchade from Turson and Domaine Banette from Collioure are two of the more unusual finds.

Italy is another tremendous source of individual style at reasonable cost. The full-flavoured wines of Lungarotti feature along with a fair selection of Barolo, Barbaresco and Chianti. Portugal offers Bairrada, Borba and Redondo, not just as reds but whites too; Bulgaria is here as a full set from basic gluggers to Special Reserves – all excellent value. From South America there are Chilean wines from Concha y Toro and Torres, while North America is represented by three unusual wines from Palmer in New York State and Columbia in Washington State. Australia, New Zealand, South Africa and even China are all here in this well-priced list.

Ravensbourne takes organic wine seriously and dotted throughout the list are little symbols indicating organic production. The two directors also enjoy speaking and spend many evenings running Wine Workshop Roadshows, which are an attempt to educate and inform the drinking public about wine. From the letters of praise we have seen, these evening sessions seem to be well received.

Best buys

Montepulciano d'Abruzzo 1990, Thaulero Orsetto Oro, £
Côtes-du-Rhône 1992, Domaine Perrin, £
Sauvignon Blanc 1993, Grove Mill, New Zealand, ££
Manso de Valesco Cabernet Sauvignon 1987, Miguel Torres, Chile, ££

Reid Wines (1992)

The Mill, Marsh Lane, Hallatrow, Nr Bristol,   *Tel* (0761) 452645
Avon BS18 5EB

Case sales only   **Open** Mon–Fri 10–6 (other times by appointment)
Credit cards None accepted; personal and business accounts   **Discounts** Not available   **Delivery** Free in central London and within 25-mile radius
Glass hire Free with order   **Tastings and talks** Regular tutored tastings by invitation   **Cellarage** Not available

---

A year after the relaunch of this company it is now looking very healthy. Fine and rare wines have always been a speciality here and the team has managed to buy up some interesting cellars of claret, burgundy, port and German wines. These include clarets going back to 1929, a fine collection of Yquem, and ports and madeiras rolling back through the years.

There are drinking wines here as well as special-occasion wines. Italy has seen lots of new additions, such as Rocca Rubia from Sardinia and Capello di Prete from the south; the Australian selection has blossomed with wines from Charlie Melton, St Hallett, Shaw and Smith and Vasse Felix; California now provides interesting flavours from Qupé, Au Bon Climat and Neibaum Coppola. Monthly tastings are free.

Best buys

Ch. de Gaurgazaud 1990, Minervois, £
Ch. les Ollieux Romanis 1990, Corbières, £
Niebaum Coppola Rubicon 1982, California, ££
Poggio alle Gazze 1991, Ludovico Antinori, Italy, ££

La Reserva (España)

Unit 6, Spring Grove Mills, Manchester   *Tel* (0484) 846732
Road, Linthwaite, Huddersfield, West
Yorkshire HD7 5QG

Open Mon–Fri 9–5.30; Sat 9–6 **Closed** Sun, Chr **Credit cards** Access, Amex, Visa; personal and business accounts **Discounts** 10% on 1 mixed case **Delivery** Free within 20-mile radius (min 2 cases); mail order available **Glass hire** Free with order **Tastings and talks** Free weekly tastings (Sat); free tastings by invitation; tutored tastings (£10 per person); theme dinner events **Cellarage** Not available

Major changes here in Huddersfield. Keith Gomersall has taken on a new partner and changed the name of the company slightly. The range is still biased towards Spain but will increase to include other wines from Europe as well as Chile, Australia and New Zealand.

Riojas start off the range with crianza, reserva and gran reserva wines from endless bodegas. CUNE and Martínez Bujanda are the major players but there are wines from Navajas, Lagunilla, Marqués de Riscal and La Rioja Alta. Moving on to Navarra, wines from Chivite and Ochoa provide big flavours at reasonable prices. There are the wines of René Barbier from Penedès, plus a complete range from Torres.

Cork is the thick outer bark of the cork oak *Quercus suber.* It takes nine years for the cork oak to produce the bark which is stripped off and seasoned before cylinders of cork are cut out.

The mission to unearth wines from every region continues into Ribera del Duero, Valladolid, Valdepeñas and La Mancha. Sherry is taken almost as seriously as Rioja, with Lustau, Garvey and Valdespino featuring. New this year is a range of Spanish country wines, including the good value Don John red and white.

There is a tasting room/restaurant on the premises which was in regular use for formal tastings and dinners. We hope that the change in company structure will not affect these events, since they sounded great fun.

Best buys

Don John Red, £
Don John White, £
Valdespino Manzanilla, ££
Viña Ardanza 1985, La Rioja Alta, ££

La Réserve

56 Walton Street, London SW3 1RB	*Tel* 071-589 2020
Le Picoleur, 47 Kendal Street, London W2 2BU	*Tel* 071-402 6920
Le Sac à Vin, 203 Munster Road, London SW6 6BX	*Tel* 071-381 6930
The Heath Street Wine Co, 29 Heath Street, London NW3 6TR	*Tel* 071-435 6845
Clapham Cellars (wholesale/by the case only), 7 Grant Road, London SW11 2NU	*Tel* 071-978 5601

Open Times vary from store to store **Credit cards** Access, Amex, Visa; personal and business accounts **Discounts** 5% on 1 case **Delivery** Free in central London (min 1 case); elsewhere free (min 4 cases); mail order available **Glass hire** Free with order **Tastings and talks** Regular programme of tastings; to groups on request **Cellarage** £5 per case per year

---

There are four retail outlets and a wholesale warehouse in this Mark Reynier organisation. Although they all have a similar core of wines, each outlet is allowed to develop its own personality according to its location and customers. None of the shops issues a full list but there are regular updates showing new wines and vintages. One marvellous way to find out what you like is to visit the cellar at La Réserve and drink a bottle there, accompanied by pâté and cheese – the wine comes at normal shop prices.

La Réserve concentrates on up-market wines – burgundies, top Californians and Australians. *En primeur* offers of Rhône, burgundy and Loire wines are made under the La Réserve name, as is an offer of *en primeur* (if that is the right phrase) malt whisky. This is a scheme where you pay now for your cask of Springbank whisky and leave it maturing and evaporating gently for the next 10, 20 or even 40 years. This idea is not for the impoverished, since the cask plus distillate costs £850 and duty will eventually set the purchaser back around £2000.

The Heath Street Wine shop has a broad range of wines, good clarets in the lower and mid-price ranges with access to La Réserve's 'old and rare' stocks for anything a bit special (such as 1961 Margaux or six vintages of Yquem). Portugal, Spain and Italy are favourite areas here, with manager Geoff Merrick stocking up the shelves with various Chiantis and interesting little gems such as Salice Salentino from Apulia. Le Picoleur is more biased towards California and white burgundy while Sac à Vin concentrates on foreign beers. Clapham Cellars acts as the central warehouse for the business and sells by the mixed cases.

Best buys

Comte de Feynes nv, Côtes de Gascogne, £
Tuilerie du Bosc 1990, Côtes de St Mont, £
Bourgogne Blanc 1991, Etienne Sauzet, ££
Gewurztraminer 1990, André Kientzler, Alsace, ££

Reynier Wine Library

See Eldridge Pope

Richmond Wine Warehouse

138 Lower Mortlake Road, Richmond, Surrey   *Tel* 081-948 4196
TW9 2JZ

Case sales only   **Open** Mon–Sat 10–7 (open Sun in Dec only)   **Closed** Sun, public holidays   **Credit cards** Access, Amex, Visa; business accounts **Discounts** Negotiable   **Delivery** Free within 5-mile radius (min 1 case); mail order available   **Glass hire** Free with order   **Tastings and talks** Every Saturday from 11–6   **Cellarage** Can be arranged

There are tastings every Saturday at Richmond Wine Warehouse between 11 and 6. With parking right outside and a large airy warehouse to wander around, this seems like a pleasant way to get out of doing the Saturday shopping. It is based in a former Victorian school but the desks have gone and most of the internal walls too, leaving a big floor area stacked high with a tremendous range.

France is strong, with a good collection of clarets in one corner of the schoolroom. Richmond Wine Warehouse makes a feature of larger bottles and so you can buy magnums and double magnums of many wines right up to a monster 18-litre bottle of Ch. Lamothe-de-Bergeron 1986 priced at £395. Apparently, they do a roaring trade in big bottles but if anyone knows the correct name for the 18-litre monster please let Stephen Addy know. He does all the buying, casting an eye to the traditional French regions, backed up by a good range of regional wines under £5.

Italy and Australia are the two regions that have seen most changes this year. Many more Italian wines are now imported direct, providing a balanced range of affordable drinking as well as the big names of Antinori, Borgogno and Frescobaldi. Australian wines concentrate on sound winemaking, with Oxford Landing, Nottage Hill, Goundry and Mount Barker.

Spain provides bags of flavour, all under £10, while Portugal does the same under the £5 price mark. A clutch of wines from New Zealand, California and South Africa adds to the variety.

For those keen to go back to school, start here.

Best buys

Cuvée St Jacques Vin de Table nv, £
Domaine de Richard 1989, Saussignac, £
Chablis 1990, Georges Forget, ££
Ch. Léoville-Barton 1988, St Julien, ££

Howard Ripley

35 Eversley Crescent, London N21 1EL   *Tel* 081-360 8904
Mainly mail order

Case sales only   Open Mon–Sat 8–10; Sun, public holidays 8–12
Credit cards None accepted; personal and business accounts   **Discounts** Not available   **Delivery** Free in London (min 5 cases); otherwise £9.40 per case
Glass hire Free   **Tastings and talks** To groups on request   **Cellarage** Not available

---

What is it about dentists that attracts them to wine? Not content with tricky bridgework and crowns, Howard Ripley has got to grips with the complicated world of domaines, winemakers and vintages which, to the uninitiated, makes burgundy more of a gamble than the 2.30 at Doncaster. There is no doubting his enthusiasm. Comparing the quality of the 1990 vintage to the overdrive of a long-ago loved sports car, he sweeps you along in a rush of anticipated pleasure.

The list is full of mouthwatering names: Bachelet, Dujac, Bize, Rousseau and Jean-Marc Boillot, who is one of the inheritors of the fabulous Sauzet estate. These are but an introduction; there is a dazzling choice of 55 red burgundies from 15 domaines from the 1990 vintage alone. The whites are less extensive but no worse for that. Older vintages compete for attention, going back to magnums of Romanée-Conti 1966. The best way to make your selection is to go along to Howard Ripley, even on a Sunday morning, and enjoy a glass or two as he signposts your way through the range. Given the price of burgundy (no one could ever accuse this region of producing cheap wine), you might be advised to rob a bank on the way there or at least cancel any major dental work you had planned.

Best buys

Savigny-lès-Beaune Premier Cru Vergelesses, 1986, Domaine Simon Bize, ££
Nuits-St-Georges Premier Cru, Clos des Forêts, 1987, Domaine de l'Arlot, ££
There are no wines in this range under £5

Roberson

348 Kensington High Street, London   *Tel* 071-371 2121
W14 8NS

Open Mon–Sat 10–8; Sun and public holidays 12–3   **Credit cards** Access, Amex, Visa; Switch; personal and business accounts   **Discounts** 5% on 1+ case (paid for by cash or cheque); negotiable on larger quantities   **Delivery** Free in West and Central London (min order 1 case) and locally for smaller quantities; elsewhere at cost   **Glass hire** Free with order   **Tastings and talks** Monthly tutored tastings to groups (from £9.50 per person)   **Cellarage** Not available

No one can accuse Cliff Roberson of setting his sights too low. He aims to become the best wine retailer in London and has got off to a flying start. This shop opened in November 1991 and even as it was being converted from a kitchen showroom, the papered-over windows managed to look more stylish than many wine merchants do when they are open for business.

Stylish is a word which frequently springs to mind when thinking about Roberson. The interior design is like no other wine shop. It is big, with space to walk around, and the wines are not standing on shelves but are displayed on the slant on racks, with spare bottles tucked below. The walls are a muddy putty colour and the curved counter seems to well up from the floor. Stairs leading down to the tasting-room would look more at home on the set of *Dr Who*. A few steps, flanked by elaborate handrails, lead up to another display area – there was no practical reason for this expensive addition but as manager

Chris Donaldson admits, it does look good. His presence is another plus point which makes Roberson different from most merchants. He used to be assistant wine buyer for Harrods and passed the Master of Wine exams in 1991. Now he buys for Roberson and since he is based at the shop, is frequently to be found behind the counter. No doubt he dispenses sound wine advice if asked.

The range is huge, around 1000 wines from Bordeaux to Peru, and spans from under £3 to over £600. There are no particular specialist areas, all are pretty good. One eye-catching feature is the old and venerable bottles that are either locked away behind bars or displayed like works of art in glass cases.

Clarets start among the petits châteaux and climb steadily to the first growths. The choice does not fizzle out after a few vintages but keeps on going: 30 from the 1985 vintage, 18 from 1982, 17 wines from 1970 – it even rolls back to a 1928 Ch. Haut-Brion for just £395. The white Bordeaux range is startling for its choice of eight vintages of Yquem but there are plenty of wines to enjoy without taking out a second mortgage. Burgundy offers wines from Jean Gros, Henri Gouges, Armand Rousseau among others, as well as a collection from Domaine de La Romanée-Conti.

The New World merits special mention, with an exciting range from good winemakers – Pipers Brook from Tasmania, Australian Yarra Yering, Petaluma and Bannockburn are just a few of the attractions. With Californians from Sanford, Bonny Doon and the fabulous Au Bon Climat competing for attention, decision-making is difficult. Italy is taken seriously: Barolos from Oddero and Borgogno, and good-value Chianti from Pagliarese, as well as the more expensive Isole e Olena and Castello di Volpaia. Spain and Portugal are well worth serious sampling. Extensive ports, endless malts and a fair selection of cognac round off an impressive range.

Frequent organised tastings provide the opportunity to learn as you taste, and a few bottles are open in the shop at weekends. Roberson offers nationwide delivery but if you can struggle into Kensington you will enjoy the whole wine-buying experience.

Best buys

San Pedro Merlot 1990, Chile, £
Côtes-du-Rhône Blanc, Le Palaison 1991, Martenot, £
Vin Sauvage Brut Sparkling nv, ££
Chablis 1991, Martenot, ££

C A Rookes

Unit 7, Western Road Industrial Estate,   *Tel* (0789) 297777
Stratford-upon-Avon, Warwickshire
CV37 0AH
(See also Halves)

Open Mon–Fri 8–7; Sat 9–2; other hours by arrangement   **Closed** Sun, public holidays   **Credit cards** Access, Visa; personal and business accounts **Discounts** Negotiable   **Delivery** Free within south Warwickshire and surrounding areas   **Glass hire** Free with order   **Tastings and talks** Tutored and untutored tastings throughout the year on request   **Cellarage** Negotiable

This independent merchant operates on a retail and wholesale basis from an industrial site on the edge of town. Enthusiasm runs high here, even on the pocket list (a mere shadow of the main effort) there are important snippets of information – like the producers' names for all the German wines and the percentage of component grapes for a whole range of champagnes. There is also the guess that Australian poet Banjo Patterson used to drink Jamieson's Run – unlikely but a fun suggestion!

The range covers all the regions but dwells longest on two favourite areas, France and Australia.

France enjoys a fine run of petit-château claret from Fronsac, Premières Côtes and St-Emilion satellites. There is no attempt to run up the Médoc classification ladder. Burgundies are mainly from *négociant* Moillard, with a handful of small domaine wines. Beaujolais seems to be popular, with an assortment of 12 wines from different crus and growers. In comparison, the Rhône and Loire seem sparse but reliable.

The rest of Europe is dismissed in just a few wines per country. Spain merits just four, all Riojas from Martínez Bujanda and Bodegas Bilbainos, good choices but hardly comprehensive. Portugal is allowed one wine, the full-flavoured Dão Terras Altas, while Italy squeezes a Barolo from Giacomo Ascheri and Isole e Olena's Chianti into a selection of just six wines.

Only in Australia does the list lengthen a little. There is the good-value Seppelt Moysten range, Jamieson's Run, Krondorf, Mount Avoca and the brilliant Tarra Warra wines. South Africa has a glazed look to it with all varieties from Simonsig Estate.

A fine collection of 'Vintage' Scotch whiskies, including a few pure grain whiskies, adds variety here in Stratford.

Rookes is now home to the vast stock of half-bottles sold by Halves (*q.v.*). Halves' customers may buy these at the warehouse or order from Halves.

Best buys

Clos Lamothe Cuvée Chloe Clairet 1992, £
Clos Lamothe Cuvée Jérôme Bordeaux Rouge 1992, £
Ch. Lamothe de Haux Blanc Sec 1992, Premières Côtes de
Bordeaux, ££
Ch. Lamothe de Haux Rouge 1989, Premières Côtes de
Bordeaux, ££

Russell & McIver

Office
The Rectory, St Mary-at-Hill, London   *Tel* 071-283 3575
EC3R 8EE
Cellars
Arch 73, St Thomas Street, London SE1   *Tel* 071-403 2240

Open Mon–Fri 9–5.30 **Closed** Sat, Sun, public holidays **Credit cards** None
accepted; personal and business accounts **Discounts** Not available
Delivery Free on UK mainland (min 1 case in London, 4 cases elsewhere);
otherwise £5.99 per consignment; mail order available **Glass hire** Free with
order **Tastings and talks** 5 major annual tastings nationwide; 10 smaller tastings
held at the Rectory; to groups on request **Cellarage** £4.70 per case per year

'No reflection on our rivals, of course,' says Direct~~ ~~ ~~ ~~ristopher
Davey, 'but we think we offer a good sense of ~~ ~~ ~~d a
lack of pomposity here.' In the serious Squa~~ ~~kes
up the City of London, a lack of pompos~~ ~~ as a
great relief to all. Perhaps this is why ~~ ~~ ~~s
survived in such a competitive pa~~ ~~ a
century.

There is no shop; the bus~~ ~~ a rectory in St
Mary-at-Hill, but the log~~ ~~mmemorates the
now demolished Coa¹~~ ~~tution which had a
prominent role in ~~ ~~e company. The range is
traditional as ~~ ~~plying City institutions but
there is a w~~ ~~ent, too. The list is just the
right siz~~ ~~case and would make good reading
on th~~ ~~ suburbs. It is informative but informal
w~~ ~~growers and a few labels to help steer you
t~~

l~~ ~~ section, cru bourgeois, Fronsac and Côtes de
Bour~~ ~~xplored before starting to climb the classification
ladder. ~~oth here and in the selection of growers' burgundies,
there seems to be more emphasis on satisfactory, quality

As we went to press, Russell & McIver was taken over by Mayor Sworder and now operates solely from the address on p. 374

drinking than collecting a top label. The Rhône, Alsace and Loire are all sound but the French country wines deserve a special mention for value. Germany goes for quality producers such as Paul Anheuser and Max Ferd. Richter. Italy and Spain play fairly safe with familiar names, apart from an oak-matured Almansa wine from Bodegas Piqueras which probably livens up a City lunch tremendously. The New World is welcomed in this list with a few wines from Fetzer and Clos du Bois in California, and Hardy and Yalumba representing Australia. South Africans come from Boschendal, and New Zealand makes a token appearance with Delegat's.

Port, as you might expect, is here in depth and there is a fine range of own-label cognacs, ports and sherries. Madeira must go down well in the Square Mile with Henriques & Henriques 10-Year-Old in force. Purchases can be collected from the offices or the cellars with a little notice, but delivery is free within London for a mixed case.

Best buys

Domaines Virginie Chardonnay 1991, Vin de Pays des Coteaux d'Enserune, £
Domaine du Gouyat 1988, Bergerac, £
Mâcon Uchizy 1991, Domaine Talmard, ££
Pouilly Fumé 1991, Domaine Guy Michot, ££

Le Sac à Vin

See La Réserve

Safeway

Head office
Safeway House, 6 Millington Road, Hayes,   *Tel* 081-848 8744
Middlesex UB3 4AY
349 branches nationwide

Open Mon–Sat 8–8; (Sun 10–4 in half the number of stores) **Closed** Public holidays **Credit cards** All accepted **Discounts** Multibuy facility **Delivery** Not available **Glass hire** Free in some stores **Tastings and talks** Occasional in-store tastings **Cellarage** Not available

With 24 stores added to the chain last year and another 24 scheduled for 1993/94, Safeway is keeping up the pressure on the other big supermarkets. The wine department has also been busy, consolidating the huge progress made last year and finding yet more new wines. It has also come up with some new ideas, such as the Safeway Wine Fair held in May this year. Sixty new lines were added specially for the occasion and prices

411

on many regular lines were cut. Tastings in larger stores helped focus attention on this splendid department.

Many new wines have appeared during the year and value for money is an overriding consideration. 'Wines of the Danube' is a good description for a whole set of value wines from Eastern Europe. Young Vatted Merlot and Young Vatted Cabernet Sauvignon come from Bulgaria and have a youthful freshness and exuberance not found before in wines from this country. In Hungary, an Australian winemaker has been finding new depths of flavour in Lake Balaton Chardonnay, and the now almost ubiquitous Hugh Ryman has been continuing his good work at the Gyöngyös Estate, also in Hungary. All these wines are under £3.50, which is great value in anyone's language. Hugh Ryman has also set to work on Safeway's own-label Côtes du Lubéron with dramatic results.

In the southern hemisphere, Chile and Argentina provide some big flavours at reasonable prices. Casa del Campo Syrah from Mendoza in Argentina stands out in the range and so does Santa Rita Medalla Real from Chile. Wines from Australia start with good-value own-labels, and climb via Moondah Brook Chenin Blanc and Michelton Marsanne to the top end of the Penfolds range and Rosemount Roxburgh wines.

Europe has not been forgotten in this world-wide search for good value. There are a few good clarets, including some second wines of respected châteaux; Spain has the glorious Viña Ardanza from Rioja as well as some Raimat wines, and Italy provides a great-tasting Montepulciano d'Abruzzo, plus Chianti from Rocca delle Macie and Salice Salentino from the south. Germany tries hard to win converts with some better-quality wines, including an organic wine from Bruder Dr Becker.

Closer to home, Safeway has introduced a range of English wines, with some available nationally and others directed at those stores nearest the vineyards. So, Devon Safeway stores have the lovely Sharpham Vineyards wine, while East Anglia gets a taste of Elmham Park Madeleine Angevine.

Safeway has pioneered the movement of organic wines out of health-food shops and into the supermarket. It sponsors the Organic Wine Fair and it is not surprising that it has some of the best examples – such as a crisp, dry Ch. Canet from Entre-Deux-Mers and the chunky Domaine Richeaume from Côtes de Provence. Millton vineyard from New Zealand also features in the Safeway range, towards the top of the price band, but at the bottom is a very acceptable glugger under the simple label of Safeway Organic Vin de Table.

Now that the quality of the wine inside the bottles is so much improved, perhaps it is time for a re-think on the narrow aisles and tall displays that can make some Safeway stores seem rather cluttered.

Best buys

Young Vatted Merlot 1992, Russe, Bulgaria, £
Safeway Côtes du Lubéron 1992, £
Viña Ardanza 1985, Rioja, ££
Wairau River Sauvignon Blanc 1992, New Zealand, ££

J Sainsbury

Head office
Stamford House, Stamford Street, London   *Tel* 071-921 6000
SE1 9LL
325 licensed branches; 9 licensed SavaCentres

Open (Generally) Mon–Thurs 8.30–8, Fri 8.30–9; Sat 8–6; Sun 10–4 (off-licence) 12–3; public holidays 9–4   **Closed** Chr Day, Boxing Day, Easter Sun
Credit cards Access, Visa   **Discounts**, **delivery**, **glass hire** Not available
Tastings and talks On request; in-store tastings at various times   **Cellarage** Not available

Ever since shoppers have been able to pick up a bottle of good-quality, reliable wine with their weekly pile of groceries, sales have rocketed. It is supermarkets like Sainsbury's which have pioneered this attitude and brought wine on to the same shopping list as the meat and two veg it eventually partners. Sainsbury's is still forging ahead in wine and now has a massive selection. Over 450 wines are listed, ranging in price from 99p for a can of vin de pays to up-market Chablis at £18 a bottle – vintage champagnes take the upper price limit even higher.

There has been some very serious thinking done at Sainsbury's this year. Until now, all bottles were emblazoned with the Sainsbury's name, to the extent that classy châteaux had to consent to having their beloved labels 'endorsed' with the special seal before they could appear on their shelves. Many labels were redesigned to squeeze 'Sainsbury's' in large letters across the top. But now there has been a change of heart and gradually the name will disappear from the front label. This is because the buyers realise that customers no longer need the reassurance of a supermarket name on their bottle. The fact that the wine was selected and put on the shelves is enough, it does not need to shout out where it was bought when it reaches the table. There will still be a range of own-label wines which will continue to travel under the Sainsbury's colours.

Not only have the buyers been thinking, but they have been rather busy pulling their socks up. Some of the range had become a little tired and sad, so they have gone out and refreshed old blends and found new ones to give the whole range a lift. Basics have been improved, such as the own-label Muscadet and Côtes-du-Rhône. Lots of new wines have joined the range, many in the good-value slot below £4: a lively Sauvignon Vin de Pays d'Oc, a terrific Sicilian white and a big flavoured Romanian Cabernet Sauvignon.

Further up the price scale there are more additions: Nuits St Georges and Gevrey-Chambertin from Burgundy, Les Galets Blancs from Châteauneuf-du-Pape and Tokay Pinot Gris from Alsace.

There are no real weaknesses in the range but particular strengths include wines from Hugh Ryman, such as the Gyöngyös Hungarian wines, and the Spanish range, with a Navarra Tempranillo/Cabernet Sauvignon.

New Zealand wines are good, providing Chardonnays from Montana Church Road and Oyster Bay.

Sainsbury's has responded to our call for more staff training. With such a wide range on the shelves it is a shame when staff cannot direct customers to particular wines or even pronounce the important wine names. Department managers have started a programme of one-day courses, which even include some tasting, and other staff will learn more about the range from a cassette and book.

It will be a long time before you can rely on getting sensible advice in a supermarket, but Sainsbury's is setting out in the right direction.

Best buys

Sauvignon Blanc Rueda 1992, Hermanos Lurton, £
Chais Baumière Merlot 1990, Languedoc-Roussillon, £
Castello di San Polo in Rosso 1986, Chianti Classico Riserva, ££
Quinta da Bacalhôa 1989, Portugal, ££

Wine comes in at the mouth
  And love comes in at the eye;
  That's all we shall know for truth
  Before we grow old and die.

W B Yeats, *A Drinking Song*

Sandiway Wine Company

Chester Road, Sandiway, nr Northwich, *Tel* (0606) 882101
Cheshire CW8 2NH

Open Mon–Fri 9–1, 2–5.30, 6.30–10; Sat 9–10 **Closed** Wed pm, public holidays
Credit cards Access, Visa; business accounts **Discounts** 5% on 1 case
Delivery Free within 10-mile radius **Glass hire** Free; breakages charged for
Tastings and talks Approximately 1 in-store tasting a month; tutored tastings
Cellarage Not available

This shop is not just the local wine shop but it is the grocery
store and post office too. It is run by Graham Wharmsby, whose
interest in wine started about ten years ago – to add to the
rock-climbing, classic cars and motor-racing which also claim
his attention.

Now with around 250 wines, he offers a sound, interesting
range, not by way of an annual list but by regular newsletters
and offers. Italy and Australia are the areas of strength but there
are treats from all around, such as affordable clarets, burgundies
from Rion and Californians from Qupé and Bonny Doon.

From Australia there are top quality wines from Petaluma, St
Hallett and Rockford and good value wines from Rosemount,
Tyrrell's and Salisbury Estate. The range also adds a little fun
with Charlie Melton's Sparkling Shiraz, a wine almost
guaranteed to start a conversation. The Italian selection manages
good value with Breganze Rosso and a super Vespaiola and
climbs to the high points with wines from Pieropan and
Allegrini.

Regular tutored tastings with winemakers from around the
world are held here at Sandiway. Not to be missed!

Best buys

Salice Salentino Riserva 1986, Taurino, £
Salisbury Estate Chardonnay 1992, Victoria, £
Passito della Rocca 1988, Pieropan, ££
Bourgogne Chardonnay 1992, Daniel Rion, ££

Ashley Scott

P O Box 28, The Highway, Hawarden,   *Tel* (0244) 520655
Clwyd CH5 3RY

Case sales only **Open** 24-hour answering service (orders delivered although collection may be arranged from warehouse) **Credit cards** None accepted; personal and business accounts **Discounts** Available **Delivery** Free in North Wales, Cheshire, Merseyside (min 1 case) **Glass hire** Free with order **Tastings and talks** Annual tasting in November by invitation (available on request); talks and tastings provided for local organisations **Cellarage** Not available

No shop, not even an address for this Welsh merchant who deals solely by mail order. But with free delivery over a wide area it is perhaps worthwhile braving the impersonal treatment to check out the range.

France is the main attraction. Among the clarets are a fair number of petits châteaux with a particularly good Grand Cru St-Emilion, but still with a price tag below £9. Alsace wines come from the splendid co-operative at Turckheim, but the Burgundy section is too *négociant*-dependent to be really interesting. Vins de pays provide a reasonable choice at good-value prices. Elsewhere, there are pockets of interest: Recioto Amarone from Quintarelli in Italy and the powerful Sassella made from the Nebbiolo grape, Sutter Home in California and Bodegas St Emiliana from Chile. German wines from Guntrum and madeira from Henriques add to this reliable and reasonably priced range.

Best buys

Dos Cepas Tinto Vino de Mesa, Spain, £
Domaine Chamfort nv, Vin de Pays de Vaucluse, £
Chablis 1989, Domaine Rottiers-Clotilde, ££
Yaldara Reserve Cabernet/Merlot 1988, Australia, ££

Sebastopol Wines

Sebastopol Barn, London Road, Blewbury,   *Tel* (0235) 850471
Oxfordshire OX11 9HB

Case sales only **Open** Tue–Sat 10.30–5.30 **Closed** Sun, Mon
Credit cards Access, Visa; business accounts **Discounts** By negotiation on 10+ cases **Delivery** Free within 10-mile radius (min 1 case); mail order available **Glass hire** Free **Tastings and talks** At least once a month on Saturdays; bottles open on premises **Cellarage** Not available

There is a limited but stylish range from this partnership in Blewbury. France is the main focus with a select parcel from

Bordeaux, including several vintages from Chasse-Spleen and Haut-Bages-Libéral. The splendid (in both name and flavour) Ch. Tertre-Rôteboeuf from St-Emilion also makes an appearance. Burgundies head speedily for the high notes with only one wine below £10, but a reasonable collection of regional wines provides value drinking whilst you are saving up. Jean Baumard's Quarts de Chaumes can be seen nestling in the Loire section and the Rhônes are heavily biased towards the excellent Ch. de Beaucastel and Jaboulet. Italian wines make a first appearance with Chiantis from quality producers such as Isole e Olena, Felsina Berardenga and Fontodi. Spain is explored with the help of Torres, Marqués de Murrieta and four vintages of Pesquera.

The Australian range has expanded to include the brilliant wines of Stephen and Pru Henschke from the Adelaide Hills, as well as Shaw and Smith, Penfolds and Moss Wood. A limited selection of California wines includes the delicious Carmenet Vineyard.

Best buys

La Vieille Ferme 1990, Côtes du Ventoux, £
Seaview Chardonnay 1992, South East Australia, £
Mount Edelstone Shiraz 1989, Henschke, South Australia, ££
Ch. de Beaucastel 1990, Châteauneuf-du-Pape, ££

Seckford Wines

2 Betts Avenue, Martlesham Heath, Ipswich,   *Tel* (0473) 626681
Suffolk IP5 7RH

Case sales only   Open Tues–Sat 10–6   **Closed** Mon, Sun, public holidays (exc Good Friday 10–6)   **Credit cards** Access, Visa   **Discounts** Not available   **Delivery** Free within 20 mile radius of Martlesham; elsewhere £5; mail order available   **Glass hire** Free with order   **Tastings and talks** Available by arrangement   **Cellarage** Not available (cellar valuation service available)

Between 20 and 40 wines open and ready for tasting sounds like a good excuse to visit this wine warehouse between Ipswich and Woodbridge. It is case sales only but mixing is encouraged, and the warehouse itself is not the vast cavernous type, but small and well laid out, with the wines neatly displayed.

The range takes a waltz through the classic areas of France. Burgundies are not extensive but the names are good. Clarets are stacked up in the middle of the floor and provide a selection from recent vintages. Alsace wines are all from Wolfberger and Rhônes include delicious Ch. de Beaucastel from the Perrin family and Côte Rôtie from Guigal.

Spain is represented by just two Riojas and a range of Barbadillo sherries; Italy fares much better with an expanded selection, mainly from Piemonte and Tuscany. However, Australia is the main feature with quality producers such as Pipers Brook from Tasmania and Cape Mentelle, Moss Wood and Shaw and Smith. New Zealand puts up a good show with Montana, Selaks, Palliser Estate and Matua Valley.

Ready assembled tasting cases take the worry out of choosing, and fine clarets are offered in unbroken cases at a discount.

Best buys

Domaine Papolle 1992, Vin de Pays des Côtes de Gascogne, £
Delheim Blanc Fumé 1992, Stellenbosch, South Africa, £
Torreon de Paredes Cabernet Sauvignon 1986, Chile, ££
Coudoulet de Beaucastel 1989, Côtes-du-Rhône, ££

Selfridges

400 Oxford Street, London W1A 1AB   *Tel* 071-629 1234

Open Mon–Sat 9.30–7 (till 8 on Thur)   **Closed** Sun, some public holidays
Credit cards All accepted; personal and business accounts   **Discounts** 12 bottles for the price of 11   **Delivery** £3.95 in Greater London; £5.95 for rest of UK; free for orders over £100; mail order available   **Glass hire** Not available
Tastings and talks Call for details   **Cellarage** Not available

---

Selfridges has a new buyer at the helm and the range seems to be better for it. William Longstaff, who travelled around the world visiting wine regions before finally pitching up in Oxford Street, tends to favour depth and complexity in a wine over the current fashion for up-front fruit. Even so, the range at this vast emporium is wide enough to cover all tastes.

Classic French regions are covered well. Clarets start off at levels that most of us would find affordable, but swiftly climb through third and second growths to Pétrus and Latour. A rich streak of 1987 vintage wines provides good names and tolerable prices. Burgundies seem realistic with small growers to the fore (Maréchal-Jacquet, Charles Nouveau, Paulette Boyer) and a reasonable choice under £15, although it is quite easy to spend a lot more. The Rhône selection is small but good, with five reds among the Loire wines as well as Baumard's Coteaux du Layon, and Huet's Vouvray.

Italy is the country of thousands of local grapes, plus a fair share of international styles. Here the range includes Teroldego, Rosso Conero and a collection of Veneto wines from Guerrieri-Rizzardi. Spain heads for reliable names such as Torres and Ochoa, but there is also Pesquera and good Riojas from La Rioja

Alta and Murrieta. The Australian range is extensive. Basic Penfolds are joined by Taltarni, Cape Mentelle and Yarra Yering. New Zealand, California, Chile, Moldova and a range of Kosher wines mean there is something for everyone here.

Plans are afoot to have a wine club here with organised tastings, and even trips to the vineyards.

Best buys

Abbaye Saint Hilaire, Coteaux Varois 1990, £
Quinta de la Rosa Tinto 1991, Douro, £
Clos de la Cure 1990, Chinon, ££
Clos Mogador 1989, Costers del Siurana, Barbier, ££

Edward Sheldon

New Street, Shipston-on-Stour,   *Tel* (0608) 661409/661639/
Warwickshire CV36 4EN   662210

Case sales only **Open** Mon 9–5.30; Tues–Fri 9–7; Sat 9–5 **Closed** Sun, public holidays **Credit cards** Access, Visa; personal and business accounts
Discounts Available depending upon size of order **Delivery** Free within north Birmingham, Northampton, Oxford and Bath areas (min 1 case); elsewhere at cost; mail order available **Glass hire** Available **Tastings and talks** Various free in-store tastings; tutored tastings **Cellarage** £4 per case per year

Medicinal wine was the start of this business way back in 1842, when pharmacist Richard Badger decided that wine was good for his customers. 150 years later, medical opinion is unchanged but the range here is enough to challenge anyone's constitution. Tradition counts for a lot here at Shipston-on-Stour, at least from the look of the list, which concentrates on the classics. There is an abundance of clarets, from cru bourgeois to classier wines, and bottles going back to 1966. Burgundies make the clear distinction between domaine and *négociant* wines, with Voarick, Sauzet and Jayer-Gilles weighing in for the domaines and Chanson and Moillard among the *négociants*. In comparison, the Rhône and Loire appear almost neglected, although the French country section has recently expanded.

Spain has plenty to interest customers, with a strong range from La Rioja Alta, Ochoa and Torres. A 1975 Vega Sicilia provides claret-style drinking from Spain. The Italian range is not extensive but Germany, being a more traditional area, extends over two pages with a fair sprinkling of good names and even a few trocken wines. The New World range is steadily expanding: a reasonable collection from Australia and a clutch of good wines from New Zealand. California is almost a Mondavi monopoly with a little help from Riverside Farm and

Quady. Ports on the list are extensive and there are even more in the cellars which have not made it to the list.

Mixed cases are available here but have to be in multiples of three bottles. Do customers like this restriction?

Best buys

Ch. Combe Lubière 1992, Corbières, £
Chardonnay Vin de Pays d'Oc 1992, Lurton, £
Chablis Cuvée Centcinquantenaire 1990, Domaine des Malandes, ££
Cloudy Bay Sauvignon Blanc 1992, New Zealand, ££

Sherborne Vintners

The Old Vicarage, Leigh, Sherborne, Dorset   *Tel* (0935) 872222
DT9 6HL

Case sales only   **Open** Mon–Sat 10–6; Sun and public holidays 10–6 by appointment; 24-hour answerphone   **Credit cards** None accepted; personal and business accounts   **Discounts** Variable over 4 cases   **Delivery** Free within 20-mile radius of Sherborne (min 2 cases) and UK mainland at cost; mail order available   **Glass hire** Free with 2-case order; breakages charged for   **Tastings and talks** Four tastings per year; to groups on request   **Cellarage** Not available

If medal-winning wines impress you, and (let's be honest) it is always special to taste wines that have impressed the International Wine Challenge judges, this is the list for you. A wide selection of wines is available from this two-man band in Dorset and all have been awarded medals or commendations in the marathon competitive tastings. From Australia, all the right names are here: Coldstream Hills, Wynns, Hardy, Brown Brothers, and lots more. The California section includes Swanson Chardonnay and Far Niente Cabernet Sauvignon. This list is fairly fat and manages to capture a representative sample of Gold, Silver and Bronze medal winners as well as commended wines in all sections. The disadvantage is that the wines are only available by the unmixed case.

Another list from the same company revolves around Spanish wines. This is a wonderful in-depth study of the region with some big names such as Raimat and Torres, but most wines are from smaller companies such as Marqués de Griñon from Rueda and Bodegas Inviosa from Estremadura. Again, these wines are available only by the unmixed case.

Yet another list (can customers cope with all this?) gives some wines from both previous lists which are available by the mixed case. This is quite a complicated arrangement and it would be sensible to see mixed cases extended to all the range. Perhaps the clinical psychologist who is consultant here could find out how customers feel about the situation.

Best buys

Lar de Barros Blanco 1991, Spain, £
Errazuriz Sauvignon Blanc 1992, Chile, £
Raimat Tempranillo 1988, Spain, ££
Lar de Lares Gran Reserva 1982, Spain, ££

André Simon

See Laytons

Smedley Vintners

Rectory Cottage, Lilley, Luton, Bedfordshire   *Tel* (0462) 768214
LU2 8LU

Case sales only   **Open** Mon–Sat 9–6; Sun and public holidays 10–5
Credit cards None accepted; personal and business accounts   **Discounts** £1.20 on
1 case   **Delivery** Free within 50-mile radius of Lilley (min 1 case); otherwise £7 on
first case and £1 on next 3 cases; mail order available   **Glass hire** Free with order;
breakages at market price   **Tastings and talks** Two main tastings annually; also
smaller tutored tastings   **Cellarage** Available

Derek Smedley has been a Master of Wine for 25 years and has worked with some of the big companies in the wine trade. He now runs this business from home, offering fast, efficient and friendly service and a good range of wines.

The list tries hard to look comprehensive but it really focuses on quality partnered with value. So Italy gets a good airing with a full set from Antinori, including the delightful Peppoli Chianti and featuring the serious Barolo producer, Alfredo Prunotto. Spain takes in the wines of Marqués de Riscal for both Rioja and Rueda as well as the good-value Altos de Pio from Jumilla. Chile is another well-researched area with the Montes wines, while Argentina provides delicious wines from Caves de Weinert. France is not neglected and should provide plenty of choice, particularly among a splendid collection of country wines. South Africa is a new addition to the range, with wines from Julius de Lazlo under the Montestell label.

This is a personal list, well chosen and well priced. Lilley does not sound like a big place but Smedley Vintners really puts it on the map.

Best buys

Orvieto Classico Secco 1992, Antinori, £
Montes Cabernet Sauvignon 1990, Chile, £
Bourgogne Chardonnay 1990, Vieilles Vignes, Antonin Rodet, ££
Jackson Estate Sauvignon Blanc 1992, New Zealand, ££

La Solitude

The Cellar, 4 The Street, Wittersham, Kent   *Tel* (0797) 270696
TN30 7ED

Open Mon–Sat 9.30–6 (till 6.30 on Fri, Sat)   **Closed** Sun, public holidays
Credit cards Access, Visa; personal and business accounts   **Discounts** 8% on
unmixed cases; 5% on mixed cases   **Delivery** Free within 10-mile radius of
Wittersham (min 1 case); mail order available   **Glass hire** Free with order
Tastings and talks Four major tastings per year   **Cellarage** Not available

If you can tear yourself away from the list of delicious food that
this company sells (gourmet duck pâté, foie gras and cassoulet),
then you might notice that it sells a lot of wine as well.

France is the main area of interest, with an extensive range of
petits châteaux from Bordeaux claiming much of the action. The
burgundy section also remains affordable with careful buying
from the Mâconnais and a lot of help from Cellier des Samsons
in Beaujolais. French regional wines supply even more good-
value drinking, with the Rhône, Alsace and Loire adding to the
variety. Nine red Riojas and two whites are the mainstay of the
Spanish list, Portugal is blessed with four Moscatels and Italy
provides Umani Ronchi's up-market Vino da Tavola Cumaro, as
well as some well-priced drinking wine. The New World
provides a good choice with Undurraga from Chile, Hamilton-
Russell from South Africa and Belvedere Grove from California.
Australia seems slightly sparse in comparison, with just a
handful of wines from Tyrrell's, Rouge Homme and good-value
Jacob's Creek.

Regular newsletters keep customers in touch with the range,
and the planned 'Gourmet Club' with wine and food means that
this company is unlikely to be as lonely as its name suggests.

Best buys

Ch. du Barrail 1990, Bordeaux, £
Domaine du Tariquet Gros Manseng Cuvée Tardive 1990, Côtes
de Gascogne, £
Ch. Les Hauts de Palette 1988, Premières Côtes de Bordeaux, ££
Mâcon-Villages 1990, Cave Charney Les Mâcon, ££

Somerfield

See Gateway

Sommelier Wine Company

The Grapevine, 23 St George's Esplanade,   *Tel* (0481) 721677
St Peter Port, Guernsey

Open Tue–Fri 10–5.30 (Fri till 6); Sat 9–5.30; 24-hour answerphone and delivery
Closed Mon, Sun and public holidays **Credit cards** Access, Visa; personal and
business accounts **Discounts** 5% on mixed cases **Delivery** Free within Guernsey
(min 12 bottles) **Glass hire** Free **Tastings and talks** Two general tastings per
year; regular tutored tastings to groups on request **Cellarage** Not available

The Sommelier Wine Company serves the wine drinkers of
Guernsey with skill. It is run by six wine enthusiasts who each
manage to hold down a day-time job as well as open their new
shop in St Peter Port five days a week. One of the partners,
Richard Allisette, is a full-time journalist and, as you might
expect, he has plenty to say about the wines he sells; however,
his tasting notes are accurate, informative and to the point.

The range is wide, with favourite producers and suppliers
representing far-flung regions. Australia has a much bigger
selection this year, with Salisbury Estate and Penfold's Dalwood
looking after the value end of the range and Mountadam, St
Hallett and the super wines of Charlie Melton at the top end.

Italy has seen some work as well with well-known wines such
as Valpolicella coming from quality producers Allegrini and
Tedeschi. Even the everyday Valpolicella comes from the best co-
operative under the label Rocca Sveve. There are the less well-
known names too, such as Ceppi Storici, Ronco di Mompiano and
Capello di Prete, all good wines and well worth a try. France has
its new faces too with the south providing good value, a new
selection of affordable domaine burgundies and the complete
range of Pol Roger champagnes. With wines from Spain, Portugal,
New Zealand and California you may not have chance to move on
to the oddly-named Nymburk Slovakian beer.

Delivery on this sunshine island is free for 12 bottles or more.

Best buys

Colombelle 1992, Plaimont, Vin de Pays des Côtes de Gascogne, £
Domaine de Vallongue 1990, Coteaux d'Aix en Provence, £
Morgon, Domaine des Roches 1991, Marcel Jonchet, ££
Pouilly Fumé 'Tradition Cullus' 1990, Domaine Masson-
Blondelet, ££

Spar

Head office
32/40 Headstone Drive, Harrow, Middlesex   *Tel* 081-863 5511
HA3 5QT
2000 licensed branches

Open Hours vary from store to store   **Credit cards** None accepted
Discounts Available   **Delivery** Varies from store to store   **Glass hire** Available
Tastings and talks In-store tastings and tutored tastings   **Cellarage** Not available

The Spar chain of corner shops and small food stores is made up
of 2000 independent retailers. The word independent is important
since there is nothing to stop each proprietor going to his or her
local cash & carry and stocking up with the bargain of the week.
But this has been happening less and less since Philippa Carr,
Master of Wine, has been in charge of buying for the group. She
started by improving the quality of the basic own-label lines (a lot
of Liebfraumilch and Lambrusco is sold through these outlets),
and then set about introducing better-quality wines under
shippers' labels. So from Bordeaux there is a good, keenly priced,
basic fruity claret, and the range climbs via Cordier's reliable
generic St-Emilion and Médoc to rather classy Baron Villeneuve
de Cantemerle from the Haut-Médoc. The rest of the French
section is also growing in confidence and style: there is Chablis
from La Chablisienne, Alsace wines from the co-operative at
Turckheim and Loires from Guy Saget. Regional French wines
have been expanded by introducing St-Chinian, Fitou and a
clutch of vins de pays.

Further afield, the picture looks promising. Basic Italian wines
are topped off with a Montepulciano d'Abruzzo, a couple of
Slovakian wines liven up the Eastern Europe section and the New
World is home to a few favourite names. Australia provides
Lindemans and Jacob's Creek. There is Errazuriz Merlot
representing Chile, Cook's Hawkes Bay wines from New Zealand
and a couple of new South Africans under the Oak Village label.

The best Spar stores are members of the group Wine Club,
which allows them to stock a better range and there will be more
interest shown behind the counter. Meanwhile, Spar is coming
out of the cold and into the cellar. Watch this space.

Best buys

Spar Coteaux du Languedoc, £
Chardonnay, Vin de Pays d'Oc, £
Ch. Prieuré des Mourgues, St-Chinian, ££
Cook's Sauvignon Blanc, New Zealand, ££

Frank E Stainton

3 Berry's Yard, Finkle Street, Kendal, Cumbria   *Tel* (0539) 731886
LA9 4AB

Open Mon–Sat 8.30–6   **Closed** Sun, public holidays   **Credit cards** Access, Visa;
personal and business accounts   **Discounts** 5% on 1 mixed case (for payment by
cash/cheque only)   **Delivery** Free within 30-mile radius (min 1 mixed case);
elsewhere at cost; mail order available   **Glass hire** Free with orders over £150;
otherwise £1 per dozen   **Tastings and talks** Tasting suite available (from £10 per
person), includes wines and tutoring   **Cellarage** Free for regular customers

This business has acquired large underground cellars that must
be the envy of merchants everywhere. Frank Stainton puts them
to good use with a fine range of wines which concentrate on the
classics. Bordeaux wastes very little time on generics and petits
châteaux before heading for the big names, although there are a
few second wines to help keep costs down. Burgundies are
extensive and concentrate on the good *négociants* of Drouhin,
Sapin and Louis Latour rather than growers. The Loire and Rhône
provide substantial choices, with Jaboulet featuring at all levels
from Côtes-du-Rhône up to Hermitage. Alsace is taken seriously
with a wide selection from Hugel and Schlumberger, and
Germany includes two Franconian wines in its range.

Italy and Spain are sound, and there is plenty of interest among
the New World wines, particularly in the New Zealand reds, with
Stonyridge Cabernet and Célèbre from Ata Rangi Vineyards. Only
the vins de pays and Southern French selections disappoint at
Berry's Yard, although there are good-value wines from
elsewhere, particularly South Africa and Chile.

Best buys

Aotea Sauvignon Blanc 1992, New Zealand, £
Montepulciano d'Abruzzo 1992, Umani Ronchi, £
Rippon Pinot Noir 1990, New Zealand, ££
Louis Roederer Brut Premier Champagne, ££

Summerlee Wines

64 High Street, Earls Barton, Northamptonshire NN6 0JG	*Tel* (0604) 810488
London Office	
Freddy Price, 48 Castlebar Road, London W5 2DD	*Tel* 081-997 7889

Open Mon–Fri 9–2 **Closed** Sat, Sun, public holidays **Credit cards** None accepted; personal and business accounts **Discounts** Not available **Delivery** Free within area of London, Oxford, Northamptonshire and Cambridge (min 2 cases) **Glass hire** Free with order **Tastings and talks** Occasional in-store tastings; tastings at colleges in Oxford and Cambridge by invitation; monthly meetings; annual tours **Cellarage** £3.70 per case per year

Summerlee Wines has the edge on most other retail shops: it has Freddy Price, with all his 30 years' experience in the trade, as consultant and buyer. German wines are his speciality and at Summerlee the range is as far away as anyone could wish from Liebfraumilch and Hock. The delicious, racy flavours of Riesling grapes, ripened in the Mosel, Nahe, Saar or Rheingau, give you as good a tour as any coach trip could. The producers are paramount: there is Paul Anheuser from the Nahe, Max Ferd. Richter from the Mosel and Schloss Saarstein from the Saar. Three Franconian wines from Juliusspital show just how good Silvaner can be.

However, there is more to this merchant than just Germany. Pockets of wine are explored rather than the more usual broad-brush approach. Petits châteaux from Bordeaux inspire confidence as Freddy's tastebuds have been involved in the selection. Domaine burgundies are from Patrick Javillier and Georges Clerget. Five wines from Ch. d'Arlay in the Jura, a selection of domaine wines from the south of France and Kuehn wines from Alsace give this list a feeling of restrained quality. Australia, New Zealand and Chile provide a few unusual names to try.

Summerlee holds tastings at Oxford and Cambridge colleges and there is a local wine society which receives support, usually in the form of Freddy himself as a tutor.

Best buys

'Cuvée Constantin' Rivaner Trocken 1991, Max Ferd. Richter, £
Ch. Bauduc 1989, Bordeaux Supérieur, £
Ch. d'Arlay Corail 1990, Jura, ££
Mülheimer Helenenkloster Riesling Eiswein 1990, Max Ferd. Richter Weingut, ££

Sunday Times Wine Club

Mail order wine club
New Aquitaine House, Paddock Road,   *Tel* (0734) 481711
Reading, Berkshire RG4 0JY   (enquiries)
                                                  Tel (0734) 472288 (orders)

Open Mon–Fri 9–7; Sat, Sun 10–4; answerphone outside these hours
Credit cards All accepted; business accounts **Discounts** Available **Delivery** Free
nationwide for orders over £50; mail order available **Glass hire** Available
Tastings and talks Approx 6–8 tastings a year **Cellarage** Not available

This is the other face of Direct Wines of Windsor, the first being
Bordeaux Direct (*q.v.*). Although it is essentially a mail-order
company, it generates more of a club feel by organising regular
activities not just in London but around the country. Highlight of
the year is the Vintage Festival held in the Horticultural Hall in
Westminster, where the people who make the wine meet the
people who drink it, and a lot of tasting gets done. This club was
also one of the first to organise charabanc trips to the vineyards.
By all accounts, these are fairly liquid occasions and recent trips
have included Oporto, Bordeaux and Verona.

A quarterly magazine, *Wine Times*, brings entertainment and a
little education to members. Special offers and wine-drinking
suggestions, such as Summer Party Mix, Barbecue Reds or Club
Clarets, will land on your doormat with amazing regularity. Many
of the wines are the same as supplied by Bordeaux Direct,
although both operations have some exclusivities. Hugh Johnson
is the Club president and therefore appears to endorse the wines,
although his photo doesn't seem to be splashed around quite as
liberally as it used to.

Membership costs £10 a year, so if you don't want the Club
activities you might just as well deal with Bordeaux Direct, but
you get a lot of entertainment for your money. Delivery for both
organisations is free for orders over £50, a welcome alternative to
all those other companies who insist on two or three cases no
matter how much you spend.

Best buys

Traminer 1991, Moravenka, Czech Republic, £
Cabernet Sauvignon Domaine de la Durançole 1992, Vin de Pays
des Bouches-du-Rhône, £
La Barque Vieille 1991, Côtes-du-Rhône, ££
Vinavius Oak-aged Chardonnay 1990, Vin de Pays de la Haute
Vallée de l'Aude, ££

Supergrape

81 Replingham Road, Southfields, London
SW18 5LU

Tel 081-874 5963

Open Mon–Fri 10–2, 5–9.30; Sat 10–9.30; Sun, public holidays 12–2, 7–9
Closed Chr Day, Boxing Day, Easter Sun **Credit cards** Access, Visa; personal and business accounts **Discounts** 5% on 1 case **Delivery** Free in Greater London (min 1 case) **Glass hire** Free with 1-case order **Tastings and talks** Four annual tastings for club members (£20 per person per year) **Cellarage** Not available

Reliable names and careful selection are the hallmarks of this little shop south of the river. At the top end of the price range, Corton Charlemagne, Premier Cru Chablis and a clutch of classy clarets are attractive. There are good Rhônes, with Ch. de Beaucastel and Jaboulet in attendance and, if you are serious about champagne, there is a fine selection here. But weekday drinking is not forgotten, with sensible country wines from France, a reasonable number of petits châteaux from Bordeaux and a lively choice from Spain, Chile and Australia.

Port seems to be a speciality here with a wide variety of shippers and vintages, including the glorious 1963.

The Wine Club costs a hefty £20 to join but you get four tastings a year and around five per cent discount on all purchases. With seven-day opening and free delivery around Greater London, this business is trying hard.

Best buys

Sutter Home Sauvignon Blanc 1990, California, £
La Vieille Ferme 1990, Côtes du Ventoux, £
Ch. De Parenchère 1989, Bordeaux, ££
Chablis Premier Cru 1990, 'Beauroy', Fromont, ££

Tanners Wines

26 Wyle Cop, Shrewsbury, Shropshire SY1 1XD	*Tel* (0743) 232400 *Tel* (0743) 232007 (sales order office)

Outlets

72 Mardol, Shrewsbury, Shropshire SY1 1PZ	*Tel* (0743) 366389
39 Mytton Oak Road, Shrewsbury, Shropshire SY3 8UG	*Tel* (0743) 366387
36 High Street, Bridgnorth, Shropshire WV6 4DB	*Tel* (0746) 763148
4 St Peter's Square, Hereford, Hereford & Worcester HR1 2PG	*Tel* (0432) 272044
The Old Brewery, Brook Street, Welshpool, Powys SY21 7LF	*Tel* (0938) 552542

Open Mon–Sat 9–5.30 (9–6 at Wyle Cop branch; 9–1 only on Sat at Welshpool branch) **Closed** Sun, public holidays **Credit cards** Access, Visa; personal and business accounts **Discounts** 5% on 1 case cash and collection; 5% on 5 cases if delivered **Delivery** Free on 1 case locally; free for order over £75 for delivery to any one address nationwide **Glass hire** Free if wine purchased from shop **Tastings and talks** Wine always available in all shops; tutored tastings for customers 5–6 times a year; to groups on request **Cellarage** Available for small amounts

Tanners is still a family business (established in 1872), now with Richard Tanner at the helm. With its long family tradition and even more ancient premises, this company ought to belong to the stuffy, dusty brigade of wine merchants that sometimes inhabit rural areas – but it doesn't. It is traditional in the quality of its wines and certainly in the efficiency of its service but stuffy and dusty just don't apply here.

The list is a chunky paperback, no glossy photos, but a working document full of information about growers and regions. Quality is a keynote at Tanners but that doesn't mean that the range is full of esoteric wines at outrageous prices. It quietly strikes the middle path with a variety of good-quality wines at reasonable prices. For a change the list starts with a round-up of vins de table and the south of France – sensible drinking at sensible prices. The rest of France has been selected with skill and style. There are Gisselbrecht, Hugel and Schlumberger from Alsace and a luscious selection of Barsac and Sauternes, particularly from the 1988 vintage; some of them are available in half-bottles. Clarets are selected 'with painstaking care' the list tells us, and tasting notes are available for each one on request. The same degree of care obviously goes into Burgundy, and the Rhône is surprising for having 14 white wines as well as a wide range of reds. Further afield, the Tanners team has built up an admirable range: Shaw and Smith,

429

Basedow and Cape Mentelle from Australia, with Hamilton-Russell and Vriesenhof in South Africa. Also from South Africa are the wines of Dieu Donné, an estate managed by Mark Tanner, cousin to Richard.

California provides wines from Simi and Mondavi and there is Mexico, Argentina and New Zealand to add to the variety.

On the service front Tanners gets the most applause from our readers, with this merchant regarding most of the West Midlands and much of Wales as its local delivery area.

Best buys

Tanners Claret, AC Bordeaux, £
Tanners Sauvignon, Vin de Pays d'Oc, £
Tanners Champagne nv, ££
Tanners Mariscal Manzanilla, ££

Tesco

Head office

New Tesco House, P O Box 18, Delamare   *Tel* (0992) 632222
Road, Cheshunt, Hertfordshire EN8 9SL
For wine enquiries write to: Head office,   *Tel* as above
Bentley House, Pegs Lane, Hertford,
Hertfordshire SG13 8EG
388 licensed branches

Open Varies from branch to branch, but usually Mon–Sat 9–8 (Sat till 7); Sun 10–4; public holidays 9–5 **Closed** Chr Day, Boxing Day **Credit cards** All accepted **Discounts** Multisaver offers **Delivery, glass hire** Not available **Tastings and talks** Regular in-store tastings **Cellarage** Not available

No one can have failed to notice just how good Tesco is at wine – there is always something new to look at. 'New Line' stickers sprout up regularly, and there are the Multisaver offers where you can buy two bottles (or sometimes six) and save a little. Occasionally, little yellow stickers indicate a £1 or so off discontinued lines to make way for new stock. In the big, newer stores they have moved away from the long straight shelves which end up looking like soldiers in a row, and instead the display units form bays giving a more relaxed, less 'supermarket' look.

There are over 380 licensed Tesco stores. Not all carry the full range and that is one of the complaints we hear most about. If you want a wine that a bigger branch has but yours doesn't, it can be ordered but only by the full case, which could be fairly expensive if you only want to try it. Tesco is good at keeping its customers informed. Leaflets around various themes appear on the shelves: summer drinking, grape varieties, they all help to interest customers and encourage them to try something new. Sadly, there does not seem to be much progress on staff training. The chances of finding someone in a store wine section who can answer a simple question – such as: 'How do you pronounce Montepulciano?' – depends more on an individual's out-of-hours enthusiasm rather than proper training at work. But if you can cope with that there is plenty at all price levels to attract you to the shelves. Own-label wines tend to be great value and it is interesting to see just how many ways you can spend £4. Among the Italian range, Colli Albani Superiore and Cabernet del Veneto have all the right flavours, and both are under £3.50. There is a tangy, fruity Cape Colombard from South Africa, and a soft gentle Bairrada at around £3 a bottle.

Tesco is not afraid to sell expensive wines such as Penfolds Bin 707 Cabernet Sauvignon or classy clarets such as Forts de Latour and Pavillon Rouge. It also has one of the best supermarket selections of champagnes – but bargain-basement special offers sit alongside the established house names. In such a huge range there are really no gaps. A good basic claret; country wines; the Rhône looks interesting and manages an upmarket Côtes-du-Rhône from La Vieille Ferme, as well as a more ordinary one. There is a Chinon from the Loire and a much improved Muscadet. From Spain, Marqués de Chive from Utiel Requena has joined the range and a new range of four Chiantis offers the choice between the various hillsides of Tuscany. Australian wines do well – all the reliable names are here, Jacob's Creek, Penfolds and Rosemount and many more, but there is also a splendid Tesco Coonawarra Cabernet Sauvignon, a pair of wines from Ryecroft and St Hallett Old Block Shiraz. German wines battle on valiantly in the hope that people will eventually go back to the better quality wines they missed the first time round.

With such a wide range there are bound to be some mistakes, but Tesco is trying hard to lead the way and certainly seems to be going in the right direction most of the time.

Best buys

Tesco Australian Sparkling Wine, £
Tesco Robertson Chardonnay 1992, South Africa, £
Tesco Champagne nv, Brut Premier Cru, ££
Penfolds Bin 707 Cabernet Sauvignon 1989, Australia, ££

Thresher Wine Shops/Wine Rack/Bottoms Up

Head office
Sefton House, 42 Church Road, Welwyn *Tel* (0707) 328244
Garden City, Hertfordshire AL8 6PJ
Over 1600 branches nationwide, including 117 Wine Rack and 61
Bottoms Up outlets

Open Mon–Sat 10–10; Sun 12–3, 7–10 **Closed** Chr Day **Credit cards** Access,
Visa; personal and business accounts **Discounts** Available **Delivery** Free within
20-mile radius of each branch **Glass hire** Free **Tastings and talks** Occasional
tastings **Cellarage** Not available

It should have been a quiet year for the people at Thresher. Last
year they swallowed up the Peter Dominic chain, dividing the
spoils between the major brand names of this group, Thresher
Wine Shops, Bottoms Up and Wine Rack. So, have they rested
on their laurels this year? Not a bit of it. They have chased
around the world bringing back more and more variety to thrill
the palates of their customers.

First, a word about the different styles of shops. Thresher is
the biggest name, with 856 stores called Thresher Wine Shops.
There are also Drinks Stores from Thresher and Food and
Drinks Stores, but these have a very limited range of wines.

Wine Rack is the specialist wine-shop chain with 117 shops,
and Bottoms Up are larger stores with 61 shops. Each type of
shop has its role in the great order of things but for the *Guide*
we concentrate on the three names, Thresher Wine Shop, Wine
Rack and Bottoms Up.

All three types of shop work from the same core range, but
Wine Rack and Bottoms Up have their own exclusivities. They
can also take on board parcels of wine which would be too
small to spread around the whole Thresher estate.

The core range at Thresher is good, with sound choices in
most areas. Bordeaux has second wines from the great châteaux,
including Clos du Marquis and Carruades de Lafite Rothschild,
as well as a reasonable choice of generics and petits châteaux. In
comparison, burgundy is less exciting, but French regional
wines are just how they should be – crisp, lively whites such as
Ch. le Bost from Bergerac and warm full-flavoured reds such as
Domaine de Rivoyre Cabernet Sauvignon from Hugh Ryman in
the south.

From Spain, there are the brilliant Bujanda Riojas and Italy
provides a good collection of Chiantis, including Peppoli from
Antinori and Villa di Vetrice. The New World is a major feature
of this range, particularly New Zealand, but Australia, Chile and
California all contribute splendid wines. Only South Africa
looks a little dull.

Wine Rack takes on the whole of the Thresher range and more, the most significant element being Alsace. Wine Rack (and Thresher) have been promoting the wines of Alsace for the past few years with remarkable results. Sales have increased dramatically, so now, as well as having a huge range in the shops, Wine Rack has also launched 'Exclusively Alsace'. This is a mail-order club just for the rare and wonderful wines of Alsace. New Zealand is also a special feature for Wine Rack, with a vast range of crisp, gooseberry-like Sauvignon Blancs, elegant Chardonnays and delicate Pinot Noir wines. Wine Rack has a definite wine-merchant feel, and staff training is a priority in these shops, so advice here should be good.

The Bottoms Up chain takes on most of the Wine Rack range with a few specialities, such as growers' champagnes and more wines from Spain and Portugal. It also seeks to offer the best value on case sales, backed up by a refund promise.

In the wine trade, the quality of a company is often inversely proportional to its size. Thresher and its other faces has set out to prove that rule totally wrong.

Best buys

Gyöngyös Chardonnay 1992, Hugh Ryman, Hungary, £
Tollana Dry White 1992, South East Australia, £
Collards Rothesay Vineyards Sauvignon Blanc 1992, New Zealand, ££
Tokay Pinot Gris 'Vieilles Vignes' Zind Humbrecht 1990, Alsace, ££

Turville Valley Wines

The Firs, Potter Row, Great Missenden,   *Tel* (02406) 8818
Buckinghamshire HP16 9LT

Case sales only **Open** Mon–Fri 9–5.30 **Closed** Sat, Sun, public holidays
Credit cards None accepted; personal and business accounts **Discounts** Not
available **Delivery** Locally and in London (min 1 case); elsewhere at cost; mail
order available **Glass hire** Not available **Tastings and talks** Three/four times
a year **Cellarage** Can be arranged

The front cover of the Turville Valley list says it all. With a copy
of a 1982 Cheval Blanc label on show, this company tells us loud
and clear that this is not the place to come to for everyday vins
de pays. The range is almost exclusively top names from
Bordeaux, Burgundy, Rhône, and ports. For those whose
tastebuds travel a little further afield there is a miscellaneous
assortment at the back of the list, but still only exclusive names:
Vega Sicilia from Spain, Grange from Australia, Mondavi and
Dominus from California and Musar from Lebanon. The real
business is classy names, from the 1930s to the most recent
vintages. So if you have need of a magnum of 1945 Château
Margaux or even a 1978 La Tâche, this is the place to come. Be
prepared to spend serious money – since Turville has no retail
licence the minimum purchase is an assorted case. VAT is not
included in the list but, even so, prices seem comparable with
others who also trade in the great and the glorious.

Having bought your piece of history we hope that you pull
the cork and enjoy it, and do not send it yet again around the
saleroom circuit.

Best buys

Côtes-du-Rhône, 1990, Guigal, £
1967 Cockburn Port, ££
Côte Rôtie 1985, Guigal, ££

T & W Wines

51 King Street, Thetford, Norfolk IP24 2AU   *Tel* (0842) 765646

Open Mon–Fri 9.30–5.30; Sat 9.30–1 **Closed** Sun, public holidays
Credit cards All accepted; business accounts **Discounts** Not available
Delivery Free within 15-mile radius of Thetford (min 1 case) and elsewhere (min 4
cases); otherwise 1–3 cases £8.95; mail order available **Glass hire** Free with 1-case
order **Tastings and talks** Monthly in-store tastings (normally free)
Cellarage £4.98 per case per year

Not only is T&W's list a splendid collection of wonderful wines,
but it has been designed by Thetford Grammar School's desk-

top publishing enterprise. School projects seem to have taken a welcome new direction recently.

Trevor Hughes, once a hotelier, is the force behind this business. He found his interest lay more and more in creating a good list for his restaurant and eventually this interest grew until there was no time for anything else. The range here is amazing. Three thousand wines is the claim but we didn't stop to count them. Not all are included in the chunky A4 list but there is enough within its pages to keep most of East Anglia busy for years.

Quality is the sole criterion for inclusion in this document. 'I never buy on price, only on quality,' Trevor assures us, and the list is his evidence. He starts off with a personal selection of reds and whites: an Italian red made from the unusual Ruche variety, Hollick Coonawarra Pinot Noir and a white Rioja from Bodegas Palacio. These are just a few of his favourite things but there are lots more.

There are growers' champagnes and a hefty contribution from Krug for days when funds are good. Clarets and burgundies go on for pages. Guigal features in the Rhône with Jaboulet standing by to lend assistance. The Californian selection has expanded a little, with a Pinot Noir from Kent Rasmussen in Carneros and a wide choice of Napa Valley wines from Silver Oak, Flora Springs, Far Niente and Duckhorn. The Australian range has doubled to include ranges from Hollick and Taltarni. Italy concentrates on top producers Gaja and Bava, with Chianti from Villa Vistarenni. Also available are Austrian wines from Willi Opitz and museum pieces from the Massandra Collection.

Half-bottles merit an extensive separate section and apparently run to 300 different wines. Free tastings in the shop every month provide a good reason for moving to Thetford.

Best buys

Domaine de la Bon Gran 1990, Thévenet, ££
Silver Oak Cabernet Sauvignon 1988, Alexander Valley, California, ££
Grand Cru Champagne Brut, Michel Arnould, ££
Hardly any wines are under £5

Ubiquitous Chip Wine Shop

8 Ashton Lane, Hillhead, Glasgow G12 8SJ   *Tel* 041-334 5007

Open Mon–Fri 12–10; Sat 11–10   **Closed** Sun, Chr Day, New Year's Day
Credit cards All accepted; personal and business accounts **Discounts** 5% on
1 case **Delivery** Free within 10-mile radius of Glasgow (min 2 cases); mail order
available **Glass hire** Free with 1-case order **Tastings and talks** Occasional
tastings (small charge per person) **Cellarage** Available

This shop started out as a way for customers of the restaurant
next door to buy wines they had enjoyed with a meal. It is now
a wine shop in its own right.

The list is a breeze through some of the most interesting
names in wine, with the added attraction of reasonable prices.
Clarets include a fair selection of classed growths but a few
unfashionable vintages and a clutch of crus bourgeois keep
many prices within reach. Burgundy sports names such as
Tollot-Beaut, Domaine Leflaive and Louis Trapet. There is
Jaboulet and Emile Florentin in the Rhône and Gaston Huet
providing his brilliant Vouvray in the Loire. Alsace is a
favoured area with wines from Rolly Gassmann and Dopff &
Irion providing most of the interest.

From Italy there are good wines at both ends of the price scale
and a few in between. Montepulciano d'Abruzzo from Umani
Ronchi weighs in for weekday nights while Angelo Gaja's
Barbaresco probably has to wait for high days and holidays.
Spain takes in La Rioja Alta, Torres, Ochoa and León.

Romanian wines are big sellers here – six reds and six whites,
none over £4. Australia builds on the firm foundations of
Barramundi and Orlando with Penley and Vasse Felix providing
the high notes. Bannockburn from Victoria surely feels quite at
home in these Scottish surroundings.

Quality German wines are the most difficult to sell here,
which is a shame considering the splendid selection from
Schloss Vollrads, Bürklin-Wolf and Matuschka-Greiffenclau.
Probably easier to find homes for are the 130 or so malt
whiskies, including a 54-year-old Glen Grant, that also grace
the shelves of this Ubiquitous Chip.

Best buys

Vin de Pays des Côtes Catalanes 1992, Rivesaltais, £
Romanian Pinot Noir 1986, Classic Collection, £
Pata Negra Gran Reserva 1982, Valdepeñas, ££
St-Véran 1991, Louis Tête, ££

Unwins Wine Merchants

Head office
Birchwood House, Victoria Road, Dartford, *Tel* (0322) 272711
Kent DA1 5AJ
Approximately 300 branches in south-east England

Open Mon–Sat 10–10; Sun, public holidays 12–3, 7–10 **Credit cards** All accepted;
personal and business accounts **Discounts** 10% on case lots **Delivery** Free in
south-east England (min 1 case); mail order available **Glass hire** Free with
orders; returnable deposit; charge for breakages **Tastings and talks** Occasional
branch tastings; to groups on request **Cellarage** Not available

After 150 years in the wine business, Unwins is starting to get
its act together with a coloured list, a range that is very good in
places and reasonable prices. If the shops could shake off their
Lambrusco and British Sherry image they could be a serious
force in the High Street.

As with many chains, not all the shops have all the wines but
managers can call on the rest of the range if you want it. Clarets
are here in depth, from a respectable Yvon Mau Bordeaux
Supérieur 1990 to Mouton-Rothschild 1983. Good clarets are
bought *en primeur* by Unwins and matured in their corporate
cellars until ready to go on the shelves. Wines from 1984 and
1985 have emerged from storage this year. Burgundies are less
exciting, most wines come from Bichot, although there are a few
new faces in this section. Regional French wines are improving.
Italy has Frescobaldi Chiantis and Spain sticks to reliable names
such as Torres, Berberana, Faustino and Riscal. With Penfolds
and Lindemans from Australia, Fairview Estate from South
Africa and Undurraga from Chile, the New World collection is
worth browsing through.

Unwins managers are encouraged to take the various wine
exams, so advice from behind the counter should be good.

Best buys

Blauer Zweigelt 1991, Weinviertel, Austria, £
Bianco di Custoza 1992, Prod. Assoc. Soave, £
Ch. Ducla, Entre-Deux-Mers 1992, Yvon Mau, ££
Ch. de Crouseilles 1987, Madiran, ££

Valvona & Crolla

19 Elm Row, Edinburgh EH7 4AA   *Tel* 031-556 6066

Open Mon–Sat 8.30–6 **Closed** Sun, 1–7 January **Credit cards** Access, Visa;
business accounts **Discounts** 5% on 1 case **Delivery** Free within Edinburgh
(min £25 order); natiowide at cost; mail order available **Glass hire** Free with any
reasonable order **Tastings and talks** Tutored and informal tastings for customers
in-house (from £5 per person) **Cellarage** Not available

Wine drinkers of Edinburgh should move away from this city
just so they can return and really appreciate how lucky they are
to have so many enthusiastic and well-stocked merchants.
Valvona & Crolla is one of these, specialising in Italian wines.
The shop has recently been extended to around three times its
original size, so now there is more room to display the stock of
550 wines and the Italian delicatessen. Before starting on the
wines it is worth mentioning the range of estate olive oils,
many bearing names like Lungarotti, Guerrieri-Rizzardi and
Capezzana, which are more usually seen on bottles of wine.

The list of wines is a compact working document, not given
to descriptions of the regions or the producers, but the range is
certainly here. Barolos in vast array, from a 1961 Borgogno to a
choice of 9 different wines from 1985. Angelo Gaja contributes
14 wines from Barbaresco and his Barbera d'Alba, Vignarey.
Tuscany is equally comprehensive, with a splendid range of
Chiantis and Super Tuscans. But work has gone into finding
wines from all parts of this country: Rocca Rubia from Sardinia,
Barbarossa from Emilia Romagna and dessert wines from
Pantelleria. There is even a cry for help in sourcing a wine from
the Valle d'Aosta, to fit in with Philip Contini's price/quality
standards.

Tutored tastings and cookery demonstrations are held in the
newly built function room at the back of the shop, and on any
day there are at least four or five bottles open for tasting.

Best buys

Barbera d'Asti 'Ceppi Storici' 1990, £
Chardonnay Le Veritiere 1992, £
Rocca Rubia, Santadi 1989, Sardinia, ££
Pinot Bianco 1991, Jermann, ££

Why not club together with friends to enjoy volume discounts and
free delivery?

Helen Verdcourt Wines

Spring Cottage, Kimbers Lane, Maidenhead, *Tel* (0628) 25577
Berkshire SL6 2QP

Case sales only **Open** All hours (24-hour answering machine)
Credit cards None accepted; personal and business accounts **Discounts** 5% for
1 case order **Delivery** Free in southern England (min order 1 case)
Glass hire Free **Tastings and talks** Regular tastings **Cellarage** Free (though very
limited space)

Helen Verdcourt still devotes a big section of her list to some of
the best wines from Australia. Glorious flavours abound from
Charlie Melton, St Hallett, Rothbury, Moss Wood and The
Tasmanian Wine Company. New Zealand does well too with
Martinborough, Cloudy Bay, Esk Valley and Hunters. Other
New World areas are included, with a selection from South
Africa, California, Oregon and Chile.

This is a serious one-woman business, launched by Helen
13 years ago after successful careers as both a biologist and a
mushroom grower. She works hard: first educating her
customers through talks and tastings at every opportunity and
then by selling a surprisingly large range of quality wines.

The Rhône is a favoured area. There are the splendid good-
value Southern French wines of La Vieille Ferme from Perrin
and the delicious Côtes-du-Rhône-Villages, Clos du Caillou
from Pouizin. The real gems of the Rhône are Guigal's far-from-
basic Côtes-du-Rhône, also his Condrieu, Jaboulet's Vin de
Paille and a collection of vintages of Ch. de Beaucastel.

Bordeaux concentrates on quality and affordability and
burgundies are select but good. Italy gets straight down to
business with Chianti from Villa di Vetrice and Isole e Olena,
Barolo from Ascheri, and the delicious Ghiaie della Furba from
Tenuta di Capezzana. Spain explores the ranges of Torres,
CUNE and Raimat, but also includes a distinguished oak-aged
Ribero del Duero from J Arroya. Fortified Spanish wines are for
true aficionados – just Scholtz Solera Málaga and a rich dry
oloroso from Díez Hermanos.

Helen Verdcourt runs three wine clubs that meet monthly in
the Berks/Bucks areas and, as yet another example of her tireless
energy, local delivery to her means most of the southern
counties. We sit back in exhausted admiration!

Best buys

Cahors, Les Côtes d'Olt 1990, £
Les Terrasses de Guilhem 1991, Vin de Pays de l'Hérault, £
Clos de Caillou, Châteauneuf-du-Pape 1990, ££
Maranges, Premier Cru Clos les Loyères 1990, Vieilles Vignes,
Girardin, ££

Victoria Wine Company

Head office
Brook House, Chertsey Road, Woking,   *Tel* (0483) 715066
Surrey GU21 5BE
Nearly 1000 branches nationwide; also approx 140 branches of Haddows
in Scotland

Open Hours vary from branch to branch; most are open from 10–10
Credit cards Access, Visa; personal and business accounts   **Discounts** 5% on 12
bottles or more; 7 for 6 on most champagnes   **Delivery** Local delivery (charges
vary from branch to branch); free delivery per £50 consignment (selected
branches)   **Glass hire** Free on large orders   **Tastings and talks** Promotional
tastings in selected branches   **Cellarage** Not available

Victoria Wine shops all look the same from the outside, but
once you are through the door, you will notice whether you are
in a 'Wine Shop', an 'Off Licence' or a 'Local'. These are the
names of the different grades of shops and, while they all carry
the same core range, Wine Shops carry a much bigger selection
than the Off-Licence shops, which in turn have more than the
locals. All is not lost if you are near a beer and fags variety, just
ask for a list and the whole range is available to you at a few
days' notice.

The range at Victoria has been steadily improving. The buyers
here tend to work on themes. Last year it was Czechoslovakia
and a collection of good-value, ripe-flavoured Czech wines
swept on to the shelves and straight out of the doors as soon as
customers tried them. These wines are now part of the
established range but this year Italy has been one of the
projects. Twenty new wines have been added, from basic
everyday wines up to classy Chiantis. Among the new good-
value wines is Basilicata White, which comes from the south of
Italy and is made by French winemaker Jacques Lurton from
local grapes. Also worth checking out is a Tuscan red, Vermiglio
di Ripanera and up-market Chianti from Rocca delle Macie,
Riserva di Fizzano.

Spain has some new arrivals, Marqués de Vitoria is a fruity
white with a touch of oak, Palácio de León is full and fruity and
Viña Pilar from Ribero del Duero has bags of concentrated
flavour. All are great value.

Classic areas have not been neglected. Victoria has always
been good at claret, and if you want a particular wine it may be
best to order in advance. Even the big stores don't carry the
whole range. Petits châteaux to first growths are here, with a
fair contribution from the 1985 vintage.

New World wines are strong. Rosemount Rosé makes an
exclusive appearance from Australia and Chilean Montes
Sauvignon Blanc joins the South American range.

Training has always been a priority at this chain, so advice from behind the counter should be good.

Best buys

Stratford Pinot Noir, California, £
Willow Court 1991, England, £
Coopers Creek Sauvignon Blanc 1992, New Zealand, ££
Pomino Rosso 1989, Frescobaldi, Italy, ££

La Vigneronne

105 Old Brompton Road, London SW7 3LE   *Tel* 071-589 6113

Open Mon–Fri 10–9; Sat 10–7 **Closed** Sun, public holidays **Credit cards** All accepted **Discounts** 5% on 1 case **Delivery** Free locally (min 1 case); mail order available **Glass hire** Free with order **Tastings and talks** Up to 2 tastings per week **Cellarage** £7.80 per case per year

La Vigneronne is run by Master of Wine Liz Berry and her husband Mike. Liz's enthusiasm is Alsace (she has written a book on the subject) and the variety of wines from that area fills a whole page of the list. The usual variations of grape variety and producer are made infinitely more complex by the endless choice of grand cru wines. The Alsace section comprises just over 100 wines.

The shop is a haven for those tired of slick corporate images. It is more like a library of wine which just happens to sell a bottle or two. Disconcertingly, some of those bottles, usually the better ones, are empty, which might lead you to think that you have just missed the best bring-a-bottle party in London. Instead, it shows that there is stock of that wine but rather than keep such quality on the shelf it is tucked away in the depths of the cellar to mature gently.

Alsace is not the only gem – the shop is stuffed with mouthwatering temptation. Bourgogne Grand Ordinaire sits easily on the shelves near to Echézeaux from Domaine de la Romanée-Conti, and a splendid range of Spanish wines is given depth by seven vintages of Vega Sicilia. But La Vigneronne is not just for treasure-trove wines. There are well-chosen drinking wines from Australia, South Africa, Italy and France.

Regular tastings add to La Vigneronne's attractions. These may be tutored by Liz or other experts and, considering the wines that are tasted, they represent good value. Some are even free if you decide to order those wines on the day. For £10 a year you can subscribe to La Vigneronne's *Wine Journal.*

Best buys

Rolle, Domaine Conjan 1992, Vin de Pays des Coteaux de
Murviel, £
Merlot, Domaine Terre Mégère 1991, Vin de Pays d'Oc, £
Ch. Carsin 1990, Premières Côtes de Bordeaux, ££
Merrick's Estate Shiraz 1990, Mornington Peninsular,
Australia, ££

Villeneuve Wines

27 Northgate, Peebles, Borders EH45 8RX   *Tel* (0721) 722500

Open Mon–Fri 10–8 (till 9 on Fri); Sat 9–9 **Closed** Sun, public holidays
Credit cards Access, Visa; personal and business accounts **Discounts** 5% on 1
case **Delivery** Free within 50-mile radius of Peebles; otherwise £5 per case
Glass hire Free **Tastings and talks** Two major annual tastings (£4 per person);
tutored tastings to groups on request **Cellarage** Free for personal customers; 4p
per case per week for wine bought elsewhere

Good value for money is what Villeneuve's customers seek and
they shouldn't be disappointed. Director Alistair Rae and his
team have selected a wide range of wines with the emphasis on
positive flavours.

Australia shows this with the Penfolds Dalwood range,
Rosemount and Wolf Blass. Len Evans' Rothbury Estate and the
new Margaret River collection from Sandstone add to the
variety. Other New World wines follow suit with Cousiño
Macul and Viña Carmen from Chile and the Trapiche wines
from Argentina, both providing good value for money. From
California, Firestone and Fetzer rarely disappoint and South
Africa includes the lovely wines of Hamilton-Russell. In Europe,
France takes the biggest share. Guy Saget features in the Loire
with Langlois-Château contributing its Chinon. Trimbach and
the co-operative at Ribeauvillé provide a good range from
Alsace. Burgundies are mainly from Faiveley with two splendid
organic wines from Jean Musso. Interesting offerings come from
Clos Guirouilh in Jurançon and a single-vineyard Minervois
owned by the Bishopric of Carcassonne.

Italy does a comprehensive tour of good areas and producers
such as Borgogno's Barolo and Frescobaldi's Chianti; Spain goes
back to favourites such as Torres, La Rioja Alta and Murrieta.
New this year are regular mailshots with special offers and keen
prices on a selection of the range, including some of the
hundred or so malt whiskies in stock.

Best buys

Domaine de Monluc 1992, Vin de Pays des Côtes de Gascogne, £
Salice Salentino Riserva 1986, Taurino, £
Fermoy Estate Chardonnay 1991, Western Australia, ££
Ch. de Sours Rosé 1992, Bordeaux, ££

Vinceremos Wines

65 Raglan Road, Leeds, West Yorkshire   *Tel* (0532) 431691
LS2 9DZ

Case sales only   **Open** Mon–Fri 9–5   **Closed** Sat, Sun, public holidays
Credit cards Access, Visa; business accounts   **Discounts** 5% on 5+ cases; 10% on
10+ cases   **Delivery** Free nationwide on 5+ cases; mail order available
Glass hire Free locally with order   **Tastings and talks** Summer and Christmas in
Leeds; periodically at Ryton Gardens, Coventry   **Cellarage** Not available

Vinceremos specialises in organic wine and the company is run
by Jerry Lockspeiser, co-author of *Thorsons Organic Wine Guide*.
Organic wine is not just for cranks. There are many people who
are keen to avoid unnecessary chemicals and pesticides. The
term organic has now been defined by the EC and producers
claiming organic status must belong to a recognised
organisation that controls standards of production.

A primary consideration behind organic wine is that it must
taste good first and be organic second. Vinceremos manages this
with quite a few wines in its range. The Millton Vineyard wines
from New Zealand are a prime example: crisp, lively wines, full
of flavour – and the fact they are organic comes as a bonus. The
same goes for Domaine Richeaume from the Côtes de Provence.

In a specialised list such as this the range is bound to be
more limited than in a normal list but Jerry has discovered
splendid Alsace wines from Pierre Frick, a robust Châteauneuf
from Pierre André and a collection of good-value wines from the
south of France. At the back of the list are a few non-organic
offerings including a Moroccan Kosher wine, Zimbabwean
Pinotage and a comprehensive range of neutral and flavoured
vodkas.

Best buys

Ch. la Blanquerie 1989, Bordeaux Supérieur, £
Vignoble de la Jasse 1990, Côtes-du-Rhône, £
Millton Vineyard Chardonnay 1992, Gisbourne, New
Zealand, ££
Domaine Richeaume 1991, Châteauneuf-du-Pape, ££

Vintage Roots

Sheeplands Farm, Wargrave Road, Wargrave,   *Tel* (0734) 401222
Berkshire RG10 8DT

Case sales only   Open Mon–Fri 9–6; Sat, Sun, 24-hour answerphone, public
holidays by prior arrangement **Closed** Chr **Credit cards** Access, Visa; personal
and business accounts **Discounts** Collection discount £1.50 per case; quantity
discount on 5+ cases **Delivery** Free within 30-mile radius of Wargrave and on 6+
cases; otherwise 1 case £3.95, 2 cases £5, 3–5 cases £6; mail order available
Glass hire Free with order **Tastings and talks** To groups on request
Cellarage Not available

Everyone has heard of organic wine, but not everyone knows
what it is. This list starts off by explaining just how it is made
and why organic might mean fewer headaches for some people.
All things organic (at least in the liquid line) is the theme of
this list, with wine as the main component.

The range now stands at 135-plus wines from around the
world. Most are from family domaines where the size of the
business is small enough to devote the extra time and care
needed for organic culture.

France is a major contributor – it has the greatest number of
organic growers. Amongst the selection are some good
burgundies from Jean-Claude Rateau and Ch. de Puy from
Bordeaux. Italy contributes Chiantis from Villa Angiolina and
California provides wines from Frey Vineyards and Orleans
Hill. From Australia come the massively flavoured Botobolar
wines from New South Wales and the elegant, fruity Eden
Ridge wines made by Adam Wynn. Vintage Roots has
unearthed organic beers, liqueurs and cognac as well as ciders
from the delightfully named Dunkerton Cider Company.

Best buys

Ch. Moulin de Romage 1992, Bordeaux Sec, £
Domaine de Dreuillé 1990, Coteaux du Layon, £
Botobolar Shiraz 1990, Australia, ££
Pineau des Charentes, Brard-Blanchard, ££

The Vintner/Viticulteur

See Arthur Rackhams

For merchants who sell a minimum of twelve bottles, we say 'Case
sales only' in the details at the head of an entry.

The Vintry

Park Farm, Milland, Liphook, Hampshire GU30 7JT	*Tel* (0428) 76389
Outlet	
Malthouse Farm, Ecchinswell, Newbury, Berkshire RG15 8TT	*Tel* (0635) 298842

Case sales only   Open By appointment only   **Credit cards** None accepted; personal and business accounts   **Discounts** Available on 10+ cases   **Delivery** Not available   **Glass hire** Free   **Tastings and talks** Six formal tastings a year in Liphook, Newbury and London   **Cellarage** Not available

The Vintry looks a lot more established this year. It is run by Nigel Johnson-Hill and for those who read the small print on bottle labels, that name may sound familiar and with good reason. Nigel is the brother of Alan Johnson-Hill, proprietor of Ch. de Méaume in Bordeaux. This wine is well liked and widely stocked but it provided the Vintry with the germ of a good idea.

There are many English/British people busy growing grapes in Bordeaux and elsewhere in France. Nigel J-H concentrates on importing these wines, not because he can't speak French but because he thinks that the Brits have a more searching, less traditional approach to winemaking(!). There is Ch. Bauduc from David Thomas in Bordeaux and Ch. de Sours owned by Esme Johnstone. Peter Sichel contributes not only his glorious Ch. d'Angludet but also second wines from there and from Ch. Palmer. He also supplies the basic claret and a wine from Corbières, Domaine du Révérend, run by Sichel Junior. Latest addition to the Brits collection is Ch. du Seuil from Graves, run by Bob and Susan Watts. Just to show he has an open mind, Nigel lists a number of wines from French winemakers too, with Olivier Leflaive and the Cave de Lugny among them. From further afield, there are Rosemount wines from Australia and a Sauvignon Blanc from California.

Best buys

Johnson's Claret, £
Resplandy Chardonnay 1991, Vin de Pays d'Oc, £
Ch. Méaume 1989, Bordeaux Supérieur, ££
Ch. de Sours Rosé 1992, Bordeaux, ££

Waitrose

Head office
Doncastle Road, Southern Industrial Area,   *Tel* (0344) 424680
Bracknell, Berkshire RG12 8YA
107 licensed branches in London, Midlands and the Home Counties

Open Mon, Tues 8.30–6; Wed, Thurs 8.30–8; Fri 8.30–9; Sat 8.30–6 **Closed** Sun,
public holidays **Credit cards** None accepted **Discounts** 5% on 1 unmixed case
or purchases of £100+ **Delivery** Not available; some wines available by mail
order through Findlater Mackie Todd **Glass hire** Free (deposit required)
Tastings and talks Occasional evening tastings for invited customers
Cellarage Not available

Waitrose shops are not like other supermarkets. They generate a
degree of loyalty that makes customers drive past Sainsbury and
Tesco to get to them. They have a higher ratio of Volvos and
BMWs in the car parks and, as one of our readers pointed out,
they are the sort of shops where you come across mothers
talking about their children's university progress over the meat
counter.

The wine section is different too. These departments are part
of the main store but they still manage to retain a separate
'wine merchant' image. They usually have a door to the outside
world so you can nip in and out for a bottle of wine without
queuing at the main checkout. Very few of the Waitrose range
are own-labels. There are the basics in each area, such as Good
Ordinary Claret which stands out on the shelf like a neon sign,
but generally bottles nestle under their own colours, giving a
lively individual look. The range is surprisingly wide, around
400 wines, and of good quality – with four Masters of Wine on
the buying team it should be. Value for money seems to be the
theme running through the range. There are a lot of wines
under £5 here and they score bulls-eyes on flavour most of the
time. Domaine de la Présidente, a Vin de Pays de la Principauté
d'Orange is just right, with soft peppery flavours, for just over
£3. The same goes for Domaine de Beauséjour from Côtes de la
Malepère. Among the whites, Ch. Haut Rian from Bordeaux
stands out, with zingy, grassy flavours, and a Cabernet Rosé
from Haut Poitou is clean, light and stylish.

If you do decide to spend more, there is plenty to work at.
Clarets start at the Good Ordinary level and work up to Forts de
Latour, which should go down well at any dinner party.
Burgundies manage a lot of the right flavours with Chorey-lès-
Beaune from Moillard, but you can invest in a bottle of
Drouhin's Chambolle-Musigny if funds permit.

Australia has Brown Brothers' lively Tarrango and South
Africa provides the lovely Fairview Merlot and Avontuur
Chardonnay.

446

Good news for those who live miles away from the Waitrose chain – it has joined forces with Findlater Mackie Todd and now offers wine by mail order to John Lewis card holders.

This is great news for everyone north of Peterborough.

Best buys

White Burgundy 1992, Bourgogne, £
Oxford Landing Sauvignon Blanc 1992, Australia, £
Waitrose Champagne Brut nv, ££
Baron Villeneuve de Château Cantemerle 1990, Haut-Médoc, ££

Waterloo Wine Company

61 Lant Street, Borough, London SE1 1QL   *Tel* 071-403 7967

Open Mon–Fri 10–6.30; Sat 10–5 **Closed** Sun, public holidays
Credit cards Access, Visa **Discounts** Not available **Delivery** Free to London (min 5 cases); otherwise a £5 surcharge **Glass hire** Free; breakages charged for
Tastings and talks Monthly tutored tastings **Cellarage** Not available

New Zealander Paul Tutton runs this business but also has a hand in a vineyard near Waipara Springs back home. The vineyard has been planted only recently so it could be some time before this wine warehouse is totally self-sufficient.

Meanwhile, the range has a strong Antipodean slant. Penfolds, Geoff Merrill, Coldstream Hills and UK new-comers Stonier's Merrick provide most of the Aussie wines, with Waipara Springs, Montana and Redwood playing for the Kiwis. France is taken seriously, with a strong selection of good-value country wines. The Loire provides rich pickings from Gaston Huet in Vouvray, as well as a good crop of reds, such as four Domaine Chinons and a 1976 Bourgueil. Alsace wines are all from A. Seitz in Mittelbergheim.

A good collection of names from Italy, Spain and Germany adds to the variety.

Despite looking like a wine warehouse, Waterloo has a retail licence so you can buy by the single bottle. Delivery is only free if you buy five cases or more, even within London.

Best buys

Domaine de Soubremont Sauvignon Blanc 1992, Vin de Pays d'Oc, £
Domaine la Tour Boisée 1990, Minervois Rouge, £
Waipara Springs Pinot Noir 1991, New Zealand, ££
Stonier's Merrick Cabernet Sauvignon 1989, New Zealand, ££

Weavers of Nottingham

1 Castle Gate, Nottingham, Nottinghamshire   *Tel* (0602) 580922
NG1 7AQ
17 Castle Gate (tasting room)

Open Mon–Sat 9–5.45 **Closed** Sun, bank holidays **Credit cards** All accepted;
personal and business accounts **Discounts** 10% on 1 case; larger discounts by
arrangement **Delivery** Free within 30-mile radius of Nottingham (min 1 case)
Glass hire 10p per dozen, plus breakages **Tastings and talks** Monthly tastings for
groups (some tutored) **Cellarage** £1 per case per year

The Weavers shop may be small but it is stuffed to the ceiling
with well-chosen wines. Further up the road is a beautiful
Georgian house, 17 Castle Gate, which Weavers is gradually
restoring to its original splendour. It is here that the Wine
School and tastings are held.

Personal, friendly service is the keynote at this company –
and this is evident if you contact them by phone or just walk
into the shop. Directors Alan Trease and Keith Whitehead are
frequently available for advice but training features large so you
can get sound recommendations from the staff, too.

The range is comprehensive. Good champagnes and clarets
are followed in the list by an interesting group of Alsace wines,
mainly from Domaines Schlumberger. Burgundies come from a
variety of *négociants*, including Louis Latour and Chanson, with
Domaine Rousseau providing his excellent Chambertins. There
are many more French country wines this year, providing bags
of flavour at very reasonable prices.

Spain and Italy are full of reliable names such as Torres,
CUNE and Antinori, while the New World sees some new faces
in St Hallett and Rowlands Brook from Australia, and Foppiano
from California.

A good range of sherries and ports rounds off this well-
balanced list.

Best buys

Ch. du Grand Moulas 1992, Côtes-du-Rhône, £
Orla Dorada Tinto Crianza 1989, Rioja, £
Hunter Estate Shiraz 1990, Australia, ££
Domaine de Vieux Télégraphe 1991, Châteauneuf-du-Pape
Blanc, ££

Please write to tell us about any ideas for features you would like to
see in the next edition of *The Which? Wine Guide* or in *Which? Wine
Monthly.*

Wessex Wines 　　　　　　　　　　　　　　　　　　　　🖵

197 St Andrews Road, Bridport, Dorset 　　　　　　　*Tel* (0308) 23400
DT6 3BT

Case sales only **Open** Mon–Sat 8.30–9.30 **Closed** Sun, some public holidays
Credit cards None accepted; personal and business accounts **Discounts** 5% on
minimum of 6 bottles (unmixed); 7.5% on 7+ cases (COD) **Delivery** Free within
20-mile radius of Bridport (min 1 case) **Glass hire** Free **Tastings and talks** One
large Christmas tasting; other tastings to groups on request **Cellarage** Not
available

Michael Farmer is hoping to expand his by-the-case business to
a wine-warehouse operation. His collection of wines, with the
emphasis on impressive flavours at good-value prices, would
certainly suit that kind of outlet. Very little in this range strays
over the £10 mark and then only with good reason, such as
domaine-bottled Chambolle-Musigny and Volnay. The south of
France, Bordeaux and Rhône provide plenty of choice. There are
reliable Alsace wines from the co-operative at Turckheim and
two red Loire wines among a handful of whites. Italy and Spain
provide reliable drinking from familiar names, while the
German range remains fairly modest. Bulgaria contributes its
good-value range but for a little more money the Undurraga
wines from Chile come into sight.

　　Australia is represented by the Bosanquet Estate, for which
Wessex are the agents, and the familiar Rosemount. Michael
Farmer claims to work 'elastic' hours which expand to fill the
needs of his customers.

Best buys

Cuvée Jean-Paul Blanc Sec, Paul Boutinot, £
Bourgogne Pinot Noir 'Louis Alexandre' 1991, £
Ch. la Garde 1986, Pessac-Léognan, Bordeaux, ££
Tarrawarra Tunnel Hill Pinot Noir 1990, Victoria, Australia, ££

Whiclar & Gordon Wines

The Bunker, Glebelands, Vincent Lane, 　　　　　　*Tel* (0306) 885711
Dorking, Surrey RH4 3YZ 　　　　　　　　　　　　　　(orders/queries)

Open Mon–Fri 9–5.30; Sat 9–4 **Closed** Sun, public holidays **Credit cards** Access,
Visa **Discounts** 5% on 1 unmixed case **Delivery** Free within a 10-mile radius;
otherwise £1.50 per case for 1–11 cases (minimum charge £6.50); mail order
available **Glass hire** Free **Tastings and talks** Available **Cellarage** Not available

Whiclar & Gordon is a major wholesaler but has created a shop
in its entrance hall and also operates a fairly energetic mail-
order service. It is part of the Australian Hardy group and so
the range here in the Bunker concentrates on wines imported by

the parent company. The overall impression is of a well-made collection of wines at reasonable prices. Alsace provides a range from the Bennwihr co-operative under the Victor Preiss label, from Burgundy there is Cave des Haut Côtes and Cave de Buxy, and Chablis is represented by La Chablisienne. There is a fair selection of clarets, mainly petits châteaux and a few classed growths from 1980s vintages. In the south of France the Hardy-owned Domaine de la Baume has developed a splendid range of varietal wines made by Australian winemakers. These are available here, almost at source, so to speak.

The Australian range is dominated by Hardy with the Bird series, Hardy Collection and top-flight Eileen Hardy Reserve wines providing good quality at all price points. Moondah Brook makes an appearance, as does Ch. Reynella from McLaren Vale.

From further afield, Caliterra gives good flavour for your money from Chile, Franciscan estates provide the Californian wines and there is a small selection from South Africa.

Finding the Bunker is not easy so be prepared to take a couple of shots at it round Dorking's delightful one-way system.

Best buys

Domaine de Puget Merlot 1991, Vin de Pays l'Aude, £
Nottage Hill Chardonnay 1992, Australia, £
Ch. Lyonnat 1988, Lussac St-Emilion, ££
Ch. Reynella, Stony Hill Shiraz 1989, ££

Whighams of Ayr

8 Academy Street, Ayr, Ayrshire KA7 1HT   *Tel* (0292) 267000

Open Mon–Sat 9.30–5.30 **Closed** Sun, public holidays **Credit cards** Access, Amex, Visa; Switch; personal and business accounts **Discounts** Available **Delivery** Free in central Scotland (min 1 case); mail order available **Glass hire** Free with order **Tastings and talks** Major tastings held through wine society; tutored tastings **Cellarage** £4.11 per case per year

Whighams can trace its history back to 1766 when the company, then called Alexander Oliphant & Co, built its cellars on a sandbank, engaged a cooper and ordered a sloop to be built by shipbuilder John Fraser. The *Buck* brought madeira, port, Málaga and especially claret direct to the docks at Ayr.

Times have moved on and Whighams is still busy shipping wine, although not in its own sloop any longer. It has a range of clarets, including Ch. Beychevelle and its second wine Amiral de Beychevelle, plus a Bordeaux Supérieur from Ch. Puyfromage and some petit-château wines. Burgundies come through *négociants* Chanson and Lamblin, reliable enough but not exciting, and Chanson crops up again in the Rhône with Paul Sapin, who also provides the Beaujolais. Most unusual in this bastion of tradition is the range of Swiss wines, including four from the Ville de Lausanne, and a range from Slovakia. Italy lets its hair down a little with a reasonable choice from Veneto, Piemonte and Tuscany.

Lustau sherries, Smith Woodhouse ports and Cossart and Gordon madeiras round off this fairly limited list. Apparently there is a greater choice of wines in the shop than on the list. We hope so.

Best buys

Frankovka 1991, Slovakia, £
Réserve de l'Oratoire Bourgogne Grand Ordinaire 1991, Chanson, £
Chianti Classico Riserva 1980, Pignatelli, ££
Scottish Gentleman's Collection, ££

Whitesides Wine Merchants

Shawbridge Street, Clitheroe, Lancashire
BB7 1NA
Tel (0200) 22281

Open Mon–Sat 9–5.30 (Sat from 9)   **Closed** Sun, public holidays
Credit cards Access, Visa; personal and business accounts   **Discounts** 5% on 1 unmixed case   **Delivery** Free within Lancashire, North and West Yorkshire and Cumbria; elsewhere at cost (e.g. £7.50 per case on mainland UK)   **Glass hire** Free
Tastings and talks Occasional in-store tastings; other tastings on request (average charge £5 per person)   **Cellarage** Not available

This is the other half of the Clitheroe phenomenon. Whitesides manages more of a traditional wine-merchant approach against D Byrne's rather more adventurous outlook. Even so, there is a wide choice here. Sadly, the list has lost its few tasting notes of last year which are now reduced to fairly meaningless comments of 'Recommended' and 'Good value'.

Classic France is taken seriously, with good clarets from the 1980s and burgundies from *négociants* and growers. There are Alsace wines mainly from Sipp, and the Rhône includes a fair showing from Jaboulet. White Loire wines are good but six reds add a touch of zest to the range. Regional French wines include Ch. Val-Joanis from the Lubéron and the Australian-influenced Chais Baumière from Languedoc-Roussillon.

Most wine merchants will supply wine for parties on a sale or return basis.

The Spanish range includes reliable names such as Torres, CUNE and Murrieta but Italy provides little excitement beyond Frescobaldi Chiantis and two organic wines from Fugazza. Germany has some good Mosel wines from Schneider. Australia is one region where caution is thrown to the wind, with collections of wines from Penfolds, Rosemount and Brown Brothers laying strong foundations for more adventurous buying from Coldstream Hills, Rothbury and Taltarni. New Zealand takes in a tour of ten wineries with several wines from each, while South Africa provides a wide range of KWV wines and two from Hamilton-Russell.

Chilean wines are from Santa Rita, and a good collection of ports rounds off this list.

Best buys

Sauvignon de Touraine Comte d'Ormont 1992, Saget, £
Bosanquet Semillon/Chardonnay 1991, Australia, £
Chardonnay de Vieilles Vignes 1990, Rodet, ££
Taltarni Sparkling Brut nv, Australia, ££

Willoughbys

53 Cross Street, Manchester M2 4JP   *Tel* 061-834 6850

Open Mon–Fri 9–6, Sat 9–5   **Closed** Sun   **Credit cards** Access, Visa; personal and business accounts   **Discounts** 5% on 1 case   **Delivery** Free in Greater Manchester; mail order available   **Glass hire** £5 per dozen   **Tastings and talks** Regular weekend tastings held in-store; specific tastings for regular customers; to groups on request   **Cellarage** £5 per case per year

Classic French wines are here in depth and variety at Willoughbys. Claret is the first region to grab the attention. Nearly 50 from the 1988 vintage alone – starting at Willoughbys Daily Claret and travelling up to second and third growths. It is the same picture for older vintages, with petits châteaux providing a fine selection without breaking the bank. Burgundies are almost as many in number: *négociants* Emile Chandesais, Jacques Parent and Antonin Rodet take a lot of the credit but a rich seam from the Hospices de Beaune and Domaine de la Romanée-Conti provide exciting and expensive drinking. After all this glory the Rhône comes as a disappointment and is mainly single sourced though Alexis Boisselet, but Alsace looks bright.

Spain is sound if a little unadventurous with a full set from Torres and Riojas from Berberana, Murrieta and the delicious Muga. Portugal is represented by the good wines of Fonseca, and Germany is extensively explored with the help of Deinhard,

Guntrum and the family firm Michel Schneider. The New World is brought to Manchester in sturdy blocks from big but reliable names: Fetzer and Firestone from California, Seppelt and Brown Brothers from Australia. Champagnes are worth a special mention for the sheer variety that is missing elsewhere. Endless permutations of bottle size and vintage from Bollinger, Krug, Pol Roger, Roederer and so on.

Best buys

Willoughbys Daily Claret nv, £
Middleton Grange Shiraz/Cabernet 1990, Australia, £
Willoughbys Red Burgundy 1989, ££
Ch. Musar 1986, Lebanon, ££

Winchcombe Wine Merchants

21 North Street, Winchcombe,   *Tel* (0242) 604313
Gloucestershire GL54 5LH

Open Mon–Sat 9–9; Sun 12–2   **Closed** Chr Day, Boxing Day, New Year's Day   **Credit cards** Access, Visa; personal and business accounts   **Discounts** 5% up to £50, 7.5% on £50+   **Delivery** Free to north Cotswolds area   **Glass hire** Free; breakages charged for   **Tastings and talks** To local groups on request   **Cellarage** Not available

A big extension to the shop has, surprisingly, cut down on the shelf space available to wine. Other more edible goodies are now stocked but if you are looking for some wine to go with your gourmet frozen dinner here is what you might find.

Spain is still a major attraction, although not as much as before. Riojas have held their place, with a good range of crianza, reserva and gran reserva wines from a number of bodegas, but some of the more obscure wines have gone. Sherries are still holding on with a fine range from Williams and Humbert, Gonzalez Byass and Garvey.

France sports a reasonable selection of clarets, mainly petits châteaux and includes the delicious Ch. Monbousquet from St-Emilion on the way up to a few third- and fourth-growth Médocs. Burgundies have faded away recently through lack of demand, but in their place have come some Australian and California wines. New Zealand is strangely absent; partner Mr Adlard is unable to find anything he likes from this splendid country.

Cellarage is generally provided at the rates quoted only when the wines have been bought from the merchant concerned.

Best buys

Claret Dubosq nv, £
Hill-Smith Riesling 1992, Australia, £
Hill-Smith Estate Cabernet/Shiraz 1988, Australia, ££
CUNE Imperial 1986, Rioja, ££

Windrush Wines

Wholesale outlet
The Ox House, Market Square, Northleach,   *Tel* (0451) 860680
Gloucestershire GL54 3EG
Retail outlet
3 Market Place, Cirencester, Gloucestershire   *Tel* (0285) 650466
GL7 2PE

Open Mon–Fri 9–6 (shop till 5.30); Sat 10–1 (shop 9–5.30) **Closed** Sun, public
holidays **Credit cards** Access, Visa; personal and business accounts
Discounts By arrangement **Delivery** Free within 20-mile radius of Northleach;
and nationwide for 3+ cases; otherwise £5 for up to 2 cases; mail order available
Glass hire Pay for breakages only **Tastings and talks** 4 free tastings per year for
customers; tutored tastings on request **Cellarage** £4.70 per case per year

Windrush has moved out of its barracks and into a fine listed
building in the Market Square at Northleach. The retail shop
remains in Cirencester, a mini food hall of gastronomic delights
with cheese, charcuterie and patisserie.

Mark Savage MW, the man behind Windrush, has steered it
towards being one of the most interesting merchants in the
country. The range is not huge but each wine has earned its
place in terms of quality, style and personality.

France is a major feature, with a careful collection of clarets;
people are more important than classification and family
domaines abound – from the Rhône, Loire and South of France.
Pinot Noir is something of a passion, with examples from
around the world. North America is taken very seriously with
Eyrie Vineyards and Stags Leap typical of the quality of
producer that Mark Savage tends to deal with. Mainland
Australia is limited to Hutt Creek and Cape Mentelle, with the
delightful Piper's Brook from Tasmania showing off its terrific
Pinot Noir. Italy and Spain are selective but good.

Hidalgo sherries, fruit brandies (from Alsace and Oregon) and
farm calvados are just some of the other attractions.

A new sister company has been launched in Paris from which
UK customers can collect wines by arrangement.

Best buys

Domaine de Roudene Syrah 1991, £
Quinta de la Rosa 1991, Douro, Portugal, £
Domaine Tempier 1990, Bandol, ££
Ch. Le Tertre Rôteboeuf 1992, St-Emilion, ££

Winecellars

153/155 Wandsworth High Street, London   *Tel* 081-871 2668/3979
SW18 4JB

Open Mon–Fri 10.30–8.30; Sat 10–8.30   **Closed** Sun, Chr Day, Boxing Day, Easter
Mon   **Credit cards** Access, Visa; Switch; personal and business accounts
Discounts £1 per case on 5+ cases   **Delivery** Free within M25 (min 1 case);
elsewhere free (min 2 cases); mail order available   **Glass hire** £5, plus 75p deposit
per glass   **Tastings and talks** Tutored tastings   **Cellarage** Not available

If there was ever a wine-producing country that needs a
specialist wine merchant, it is Italy. And so, riding to the
rescue, come David Gleave and Nick Belfrage, both MWs and
Italian specialists and both able to unravel the intricacies of
these fascinating wines. Winecellars is big in supplying to the
trade but there is also a retail shop and a mail-order business.

The list is a gem and essential reading for anyone preparing
to tackle Italian wines seriously. At first sight it might look a
little daunting, with descriptions of regions, winemakers and
their styles, but it is worthwhile spending the time before
spending the money. To start with, there is Barolo – 47 wines
from 19 vintages and no fewer than 14 producers – which is
when you need to look back at the notes, all written in an easy,
understandable style. Piemonte goes on to include six Dolcettos,
nine Barbarescos and a collection of other wines made from the
Nebbiolo grape. Moving on to the Veneto, Winecellars has
discovered excellent-value Valpolicella and Soave under the
Rocca Sveva label and a range of inexpensive varietals from
Puiatti. Allegrini and Pieropan provide the top-notes.

The Tuscan section is a delight, with Chiantis from 11
producers, including the splendid Felsina Berardenga and Isole
e Olena. Super Tuscans are here in abundance, including two
vintages of Ornellaia and the magnificent Merlot-based Maseto,
both new wines from Ludovico Antinori made on an estate next
door to Sassicaia at Bolgheri.

The South has been explored with great success, producing
Salice Salentino from Francesco Candido in Puglia and
Ramiletto from Di Majo Norante in Molise.

Winecellars is so expert at Italian wines it is easy to overlook
the rest of the range but France is worthwhile, particularly on

good-value southern wines. Australia takes in a personal selection from notable winemakers such as Shaw and Smith, Charlie Melton, Adam Wynn and Brian Croser. Salisbury Estate is a new good-value addition. If this wonderful selection of wine is not enough you can stock up on olive oils from selected Tuscan estates. Villa di Vetrice, Tenuta di Capezzana and Ornellaia are all on offer at serious prices but the flavours will convert you from supermarket stuff for ever.

Best buys

Salice Salentino Riserva 1988, Candido, Puglia, £
Barbera d'Asti 'Ceppi Storici' 1990, C S Nizza Monferrato, £
Sauvignon Blanc 1992, Shaw and Smith, South Australia, ££
Chianti Classico 1990, Isole e Olena, ££

The Wine Emporium

7 Devon Place, Edinburgh EH12 5HJ   *Tel* 031-346 1113
also Cockburn's of Leith, 1–2 North West   *Tel* 031-225 2833
Circus Place, Edinburgh EH3 6ST

Case sales only   Open Mon–Sat 10–6; Sun, public holidays 11–5 **Closed** Chr Day, Boxing Day, 1 & 2 Jan **Credit cards** Access, Visa; personal and business accounts **Discounts** Available on application **Delivery** Free within Edinburgh district; mail order available **Glass hire** Free with order
Tastings and talks Wine course throughout the winter months; regular tutored tastings; in-store tastings on Sat **Cellarage** £2.50 per case per year

The Wine Emporium remains a case-sales only business but a retail shop has now joined the family under the Cockburn's of Leith banner. The range is much bigger and better than last year. France has emerged as the main attraction, clarets are the affordable sort, with a rich seam of young second and third growths offered as 'wines for laying down'. There is a short selection of burgundies, most from top-name growers such as Tollot-Beaut, Armand Rousseau, Yvon Clerget and Bruno Clair. Rhônes have a sprinkling of Perrin at both ends of the price scale, with his Châteauneuf-du-Pape, Château de Beaucastel and his good-value Vieille Ferme wines. French country wines are limited but good.

Further afield, Spain, the highlight of last year's list, is still very good, focusing on just a few producers such as Ochoa, Barbier and CUNE. Italy is less extensive but highlights include Umani Ronchi's Montepulciano d'Abruzzo. The 'key-suppliers' approach is particularly evident in Australia with Taltarni and Wyndham seeing most of the action. The Californian range has dwindled to just Riverside Farm plus small parcels of wine which are not included on the list.

Germany remains in all its glory, a fine collection from Prüm, Bürklin-Wolf, Guntrum, and Prinz zu Salm-Dalberg, plus a special collection of Treasure Room rarities.

Other specialities here include vintage cognacs from Hine, single-domaine armagnacs and a wide range of Warre's port.

Best buys

St Giles Rouge Vin de Table, £
Chenin Blanc Cape Selection 1992, South Africa, £
Mâcon-Lugny 1991, Raymond Mathelin, ££
Ch. Haut Rian 1991, Entre-Deux-Mers, ££

Wine Growers Association

See Les Amis du Vin

The Wine House

10 Stafford Road, Wallington, Surrey SM6 9AD   *Tel* 081-669 6661

Open Tue–Sat 10–6; Sun 12–2; public holidays variable   **Closed** Mon
Credit cards Access, Visa; personal and business accounts   **Discounts** 10% to members of Wine Circle only   **Delivery** Free within 5-mile radius (min 1 case); elsewhere at cost; mail order available   **Glass hire** Free   **Tastings and talks** Two large tastings a year (all ticket) and occasional smaller tastings (also all ticket); tastings and talks to groups on request   **Cellarage** Not available

There are some wine shops where the proprietors are very much in control of the stock, where lots of wines come from the same suppliers and where there is no duplication. The other type of shop is where the stock seems to have the upper hand and more and more variety is squeezed on to the shelves and easy buying is cast to the winds. The Wine House is firmly in the second category. This year we mourn the demise of the list which had become one of the mega-productions of the wine world, with lots of information on the regions and the wines. Apparently the whole thing got out of hand and, as proprietor Morvin Rodker says, 'true customers seem to prefer to browse along the shelves rather than compare prices at home'. Even so, the list may re-appear when time permits.

There are no real gaps in the range and if they appear they are swiftly plugged by Mr Rodker's relentless enthusiasm to find new flavours and better value.

Spain has seen some new additions this year – more wines from Somontano, yet another range of Riojas (Navajas) and some fresh faces from Priorato. Portugal has lots of new wines, all under £4.50. Italy has changed a little, new wines from Masi and Castello Vicchiomaggio, and there's Moldova, California, Australia, not to mention a vast range of French wines. £5 gets

457

you into the Wine Club which allows a 10% discount on mixed cases. Selecting that dozen is not difficult.

Best buys

Quinta de Folgorosa White 1991, Torres Vedras, Portugal, £
Ochoa Rosado 1991, Navarra, £
Givry 1990, Domaine Chofflet Valdenaire, ££
Châteauneuf-du-Pape Cuvée des Celestins 1989, Henri Bonneau, ££

Wine Rack

See Thresher

The Wine Schoppen

1 Abbeydale Road South, Sheffield, South Yorkshire S7 2QL	*Tel* (0742) 365684
Associated outlet	
Barrels & Bottles, 1 Walker Street, The Wicker, Sheffield, South Yorkshire S3 8GZ	*Tel* (0742) 769666

(Contact main outlet for details of new warehouse in Heeley)

Open Mon–Fri 9.30–6; Sat 9.30–5 **Closed** Sun, public holidays
Credit cards Access, Visa; Switch; personal and business accounts **Discounts** 5% on 1–2 unmixed cases; 6% on 3–5 unmixed cases **Delivery** Free to UK (min 3 cases); otherwise £5.80 per consignment **Glass hire** Free with order
Tastings and talks In-store tastings held every first Saturday of the month; tastings by invitation 4 times per year; wines always available for tasting in-store; monthly tastings through wine tasting club; to groups on request **Cellarage** £2.50 per case per year

This company has grown yet again with the acquisition of a new hotel and restaurant, plus a case-sales warehouse in the Sheffield suburbs. The range at all premises is much the same, with German wines taking centre stage. There is a fine selection from growers in the Mosel, Rheinhessen and Rheinpfalz areas, and a collection of 21 Franken wines, including a fairly unusual Trockenbeerenauslese. But no matter how good German wines are, they are difficult to sell at the moment and so a wide variety from the rest of the world adds to the range. France includes a reasonable collection from Bordeaux, Burgundy and the Rhône, with three vintages of Mas de Daumas Gassac adding interest. There is Vega Sicilia from Spain, a good-value selection from Portugal and wines from Australia, Chile, Mexico, Brazil and California. New this year is a range of malt whiskies from Gordon & MacPhail.

Training is a priority, so advice behind the counter should be reliable.

Best buys

Kerner Kabinett 1991, Kuehling Gillots, Rheinhessen, £
Castillo de Almansa Reserva 1986, Spain, £
Ch. de Canterrane 1978, Côtes du Roussillon, ££
Pirramimma Shiraz 1987, McLaren Vale, Australia, ££

The Wine Shop

7 Sinclair Street, Thurso, Caithness   *Tel* (0847) 65657
KW14 7AJ

Open Tue–Sat 10–1, 2.30–5.30   **Closed** Sun, Mon, Chr and New Year
Credit cards Access, Visa; personal and business accounts   **Discounts** Available
on unmixed case   **Delivery** Free within 10-mile radius of Thurso (min 6 bottles);
otherwise £1.50 per case or part case within Caithness; quotes given for
Sutherland   **Glass hire** Free with order   **Tastings and talks** Available on request
Cellarage Not available

This wine shop in Thurso is just about as far north as you can
go without getting on a boat. The proprietors are Jan and
Martine Hughes and, when not behind the counter, Jan works
as a chemist at the Dounreay Nuclear Establishment.

The range of wine is surprisingly wide and very well chosen
with a keen eye on value. From France there is a reasonable
collection of clarets, with Côtes de Bourg and Fronsac at the
value end and Ducru and Pichon-Lalande for special occasions.
Bouchard Père features among the burgundies and there are
small but sound selections from the Rhône, Loire and Alsace.
The German range goes straight for style with Guntrum, Prüm,
Dr Loosen and Robert Weil. Italy includes the delightful Peppoli
Chianti from Antinori and Tedeschi's sturdy Recioto della
Valpolicella. There is a splendid Spanish selection with the well-
known names of Torres, CUNE and Ochoa providing most of
the flavours and two Priorato wines from Masia Barril adding
interest. Australia and New Zealand are well represented by
Brown Brothers and a few Penfolds wines, and there is a clutch
of good wines from Chile. In a major town, the quality of this
selection would be commendable, but in such a remote part of
the country it indicates a singleminded determination to do
things properly.

Best buys

Domaine du Tariquet 1991, Vin de Pays des Côtes de
Gascogne, £
Chardonnay, Concha y Toro 1992, Chile, £
CUNE Viña Real 1988, Rioja, ££
Erdener Treppchen Spätlese 1983, Dr Loosen, ££

The Wine Society

Registered office (mail order only)
Gunnels Wood Road, Stevenage,   *Tel* (0438) 741177
Hertfordshire SG1 2BG   (enquiries)
                                          Tel (0438) 740222 (24-hour
                                                  answering service)

Open Mon–Fri 9–5; Sat 9–1 (1 retail outlet in Stevenage); showroom open for
collections **Closed** Sun, public holidays **Credit cards** Access, Visa; personal and
business accounts **Discounts** £1.20 on 1 unmixed case; also £1 per case on 5–9
cases, £2 per case on 10 cases or more **Delivery** Free in UK (min 1 case or for
orders of over £75); otherwise £3 **Glass hire** Free with 1-case order
Tastings and talks Series of tastings for members (monthly in Stevenage and
London); 30 tastings per year nationwide; also wine weekends in England, Italy
and France **Cellarage** £4.08 per unmixed case per year

Formed in 1874, the International Exhibition Co-operative Wine
Society Ltd, to give it its full name, exists as the oldest and
largest 'wine club' in the world. A single £20 payment buys you
membership for life and when you move on to that great
vineyard in the sky, your grieving relatives can pick up the
dividend which has accrued. In fact, you purchase a share in the
business and from then on you can vote at meetings, elect the
officials and even stand for the Committee of Management.

Membership also brings you three well-annotated lists per
year and monthly newsletters focusing on different regions and
wines. You can also attend one of the many tastings held at
venues around the country.

The wines are well chosen, each one a good representative of
its region. Claret has always been a sound area. Most of the
wines on the main list are ready to drink, those for laying down
are noted in a separate section at the back. The Rhône is a
satisfying selection from Jaboulet, Guigal and Chave with a few
extras such as the Domaine Font Michelle Châteauneuf-du-Pape.
French country wines merit a large section, most wines are
below the magic £5 mark and represent as good a selection as
you are likely to find anywhere in the UK. Sherry has long been
a strong point, and the Society's own-label wines are
particularly impressive. Alsace, Hungary, Moldova and Italy all
contain new additions this year.

En primeur offers have been growing in recent years and now Rhônes, burgundies, Sauternes and clarets are offered in this way. The selection is wide, prices are reasonable and often there is the chance to buy six bottles instead of a whole case. Mixed cases are also available.

This year the Wine Society was one of the first merchants to take advantage of the new customs allowances by opening a collection facility in France, near the Channel ports. Members can now order a selected range of wines for collection at Hesdin. Payment can be made in advance in sterling or French francs. So far, only unmixed cases are available this way but with savings of around £14 a case it seems very worthwhile. One of our readers summed it up so well: 'A society that is well worth belonging to.'

Best buys

Ch. Bel Air 1992, Bordeaux Blanc, £
Minervois, Domaine de Moulin Rigaud 1991, £
The Society's Riesling, Niedermenniger Herrenberg, Von Kesselstatt, ££
Ravenswood Vintners Blend Merlot 1990, California, ££

Wines of Interest

46 Burlington Road, Ipswich, Suffolk IP1 2HS   *Tel* (0473) 215752

Open Mon–Fri 9–6; Sat 9–1   **Closed** Sun, public holidays   **Credit cards** None accepted; personal and business accounts   **Discounts** 5% on 1 unmixed case **Delivery** Free in City of London, Ipswich and central Norwich (min 1 case) and elsewhere (min 6 cases); otherwise at cost; mail order available   **Glass hire** Free with suitable order   **Tastings and talks** Regular series of tastings in London, Clacton and Norwich (approx £15 per person)   **Cellarage** Not available

To persuade customers to try something different Wines of Interest has started a Sampling Club. Not the usual idea of a sip in the shop: here the customer joins the Club for a £12 annual subscription and can then buy a single bottle of one or two selected wines per month at half price.

Tim Voelcker, MD of Wines of Interest, has assembled a good collection of wines and has tried to find a few from off the beaten track, such as a Côte Roannaise wine, made from Gamay, in the upper reaches of the Loire not too far from Beaujolais, and a Collioure from the South of France. Both are worth sampling. Generally, the range takes a fairly conventional tour around the vineyards adding one or two less usual wines here and there. So, in a small Italian range we find a wonderful Rocca Rubia made from Carignano grapes in Sardinia and a stylish Salice Salentino. Spain includes Pata Negra, the big brother version of Señorio de los Llanos from Valdepeñas, and there is a single quinta Vinho Verde from Portugal. From Australia, a few unusual names are included such as Blewitt Springs, St Leonards and Wirra Wirra, as well as Peter Lehmann, Brown Brothers and Salisbury.

Most of the main list concentrates on providing value and flavour at under £10 but there is a Fine Wine list to keep the interest going: classic clarets and burgundies, along with older vintages of estate German wines, and ports and madeiras rolling back through the years.

Best buys

Salice Salentino Riserva 1988, Candido, Puglia, Italy, £
Shawsgate Dry, Framlingham 1990, Suffolk, England, £
Wirra Wirra Cabernet Sauvignon, The Angelus 1991, McLaren Vale, Australia, ££
Chardonnay de Franche Comté 1992, Guillaume, ££

Wines of Westhorpe

Birch Cross, Marchington, Staffordshire ST14 8NX	*Tel* (0283) 820285
Bond address for collections	
Cargo Bonding Ltd, Derby Turn, Derby Road, Burton on Trent, Staffordshire DE14 2QD	*Tel as above*

Case sales only **Open** Mon–Fri 9–6.30; also open at various times on Sat, Sun and some public holidays **Closed** Chr Day (and possibly between Chr and New Year) **Credit cards** Access, Visa **Discounts** Available, £2.60 on 5–10 cases, £3.20 on 11–20 cases etc. **Delivery** National delivery, £3.90 for 1 case, free on 2+ cases **Glass hire** Not available **Tastings and talks** Occasionally to groups on request **Cellarage** Not available

With its limited range (just 85 wines from 5 countries) and case-only sales, newcomers to Wines of Westhorpe might think it has very little to offer, but try comparing prices and you will soon see the attraction.

The whole Bulgarian range is available, from the basic but good country wines right up to Special Reserves. On every wine the bottle price is less than at most high street shops – by 25p or so at the bottom end but at the top end the difference can be as much as 80p a bottle. This is for exactly the same wines as those widely available.

A man cannot make him laugh; but that's no marvel; he drinks no wine.

Shakespeare, *Henry IV (Part II)*

Chilean wines are from Peteroa, Australians from Tatachilla Hill and new this year is a range of Portuguese wines from the Alentejo region. You may not have heard of the producers before, but the wines are generally full-flavoured, well made and great value. Mixed cases are available but these are pre-selected as 'tasting cases'.

Best buys

Reserve Oriachovitza Cabernet Sauvignon 1989, Bulgaria, £
Tatachilla Hill Grenache nv, Australia, £
Peteroa Sauvignon Blanc 1992, Chile, £
Special Reserve Stambolovo Merlot 1988, Bulgaria, £

Wright Wine Company

The Old Smithy, Raikes Road, Skipton,
North Yorkshire BD23 1NP

Tel (0756) 794175/700886

Open Mon–Sat and public holidays 9–6   **Closed** Sun   **Credit cards** None accepted; personal and business accounts   **Discounts** 5% on mixed/unmixed cases   **Delivery** Free within 30-mile radius of Skipton; elsewhere at cost **Glass hire** Free   **Tastings and talks** Not available   **Cellarage** Available free for 1–2 years, after that negotiable

Bob Wright is forever reviewing his range and seeking to improve the quality and value of the wines he stocks. From the look of his existing selection he does a good job. Clarets are here in a variety of vintages, with a sizable proportion below £10 as well as above. Burgundies have changed allegiance over the years and now come mainly from quality domaines such as Emile Voarick and Marchand. Alsace goes straight for style with wines from Schlumberger and Hugel, while a handful of grand cru wines shows just how good this region can get. The rest of France is good, particularly the 'French Provincial' section which provides value drinking as well as a choice of four vintages of Mas de Daumas Gassac.

There is a serious attempt to show the style and variety of good German wine, Anheuser and Guntrum feature here while Spain and Italy cover the ground with a reasonable selection. Australia is favoured with a review of good drinking under £10, including the delightful Tasmanian Wine Company Pinot Noir. With New Zealand, Chile, South Africa and California all providing a well-thought-out range, it seems like Bob Wright has been working hard.

Best buys

Jeunes Vignes au Château Cissac nv, £
Neethlingshoff Estate Wine 1990, Stellenbosch, £
Bairrada Reserva, Frei-João 1982, Portugal, ££
Hautes Côtes de Nuits Blanc, Pinot Beurot 1990, Thévenet le
Brun, ££

Peter Wylie Fine Wines

Plymtree Manor, Plymtree, Cullompton,   *Tel* (0884) 277555
Devon EX15 2LE

Open Mon–Fri 9–6; Sat (by appointment) **Closed** Sun, public holidays
Credit cards None accepted; personal and business accounts
Discounts Available **Delivery** 1 case at £10, 2 cases at £6.50 per case, 3 cases at £5
per case **Glass hire** Not available **Tastings and talks** Tastings by invitation
only **Cellarage** £6 per case per year (plus VAT and insurance)

If we had to nominate a favourite cellar to get lost in, the one at
Peter Wylie's home in delightful Devon would probably be it.
With a choice of 15,000 classic wines from assorted vintages
back to 1890 and beyond, there is a lifetime's tasting homework.

Peter Wylie specialises in fine and rare wines from Bordeaux,
Burgundy and Champagne and in vintage port. The list
concerns itself not just with the château name and vintage but
with the liquid level of the wine – base of neck, upper shoulder
and so on – and the condition of the label. For those of us who
would drink the contents, the level in the bottle is important
and gives an indication of the condition of the wine. The state
of the label is more the concern of collectors, who would no
more pull the cork than stick a Penny Black on an envelope. On
any list of old wines it is the great names, such as Yquem, Lafite
and Latour, that dominate and these antique gems don't come
cheap, though there are some bottles at less than £100. Peter
Wylie does not just deal in history, he has quite a collection of
clarets, Sauternes and burgundies from recent vintages.

Best buys

Not really appropriate here, considering the individual nature of
the stock

---

*I think the British have the distinction above all other nations of being
able to put new wine into old bottles without bursting them.*

Clement Attlee, *Hansard*, Oct 1950

Yapp Brothers

The Old Brewery, Mere, Wiltshire BA12 6DY   *Tel* (0747) 860423

Case sales only   Open Mon–Fri 9–5; Sat 9–1   **Closed** Sun, public holidays
Credit cards Access, Diners Club, Visa; personal and business accounts
Discounts Quantity and collection discounts available   **Delivery** Free locally
(Wiltshire, Dorset, Somerset); free on UK mainland (min 2 cases); otherwise 1 case
£3; mail order available   **Glass hire** Free   **Tastings and talks** Occasional tastings,
£5 per person (refundable on purchase)   **Cellarage** £5 per case per year

Robin Yapp is a specialist. He concentrates his time and tastebuds on two areas of France that in many lists get only cursory treatment, the Rhône and Loire. He deals not just with suppliers but with people; he knows every bump in the road, every garden gate and this kind of knowledge brings dividends.

Starting off in the centre of France with a fairly obscure but very good-value St-Pourçain-sur-Sioule, he travels this long, languid river calling in at vineyards where the people are friendly and the wine quality is paramount.

There are the well-known names, such as Sancerre, which comes in a choice of four whites, two reds and a rosé. Orléannais, Jasnières, Chinon and Bourgueil follow. Coteaux du Layon from four different cuvées of the same property shows just how good this wine can get. Quarts de Chaume continues the tasting exercise and a 1935 Bonnezeaux demonstrates that these Loire whites can last for years. There are 10 wines from Savennières, a fine collection of Saumur Champigny and Vouvray in all its forms: sec, demi-sec, moelleux and sparkling.

The Rhône is explored with the same level of dedication. Condrieu and Ch. Grillet are listed in a choice of vintages, Gérard Chave provides his wonderful Hermitages, Crozes comes from Alain Graillot. Nine wines from Cornas, a hefty chunk from Châteauneuf-du-Pape and three wines from Brézème, a fairly rare and exciting discovery, add to the variety. One small criticism is that some wines in the list lose their growers' name, though these are often hidden in the text and where there is more than one supplier it can get confusing.

There is some good Côtes-du-Rhône as well as domaine wines from Lirac, Côtes du Ventoux and Tricastin. Robin Yapp strays a little from his chosen path with a collection of Alsace wines from Schléret and the splendid Jacquesson champagnes.

Best buys

Gamay de l'Ardèche 1992, Les Vignerons Ardéchois, £
St-Pourçain-sur-Sioule 1992, Union des Vignerons, £
Pouilly Blanc Fumé, Les Loges 1990, ££
Châteauneuf-du-Pape, Le Vieux Donjon 1990, ££

York House Wines

See John Ford Wines

Yorkshire Fine Wines

See Bibendum

WHO'S WHERE

This is a gazetteer of individual wine stockists listed in the *Guide*. See also the directory of chains and supermarkets that follows.

London

EC1
Cantina Augusto 274
Corney & Barrow 288

EC3
Russell & McIver 410

EC4
The Vintner 329

N7
Le Nez Rouge 385

N10
The Hermitage 347

N21
Howard Ripley 406

NW1
Bibendum 260
Laytons 365

NW3
Heath Street Wine 404

NW5
Fine Wines of New
  Zealand 309

NW6
Grape Ideas 324

NW10
Les Amis du Vin 241

SE1
Russell & McIver 410
Charles Taylor Wines
  19
Waterloo Wine 447

SE10
Ravensbourne 401

SE11
Alex Findlater 308
London Wine
  Emporium 368
Mayor Sworder 374

SW1
Berry Bros & Rudd
  257
Farr Vintners 305
Harrods 339
Harvey Nichols 342
Justerini & Brooks 361
Laytons 365
Morris & Verdin 382

SW3
Nicolas 388
La Réserve 404

SW5
Nicolas 388

SW6
Friarwood 314
Fulham Road Wine
  Centre 315
Haynes Hanson &
  Clark 343
La Sac à Vin 404

SW7
La Vigneronne 441

SW8
Adam Bancroft 249

SW10
Lea & Sandeman 366

SW11
Clapham Cellars 404

SW12
Benson Fine Wines
  256
Fernlea Vintners 19

SW13
Barnes Wine Shop 250

SW18
Supergrape 428
Winecellars 455

SW19
Findlater Mackie Todd
  309

WC1
Domaine Direct 299

WC2
Australian Wine
  Centre 246

W1
Les Amis du Vin 241
Fortnum & Mason 312
Harcourt Fine Wine
  334
Laytons 365
Nicolas 388
Selfridges 418

W2
Champagne House
  279
Moreno Wines 381
Le Picoleur 404

W5
Côte d'Or Wines 290
Summerlee Wines/
  Freddy Price 426

W6
Bin Ends 17

W8
Haynes Hanson &
  Clark 343
Lea & Sandeman 366
Nicolas 388

W9
Les Amis du Vin 241
Moreno Wines 381

W11
John Armit Wines 242
Corney & Barrow 288
Holland Park Wine
  352
Nicolas 388

W14
Roberson 407

England

Avon

Bath
Great Western Wine 327

Bristol
Averys of Bristol 247
Clifton Cellars 285
John Harvey 340
The Vine Trail 21

Hallatrow
Reid Wines (1992) 402

Bedfordshire

Bedford
Bedford Fine Wines 252

Luton
Smedley Vintners 421

Berkshire

Hungerford
Hungerford Wine 356

Maidenhead
David Alexander 239
Helen Verdcourt 439

Newbury
The Vintry 445

Reading
Bordeaux Direct 264
Harvest Wine Group 340
Milton Sandford 377
Sunday Times Wine Club 427

Wargrave
Vintage Roots 444

Warren Row
Milton Sandford 377

Buckinghamshire

Amersham
Philip Eyres 304

Aston Clinton
Gerard Harris 336

Great Missenden
Turville Valley 434

Taplow
Half Yard Wines 330

Cambridgeshire

Cambridge
Bin Ends 17

Ramsey
Anthony Byrne 269

Cheshire

Alderley Edge
Eaton Elliot 300

Chester
Classic Wine Warehouses 285

Macclesfield
Portland Wine 398

Nantwich
Rodney Densem 297

Sandiway
Sandiway Wine 415

Cornwall

Camborne
Cornwall Wine Merchants 290

Falmouth
Constantine Stores 20

Truro
Laymont & Shaw 364

Cumbria

Carlisle
B H Wines 259

Cockermouth
Garrards 318

Kendal
Frank E Stainton 425

Penrith
Cumbrian Cellar 293

Derbyshire

Burton on Trent
Colombier Vins Fins 286

Buxton
Mi Casa Wines 375

Devon

Axminster
Justerini & Brooks 361

Cullompton
Peter Wylie 464

Doddiscombsleigh
The Nobody Inn 389

Exeter
Christopher James 358

Ottery St Mary
Christopher Piper 395

Dorset

Blandford Forum
Woodhouse Wines 20

Blandford St Mary
Hicks & Don 348

Bridport
Wessex Wines 449

Christchurch
Christchurch Fine Wine 283

Sherborne
Sherborne Vintners 420

Wareham
Richard Harvey 341

Co Durham

Darlington
Pease & Wrightson 393

Shropshire

Bridgnorth
Tanners Wines 429

Ludlow
Halves 332

Shrewsbury
Tanners Wines 429

Somerset

Chard
Abbey Cellars 237

Taunton
Châteaux Wines 280

Staffordshire

Burton on Trent
Wines of Westhorpe
462

Marchington
Wines of Westhorpe
462

Suffolk

Halesworth
Alex Findlater 308

Ipswich
Seckford Wines 417
Wines of Interest 461

Newmarket
Corney & Barrow 288

Southwold
Adnams 238

Sudbury
Ameys Wines 240

Surrey

Brockham
Ben Ellis 302

Burpham
Guildford Wine
Market/The Vintner
329

Cranleigh
A & A Wines 236

Dorking
Whiclar & Gordon 449

Gomshall
Lorne House Vintners
369

Guildford
The Vintner 329

Kew
Nicolas 388

Richmond
Richmond Wine
Warehouse 405

Wallington
Wine House 457

Woking
The Vintner 329

Sussex (East)

Alfriston
English Wine Centre
303

Brighton
Butlers Wine Cellar
268

Hove
John Ford Wines 311

Sussex (West)

Arundel
Pallant Wines 392

Billingshurst
Charles Hennings 347

Chichester
Pallant Wines 392

Horsham
King and Barnes 362

Midhurst
Midhurst Wine
Shippers 375

Petworth
Charles Hennings 347

Pulborough
Charles Hennings 347

Tyne & Wear

Newcastle upon Tyne
Dennhöfer Wines 296

Warwickshire

Shipston-on-Stour
Edward Sheldon 419

Stratford-upon-Avon
C A Rookes 409

Warwick
Broad Street Wine 266

West Midlands

Birmingham
Connolly's 287
John Frazier 313

Cradley
Nickolls & Perks 387

Lye
Nickolls & Perks 387

Solihull
John Frazier 313

Stourbridge
County Wines of
Hagley 291
Nickolls & Perks 387

Sutton Coldfield
John Frazier 313

Wiltshire

Mere
Yapp Brothers 464

Salisbury
Nadder Wine 384

Westbury
Hicks & Don 348

Yorkshire (North)

Ripon
Great Northern Wine
Company 326

Skipton
Wright Wine 463

Thirsk
Playford Ros 397

York
Bywater & Broderick
271
Cachet Wines 272
Chennell &
Armstrong 281
Patrick Toone 262
Yorkshire Fine Wines
260

Yorkshire (South)

Rotherham
Bin Ends 262

Sheffield
Barrels & Bottles 458
Bin 89 Wine
Warehouse 261
Mitchells Wine
Merchants 379
Penistone Court Wine
Cellars 22
The Wine Schoppen
458

Yorkshire (West)

Huddersfield
La Reserva España 403
Springfield Wines 22

Leeds
Bywater & Broderick
271
Cairns & Hickey 273
Great Northern Wine
326
Vinceremos Wines 443

Otley
Chippendale 282

Scotland

Borders

Peebles
Villeneuve Wines 442

Dumfries &
Galloway

Moffat
Moffat Wine Shop 380

Fife

Cupar
The Wine Byre 23

Grampian

Elgin
Gordon & MacPhail
323

Highland

Thurso
Wine Shop 459

Lothian

Edinburgh
Peter Green 328
J E Hogg 351
Justerini & Brooks 361
Raeburn Fine Wines
400
Valvona & Crolla 438
Wine Emporium 456

Strathclyde

Ayr
Whighams of Ayr 450

Glasgow
Ubiquitous Chip 436

Rothesay, Isle of Bute
Bute Wines 267

Tayside

Perth
Matthew Gloag 322

Wales

Clwyd

Hawarden
Ashley Scott 416

Dyfed

Llanwrda
A Case of Wine 276

Gwynedd

Llandudno Junction
Terry Platt 396

Powys

Welshpool
Tanners Wines 429

West Glamorgan

Swansea
The Celtic Vintner 278
CPA's 21

N. Ireland

Co Antrim

Belfast
Belfast Wine 253
Direct Wine
Shipments 298

Co Down

Crossgar
James Nicholson 386

Republic of Ireland

Dublin
Mitchell & Son 378

Channel Islands

Guernsey

St Peter Port
Sommelier 423

Jersey

St Helier
Bergerac 256

St Saviour
Victor Hugo 355

CHAINS AND SUPERMARKETS

Space does not permit us to list the addresses of all the branches of each chain, but details of the entry include the address and telephone number of the company's head office, from whom you will be able to find out your nearest branch.

ASDA 244
Augustus Barnett 251
Booths 263
Cellar 5 277
Davisons Wine Merchants 294
Eldridge Pope 301
Fullers 316
Gateway/Somerfield 319
House of Townend 353

Leo's/Stop & Shop 367
Wm Low 370
Majestic Wine Warehouses 371
Marks & Spencer 372
Morrisons 383
Oddbins 391
Thos Peatling 394
Arthur Rackhams 399
Safeway 411

J Sainsbury/ SavaCentres 413
Spar 424
Tesco 430
Thresher/Wine Rack/ Bottoms Up 432
Unwins Wine Merchants 437
Victoria Wine Company 440
Waitrose 446

Part IV

Find out more about wine

Find out more about wine

There is more activity than ever before for those who want to find out more about wine. You can join wine clubs and societies, you can go on wine courses, or you can travel to the vineyards in the company of like-minded wine lovers.

Some wine societies are independent organisations run by enthusiasts who arrange events throughout the year for their members, and they will often sample wines from several merchants. There are also some 'wine clubs' which are really just mail-order merchants, these are to be found in the main WHERE TO BUY section of the *Guide* under their trading names.

WINE CLUBS

Association de la Jurade de Saint-Emilion (Grande Bretagne)
Peter Shamash, 7 Tower Court, Overstone Park, Northampton, NN6 0AS TEL (0604) 64379 FAX (0604) 588889 A regular series of gastronomic dinners, lunches and visits to St-Emilion, all with the aim of increasing knowledge and appreciation of the wines of this region.

Bramhope Wine Appreciation Group Kelvyn Chapman, 20 Ayresome Avenue, Leeds, W Yorks LS8 1BE TEL (0532) 666322 Tutored tastings are held twice a month with the cost of wines shared (usually £3-£5 per session for six wines). Activities include visits from guest speakers, occasional visits to merchants, dinners and tours of wine-making regions abroad. Annual subscription £15. A smaller group also meets every Monday at the Garforth School Evening Centre during term-time.

Capital Wine Appreciation Group (CWAG) R & A Sperry, 67 Wentloog Road, Rumney, Cardiff CF3 8HD TEL (0222) 791088 Limited membership of up to 20 people. No membership fee but there is a supplement of £4 per meeting attended (held once a month) to cover the cost of the wines. Members are asked to make an annual contribution (£1) towards postal costs.

Cornwall Wine Tasting Group Christopher James, 20 Lodge Drive, Truro, Cornwall TR1 1TX TEL (0872) 71912 Although the group is affiliated to the Wine Society, membership is open. There is a one-off joining fee of £10 but a supplement is charged for each tasting attended. Meetings usually take place every six weeks.

The International Wine & Food Society 9 Fitzmaurice Place, Berkeley Square, London W1X 6JD TEL 071-495 4191 FAX 071-495 4172 Membership terms on application; special rates for members under 25. The International Secretariat in London has a library and club and hotel facilities. Nearly 200 regional branches organise dinners, tastings, lectures and visits. The annual *Food & Wine*, regular newsletters and annual vintage guide to wine-buying are free to members.

The Lincoln Wine Society Norman Tate, 8 Green Lane, North Hykeham, Lincoln, Lincolnshire LN6 8NL TEL (0522) 680388 Meetings are held once a month and activities include guest experts and wine merchants, fine wine and food evenings, trips to merchants and wine areas, and a grand annual dinner. Membership is £7 annually (£12 joint). (See also **The Lincoln Wine Course**.)

North East Wine Tasting Society Nigel Ellam (Secretary), 1 East View, High Heworth, Gateshead, Tyne & Wear NE10 9AR TEL 091-438 4107 Monthly meetings are held in Newcastle. Tastings are aimed at improving knowledge of wine-producing areas, grape varieties and the wines themselves. Annual membership £15 (£27 joint).

Northern Wine Appreciation Group D M Hunter, 21 Dartmouth Avenue, Almondbury, Huddersfield, W Yorks HD5 8UR TEL (0484) 531228 Weekly meetings are held from September to June. Graded tutored tastings and special events are held for new members. Activities include visits to merchants for tastings and the planning of meals.

Ordre Mondial des Gourmets Dégustateurs Martin Mistlin, 41 Kingsend, Ruislip, Middlesex HA4 7DD TEL 081-427 9944 (day) This is a French wine guild with a British chapter (the headquarters are in Paris). Varied, regular tastings and dinners are held with access to meetings abroad. Annual subscription is £65 for professionals, £45 for amateurs. Martin Mistlin also runs Fine Wine Dining Club (subscription £5) and Wine and Gastronomic Societies (joining fee £10), specialising in wine and food events, wine weekends and wine tours abroad.

The Petersham Wine Society John Trigwell, Tanglewood House, Mayfield Avenue, New Haw, Addlestone, Surrey KT15 3AG TEL (0932) 348720 FAX (0932) 350861 Regular tastings are held in the cellars of the Petersham Hotel in Richmond (Surrey), followed by a small regional dinner. Annual membership £7.50 (£12 joint at the same address). A charge is made for each tasting (about £20 per head).

Tanglewood Wine Society Tanglewood House, Mayfield Avenue, New Haw, Addlestone, Surrey KT15 3AG TEL (0932) 348720 FAX (0932) 350861 The Society has branches in Cobham, Ashtead, Woking and East Grinstead holding regular monthly tastings and social events. Annual membership costs £7.50 (£12 joint at the same address). A charge is made at each tasting, averaging £9 per head. (See also **Tanglewood Wine Tours**.)

The Wine & Dine Society 96 Ramsden Road, London SW12 8QZ TEL 081-673 4439 Weekly tastings, including tasting workshops and 'vertical and horizontal tastings' with guest speakers. Dinners in London follow an ethnic theme.

The Winetasters P N Beardwood (Secretary), 44 Claremont Road, London W13 0DG TEL 081-997 1252 This is a non-profit-making club which organises tastings, seminars, dinners and tours. Annual subscription £10 (£3 if you live more than 50 miles from London).

WINE COURSES

Camberley Wine Courses Lindum House, 27 Cambrian Close, Camberley, Surrey GU15 3LD TEL (0276) 23964 Introductory and fine wine courses are held generally in autumn and spring terms at Camberley Adult Education Centre. The Wine & Spirit Education Trust Higher Certificate course is also offered at Brooklands Technical College, Weybridge.

Christie's Wine Course Caron Williamson (Secretary), 63 Old Brompton Road, London SW7 3JS TEL 071-581 3933 FAX 071-589 0383 On offer is an Introduction to Wine Tasting course, concentrating on the principal wines of France. It runs on five consecutive Tuesday evenings, six times a year, price £155. Christie's also offers Master Classes: specialist tastings of fine and rare wines. There are places for 14-45 people, cost £55-£65.

Ecole du Vin, Château Loudenne, Bordeaux Ecole du Vin, Château Loudenne, St-Yzans-de-Médoc, 33340 Lesparre, France TEL 010 33 56.09.05.03 FAX 010 33 56.09.02.87 Six-day courses are held at the château for a dozen students five times a year. Aimed at the public and professionals in the trade, the lectures and tastings cover all aspects of viticulture and vinification. Price in 1993 was 12900FF inclusive. A short course is also available (5750FF in 1993) for both intermediate and advanced levels.

Fulham Road Wine School The Fulham Road Wine Centre, 899-901 Fulham Road, London SW6 5HU TEL 071-736 7009 FAX 071-736 6648 A selection of courses on offer, from a straightforward introduction to wine tasting to identifying styles; also how to match food and and wine, and Saturday workshops (January to May) consisting of blind tastings for people studying for the Wine & Spirit Education Trust Diploma or Master of Wine exams. (See also the **Where to buy** section.)

German Wine Academy German Wine Information Service, Chelsea Chambers, 262a Fulham Road, London SW10 9EL TEL 071-376 3329 FAX 071-351 7563 A twelfth-century German monastery is the setting for courses (delivered in English), which include lectures by wine experts, vineyard visits and tastings. The basic 7-day course is run in May, September and October, price £625. This is supplemented by more advanced courses and an extended, culturally oriented course conducted at a more relaxed pace.

Lay & Wheeler Hugo Rose MW, 6 Culver Street West, Colchester, Essex CO1 1JA TEL (0206) 764446 FAX (0206) 564488 Approximately 100 wine workshops are held throughout the year covering varying themes from wine regions to general interest and blind tastings. The tutored tastings are for a maximum of 50 people and are followed by a two-course supper. Prices range from £18.50 for workshops aimed at the novice to £85 for the flagship tastings held at outside venues. (See also the **Where to buy** section.)

Leith's School of Food and Wine 21 St Alban's Grove, London W8 5BP TEL 071-229 0177 Two evening courses are available to outsiders leading to either the award of Leith's Certificate or Leith's Advanced Certificate of Wine (roughly analogous to the Wine and Spirit Education Trust's Higher Certificate, without the sessions on licensing and labelling laws). Price £190 and £315 respectively. Other courses are also sometimes available.

The Lincoln Wine Course Norman Tate, 8 Green Lane, North Hykeham, Lincoln, Lincolnshire LN6 8NL TEL (0522) 680388 A wine appreciation course is offered at North Hykeham Evening Institute and at Yarborough Adult Education Centre, Lincoln, starting in September each year. This is a two-term course (two hours a week) with the emphasis on tasting as well as gaining a good general knowledge of wine. The cost is divided between the course fee (£28.40) and a weekly supplement to cover the cost of the tastings. (See also **Lincoln Wine Society**.)

Sotheby's Annabel Wingfield, Sotheby's Wine Department, 34-35 New Bond Street, London W1A 2AA TEL 071-408 5051 FAX 071-499 7091 (Booking office: Sotheby's Educational Studies, 30 Oxford Street, London W1R 1RE TEL 071-323 5775 FAX 071-580 8160) Varietal and Regional Wine Courses alternate and run throughout the year, on consecutive Wednesday evenings, £160 per course of five sessions. Regular Wine Dinners are also held, as well as tutored tastings with top wine producers.

Tante Marie School of Cookery Woodham House, Carlton Road, Woking, Surrey GU21 4HF TEL (0483) 726957 Conal Gregory MW MP organises wine appreciation courses, generally during the autumn and winter, on three weekday evenings (lasting two hours), aimed at those with modest knowledge, including extensive tutored tastings.

The Wine School at Roberson 348 Kensington High Street, London W14 8NS TEL 071-371 2121 FAX 071-371 4010 Tastings are held on a regular monthly basis, lasting approximately one and a half hours, and the programme consists of tutored tastings by specialists in their various fields. There is a maximum of 16 people per course, price from £10 to £25. (See also the **Where to buy** section.)

The Wine Schoppen Wine Tasting Circle Mrs Anne Coghlan (Managing Director), 1 Abbeydale Road South, Sheffield, S Yorkshire S7 2QL TEL (0742) 365684 FAX (0742) 352171 A wide range of tutored tastings is hosted by guest speakers. Also included in the programme are 'open days' (held on the first Saturday of each month, tasting one special or rare wine), cheese and wine tastings, and dinners. A wine tour abroad and a wine weekend are organised annually. Annual fee is £5.50 (£10 joint).

Winewise Michael Schuster, 107 Culford Road, London N1 4HL
TEL 071-254 9734 Regular tastings include two wine courses: a
Beginners' Course (£100 for six evenings) and an Intermediate
Course (£145 for six evenings). Each course is limited to 18
participants. Other tastings are held to examine the wines of
individual properties and vintages from around the world. There
are blind tastings each spring, workshops on Saturday mornings,
wine and food events, and fine wine tastings on late Sunday
afternoons.

Wine World Lilyane Weston, 'Owlet', Templepan Lane, Chandlers
Cross, Rickmansworth, Hertfordshire WD3 4NH
TEL/FAX (0923) 264718 The programme includes fine wine tastings,
workshops on individual wines, and external tastings and
lectures; 10-12 wines tasted on average, cost £15-£18 per session.
Training also offered to restaurant staff to improve their wine
knowledge. Tutorials given to candidates sitting for the Wine &
Spirit Education Trust Diploma (£15 per session). Visits organised
to UK and French vineyards.

WINE TOURS

Allez France 27 West Street, Storrington, West Sussex RH20 4DZ
TEL (0903) 745793/742345 Allez France offer wine holidays for the
independent traveller to France based in hotels chosen for their
setting, cuisine, character and comfort, including a 'unique'
selection of hotels with their own vineyards. Travel arrangements
are flexible, and tailor-made wine tours for groups, clubs or
associations can be arranged.

Arblaster & Clarke Wine Club Tours 104 Church Road, Steep,
Petersfield, Hampshire GU32 2DD TEL (0730) 266883
FAX (0730) 268620 Tours are made to the major wine-growing
regions of the world, including a visit to Prague for a specially
organised wine festival, a journey on a Tall-Ship from Oporto
tasting port, and weekends in Champagne tasting 25 different
champagnes. Prices start from £199, and individual or group
itineraries can also be arranged.

Australian Tourist Commission Gemini House, 10-18 Putney Hill,
London SW15 6AA TEL 081-780 2227 The Tourist Commission can
provide information on tours and holidays available through
Australian travel firms (for a free Travellers Guide call 081-780
1424). For more specific information on wine tours, contact The

Australian Wine Centre, South Australia House, 50 Strand, London WC2N 5LW (071-930 7471).

Blackheath Wine Trails Carol and Desmond Pritchett, 13 Blackheath Village, London SE3 9LA TEL 081-463 0012 FAX 081-463 0011 In 1993 wine tours were offered to northern Italy, Portugal, Spain, France and Israel. Prices start at £259 and tours vary from 4 to 20 days. For the independent traveller, fly-drive and self-catering options are also available.

Classic Wine Tours Helen Gillespie-Peck, HGP Travel Services, 103 Queen Street, Newton Abbot, Devon TQ12 2BG TEL (0626) 334233 FAX (0626) 334749 Tours offered around France, from 5 to 14 days, price £245 to £580. There are some visits to other European wine regions as well as gastronomic weekends in northern France (Le Touquet and surrounding region). Travel is by luxury coach and numbers are limited to a maximum of 32 per trip.

DER Travel Service Ltd 18 Conduit Street, London W1R 9TD TEL 071-408 0111 FAX 071-629 7442 As well as Rhine cruises, DER arranges air and rail holidays in German and Austrian hotels, guesthouses or apartments in wine-growing areas, and with your own car you can tour the wine-growing areas of the Rhine and Mosel on its 'Wine Regions Tour'. An 8-night tour in 1993 cost from £235 to £284.

English Vineyards Association 38 West Park, London SE9 4RH TEL 081-857 0452 Many English vineyards are open to the public and offer guided tours, tastings and sales. A free pamphlet giving all these details is available from the address above (send an s.a.e.).

Eurocamp Canute Court, Toft Road, Knutsford, Cheshire WA16 0NL TEL (0565) 626262 (Reservations only: 28 Princess Street, Knutsford, Cheshire WA16 6BG) Eurocamp arranges self-drive camping and mobile home holidays at over 250 sites in Europe, many of which are 'almost among the grapes'. These include Bergerac, Cahors, Bordeaux, Mosel and Rhineland. 'Eurocamp Independent', tel (0565) 755399, offers a ferry/pitch reservations 'package' for campers and touring caravan-owners.

Francophiles Ron and Jenny Farmer, 66 Great Brockeridge, Westbury-on-Trym, Bristol BS9 3UA TEL (0272) 621975 Personally escorted 'holidays of discovery in the regional heartlands' on offer to Alsace, Provence, Cévennes, Auvergne, Tarn, the Dordogne, the Jura and the Beaujolais region.

Hide-a-Way Holidays in Burgundy Maureen and Ken Deeming, Greenbank, Penrith Road, Keswick, Cumbria CA12 4LJ TEL (07687) 72522 (Oct-Mar) and The Hide-a-Way, Lampagny, Gigny sur Saône, 71240 Sennecey le Grand, France TEL (010 33) 85.44.71.27 (Apr-Sept) One week 'Wine Appreciation Holidays' are offered from May to September, based in a renovated 200-year-old cottage in southern Burgundy. Price starts from 1060F to 2250F per person. Also included are conducted visits to vineyards for tastings.

KD German Rhine Line G A Clubb Rhine Cruise Agency, 28 South Street, Epsom, Surrey KT18 7PF TEL (0372) 742033 FAX (0372) 724871 In 1993, a week-long 'Floating Wine Seminar' (cost from £660) visited six famous wine-growing areas from the Mosel, the Rhine, Alsace and Baden, and included lectures, tutored tastings and optional sightseeing tours.

Moswin Tours Moswin House, 21 Church Street, Oadby, Leicestershire LE2 5DB TEL (0533) 719922/714982 FAX (0533) 716016 Wine tasting tours, of 4 to 11 days, by air or coach to the Mosel, Rhine and Ahr Valley, Franconia, Baden, Elbe Wineland and Saale-Unstrut Wineland, as well as wine weekends, autumn visits to vineyards and trips to wine festivals. Tailor-made specialist wine tours can also be arranged for individuals and groups.

Sonata Travel 227 Umberslade Road, Selly Oak, Birmingham B29 7SG TEL 021-472 8636 This specialist coach company offers group tours to French and German wine regions from 4 to 7 days. Joining points are in the Midlands and London.

Tanglewood Wine Tours Tanglewood House, Mayfield Avenue, New Haw, Addlestone, Surrey KT15 3AG TEL (0932) 348720 FAX (0932) 350861 This company specialises in coach tours to vineyards in France. A highlight of the programme is a special tour in November to Beaune for the Hospice de Beaune wine auctions. (See also **Tanglewood Wine Society**.)

Tourism Victoria Gemini House, 10-18 Putney Hill, London SW15 6AA TEL 081-789 7088 FAX 081-780 1496 Tourism Victoria produce a wine and food guide to Victoria with helpful notes on wineries and ideas for self-drive visits. They also have details of various tours including Peter Heath's Unique Winery Tours, Winery Walkabout and Bogong Jack Cycling Winery Tours.

Wessex Continental Travel PO Box 43, Plymouth, Devon PL1 1SY
TEL (0752) 846880 FAX (0752) 845547 Described as 'holidays with
wine', a range of 9-day coach tours are offered around France.
Prices are from £355 to £385 and there is a maximum of 36 people
per tour. For private/corporate groups, independent arrangements
can be made to other wine regions of the world. Pick-up point is
in Portsmouth.

Wine Journeys Alternative Travel Group, 69-71 Banbury Road,
Oxford, Oxfordshire OX2 6PE TEL (0865) 310244 FAX (0865) 310299
A wide range of wine tours is offered, each lasting from 4 to 8
days, to top wine estates and châteaux in France, Italy, Spain and
Portugal. A maximum of 20 bookings accepted on any one tour
and prices start from £595. Specially tailored tours can be arranged
both for private groups of wine enthusiasts and as corporate
incentives/hospitality.

Wine glossary

abboccato (Italy) medium-dry

abocado (Spain) medium-dry

adega (Portugal) winery

almacenista (Spain) a small-scale sherry stockholder

amabile (Italy) medium or medium-sweet

amarone (Italy) dry passito (*q.v.*) wine from Valpolicella

amontillado (Spain) an aged fino (*q.v.*) sherry on which yeast flor (*q.v.*) has ceased to grow but which is matured further without flor to develop delicate nutty flavours; commercial 'medium amontillados' are not made in this way, but are blended, sweetened sherries

amoroso (Spain) medium-sweet style of sherry

Anbaugebiet (Germany) growing region

appassimento (Italy) drying of grapes to concentrate their sugars

appellation contrôlée (France) the best category of French wine, with regulations defining the precise vineyard area according to soil, grape varieties, yields, alcohol level, and maybe vineyard and cellar practices

Ausbruch (Austria) dessert wine, between Beerenauslese and Trockenbeerenauslese, from nobly rotten grapes

Auslese (Germany) wine from selected ripe grapes, possibly with noble rot (*see* botrytis)

barrique 225-litre barrel, usually of French oak, in which both red and white wines are matured and white wines sometimes fermented. Normally replaced every 2-3 years, as new barriques have more effect on taste

Beerenauslese (Germany) wine from specially selected ripe berries, probably with noble rot

Bereich (Germany) region, larger than Grosslage, smaller than Anbaugebiet (*q.v.*)

blanc de blancs white wine or champagne made from white grapes only

blanc de noirs white wine or champagne made from red grapes vinified without skin contact (the juice of most red grapes is colourless; all the colouring matter is found in the skins)

bodega (Spain) cellar, winery

botrytis cinerea a form of rot that shrivels grapes and concentrates their sugars ('noble rot')

botte/i (Italy) large oak or chestnut barrel/s

brut (Champagne) dry or dryish (up to 15g sugar/litre)

bual (Madeira) smokily sweet madeira

cantina sociale/cantine sociali (Italy) co-operative winery/ies

carbonic maceration fermentation of whole bunches of grapes in vat filled with carbon dioxide to give fruity wines with low tannin

cava (Spain) champagne-method sparkling wines; now a DO in its own right

chaptalisation the addition of sugar to the must to increase the final alcohol content of the wine

classico (Italy) heartland of a DOC zone, producing its best wines, e.g. Soave

clos (Burgundy) vineyard site that was walled in the past, and may still be walled

colheita (Portugal) vintage (table wine); single-vintage tawny (port)

cosecha (Spain) vintage

cream (Spain) sweet sherry

criadera (Spain) literally 'nursery'; signifies a stage in a sherry solera system (*q.v.*)

crianza, sin (Spain) without wood-ageing

crianza, vino de (Spain) basic wood-aged wine, with one year's oak-cask ageing and one year's bottle- or tank-ageing

cru (France) literally 'growth', meaning either a distinguished single property (as in Bordeaux) or a distinguished vineyard area (as in Beaujolais or Burgundy)

cru (Italy) wine from grapes of a single vineyard, usually of high quality. Term is in common use but not officially permitted

cru bourgeois (Bordeaux) 'bourgeois growth', indicating a wine from the bottom tier of the Médoc region's secondary classification system

cru classé (Bordeaux) 'classified growth', indicating a wine from the Médoc's primary classification system, divided into five strata (premiers, deuxièmes, troisièmes, quatrièmes and cinquièmes crus classés); or from the classification systems of the Graves, Sauternes or St-Emilion

cru classé (Provence) estates bottling their own wines since 1953 (of little significance)

cru grand bourgeois (Bordeaux) 'a fine bourgeois growth', indicating a wine from the middle tier of the Médoc's secondary classification system

cru grand bourgeois exceptionnel (Bordeaux) 'exceptionally fine bourgeois growth', indicating a wine from the upper tier of the Médoc's secondary classification system

crusting/crusted (Portugal) a blend of port of different years for short-term cellaring; needs decanting

cuve close a method of making sparkling wines by carrying out the second fermentation inside a sealed tank rather than in bottle. Also known as the 'tank method' and 'Charmat method'

cuvée (France) vat or tank; sometimes means a 'selected' wine, but the term has no legal status on labels

demi-sec (Champagne, Loire) sweet (up to 50g sugar/litre)

Denominación de Origen (DO) (Spain) wines of controlled origin, grape varieties and style

Denominación de Origen Calificada (DOCa) (Spain) as DO, but entails stricter controls including bottling at source; so far, only Rioja has been given a DOCa status

Denominazione di Origine Controllata (DOC) (Italy) wine of controlled origin, grape varieties and style

Denominazione di Origine Controllata e Garantita (DOCG) (Italy) wine from area with stricter controls than DOC

domaine (Burgundy) estate, meaning the totality of vineyard holdings belonging to a grower or *négociant*

dosage (Champagne) the sugar added with wine to champagne after disgorgement, to determine the degree of sweetness of the final blend, from brut, through extra sec, sec, demi-sec to doux. Extra brut has no dosage

doux (Champagne, Loire) sweet to very sweet (over 50g sugar/litre)

Einzellage (Germany) single vineyard site

Eiswein (Germany) wine made from frozen grapes

English table wine (England & Wales) all English wines, including the very best, are, as yet, classed as 'table wine' by the EC. A pilot scheme for quality wine is being introduced

Erzeugerabfüllung (Germany) estate-bottled (co-operative cellars may also use this term)

extra brut (Champagne) absolutely dry (no added sugar)

extra dry (Champagne) off-dry (12-20g sugar/litre)

fino (Spain) light, dry sherry matured under flor (*q.v.*)

flor (Spain) a layer of yeast growing on sherry in a part-empty butt; gives fino (*q.v.*) its character

frizzante (Italy) lightly sparkling

fusto/i (Italy) oak or chestnut barrel/s

garrafa (Portugal) bottle

garrafeira (Portugal) better-than-average table wine given longer-than- average ageing; a producer's selection of his best wine; a colheita port given bottle as well as cask age

generoso (Portugal, Spain) fortified wine

grand cru (Alsace) classified vineyard site

grand cru (Burgundy) finest category of named vineyard site

grand cru classé (Bordeaux) 'fine classed growth', indicating a wine from the second level of the St-Emilion classification system

grand vin (Bordeaux) 'fine wine': the top wine of a Bordeaux château, blended from selected cuvées only, as opposed to the 'second wine', which is blended from less successful cuvées and perhaps the wine of younger vines, and which is generally sold at a lower price; in other regions the term is used more loosely

gran reserva (Spain) red wine aged for a minimum of two years in oak casks and three in bottle; white (or rosé) wine aged for a minimum of six months in oak casks and three and a half years in tank or bottle

Grosslage (Germany) collective vineyard site

halbtrocken (Germany) semi-dry

Kabinett (Germany) first category of Prädikat wine (*q.v.*), light and delicate in style

kolektziono (Bulgaria) reserve

Landwein (Germany) country wine

Late-Bottled Vintage (LBV) (Portugal) a medium-quality red port of a single year

late harvest (Australia, New Zealand, North America) sweet wine made from grapes picked in an over-mature or maybe botrytised condition

lieu-dit (Burgundy) named, but unclassified, vineyard site

liquoroso (Italy) wines fortified with grape alcohol

maduro (Portugal) a term, meaning 'matured', used loosely of any non-verde (*q.v.*) young wine

malmsey (Madeira) the most sweet and raisiny of madeiras

malolactic fermentation a secondary, non-alcoholic 'fermentation' that converts malic acid into lactic acid. The process is accomplished by bacteria rather than yeast

manzanilla (Spain) salty fino from Sanlúcar de Barrameda

manzanilla pasada (Spain) aged manzanilla (*q.v.*)

méthode traditionnelle (France) replaces méthode champenoise in France to describe the champagne method

metodo classico (Italy) champagne-method sparkling wines

método tradicional (Spain) champagne-method sparkling wines

mis en bouteille par (France) bottled by

moelleux (France) medium-sweet to sweet

mousse (France) term used to describe the effervescence in sparkling wine

mousseux (France) sparkling

muffa nobile (Italy) noble rot

naturale (Italy) natural; describes non-sparkling or slightly sparkling Piemontese Moscato wines with lowish alcohol

négociant (France) wholesale merchant and wine trader

noble rot *see* botrytis

non-vintage (nv) a wine or champagne made from a blend of wines of different years

normale (Italy) non-riserva; most commonly mentioned for Chianti

nouveau (particularly Beaujolais) new wine sold from the third Thursday in November after the harvest. Other areas may be earlier

novello (Italy) new wine, for drinking very young, on sale from October or November

Oechsle (Germany) measure of sugar in grape must; determines quality of wine in Germany and Austria; also used in New World

oloroso (Spain) sherry aged oxidatively rather than under flor (*q.v.*)

Palo Cortado (Spain) light and delicate style of oloroso (*q.v.*)

passerillage (France) the process of leaving grapes to dry and dehydrate on the vine with the eventual aim of producing a dessert wine from them

passito (Italy) dried or semi-dried grapes or wine made from them

perlant (France) with a slight prickle of gas, visible on the side of the glass

pipe (Portugal) a port cask containing between 534 litres (shipping pipe) and 630 litres (lodge pipe)

Port with an Indication of Age (Portugal) true tawny port, in four styles: 10 Years Old, 20 Years Old, 30 Years Old, over 40 Years Old

Prädikat (Germany and Austria) a category of wine with a 'special attribute' based on natural sugar levels in must, such as Kabinett, Spätlese, Auslese, Beerenauslese, Trockenbeerenauslese or Eiswein

predicato (Italy) category of merit used for new-style Tuscan wines

premier cru (Burgundy) second highest category of named vineyard site. If no vineyard name is specified, wine made from a number of different premier cru sites

premier grand cru classé (Bordeaux) 'first fine classed growth', indicating a wine from the top level of the St-Emilion classification system

propriétaire (France) vineyard owner

puttonyos (Hungary) in practical terms, an indication of sweetness of Tokaj Aszú wines (*q.v.*). The more puttonyos specified (3-6), the sweeter will be the Tokaj

Qualitätswein (Germany) quality wine

Qualitätswein bestimmter Anbaugebiet (QbA) (Germany) quality wine from a specific region

Qualitätswein mit Prädikat (QmP) (Germany) quality wine with a 'special attribute' (*see* Prädikat)

quinta (Portugal) farm, estate. In the port context, any style may be branded with a quinta name, but 'Single Quinta' port generally refers to a single-farm port from a lesser year

rainwater (Madeira) a medium-dry madeira based on the Tinta Negra Mole variety

recioto (Italy) sweet passito (*q.v.*) wine from the Veneto

récolte (France) harvest

reserva (Portugal) better-than-average wine; slightly higher (0.5%) in alcohol than legal minimum; at least one year old

reserva (Spain), red wine aged for a minimum of one year in oak casks and two years in bottle;

white (or rosé) wine aged for a minimum of six months in oak casks and one and a half years in tank or bottle

reserve (Bulgaria) wine which has spent two years (white) or three years (red) ageing in wood

reserve (Madeira) madeira with a minimum age of five years

réserve (France) 'reserve': this term has no legal status on labels

riserva (Italy) wines aged for longer than normal. If DOC wines are riserva, then a minimum (but variable) ageing period is laid down. Usually the best wines are held back for riserva

sec (Champagne, Loire) medium-dry (17g–35g of sugar per litre of wine); (other wines) dry

secco (Italy) dry

seco (Portugal, Spain) dry

second wine (Bordeaux) *see* grand vin

Sekt (Germany) sparkling wine

sélection de grains nobles (Alsace) wine made from botrytis-affected grapes (*see* botrytis)

semi-seco (Spain) medium dry

sercial (Madeira) the driest madeira, though cheap examples are rarely fully dry

solera (Spain) sherry ageing system which, by fractional blending, produces a consistent and uniform end product

sous-marque (France) a wine sold or labelled under a secondary, possibly fictional, name

Spätlese (Germany) wine from late-picked grapes, possibly with noble rot

special reserve (Madeira) madeira with a minimum age of ten years

spumante (Italy) sparkling

stravecchio (Italy) extra old

sulfites (US) sulphur dioxide, present in all wines (including organic wines), used as a preservative and disinfectant

supérieur (France) higher alcohol content than usual

'sur lie' (Loire) this should refer to a wine (generally Muscadet) bottled directly from its lees, without having been racked or filtered. The term has, though, been used in a lax fashion in recent years; grant it credence only in conjunction with an indication of domaine-bottling, such as 'mis en bouteille au domaine'

superiore (Italy) wine with higher alcohol, and sometimes more age

Super Tuscan (Italy) non-DOC wine of high quality from Tuscany

Süssreserve (Germany) unfermented grape juice which may be added to fully fermented wine to sweeten it; the process is known as 'back-blending'

Tafelwein (Germany) table wine

tank method *see* cuve close

tawny port (Portugal) basic light port. True wood-aged tawny ports are either marketed as colheitas (*q.v.*) or as Ports with an Indication of Age (*q.v.*)

transfer method a method of making sparkling wines in which the second fermentation takes place in bottle, but the sediment produced by this process is eliminated by decanting and filtering under pressure. The wine is then rebottled

trocken (Germany) dry

Trockenbeerenauslese (Germany) very sweet wine from raisined grapes affected by noble rot

varietal a wine based on a single grape variety

vecchio (Italy) old

velho (Portugal) old

vendange tardive (Alsace) 'late harvest', meaning wine made from especially ripe grapes

verde (Portugal) 'green', meaning young

verdelho (Madeira) medium-dry madeira

viejo (muy) (Spain) old (very)

vigna (Italy) vineyard or 'cru' (*q.v.*)

vigneto (Italy) vineyard or 'cru' (*q.v.*)

viña (Spain) vineyard

vin de pays (France) literally translates as country wine, and describes wine that is better than basic vin de table, with some regional characteristics. Usually vins de pays are determined by administrative geography, with more flexible regulations than for appellation contrôlée (*q.v.*)

vin de table (France) the most basic category of French wine, with no precise provenance other than country of origin given on the label

vin gris (France) pale rosé wine

vinifera (North America) a grape variety that is a member of the European *Vitis vinifera* family, as opposed to some of the other vine families (such as the native American *Vitis labrusca* family)

vinificato in bianco (Italy) juice from black grapes fermented without skin contact to make white wine

vino da tavola (VdT) (Italy) table wine: wine that is neither DOCG, DOC nor fortified nor sparkling nor low in alcohol. Quality may be basic or exceptionally fine

vino de la tierra (Spain) country wine

vino de mesa (Spain) table wine

Vino Kontrolirano (Bulgaria) Controliran wine, made from certain grape varieties in certain DGOs (*see below*)

Vino ot Deklariran Geografski (Bulgaria) Wine of Declared Geographic Origin (DGO)

vin santo (Italy) type of passito (*q.v.*) wine from Trentino, Tuscany and Umbria

vino tipico (Italy) new category for vino da tavola with some regional characteristics

vintage champagne champagne made from a blend of a single year, sold after at least three years' ageing

Vintage Character (Portugal) medium-quality red port. This style may cease to exist in the near future

vintage madeira (Madeira) the finest madeira; declared only after 20 years' maturation

vintage port (Portugal) very fine port, bottled young and requiring long cellaring (8 to 40 years); needs decanting

vitivinicoltura (Italy) the whole process of wine-making, from the vineyard through to the finished wine

VDQS (France) (Vin Délimité de Qualité Supérieure) covers the very much smaller category, below appellation contrôlée (*q.v.*), with very similar regulations

VQPRD (Italy) 'quality wine produced in a specified region'; EC term indicating appellation contrôlée, DOC, DOCG, DO, DOCa and other similarly controlled quality categories

Weinbaudomäne (Germany) wine estate

Weingut (Germany) wine estate

Weinkellerei (Germany) wine cellar

Weissherbst (Germany) rosé

Winzergenossenschaft (Germany) growers' co-operative

INDEX

The index covers mainly the **Taste of wine** section and includes principal areas, grapes and wine characteristics, as well as the names of some wines themselves. See also the **Glossary** on page 483.

INDEX